W9-CUN-067

Urban Land Use Planning

Fourth Edition

Urban Land Use Planning

Edward J. Kaiser, David R. Godschalk, and F. Stuart Chapin, Jr.

University of Illinois Press Urbana and Chicago

© 1995 by the Board of Trustees of the University of Illinois
Manufactured in the United States of America
C 5 4 3

This book is printed on acid-free paper.

Contents

List of Tables and Figures ix

Preface xiii

Part 1: Conceptual Framework 1

1. The Land Planning Arena 5

Land Planning as a Serious Game · Land Planning and Development
Markets · Land Planning and Governments · Land Planning and
Special Interests · Planning Practice Trends · Pressures on Local
Planners · Countervailing Planning Responses

2. Concepts of Land Use Change Management 35

Managing Land Use Change as Practice Rationale · Three Sets of
Land Use Values · Integrating Land Use Values

3. A Local Government Land Use Planning Program 61

The Four Functions of a Land Use Planning Program · Roles
of Planners, Elected Officials, Appointed Officials, Market Participants,
Interest Groups, and Citizens in the Planning Program · Organization
of a Planning Program · Linking Goals and Action

Part 2: Planning Intelligence 85

4. Planning Information Systems 89

Definition and Purpose · Management Issues · Information System
Design · Information Module Design · Illustrative Land Records
Management Program · Illustrative Land Supply Monitoring
Program · Planning Information as Strategic Intelligence

5. Population 115

Economic and Population Information in Land Use Planning ·
Important Characteristics of Population and Economy to Study ·
Ways to Obtain Data · Sources of Population Data · Methods and
Techniques for Population Projection and Estimation

6. The Economy   145

Economic Data · Methods of Analysis · Component Methods · Joint Economic-Population Approach · Normative Economic Projection · Conversion of Population and Employment Projections into Socioeconomic Characteristics for Land Use Planning

7. Environment   172

Environmental Information in the Planning Program · Inventorying and Mapping Environmental Information · Analyzing Environmental Information

8. Land Use   196

Land Use Information in the Planning Program · Inventorying and Mapping Land Use Information · Analyzing Land Use Information

9. Infrastructure and Community Facilities   228

Infrastructure and Facilities Planning Information · Transportation · Sewerage · Water Supply · Stormwater · Schools · Recreation

Part 3: Advance Planning   249

Purposes of Plans · Major Stages and Products in Advance Planning · Advance Planning as a Community Activity Involving Planners, Publics, and Elected Officials · Making a Work Plan · Plan-Making as an Integrated Process of Analysis, Synthesis, and Implementation

10. Direction-Setting   257

The Fact Component · The Values Component · The Policy Component

11. Overview of the Land Use Design Process   278

The Land Use PLan-Making Process · An Appropriate Progression of Attention among the Various Land Uses

12. Land Classification Planning   290

The Overall Process for Land Classification Planning · Delineating Open Space · Allocating Urban Growth · Formulating Implementation Policies · Bringing It Together

13. Commercial and Employment Centers   316

Types of Land Use and Activity Centers · The Plan-Making Process for Employment and Commercial Uses and Activity Centers

14. Residential Areas 341

Residential Design Concepts · The Planning Process · Beyond the Preliminary Plan

15. Integrating Community Facilities with Land Use 368

Important Traits of Community Facilities · The Community Facilities Planning Process · Transportation Facilities · Water and Sewer · Schools · Recreation Facilities

16. Development Management Planning 398

Description of a Development Management Plan · Overview of a Planning Methodology · Stage 1: Initial Steps · Stage 2: Direction-Setting · Stage 3: Design, Assessment, and Adoption

Part 4: Development Management and Problem Solving 421

17. Evaluation and Impact Mitigation 425

Plan Evaluation · Development Proposal Evaluation · Impact Mitigation

18. Implementation 454

Capital Budgeting · Small-Area Planning · Conflict Resolution · Problem Solving · Legal Challenges

Index 475

Tables and Figures

Tables

3-1	Content of the Development Management Plan	74
3-2	Hybrid Plan Table of Contents	75
3-3	Steps and Methods in the Problem Solving Process	77
4-1	Computer Software Types and Functions	94
4-2	Illustrative Parcel Data File	107
6-1	Illustrative Base Multipliers for Some U.S. Areas	151
6-2	Classes of Predictor Variables for Models for Export-Oriented Industries	162
6-3	Classes of Predictor Variables for Models for Local-Serving Industries	163
7-1	Illustrative Trade-Off Matrix	188
7-2	Illustrative DRASTIC Model	190
8-1	Functional Space Characteristics	197
8-2	Planning Units	203
8-3	Land Use and Land Cover Classification System for County or Small City	207
8-4	Suitability Analysis Procedure	217
9-1	Functional Route Classification	233
9-2	Transportation Levels of Service	234
10-1	Selected Statewide Goals Mandated for Local Planning in Oregon	265
10-2	A Policy Statement That Shows the Linkage among Findings, Policy, and Implementation Strategies	275
11-1	Recommended Order of Consideration for Categories of Land Uses for Land Classification and Urban Land Use Design	287
12-1	Open-Space Requirements by Type of Open Space, by Planning District	304
12-2	Summary of Land Classifications	313
13-1	Typical Characteristics of Industrial and Office Parks	320
13-2	Shopping Center Types and Characteristics	322
13-3	Allocation of Future Economic Base Employment by Type of Employment, Employment Center, and General Location	328
13-4	Employment Densities for Industrial Activities	330
13-5	Density Standards for Employment in the Land Use Plan by Type of Employment, Employment Center, and Location	331
13-6	Estimated Space Requirements (in Acres) for Employment Areas in the Land Use Plan	332

13-7 Estimating Retail and Office-Floor Area Requirements for the Land Use Plan and Allocating Them among Commercial and Employment Centers 334

13-8 Calculating Ground-Area Requirements for Land Use Design, Central Business District 336

13-9 Work Table of Space Allocation for Employment and Commercial Centers 339

14-1 Current Stock of Dwellings, Acreage in Residential Use, and Net Densities by Housing Type 352

14-2 Recent Trends in New Additions to Housing Stock 353

14-3 Derivation of Total New Dwelling Units Required 354

14-4 Allocation of New Dwelling Units by Housing and Density Types 355

14-5 Typical Residential Densities for Common Housing Types 356

14-6 Approximate Holding Capacity of Vacant-Renewable Land Suited for Residential Development by Several Types of Dwellings, by Planning District 358

14-7 Spatial Allocation of New Dwelling Unit Requirements, by Density Type 360

14-8 Future Distribution of Population by Planning Sub-area 361

14-9 General Space Requirement Standards for Neighborhood and Community Shopping Centers 362

14-10 Allocation of Land to Local Community Facility Uses, by Planning Sub-areas 364

14-11 Derivation of Gross Space Requirements for Entirely New Residential Communities in Selected Planning Districts 365

15-1 Illustrative General Policies for Community Facility Planning 371

15-2 Suggested Standards for Siting Schools 386

15-3 Recreation and Open Space Standards Suggested by the National Recreation and Park Association 390

15-4 Summary of Recreation Standards for the District of Columbia 392

16-1 Development Management Measures 402

16-2 The Five Dimensions of a Development Management Plan 404

16-3 Illustrative Land Requirements, in Acres, for Full-Service Urban Development 414

17-1 Evaluation Methods Selection Factors 426

17-2 Illustrative Land Development Impact Measures 430

17-3 Illustrative Numerical Indicator Targets 432

17-4 Illustrative Goals-Achievement Matrix 432

17-5 Illustrative Wetland Mitigation Checklist 447

17-6 Tools and Hazards Matrix 451

18-1 Illustrative Stakeholder Analysis Framework 467

Figures

1-1 The Land Planning Game 7

2-1 The Rational Planning Model 38

2-2	Land Use Change Management as a Three-Legged Stool	52
2-3	Planning Discourse Model	54
3-1	The Four Functions of a Land Use Planning Program	62
3-2	Verbal Format Policy Plan	67
3-3	A Land Classification Plan	68
3-4	Howard County, Maryland, Land Use Design and Policy Maps	71
4-1	Information System Organization Alternatives	96
4-2	Layered Land Information System	100
5-1	The Geometric Growth Curve	126
5-2	The Modified Exponential Curve	127
5-3	Three Possible Chains in the Multiple Step-Down Approach	129
5-4	Population Pyramid	134
5-5	Surviving Population over One Period in the Cohort-Component Model	135
5-6	Projecting the Youngest Cohort in the Cohort-Component Model	136
5-7	Migration in the Cohort-Survival Model	137
6-1	Transactions Table Format	156
6-2	An Overview of the Single Equation Methodology	160
7-1	Slope and Watershed Maps	178
7-2	Digitized General Soils Map and Digitized Hydric Soils Map, Durham County, N.C.	180
7-3	Flood Hazards Map	183
8-1	Levels of Developability	198
8-2	Traditional Existing Land Use Map and Computerized Existing Land Use Map	210
8-3	Impact of Traffic on Neighboring and Visiting	214
8-4	Development Simulation Model Structure	222
8-5	Evaluative Image Map	224
9-1	The Urban Hierarchical System of Roadways	232
9-2	Schematic Diagram of Sewerage Systems	237
10-1	The Role of Direction-Setting in Advance Planning	258
10-2	Five Sources of Community Goals	263
11-1	The Five Tasks for Land Classification and Urban Land Use Design	280
12-1	A Hierarchy of Land Classification Categories	293
12-2	Diagram of the Steps in Estimating Space Requirements	307
12-3	Functional Planning Areas Concept	311
13-1	The Three-Part Challenge of Designing the Fit between Use, Activity Center Type, and Location	317
14-1	Versions of the Neighborhood Unit Concept	343
14-2	The Transportation-Oriented Development Concept	346
14-3	A Hierarchical Nested Pattern of Residential Community Units	347
15-1	A Joint Land Use and Transportation Planning Process	377
15-2	Diagrammatic Layout and Characteristics of a Transit System's Components	379
16-1	The Three Stages of Development Management Planning	407

17-1   Conventional Development Alternative   428
17-2   Cluster Development Alternative   429
17-3   Generalized Volusia County Coastal Land Use Plan   435
17-4   Monitoring and Evaluation Activities   437
17-5   Cumulative Impact Analysis Approach   443
17-6   Exactions and Land Use Objectives   448
17-7   Social Impact Relationships   449
18-1   Facility Investment Decision Environment   456
18-2   Small-Area Planning Process   459
18-3   Illustrative Small-Area Plan   461
18-4   Spiral of Unmanaged Conflict   463
18-5   Linked Conflict Management Approach   464
18-6   Decision Tree Graph   470

Preface

This fourth edition of *Urban Land Use Planning* presents methods and techniques for land use plan-making within a holistic planning process. It lays out a framework for organizing a local planning program, explains planning techniques and their strengths and weaknesses, suggests specific standards and criteria, and indicates sources for further information. It is designed as a text for graduate and advanced undergraduate planning methods courses and as a reference for practicing planners.

The methods we lay out emphasize a how-to-do-it approach to urban land use plan-making in a local U.S. context. The professional practice perspective is aimed at land use planning in the 1990s, given the current and emerging context of issues, technology, intergovernmental relations, and societal trends. The focus on U.S. local governmental planning is also relevant for state and regional land use programs, particularly as they relate to urbanizing regions, and for other countries, with adjustments. While focusing on land use planning, we also discuss ties to comprehensive planning, environmental planning, and infrastructure planning. The urban orientation incorporates environmental values and factors and regards agriculture, forestry, and natural environmental processes as suitable uses of land in plans for urban regions.

The book has four parts. In Part 1, "Conceptual Framework," we present land use planning in the context of societal, governmental, and technological trends as well as planning theory, describing that context as a big-stakes game of multiple-party competition over the community's future land use pattern. It also proposes our model planning program for local government, which is then filled out in the remainder of the book. In Part 2, "Planning Intelligence," we set out a computerized local government information system to support a land use planning program. We pay particular attention to population and economic projections and also to inventories and analyses of environmental processes and features, land and land uses, and community facilities and infrastructure. In Part 3, "Advance Planning," we describe how to make a plan for the future development of an urban community. We cover goal-setting, land use design, land classification plans, planning for commercial and employment centers, residential areas, community facilities and infrastructure, and, finally, planning a development management program. In Part 4, "Development Management and Problem Solving," we discuss techniques used in implementing plans, operating the development management program, and solving problems unforeseen during advance planning. The unifying thread in this part is the notion of implementation as a process of ongoing evaluation and mitigation, budgeting and planning, conflict resolution and problem solving within the context of the land use game.

The fourth edition of *Urban Land Use Planning* reflects the continued evolution of land use planning methods since 1957, when Chapin wrote the first edition. In a way, the four editions constitute a history of land use planning methodology in the United States. The first edition in 1957 organized and synthesized the techniques that characterized the craft of planning as it had evolved and was practiced during the 1950s. It also explored the emerging theory of a young and growing profession.

The second edition in 1965, also by Chapin, contained a distinct shift in emphasis from the use of "craftsman's" methods to more scientific approaches, such as automatic data processing and mathematical models. It also reflected the stronger basis in planning theory and urban theory that had developed by the 1960s, specifically introducing the notion of activity patterns of households and firms as the underlying basis of land use.

The third edition in 1979, by Chapin and Kaiser, emphasized the increased importance of a federal and state planning context for local planning, an integrated information system instead of a collection of files and analytic studies, land use projection models, and the idea of a development guidance system instead of the traditional long-range land use design as the output of planning.

This fourth edition, now by Kaiser, Godschalk, and Chapin, reflects (1) the use of microcomputer technology in the organization and analysis of information and the presentation and evaluation of plans; (2) modern planning theory that features participation and negotiation in addition to integration of plan and action; (3) extension of the planning process beyond advance planning to development management and problem solving; and (4) the evolving governmental context for local planning, which features greater state influence and more attention to the consistency between plans and action, and between local and regional plans. But even so, we cannot capture all anticipated change in land use practice. For example, computer technology continues to evolve at a dizzying rate, and even our familiar measurement system is scheduled to go metric by the end of the 1990s.

The evolution of this text as it seeks to keep abreast of change demonstrates how important it is for the planner to continually up-date techniques. Nevertheless, in spite of such sea changes in methods and context, we have sought to continue the coherence of earlier editions by presenting techniques as parts of a holistic technical planning process and an overall community planning program. The framework has evolved to include short periods as well as long, the development of a management plan as well as land use design, and management of change as well as specification of a long-range future urban form. Still, the vision of an ideal planning approach remains a fundamental contribution of *Urban Land Use Planning*.

This Preface would be incomplete without acknowledgment of the contributions of many people who helped us complete this new edition. We thank our students for challenging us to keep improving the methodology and its explanation, and in many instances suggesting better methods. Becky Crane, Michael Delaney, Jillian Detweiler, Sally Loveland, Toby Millman, Jeanine Stevens, and Carolyn Turner helped edit drafts of the manuscript and refine tables and figures. Colleagues at the University of North Carolina and other universities gave us feedback on the previous edition and drafts of chapters in this edition; in particular we thank Eric Strauss, Raymond Burby, William Drummond, Peter Flachsbart, Harvey Goldstein, Deborah Howe, Richard Klosterman, Gerard McMahon, Isaac Megbolugbe, Francis Parker, and Brian Taylor. Practitioners provided examples of plans and studies that helped us illustrate our explanations and provide references to professional work; without them, the methods described here would be less credible. Finally, thanks to Pat, Lallie, and Mildred for their support in this endeavor and all the others.

PART 1

Conceptual Framework

We start the book by exploring the societal, governmental, technological, and planning theory contexts for land use planning. We also propose our vision of a planning program for a local government and provide the framework that will be used to organize the methods and techniques in the rest of the book.

In chapter 1, "The Land Planning Arena," we describe the current status and trends in society, government, and technology that affect the practice of land use planning in the United States. These trends constitute a context to which local land use planning must adapt. Some occur in the intergovernmental organization for planning, including the growing use of state mandates for local governments to plan in prescribed ways consistent with state plans, local regulations, and capital improvement programs. Converging with those top-down influences are grass-roots influences from pluralist constituencies within the community. Land use planners in local agencies also must attune their methods and techniques to changes in planning technology, including the increased availability, power, and speed of computers and software. Geographic information systems (GIS), in particular, are changing planning methods.

These contexts comprise what we call a serious, big-stakes, land use planning and management game with multiple-party competition over a community's growth, future land use pattern, and environmental quality. The game is in constant flux, and players include individuals involved in land market issues, as well as government officials, advocates of various interests, and also the planner, who is both a player and a game manager.

We provide the theory base for land use planning in chapter 2, "Concepts of Land Use Change Management." Our discussion draws from both planning theory and urbanization theory to develop the idea of land use change management as a rationale for planning practice. Under planning theory, we explore various prescriptions about how planning ought to be done. Our proposed planning model is based on rational planning, which was also the primary planning theory base for earlier editions of this text. But it now incorporates critical theory and communicative competence, dispute resolution, and adaptive planning concepts within a broader model of discourse and consensus-building among the players in the land use planning game.

A second source for constructing a planning rationale is drawn from theories of how and why urban change occurs and theories of values associated with urban form and urban change. We argue that the planner's task is to balance three competing sets of values or perspectives on urban change: social, market, and environmental. People using the community as a setting for living their lives ascribe social values to land use arrangements. They see land use as facilitating their activities and representing their social ties and place in the community. Market values express the weight people and institutions give to land as a commodity, that is, real estate to be bought, sold, and developed for profit. Such values dominate the urban growth and change process in the absence of planning but must also be accommodated even with planning. Environmental values express the weight people give to natural features and natural systems that occur in the landscape.

The third and final chapter in Part 1 presents our recommended model land use planning program for a local government. It describes the services a planning program should provide to local government and the community; outlines the types of plans and other products the program should produce; specifies the roles of professionals, community officials, and citizens; and suggests appropriate relationships between land use planning and other types of planning. The land use plan is only one element, although a critical one, of the overall comprehensive plan, which includes detailed transportation, community facilities, economic development, housing, and other elements. However, the land use plan is the cornerstone in formulating a comprehensive community development strategy. The third chapter translates the context and theory of land use planning into practice, and outlines the approach followed in the remainder of the book.

1

The Land Planning Arena

Because each actor's reward depends on the actions of others, he will maximize his rewards if he can anticipate the actions of other players and devise a plan of action which enables him to benefit from their actions. . . . These observations suggest that game theory may help explain interactions between landowners as they struggle in an evolving context to benefit from changes in land use.

—Rudel 1989, 19

Local land use planning and decision-making can be seen as a big-stakes game of serious multiparty competition over an area's future land use pattern. To win the game is to gain adoption and implementation of the future land use plan, development regulations, and development decisions that most benefit your role or organization. Land planners play the land use game in an arena with other players, each with resources and influence over decisions. However, planners also act as game managers, drafting and enforcing the rules of the game and advocating community cooperation to achieve multiparty benefits. Mindful of the inherent tensions between the player and manager demands of their roles, they must walk a tightrope between advocacy and neutrality. Effective land planners carefully watch and respond to the interests, actions, and alliances of the other players. Not to understand the game at every stage is to risk losing the planners' credibility and authority, and the broader public's stake in the community's future.

In this chapter, we discuss the structure, content, and dynamics of the land planning arena as the stage upon which the local land use game is played. The purpose of our discussion is to illustrate the *context* for land use planning in order to alert planners to the ways that the institutional environment can affect their work.

Land Planning as a Serious Game

The land planning arena can be confusing and frustrating to the novice planner. Rather than an orderly and rational procedure of adopting land plans and policies based upon systematic technical studies aimed at the overall public interest, it often appears to be an ad hoc, political process based on influence and narrow interest group bias responding to the issue of the moment. The theories and statistical analyses taught in planning school may carry less weight with elected officials than the self-serving demands of a mob of angry speakers at a public hearing. The long-range projections of plans may fail as guides to decision-making due to unforeseen changes in economic or social conditions. How can there be an art and science of land use planning in the face of such a politicized decision-making process and such an unpredictable future?

One premise of this book is that land use planning and decision-making resemble a high-stakes *competition* over an area's future land use pattern. However, the players are locked together in a framework of interdependence in which they must gain agreement from other players in order to achieve their goals. Thus, the process's competition is tempered with the need for *cooperation* as well. Characterizing planning as a serious game helps to visualize the dynamics of the process and to see how to apply land use planning techniques to improve overall game outcomes.[1] Understanding the nature of the land use game is the first step toward developing an art and science of land use planning and development management.

A second premise is that the land use plan is a key tool in coordinating community development activities. We disagree with those who hold that land use planning is *only* a process. We see it as a *process guided by a plan.* The plan fulfills many needs. It helps to turn competitors into collaborators through involvement in its preparation. It records a series of agreements among the players about ways to deal with their different objectives, serving as a community dispute resolution mechanism. It ensures that public interest goals are not overlooked in the rush to realize narrower aims, preventing the "tragedy of the commons" in which a valued community resource is destroyed by unbridled self-interest. It creates joint gains shared by various interest groups as well as the community as a whole. It acts as a platform for the application of analyses and technical studies. It lays out a vision of the area's future and a strategy for achieving it. As game conditions change, the plan is regularly revised in order to maintain currency and consensus. Just as the most successful athletic teams are those with effective game plans, so the most successful communities are those with effective land use plans.

In the land use game, planners are not only players, they are also game managers, drafting and enforcing the rules of the game and advocating cooperation among the players in order to achieve communitywide goals. Because of their responsibility for recommending and administering not only plans and regulations but also public participation processes for plan and policy review, planners have a unique position at the center of the land use game. They have inside information and privileged access to the other players. Land planners are expected to keep careful track of all stakeholders' interests, actions, and alliances. To lose track of the game status is to risk losing planners' credibility as experts, their authority as land use change managers, and their opportunities to facilitate cooperation among competing interests in building a better community.

In addition to planners, the major types of institutional stakeholders attempting to influence the direction of future urban growth and change are development market players, government officials, and advocates of various interests (Figure 1-1). *Market-oriented* players include private-sector land owners, developers, builders, realtors, and others who seek to profit from land use change. *Government* players include public-sector elected and appointed officials at the federal, state, regional, and local levels, who frame laws and make governmental land use decisions aimed at the overall public interest. *Interest group* players include representatives of special interests—neighborhood preservation, environmental conservation, economic development, farming, minority groups, and others—who view land use through the lens of their group's particular values. *Land planners* include those in government concerned with both current and future land use issues. These stakeholders compete over the content and procedures of land use regulations, plans, and development decisions. Sometimes they work together and sometimes they oppose each other in an ecology of games in which coalitions are framed by

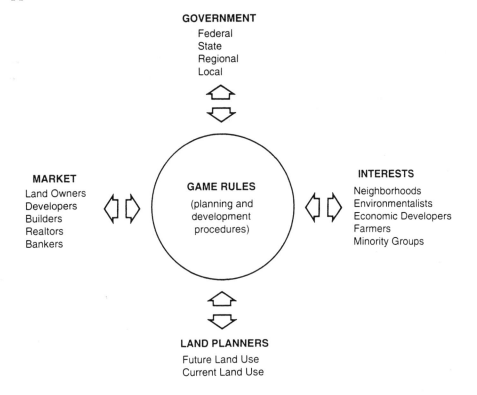

Figure 1-1. The Land Planning Game: Stakeholders, Planners, and Rules

the issue at hand.[2] The planner must understand the goals and interests of these institutional actors in order to be an effective player and manager of the land use game.

In theory, land use stakeholders are continuously in conflict, causing inherent tension for land planning. In practice, this conflict is moderated by the legal and governance systems—"the rules of the game." The rules turn conflict into regulated competition. Their constitutional provisions, laws, regulations, planning powers, and decision processes seek to protect overall public interests from the extremes of unregulated maximization of market, social, or environmental values. The planner must rely upon legal and governance systems to balance conflicts among values, to make hard choices about community priorities, and to ensure fairness in land use decisions. The planner is both a drafter and an enforcer of the game rules (in the form of development regulations and community objectives) but is not their final arbiter. That role is reserved for the elected officials of the community or the courts if the elected officials' decision is challenged. But the planner must understand the influences of legal and constitutional checks and balances upon the powers of land use plans to achieve community goals.

Land Planning and Development Markets

The bottom line for land planning is its influence over the outcome of the land development process by which projects, neighborhoods, communities, and cities are built. A "good" land use plan with "good" implementation produces a "good" built environment. What is built, where it is built, and when and how it is built are all critical questions whose answers depend upon many actors, each with different definitions of what is good (Jacobs 1978; Lynch 1981; Calthorpe 1989; Beauregard 1990). The goal of the land planner is not simply to accommodate market demand for development, but to guide the market toward producing good communities.

In a democratic, capitalist society, business entrepreneurs assemble the land and capital to build the private-sector portions of communities. They are the "engines" of community-building, adding value to land through the improvements they place upon it.[3] The most obvious measure of their winnings at the land use game is their profit from the sale of land and buildings. They gamble that they can anticipate market demand, producing developed urban space that the market will value at a higher level than its cost to them. They are risk-takers, willing to face financial losses and even bankruptcy in order to profit from their gambles. A more subtle measure of their success is their reputation as public-spirited "community builders" who create desirable living and working environments rather than simply market commodities.[4]

Landowners, builders, and developers scrutinize land policies, regulations, and plans for their impacts on the monetary values of land. Landowners often include those whose land is presently in nonurban use, such as farms and forests, but who wish to preserve the option of conversion to urban use that would bring an increase in market value. Developers who make their livelihood from the conversion of land to more intense uses are also concerned with the effects of public actions on land price. This group may be joined at times by other business interests affected by land policies, such as financial institutions, and by those who simply advocate the lessening of government intervention into the market as an ideological position.

Developers are constrained by both land planning and market demand. To succeed, their projects must pass both a government test and a market test. They must satisfy the intent of governmental plans and regulations adopted by the local elected representatives in order to get a development permit. They must satisfy the consumer's taste in order to sell and make a profit. They operate in a market of buyers and sellers that is influenced by public plans and service programs but not driven by them. For them, the driving forces are the growth of the population, the economy, and interest rates, which affect demand and capital availability.

In a nonmarket society, the state plays both regulator and developer roles. This does not necessarily mean that land plans are always well done and well implemented, that the resulting cities are always well built, or that the environment is always well protected. In these cases, the state's ideology and economic health, determining what the government wants and can afford to build, are critical determinants of the quality of development. Even though the government controls and monopolizes the development market, recent government-built cities have often been less attractive and efficient than those built under market conditions.

Governments in both market and nonmarket societies take responsibility for seeing that the necessary community infrastructure—roads, water and sewer systems, schools, parks, and the like—gets produced. This infrastructure framework supports residential, commercial, and industrial development. And its influence over development's type, location, and timing is often more direct than that of land use plans or regulations alone. However, government infrastructure alone also does not drive development; that driving force comes from demand for the product of development—developed land in the form of building lots, houses, offices, factories, and stores.

Active land use planning affects the development market by identifying land that is available or planned for development; by limiting the type, location, timing, and density of development that can take place; by programming the infrastructure to support development and allocating its costs between the public and private sectors; and by specifying the standards under which development proposals will be reviewed. These actions define the supply of developable land and what can be built upon it. They have been described as "managing the market." Although that description is too extreme for most cases, it is clear that the active land planner is attempting to guide the process of structural change in accordance with community goals. In that sense, the land planner can be seen as both a "growth manager" and a "manager of change."

This book focuses on land planning in market-oriented societies, with U.S. practice as its basis. The U.S. setting is distinguished both by active local real estate markets and by extensive local government autonomy over land use decisions. Thus our concern in this book is not only with the techniques of analyzing local values, land use trends, and needs as the bases for land use plans, but also with the related processes of public participation and open government plan review, adoption, and implementation. These related participatory processes are requirements in a democratic, market-oriented system; they cannot be overlooked. We believe that they also should be relevant in non-market societies in order to ensure better plans. Whether or not a private land market exists, a broad spectrum of contending interests must inevitably be integrated into land use and development management plans. Planners must reconcile these interests with feasible and desirable objectives, as well as with responsive and defensible implementation. Effective land use planning is always both a technical process and a broadly political process.

Land Planning and Governments

Government officials are major players in the politics of U.S. land use. Land planners must account not only for the policies of their individual governments, but also for the policies of governmental agencies at the federal and state levels and within multijurisdictional regions.

Federal Government Policy

The federal government sets national policy in response to perceptions of nationwide problems. This policy, expressed in laws and programs, results from debates and compromises among contending parties, public and private, over the appropriate solutions to such problems and the appropriate roles of federal, state, and local governments. It is measured against the Constitution's broad framework and the specifics of legal principles and precedents (Blaesser and Weinstein 1989). It is adopted and carried out within a system of checks and balances in which the legislative, administrative, and judicial branches are counterbalanced to prevent abuses of power. Because of the complexity and competition within the federal establishment, federal policy affecting local land use is often fragmented and inconsistent.

The fragmentation of federal policy does not mean that it has nothing to say about land use decisions. As Maranda et al. (1980, 15) note, "The multitude of federal housing, community development, transportation and environmental programs have both direct and indirect land use policy implications.

In sum, these programs provide the national perspective on land use—a patchwork land use policy that is neither comprehensive nor without major contradictions." Thus, the local land planner must maintain familiarity with a variety of federal programs, including their sometimes contradictory mandates.

Implementation of federal programs generally uses one or more of the following techniques:

1. setting uniform national requirements that state and local governments must follow or be penalized;
2. awarding grants and incentives to encourage state and local governments to voluntarily develop plans and programs to meet federal objectives;
3. withdrawing federal subsidies or assistance or leaving program costs to state and local government actions;
4. regulating certain types of development through required permitting programs; or
5. building certain types of public development projects.

Uniform national standards are typically used to implement environmental protection policies. For example, the Environmental Protection Agency (EPA) sets national standards for clean air, clean water, and safe disposal of solid and hazardous waste. Cities and states must meet these standards, often by means of land use regulations, or face penalties. Sometimes, environmental protection goals conflict. For example, in the Los Angeles metropolitan area, the EPA has imposed sanctions for the failure to meet federal air quality standards, particularly for ozone, and has suggested that new sewage treatment facilities not be federally funded because they induce growth. At the same time, Los Angeles is attempting to meet a goal of "no discharge" into Santa Monica Bay by sewage treatment plant improvements that will reduce the level of toxins in sewage effluent. As a recent report notes, "The conflict between these environmental mandates ('clean the Bay' versus 'clean the air') is a clear example of intermedia tradeoffs that are difficult to make in the current regulatory system" (Los Angeles 2000 Committee 1988, 31).

Planning and management incentives are also used to implement environmental and land use policy. Federal grants are available for affordable housing subsidies, community development improvements, metropolitan transportation planning, and transit programs. Federal flood insurance is available to property owners in communities that implement floodplain regulations. Federally guaranteed mortgages have encouraged suburban development, and federal tax breaks have encouraged preservation and adaptive reuse of historic buildings. The Coastal Zone Management Act of 1972 offers planning and management grants to encourage individual states to develop and carry out coastal plans. Twenty-nine of the thirty-five eligible states and territories participate in this program, which offers flexibility to meet the differing needs of coastal areas.

Withdrawal of subsidies is another implementation method. For example, the Coastal Barrier Resources Act of 1982, administered by the Department of the Interior, identified coastal areas where further development should be discouraged. To reduce future federal losses from coastal storm damage on these hazardous coastal barriers, the program removes federal subsidies to development in the form of federal flood insurance and infrastructure funding.

Permitting of certain types of development involves federal agencies directly in land use decisions. For example, the Army Corps of Engineers issues permits for dredge and fill of waterways and for alteration of wetlands, requiring applicants to analyze and mitigate the impacts of their proposals upon these areas. Under section 404 of the Clean Water Act, no discharge of dredge or fill material into waters of the United States is allowed without a Corps permit. These permits are also reviewed by the Environmental Protection Agency for wetlands impacts. Under the Endangered Species Act, the U.S. Fish and Wildlife Service can also require an environmental impact assessment if endangered species are present on the project site.

Construction of public works also involves federal agencies in land use actions. The most prominent examples are the interstate highway system built by the U.S. Department of Transportation and the system of dams and flood control structures built by the Army Corps of Engineers. However, there are many other federal construction programs, ranging from military bases and installations to post offices and national parks.

State Government Policy

State government policy-making processes rely primarily on state constitutions and state laws. Like the federal government, states also work within systems that balance the powers of the legislative, administrative, and judicial branches of government and often result in interagency competition. In terms of land policy, states fall roughly into two types: (1) growth-managing states, where fast growth and a high degree of development change have stressed local capabilities to the extent that new state growth management laws have been passed, and (2) growth-accommodating states, where growth and change have not been perceived as state problems (Brower, Godschalk, and Porter 1989).

Growth-managing states mandate actions by their local governments to manage development in accordance with state goals and objectives. During the 1960s and 1970s, five states enacted statewide growth management policies: Hawaii (1961), Vermont (1970), Florida (1972), Oregon (1973), and Colorado (1974). (Colorado did not continue to pursue growth management.) These were followed in the 1980s by five new state initiatives and one revised program: Florida (revisions 1984–86), New Jersey (1986), Maine (1988), Vermont (1988), Rhode Island (1988), and Georgia (1989). (Maine's program was cut back in 1992 for budgetary reasons.) The state of Washington joined this group with the enactment of growth management legislation in 1990 and 1991, along with Maryland in 1992. Eight other states considered statewide legislation in the early 1990s: California, Colorado, Massachusetts, New York, North Carolina, Virginia, Pennsylvania, and West Virginia.

In addition to states with statewide growth management mandates, other states require local planning and growth management in specific regions or types of areas. Twenty-four have adopted coastal management programs under the Coastal Zone Management Act of 1972 in the form of state standards and procedures for local land use and environmental management and planning in designated coastal areas (Godschalk 1992).[5] Several have adopted mandates for protection of specific natural areas, including California and Nevada's Tahoe Regional Planning Agency (1970), New York's Adirondack Park Agency (1971), New Jersey's Pinelands Commission (1978), and Maryland's Chesapeake Bay Critical Area Commission (1984). Other states have adopted mandates for metropolitan area planning, including Minnesota's Metropolitan Council of the Twin Cities Area (1967), Georgia's Atlanta Regional Commission (1971), and Oregon's Portland Metropolitan Service District (1979).

As De Grove (1989, 41) states, "Most of the growth management systems . . . have in common a change in the allocation of authority and responsibility vertically; and, at a minimum, new coordination requirements horizontally between and among state agencies, and between and among cities and counties where both are players in the growth management process." His point is that the systems change the traditional permissive local planning statutes to new requirements for local governments to plan and manage growth. Under these state growth management programs, the states themselves take an active role in guiding local planning by establishing goals, procedures, and standards and by taking an oversight role.

Local planners in growth-managing states must plan by state rules, which in some cases put them in an adversarial position with the state planning agency. De Grove (1992) notes that state mandates may require local plans to:

1. include certain elements—a content requirement;
2. be consistent with state goals and policy—a consistency requirement;
3. require infrastructure to be provided concurrently with development—a concurrency requirement;
4. be coordinated with plans of neighboring governments—a coordination requirement;
5. contain urban sprawl—a containment requirement;
6. provide for affordable housing—an affordability requirement;
7. broaden growth management to include promotion of economic development—a growth encouragement requirement; and
8. protect natural resources—a conservation requirement.

The advantage of state guidance is that it can overrule local political decisions that do not meet statewide standards for sound land planning practice. For example, Florida insists that local plans either set standards for, and provide infrastructure concurrently with, new development or face a moratorium. Sprawl is discouraged by drastically limiting outlying rural densities (DeGrove 1989; Audirac, Shermyen, and Smith 1990). The disadvantage of state guidance is that it can reduce local initiative and creativity through the necessity of meeting uniform standards and timetables, resulting in local frustration with planning.

Growth-accommodating states follow the traditional role of providing a statutory base of planning and regulatory powers for those local governments that choose to exercise them. Enabling acts for planning, zoning, subdivision regulation, and health and building codes are enacted as permissive laws. The state government does not involve itself in local land use decisions, which are seen as the prerogative of the local governments. Either due to a lack of growth problems or to a political culture that stresses minimal government intervention into the market, the majority of states fall into the growth-accommodating camp.

Local planners in growth-accommodating states have considerable freedom to define planning content and processes. However, they lack the backbone of state-mandated principles and standards for acceptable plans, as well as the importance accorded to planning through state legislative attention. They also lack the potential coordinating power of required consistency between state, regional, and local plans, a particularly valuable power for planning infrastructure or environmental systems that cross jurisdictional boundaries.

Local Government Policy

Local governments are creatures of their states, deriving their power and authority from state legislatures. Standard state enabling acts, adopted throughout the United States, make planning and development regulation legitimate functions of local governments. However, their ability to innovate beyond the standard powers is limited by the necessity to gain state legislative approval for major changes in their functions. Still, within the realm of the authority granted to them, they have considerable freedom to make decisions and considerable power to guide development. Without the built-in checks and balances, agency competition, and program fragmentation that federal and state governments face, they can be more consistent in implementing land policies. More important at the local level, however, is where, between the poles of strict management and laissez-faire accommodation, the community stands on growth.

Growth-managing localities seek to influence the location, amount, type, timing, quality, and/or cost of development in accordance with public goals (Godschalk et al. 1979). These cities and counties place community and environmental goals on par with goals of the development market. They allocate land for development by means of a public calculus based not only on development demand, but also on environmental protection, fiscal efficiency, neighborhood compatibility, limitation of sprawl, and esthetic appeal. They carry out their land use plans with a wide range of tools— impact fees, urban limit lines, design guidelines, development agreements, capital improvements programs, and adequate public facility ordinances—as well as traditional zoning and subdivision controls.

Growth-accommodating localities seek to ensure a steady, unrestricted supply of land for development so that the market is not constrained. These areas limit the amount of regulation to that necessary for minimum health and safety protection. They allocate land for development by means of a marketability calculus based on ensuring a wide selection of sites sufficient to meet projected development demand with a generous margin for choice. Many carry out their land use plans with minimum zoning and subdivision regulations and also liberal terms for infrastructure provision.

Conflicts often occur between local governments whose growth policies are not compatible. These may be between adjacent local governments whose boundaries are coming together and who get into disputes over annexation or who differ on the growth management versus accommodation issue. They may be between cities and their parent county over differing urban and rural perspectives toward growth management. They may be between upstream and downstream areas over protecting water quality and maintaining stream flows in shared water bodies. Increasingly, local governments with overlapping jurisdictions, shared boundaries, or interests in areawide resources are coordinating their development plans and policies through techniques ranging from informal staff consultation to multijurisdictional forums to formal intergovernmental agreements.

Policy Dynamics

Elected and appointed policymakers at all three levels of government seek to influence land use in different ways, depending upon the problem of concern. For example, the federal government may pass a coastal zone-management law offering grants to states to attack the problem of uncoordinated land use in coastal areas. Coastal states may respond by passing new state coastal management laws that establish procedures for local plans and for state review of certain land use proposals in critical coastal areas. Local governments in coastal areas must then incorporate the state and federal policies into their local land use plans. Then the federal law may be amended to deal with a new problem, such as the impacts of energy developments on coastal environments, and the state and local responses are modified accordingly. The content of intergovernmental land policy changes over time, as the perceived problems change.

While land policies come and go with social change, land policy institutions are more stable. The structure and procedures of federal, state, and local legislatures change infrequently. Government agencies concerned with land use, such as the federal Environmental Protection Agency or a state department of community affairs, change more frequently but typically on a time scale measured at least in decades. Institutional stability, however, can mask major policy swings, particularly as new administrations set new priorities and install new agency staff. For example, the Reagan administration tried for eight years to dismantle national funding for the coastal zone management program, which was only saved from extinction by repeated congressional actions (Godschalk 1992).

For the local planner, one of the most critical policy dynamics is the election of new local government representatives. Because of the power of local elected officials over the planning and development management processes, the outcomes of the elections that occur every two or four years can spell defeat or victory for a local planning effort. The knowledge, experience, and attitudes of elected officials about planning issues vary radically. Although the literature typically characterizes decision-making groups as homogeneous, in practice the members of elected bodies often disagree among themselves over planning proposals. Planners often find themselves acting as educators for elected officials who are unaware of the potential impacts of their planning decisions (Lucy 1988).

Land Planning and Special Interests

In a democracy, land planning by law must afford opportunities for public participation in governmental decision-making. Because land values—market, social, and environmental—are so pervasive, a variety of interests or publics have broad interest in land use decisions. As the impacts of both private and public development projects grow larger and more pervasive, more public constituencies are motivated to participate in the review process.

Market value advocates have already been discussed in terms of their advocacy for specific projects where they hold a financial interest and for community plans and regulations that favor market values. A broader type of public is also concerned with market values. This group may bring together businesses, chambers of commerce, economic development organizations, and citizens concerned with the monetary value of their land investments. Depending upon the issue, the group may include some strange bedfellows, as in the case of developers and low-income individuals joining together to oppose large lot exclusionary zoning.

Neighborhood residents typically advocate the preservation and enhancement of the social use values of communities. They scrutinize land policies and plans for impacts on their quality of life while also keeping an eye on impacts on the market value of their property. In the absence of an informed community consensus about future growth, these groups may mobilize to block or modify development. Neighborhood groups sometimes include those who seek to prevent any new development, or at least to prevent adjacent development at densities higher than theirs (Babcock and Siemon 1985). In an interesting about-face, some neighborhood groups have banded together to sell their properties as a group to a developer in order to benefit uniformly from new development (Logan and Molotch 1987, 117–18).

Environmental groups range from those who seek to protect critical environmental areas to those who would stop growth altogether. Often these groups are local chapters of such national environmental advocacy groups as the Sierra Club. They view land policies and plans through an ecological lens, seeking the maximum preservation of existing natural environmental features such as wetlands, streams, and forests. They may form coalitions with neighborhood groups opposed to growth and even with business groups opposed to specific projects seen as antithetical to existing businesses.

Other special interest groups advocate other values. Low- and moderate-income housing groups seek less expensive, higher-density sites for housing projects. Farmers seek the flexibility to sell their land for urban development when they leave farming. Mass-transit groups seek plans with feasible transit corridors accessible to higher-density housing and employment destinations. Representatives of institutions, such as hospitals or universities, seek space for institutional expansion with good access to their activities.

Local land planners must work with many publics. To be acceptable and effective, land use plans must recognize and reconcile the pluralistic interests of these publics with those expressed by governments and markets. It is a major challenge to design a fair and orderly forum for expressing and reconciling the interests of those affected by land use decisions. Managing this complex public participation process makes land planning as much an art as a science, especially when planning concerns change so often.

Planning Practice Trends

The content of U.S. planning practice has been characterized by continuing turbulence, as planners have responded to a changing institutional and policy environment. As the rate of social and technological change has increased, our ability to predict or guide that change has decreased. Instead, planning has been forced to invent new programs and techniques to deal with a changing slate of urban problems.

Past Trends

Perloff (1974, 163–64) demonstrates how planning responded to social trends in the decades of the 1940s to the 1970s. Advancing technology, the increasing importance of service employment, greater affluence, and increases in urbanization and metropolitanization during and after World War II created new planning problems. The federal government responded initially with physical and financial programs of mortgage insurance, public housing subsidies, urban highways, and urban renewal, including the 701 program of funding local plan preparation. These were followed by socially based programs aimed at reducing poverty, increasing citizen participation, and protecting civil rights and by environmental programs aimed at reducing impacts on natural resources. At the same time, the number of professional planners underwent an exponential increase, and planning skills broadened from design and apolitical physical planning to include social science concepts and methods, quantitative methods and models, politically focused program planning, budgeting and implementation, and interactive skills.

During the 1970s and 1980s, some of the earlier planning approaches, such as urban renewal, 701 planning assistance, and poverty programs, faded away. In their place, local efforts increased to manage growth and economic development, along with deepening federal and state efforts to mitigate environmental hazards and damages through clean air, water, and hazardous waste management programs and efforts to stimulate urban rehabilitation through tax incentives for historic preservation and grants for community development. Cities found themselves either competing for new enterprises or fighting to keep out undesirable uses.

Local planning adapted to include each new range of concerns. In an effort to cope with the issues of the fifties and sixties, local plans added sections on blight and redevelopment, neighborhood planning, transportation, and citizen participation. To meet the demands of the seventies and eighties, local plans broadened to include sections on growth management, economic development, environmental protection, waste management, historic preservation, development finance, affordable housing, and community development. The goals grew from accommodation of urban growth to include urban development management with specific mandates of social, environmental, and fiscal sensitivity.

In the process of change, the land use game has become more complex. No single set of problems or type of solution dominates; instead, the planner faces a complicated agenda of interlinked issues. In comparison with earlier periods when beauty or functionalism were the primary planning concerns, Hall (1989) characterized planning during the 1980s in terms of three sets of concerns: "The City Enterprising," featuring planning as real estate development; "The City of Ecologically Conscious NIMBYism," featuring special interest groups devoted to protecting the environment and stopping development; and "The City Pathological," featuring the problems of the urban underclass.

Current Trends

The local land use game continues to change in response to trends in national concerns, shifts in government programs, advances in technology, and the appearance of new ideas. Trends affecting the play of the game during the 1990s continue and extend those of the recent past, including state and local responses to federal devolution and deregulation, the deepening global environmental crisis, a worsening national infrastructure deficit, increasing organized opposition to development, widening urban social disintegration, and growing interdependence of all spheres of life.

Federal Devolution and Deregulation During the 1980s, the federal government devolved responsibility for a number of public programs affecting land use from national agencies to state and local governments. The increase in the number of growth-managing states is at least in part related to this trend. But the trend is much broader than this. Passing down responsibility for land use-related programs to state and local governments has taken place in many policy areas. One clear example is urban planning policy. In the past, the Department of Housing and Urban Development (HUD) administered a slate of programs ranging from funding for local comprehensive planning (the 701 program) to federally subsidized urban renewal and redevelopment. Under the Reagan and Bush administrations, these programs were phased out at the federal level, and states and local governments were expected to take them over.

Devolution also has taken place in many infrastructure programs, with the federal government setting standards for such functions as wastewater treatment but no longer providing sufficient funding for the necessary treatment plants. During the 1970s, some planners built their reputations as grants-writers who could shake the federal money tree for their jurisdictions. Since then, federal grants have become much scarcer.

With the federal government facing a large deficit that contributes to a fiscally conservative federal philosophy, it is unlikely that the devolution trend will change greatly in the future. For local planners, this means that Washington will be the source of standards, such as air and water quality criteria, but not the primary source of dollars to pay for meeting those standards. One response has been the "fiscalization" of local urban development policy, in which local governments have scrutinized all their capital expenditures for possible recapture from developers or other benefiting groups.

The federal deregulation of development finance institutions during the 1980s also triggered a number of changes in private land use investments as capital freed from past constraints was invested in more speculative projects, for example, the boom in suburban office and retail projects. A response to federal deregulation has been an increase in state and local development regulations and growth management initiatives.

State and Local Initiatives in Managing Growth Growth management appeared during the 1970s as a way for state and local governments to cope with development that outstripped public resources and infrastructure, at least partly in response to federal devolution. Growth management has become established as a way of interjecting quality of life, fiscal, equity, and other concerns into local development market processes (Brower, Godschalk, and Porter 1989). As state and local governments continue to wrestle with these problems, the natural tendency is to invent new methods of regulating the development market. Despite studies that have shown that new regulations are sometimes counterproductive, as in the effects of excessive building regulations on raising housing costs or of the exclusionary effects of lowering densities, the trend of increasing development market regulation is likely to continue. The implication for land planning is that advance analyses of new regulations' legal and constitutional impacts should be made, along with continuing efforts to monitor and evaluate their implementation, to ensure that they have no unforeseen negative consequences.

As land planning becomes more precise through improved information and coordination, and more directive through growth management programs, the debate over planning standards becomes more intense. One facet of this trend is the argument over whether to use performance standards that allow design flexibility or specification standards that define design requirements. For example, performance standards would permit a developer to achieve the desired rate of stormwater runoff through a variety of best-management practices; specification standards would require the developer to use a certain management practice, such as on-site detention ponds. Another facet is the discussion about the appropriate standard level to set as a planning target, as for example in choosing among alternative traffic capacity levels for local arterial streets. Finally, local governments may need to devise standards to reflect the impacts of more complex proposals, such as the addition of an assembly plant or a corporate headquarters, on the local economy. Planners are discovering that there is a great deal more to setting standards than simply picking a standard from a handbook.

Among the responses to the new regulatory climate are the increased use of public/private partnerships for large-scale development projects (Frieden and Sagalyn 1989). Developers see these partnerships as ways to negotiate the regulatory maze and build more certainty into project approvals. Governments see them as ways to supplement scarce capital resources and build more community objectives into project designs. Another trend, partially linked to the new regulatory climate, is a rash of overbuilding, especially of commercial and office projects, in rapidly developing "hot" local markets. This boom and bust phenomenon, leaving large inventories of underused space to be slowly absorbed by the market, complicates orderly local planning and forecasting of needs. Some observers believe that growth management could be an effective guard against the perennial problem of overbuilding (Leinberger 1993). Finally, the new climate has prompted a great deal of litigation as developers and those with land to sell challenge the restrictive land and development market controls that local governments have adopted (Babcock and Siemon 1985; Blaesser and Weinstein 1989).

Environmental Threats The national awareness of environmental threats that was launched with passage of the National Environmental Policy Act of 1969 and Earth Day in 1970 has gathered momentum with the discovery of more and more serious chemical hazards, along with the recognition of the progressive loss of species diversity and the possibility of accidental pollution due to human actions. The planning response has proceeded broadly from the enactment of new requirements in such federal laws as the Clean Air and Clean Water acts and Superfund (the Comprehensive Environmental Response, Compensation and Liability Act of 1980) to the setting of state and local goals for increases in recycling and the reduction of solid waste disposal in landfills. Attention to the global impacts of environmental disruptions, proceeding from the 1992 UN Conference in Rio and the signing of the Agenda for the 21st Century (Agenda 21), will likely result in further regulations and guidelines affecting local plans (UNDP 1993).

Recent public policy is recognizing what planners have long known—that land use and environmental quality are two sides of the same coin. The land use pattern affects air and water quality in numerous ways, from development in critical environmental areas to emissions of commuter automobiles to storm-water runoff from shopping centers. Early environmental protection programs focused on engineering solutions to pollution management rather than land planning solutions to pollution source reduction. More recent understanding of the land use-environment linkage appears in water quality programs that recognize "nonpoint sources" (overland flows) as critical contributors to stream pollution.

Recent air quality programs also recognize that excessive auto travel due to inefficient land use patterns separating home, work, and service areas contributes to air pollution. Long-term implications of the linkage show up in concern over global warming from the greenhouse effect—the most serious environmental threat of the twenty-first century. Depletion of the protective ozone layer is a function of the use of materials like chlorofluorocarbons, which are built into present life-styles. Should global warming not be halted, then one potential effect would be an increase in the rate of sea-level rise from the melting of the polar ice caps, which could flood many coastal areas. This flooding would not only endanger developed shorelines, but it would also destroy valuable coastal wetlands (Titus 1990).

This trend of recognizing the connections between land use and environmental quality should intensify as more scientific knowledge of environmental systems dynamics is accumulated and translated into public policy findings. At the local level, this is likely to result in more sophisticated environmental quality monitoring, the setting of more precise performance standards, and the development of new environmental impact methods.

Infrastructure Deficits   Many rapidly growing areas of the country face a serious infrastructure deficit. A recent report card on the nation's public works (National Council on Public Works Improvement 1988) graded no type of infrastructure higher than B, with several grades of C or less:

Highways C+
Mass transit C-
Aviation B-
Water resources B
Water supply B-
Wastewater C
Solid waste C-
Hazardous waste D.

Public works outlays on capital investment, relative to the Gross National Product, peaked in the 1960s at about 2.4 percent, and declined to around 1.3 percent in 1985.

A large sector of recent planning literature focuses on paying for growth, which involves looking for such alternative infrastructure funding sources as impact fees and other developer exactions (Frank and Rhodes 1987). Whether or not the federal government increases its infrastructure funding through use of the "peace dividend" resulting from the end of the cold war, state and local governments will continue to struggle with ensuring that development does not outstrip the capacity of supporting roads, water and sewer systems, schools, storm drainage, and other community facilities. The most stringent state measure to deal with this problem is Florida's concurrency system, under which the state requires that future land use plans ensure that infrastructure is available concurrently with projected development or the state can impose a development moratorium (De Grove 1989). Some local governments also mandate concurrency, as in the Adequate Public Facilities ordinance of Montgomery County, Maryland. One of the important effects of this "fiscalization" of land use planning is to highlight the connection between the future land use plan, the transportation and public facilities plans, and the capital improvement program (CIP).

Development Opposition and Dispute Resolution   In the United States, as well as in Britain and other developed countries, opposition to development has deepened in recent years. Citizen groups have learned to mobilize in opposition to private development proposals as well as to proposed public facilities. Taking advantage of laws that encourage public participation, of lessons from political campaigns, and of environmental concerns, anti-growth groups have stopped highways, dams, public housing projects, shopping centers, mixed use projects, and subdivisions. In response, alliances of landholders and developers have mounted counterattacks on land use and environmental regulations. Insisting that these regulations constitute a "taking" of their property, these groups have brought lawsuits demanding just compensation under the Fifth Amendment. Land use plans have been held up for years as interest group-dominated planning task forces have battled over each line of text and each area boundary. Planning has had to account for a new sort of public participation that has expanded far beyond the involvement of poor and minorities of the participation programs of the 1960s to include combative interest groups of every possible type.

One outcome of the higher intensity of public participation has been the creation of the alternative dispute resolution field, which is dedicated to finding ways around the impasses that public conflict creates. The implication is that local land use planning must include ways of involving community interest groups and dealing with their concerns, not just at the end but throughout the plan-making process, if the proposed plan is not to founder in a sea of controversy. It implies rethinking the traditional planning process as not only a technical effort but also a consensus-building effort (Susskind and Cruikshank 1987; Dotson, Godschalk, and Kaufman 1989). As these techniques have gained credibility for their fairness and effectiveness, more and more interest groups have accepted them as ways to settle planning disputes.

Negotiating consensus does not settle all disputes. Use of initiative and referendum tactics to defeat growth proposals is increasing, especially in rapidly growing western states like California, where 132 local growth referenda were held between 1971 and 1986. Interest groups still turn to the courts to challenge both private and public development projects, requiring land use planners to school themselves in legal and constitutional principles in order to practice. The implication is that local plans must take the interests of affected groups into careful account and must be constructed to withstand strict judicial scrutiny.

Urban Social Disintegration   Urban poor and minority groups continue to suffer from a slate of ills that have resisted planning solutions. Ghettos of poor, Hispanic, and black households are characterized by rising problems of crime, drugs, unemployment, school dropouts, and substandard housing. Despite Affirmative Action, Head Start, subsidized housing, and other targeted programs, these problems persist. Poor ethnic groups, concentrated in deteriorated inner-cities, poorly educated, without job skills, and strained by deteriorating family structures, make up an urban underclass that is isolated from mainstream society and its opportunities. As the Los Angeles riots of 1992 illustrate, these neighborhoods are potential tinder boxes waiting to erupt.

These problems of the poor are typically seen as the province of economic development programs. Types of local economic development approaches are distinguished by whether they simply attempt to facilitate private investment to generate growth ("corporatism") or to use public policy to encourage private investment that benefits low-income and ethnic minority groups (Robinson 1989). The type of approach used can have major implications for local land planning in terms of public land use policies applied to different parts of the urban area. For example, under a corporate approach, land plans might emphasize provision of opportunities for new branch plants, high-tech industries, or tourism through creation of industrial and theme park areas with ample infrastructure and development incentives. Under an approach aiming to benefit local workers, land plans might emphasize provision of opportunities for expansion of existing local enterprises and directing economic growth toward underdeveloped urban areas.

Technological and Organizational Interdependence Closer interdependence among organizations, businesses, and governments at all levels has been encouraged by the increase in access to computers and control and communications technology (Perloff 1980). The urban realm has expanded to a regional or global realm in many cases. Not only does this imply that local real estate development decisions may be made in foreign capitals, but it also implies that local manufacturing and retailing decisions may come from abroad as well, and that U.S. government policies may be based on international conditions as much as on national conditions. The implication for the local planning game is that its intelligence borders must be widened to encompass a broad realm of external factors and its processes must account for the internationalization of development and capital investment.

New developments in communications technology have released both the corporate headquarters (Heenan 1991) and the individual household from dependence on an urban location. With the freeing of locational choice, there is a diffusion of population and employment to small cities, towns, and rural areas. People are moving away from the traffic congestion, air pollution, crime, and drug problems of large cities in order to seek more attractive and secure living environments. In some cases, this results in movements to the outer edges of metropolitan areas. In other cases, it results in migration to different states, such as those in the Northeast, South, and Southwest (Kasarda 1992).

Many past land use plans have rested on slim information bases. The demands of developing and keeping current a comprehensive land information system have overwhelmed many local planning departments, especially in high-growth areas. With the advent of database management programs and the increasing availability of geographic information systems (GIS) on personal computers as well as larger computers, the new technology has made possible much greater information management capability.

Issuing the 1990 U.S. Census in digital format in the TIGER GIS system permits a higher level of spatial analysis of demographic data by local governments. Although converting a local government to this new technology entails many problems, including digitizing and linking to coordinate systems, the long-term prospect is for more effective land use analysis and decision-making, including the ability to monitor actions of absentee owners and transnational corporate citizens. An intriguing potential effect of government databases is the possibility for raising the level of public discourse over local policy proposals, such as impact fees, through increased public access and use.

Future Trends

As we near the end of the twentieth century, the world is going through major transformations. Turbulence has become a global condition with powerful local effects.[6] Among the forces driving the changes are: (1) the shift from an industrial to a postindustrial order, as marked by new microelectronic computing and communications technologies; (2) the emergence of transnational issues, such as atmospheric pollution; (3) the weakening of governments and the strengthening of interest groups; and (4) the enlargement of individual analytic and mobilization capabilities.[7] Rosenau (1990, 13) argues that the enlargement of people's capacities is the most powerful shift: "with their analytic skills enlarged and their orientations toward authority more self-conscious, today's persons-in-the-street are no longer as uninvolved, ignorant, and manipulable . . . as were their forebears." Because people are developing new modes of learning and new role scenarios at the same time that they are questioning compliance with governmental authority and refocusing their loyalties, future planning policy must expect more informed and skeptical citizen constituents. This will influence not only the process but also the type of future policy outcomes.

Of the current trends, only the federal devolution and deregulation policies appear to have substantial potential to be redirected in the decade ahead. Because they reflect a conservative approach to federal governance and were put in place by a particular administration, they are less grounded in outside conditions than the other trends. However, it is difficult to foresee whether the federal government will assume a stronger planning role in the future. The most likely catalysts for such a change would be major economic or environmental crises, both of which appear possible under increasing global interdependence.

The coming years are likely to bring even more environmental threats, leading to calls for extraordinary measures locally, nationally, and internationally. These will cover a wide front, from air and water quality to resource conservation measures to mitigation of natural and manmade hazards. They will force federal and state attention to, and investment in, new and more sophisticated environmental monitoring and management systems. And they will force governments at all levels to devote more effort to behavioral changes designed to reduce environmental impacts and to creative dispute resolution to solve environmental crises.

The infrastructure deficits also may worsen, bolstering calls for more public capital investment efforts. This will open opportunities for regional planning to link public works investment programs with settlement policies, but whether these opportunities will be used will depend upon overcoming Congress's long standing reluctance to acknowledge the national interest in land use planning.[8] A more likely scenario is a series of functional initiatives to develop individual systems of transportation, solid waste disposal, sewage treatment, and water supply that are linked with environmental protection initiatives in air and water quality, perhaps through funding incentives.

Development opposition is unlikely to diminish and will probably increase in intensity and sophistication. The Green party in Europe has already emerged in the United States, and the political tactics of the Sierra Club and of neighborhood organizations have benefited from their members' experience in political election campaigns. Planners and public officials can expect higher levels of conflict over development proposals from a variety of groups, often united in coalitions on grounds of environmental, traffic, neighborhood compatibility, health, and other impacts. These NIMBY (not in my back yard) campaigns against LULUs (locally unwanted land uses) will encompass a broad range of uses, from affordable housing and shopping centers to airports and land fills.

Urban social disintegration shows no signs of lessening. Despite new social policy initiatives, the major problems appear resistant. Unless substantial advances are made in employment, education, job training, drug eradication, housing, and other such problems, success stories may be few. Land planning alone can not deal with these problems, but it can be a major part of a coordinated strategy, such as President Clinton's Empowerment Zones and Enterprise Communities program.

Technological interdependence also is likely to become more pervasive as the global economy links urban areas around the world. This will have particular effects on future population and economic projections as national borders open and cross-national interaction increases. At the state and local level, one outcome could be an increase in ethnic concentrations and businesses. Another could be a much more active public/private sphere, not only in project development but also in strategic planning and information systems. For example, private-sector computer information systems, such as the real estate industry's Multiple Listing Service, could be linked to public-sector information systems, such as tax assessors' listings and planning policies, to provide a land and housing database that reflects both the market and public policy.

A promising new federal law that recognizes several of these future trends is the 1991 Intermodal Surface Transportation Efficiency Act (ISTEA). While it places major new responsibilities on state and local planners, it also provides significant federal funding to help carry out these responsibilities (Transportation Research Board 1993). Among its innovations are the linking of land use plans with multimodal transportation plans, investment decisions, air quality standards, energy conservation, environmental protection, and infrastructure management. ISTEA boosts comprehensive planning and also gives state and local governments more flexibility in determining transportation solutions. It makes highway funds available for wetland banking, wildlife habitat mitigation, historic sites, air quality improvement, bicycle and pedestrian facilities, and highway beautification.

Under ISTEA, the local metropolitan planning organization (MPO) is responsible for developing a long-range, twenty-year transportation plan and a three-year transportation improvement program (TIP), including funding sources. The planning process must include considerations of land use, intermodal connectivity, and transit service enhancement. The MPOs geographic planning area must include the urbanized area as defined by the U.S. Census Bureau, plus the area forecast to become urbanized within the next twenty years.[9] At the state level, a statewide transportation plan and TIP are required. And states must implement six new management systems covering highway pavement, bridges, highway safety, traffic congestion, public transportation, and intermodal transportation. The act stresses citizen participation, requiring involvement of environmentalists, transit advocates, and other interest groups in the planning process.

One feature of ISTEA is its link to the 1990 amendments to the Clean Air Act, which allow the Department of Transportation to withhold federal matching funds from road and sewer projects in metropolitan areas that do not attain air quality standards (Transportation Research Board 1993). ISTEA provides Congestion Mitigation and Air Quality Improvement Program funds for transportation projects in nonattainment areas for ozone and carbon monoxide. If these nonattainment areas are in Transportation Management Areas (TMAs), areas with populations of more than two hundred thousand, then efforts must be made to decrease single-occupant vehicle travel in order to receive ISTEA funding. Some observers see ISTEA as the carrot and the Clean Air Act as the stick to force a major transition in transportation planning (Plotus 1993).

Continuing changes in federal legislation and social concerns demand that planning be a continuous learning process in order to stay abreast of the land use game. This is one of a number of pressures on the land use planner.

Pressures on Local Planners

Unlike other professionals, land use planners work in a fishbowl under constant public scrutiny. Engineers designing a bridge or surgeons doing a heart transplant do not have citizens constantly questioning their decisions. The fishbowl effect has a significant influence on land planning methods and recommendations, which must be not only technically sound but also politically acceptable.

Playing the land use game is a challenge, given the demands of other players as well as the changing trends. Player competition is often fierce. Local land use planners are expected to respond to market, government, and public demands while performing their technical duties and being stewards of the overall public interest. Pressure on local land planning is especially intense because planners can influence not only the content of proposed plans but also the rules by which development proposals are judged, the schedules and standards for provision of public facilities, the information provided to decision-makers in their deliberations over plans and projects, and the values expressed in assessments of impacts. Planners are accountable both for their own plays and for their management of the game rules under which the other players operate.

Developers expect land use planning to facilitate their difficult and risky efforts to meet the market demand for developed land. They prefer the certainty of adopted public plans that spell out the location and scheduling of infrastructure improvements and the allowable uses of land. They are uncomfortable with ambiguous exaction policies that they cannot cost out in advance of planning their projects. They fear uncertain land use policies that might downzone land after they have invested in it. Change, in the form of urban development, is their business. They like land markets with minimum constraints, regulations with maximum flexibility and certainty of outcome, and vigorous public funding of infrastructure.

Publics, particularly those in slow-growth, neighborhood protection, or environmental groups, expect land use planning to facilitate their sincere efforts to intervene in the development market on behalf of their particular interests. They too prefer adopted plans and infrastructure schedules to the extent that these are in line with their objectives. But they applaud exactions, downzonings, and moratoria that slow the pace of change. Contrary to development interests, they like land markets with maximum constraints, regulations with minimum flexibility, and private funding of infrastructure.

Federal and state government officials expect land use planning to facilitate their efforts to carry out their agencies' policies, such as transportation, education, air quality, and flood plain management. Given their specialized concerns and their distance from the local area, they are less pervasive in land use debates, but their standards often carry weight due to the sanctions that accompany them in the form of grants for compliance or penalties for noncompliance.

Local government officials also have expectations for land use planning. Host government officials expect planners to respond to their demands on plan content to meet campaign promises and constituent requests, and they use tactics ranging from public criticism to job threats to back up their expectations. The elected and appointed officials of neighboring local governments do not enjoy direct influence over planners in other jurisdictions but may attempt to use persuasion or negotiation to achieve joint solutions to shared land use problems or conflicts.

Besides the pressures from other players, planners face pressures to master the changing agendas of planning issues. It is a constant challenge to stay abreast of the technical side of planning practice as it grows in response to new issues and demands. For example, land use planners in the recent past had to learn about the legal and constitutional issues of growth management in order to survive court challenges and about the fiscal issues of exactions and capital improvement programs in order to survive local budget shortages. More recently, they have had to learn about computer databases and geographic information systems in order to manage complex planning information programs and about dispute resolution and consensus-building techniques in order to avoid decision impasses.

Countervailing Planning Responses

In the face of pressures to alter land plans to suit a changing panoply of public and private interests and trends, local planners need a strong sense of their own role values to maintain the integrity of the planning process. While the other players unabashedly advocate their own interests and often feel free to use any available means to achieve their ends, planners are expected to advocate the overall public interest and to be constrained by professional methods, ethics, and tenets to facilitate achievement of the ends of the other players. While planners can make substantive recommendations, these will be subject to intense scrutiny and attack by other players. And because planners write and enforce the rules of the game, they will be subject to constant pressure to favor one side or the other or to make exceptions for them.

Planners thus must develop some special capabilities to play the local planning game well. Among these are vision, comprehensiveness, technical competence, fairness, consensus-building, and innovativeness. Together they constitute the qualities that the public and the planning profession expect to find in planners.[10]

The *vision* to look beyond immediate concerns and issues to the needs of the future is a key attribute of the land planner. Some critics have charged that the current emphases on management and implementation detract from the long-range vision of the future that planners are expected to develop; others have complained that future visions turn out to be utopian dreams that can never be realized. We hold that the effective land planner must be willing to look ahead as well as to solve present problems. Without claiming to know exactly what the future will bring, the planner nevertheless must work to guide urban development toward future forms that embody such social values as equity, accessibility, efficiency, and environmental quality. By insisting on looking beyond immediate payoffs, the planner injects the needs of future generations into the debate about urban form and change. By systematically evaluating the outcomes of past planning attempts, the planner enables the community to learn how to plan more effectively.

The ability to *think comprehensively* is another key attribute of the land planner. The functional emphases of state and federal government policies and the demands of pressure groups all encourage fragmentation. Some planners succumb and produce one-dimensional plans that cater to a single goal or function. We hold that the effective land planner must attempt to integrate land use, transportation, public services, environmental protection, hazard mitigation, public finance, historic preservation, and other related functions into a comprehensive plan that accounts for the connections among these areas. Similarly, the interests of those affected by the plan should be taken into account. Although this makes planning more complex and less neat, it is recognition of such complexity that underlies the significant and effective plan.

Technical competence is also vital. In the emphasis on political effectiveness, it can be forgotten that the cornerstone of planning's authority is the quality of its technical work. It is acceptable for an advocate to argue for a policy or plan change on the basis of a partisan analysis, but the public planner is expected to carry out technical tasks with rigor and objectivity. In land use planning, technical competence includes analysis, with its breaking down of data to seek out trends and meaning, as well as synthesis, with its recombination of elements into proposed designs. It involves framing problems as well as developing solutions. We hold that both the analytical and synthetic work of plan-making should follow strict professional canons.

Fairness is another attribute that the land planner must emphasize. In a fair process for plan-making, all groups affected by the plan must have an opportunity to influence its content. Fairness also involves analyzing plan alternatives in terms of their effects upon different groups and seeking to equalize the costs and benefits. The courts may overturn plans that blatantly ignore the principle of equity, but many subtle ways to plan unfairly may escape legal scrutiny. We hold that equity of process and content is a critical ingredient of socially responsible land planning.

Skill at *consensus-building* is increasingly important. From their positions in the middle of land use arguments planners are bombarded with opposing views. At the same time, they are in a unique position to see common interests and to help forge consensus solutions. They can use the occasion of plan-making to build consensus through the techniques of alternative dispute resolution (Fisher, Ury, and Patton 1991). They can look beyond the use of majority power, which often leaves a residue of bitterness, and seek broader agreements that satisfy minority interests as well. Accomplishing this calls for a great deal of political sensitivity. We hold that plan-making should be a consensus-building process in which issues are recognized and resolved before they escalate into impasses.

Finally, willingness to advocate *innovation* is a necessary attribute of effective local planning. Communities look to their planners for awareness of new approaches to urban problems. Although there is always pressure to repeat tried-and-true solutions, it is also important to consider policy innovations. By their nature, innovations require more effort to launch and involve more risk than traditional means do. At the same time, social and technological change moves on, and urban problems increasingly demand new, creative solutions that are responsive to change (Teitz 1974). Innovation may take the form of efforts to devise more effective planning or growth management techniques or to create more attractive and safe urban forms. We hold that effective land planning should not be timid about advocating change in its process or content.

NOTES

1. As Rudel (1989, 18–19) notes, others (Feagin 1983; Babcock and Siemon 1985) have also made the analogy to a game but do not explain why urban land use conversion could be considered a game. Rudel finds the empirical basis in land use politics, where each participant's outcomes are dependent not only on individual actions or those of nature but also upon those of other participants whose interests are sometimes opposing and sometimes supporting. This interdependence is the defining characteristic of a game. It forces players into the cooperative/competitive process that various planning simulation games are structured around (Duke 1964; Feldt 1972; Wynn 1985). It is also at the heart of such advice books as *Winning the Land Use Game: A Guide for Developers and Citizen Protesters* (Logan 1982).

2. Long, in a provocative essay (1958), has laid out the conceptual framework of local governance as an ecology of games. We would add that present-day development ecologies extend well beyond the local area in many cases. The larger political economy could be seen as the first-tier game, the outputs of which influence local planning and project decision outcomes within the second-tier game. Decisions of large corporations and foreign investors can act as wild cards in the land use game, removed from the give and take of the local development market but having a powerful impact on it. Often these wild-card projects are located at the outer edges of the urban area in what Garreau (1991) has termed "edge cities."

3. Before the placement of development projects, the value of nonagricultural land is initially established on the basis of its location relative to public infrastructure investments—streets and transit systems, water and waste disposal systems, schools and parks, and other community facilities. Such urban infrastructure is a prerequisite to urban development.

4. The community builder concept is exemplified by James Rouse, developer of the new town of Columbia, Maryland, as well as a number of downtown redevelopment projects. The Urban Land Institute, a nonprofit real estate development education and research organization, published the first *Community Builders Handbook* in 1947 and now issues a Community Builders Handbook series devoted to such various types of development as office, residential, and shopping center. An account of the rise of community builders in the United States is provided by Weiss (1987).

5. As of 1993, the states with approved coastal management programs under the Coastal Zone Management Act of 1972 are: Washington, Oregon, California, Massachusetts, Wisconsin, Rhode Island, Michigan, North Carolina, Hawaii, Maine, Maryland, New Jersey, Alaska, Delaware, Alabama, South Carolina, Louisiana, Mississippi, Connecticut, Pennsylvania, Florida, New Hampshire, New York, and Virginia. In addition, Puerto Rico, Virgin Islands, Guam, Northern Marianas, and American Samoa have approved programs.

6. This has led planners to speculate on new ways to envision future strategies in the face of endemic uncertainty, including radical theories of planning as "fuzzy gam-

bling," where the rules of the game are largely unknown and subject to great change during the course of play (Dror 1986).

7. These forces are adapted from a list provided by Rosenau (1990, 12–16).

8. The last effort to gain congressional approval of a national land use strategy was defeated during the Nixon administration in the early 1970s. As a compromise, Congress enacted the Coastal Zone Management Act of 1972, which applied only to coastal states and territories and was based on voluntary participation.

9. There is an interesting parallel between the requirement to plan for the area forecast to become urbanized within the next twenty years and the concept of an urban growth boundary or urban transition area, where a local government seeks to guide development within a twenty-year period by means of infrastructure programs and growth plans. ISTEA may encourage many more local governments to develop official urban growth boundaries and transition areas as discussed under land classification in later chapters in this book.

10. The American Institute of Certified Planners issues a code of ethics that sets forth the professional qualities expected of the planner. These include descriptions of the planner's responsibility to the public, to clients and employers, to the profession and colleagues, and to his or her self (AICP 1990). For a more detailed discussion of land use ethics, see Beatley (1994).

REFERENCES

American Institute of Certified Planners. 1990. *AICP 1990/91 roster.* Washington, D.C.: American Institute of Certified Planners.

Audirac, Ivonne, Anne H. Shermyen, and Marc T. Smith. 1990. Ideal urban form and visions of the good life: Florida's growth management dilemma. *Journal of the American Planning Association* 56(4): 470–82.

Babcock, Richard F., and Charles Siemon. 1985. *The zoning game revisited.* Boston: Oelgeschlager, Gunn and Hain.

Beatley, Timothy. 1994. *Ethical land use: Principles of policy and planning.* Baltimore: Johns Hopkins University Press.

Beauregard, Robert. 1990. Bringing the city back in. *Journal of the American Planning Association* 56(2): 210–14.

Blaesser, Brian, and Alan Weinstein, eds. 1989. *Land use and the Constitution: Principles for planning practice.* Chicago: Planners Press.

Brower, David, David Godschalk, and Douglas Porter, eds. 1989. *Understanding growth management: Critical issues and a research agenda.* Washington, D.C.: Urban Land Institute.

Calthorpe, Peter. 1989. *The pedestrian pocket book: A new suburban design strategy.* Princeton: Princeton Architectural Press.

De Grove, John. 1989. Growth management and governance. In *Understanding growth management: Critical issues and a research agenda,* ed. David Brower, David Godschalk, and Douglas Porter. Washington, D.C.: Urban Land Institute.

———. 1992. *Planning and growth management in the states.* Cambridge: Lincoln Institute of Land Policy.

Dotson, Bruce, David Godschalk, and Jerome Kaufman. 1989. *The planner as dispute resolver.* Washington, D.C.: National Institute for Dispute Resolution.

Dror, Yehezkel. 1986. Planning as fuzzy gambling: A radical perspective on coping with uncertainty. In *Planning in turbulence,* ed. David Morlely and Arie Shachar. Jerusalem: Magnes Press, Hebrew University.

Duke, Richard. 1964. *Gaming-simulation in urban research.* Ann Arbor: University of Michigan Press.

Feagin, Joe R. 1983. *The urban real estate game.* Englewood Cliffs: Prentice-Hall.

Feldt, Allen. 1972. *The community land use game.* New York: Free Press.

Fisher, Roger, William Ury, and Bruce Patton. 1991. *Getting to yes: Negotiating agreement without giving in.* 2d ed. New York: Penguin Books.

Frank, James, and Robert Rhodes, eds. 1987. *Development exactions.* Chicago: Planners Press.

Frieden, Bernard J., and Lynne B. Sagalyn. 1989. *Downtown, Inc.: How America rebuilds cities.* Cambridge: MIT Press.

Garreau, Joel. 1991. *Edge city: Life on the new frontier.* New York: Doubleday.

Godschalk, David R., et al. 1979. *Constitutional issues of growth management.* Chicago: Planners Press.

Godschalk, David R. 1992. Implementing coastal zone management: 1972–1990. *Coastal Management* 51(3): 93–116.

Jacobs, Allan. 1978. *Making city planning work.* Chicago: Planners Press.

Hall, Peter. 1989. The turbulent eighth decade: Challenges to American city planning. *Journal of the American Planning Association* 55(3): 275–82.

Heenan, David A. 1991. *The new corporate frontier: The big move to small town USA.* New York: McGraw Hill.

Kasarda, John D. 1992. Demographic and related demand-side factors affecting longer-term commercial real estate returns. Paper presented at the Prudential Real Estate Investment Strategy Conference, Pinehurst, N.C., May 16–21.

Leinberger, Christopher. 1993. Suburbia. In *Land use in transition.* Washington, D.C.: Urban Land Institute.

Logan, Carolyn J. 1982. *Winning the land use game: A guide for developers and citizen protesters.* New York: Praeger.

Logan, John R., and Harvey L. Molotch. 1987. *Urban fortunes: The political economy of place.* Berkeley: University of California Press.

Long, Norton. 1958. The local community as an ecology of games. *American Journal of Sociology* 61(2): 251–61.

Los Angeles 2000 Committee. 1988. *LA 2000: A city for the future.* Los Angeles: Mayor's Office.

Lynch, Kevin. 1981. *A theory of good city form.* Cambridge: MIT Press.

Lucy, William. 1988. *Close to power.* Chicago: Planners Press.

Maranda, Edward et al. 1980. *Federal policy impacts on United States land use.* St. Paul: Metropolitan Council of the Twin Cities Area.

National Council on Public Works Improvement. 1988. *Fragile foundations: A report on America's public works.* Washington, D.C.: National Council on Public Works Improvement.

Perloff, Harvey. 1974. The Evolution of Planning Education. In *Planning in America: Learning from turbulence,* ed. David Godschalk. Washington, D.C.: American Institute of Planners.

———. 1980. *Planning the post-industrial city.* Chicago: Planners Press.

Plotus, F. K., Jr. 1993. Refreshing ISTEA. *Planning* 59(2): 9–12.

Robinson, Carla. 1989. Municipal approaches to economic development: Growth and distribution policy. *Journal of the American Planning Association* 55(3): 283–95.

Rosenau, James. 1990. *Turbulence in world politics: A theory of change and continuity.* Princeton: Princeton University Press.

Rudel, Thomas K. 1989. *Situations and strategies in American land-use planning.* Cambridge: Cambridge University Press.

Susskind, Lawrence, and Jeffrey Cruikshank. 1987. *Breaking the impasse: Consensual approaches to resolving public disputes.* New York: Basic Books.

Teitz, Michael. 1974. Toward a responsive planning methodology. In *Planning in America: Learning from turbulence,* ed. David Godschalk. Washington, D.C.: American Institute of Planners.

Titus, James. 1990. Strategies for adapting to the greenhouse effect. *Journal of the American Planning Association* 56(3): 311–23.

Transportation Research Board. 1993. Transportation planning, programming, and finance. Conference Proceedings. Circular no. 406. Washington, D.C.: Transportation Research Board.

UNDP. 1993. UNDP's handbook and guidelines for environmental management and sustainable development. New York: United Nations Development Program.

Weiss, Mark A. 1987. *The rise of the community builders: The American real estate industry and urban land planning.* New York: Columbia University Press.

Wynn, Martin. 1985. *Planning games: Case study simulations in land management and development.* London: E. and F. N. Spon.

2

Concepts of Land Use Change Management

> . . . a turbulent environment tends to put an organization at odds with itself: high complexity needs to be addressed with intense intellectual effort in the analysis of information and the planning for contingencies, while high dynamism calls for a great deal of sociopolitical energy, for bargaining, compromising, and mobilizing, resulting in two activities . . . inherently antithetical to each other.
>
> —Rosenau 1990, 62

American city and regional planning has been correctly described as a "turbulent" activity due to the complexity and dynamism of its social, physical, institutional, and policy environments.[1] Within this changing practice matrix, planners must learn their way into an uncertain future through a planning process that combines rational and adaptive techniques. No single theory of planning or urban change adequately describes the complex and dynamic reality of land use planning practice under these conditions of competition, change, and reciprocity.

Because change is the only constant in turbulent times, a conceptual approach based on "management of land use change" comes closest to matching the reality of planning practice. Under this approach, the goals of all land use planning activities—intelligence collection, advance planning, development management, and problem solving—are to monitor and guide continuing change to best benefit the community. To do so, land planners must balance three competing sets of land values: social, market, and environmental. This balancing takes place through community discussion or "discourse" on the content and procedures of land use change. The form of the consensus-building process influences the distribution of power and influence over land use outcomes.

Managing Land Use Change as Practice Rationale

At the core of local land use planning is the effort to influence the direction of land use change. This effort is carried out through the preparation and implementation of future land use plans and policies, through the review and approval of development projects, through the recommendation of capital improvement programs, and through participation in ongoing local government decision-making and problem solving. Both an intellectual and a sociopolitical activity, it is guided by a mixture of community values, professional standards, legal precedents, political tactics, and long-range visions. This total effort, which we call "managing land use change," is the fundamental rationale for the theory and practice of land use planning.[2]

The activity of land use planning combines analysis, synthesis, and consensus formation. On the analytical side, the methods are primarily quantitative and statistical. On the synthesis side, the methods are primarily qualitative and design-based. On the consensus formation side, the methods are primarily interactional and based on conflict management. Managing land use change is not simply preparing and adopting an "end state" master plan and expecting it to be built-out at the end of the twenty-year planning period. Although the approach includes an advance plan aimed at guiding future development, it also includes actions to monitor and respond to change, to build consensus for planning goals and objectives, and to enlist public building and spending powers in plan implementation.

Turbulence complicates change management. The history of U.S. planning exhibits continuing turbulence, as practitioners work within a complex, dynamic institutional and policy environment to solve a changing slate of urban problems. Turbulence involves not only an increasing rate of social and technological change but also an apparent decrease in our ability to guide or predict that change (Schon 1971; Michael 1973; Perloff 1974; Hall 1989; Rosenau 1990). Rather than leading events, in turbulent times planners are constantly responding to events. Morley (1986, 5) identifies the characteristics of turbulence as

—accelerating rates of change;
—increasing scale of perturbations or shifts in conditions;
—increasing unpredictability of events;
—a continuing sense of crisis;
—frequent confrontations with problems so complex as to be inaccessible to normal intervention strategies; and
—increasing time spent on responding to unanticipated consequences of previous actions.

To account for the turbulent nature of the public domain, planning can be seen as a learning process in which the future is treated as an emergent state not completely predictable from present knowledge. Instead, plans are viewed as a series of approximations to be adapted to future conditions as those conditions become more evident. Lynch (1981, 115–16) speaks of the human settlement as a "learning ecology" in which actors are capable of consciously modifying the parts of the urban system, maintaining continuity while permitting progressive change. This requires methods for generating knowledge and agreeing upon actions in the face of less-than-complete information. The goal is to recognize uncertainty without being paralyzed by it. The necessary techniques must be both *rational* in attempting to project and guide the future on the basis of factual analysis and *adaptive* in responding strategically to unforeseen changes as they occur.

In addition to sociopolitical change, land planners face continuing changes in their client communities through processes of growth and decline. They must regularly monitor and interpret these processes in order to understand the stocks and flows of urbanization and to estimate the impacts of public intervention policies. They must engage in dialogue with the other players in the land use game, adjusting rules and strategies in response to their changing demands and needs. Their land use plans rarely deal with the creation of totally new communities. Occasionally, they deal with major changes in land development programs in response to new state or federal policies, new interpretations of local conditions, or new political issues. Typically, they deal with *incremental* additions of new urban land and infrastructure at the fringe and deterioration of older neighborhoods and public facilities at the core. Ensuring that the cumulative impact of these incremental changes does not disturb community continuity but does foster progressive change, as Lynch suggests, is the land use game challenge.

No single theory of planning or urban change adequately describes the full range and complexity of land use planning practice. Neither descriptive theories that purport to explain how planning and urban change do occur nor normative theories that assert how planning and urban change should occur encompass the full dimensions of reality.[3] Most individual planners fashion their own practice guidelines, building a working synthesis from a variety of experiential and theoretical sources to respond to their working needs. Such syntheses must encompass both planning *process* theories to guide the making of plans and urban change *content* theories to guide the substance of plans.[4] As a foundation for our approach, we next review selected concepts from both the process and the content literature. Our purpose is not to recreate planning theory but simply to point out some useful ideas for land use planning.

Planning Process Theories

The science of muddling through may well give way to
the science of modeling through.
—Rosenau 1990, 324

Competing planning process theories provide important but incomplete procedural models for carrying out planning efforts. Of all these models, that best known and widely used for long-range planning is "rational planning," with its systematic forward progression from goal setting to implementation and back again through a feedback loop (Figure 2-1). Rational planning is both a normative theory in that it advocates a particular format for making planning decisions and a descriptive theory in that it describes the steps that most planning processes attempt to follow.

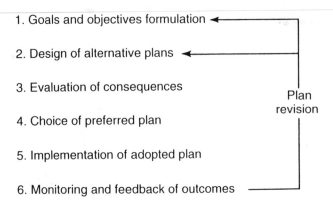

Figure 2-1. The Rational Planning Model: A Logical Progression from Goal-Setting to Implementation and Back

The rational planning approach, as applied to land use planning, consists of a series of activities:

1. goals and objectives formulation, in which community leaders and citizens help formulate a long-range vision;
2. design of alternatives, in which planners and advisory groups prepare alternative scenarios to achieve the vision;
3. evaluation of consequences, in which the projected costs and benefits of land use alternatives are considered;
4. choice of preferred alternative, in which community participants and planners settle on a consensus plan;
5. implementation, in which the land use plan is adopted and carried out, typically as part of a comprehensive plan;
6. monitoring and feedback of outcomes, in which the progress of development is compared with the objectives of the plan; and
7. plan revision, in which the plan is reanalyzed after a period of five years or so, and the re-planning process is begun, perhaps going back to a fundamental restudy of goals and objectives and/or alternatives design if major changes have occurred, or perhaps only to reconsideration of implementation if adopted techniques are not effective.

In its pure form, the rational model does not consider the necessary adaptations that land use plans must go through in order to gain community acceptance and respond to continuing change. However, procedures for citizen participation help build community acceptance of plan decisions, and day-to-day plan implementation and development management procedures respond to ongoing change. The combination could be seen as a synthetic "rational-adaptive" model. In this model, plan-making is primarily a rational analysis- and design-based activity, whereas plan implementation is primarily an incremental administrative- and political-based activity. Some examples of the land use plan preparation techniques associated with the rational model and the adaptive techniques used to carry out plans in a changing context are:

Rational Techniques	Adaptive Techniques
Data analysis	Public participation and discourse
Trend projection	Consensus-building and conflict resolution
Supply and demand derivation	Monitoring and problem solving
System modeling	Impact analysis and mitigation
Goal and objective statements	Capital budgeting and project review
Plan design	Plan evaluation and amendment

The rational model has come under fire from advocates of other descriptive process theories. It has been argued that no one follows the pure rational model because of its exorbitant demands for information, its artificial separation of the stages of decision-making, and its unreasonable expectation for consideration of all possible alternatives. Instead, it is claimed that decisions are made by "muddling through," using "incremental" theory (Braybrooke and Lindblom 1963).

We do not quarrel with the idea that incremental adjustments figure into land use planning, but we take issue with the straw man definition of a pure and unachievable rationality. We support the rational model's connection between goals, objectives, and policies; its staged progression from goal-setting to implementation; and its use of logic and deduction to analyze relevant information. In company with adaptive techniques, the rational model is the strongest available theoretical foundation for land use planning.

The rational model has also been criticized by advocates of competing normative process theories such as "strategic" planning (Bryson and Einsweiler 1988; Bryson 1988), "critical theory" (Forester 1989), and dispute resolution (Susskind and Cruikshank 1987), who all argue for the merits of their approaches.[5] We readily concede that each of these alternative approaches offers some practical advantages, but rather than seeing them as alternatives we believe that their strengths can be incorporated into our rational-adaptive model.

Strategic planning narrows the task of more comprehensive analysis by focusing on only selected critical issues. But strategic planning relies on a rational process of assessing the environment, creating a vision of success, and selecting actions in light of a range of possible futures. Critical theory insists on processes for open communication, including critiques of plans, among all affected interests. These processes are incorporated in participation and information-sharing techniques commonly used in land use planning and development management. Alternative dispute resolution calls for involving all stakeholders in negotiating consensus over plan disagreements. Consensus-building increasingly is incorporated into rational planning approaches; for example, the New Jersey state land use plan is the product of both rational analysis and negotiation with local interests in a "cross-acceptance" process (New Jersey State Planning Commission 1991; Innes 1992).

Despite its critics, we believe that the rational model still offers the most solid platform for advance plan-making when combined with techniques for participation and consensus-building. Not only is the notion of choosing means to achieve defined ends attractive to planners, but it also appeals to publics as a common-sense way to anticipate the future. A rational-adaptive approach is a workable way to achieve the linkage of knowledge to action that Friedmann (1987) sees as the hallmark of planning.

The microelectronic revolution has boosted planners' capacities to manage large bodies of information and compare alternative strategies in more systematic ways. However, simply adding analytic and consensus-building capacity to the rational model does not deal with all of the elements of effective land use change management, omitting the necessary parallel functions of intelligence collection, development management, and problem solving.

To remedy these planning process gaps, we propose at the end of this chapter a model of community planning discourse that supplements the rational model with extensive public participation, and, in the next chapter, a land planning program that includes the other necessary processes of intelligence collection, development management, and problem solving. We believe that the claims made by advocates of strategic planning, critical theory, dispute resolution, and incrementalism can be dealt with by this discourse model and planning program in combination.

We now look briefly at the potential sources of urban change content ideas important to the practice of land use change management. Each of these theories offers a lens for understanding land use change.

Urban Change Content Theories

Competing urban change theories provide important, but incomplete, models of urban change content. The most complete formulation is found in political economy theories, which explain urban development in terms of culture-driven efforts to organize urban space to serve social needs, including both use for housing and business and for profit from real estate transactions (Logan and Molotch 1987).[6] Other theories offer more specialized views. Theories of good city form propose performance dimensions for assessing the spatial form of cities (Lynch 1981). Land market theories describe the relationships between land owners, purchasers, and developers as land progresses from rural to urban (Kaiser and Weiss 1970) and suggest how regulations impact on land sales and prices (Nelson 1988; Fischel 1989).

Classical economic theories, such as those of Alonso and Wingo, explain spatial structure through the workings of the market in allocating space to users according to supply and demand relationships in an equilibrium system. These theories were used in a number of early urban development models (Chapin and Kaiser 1979, chs. 14, 15). Human ecology theories explain urban development through market-driven economic competition for urban space, in which each type of land user ends up in the location to which the user is best adapted (Hawley 1950). Marxian theories explain urban development in terms of the exploitation of workers by capitalists (Harvey 1981). Ecological theories describe the stages of natural environmental equilibrium and threats to this condition (Holling and Goldberg 1971).

The most relevant unit of analysis for the land planner is land use change. Issues of land and housing market performance, land conversion, economic competition for space, and environmental equilibrium offer various explanations of how land use change takes place and what effects that change has. However, the bottom line for the land planner is what occurs and is proposed to occur on the land. This is not to say that these broader theories are not relevant, only that they do not provide sufficient guidance to the work of land planning. For such guidance the land planner turns to middle range concepts of planned urban change such as those of Thomas Rudel.

Rudel (1989) combines a number of the social science theories into two approaches: human ecological and political-economic. He argues that both of these focus on "structural" variables and that a game theory approach is also needed to incorporate "process" variables because land use planning involves interactions among parties interested in land use. He characterizes the human ecology approach (e.g., Berry and Kasarda 1977) as assuming that market changes, often resulting from actions such as the construction of new highways, produce demographic changes and changes in land use regulations over time. "In most cases a change in land use, repeated dozens of times on different parcels of land, gradually alters the configuration of interests in a community, and this change in interests causes a change in policy. For example, the steady construction of single-family homes gradually populates rural-urban fringe communities with people who lobby for and eventually obtain restrictive land-use controls for residential areas" (Rudel 1989, 11).

Rudel characterizes the political-economic approach as adding two missing variables: the influence of powerful political interests (such as developers versus organized interest groups) and the salience of land use conflicts shaped by differences between places (such as urban versus rural areas). Within this group who see political inequalities rather than market forces determining land use policies, he includes Marxist theorists and authors of progressive case studies (e.g., Clavel 1986). He finds the model of cities as "growth machines" that Logan and Molotch (1987) expound to be the most useful of the political economy models because it discusses not only the structural variables but also interactional variables.

Rudel builds his theory on the notion of the influence on future outcomes of *sequential interactions* among land use actors. Drawing from game theory findings that show that players are more cooperative and less conflictual if they know that they will play repeated rounds with the same players, he develops the notion of "tit-for-tat" land use behavior. He then identifies three types of land use change areas: (1) slow-growing rural areas with relatively stable residents and low rates of land use conversion, where informal tit-for-tat land use agreements among neighbors predominate; (2) rapidly growing rural-urban places, where growth raises mobility and destroys recurrent relationships necessary for tit-for-tat agreements, encouraging the adoption of legal rules (such as zoning) to control land use conversion; and (3) slow-growing urban places, where stable neighbors contest each development proposal and the increase in disputes leads to more court cases and negotiated settlements, where a more formal tit-for-tat behavior is encouraged.[7] In his view, community growth leads to a rural-to-urban developmental sequence with a layering on of new types of regulatory procedures in which older procedures are not fully displaced so that informal agreements, zoning, and mediation may coexist.

Focusing on management of land use change provides a clear practice rationale in which to organize concepts from various urban theories. Justification for planners assuming this responsibility is found in the failure of both the market and political institutions to deal adequately with management of land use change. This responsibility has been assigned to planners through the standard state enabling acts that grant to local governments the power to plan for—and regulate the use and development of—their land. Although planning has not been accorded the status of a "fourth power of government" as Rexford Guy Tugwell recommended in 1940 (cited in Friedmann 1987, 106), it has been recognized as a legitimate agency for managing land use change within the constraints of democratic governance.

The content of land use change management can be described in terms of three value sets that must be brought into balance by land planning. We next review salient land use planning concepts associated with each of these value sets as an aid to the balancing task.

Three Sets of Land Use Values

In managing change, local land planners must deal with three powerful types of land values. Social use values express the weight that people give to various arrangements of land use as settings for living their lives; this view sees land use as a facilitator of desirable activity patterns and social aspirations. Market values express the weight that people give to land as a commodity; this view sees land use as a real estate profit medium. Ecological values express the weight that people give to the natural systems on the land; this view sees land use as a potential environmental threat to be mitigated. These three values are sometimes separate and competing, sometimes intermingled and supporting.

Social Use Values

Concepts of social use values include those derived from theories of urban form, activities systems, and the social neighborhood. They all consider connections between the physical environment and the quality of life, although their underlying concerns differ. Urban form theories are concerned with designing the physical environment. Activities systems theories are concerned with understanding the behavior patterns of urban residents. Neighborhood theories are concerned with both design and behavior, but at the subcity level.

In practice, social use values often are presented to the planner in the form of arguments against urban change and in support of the status quo. But social use values also can be enhanced through well-managed growth and change.

Urban Form   Lynch (1981) has proposed a theory of "good" city form, relating social use values to change and stability in urban physical structure. According to Lynch (118–19), good urban form has a number of dimensions that can be expressed in varying degrees.

1. *Vitality* is support provided by the city's urban structure for human functions, biological requirements, and capabilities.
2. *Sense* is clarity of residents' perception of the city as a structure in time and space and the connection between the urban structure and residents' values.
3. *Fit* is the match between the city's spaces, channels, and equipment and the activities of its people.
4. *Access* is the ability to reach persons, activities, resources, services, information, or places within the urban form.
5. *Control* is the control by users of use, access, and change of spaces and activities within the city.
6. *Efficiency* is the relative cost of creating and maintaining the settlement for various levels of vitality, sense, fit, access, and control.
7. *Justice* is the balance of the distribution of environmental benefits and costs among the city's people.

Lynch's view of the good city is one that encourages change in the form of continuous development of individuals or small groups and their culture:

> a process of becoming more complex, more richly connected, more competent, acquiring and realizing new powers—intellectual, emotional, social, and physical. . . . a good settlement is also an *open* one: accessible, decentralized, diverse, adaptable, and tolerant to experiment. This emphasis on dynamic openness is distinct from the insistence of environmentalists (and most utopians) on recurrence and stability. The blue ribbon goes to development, as long as it keeps within the constraints of continuity in

time and space. Since an unstable ecology risks disaster as well as enrichment, flexibility is important, and also the ability to learn and adapt rapidly. (116–17)

A narrower view of desirable urban form seeks to achieve *compact* urbanized areas and to avoid *sprawl.* The basic argument in favor of compact development stresses its fiscal efficiency in providing urban services and infrastructure, its protection of environmental resources and agricultural industries, and its maintenance of existing central cities and downtown centers (Florida Governor's Task Force on Urban Growth Patterns 1989). Another argument in favor of compact development has been made by advocates of higher-density, mixed-use urban areas that can support mass transit and reduce automobile dependency with its air pollution and commuting frustrations (Van der Ryn and Calthorpe 1986). Low-density sprawl with its leapfrog development patterns is seen to be not only ugly and wasteful of land but also fiscally inefficient, environmentally harmful, socially isolating, and exclusionary. The planning dilemma is that low-density suburban living is ingrained as an ideal for the American household seeking to escape older, high-density urban areas (Audirac, Shermyen, and Smith 1990).

Activity Systems   A second source of social use concepts is provided by F. Stuart Chapin, Jr.'s work with "human activity systems," the patterned ways in which households, firms, and institutions use urban areas (Chapin and Kaiser 1979). This draws on time budget studies, which construct descriptions of the duration and location of such household activities as child care or socializing and explore moving plans and location preferences. It also draws on analyses of the current and preferred activity patterns and site qualities of firms and institutions. Activity systems analyses are designed to provide the planner with a method of monitoring activity and space choice patterns as an input into land use plans, projections, and forecast models.

In terms of Lynch's urban form performance dimensions, activity systems analyses would be most concerned with the fit between the physical parts of the city and the activities of its users. Chapin proposes a qualitative, micro perspective that searches for archetypal households, firms, and institutions and relates their activities and spatial choices to locational requirements for land plans. Underlying his work is the notion that planners should monitor social change in order to plan cities more responsive to residents' needs.

Given the dramatic changes in household composition, female participation in the work force, and location of offices during the past decade, activity systems information would be invaluable. Unfortunately, the periodic surveys and inventories needed for activity analyses are rarely conducted by local planning offices, which must rely upon more fragmented and subjective information. However, metropolitan transportation surveys regularly collect some activity information related to communications behavior (which Chapin views as the second element of metropolitan interaction, along with activities) for sub-areas called transportation analysis zones (TAZs). Transportation planners also allocate projected residential and employment growth to TAZs. These transportation surveys provide a useful source of urban behavioral and planning information and could be expanded to include even more activity questions.

Neighborhoods   The social neighborhood is a third source of social use concepts. In a review of the theoretical underpinnings of neighborhood planning, Rohe and Gates (1985, 51–52) observe: "The social functions of neighborhoods include the development of significant primary social relationships; the socialization of children and the development of informal social control; the provision of personal support networks; and the facilitation of social integration into the larger society." They note that, in addition to other benefits, decentralized neighborhood planning also can be more responsive to local needs, increase citizen participation, result in more physical improvement projects, widen the scope of problems addressed and improve public services, and result in more social interaction and a stronger sense of community.[8]

Physical planners have used the neighborhood as an organizing device. Organic models view the physical pattern of the city as comprised of a number of neighborhood "cells," each with their own houses, schools, shops, and recreation areas (Lynch 1981, 400–402). In this view, each neighborhood is a small bounded area where the residents are in face-to-face contact and on intimate terms, creating a sense of community. Clarence Perry proposed that neighborhood units be focused around elementary schools in the first regional plan of New York, an idea followed in many other plans, especially for such new towns as Columbia, Maryland (Hoppenfeld 1967). Survey respondents in cities typically can define their social neighborhoods. However, social neighborhoods are normally limited to twenty or thirty households rather than the larger units that planners define as elementary school catchment areas. Too, since busing has been used for school integration, elementary school districts no longer necessarily fit the space adjacent to school buildings. Meanwhile, as questions have arisen about the validity of the social function of the neighborhood unit, growth has also occurred in the political function of the neighborhood as an organizing force for lobbying against projects that change its predominant character (Babcock and Siemon 1985).

Logan and Molotch (1987, 99) put the neighborhood into the context of the larger city value system: "The city is a setting for the achievement of both exchange values and use values; and the neighborhood is the meeting place of the two forces, where each resident faces the challenge of making a life on a real estate commodity." They see the creation and defense of the use values of neighborhoods as the central urban issue for residents and identify six major categories of neighborhood use values.

1. The daily round involves the neighborhood as the setting for routine activities centered on the residence.
2. Informal support networks are the neighborhood-based people and organizations who provide life-sustaining products and services, especially for the poor.

3. Security and trust result from membership in a neighborhood social space that is seen as orderly, predictable, and protective, especially for women with families.
4. Identity for residents and others results from neighborhood social and spatial demarcations, encouraging competition among neighborhoods for public facilities that will raise their social status.
5. Agglomeration benefits consist of the package of overlapping use values (such as identity and security) that neighborhood residents share.
6. Ethnicity, when it occurs, summarizes the overlapping benefits of neighborhood life, a shared life-style, similar needs for the daily round, and social service and interpersonal support boundaries.

To Logan and Molotch (111–24) the neighborhood is both a viable social network and a demographic-physical construct. They identify the threats to neighborhoods from firms and government bureaucracies whose routine functioning reorganizes urban space. Thus planners attempting to revive poor neighborhoods by urban renewal, gentrification, or infrastructure placement, or to provide new land for urban growth by converting rural areas, often disrupt existing neighborhood values. Similar threats are posed by bankers, property managers, and developers who raise rents, renovate, convert, sell property, or assemble land for new projects. "Whether among rich or poor neighborhoods, in the central city or the urban fringe, neighborhood futures are determined by the ways in which entrepreneurial pressures from outside intersect with internal material stakes and sentimental attachments" (Logan and Molotch 1987, 123).

Others have observed different uses of neighborhoods. Perin (1977) found that residential environments are linked to the notion of a "ladder of life" that people climb as they move up the social order, going from small rental apartments to ownership of detached single-family houses. Appleyard (1981) notes the emergence of a new attitude toward neighborhoods based on the mobile population's search for roots. In this view, the new neighborhood, unlike the old, working-class neighborhood, is one of choice and limited commitment.

Feminist urban theorists (Hayden 1980; Markusen 1980; Spain 1992) assert a different view of urban spatial structure, in which gender is an organizing force equal to class and race. Gender does not lead to spatial segregation but to different urban forms within areas defined by class and ethnicity. In this view, current urban forms, oriented to male activity patterns, do not meet the needs for women's daily activity mixes combining waged and domestic labor. Separation of workplaces and residential areas, as in large-lot suburban developments, isolates women's space and lengthens their travel times for work and household activities. One planning response to promote the economic efficiency of the household is to change land use plans and zoning regulations to encourage mixed-use development bringing together shopping, employment, education, and child-care centers. Another is to provide for decentralization of jobs to bring work opportunities closer to existing residential areas.

Land planners, who are centrally concerned with reorganizing urban space to provide for changing urban needs, face continual conflicts with those who want to maintain the status quo because of existing social use values. Neighborhood planning has been one response although it has encountered both conceptual and practical difficulties.[9] It is clear, however, that some type of planning units smaller than the city, whether neighborhoods, planning districts, or groups of TAZs, are needed to deal with place-oriented social use values. Social use values also are embodied in the more holistic concept of quality of life, a perceptual measure of individual rankings of various urban functions and elements (Myers 1989). Both neighborhood planning and quality of life surveys can inform the land planning process concerning social use values.

Market Values

Commodity values of land drive the business side of urbanization, providing incentives to developers and financiers as well as measures of locational advantage for firms and organizations. In this view, land should be put to its "highest and best use" as determined by the operations of the market. However, unfettered market competition fails to meet all the needs of desirable communities.

At the extremes, land use planners find two opposing sets of ideas about the relationship of planning and the market. One view is that the market is an effective mechanism for organizing transactions, which should only be fine-tuned by government regulation and planning to correct minor distortions. This view focuses on correcting market failure. The other view holds that public intervention should substitute for market processes in order to redistribute wealth and opportunities. In between is the new and still somewhat uneasy merger of the market and government in public-private partnerships. As usual, land use planning practice operates in a terrain that is broad and responsive to changing urban conditions.

Correcting Market Failure   Lee (1981, 150) states that "most land use outcomes are determined by private markets, indirectly influenced by government policies and related private sector actions. . . . The initiative lies primarily with the private sector. Land use decisions can be thought of as the output of land markets, which take as inputs various factors of supply, demand, and public policies."[10] He asserts that the objective of land use planning should be to foster those aspects of private market processes that work well and to compensate for market failures. These failures include negative externalities that have adverse side-effects for those who do not benefit. Thus the market price does not reflect the full costs; for example, an apartment project can create additional traffic impact. However, Lee warns that the cost of government programs to correct failures may exceed the benefits of greater efficiency and equity.

Lee's view that growth controls may be inefficient in the market sense is generally supported by economists (for a review of the literature, see Fischel 1989). For example, Dowall (1984) concludes that land use controls in some places have produced more costs than benefits, resulting in a "suburban squeeze" that has stifled growth, reduced the supply of developable land, and driven up the cost of housing. Land use policies have reduced development potential through downzoning and other means of limiting the intensity of use and also by reducing the supply of land through purchase or imposition of urban service districts or other growth limits. Owners of developable property in real estate markets where land is viewed as being in tight supply have held their parcels off the market until prices have been bid to a maximum. In order to provide more affordable housing, Dowall believes that land use policies will have to become more sensitive to market effects through such techniques as tax-exempt bond financing for infrastructure, lowered subdivision standards, higher-density and mixed-use development, and streamlined land use regulations.

Redistributing Wealth and Power Logan and Molotch (1987, 50) argue that "the city is a growth machine, one that can increase aggregate rents and trap related wealth for those in the right position to benefit." They are skeptical about the contribution of market-oriented urban growth to social values, focusing on the way that elites influence local political decision-making to further their profits through supposedly "value-free" economic growth. Supporting this economic growth perspective they see a coalition of business, politicians, the media, independent utility agencies, organized labor, corporate officials, and cultural institutions. The coalition claims that growth strengthens the local tax base, creates jobs, provides resources to solve social problems, meets housing needs, and allows the market to serve public tastes in housing, neighborhoods, and commercial development. However, critics believe that the growth coalition's power needs to be counterbalanced with public programs to redistribute wealth and ensure equity in land use decision-making.

Public-Private Partnerships At one time, public planning was defined solely as a governmental function that was separate from the market. During recent years, however, local governments in many areas have entered the market in company with private development firms in "public-private partnerships." Focusing on large projects, such as downtown redevelopment projects like San Diego's Horton Plaza and New York's Battery Park City, these new partnerships have changed the assumptions about the legitimate role of planning and have led to a new era of public and private "deal making." According to Frieden and Sagalyn (1989, 315–16):

> Deal making for downtown projects was in line with the 1970s idea that financial incentives could get private interests to serve public purposes. This approach led both cities and developers to cross the boundary that used to separate public from private responsibilities. Developers ended up owning and managing public spaces, an arrangement that produced conflicting claims over public rights of access and political expression. City officials in turn ended up with a major voice in decisions that used to be private, including details of design, management, and the uses of rental income.

Ecological Values

Ecological values stem from various conceptions of the role of the natural environment in human affairs. Not all ecological values stem from the same root. At least three conceptions can be identified (Ortolano 1984, 5–18).

1. Efficient use of natural resources, formulated by Gifford Pinchot, the first head of the U.S. Forest Service, as the basis for scientific forest management and exemplified in the resource economist's utilitarian economic efficiency objective.
2. Maintaining integrity of natural systems, advocated by ecologists who argue for harmony between the actions of people and nature's processes to avoid irreversible damage to ecological functions that support human life.
3. Pure preservation of nature, advocated by philosophers who believe that wilderness is a source of spiritual and esthetic renewal to be preserved for its own sake and that plants and animals have an ethical right to exist.

Environmentalists' arguments may contain elements of all three conceptions. However, it is possible to link efficient use values to views of the environment as an asset; natural systems functional integrity values to carrying capacity, land suitability, and sustainable development approaches; and preservation values to endangered species and natural preserve approaches.

There is a tendency to politicize the environment as a means of accomplishing such other ends as stopping a project or slowing urban growth. Where environmental values are in conflict with market or social use values and scientific evidence is ambiguous, then conflicting testimony on the predicted impacts may be offered. For example, experts differed over the potential health effects on an adjacent neighborhood of a new incinerator proposed for the Brooklyn Navy Yard (Klapp 1989). But under any of the three conceptions, environmental values need not be viewed as antithetical to land use planning.

Environmental Assets Traditional approaches to environmental values have linked them to the environment as an economic asset in which pollution is defined as a "residual," manageable leftover from production and consumption. The evaluation of environmental impacts, in which benefit-cost analysis is used as a basis for choice among alternatives, is another economic approach to valuing the environment (Ortolano 1984). A third approach stresses the protective features of the environment in protecting people and property from natural disasters, such as floods and hurricanes (Pilkey et al. 1980). In all three approaches, environmental assets are to be efficiently managed for human benefit through plans, management programs, regulations, and project evaluations.

Environmental Integrity Land planners have incorporated environmental integrity values into their plans through the use of concepts that link characteristics of land areas with environmental processes and human uses. Three such concepts are carrying capacity, a measure of "capability"; land suitability, a measure of "desirability" for a particular use; and sustainable development, a measure of "feasibility" for balancing environmental, economic, and social functions.

Carrying capacity analysis describes the amount of development an area can accommodate without undergoing irreversible ecological change or damage due to some threshold limits to growth. Limits may be environmental (air and water quality, ecosystem stability, soil erosion), physical (infrastructure capacity), or psychological (e.g., perceptions of crowding or esthetics). As Clark (1981, 81) notes, the natural carrying capacity of an ecological system is variable not fixed, and "the analysis of carrying capacity is a method for testing the effects of policies, not for making them." He states that among the proper tasks of natural environmental carrying capacity analysis are allocation of predetermined amounts of growth, determination of ecological impacts from human actions, identification of critical areas, prediction of effects of alternatives, restoration of ecosystems and renewable resources, specification of performance standards for development, and determination of consequences of various levels of resource utilization.[11] Carrying capacity analysis links environmental values and social use values by identifying threshold of use limits that respect the capability of land and ecology.

Land suitability analysis describes the uses to which a particular land parcel is inherently suited due to such characteristics of the parcel as its soils, slope, vegetation, and hydrology. Applications of land suitability analysis are associated with the work of McHarg (1969), who used map overlays to define areas best suited for particular land uses based on constraining as well as accommodating factors. A simple land suitability analysis for potential industrial use might include parcels with flat to moderate slopes, soils with good bearing capacity, nonthreatened habitats, and few wetland areas. In practice, most areas will be suitable for more than one type of use, requiring the addition of such other factors as infrastructure availability and compatibility with adjacent parcels in order to assign desired land uses.

Sustainable development is a more recent concept linking environmental, economic, and social use values. The goal is to identify the level of development that can be sustained without critical environmental damage, while meeting economic and social needs of present and future generations (Breheny 1992). Taking capability and suitability analysis a step further, sustainable development analysis recognizes not only that the environment produces valuable resources and that environmental stress is a product of human use but also that environmental preservation has costs. An underlying premise is that a certain level of economic development is necessary in order to pay for sustaining ecological diversity and stability. Without adequate economic development, natural resources may be overexploited and destroyed, as in cases of deforestation in developing countries where people had no alternative source of livelihood. Another premise is that sustainability depends on reducing consumption of materials and energy. Arising from work at the United Nations (1993), the concept has potential for application in developed as well as developing areas where environmental resources sustain social systems and economies, as in agricultural, silvacultural, and maricultural areas dependent on renewable resources and in tourist and recreation areas where the environment is the attraction (Ascher and Healy 1990). Sustainable development analysis looks at the feasibility of environmental management strategies in light of related economic and social needs rather than in isolation. It recognizes the need to conserve natural (ecological) capital and to develop human capital through wise use of economic capital. For example, the 1992 New Zealand Resource Management Act requires local planning to follow sustainable development principles (Monty and Dixon 1993; Berke 1994).

Preservation of Nature   One strong set of environmental values insists on the preservation of nature as a basic purpose. This view appears in legislation to preserve endangered species of plants and animals in order to maintain species diversity and in programs to preserve wetlands and rain forests. It defends its position on the grounds that human activities are reducing diversity and that intergenerational equity demands that future generations not be deprived of the same level of diversity that present generations enjoy as well as on the grounds that nature has inherent value to be preserved for its own sake. It also appears in the arguments of animal rights activists and landscape preservationists. Land use actions to support preservation values include designation of protected nature preserves; maintenance of endangered species habitats; protection of water supply watersheds and aquifers; and reduced densities in buffer areas adjacent to parks, waterways, viewsheds, and natural open spaces.

Planners confront the tension between development and conservation as they do the tension between development and social use—with an effort to strike a working balance. If all environmental impacts were stopped, then most human activities would have to stop as well. Yet to ignore environmental impacts is to risk human health and safety as well as economic and esthetic contributions of natural features. What is needed is a theory of practice broad enough to incorporate the necessary elements yet effective in achieving a balance.

Integrating Land Use Values

Effectiveness in land use change management as a local government responsibility depends upon integrating the use, exchange, and ecological views of land into a balanced system. Our proposed system is made up of two parts: (1) a land use change management model that incorporates structural concerns of human ecology and political economy theories through land use planning concepts, and (2) a planning discourse model that incorporates process concerns of game theory through participation and dispute resolution concepts. It recognizes not only the values of the major stakeholders in the land use game, but also the values of the planner as both a technical expert and a player.

A Model of Land Use Change Management

To use a simple structural analogy, land use change management can be visualized as the seat or main integrating framework of a stool whose three legs are social use, market, and ecological values. Further joining the legs is the overarching concept of sustainable development (Figure 2-2). For the stool to stand, every part must be in place, equally proportioned and properly joined.

Each leg—or value—is necessary. If social use values, as exemplified by neighborhoods and activity patterns, are not accounted for, then citizens will not accept planning. If market values, as exemplified by profit-seeking real estate development, are not accounted for, then city building cannot take place. If ecological values, as exemplified by natural resource conservation, are not accounted for, then development cannot be sustained.

If the three legs have no integrating structure, there will be no way to resolve their conflicting claims through the land use change management process. Because of the inherently selfish nature of interest group advocacy of individual values, a strong coordinating process is necessary to provide the analytical, synthetic, and sociopolitical efforts needed to balance and coordinate competing interests. Public leadership in land use change management provides the primary coordinating process. Sustainable development can be an important guiding principle in the search for balance among the three legs.

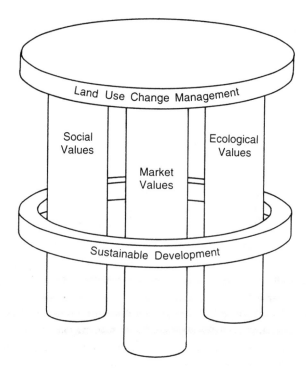

Figure 2-2. Land Use Change Management as a Three-Legged Stool

Land use change management as the integrating structure also leads the social learning process necessary for the community to understand the impacts, opportunities, and pitfalls of change. Without the sense of continuity that planning provides and that connects the past, present, and future, the community is unable to connect events into trends and to interpret patterns of change. Collecting and analyzing information are central to this effort, as are making and implementing advance plans.

Finally, the land use change management process operates in the arena where consensus is hammered out over the direction and meaning of change and desirable community response. This consensus-building process is as critical as technical analysis and design solutions. The next section proposes a model of community consensus-building organized around discourse over planning issues.

A Model of Planning Discourse

Every land planner depends on a working community consensus over desired ends and means in order to achieve action in line with plan proposals. The cliché about plans that gather dust on the shelf, unconsulted by public or private decision-makers, stems from the days in which planning was viewed as an independent, autocratic, and self-fulfilling exercise. Contemporary planners realize that gaining community support, understanding, and "ownership" of plans through a broad-based consensus formation effort is a necessary but not sufficient condition of successful implementation. It must be followed by systematic programs to ensure that adopted plans are used in operational decisions. The process must also continue over time, building new consensus to deal with changed conditions and needs.

To achieve consensus, the land planner engages in a community discourse with market-oriented developers, social use interests, and government officials, regularly exchanging information, involvement, influence, and proposals in order to find solutions to development problems and needs (Godschalk and Stiftel 1981). This planning discourse model is a central feature of the land use game, with elements of public education, bargaining, persuasion, and reciprocal trades, in addition to its technical and analytical features (Figure 2-3). Besides doing technical planning work, the land planner maintains and participates in this discourse process which debates proposals for land use change, considering land as a community resource to be allocated in accordance with consensus values during the city building process.

For the land planner, the basic ends of planning discourse are plans, policies, and community development actions that balance the three major values—social, market, and environmental. Other players in the land use game may see the ends and means more narrowly. Enlivening the discourse are the contrasting perspectives of those who view land primarily as a homeplace or neighborhood for living and working, as a commodity to be exchanged for profit on the real estate market, or as an irreplaceable environmental resource to be conserved in its natural state.

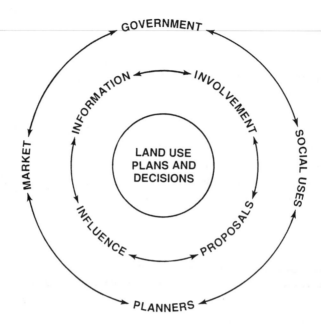

Figure 2-3. Planning Discourse Model: Exchange among Land Use Game Players

It is planning discourse that humanizes the rational planning model and transforms it into a community learning and consensus-building process. Discourse will pass through varying levels of intensity over time as major planning and community development decisions rise to the top of the community agenda. Because planmaking is a cyclical process, planning discourse can be anticipated to peak in regular five- to six-year periods. However, external events may force a less predictable cycle. For example, if a community faces a significant loss due to a military base closing or a natural disaster, then discourse will be initiated to formulate a strategic response.

Planning discourse not only keeps the planner and other players abreast of current issues and proposals, but it also serves as a forward-looking process. By aggregating the knowledge of stakeholders about potential changes in their various realms, the discourse process enables the community to forecast likely future scenarios and explore alternative land use and other planning strategies.

Recognizing the Planner's Values

Like the other players in the land use game, planners also bring values to the table. These are typically a mix of personal and professional values that embody the reasons why the person chose to become a planner and what the planning peer group expects its members to strive for.[12] Reflective planners, who are aware of the values that underlie their recommendations and analyses, make them explicit parts of their practice (Schon 1983). The integration of planning values with practice methods is expressed through planning ethics, adding a moral dimension to professional activity (Beatley 1984).

Planners' concepts of practice stress the priorities of various ends and means. For example, as general ends, most planners strive for cities that are efficient, equitable, and esthetically pleasing, but when dealing with a particular proposal one goal may take on a higher priority. At the level of general means, most planners strive to ensure that all affected parties have opportunities to participate in decisions and that results are capable of effective implementation. Again, however, the means may be influenced at the stage of dealing with a particular process by such other factors as power imbalances or deadlines. In other words, practice values often are necessarily conditional and situational rather than general.

All plans rest on values. The best plans attempt to make those values explicit and subject them to public discussion. The difficulty is that once the values go beyond such abstract statements of the public interest as furthering public health, safety, convenience, efficiency, and the like, they are subject to intense disagreement.

One response has been to construct alternative plans that accomplish different blends of values and to let the public and decision-makers choose the desired alternative. For example, the 1990 Volusia County, Florida, Coastal Management Plan considered a series of alternative land use schemes ranging from a continuation of past development practices—which was found unacceptable from an environmental and urban service perspective—to a prohibition on development outside the urbanized area—which was found unacceptable politically and economically. The compromise solution permitted the expansion of the urban area, but only in limited areas adjacent to the coastal cities where natural resource losses could be adequately mitigated (Sedway Cooke Associates 1989). In that case, the practical factors of the situation tempered the sharply defined abstract values of the alternative plans.

As with other parts of land planning, we return to the importance of balance in the planner's value schema. The planner is only one player in the land use game. Despite the knowledge and expertise of the planner, the other players' values and knowledge must also be recognized. The great mistakes of planning often have stemmed from a professional arrogance that did not recognize competing views (Hall 1982). Our approach to land use change management takes a more open and balanced direction.

NOTES

1. See, for example, the chapters in Godschalk (1974) and Morley and Shachar (1986).

2. The contemporary literature of planning includes several works oriented toward the notion of change management. See Yaro et al. (1989) and McClendon and Quay (1988).

3. Giuliano (1989) has critiqued traditional economic-behavioral theories of urban change that use economic principles of utility and profit maximization to explain land use and transportation relationships. She points out that changing conditions, such as employment decentralization, the increase in two-worker households, and improvements in ac-

cessibility due to well-developed transportation systems, have contributed to the inability of existing theory to capture major explanatory factors of land use change in today's metropolitan areas. Hall (1989) has described the competing approaches to planning theory. Marxists argue that planners are mere agents of the capitalist local state. Urban political economists argue that economic and social structures dominate planning. Critical theorists argue that planners should communicate with people over the crucial issues of urban development. Hands-on planners stress dealing with current issues such as economic development for distressed areas, project finance, affordable housing, and the use of computers and geographic information systems to help solve problems.

4. Lynch (1981, ch. 2) identifies three types of theories: (1) decision theories, which correspond to our planning process theories; (2) functional theories, which are empirical explanations of urban development; and (3) normative theories, which connect human values and settlement form.

5. Strategic planning advocates assert that the rational model is too inclusive and cumbersome to be effective, that it fails to consider external conditions, and that it does not gain agreement from the actors with the necessary power to implement its recommendations (Bryson and Einsweiler 1988). Critical theory advocates argue that the rational model is too elitist and bureaucratic, failing to achieve the necessary communicative competence and ethics (Forester 1989). Dispute resolution advocates claim that the rational model does not recognize the disputes inherent in plans and planning and thereby sets the stage for either conflict over planning proposals or rejection of the legitimacy of the plan when it fails to deal with the interests of affected parties (Susskind and Cruikshank 1987).

6. Content theories can be both descriptive and normative. Most political economy theories have a normative component allied with a descriptive component.

7. Rudel (1989) calls these three patterns of land use control: (1) bilateral relational control in rural areas; (2) rule-based control in rural-urban fringe areas; and (3) trilateral relational control for urban areas. Under bilateral control, land owners deal directly with each other. Under rule-based control, local elected officials decide on land use changes. Under trilateral relational control, a third-party decision-maker is involved in the form of a judge or a mediator.

8. However, see de Neufville (1981, 44–46) on the parochial and protectionist tendencies of making decisions on a neighborhood scale and on the unequal power of rich and poor neighborhoods.

9. See Webber's essays on "community without propinquity" (1963) and the "nonplace urban realm" (1964), which attack the idea that urban social networks are the result of, or confined to, physical neighborhoods.

10. Although the initiative of the private sector is critical, the public sector can also play various growth-guiding cards in the form of infrastructure policies and decisions. Expressway and interchange locations, trunk sewers, large water mains, school locations, and the like heavily influence private-sector development decisions.

11. Clark believes that policymakers, not technical experts, should resolve questions of population limits, density of structures, type and mix of uses, optimal rate of development, and optimal rate of return on investment. He sees carrying capacity analysis as an adjunct to, not a substitute for, political processes.

12. Lynch (1981, 366–67) derived the following list of planners' values about settlement form from his review of the literature:

1. Enjoy the city for its urbanity—diversity, surprises, picturesqueness, and high interaction levels.
2. The city should express and reinforce society and the nature of the world, including symbolism, cultural meanings, history, and traditional form.
3. Order, clarity, and expression of function are the principal criteria.
4. City design is the efficient provision and maintenance of facilities and services, for example, good engineering.
5. The city is a managed ongoing system whose key elements are the market, institutions, communications, and the decision process—the view from above.
6. The principal values are local control, pluralism, advocacy, behavior settings, and the small social group—the view from below.
7. The environment is to be valued by its individual experience, for its openness, legibility, meaning, educativeness, and sensory pleasure.
8. The city is a means for profit or power through competition, appropriation, and exploitation and division of resources.
9. The environment is a given, to be survived in and observed.

REFERENCES

Appleyard, Donald. 1981. Place and nonplace: The new search for roots. In *The land use policy debate in the United States,* ed. Judith de Neufville. New York: Plenum Press.

Ascher, William, and Robert G. Healy. 1990. *Natural resource policymaking in developing countries: Environment, economic growth, and income distribution.* Durham: Duke University Press.

Audirac, Ivonne, Anne H. Shermyen, and Marc T. Smith. 1990. Ideal urban form and visions of the good life. *Journal of the American Planning Association* 56(4): 470–82.

Babcock, Richard, and Charles Siemon. 1985. *The zoning game revisited.* Boston: Oelgeschlager, Gunn and Hain.

Beatley, Timothy. 1984. Applying moral principles to growth management. *Journal of the American Planning Association* 50(4): 459–69.

Berke, Philip. 1994. Evaluating environmental plan quality: The case of planning for sustainable development in New Zealand. *Journal of Environmental Planning and Management.* In press.

Berry, B. J. L., and John D. Kasarda. 1977. *Contemporary urban ecology.* New York: Macmillian.

Braybrooke, David, and Charles Lindblom. 1963. *A strategy of decision.* New York: Free Press of Glencoe.

Breheny, M. J., ed. 1992. *Sustainable development and urban form.* London: Pion.

Bryson, John. 1988. *Strategic planning for public and nonprofit organizations.* San Francisco: Jossey-Bass.

Bryson, John, and Robert Einsweiler, eds. 1988. *Strategic planning: Threats and opportunities for planners.* Chicago: APA Press.

Chapin, F. Stuart, Jr., and Edward J. Kaiser. 1979. *Urban land use planning.* 3d ed. Urbana: University of Illinois Press.

Clark, John. 1981. The search for natural limits to growth. In *The land use policy debate in the United States,* ed. Judith de Neufville. New York: Plenum Press.

Clavel, Pierre. 1986. *The progressive city: Planning and participation.* New Brunswick: Rutgers University Press.

de Neufville, Judith, ed. 1981. *The land use policy debate in the United States.* New York: Plenum Press.

Dowall, David. 1984. *The suburban squeeze: Land conversion and regulation in the San Francisco Bay area.* Berkeley: University of California Press.

Forester, John. 1989. *Planning in the face of power.* Berkeley: University of California Press.

Fischel, William A. 1989. What do economists know about growth controls? A research review. In *Understanding growth management: Critical issues and a research agenda,* ed. David Brower, David Godschalk, and Douglas Porter. Washington, D.C.: Urban Land Institute.

Florida Governor's Task Force on Urban Growth Patterns. 1989. *Final report.* Tallahassee.

Frieden, Bernard, and Lynne Sagalyn. 1989. *Downtown, Inc: How America builds cities.* Cambridge: MIT Press.

Friedmann, John. 1987. *Planning in the public domain: From knowledge to action.* Princeton: Princeton University Press.

Giuliano, Genevieve. 1989. New directions for understanding transportation and land use. *Environment and Planning* 21: 145–59.

Godschalk, David R., ed. 1974. *Planning in America: Learning from turbulence.* Washington, D.C.: American Institute of Planners.

Godschalk, David R., and Bruce Stiftel. 1981. Making waves: Public participation in state water planning. *Journal of Applied Behaviorial Science* 17(4): 597–614.

Hall, Peter. 1982. *Great planning disasters.* Berkeley: University of California Press.

———. 1989. The turbulent eighth decade: Challenges to American city planning. *Journal of the American Planning Association* 55(3): 275–82.

Harvey, David. 1981. The urban process under capitalism: A framework for analysis. In *Urbanization and urban planning in capitalist society,* ed. M. Dear and A. Scott. New York: Methuen.

Hawley, Amos. 1950. *Human ecology: A theory of community structure.* New York: Ronald Press.

Hayden, Dolores. 1980. What would a non-sexist city look like? Speculations on housing, urban design, and human work. *Signs: Journal of Women in Culture and Society* 5(3) Spring Supplement: S170–87.

Holling, C. S., and M. A. Goldberg. 1971. Ecology and planning. *Journal of the American Institute of Planners* 37(4): 221–30.

Hoppenfeld, Morton. 1967. A sketch of the planning-building process for Columbia, Maryland. *Journal of the American Institute of Planners* 33(5): 398–409.

Innes, Judith. 1992. Group processes and the social construction of growth management: Florida, Vermont, and New Jersey. *Journal of the American Planning Association* 58(4): 440–53.

Kaiser, Edward J., and Shirley F. Weiss. 1970. Public policy and the residential development process. *Journal of the American Institute of Planners* 36(1): 30–37.

Klapp, Merrie. 1989. Bargaining with uncertainty: The Brooklyn Navy Yard incinerator dispute. *Journal of Planning Education and Research* 8(3): 157–66.

Lee, Douglass, B., Jr. 1981. Land use planning as response to market failure. In *The land use policy debate in the United States,* ed. Judith de Neufville. New York: Plenum Press.

Logan, John, and Harvey Molotch. 1987. *Urban fortunes: The political economy of place.* Berkeley: University of California Press.

Lynch, Kevin. 1981. *A theory of good city form.* Cambridge: MIT Press.

Markusen, Ann. 1980. City spatial structure, women's household work, and national urban policy. *Signs: Journal of Women in Culture and Society* 5(3): 20–41.

McClendon, Bruce, and Ray Quay. 1988. *Mastering change.* Chicago: APA Planners Press.

McHarg, Ian. 1969. *Design with nature.* Garden City: Doubleday.

Michael, Donald. 1973. *On learning to plan—and planning to learn.* San Francisco: Jossey Bass.

Monty, B. E., and J. E. Dixon. 1993. From law to practice: EIA in New Zealand. *Environmental Impact Assessment Review* 13(2): 89–108.

Morley, David. 1986. Approaches to planning in turbulent environments. In *Planning in turbulence,* ed. David Morley and Arie Shachar. Jerusalem: The Magnes Press, Hebrew University.

Myers, Dowell. 1989. The ecology of "quality of life" and urban growth. In *Understanding growth management: Critical issues and a research agenda,* ed. David Brower, David Godschalk, and Douglas Porter. Washington, D.C.: Urban Land Institute.

Nelson, Arthur. 1988. An empirical note on how regional urban containment policy influences an interaction between greenbelt and exurban land markets. *Journal of the American Planning Association* 54(2): 178–84.

New Jersey State Planning Commission. 1991. *Communities of place: The interim state development and redevelopment plan for the state of New Jersey.* Trenton.

Ortolano, Leonard. 1984. *Environmental planning and decision making.* New York: John Wiley and Sons.

Perin, Constance. 1977. *Everything in its place.* Princeton: Princeton University Press.

Perloff, Harvey S. 1974. The evolution of planning education. In *Planning in America: Learning from turbulence,* ed. David R. Godschalk. Washington, D.C.: American Institute of Planners.

Pilkey, Orrin H., Sr., et al. 1980. *Coastal design: A guide for builders, planners, and home owners.* New York: Van Nostrand Reinhold.

Rohe, William, and Lauren Gates. 1985. *Planning with neighborhoods.* Chapel Hill: University of North Carolina Press.

Rosenau, James. 1990. *Turbulence in world politics: A theory of change and continuity.* Princeton: Princeton University Press.

Rudel, Thomas K. 1989. *Situations and strategies in American land-use planning.* Cambridge: Cambridge University Press.

Schon, Donald. 1971. *Beyond the stable state.* New York: Random House.

———. 1983. *The reflective practitioner: How professionals think in action.* New York: Basic Books.

Sedway Cooke Associates. 1989. *Volusia County coastal management element.* San Francisco: Sedway Cooke Associates.

Spain, Daphne. 1992. *Gendered spaces.* Chapel Hill: University of North Carolina Press.

Susskind, Lawrence, and Jeffrey Cruikshank. 1987. *Breaking the impasse: Consensual approaches to resolving public disputes.* New York: Basic Books.

United Nations. 1993. *The global partnership for environment and development: A guide to Agenda 21.* New York: The author (post Rio edition).

Van der Ryn, Sim, and Peter Calthorpe. 1986. *Sustainable communities.* San Francisco: Sierra Club Books.

Webber, Melvin. 1963. Order in diversity: Community without propinquity. In *Cities and space: The future use of urban land,* ed. Loudon Wingo. Baltimore: Johns Hopkins University Press.

———. 1964. The urban place and the nonplace urban realm. In *Explorations into urban structure,* ed. Melvin Webber et al. Philadelphia: University of Pennsylvania Press.

Yaro, Robert, et al. 1989. *Dealing with change in the Connecticut River Valley: A design manual for conservation and development.* Cambridge: Lincoln Institute of Land Policy.

3

A Local Government Land Use Planning Program

In order to be useful in local government decision-making about land development, the land use planning program should provide three types of services:
1. Intelligence—the gathering, organization, and dissemination of information
2. Advance plan making—the formulation of coordinated land use and guidance system proposals . . .
3. Action planning—active, on-line participation in ongoing decisions about land use issues

—Chapin and Kaiser 1979, 69

This chapter prescribes the set of activities, products, and players that constitute a land use planning program. The land use planning program is how the planner manages the land use game and provides useful services to the various land use game players. In many ways it formalizes the planner's role in local government. The program we describe is intended as both an ideal model and as the framework for the studies described in later chapters, showing how they fit together to form an effective force in the community.

The Four Functions of a Land Use Planning Program

We see land use planning as serving four functions in the community's management of change—intelligence, advance planning, problem solving, and operating the community's development management system (Figure 3-1). Those four services should be provided to both public and private decision-makers to improve community discourse and land use decisions and to achieve a more desirable future in which social use, market values, and environmental values are in balance.

Intelligence consists of gathering, organizing, analyzing, and disseminating information to stakeholders in the use and development of land. Intelligence alerts decision-makers to conditions, trends, and projections as well as the social, economic, and environmental impacts of those projections and proposed alternative decisions (i.e., impact assessments). It aims to serve public officials and agencies primarily but also provides information to private firms, organizations, and individuals. The presumption is that better information will lead to improved public discourse, more equitable and effective policy, and better land use decisions.

Advance plan-making, the most traditional function of a land use program, consists of making long-range and intermediate-range plans. That involves formu-

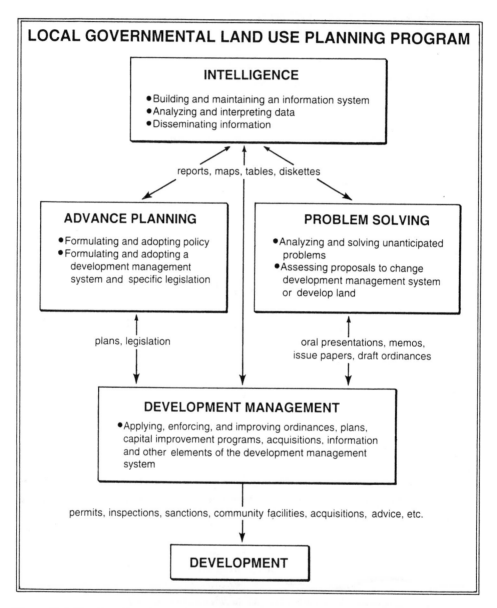

Figure 3-1. The Four Functions of a Land Use Planning Program, Their Sub-elements, and Their Linkages

lating goals; defining desirable future land use patterns that balance social, market, and environmental values; devising policies and action programs to achieve them; and getting such policies and programs adopted.

Problem solving assists the community in addressing issues not anticipated adequately in advance planning. Sometimes referred to as "brush fires," these issues call for a "firefighting" capacity in local government. In contrast to advance plan-making, problem solving is responsive rather than anticipatory and isolates salient features of individual problems rather than coordinating solutions across many community issues.

Managing development, the fourth function of a land use planning program, involves the day to day administering, enforcing, and revising of policies, regulations, public investments, and other measures that constitute the actual (as opposed to proposed) development management system. Included are such activities as negotiating stipulations in permitting procedures, monitoring and enforcing permits and public investment policies, invoking sanctions where necessary, and seeing to funding, site selection, and site planning for community facilities. In other words, this function includes all aspects of implementation after adoption. This is where the planner plays one on one with the other players in the land use game.

The Intelligence Function

The capacity to provide intelligence begins with building and maintaining an information system, which is also necessary for advance planning, problem solving, and managing land use controls. The planner must design and build the database, maintain it, obtain suitable hardware and software, assemble people with information processing skills, and, finally, employ that information system creatively and effectively. Thus, an information system is much more than data files, maps, and computer hardware and software, although computer technology is a virtual necessity today. Rather, a planning information system is the entire approach to obtaining, storing, retrieving, and analyzing data and presenting information in response to specific intelligence needs of the planning program, elected and appointed officials, and other players in the community land use game. The information system should be designed to provide facts and values about all three aspects of land use and development systems—social, market, and environmental. That includes past conditions, present conditions, trends, and alternative projections of future conditions based on varying scenarios.

Several tasks are involved in building an information system. They include identification of key information files to be included (e.g., files on the economy, population, land use, land supply, status of land undergoing development, environmental features and systems, community facilities and infrastructure, and existing land use controls and policies). Data for those files must be specified. Where appropriate, the data should be geographically referenced by grid coordinates, census block, census tract, watershed, and other spatial identifiers. The planner must assemble the data, update it regularly, and maintain the system. Models and procedures must be developed for summarizing and analyzing data, projecting conditions, and putting it into appropriate forms for better communication.

After constructing the information system, the planner faces the tasks of actual data retrieval and analysis to convert it to useful information. These tasks involve the presentation of summary statistics, including maps showing spatial variation in those statistics and graphs showing trends over time. The planner must also be able to identify current and projected deficiencies and current and future needs of the community and various groups within it. Anticipating and interpreting social, market, and environmental effects of specific policies and ordinances is also required.

More complex inferences about present and future conditions relating to land use, environment, and infrastructure require simulation models. At its highest level, intelligence transforms data into patterns of facts, estimates, projections, values, and criteria for decision-making. It also includes building an understanding of cause-and-effect relationships, which requires data on causes as well as conditions, and data from the past that can be analyzed to establish trends and cause-and-effect relationships.

Finally, intelligence includes the important step of disseminating information to the various players in the land use game. That means publication of current conditions, status of government programs, and projections of future conditions. It also means making information available upon request to participants in the land planning and development game when they need it, during advance planning procedures, during problem solving, and during permitting procedures. Players may also be provided their own access to the information system and their own means of analyzing data.

The Advance Planning Function

Two main types of advance plan-making are advocated in this text: policy planning and development management planning. These two types of plans are not mutually exclusive, and in fact we argue for a hybrid plan. The policy plan element features a future goal form—expressed as a map of the future land use pattern—and general policies about governmental action to achieve the goal form. The development management plan is a program of procedures and standards for regulating development, a schedule for funding and building community facilities and infrastructure, and a set of incentives for development decisions. It is shorter-range, more specific than a policy plan, and obviously more oriented toward means than ends.

The two types of plans are associated with two branches of planning theory and planning history. The goal form and policy plan is associated with the planning profession's roots in the design professions. A plan is a proposed physical design, a vision of a future land use pattern as a goal form to be pursued. The development management plan draws more from later planning theory that took root in the 1950s and 1960s, wherein a plan is conceived more as a proposed course of action than a vision of the future. This perspective borrows more from the social sciences and the fields of systems analysis, policy analysis, and business administration rather than from architecture and landscape architecture. Thus, the development management system plan is a proposed mix of regulations, community investments, and other actions.

What we propose is a merging of the two perspectives, a plan that is both a vision of the future *and* a course of action and has general and specific components as well as long-range and short-range proposals. We also propose that the general, long-range, vision-oriented, mapped policy planning precede and guide the shorter-range, specific, action-oriented development management planning.

Plans, whether policy-oriented, action program-oriented, or a hybrid, should have four components: a fact component, a goals component, a solution component, and an evaluation component. The fact component or fact basis consists of an analysis of relevant past, current, and projected facts about the community, its problems, and their causes. The goals component represents the values of the community in the form of goals and objectives and policies from state and local government that must be followed. The solutions component consists of at least one and sometimes several alternative goal forms, policies, and combinations of development management measures. The evaluation component consists of an assessment of alternatives, including the no-intervention or no-change-in-policy alternative. It is sometimes missing from the final plan but should be a formal step in the design and adoption process. no option - option - "do-nothing option" • do we really need to address this?

The Policy Plan   Various meanings have been ascribed to the terms *development policies, land use policies,* or *land and environmental policies.* Some policies are input policies; they have been previously determined by state or federal governments, agreed to by a regional association of local governments, or adopted previously by community officials. Input policies are in the form of legislation, administrative rules and guidelines, resolutions, or plans. Such policy inputs are important and may be incorporated into advance plans, problem solving proposals, and development management, but they are inputs to, not outputs of, advance planning.

The policies of primary concern here, however, are output policies resulting from advance planning. Output policies are explicit public decision guides designed to provide consistency in development guidance decisions over time. A land use goal form is itself a policy statement and is usually supported by other policies designed to encourage achievement of that goal form.

Plans do not become meaningful policy, however, until elected and appointed officials adopt them and employ them consistently. A policy plan might state where and when sewers will be extended, for example, and under what conditions, and who would pay for them, but it remains "potential" policy until actually employed in sewer extension decisions. Thus, to the extent that policy continues to be defined as it is being interpreted and enforced, policy design continues into implementation. In that sense, planning does not stop with adoption of the plan, but continues through implementation. Hence, the inclusion of development management as one of the four components of the planning program.

Policy Plan Formats The policy planning track of advance planning begins with a problem analysis and goal-setting element and a review of input policies. It then seeks to transform the goals and input policies into output policies that also reflect the conditions, causes, and projections that problem analysis highlights. The policies are expressed in one of three forms, or in a mix of them.

1. A verbal statement.
2. A land classification plan, which maps areas where development should occur and other areas where it should be discouraged over some specific period and where natural resources are to be protected. Both areas for development and areas not to be developed are mapped and accompanied by policies that encourage the outcome specified by the land classification.
3. A land use design, which maps more detailed designations of land uses than does the land classification plan and constitutes the desired future spatial organization of land uses—a goal form.

The three formats are quite different, each with its own advantages and limitations.

The verbal policy format focuses on written statements of policy without mapping or committing to a specific spatial goal form for future development. The policy excerpts in Figure 3-2 are taken from the 1983 Calvert County (Maryland) Comprehensive Plan, which won an award from the American Planning Association in 1985. The policies are concise and easy to grasp, and they are grouped in sections corresponding to the six divisions of county government assigned to implement the policies. The Calvert County plan contains no land use map.

The verbal policy format is the easiest, quickest, and most flexible of the three policy plan formats. Some planners also claim that it avoids people's inclination to rely too heavily on maps, which are difficult to keep up to date to reflect current interpretation of basic policy (Hollander et al. 1988). However, verbal statements in the absence of maps provide little spatial specificity, and therefore lack teeth. Our judgment is that the plan should supplement verbal policy with policy maps. In fact, the verbal policy statement is a good first step in formulating a land classification or land use design plan and is often a part of those type plans.

The land classification format can be a follow-up to the verbal policy statement approach, or combine the verbal policy and land classification formats. It focuses on specifying the location and timing of future urban development and on protecting "critical" areas, particularly environmentally vulnerable areas, productive agricultural, and forest lands, from development. Both the areas earmarked for development and those to be protected from development are mapped.

In format, the land classification plan divides the region into districts, with separate policies for each district type. The number and types of districts vary from case to case. In its simplest, or level-one, format, three types of policy districts

INDUSTRIAL DISTRICTS

Industrial Districts are intended to provide areas in the county which are suitable for the needs of industry. They should be located and designed to be compatible with the surrounding land uses, either due to existing natural features or through the application of standards.

> **RECOMMENDATIONS:**
> 1. Identify general locations for potential industrial uses.
> 2. Permit retail sales as an accessory use in the Industrial District

SINGLE-FAMILY RESIDENTIAL DISTRICTS

Single-Family Residential Districts are to be developed and promoted as neighborhoods free from any land usage which might adversely affect them.

> **RECOMMENDATIONS:**
> 1. For new development, require buffering for controlling visual, noise, and activity impacts between residential and commercial uses.
> 2. Encourage single-family residential development to locate in the designated towns.
> 3. Allow duplexes, triplexes, and fourplexes as a conditional use in the "R-1" Residential Zone so long as the design is compatible with the single-family residential development.
> 4. Allow home occupations (professions and services, but not retail sales) by permitting the employment of one full-time equivalent individual not residing on the premises.

MULTIFAMILY RESIDENTIAL DISTRICTS

Multifamily Residential Districts provide for townhouses and multifamily apartment units. Areas designated in this category are those which are currently served or scheduled to be served by community or multi-use sewerage and water supply systems.

> **RECOMMENDATIONS:**
> 1. Permit multifamily development in the Solomons, Price Frederick, and Twin Beach Towns.
> 2. Require multifamily projects to provide adequate recreational facilities— equipment, structures, and play surfaces.
> 3. Evaluate the feasibility of increasing the dwelling unit density permitted in the multifamily Residential Zone (R-2).

Figure 3-2. Verbal Format Policy Plan. Excerpted from *The Calvert County* [Maryland] *Comprehensive Plan* (1983), it contains no land use design map and is written in newspaper style; the recommendations constitute the policy content.

would be mapped: an urban district, a rural district, and special consideration/ critical area districts. The special consideration areas may penetrate or overlay the urban and rural districts, delineating sensitive natural environment areas or built-up neighborhoods where special policies would either preclude development or allow it only if it met stipulated conditions.

More detailed classification systems designate additional policy areas within those three major distinctions. The urban area, for example, might be divided into a developed area consisting of the built-up central city and older suburbs and an urban growth or transition area only partially developed or undeveloped at the time of the plan and where future urbanization is encouraged. The rural area might be divided into agricultural districts where long-range commitment is made to agricultural and forest uses, with the remaining land being classified into less crit-

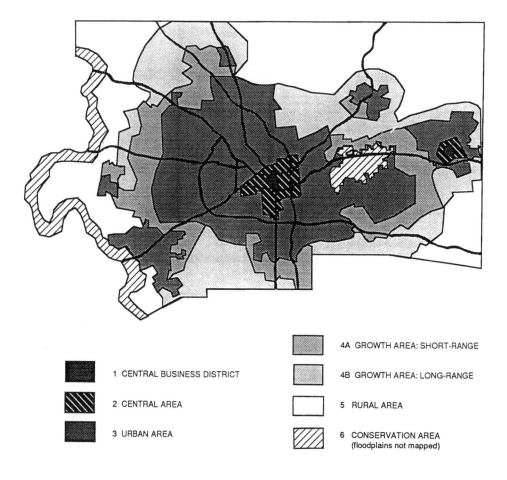

1 CENTRAL BUSINESS DISTRICT

2 CENTRAL AREA

3 URBAN AREA

4A GROWTH AREA: SHORT-RANGE

4B GROWTH AREA: LONG-RANGE

5 RURAL AREA

6 CONSERVATION AREA (floodplains not mapped)

Figure 3-3. A Land Classification Plan. The map, adapted from the Forsyth County, North Carolina, growth management plan, illustrates the land classification format. The accompanying table summarizes the character, problems, and policy objectives of each classification area on the map. Adapted from City-County Planning Board, Vision 2005, 1988.

	Character	Attributes	Problems	Policy Objectives
1. Central Business District	Core area and focal point of the community Most intensive land uses Downtown office/business district Concentration of prime architectural resources	Major employment center Location is major attraction for business Solid market for office space	Loss of retail magnets and daily shopping facilities Negative perceptions of safety Perception of lack of parking In competition with suburbs for office space	Office and employment center for major corporations Promotion as the focus of urban development in Forsyth County
2. Central Area	First ring of older neighborhoods surrounding downtown Predominantly residential with some mixed use High concentration of historically and architecturally significant homes	Close proximity to CBD attractions (theater, galleries, restaurants, events, etc.) Recent interest in inner city housing (new and rehab) Small lot residential areas more conducive to social interaction	Loss of population Aging population Residential structures in need of repair or rehabilitation Conflicts with infill development	New housing that will attract middle- and upper-income people Rehabilitation of existing housing
3. Urban Area	Contains major commercial, industrial, and office employment centers Has large undeveloped tracts of land adjacent to existing neighborhoods	Stable residential areas Convenient retail services Has employment centers Significant vacant land remains	Rapid growth and development Congested road system Conflicting land uses due to mix of zoning types	Development of activity nodes at planned locations Improved transportation system Preservation of stable neighborhood areas
4. Growth Area	Predominantly rural area with some subdivisions adjacent to farms Most land is undeveloped Lies within drainage basins that can be sewered efficiently	Directly adjacent to existing developed areas and services With proper planning contains prerequisites to accommodate future growth (roads, sewer interceptors, large vacant tracts)	Inadequate rural roads to accommodate future development Large investment needed in sewers, parks, etc., to serve expected growth Lacks retail services	Provision of sewer service in an orderly fashion to serve development Build adequate highway network to serve planned development Employment concentrations and major retail at defined activity nodes
5. Rural	Rural with little or no development Major land use is scattered low-density residential along secondary roads Farming a major activity	Prime farmlands Rural life style Attractive natural environment	Cannot be efficiently served with sewer Development will cause loss of prime farmland and contribution of agriculture to economy	Limited residential and commercial development Retention of farming activities Preservation of natural environment
6. Conservation	Lands adjacent to the Yadkin River, Salem Lake, and flood-prone streams	Environmentally sensitive areas Adjacent to public water supplies Important recreational resources	Development may negatively affect water supply resources Development may cause recreational and historical attributes to be lost	Establishment of a linear park along the Yadkin River Protection of conservation areas from development Retention of aesthetic characteristics

ical "rural" districts, perhaps considered as the long-range supply of land for future urbanization. The special consideration areas might be divided into areas for different critical environmental processes, for example, wetlands being separate from water supply watersheds, each with its own proposed policies, standards, and procedures for allowing future development.

The land classification plan shown in Figure 3-3 is from a plan for Winston-Salem–Forsyth County, North Carolina. Published in 1988, it won honorable mention from the American Planning Association in 1989. Six districts, called growth-management areas, are shown, as well as general locations for activity centers. The accompanying table describes the character, problems, and objectives for each of the policy districts. Policies about development densities and public capital improvements scheduled for each district are provided elsewhere in the plan. For example, the density range for residential development in the central business district is fifteen to twenty-five dwellings an acre compared to two to ten dwellings an acre in the short-range growth area.

Compared to the verbal policy format, land classification is more specific about the desired location of growth and other change, and about what areas should be protected from change. It is therefore less flexible in implementation. It requires more sophisticated analysis in its preparation.

The land use design format is the more traditional format of land use plans. It is more specific than the land classification plan about the future land use pattern as a goal form. For example, the urban land classification district is divided into retail, office, industrial, residential, or public/institutional use, and the map of the goal form specifies the locations for each. Figure 3-4 illustrates the land use design format. The maps in the figure are from the Howard County (Maryland) 1990 General Plan, which won an award from the American Planning Association in 1991. Figure 3-4a is Howard County's vision of the desired land use pattern for the year 2010. The policies map in Figure 3-4b summarizes strategies, consistent with the land use design, that are elaborated in strategy maps throughout the plan. Both maps are multicolored and more complex in their original form. They have been simplified for inclusion in this text.

The spatial specificity of the land classification plan and land use design serves several purposes. One is to promote efficiency by coordinating the size and location of future public facilities with the location and intensity of future residential, commercial, and industrial development. For example, the land use plan suggests where to acquire land and build schools, parks, and other community facilities to best serve future as well as present residential areas. It suggests where to locate expressways and transit to best accommodate future and present travel demand, where to construct sewer lines, and how large they must be to serve anticipated growth.

A second purpose of the land use design is to specify the most suitable long-range pattern to counteract the short-sighted misallocation of land through an unplanned market. For example, through the plan a city can encourage industrial development on sites with lower long-run municipal costs, adequate future

a. Land Use Map 2010

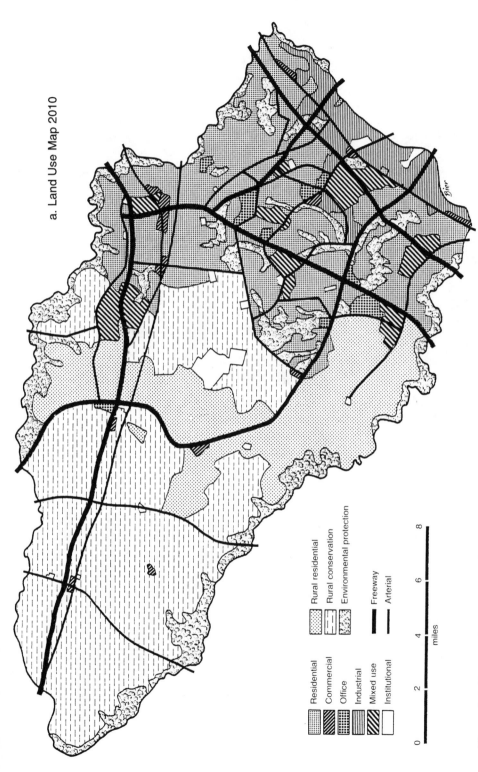

Residential
Commercial
Office
Industrial
Mixed use
Institutional

Rural residential
Rural conservation
Environmental protection

Freeway
Arterial

0   2   4   6   8
miles

Figure 3-4. Howard County, Maryland, Land Use Design and Policy Maps. The Land Use 2010 map (a) illustrates the land use design format, while the Policies Map 2000/2010 (b) summarizes more detailed strategy maps from the plan. Howard County, Maryland, 1990.

b. Policies Map 2000/2010

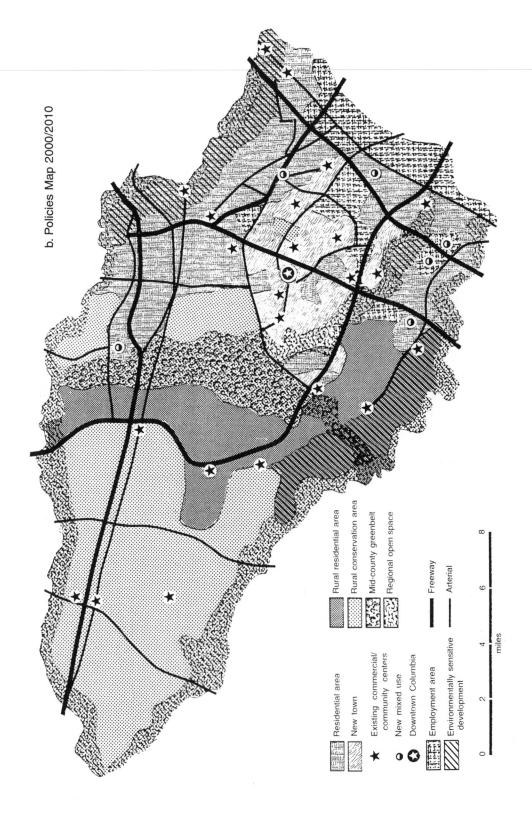

Residential area

New town

Existing commercial/ community centers

New mixed use

Downtown Columbia

Employment area

Environmentally sensitive development

Rural residential area

Rural conservation area

Mid-county greenbelt

Regional open space

Freeway

Arterial

0   2   4   6   8
miles

transportation, and suitable slopes and soils for construction of industrial plants or offices. The city can then protect such sites from premature development in housing that would preclude more efficient long-term use as an industrial park. Or, a community can preserve the capability of a watershed to serve as a future water supply and avoid irreversible damage from premature industrial, commercial, or other land uses that would jeopardize water quality.

A third purpose of the land use design can be to provide a large-scale urban design—an imageable community of vistas, skylines, distinguishable neighborhoods, and interesting entranceways.

The policy planning methodology presented in chapters 10 through 15 is aimed at producing a policy plan in both the land classification and land use design format, which are both assumed to incorporate the verbal format as an initial section.

The Development Management Plan A community cannot make a quantum leap into the future depicted by the long-range goal form of the land classification or urban land use plan. The future can only be achieved through consistent application of the policies in the plan through development management measures and programs of community action. A community therefore needs a development management plan to help implement longer-range, general policy planning. In other words, a community needs both the long-range, general, goal-oriented plan and the shorter-range, means-oriented plan. They complement each other. Without roots in long-range policy, the development management system plan runs the danger of nearsighted suboptimization, long-run inconsistency, and inadvertent creation or aggravation of future land use problems. Conversely, without the shorter-range development management plan, it is more difficult to achieve the long-range plan.

The development management plan is a proposed sequence of actions by specific organizations of the community over a three-to-ten-year period to improve the community's development management system. Such a plan might include for example, deletions, modifications, and additions to environmental and land use regulations, development fees, preferential tax ordinances; specifications of land to be acquired and community facilities to be constructed; and specific purpose programs for affordable housing, community development, economic development and historic preservation. It is aimed at alleviating current and projected problems as well as attaining long-range goals, policies, and the goal form specified in the policy plan. It includes a time schedule for implementing various components of the plan and a financial and organizational plan to generate necessary revenues to carry out the plan. It also contains a more explicit analysis of the social, economic, and environmental consequences of implementing the plan than is possible in the policy plan (Table 3-1). The plan format, adapted from that proposed by the American Law Institute (1976), features a program of specific actions guided by a statement of goals and an analysis of conditions. Note that it does not necessarily include a long-range goal form.

Table 3-1. Content of the Development Management Plan

1. A section identifying present and emerging conditions.
2. A section of goals, objectives, standards, and input policies.
3. A program of specific actions, including deletions, modifications, and additions to regulations; the amounts and general locations of land to be acquired or otherwise reserved; characteristics and general locations of community facilities and infrastructure; affordable housing and community development actions; and other special purpose programs (e.g., central business district revitalization program).
4. A time schedule for implementing the actions.
5. Estimates of personnel and other resources required to implement the plan, including costs of capital improvements and property acquisitions.
6. A financial plan to generate the revenues to pay for the implementation of proposed actions, particularly capital improvements.
7. An assessment of financial, social, economic, and environmental costs and benefits of implementing the actions, and their distribution among segments of the community.

Source: Adapted from American Law Institute 1976.

While the development management plan remains a statement of intent, it makes a decisive step toward action. It translates goals, land use and environmental policies, and longer-range land use goal form into a specific action program. It addresses costs, priorities, scheduling, financing, assignment of responsibilities among agencies, and assessment of impacts. It is designed to obtain a commitment by decision-makers to a coordinated set of actions beyond adoption of general policy guidelines. Also, by bringing the plan into a specific short-to-intermediate-range timeframe in which projects can be completed and credit claimed within an elected official's anticipated term of office, this approach can improve the feasibility of the long-range plan.

The advance planning process should not postpone consideration of development management actions until after completion of more general policy plans. The policy plan should generally include at least an outline of a development management strategy. In the land classification plan, for example, the policy bundles for each land classification district might suggest development management measures. By explicitly including development management considerations, even if only in outline form, the long-range land use design plan and land classification plan envisioned in this text differs in an important way from the traditional land use plan, which focuses almost solely on the goal form and not the means to bring it about (Kent 1964, 1991).

The plan for Gresham, Oregon (1980), provides an example of a plan that combines both long-range policy and specific development management proposals in a hybrid plan. It integrates an analysis of facts (called "findings" to reinforce the legal defensibility of the plan), a specification of goals and corresponding policies, a combination of land classification and urban land use design on a map, a capital improvements program, and standards and procedures for a unified development code. Furthermore, the land classification plan and goal-form land use design are integrated into regulations as explicit criteria; they determine which procedures and standards of the development code apply to a specific property. By adopting such an omnibus plan, the local government adopts at the same time the essentials of the development management system; there is no separate subsequent interpretation and implementation of the plan into a development code. When adopted as local legislation, the code becomes the land use regulation, which directly incorporates the plan. Table 3-2 is an illustrative contents page for an omnibus plan like Gresham's (Gresham Planning Division 1980).

Table 3-2. Hybrid Plan Table of Contents

1. Findings.
2. Policies, including both a land classification plan and urban land use design plan as goal form statements.
3. Development code, including procedures for obtaining development permits; procedures vary according to land classification district and land use proposed in the land use design for the property.
4. Standards that development must meet; standards vary according to land classification district in which the property is located and the land use indicated in the land use design for the property.
5. Capital improvements plan
6. Special functional plans, such as sewerage plan, water system plan, transportation plan, or parks and open space plan, for example.
7. Special area plans, such as central business plan, transit station area plans, or neighborhood conservation plan.

Note: This hybrid format integrates the land use design, land classification, and development management formats into the plan, and then goes a step further by incorporating those elements into specific procedures and standards that constitute a development code. When adopted as local legislation, the code becomes the land use regulation, which incorporates the plan directly.

Source: Adapted from Gresham Planning Division 1980.

Advance planning should include annual reports and periodic revisions to adopted plans. The annual reports should summarize current development, land use, and environmental conditions. They should also report on the status of the development management system and its effectiveness and suggest adjustments to long-range policy and to procedures and standards of development management measures for study and action in the forthcoming year. More fundamental reexaminations and revisions can be made less often, as need and opportunity permit, but preferably every five to ten years.

The Problem Solving Function

Problem solving is addressed to situations in the land use game that are not anticipated adequately through advance planning. For example, a problem not addressed in the plan might emerge, such as the declining water quality in the water supply watershed or a growing concern about the decline of a neighborhood. A second type of situation occurs when one of the players in the land use game proposes a significant modification to the community's development management system. For example, the mayor proposes an aggressive annexation program, an economic developer proposes an industrial park, or the chamber of commerce proposes revisions in central business district development regulations.

In the first type of situation, the question is what to do about the newly perceived problem on the community's agenda. The planner's task is to transform an expression of discontent or need into an explicit problem statement that provides land use game players more useful models of the situation; the planner must also propose and evaluate solutions that players may consider. In the second type of case where the stimulus is a non-planned proposal by a game player to change the land use management system, the planner's role is focused on evaluation of the proposal. That means analyzing its impacts with respect to adopted goals, policies, plans, and standard policy analysis criteria (equity, effectiveness, efficiency) and with respect to the way the proposal would interact with other elements of the development management system. The planner may, of course, suggest alternative solutions to the implied problem and even suggest redefinitions of the problem.

The problem solving function draws from the information system and the intelligence produced through it, as well as from goals, policies, proposed goal-form land use patterns, and the planned development management system specified in adopted plans. Rational analysis and community discourse are employed, as in advance planning, but are adapted to the constraints of time and the less-comprehensive nature of the inquiry. More specifically, problem solving includes the following tasks:

1. *Problem definition.* In this step, the planner gathers, verifies, and organizes relevant information and states the problem situation in simple, precise, meaningful terms and in sufficient detail to provide a clear, accurate picture of the problem situation.
2. *Specification of goals and evaluation criteria.* There should be a statement of what should be achieved by solving the problem and what additional evaluation criteria (e.g., cost, equity, administrative difficulty, political feasibility) will be used in evaluating proposals and alternative solutions.
3. *Identification and refinement of alternatives.* Alternative solutions are explored, including variations on the no-action or status-quo alternative.
4. *Evaluation of alternatives.* The consequences of alternatives are assessed with reference to previously developed goals and evaluation criteria. This evaluation may be as modest as a listing of advantages and disadvantages of each choice and an estimation of costs. The distribution of costs and benefits over space and population groups is often critical.
5. *Recommendations.*

Tasks 1, 2, and 3 are deemphasized when problem solving is stimulated by a specific proposal rather than a problem.

The outputs of problem solving differ in several ways from those of advance planning. Memoranda and oral reports, issue papers, or draft legislation or decision rules are more likely than substantial publications. There is no ideal format.

Still, we advocate adherence to the components of a plan—a section about conditions and problem structure, a section on goals and evaluation criteria, a section on alternative policies or actions, a section on assessments of alternatives, and a section on recommendations.

Relevant planning theory and methodology for action planning or problem solving are underdeveloped, and practice is largely catch-as-catch-can. The art of personal relations and politics plays a large role. Friedman (1969) has suggested some of the characteristics necessary to improve professional practice in so-called action planning: sharpened self-knowledge and perception of the planner in interpersonal situations together with a capacity for empathy to see the situation as other actors in the land use game see it; capacity to learn about a situation quickly and rapidly integrate this learning with knowledge, plans, and policies already on hand; knowledge about conflict, power, and the political process; and skills in the art of getting things done on time. *[handwritten: The public has an obligation to question the planner]*

Sawicki and Patton (1986) also suggest a methodology for "quick policy analysis" based on a variation of the rational model and comprising quickly applied but theoretically sound methods and techniques to address public policy problems or analyze proposals of others. Table 3-3, adapted from Patton and Sawicki (1993), indicates the basic methods of quick policy analysis as they relate to the steps in the problem solving process.

Table 3-3. Steps and Methods in the Problem Solving Process

Steps in the Process	Appropriate Methods
All steps	Identifying and gathering data Library search methods Interviewing for policy data Basic data analysis
1. Problem definition	Communicating the analysis Back-of-the-envelope calculations Quick decision analysis Creation of valid operational definitions Political analysis The issue paper/first-cut analysis
2. Specification of goals and other evaluation criteria	Technical feasibility Economic and financial possibility Political viability Administrative operability
3. Identification and refinement of alternatives	Researched analysis No-action analysis Quick surveys Literature review Comparison of real-world experiences Passive collection and classification Development of typologies Analogy, metaphor, and synectics

Table 3-3, continued

Steps in the Process	Appropriate Methods
	Brainstorming Comparison with an ideal Feasible manipulations Modifying existing solutions
4. Evaluation of alternatives	Extrapolations Theoretical forecasting Intuitive forecasting Discounting Sensitivity analysis Allocation formulas Quick decision analysis Paired comparisons Satisficing Lexicographic ordering Nondominated-alternatives method Equivalent-alternative method Matrix display systems Political analysis Implementation analysis Scenario writing

Source: Adapted from Patton and Sawicki 1993, Figure 2-3, 65.

The Development Management Function

Lay citizens, many elected officials, and even some planners look at drafting and adoption of a land use or a comprehensive plan as the solution to managing land use change. They do not understand that ordinances, capital improvements, and other governmental actions must be enacted before a community has an effective planning program. Moreover, beyond the adoption of ordinances, development management includes the ongoing process of reviewing and approving the location, type, size, density, timing, mix, and site design of proposed developments. It also includes enforcing the ordinances and otherwise playing an active role in the land use game. In addition, it includes making decisions about water and sewer extensions, transportation corridors and facilities, parks and recreation, and other public facilities. Finally, development management involves feedback to the intelligence, advance planning, and problem solving functions, as well as adjustment of land use controls in response to experience. In short, we see direct involvement in development management as an extension of planning. Planning becomes action, and action is the final step in the design of policy.

Planners have greater need to be involved directly in operating the development management system the more sophisticated its strategy, the greater its reliance on performance standards, the more flexibility allowed of developers, the more negotiation expected of local government officials, and the greater the extent of joint public-private development of major projects.

Figure 3-1 illustrates both the relationships among the four functions of the planning program and the major parts of each function. The planning program begins with intelligence, which feeds into all three of the remaining functions. Advance planning draws on intelligence. Problem solving draws on both intelligence and on plans produced through advance planning. Development management, the culmination of planning, draws on all three. Development management may, for example, incorporate a program to influence behavior and development through dissemination of intelligence; that is, providing systematic intelligence and responding to needs of development decision-makers. It may incorporate policy plans as explicit criteria for development permits and infrastructure extension. Furthermore, there is also feedback from problem solving and development management to advance planning and intelligence. Monitoring and assessment of development management, for example, are a part of intelligence. Thus, the four functions operate simultaneously at different levels of refinement perhaps but all supporting one another, and all providing important services in the land use game.

Roles of Planners, Elected Officials, Appointed Officials, Market Participants, Interest Groups, and Citizens in the Planning Program

The professional planner organizes and manages the planning program to fulfill the four functions of land planning in the land use game. As stressed in chapters 1 and 2, however, land use and environmental planning is a merging of technical and sociopolitical competencies and involves many participants in addition to the planner. Governmental officials—elected officials, citizens and experts appointed to various community boards, and city staff such as city attorneys, public works engineers, and inspectors—play important roles. Nongovernmental representatives, such as developers, landowners, and associated land market players, also participate, as do special interest groups such as environmental advocates, neighborhood associations, and individual citizens. All four functions—intelligence, advance planning, problem solving, and operation of the development management system—require substantial participation from these other participants. Without them, planning will be ineffective no matter how technically competent.

The planner plays several roles, using the skills and qualities called for in chapter 1. She or he serves as a visionary and creative innovator with the responsibility to look beyond present conditions and near-term projections and invent and visualize possibilities. The planner also advocates on behalf of future citizens, firms, and organizations as well as current residents who otherwise have little voice in the land use game. In addition, the planner contributes a comprehensive perspective required for coordinating multiple interests, objectives, policies, and programs of action. A good planner is also a consensus-builder who facilitates group planning, problem solving, and decision-making, emphasizing the more comprehensive and shared public interests.

It is also important for the planner to be a communications expert, not only in the sense of communicating technical analyses and recommendations, but also in the sense of organizing, facilitating, and managing the planning and development management process as an effective communication process, enabling all participants to reach better decisions. In other words, the planner manages community discourse. Thus, in the land use game, the planner provides technical leadership but depends on a team of diverse players. Of course, the planner should also be professionally competent in the technical aspects of analysis, projection, design, and evaluation.

Elected officials play different roles. They must lead in the broader sense of setting the agenda of issues and priorities to be addressed. They determine the scope of the planning program and the size of the planning agency. In the process of adopting and implementing the development management system, they are among the most important consumers of intelligence, advance planning, problem solving, and other advice from planners. Beyond being consumers, however, elected officials should participate throughout the advance planning and problem solving processes to assure their sense of ownership and commitment to the plans that result. They will then be less likely to ignore them or misuse the plans in their decisions.

Elected officials also determine the allocation of responsibility and authority in making development permit decisions and public investments among planners, other local officials, appointed boards, and citizens. In fact, elected officials often retain much project review and public-investment decision prerogatives for themselves and thereby play a major role in day-to-day development management, not just in setting policy and adopting legislation.

Appointed officials—both government employees and the lay people who serve on various advisory, administrative, or quasi-judicial boards—also play significant roles. They serve as sounding boards and advisors, as well as decision-makers on permits required for some development proposals. It is important for inspectors, attorneys, public works engineers, and operating department heads to also participate in the advance planning, problem solving, and intelligence functions. They should help define problems, formulate goals and policies, specify legislation and other actions, and evaluate alternatives as well as administer development regulations and build infrastructure.

Interest groups, including those representing the natural environment, the development industry, landowners, neighborhoods, business owners, and other development market players, are consumers of intelligence services, advance planning, problem solving, and development management decisions. Interest groups also advocate their views during goal-setting, policy formulation and evaluation of alternatives in advance planning, problem solving, and design and interpretation of development management system measures, as well as in development-permitting procedures and public infrastructure decisions.

Where the various land use game players have an interest, and where they play a role in influencing land development, will become more apparent in Parts 2, 3, and 4 of this book. It will become clearer in the chapters that follow when the planner, as a lead player in the land use game, involves other players and the public; gauges reactions from other players; and determines where adjustments are needed to studies and recommendations.

Organization of a Planning Program

The planning agency should be organized to accomplish the four functions efficiently while incorporating relevant participation and effective community and stakeholder discourse. At the local government level, the planning department is normally tied closely to the city or county manager's office. In addition to the planning department, the planning program would involve task forces; some temporary (for developing an approach to address flooding hazards, for example) and others that are more or less permanent (meeting regularly to review applications for development permits, for example). These groups would include expertise and perspectives from other parts of the local government, including public works, housing, community development, recreation, public safety, tax appraisal and land records, among others, as well as representatives of development interests and public interest groups.

The program should incorporate one or more planning-oriented boards of citizens to expand the resources that a planning department and professional planners can bring to the formation of policy and its implementation. A planning board, for example, is involved in all four planning functions. Usually a quasi-judicial board is needed to hear requests for variances (for hardship relief) and other appeals from permitting standards and decisions. In addition, there may be need for special boards for historic neighborhoods, appearance districts, and other special purposes. Those relatively permanent boards should systematically involve relevant neighborhood and other special interest groups.

Within the planning department, and sometimes even within the various boards associated with the department, organization should assure that each of the four functions is given appropriate attention and resources. One way to do that is to divide the department into four divisions corresponding to the four functions of planning: information, or intelligence; advance planning, or long-range planning; problem solving, or policy analysis; and development management, or current planning. Such division helps assure continued attention to advance planning, for example, to counter constant pressure to devote personnel, budget, and attention to development management and crisis management (problem solving). Sometimes the intelligence function is an interdepartmental operation involving representatives from land records as well as planning, public works, and other operating departments; then it is under more central control of the city or county manager's office. A division called current planning might include responsibility for both problem solving and administering development regulations. On the other hand, the planning director might not want to make the organizational division of the department too sharp, allowing instead for the Japanese concept of quality circles, which facilitate shifting and focusing staff efforts to meet changing community needs.

Linking Goals and Action

We might think of a community's land use planning program as establishing a chain of logic and participation for making land use and development decisions. The chain must link goals and problems at one end to actions at the other. Unless the planning and management system is logically consistent with the community's goals and input policies from regional, state, and federal governments, it will fail to achieve progress—regardless of how conscientiously regulations are implemented and public investments made. By the same token, regardless of how well plans are related to goals, the land planning program and the community will fail to achieve their potentials unless regulations and public investments follow the plans. It is important to attend to each function of the planning program and to each link in the planning chain, from goals and problems right through to the administration and enforcement of regulations.

In general, we conceive of the planning program as proceeding from ends to means, from the general to the particular, and from the long range to the short range. At the same time, the planner must appreciate and seize opportunities to work on particular problems in more detail or to implement elements of the development management system even before comprehensive policy is in place.

As for planning theory, the approach described in this chapter might be described as "more-or-less" rational planning. It falls short of the pure rational planning model in that it accepts less than perfect information and less than exhaustive listings of all alternatives. On the other hand, the proposed approach, as described in this chapter and in the methods chapters to follow, is more idealistic than the incrementalist approach. The text advocates a comprehensive perspective on urban change and the role of government and planner; systematic consideration of goals; and development of several alternatives, some of which propose basic structural changes beyond incremental adjustment and some of which are also specific actions. It also incorporates community discourse.

In describing the four functions of a land use planning program, we have purposely emphasized fundamental concepts. Similarly, in the chapters on information systems and advance planning that follow, the emphasis is on establishing a basic process, rationale, and methodology, not on the latest and most sophisticated techniques. This book is meant to provide an enduring framework. The planner can refine the simple techniques presented here and use more advanced forms of analysis as the community's program and the profession itself advances, but he or she can still rely on the basic rationale provided.

In Part 2, which follows, we discuss the intelligence function. However, we realize that direction-finding, which is covered in Part 3, is an activity that is often taken in conjunction with or even before the studies covered in Part 2. Readers may wish to consider chapter 10 on direction-setting as a chapter in Part 2.

REFERENCES

American Law Institute. 1976. *A model land development code.* Philadelphia: American Law Institute.

Calvert County, Md. 1983. *Comprehensive plan, Calvert County, Maryland.* Prince Frederick: Department of Planning and Zoning.

Chapin, F. Stuart, Jr., and Edward Kaiser. 1979. *Urban land use planning.* Urbana: University of Illinois Press.

Charlotte-Mecklenburg County Planning Board. 1985. *2005 generalized land plan.* Charlotte-Mecklenburg County.

City-County Planning Board. 1988. *Vision 2005: A comprehensive plan for Forsyth County, North Carolina.* Winston-Salem: City-County Planning Board.

Friedmann, John. 1969. Notes on societal action. *Journal of the American Institute of Planners* 35(5): 311–18.

Gresham Planning Division. 1980. *Gresham community development plan.* Gresham, Ore.

Hollander, Elizabeth L., Leslie S. Pollack, Jeffry D. Rechlinger, and Frank Beal. 1988. General development plan. In *The practice of local government planning,* ed. Frank S. So and Judith Getzels. 2d ed. Washington, D.C.: International City Management Association.

Howard County Department of Planning and Zoning. 1990. *Howard County, Maryland, the 1990 general plan . . . a six point plan for the future.* Ellicot City, Md.: Howard County Department of Planning and Zoning.

Kent, T. J., Jr. 1991. *The urban general plan.* Chicago: Planners Press. Repr. from *The urban general plan.* 1964. San Francisco: Chandler Publishing.

Patton, Carl, and David Sawicki. 1993. *Basic methods of policy analysis and planning,* 2d ed. Englewood Cliffs: Prentice-Hall.

PART 2

Planning Intelligence

This part of *Urban Land Use Planning* deals with the intelligence, or planning information base, necessary to support a land use planning program. It consists of six chapters that recommend the organization of an overall information system and the makeup of its primary functional elements: population, economy, environment, land use, and infrastructure and community facilities.

In chapter 4, "Planning Information Systems," we provide an overview of the role and techniques of the intelligence function in land use planning. We define planning information systems and describe management issues, especially those relating to the maintenance of local government computerized information systems. We discuss the design of complete information systems and of individual information modules. Finally, we present an illustrative land records management program and an illustrative land supply monitoring program.

We offer an introduction to socioeconomic analysis and growth projection for land use planning in chapter 5, "Population." It is a review of the techniques of forecasting, estimating, impact assessment, and policy preference derivation. We also cover trend extrapolation, ratio-share, indirect symptomatic and statistical association, population disaggregation, joint economic-population projection, and holding capacity.

In chapter 6, "The Economy," we continue the introduction to socioeconomic analysis and describe economic data sources and methods for economic forecasting and impact assessment, including the judgmental approach, trend extrapolation, ratio-share techniques, component techniques (economic base, input-output, regression models, econometric models), and joint economic-population projection. We also discuss the conversion of population and employment projection outputs, such as numbers of people or employees, into indicators useful for land use planning, such as number and size of households.

Chapter 7, "Environment," is a discussion of an environmental intelligence system. We describe the types of environmental information needed to preserve environmental services and biological diversity; propose a three-part framework for organizing this information, consisting of an environmental inventory, a cumulative impact assessment, and an environmental management strategy statement; and review environmental components and their mapping. Finally, we suggest three types of environmental analysis for land use planning: impact analysis, critical area analysis, and hazard analysis.

Chapter 8, "Land Use," contains our recommendation for a land use intelligence system. We describe two concepts that underlie land use change management: developability and imageability. Similar to the environmental system, the chapter's framework for organizing land use information includes a land supply inventory, a cumulative impact assessment process, and a land use management strategy statement. We review techniques for mapping land use information and monitoring land use change and suggest two analytical techniques: land suitability analysis and carrying capacity analysis.

In chapter 9, "Infrastructure and Community Facilities," we lay out an information system for keeping track of infrastructure systems. Two concepts are defined for infrastructure management: service standards and concurrency of infrastructure and land development. The chapter's organizing framework consists of an infrastructure inventory, a cumulative impact assessment process, and an infrastructure management strategy statement. We review techniques for mapping infrastructure and monitoring its change and discuss techniques for joint land use/infrastructure modeling and capacity analysis.

4

Planning Information Systems

Managers are not confronted with problems that are independent of each other, but with dynamic situations that consist of complex systems of changing problems that interact with each other. I call such problems messes. . . . Managers do not solve problems; they manage messes.
—Ackoff 1979

Planning intelligence is strategic decision-support information that enables the planner and the community to identify, understand, and deal with new and trying situations, which often appear as messes until they are systematically sorted out. Intelligence is derived from information, which consists of organized data or facts (Catanese 1979). The foundation of planning intelligence is an information system that purposefully compiles, organizes, and analyzes data on community change.

A planning information system should be able to answer, in accurate and timely fashion, critical questions about the location, nature, rate, amount, and type of land use change taking place in the community. It should be able to provide the information necessary to analyze the social, environmental, fiscal, and economic impacts of the changes and to compare historic, current, and projected changes. It should enable the planner to advise decision-makers about the potential for substituting alternative types of changes for those proposed, and about the calculus of winners and losers associated with each. The system should be able to relate these answers to more complex issues of the public interest in terms of how they affect the balance of land market values, social uses, and environmental quality.

In practice, planning information systems range from simple hand-drawn maps and manually produced report files to sophisticated computerized Geographic Information Systems (GIS). Although some manual system elements will remain in use, particularly in smaller jurisdictions, we assume that most future planning information systems will use computers, at least for record keeping and increasingly for analysis, mapping, and modeling. Advances in hardware and software technology, availability, and user friendliness, along with adoption of computer information systems in other local government departments such as tax assessment, have opened the door to exciting planning uses that appeared out of reach only a decade ago. Thus, much of the discussion in this chapter is oriented toward computerized planning information systems.

Most applications of planning information systems evolve over time from basic to advanced tasks. Case studies show that such systems are initially applied as management information systems to enhance and streamline such routine management operations as development permit tracking (Godschalk et al. 1986; Kraemer et al. 1989). This allows for the early success stories necessary to maintain political support for the new systems, which can be expensive and sometimes threatening. The systems eventually evolve into decision-support systems as top managers realize the potential for rationalizing more complex tasks, such as formulating land use plans. Ultimately, they should become public information systems supporting community discourse over land use change and helping resolve planning disputes by visually and analytically comparing different development proposals (Drummond 1989).

As they mature and evolve, governmental planning information systems are taking on the qualities of existing public information systems such as the U.S. Census. That is, they are becoming open, rather than proprietary, systems. Their information and models are becoming accessible to nongovernmental as well as governmental users. Regular users are able to subscribe to all or part of their databases. Although such openness raises a number of issues of control, privacy, and security, these issues should be manageable.

Definition and Purpose

Planning information systems are collections of spatially referenced data, studies, analyses, and models used for public planning and change management recommendations, negotiations, debates, and decisions. Planning information systems differ from other information systems in their need for relating information to space and spatial location, and in their focus on the action implications of community planning and change knowledge. In this book, we are concerned primarily with the land use change aspects of planning information, but such public information systems necessarily include a number of other categories of information.

The purposes of planning information systems are to generate knowledge and support discourse and decisions about the planning area's population, economy, environment, land use, infrastructure, and community facilities. For each of these topics, this knowledge and support is built by:

—describing its history and current status;
—forecasting its future status;
—monitoring, recording, and interpreting its changes;
—diagnosing its planning and development problems;
—assessing its supply/demand balance;
—modeling relationships, impacts, and contingencies; and
—presenting information to planners, publics, and decision-makers.

For purposes of land use planning, such systems should be able to identify the implications of local trends for land use patterns. For example, because population growth generates demand for land use change, the systems should be able to respond to questioning.

—In which planning areas is population growth occurring?
—What age groups are growing fastest, and what are the implications for housing and employment?
—When is the growth rate expected to change?
—How much population increase has occurred since the last census?
—What impacts will the new growth rate have on the demand for land and public facilities?
—What if the rate changes sooner than expected?
—Who benefits from growth in a certain location?

The ultimate purpose of the planning information system is to relate community change information back to public interest issues. Because the balance among values associated with the land market, the social use of land, and environmental quality is always subject to disruption, the information system should be able to monitor and analyze that balance in light of present conditions and to look ahead to potential future conditions.

Over time, planning information systems should evolve from in-house management information systems to full-fledged public information systems. In the process, the applications will change from dealing with the routine to dealing with the new and unexpected, and the users will expand from government to the total community. Planning information system managers will need to learn and grow with the systems, blending technical, managerial, planning, and political skills. Initially, however, the first hurdle for most local governments is figuring out how to start a system. This involves looking at questions of both system management and system design.

Management Issues

Information system management is a process of design and implementation. This is a challenging task, and its dimensions are becoming clearer as more experience is gained. Combining art and science, it involves issues of control, interests, coordination, hardware and software, system organization, system implementation, accessibility, and staffing (Godschalk et al. 1986; Kraemer et al. 1989).[1]

Locus of Control

The most fundamental issue concerns who is to be in charge of the information system. Candidates for control include:

1. the technical staff who run the equipment;
2. the heads of the departments whose operations use or are affected by the system;
3. the top government managers, such as the county administrator or city manager, who see the system as a strategic control device; and
4. a shared group that may include any of the above as well as elected officials or public interests.

Because information is a resource whose use can have major organizational and political implications, the issue of control is not trivial. Top managers who initially view information systems as purely technical services may learn of the power-enhancing capabilities of these systems through experience. Control of the generation and circulation of information within an organization is a major form of organizational power. According to Kraemer et al. (1989, 28), "previous research has demonstrated that decision-making about computing tends to occur in ways that reinforce existing political elites in organizations." To minimize the use of information systems for power enhancement, we emphasize the importance of designing the systems for broad access, including public interest group users.

From the planning department viewpoint, it is critical for the planning director and staff to have influence over and access to—if not control of—information systems. In the past, when data-processing technicians outside of planning were in control, the systems tended to be slow in responding to planning needs. Unless the planning function is an integral part of the system's operations, similar problems could arise under multiple department-controlled systems or under systems controlled by top management. Because of the specialized and extensive nature of planning information, it is desirable for the planning department to design and manage the planning information system, which may be part of an overall information system network drawing on other sources and providing information to other users.

System control tends to determine the orientation of the systems. That is, the primary interests served tend to be those of the controlling decision-makers.

Interests Served

The types of interests that planning information systems serve are related to the locus of control (Kraemer et al. 1989). If the technical staff controls the system, it will likely be oriented toward development of technically advanced hardware and software packages and leading-edge applications. If the local government department heads control the system, it will likely be oriented toward servicing departmental operations and use a variety of hardware and software to meet the administrative needs of the departments involved. If the top managers control the system, it will likely be oriented toward meeting broader, strategic organization and management goals. If control is shared with elected officials or representatives of the public, then the system is more likely to be oriented toward meeting public information needs and may stress accessibility and presentation clarity. Mixed control arrangements, in which system direction is divided between technicians and department heads or technicians and top managers, are likely to have mixes of system objectives similar to their mixes of control.

Coordinating Information Providers and Users

A variety of local government departments and private-sector groups use planning information. In some cases, the users are also the providers of the information. Because of the comprehensive nature of their responsibilities, planners tend to have wide-ranging interests in information and to depend upon many other sources to provide it. Public and private planning information-users and the types of information they use include:

Users	Information
Governmental:	
Land planner	Land supply/demand indicators (including all the following)
Tax assessor	Land value, use, amount, characteristics
Building inspector	Development permits and project status
Engineering	Public facility location, capability, status
Budget and finance	Capital improvements funding, status
Parks and recreation	Open space inventory and population growth
Public safety	Incident location, response management
Emergency management	Hazard locations, mitigation programs
Chief executive	Governmental demands, responses, policies
Elected official	Public development issues, impacts
Private-sector:	
Developer and builder	Land regulations and infrastructure
Realtor and appraiser	Land availability and development potential
Engineer and architect	Land characteristics, services, codes
Environmental advocate	Natural resource systems, development impacts
Neighborhood advocate	Social use patterns, development impacts
Nonaligned citizen	Costs/benefits of land use changes/proposals

Hardware and Software Selection

One of the more difficult decisions in starting a planning information system is how to select the right package of hardware and software. There is no universal answer to this question given the range of local government situations and the changing nature of information technology. But there are systematic ways to find answers.

The major hardware decisions have to do with whether to acquire personal computers (also called microcomputers), workstations, minicomputers, mainframe computers, or some combination. Previously this was a matter of the size of the database and programs that needed to be run, with minis or mainframes necessary for all sizeable jobs. With the growing storage capacity of personal computers and the ability to network a number of machines together with a central file server, as well as to download portions of databases in order to work with them, however, the answer is no longer that simple. Add in the fact that many local governments already have some computers on-line, and the decision about equipment could call for specialized help in designing an optimal package. This could be provided by staff, an outside consultant, or, in some cases, by a vendor, although usually it will be better to maintain an arm's length relationship with vendors.

Major software decisions have to do with which types of programs to acquire. Because well-tested and supported programs are widely available on the commercial market, there is no longer a need for major in-house program design.[2] But the array of marketed products can be confusing. All systems will need a relational database management program, which can maintain, store, and update files, such as parcel land use records, and a spreadsheet program that uses a tabular format and can perform such rapid calculations and adjustments as analyzing land use changes by type and district under various land policies. As systems develop, they will likely add a computer mapping and spatial analysis program chosen from among the three major types (Table 4-1):

Table 4-1. Computer Software Types and Functions

Types	Functions
Database management	Attribute file maintenance
Spreadsheet	Numeric analysis
Computer mapping and	Thematic mapping (fixed areas)
spatial analysis	Computer assisted design (CAD)
	Geographic information systems (GIS)
	Vector (polygon)
	Raster (grid)
	Quadtree (subdivided grid)

1. *Thematic mapping* programs, such as ATLAS Graphics, associate tabular attribute data with fixed spatial areas, such as census tracts or planning districts, in order to prepare presentation maps and figures, such as population density maps.
2. *Computer assisted design* (CAD) programs, such as AUTOCAD, allow the user to draw precise lines, points, and shapes in order to lay out designs or spatial data for architectural, engineering, site planning, facility management, or urban planning applications.

3. *Geographic information system* (GIS) programs, such as ARC/INFO, use integrated spatial and textual databases that allow the user to overlay layers of information and create new layers from the overlaid combinations in order to ask "what if" questions for presentations, analysis, modeling, and planning (Star and Estes 1990).

Computer mapping outputs are divided into two major types. *Vector* mapping programs produce *polygon* outputs, which reproduce the actual shapes of geographic areas, such as land parcels or watersheds. *Raster* mapping programs produce *grid* outputs, which show data in a square cell format. A variation of the raster, *quadtree* programs produce subdivided grids that vary the grid size to fit the individual data structure units so as to use computer data storage capacity more efficiently.

Many simple planning applications can be done at relatively low cost by linking a database management program to a thematic mapping program (Ferriera and Menendez 1988). Increasingly, all types of commercial software are expanding to become "full service" packages.[3] The capacity of hardware is also expanding. Distributed personal computer/workstation networks can handle most CAD or GIS applications. The field has moved from "smart" mapping systems to integrated, stand-alone GIS packages, to third-generation distributed systems that link various computers, data, and software packages. Future advances will add more visualization capabilities where maps are used to find and retrieve video images of particular features (e.g., buildings or bridges) or areas (e.g., neighborhoods or wetlands), facilitated by new "object-oriented" software (Weigand and Adams 1994).

System Organization

Computers for information systems can be organized in three patterns: centralized, decentralized, and distributed (Figure 4-1). Each form has its advantages and disadvantages.

1. *Centralized* organization places the main computer, a high-capacity machine such as a mainframe, in one location where it is controlled and operated by a specialized data processing, information services, or management information department. User departments may be tied in by remote access terminals. The advantage is that the equipment and database are maintained by expert technicians, where economy of effort results in lower costs and standardized procedures result in less potential for misuse or error introduction. The disadvantage is that planning and other departments are dependent on the central staff, which reduces their ability to initiate analyses independently and can introduce delays and bureaucratic frustration.

2. *Distributed* organization combines a high-capacity central computer facility acting as a data and program library serving smaller client computers distributed among the departments, providing for both remote access and re-

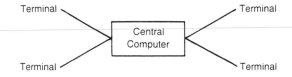

CENTRALIZED PROCESSING
(Terminals provide remote access for user
departments but not remote processing.)

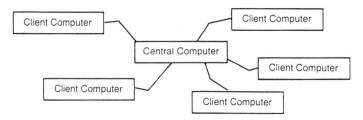

DISTRIBUTED PROCESSING
(Client computer workstations provide both remote access for
user departments *and* remote processing through downloading.)

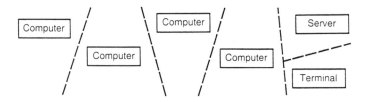

DECENTRALIZED PROCESSING
(Each user department has its own processing unit or system, and
there is no central coordination among the various
units to guard against duplication.)

Figure 4-1. Information System Organization Alternatives. From Godschalk et al. 1986, 41.

mote processing. The advantages are that analytical autonomy for users is provided without sacrificing central coordination and economy of scale. A variety of hardware, software, and data can be linked into an integrated information system. The disadvantage is that departments do not have complete operational freedom, but with proper coordination this problem can be minimized. On balance, the distributed option appears to be the most useful for a planning information system that relies on other departments for much of its data and shares hardware and software capabilities, but local conditions could dictate another form of organization.

3. *Decentralized* organization places independent computers or computer systems in the individual user departments, each with its own database, where they are controlled by department staff. The advantage is that the equipment

and databases are in the hands of the users of the information, who can set their own work priorities, customize applications, and acquire the hardware and software that they desire. The disadvantage is that without central coordination, there may be duplication of effort across departments, and useful, efficient database linkages may not be made.

System Implementation

Implementing a new computerized planning information system can be a difficult experience due to the mingling of technological complexity, political risk, and institutional change. Implementers must sort out what type of equipment package is needed, how they can persuade decision-makers to commit funding, and when they can expect to get operational results from the new way of doing things.

One way to cope with the uncertainties of implementation is to develop the new system incrementally rather than comprehensively. Incremental development can proceed by adding pieces of hardware, software, and databases over time, according to a general and flexible system design. This has several advantages: the ability to try out different types of equipment, to keep the budget manageable and the system output expectations within bounds, to allow the technical staff to learn their work gradually, and to let the system develop in accordance with the development of the technology. On the other hand, if system needs are well defined, if system funding is available at the start, and if qualified technical staff can be put in place early, then comprehensive implementation has the advantages of ensuring hardware and software compatibility, of allowing an immediate start on long-range database creation, and of initial planning for full-scale system administration and staffing.

Gaining and maintaining political support for procurement of a planning information system depends upon being able to demonstrate to decision-makers that benefits outweigh costs. This demonstration can show benefits from improved operations efficiency, from more precise and timely information for decision support, and from greater use of public information by those outside government. More accurate, timely, and widely used information should result in smoother governmental operations, better coordination of capital expenditures with development, and more credible public decision-making. Because the equipment packages are expensive, it may also help to gain political support by staging expenditures over time through an incremental or modular implementation program. Other effective tactics are to designate a "champion" to spearhead implementation and to use a pilot project to demonstrate system benefits and root out problems.

When results can be expected from new planning information systems depends upon the scale of the system, the installation and learning times for new equipment, and how long it takes to create usable databases. It is a mistake to promise very early results for systems that must be built from scratch. Larger systems, with more complex equipment and bigger databases, may take several years to reach operational levels. Among the most time-consuming tasks are creating properly registered base maps and digitizing land parcel record databases. It will also take time to reorient old data collection and management procedures to the new information system procedures. If major staff turnovers or policy changes take place in the local government, then system implementation can be further delayed. A reasonable rule of thumb on when to expect outputs from a new system is to double the initial estimates in order to allow for inevitable problems and overly optimistic schedules.

Accessibility

Decisions on who will have access to do what to various parts of the system depend on how the database is to be created and used. Some systems allow users to inspect data but not to change it. Other systems allow certain qualified users to both access and input data. For public records, accessibility raises issues of protecting the security of information from unauthorized tampering, of protecting the privacy of sensitive information about individuals or organizations, and of sharing the costs of database maintenance among users.

Computerized information systems limit access to certain users by means of passwords, "read only" files, and other techniques. To protect privacy, some information may only be available in the form of aggregated files. Cost sharing and recovery is becoming a greater problem because of the costs of computerized information systems. Some local governments charge a fee for over-the-counter data; others offer a monthly subscription for a fee to on-line access for frequent nongovernmental users and outside public agencies.

Staffing

Finding qualified staff to operate computerized information systems is a major management problem. Until more individuals are trained in this field, there will be continuing stories of systems sitting idle because the qualified operators who started them got hired away. Not only must staff be found initially, but they also must be trained in the local system, and their training must be updated as the system changes. The initial staff must be backed up with others who can take over in cases of advancement or departure from the job. Qualified staff must also be provided with sufficient incentives, in terms of learning and advancement opportunities, to keep them in place.

Information System Design

Resolution of management issues goes hand in hand with resolution of information system design issues. These range from determining the scope of the system's coverage to working out procedures for controlling the quality of the data in the system.

System Scope

Scope is usually determined through a needs analysis aimed at defining the jobs to be done by the system. In the absence of budget and staff constraints, the scope of a planning information system could be very broad because planning is concerned with relationships among many activities and functions. But when constraints are applied, it is necessary to be parsimonious about the scope of the system. Capturing and maintaining data can be expensive. Planners need to think in terms of the fundamental types of data and analyses first and to design systems that will encompass these basic needs.

Computer Mapping and Spatial Analysis

Computer mapping systems contain two basic types of data: *graphic* and *attribute*. These are linked by *geographic identifiers*. Graphic data include points (wells, spot elevations); lines (rivers, streets); areas (land parcels, drainage basins); and blocks (aquifers). Attribute data include such nongraphic characteristics as density, land use type, or address, which are stored as alphanumeric characters, usually in tabular form. Geographic identifiers relate graphic and attribute data using a standard reference scheme, such as the state plane coordinate system, to key the attributes to specific locations.

Information system design issues for computer mapping include the types of spatial units to be used, the registration system for the maps, the accuracy specifications, and the updating arrangements. Computer graphics programs can produce thematic maps based on stable designated areas like census tracts or planning districts, CAD maps based on areas digitized by the operator such as project sites, and GIS maps based either on vector systems that allow the operator to digitize areas that replicate actual shapes of areas such as parcels or watersheds (called polygons) or raster systems that produce areas divided into uniform grids (Table 4-1).

If the purpose of the maps is primarily to compare and display information, then simple thematic mapping may suffice. If the purpose is to provide engineering design precision, then CAD maps will be needed. If the purpose is for urban land use planning where recognition of irregular polygons such as parcels is necessary, then vector GIS programs, such as ARC/INFO, are most useful. If the purpose is for regional planning or large-area environmental planning or use of satellite data, then raster GIS programs, such as ERDAS, are useful. Although most mapping software was originally designed for single-purpose applications, the trend is to add capabilities to the programs as they are updated. Future programs may well include the features of thematic maps, CAD, and GIS within one software package.

Registration systems tie maps into larger location schemes such as state plane coordinates, latitude and longitude, and Universal Transverse Mercator systems. All are basically grids precisely located upon the earth's surface so that a land parcel can be located within the grid; thus its location relative to all other land parcels and grid locations can be readily determined. Planners, however, have not been accustomed to making registered maps, and the process of transferring existing planning maps to registration schemes can be troublesome. Each computerized map has to be provided with "tick" marks that place it precisely on a registration location.

The benefit of relating all spatial data and map areas to a registration system is

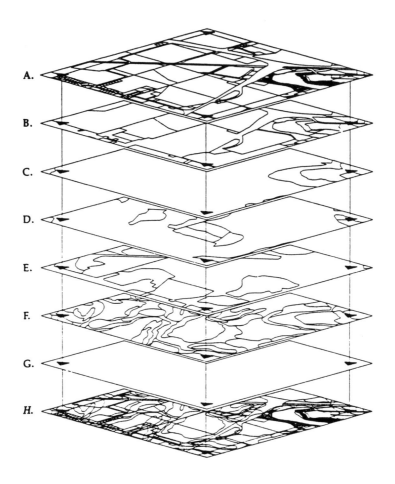

Section 22, T8N, R9E, Town of Westport, Dane County, Wisconsin

Data Layers:	Responsible Agency:
A. Parcels	Surveyor, Dane County Land Regulation and Records Department.
B. Zoning	Zoning Administrator, Dane County Land Regulation and Records Department.
C. Floodplains	Zoning Administrator, Dane County Land Regulation and Records Department.
D. Wetlands	Wisconsin Department of Natural Resources.
E. Land Cover	Dane County Land Conservation Committee.
F. Soils	United States Department of Agriculture, Soil Conservation Service.
G. Reference Framework	Public Land Survey System corners with geodetic coordinates.
H. *Composite Overlay*	*Layers integrated as needed, example shows parcels, soils and reference framework.*

Figure 4-2. Layered Land Information System. From Godschalk et al. 1986, 28.

that accurate map overlays can be produced. The land planner is interested in combining various types of information in order to analyze relationships. For example, an analysis of developable land would consider several types of environmental data together with land ownership and zoning. Individual maps of land parcels, zoning, floodplains, wetlands, land cover, and soils can be registered through a common coordinate system in order to generate a *composite map* of developable land (Figure 4-2).

Accuracy also comes into play in the process of transferring hand-drawn maps into computer maps. In most cases, the hand-drawn maps will not fit precisely together because they were drawn at different scales and degrees of accuracy. These were adequate for broad, felt-tip-pen planning overlay studies. However, the computer requires a precise fit and will not tolerate leftover areas, gaps, slivers, overlaps, or lines that do not meet. GIS programs have routines such as "rubbersheeting" and "snapping" that bring mapped areas into alignment. But it is important to record the level of accuracy of the maps involved for future measurement and analysis purposes.

Updating computer databases and maps is critical to ensure that the information used is current. Given the varying types and rates of urban change, most planning information systems lag well behind the current status of development in their jurisdiction. By considering procedures for updating during the system design phase, it may be possible to reduce the lag between the receipt of information and its incorporation into the planning database. For example, if all requests for building permits, preliminary subdivision plats, project approvals, certificates of occupancy, and the like were entered into the planning information system concurrently with their receipt, then a major source of lag would be eliminated. Similarly, if all land use changes were entered upon receipt, then computer file versions of maps would remain current.

Querying, Reporting, Analysis, and Modeling

Planning information systems contribute to better decisions on land use change through answering questions, compiling reports, conducting analyses, and modeling change impacts and alternatives. The fundamental use is to respond to such queries as the what, where, and when questions posed at the start of this chapter. For this purpose, the information system is basically a reference system, containing historic and current facts as well as future estimates. An extension of this purpose is reporting on a regular or on-demand basis of conditions or states of the urban area, such as the type and amount of development that has taken place in the past year in each planning district.

More advanced uses involve conducting analyses or modeling that relates different land use change variables. The following chapters describe analytical and modeling techniques for each major topic of planning information. These techniques attempt to discover significant trends, problems of supply/demand imbalance, or causal relationships. For example, they might model the impacts of projected future urban development upon transportation and utility system capacity, upon water and air quality, and upon the urban economy. Because these models often require large amounts of computer storage, it is useful to anticipate their requirements during the system design phase.

Expert Systems

Expert systems are computer programs that apply artificial intelligence, in the form of decision rules based on the knowledge of experts, to narrow and well-defined problems in order to provide advice in problem solving (Ortolano and Perman 1987). They rely on theories of logical deduction to generate conclusions from facts and rules, often in the form of "if this premise applies, then that consequence occurs." Expert systems are applied to "domains," such as zoning administration or site planning, using a "knowledge base" of facts, definitions, rules of thumb and computational procedures, and a "control mechanism" or set of procedures for manipulating the separately coded knowledge base. Generic software is available in the form of expert system "shells" consisting of a general control mechanism and an editing facility for entering the knowledge base for a particular domain. Knowledge bases are developed through iterative processes of refining prototype expert solutions.

Most of the applications of expert systems have been in fields such as medicine, engineering, and chemistry, but there is potential for planning uses in each of the types of activities that they perform (Ortolano and Perman 1987, 99–101):

—interpretation of situation descriptions from data, such as determining whether a proposed land use meets zoning and other local development regulations;
—diagnosis of problems and prescription of remedies, such as assisting in the operation and maintenance of physical infrastructure;
—design and planning, such as performing an analysis of a particular site;
—monitoring outcomes and controlling system behavior, such as controlling environmental conditions within a building; and
—instruction of novices, such as teaching new staff members about zoning and development regulations.

Few operating expert systems exist in the planning domain. However, a number of prototypes are being built.[4] It remains to be seen whether such systems will be able to perform as well as human planners at the really challenging tasks of the field or whether they will simply be automated tools for carrying out lower-level and routine tasks.

Information Module Design

Collections of data dealing with different functional areas, such as economy and population, have different types of content but similar structures. They also follow similar technical processing steps. These collections can be visualized and designed as "information modules." Certain basic tasks are necessary to organize each functional information collection or module: classification, data capture, data organization, and interpretation. Although the elements will differ by module, as between economy and environment, for example, the basic tasks apply across modules. Each module will develop a "database"—a structured collection of information on its subject—and will use database management software to permit users to work efficiently with the data (Star and Estes 1990, 127). It will describe the information stored in the database in a "data dictionary," a comprehensive listing of the categories of data collected. The database management system should provide efficiency in storage, retrieval, deletion, and update of large data sets; support for simultaneous access to the database by multiple users; reduction of data redundancy; and data independence, security, and integrity.

Classification

All information systems rely upon classification of data to make information intelligible and manageable. Classification schemes are typologies that assign each piece of data an identification label and a place within a data structure or hierarchy. Where more than one classification scheme is available, the choice of classification scheme is a critical information system design decision that will have far-reaching implications. For example, if land use is classified according to density (e.g., number of units per acre), then the density ranges chosen (e.g., one to two units per acre, three to five units per acre, six to ten units per acre, and eleven or more units an acre) should be compatible not only with existing land use patterns and land use plan classes but also with zoning and development ordinance classes and with environmental standards and criteria. Similar considerations apply to classifications for population, economy, and other modules.

Data Sources and Capture

Data are obtained or "captured" for information systems both through importing from outside sources and through collecting. Increasingly, standard data are available for import to local information systems from state and federal government sources.

For example, the 1990 Census of Population is being supported with an automated geographic database called TIGER (Topologically Integrated Geographic Encoding and Referencing System). The TIGER database merges all of the Census Bureau's address coding, mapping, and geographic inventory functions into a single digital database. The TIGER/Line files, available on computer tape and CD/ROM, are organized by county and contain digitized base maps. Their data include geographic coordinates for physical features such as roads, rivers, railroads, major power lines, and pipelines; political boundaries for counties, townships, and places; statistical boundaries including census tracts and blocks; and associated collection/tabulation codes, address ranges, and zip codes for street segments (in metropolitan areas only), feature names, and other information.

TIGER/Line files were developed from mosaics of U.S. Geological Survey (USGS) 1:24,000 scale maps that were photographically reduced to a scale of 1:100,000 and digitized at national map accuracy standards. These USGS digital line graphs (DLGs)[5] contain separate digital layers for roads, hydrography, railroads, and miscellaneous transportation features. The DLGs were merged with the 1980 Census GBF/DIME (Geographic Base File/Dual Independent Map Encoding) files, and 1990 census collection and tabulation digital codes were added. Uses of TIGER include county planning base maps, address-matching, emergency response and transportation routing, and site location and market analyses. To make full use of TIGER requires GIS or CAD software.

State and regional agencies also can provide digital data for planning information systems. Some state land records offices may maintain computer files of assessed land values. Land information systems may have computer maps of soils (digitized from U.S. Soil Conservation Service soil surveys), topography (from digital line graphs), and environmental conditions (such as wetlands from the National Wetlands Inventory) for some or all parts of the state. State departments of transportation often will have computer maps of road systems and small-area transportation analysis zone computer files of population, employment, and other demand factors. State emergency management offices will compile data on hazard areas. State demographic agencies maintain population data and often prepare local population projections. Regional planning agencies increasingly compile regionwide computer databases that demonstrate linkages between neighboring environmental and infrastructure systems. Often these files can be imported on computer tape to the local information system for a nominal cost.

Local government agencies are also important sources of data. As mentioned earlier, planning information is generated by agencies ranging from tax assessment to building inspection. The planning agency will originate some of the data for the planning information system in the form of existing land use surveys, environmental inventories, population and economic studies, and development application reviews. Much of the information needed for a planning information system often is already collected by such other local or regional agencies as transportation planning organizations, but it may be buried in individual file cabinets rather than being captured by the information system. Planning information system managers need to be diligent in seeking out existing information sources, as well as in creating new sources when necessary.

In addition to "hard" data sources, information systems should not overlook "soft" data, such as community surveys and quality of life studies. Myers (1989) points out the utility of quality of life information in understanding the positions of community interest groups in local development disputes and enabling planners to establish a cooperative dialogue with them.

Data Quality

The value of the information generated depends upon the quality of the data collected and maintained in the information system. Quality control is necessary to ensure the consistency and accuracy of data collected from surveys, records, and other sources. Data quality affects the reliability and validity of findings from planning analyses. Reliability is achieved when the findings from analyses are repeatable. That is, the results are the same, or only vary to a minor degree, when the analyses are rerun under similar circumstances. Validity is achieved when the analysis findings are corroborated within reasonable limits by results obtained from another established measure. That is, they are genuine measures of the condition or phenomenon they seek to measure.

It is tempting to assume that maps and tables that computerized information systems produce are error-free. However, that assumption is unrealistic, given the complex nature of the natural features on a map and the complicated procedures for entering data. Errors may be inherent in the source documents or base maps due to problems of initial inaccuracy, the age of the data, use of inappropriate scale (e.g., seeking to transfer small-scale maps to a larger scale), inadequate ground control, measurement and classification errors, and the variability of the natural features (e.g., a reservoir shoreline).

Errors also may be operational, produced by the processes of data capture and manipulation. The processes of digitizing, editing, and plotting base maps are subject to operator errors. Combining several individual maps, each with some errors, into a composite map can magnify the degree of error. Converting maps from vector to raster formats will result in the loss of some information.

To minimize the adverse effects of data quality problems, the quality of data presented on any map should be specified. Three characteristics should be reported.

1. Lineage information should contain the date and scale of the source map and an assessment of its compilation error.
2. Positional accuracy should be assessed against check plots and independent control points.
3. Attribute accuracy should be checked against samples of correctly classified information or ground-truthed areas.

Data Organization

Once the necessary data have been collected, they must be organized in a systematic fashion to facilitate access and use. The basic elements in a data module and their purposes include:

—records, basic units of organization for data collection;
—files, collections of related records to produce information;
—attributes, listings of characteristics of spatial areas;
—maps, spatial displays of geographic features and their attributes;

—registration systems, frameworks (e.g., state plane coordinates or latitude and longitude) to locate data on the earth's surface;

—parcel identification numbers (PINs), links between mapped areas and attribute data; and

—screens, preorganized menus or outlines of information requested in routine queries.

The basic unit of organization is the record, which might be an individual land parcel record or a single zoning change request record. Related groups of records are organized into files, or collections of data about a particular topic, such as all the land parcels or zoning change request records. Permanent files will be kept of certain information, while temporary files will be opened for new studies and analyses. For purpose of GIS mapping, the format of the file is important in determining the use of computer-generated overlays. Attribute data must be maintained in relational databases. Map or locational data must be maintained in topologically consistent databases and referenced to a registration system through the use of parcel identification numbers or other connectors. To facilitate repetitive inquiries, screens are constructed so users who ask for a particular type of information, such as a title search, see a menu listing the available data with a computer prompt directing attention to the potential choices.

The most fundamental type of file is based on individual land ownership records in which the parcel is the unit of ownership. The planning department will need access to a parcel file in which information on all the parcels in the planning jurisdiction is maintained (Table 4-2). Another basic unit of interest to the land planner is the project, the typical unit of development. Files on applications for rezonings, subdivision requests, and site plan approvals could be kept in a project file, where information is collected on the type of project permit or request, action to be taken, dates of action, and present status. A third type of file might be based on environmental units. This could be a natural areas file, including soils, slopes, watersheds, and land cover, where relatively stable environmental information is collected and stored for use in planning and evaluation.

Data Interpretation

Software programs can facilitate the work of going beyond the raw data to an interpretation of meaning. For example, a spreadsheet model can be used to test the impact of various best-management practices, including stormwater detention basins, large-lot zoning, and stream buffers, on the quality of water in a drinking water supply reservoir. To test the feasibility of a proposed transit system, a GIS buffer model can be used to compare the size of the populations living within various distances from the proposed transit corridor under different density assumptions.

Each information module will use its own forms of interpretation to generate knowledge about its topic. Cross-module analyses will link various topics such as

Table 4-2. Illustrative Parcel Data File

Geographic Identifiers

Parcel identification number (PIN) assigns a unique identification number to each land parcel, usually based on a state plane coordinate system.
Tax map, block, and parcel number
Site address
Census tract and block
Planning district
School district
Electoral district
Utility or service district (water, sewer, fire, police)
Traffic Analysis Zone
TIGER file identifier

Assessor's Information

Land use code identifies the basic use of the parcel (e.g., residential) and possibly more specific breakdowns (e.g., single-family detached, one dwelling unit per acre), based on a land classification system
Size: the overall acreage or square feet of the parcel, sometimes broken down for larger parcels into subareas by use type (e.g., twenty acres overall, with ten acres pasture and ten acres woodland)
Owner's name and address
Assessed value: divided into land and improvements
Tax status and legal description
Recent sales price and date
Easements, deed restrictions, or permit conditions

Planning Information

General plan designation (proposed future land use type and density)
Zoning classification
Existing land use type (see also assessor's land use code)
Intensity of use (e.g., floor-area ratio)
Infrastructure availability (water, sewer, roads)
Growth management status (e.g., "committed land" overlay where project approvals have been granted)
Hazard area (e.g., hundred-year floodplain)

Site Characteristics

Topography and slope (e.g., flat—1–2 percent slope)
Soils and septic potential
Vegetation and land cover type
Watershed and aquifer recharge area
Proximity to road

land use and environment, or economy and infrastructure. Each module also will include maps illustrating and interpreting its particular data. The land use planner must be able to interpret basic map features.

Map Features

Scale is the precise relationship between actual distance on the ground and the fractional representation of that distance on a map. The larger the scale of the map, the more extensive its representation of details on the ground. Thus a map drawn at two thousand feet to the inch shows more information than one drawn at a hundred thousand feet to the inch. The scale of the original source map is important in judging the amount of information and accuracy of a digitized map in a computer database. For example, the large-scale USGS digital line graphs (digital representations of cartographic information) are derived primarily from their 1:24,000, 7.5-minute quadrangle maps. Although accurate, these maps do not show much local detail.

Location is the placement of a feature on a map relative to placement on the surface of the earth. Maps are tied to geographic referencing systems that permit their features to be located on the ground. Among the standard referencing systems are the township, range, and section system used in early U.S. land subdivision descriptions, the state plane coordinate system used in many computerized state land records programs, the universal transverse mercator system used by USGS in their mapping programs, and the latitude and longitude system used for navigation. With the advent of geographic information systems, accurate placement of maps within a standard referencing system is required.

Area is the amount of space within a two-dimensional land surface such as a subdivision lot or a floodplain. For a rectangular surface, area is determined by multiplying length times width. Irregular surface areas can be determined by various hand methods including measurement with a planimeter; division into geometrically regular sub-areas (rectangles and triangles); using a uniformly spaced dot grid overlay; or constructing a series of equally spaced transects. Contemporary computer mapping systems calculate areas automatically.

Three-dimensional surfaces, based on area plus height, can be represented as "digital elevation models" (DEMs). For example, such continuously varying surfaces could include land topography, population density, or air pollution. The triangulated irregular network (TIN) is a special GIS technique for representing three-dimensional surface values. TIN models allow for extra information in areas of complex relief similar to the quadtree for two-dimensional areas.

Illustrative Land Records Management Program

North Carolina established the state's Land Records Management Program to provide technical and financial assistance to local governments for modernization of their land records systems (North Carolina Land Records Management Program 1987). The program sets out specifications for creating standardized, accurate land records program elements: aerial photography, orthophoto base maps, cartographic base maps, topographic maps, cadastral maps, and soil maps. It is presented here as an illustration of the content of a modern land records system.

A specification-based land records program gives consistent land records across the state. In North Carolina, the land records of two adjacent counties can be merged into one map because they both use the same PIN code system, state plane coordinates, and accuracy standards. Planners can use intergovernmental databases for regional intelligence systems with assurance that they will be dealing with land records with similar performance specifications. Because the parcel centroid is located within the PIN code, construction of large-area land use maps is facilitated. Furthermore, the North Carolina Geographic and Information Analysis office can provide state, regional, and local GIS maps and databases formatted to a standard system.

Aerial Photography

Controlled aerial photographs are flown to record the base conditions of the planning area. The contractor is responsible for establishing horizontal and, if applicable, vertical control surveys. First, existing control by the National Geodetic Survey (formerly U.S. Coast and Geodetic Survey), state geodetic survey, and state department of transportation, is located. Then the contractor marks additional control points with permanent monuments that are detectable by magnetic or electronic locators. The control points are referenced to the state plane coordinate system.

Base maps produced from aerial photographs are either line-drawn cartographic base maps or photographic-image orthophoto base maps. They are produced in series of four map scales: 1 inch equals 400 feet, 1 inch equals 200 feet, 1 inch equals 100 feet, and 1 inch equals 50 feet, with each image area bounded by state plane coordinate system grid ticks and identified by selected paired digits of the east and north coordinates.

Orthophoto Base Maps

Orthophoto base maps are prepared from rectified aerial photographs in which only the center portion of the photograph is used in order to eliminate distortion of the image. Distances on orthophoto base maps may be scaled, as with cartographic maps. They have the advantage of showing actual ground features, including vegetation and other natural features, in addition to roads and other mapped elements.

Cartographic Base Maps

Cartographic base maps are line-drawn to show planimetric features including names and boundaries of cities, towns, rivers, streams, railroads, state and federal highways, and land use features, structures, hydrographic features, and recreational facilities. They have the advantage of providing a simplified format in which the items of interest show up clearly.

Topographic Maps

Topographic maps are orthophoto or cartographic base maps containing contour lines and point of spot elevation to show changes in the vertical elevation of the ground surface. Elevations are based on the National Geodetic Vertical Datum, 1929 Adjustment. Contour interval is 2 feet on 1 inch equals 100-feet scale maps and 4 or 5 feet on 1 inch equals 200-feet maps.

Cadastral Maps

Cadastral maps depict the boundaries of land ownership parcels, each with a parcel identification number (PIN). The ten-digit PIN is constructed from the state plane coordinates for the visual center of the parcel and includes a four-digit number of the basic map module, a two-digit block number, and a four-digit lot or parcel number. PINs are included on the maps only for "active" subdivisions where the plat is filed and lots sold. Cadastral maps include names, boundaries, and identification of subdivisions and plats; governmental unit boundaries and names; streets, railroads, rivers, lakes, canals, seaports, and airports; and horizontal control monuments. In addition to the maps, the contractor must produce two computer-printed property indexes; one lists parcels by PIN in numerical sequence, and one lists parcel owners' names in alphabetical order. They also produce a list of acreages showing deed acreage, computed acreage, and assessed acreage for each parcel.

Soil Maps

Soil maps depict the detailed soil types and soil land uses (water, homesite, cemetery, wooded, cleared, right-of-way, and exempt) based on the U.S. Soil Conservation Service county soil survey. Along with the map, the contractor must generate a computer soil report for each parcel of land, including the PIN, total acreage, soil types and acreages, and soil land uses and acreages.

Illustrative Land Supply Monitoring Program

Planning information systems not only record basic data such as land records, but they also combine data in order to carry out local programs and policies. An example of a combined system is one used to monitor the balance between urban development and infrastructure in which the approval of requests for new development is based on the availability of sufficient infrastructure capacity to serve that development (Godschalk et al. 1986; Bollens and Godschalk 1987).

Montgomery County, Maryland, uses a land supply monitoring system to administer its adequate public facilities ordinance (Maryland-National Capital Park and Planning Commission 1986). The county regulates the location of residential development and employment concentrations by allocating the capacities of transportation routes to policy areas. Each policy area is assigned a threshold level of development, expressed in both residential and employment terms, which is balanced with existing and programmed transportation facility capacity. Subdivisions that add development above the threshold level may be refused approval. Approved but unbuilt projects are counted as in the development pipeline. The number of dwelling units in the pipeline, along with existing units, are subtracted from the threshold to find the number of new units that will be permitted in each policy area.

Although the adequate public facilities ordinance covers all types of facilities, including sewer systems, water systems, police stations, fire stations, and health clinics, transportation has been found to be the most constraining facility, and the methodology balances development against transportation capacity. School capacity also must be found adequate under a separate review.

Policy areas are grouped by their transportation service standard for both transit and roads. For transit, a full-service area has frequent metro service, concentrated feeder and community bus service, "kiss-'n'-ride" parking lots, and easier walk access. Frequent transit service areas have some metro, regional and feeder bus service, kiss-'n'-ride, and community bus service. Moderate transit service areas have regional bus or commuter rail access or both as well as limited metro, park-'n'-ride, and feeder bus service. Limited transit service areas have regional bus or commuter rail access or both as well as park-'n'-ride. For roads, the standard level of service ratings of A through E are used (chapter 9).

The system obtains parcel data from the assessor's files and supplements it with information from building permit applications, sewer authorizations, subdivision requests, zoning applications, and housing completions. Each project in the pipeline is monitored through the required steps of preliminary plat approval, sewer allocation review, record plat approval and recording, sewer permit granting, building permit granting, and occupancy permit.

In determining residential development amounts, each dwelling unit, single family or detached, is counted as one unit. Unless the development is unique, statistical averages are used for employment calculations for major land use categories: office (two hundred square feet per employee), retail (four hundred square feet per employee), industrial (450 square feet per employee), and other (five hundred square feet per employee). For determining whether a capital facility project is "programmed," it must be within the approved county capital improvements program or the State Consolidated Transportation Program, such that 100 percent of the funds necessary for construction or operation are scheduled for expenditure within six years.

Planning Information as Strategic Intelligence

Planning information systems are major sources of planning intelligence. They not only help players of the land use game learn and understand the effects of changes in the urban area, but they also help them manipulate their environments constructively. However, apparently neutral and objective information can become a strategic game resource used to maintain or alter power balances among the players as well as to influence decisions in favor of certain interests.

Market-oriented players often hold their own information close to the vest in order to conceal forthcoming investment strategies from business rivals. However, they are interested in tapping into planning information about changes in demographics, infrastructure, environmental conditions, and project approvals for their market and feasibility analyses.

Social use players scan planning information for early warnings about public and private projects that may affect their interests. They look for data that can be used to oppose undesired projects as well as to mitigate their impacts. They see information as a key resource in attempting to influence public policy and decisions.

Government players use planning information in the conduct of their operations as well as in the construction of plans and budgets. Functionally oriented departments look to information affecting their functions, such as zoning or public works. Management departments, such as city managers, look at information that facilitates both their internal control of their staff and their external relations with the community and elected officials.

It is the planner's responsibility to ensure that information systems are designed and used to benefit the community as a whole while at the same time supporting the planning function. In the process, there are likely to be many conflicts over the definition, collection, and distribution of planning information. As in other planning responsibilities, this requires careful attention to both fairness and efficiency.

Computerized information systems have the potential to restructure and enlarge the scope of planning analyses. However, they are complex undertakings that can require years to become operational. They also require major institutional changes to become effective. It is tempting to become dazzled by their technological potential and to underestimate the "soft" costs of implementation, including staffing, training, maintenance, and management. It is also easy to underestimate the political effort necessary to support innovative information systems.

The wise planner will pursue a conservatively staged implementation effort. Not only should simple systems be learned first, but the trajectory of the system should also be seen as a progression from serving operational needs, to serving decision-support needs, to ultimately serving public information needs. The technical aspects of the system must be mastered before the purposes are enlarged beyond the ability of the staff to support them.

During the design and implementation of planning information systems, the overall purpose should be kept in mind. The larger goal is to provide intelligence to the community to help manage change in order to maintain a working balance among the values associated with the environment, the social use of land, and land as an exchange commodity. Including representatives of each of these interests in the design process will help to ensure that the adopted system design respects this balance.

NOTES

1. See Kraemer et al. (1989) for a model of information system "management states" based on locus of control and interest served in which control by information system managers is equated with technical interests in the "skill" state, control by department managers is equated with operational interests in the "service" state, and control by top managers is equated with organizational interests in the "strategic" state.

2. Commercial software packages are developing at a rapid rate. In order to keep up with planning software changes, see the "Computer Report" section of the *Journal of the American Planning Association.* Useful "Computer Report" reviews include those by Klosterman (1986, 1990), Harris (1989), Levine and Landis (1989), Ferreira (1990), Wiggins and French (1990), and Ferguson, Ross, and Meyer (1992).

3. For example, the ATLAS thematic mapping program has been expanded to include GIS capabilities, and the AUTO/CAD computer assisted design program has been expanded by adding a spatial/textual database program, Geo/SQL, that converts it to a GIS.

4. A promising application of expert systems concepts is the BASS II metropolitan simulation model (Landis 1992), which incorporates a market clearing program replicating developer decisions about developing land parcels in the context of local growth-management regulations; projected population growth; physical characteristics such as slope and wetlands; infrastructure availability; and other parcel attributes.

5. Digital line graphs (DLGs) are digital cartographic maps based on a vector format. The USGS produced them from their 7.5-minute and 15-minute topographic map series. In addition to the map topology, the files contain attribute such data on the features of USGS topographic maps as hydrography and surface cover.

REFERENCES

Ackoff, Russell. 1979. The future of operations research is past. *Journal of the Operational Research Society* 30(2): 93–104.

Bollens, Scott A., and David R. Godschalk. 1987. Tracking land supply for growth management. *Journal of the American Planning Association* 53(3): 315–27.

Catanese, Anthony J. 1979. Information for planning. Ch. 3 in *The practice of local government planning,* ed. Frank So, Israel Stollman, Frank Beal, and David Arnold. Washington, D.C.: International City Management Association.

Drummond, William J. 1989. The design of information systems for public issues: An impact fee prototype case study. Ph.D. diss., University of North Carolina, Chapel Hill.

Ferguson, Erik, Catharine Ross, and Michael Meyer. 1992. PC software for urban transportation planning. *Journal of the American Planning Association* 58(2): 238–43.

Ferreira, Joseph, Jr. 1990. Database tools for planning. *Journal of the American Planning Association* 56(1): 78–84.

Ferreira, Joseph, Jr., and Aurelio Menendez. 1988. Distributing spatial analysis tools among networked workstations. In *Proceedings of the 1988 national conference of the Urban and Regional Information Systems Association,* 3:200–215. Los Angeles.

Godschalk, David R., Scott A. Bollens, John S. Hekman, and Mike E. Miles. 1986. *Land supply monitoring: A guide for improving public and private urban development decisions.* Boston: Oelgeschlager, Gunn, and Hain.

Harris, Britton. 1989. Beyond geographic information systems: Computers and the planning professional. *Journal of the American Planning Association* 55(1): 85–90.

Klosterman, Richard E. 1986. An assessment of three microcomputer software packages for planning analysis. *Journal of the American Planning Association* 52(2): 199–202.

———. 1990. Microcomputer packages for planning analysis. *Journal of the American Planning Association* 56(4): 513–16.

Kraemer, Kenneth L., John Leslie King, Debora E. Dunkle, and Joseph P. Lane. 1989. *Managing information systems: Change and control in organizational computing.* San Francisco: Jossey-Bass.

Levine, Jonathan, and John D. Landis. 1989. Geographic information systems for local planning. *Journal of the American Planning Association* 55(2): 209–20.

Maryland–National Capital Park and Planning Commission. 1986. *1985 report on comprehensive planning policies, including guidelines for the administration of the adequate public facilities ordinance.* Silver Spring: The Commission.

Myers, Dowell. 1989. The ecology of "quality of life" and urban growth. In *Understanding growth management: Critical issues and a research agenda,* ed. David J. Brower, David R. Godschalk, and Douglas R. Porter. Washington, D.C.: Urban Land Institute.

North Carolina Land Records Management Program. 1987. *Technical specifications for base, cadastral and digital mapping.* Raleigh: North Carolina Department of Environment, Health, and Natural Resources.

Ortolano, Leonard, and Catherine D. Perman. 1987. A planner's introduction to expert systems. *Journal of the American Planning Association* 53(1): 98–103.

Star, Jeffrey, and John Estes. 1990. *Geographic information systems: An introduction.* Englewood Cliffs: Prentice-Hall.

Weigand, Nancy, and Teresa M. Adams. 1994. Using object-oriented database management for feature-based geographic information systems. *Journal of the Urban and Regional Information Systems Association* 6(1): 21–36.

Wiggins, Lyna L., and Steven P. French. 1990. Desktop mapping and GIS. *Journal of the American Planning Association* 56(3): 370–73.

5

Population

Knowledge about past populations and assumptions about future populations are fundamental to planning decisions in every aspect of community life.
—Krueckeberg and Silvers 1974, 259

The future economy and population level of an urban area are complementary aspects of urban growth. Many players in the land use game are interested in economic and population analyses and projections. Population and employment largely determine future overall land use and community facility needs from the social use viewpoint of those who will use the land. They also determine the future levels of urban stress that will be put on environmental resources. Finally, population and employment growth underlie the amount of development pressure and the pace of urban development to be accommodated and addressed. Thus, the land development industry is interested in population and economic analyses as factors in commercial, office, industrial, and residential development decisions.

Economic and population studies are also related methodologically. Studies of the economy, particularly employment, are key elements in population forecasts because economic opportunity, or lack of it, is a basic determinant of migration into or out of the planning study area. Similarly, studies of population as a labor market and source of consumer purchasing power play important roles in economic forecasting as well as in determining the feasibility and locations of retailing centers. Furthermore, population and employment projection share similar techniques.

In this chapter, we will cover population first, not because population studies should precede economic studies (if anything, it is the other way around) but because population studies often employ simpler versions of methods, which take on more complex forms in economic analysis. Also, population forecasting has a longer history, and its role is more central in the evolution of forecasting, which is a secondary theme through this part of the book. By the 1950s, when forecasting for economic activity and land use became widespread, demographic forecasting already had evolved into the typology used to structure the discussion in this book.

Full-fledged analyses of the economy and the population usually require the skills of economists and demographers who understand economic and demographic dynamics and have solid command of theory, methods, data sources, and interpretive skills. Nevertheless, the local land use planner must know something of data requirements and the weaknesses and strengths of the various methods of analysis and projection. Beyond that, the planner should be prepared to execute limited investigations, particularly those directly related to demand for land and public infrastructure. Simple population and economic analyses are within the capacity of many local planning agencies.

Economic and Population Information in Land Use Planning

Economic and population information has several uses in planning. The first is to estimate current population and employment. Estimates of current levels indicate the need for revenue-sharing, for assessing per-capita conditions with respect to community services compared to community service standards (e.g., recreation standards about acres of parks for every thousand residents), for measuring and understanding community change, and for developing inputs for other analyses. A second purpose is to make population and economic forecasts, which determine future land use and community facility requirements. A third purpose is to trace and assess population and economic impacts of past events, proposed events, and possible future events. A fourth purpose is to establish policy preferences for population level, composition, or rate of change, that is, to choose a desired growth rate, future population level, or employment level, on the basis of community goals, rather than project trends.

Estimating Past and Present Population and Economic Indicators

State and federal grants to localities are often made on the basis of population or economic activity levels. Because censuses are taken only every ten years in the United States, it is necessary in the years after the most recent census to estimate the population of cities, counties, sub-state regions, and even states and the nation. Beyond revenue-sharing, communities want to know their population and employment levels in order to measure trends and evaluate local service requirements and levels of service. Up-to-date population estimates are so useful, in fact, to a broad range of local government purposes that many planning agencies make annual estimates. Estimates also serve as part of the database for making projections.

Forecasting Future Population and Economic Activity

Forecasting is the second—in land use planning the predominant—application of population and economic studies. Together, the economy and population determine the amount of development that will occur. A projection of how much the study area will grow, level off, decline, or change in composition of industries or population is necessary for the planner to estimate changing land and public service requirements as well as demands on the environment. An expanding economy and population means that more land is going into use. A declining economy and population, however, or one that is changing in composition, also suggests changes, if not growth, in land use requirements.

Employment and population forecasts serve two particular purposes. First, they are the basis for estimating future space requirements. Space requirements for housing are estimated by converting population forecasts into numbers and types of households; estimating the housing types that will be preferred, affordable, and suitable; converting those housing types into density requirements; and then multiplying population/housing need forecasts by those density standards. Space requirements for future levels of economic activity are estimated by multiplying employment forecasts for various manufacturing, wholesale, retail, and office sectors by appropriate employment density standards.

The second application of population and employment forecasts is in projecting the need for transportation, community facilities, and public services. Thus, estimates for the quantity and types of highways and public transportation facilities, parking facilities, water and sewer plants, schools and parks, and other community facilities are all based in part on the amount, composition, and spatial distribution of population and economic activity in the study area.

Distinctions between Projections and Forecasts   Although the terms *forecast* and *projection* are often used interchangeably, they carry a subtle but important distinction. A projection is the exact measurement of a future condition that will exist *if* the assumptions embodied in the projection approach prove true. Those assumptions may posit the continuation of current conditions, extrapolate trends, or pose departures from either existing conditions or trends, based on expert or other judgments. Whatever the assumptions, a projection is always correct if the projection technique is logically correct and is carried out without arithmetic error. Most economists and demographers do projections; they cannot be wrong.

A forecast, on the other hand, makes judgments about the likelihood of assumptions behind projections. The most unequivocal forecasts are called predictions. Sometimes a range of assumptions is used to produce a high-low range of projections. But, because judgment comes into choosing the high-low assumptions, the results still constitute a forecast. Thus, although all forecasts are projections, not all projections are forecasts; it depends on whether the analyst makes judgments about the likelihood of the projections coming true.[1]

Difficulties in Making Projections for Land Use Planning   Two aspects of forecasting for land use planning make the task more difficult than forecasting for many other policy analysis purposes. First, land use planning requires long-range forecasts. Where economic forecasting, by contrast, extends to one or two quarters, or one or two years, the land use planner must look ahead five, ten, even thirty or more years.

Second, local land use planning requires "small-area" analysis and projection. Economists and demographers tend to study economies and populations of nations or large regions, so they regard a city, county, metropolitan area, or even a state as a small area, to say nothing of neighborhoods or small towns. Planners, however, are particularly interested in those small "small areas," which makes the planner's task even more daunting because demographic and economic analyses for small areas are more difficult than for larger areas. Not only are data more difficult to obtain, but the dynamics of small areas are also much more volatile and difficult to predict. Movement in and out of the area is greater as a percentage of the population or employment; the closing or opening of a single large firm might change employment significantly.

Planners' analyses may include spatial modeling to distribute the employment and population estimated by population and economic analyses described in this chapter and the next. Thus, it extends beyond population and economic forecasting and into the realm of land use modeling, requiring simulation of the land market and other spatial behavior.

Because forecasts of population and employment for city planning are long-range and for small areas, they are often met with skepticism. At the same time, in most land use planning applications, there is latitude for inaccuracy. In the same way a civil engineer uses a safety factor in designing a bridge, the city planner uses an "industrial reserve" or "residential land reserve" as a safety factor in estimating future space requirements. Beyond that, even if we concede the possibility of economic or forecast inaccuracies being large, the effect of such inaccuracies tends to be relatively small compared to the possible error in assumptions about future employee and housing density used in conjunction with the population and employment projection to estimate land requirements. Thus, there should be as much concern for the choice of that density multiplier as there is for the projection of employment or population level.

There are additional moderating elements. Implicit in the planning process is the necessity to review plans periodically in light of unforeseen events. That provides continuing opportunities to adjust the plan long before reaching the target date for which the forecasts and land requirements are projected. Furthermore, the land use plan to some extent is not tied to a specific future date. Rather, it is for a community of a certain population and economy, factors that may occur several years earlier or a few years after the target date without unduly affecting the usefulness of the plan. Finally, land use controls and capital investments influence growth and may reinforce the forecast somewhat, particularly if there is conscious population and economic growth policy.

Socioeconomic Impact Assessment

As a third application to land use planning, a planner sometimes wants to trace the population implications, spin-off employment, or the changes in land use requirements of an event such as the closing or opening of a manufacturing plant or office park. Population and economic models provide a partial basis for estimating those consequences. Impact assessment is sometimes applied to a past event to single out the effect of that event from what would have occurred without it. More often, however, planners want to determine population or economic change of a proposed event, for example, the opening of a new plant or the decline of an existing industry.

A Normative Approach to Population and Employment Studies

A fourth application of population and economic studies, actually constituting a contrasting philosophical approach, is to determine what population or economic activity level *should* occur; what composition *should* occur; or what rate of growth *is best*. Land, environmental, and infrastructure-carrying capacity analyses; studies of alternative ways to finance and expand infrastructure; and analyses of land use design possibilities are used to help decide such economic and population policy.

This approach is in strong contrast to the more traditional approach of projecting population and employment and then designing the future land use plan to accommodate what is projected. That is, the more traditional approach is to forecast how many people would be living in the area in the future based on trends and assumptions about future factors that affect growth and then design the plan to accommodate that number of people. The normative population analysis approach asks, instead, how many people can our environment, infrastructure, and land area sustain without unacceptable harm to the environment and quality of life. The answer to that and similar questions provides a population figure and growth rate consistent with planning sustainable communities.

Important Characteristics of Population and Economy to Study

Three characteristics of population and economy are especially relevant for land use planning purposes: size, composition, and spatial distribution. Size is the basic yardstick for estimating space needs for various categories of land use—retail, office, and manufacturing in the case of employment levels, and housing in the case of population—as well as needs for infrastructure and community facilities like parks and schools. Future employment and population size determine future dimensions of urbanization.

Beyond total size of the population or employment, the planner studies their composition. By composition, we mean the sizes of specific age groups, household types, and socioeconomic levels of the population and by industry and type of firm for economic activity. Knowledge of composition assists the planner in determining future requirements of particular types of housing.

Finally, the planner studies the spatial distribution within the study area. Spatial distribution is important in planning the locations of various land uses and community facilities. For spatial analysis purposes the local population or employment estimates and projections are allocated to traffic zones, planning zones, census tracts, neighborhoods, or other such divisions of the urban area.

In addition to size, composition, and location dimensions, planners also study past, present, and future conditions. They study the past to determine trends and model the dynamics of population and economic change. That information is necessary to understand where the community has been, where it is at present, where it seems to be headed, what alternative futures are possible, and what population and economic targets might be reasonable. Data on the present are necessary in order to be precise about current conditions, to establish trends (by comparing present to past conditions), and to establish fair shares of state and federal revenue sharing and grant programs. Finally, planners need to project the future size, composition, and location of population and employment to determine the amounts and locations for space, facilities, and services that must be provided in land use plans.

Ways to Obtain Data

Some data are obtained from outside the planning agency, for example, the U.S. Bureau of the Census or a state office of economic and demographic analyses. Such data are often called *secondary data*. Secondary data may also come from other local government agencies or other sections of the planning agency, for example, from the tax office. Secondary data is available in many forms: reports, records, microfiche, and computer tapes and disks, as well as maps, text, graphs, tables, and computerized files of records. In addition to obtaining information from others, a planning agency may collect or otherwise generate its own data. Such information is called *primary data*.

Regardless of whether the data are primary or secondary, data measurements can be made in four ways: *enumeration* (100 percent survey); *sampling* (less than 100 percent survey); *estimation* based on indirect indicators (e.g., estimating population by reference to recorded school enrollment); and *projection*. The Census Bureau's decennial census is an enumeration, as would be a planning agency's 100 percent survey of a neighborhood or community. Sampling is designed to obtain data that would be too costly or time-consuming to measure by enumeration. Of course, sampling is not as accurate as enumeration.

An estimate has an explicit meaning in population and economic studies. It is an indirect measure of a condition that exists or has existed and which in principle could be, or could have been, measured directly by sampling or enumeration. An estimate is made because an enumeration or sample is unavailable, impossible, too costly, or too time-consuming. Estimates of population and economic activity are often based on utility hook-ups, housing starts, school enrollment, or voter registration, for example. These symptomatic data are recorded for other purposes, but they are accurate, readily available, and closely associated with population or employment. It is important therefore for the planner's information system to contain or have access to symptomatic data. If such data are not readily available for the study area, projection techniques are substituted as a way to estimate current conditions.

Thus, a population and economic information system contains both primary and secondary data, and data created by projection, enumeration, sampling, and indirect estimation.

Sources of Population Data

Planners turn to many sources of demographic information, and many types of information are needed. In addition to information on the level, composition, and spatial distribution of population, past, present, and projected, that information should include data on such factors of demographic change as births, deaths, and migration, space availability, and population-symptomatic data such as school enrollment. The information should cover not only the study area but also its region, state, and the nation. For some techniques, data for the region are used to help estimate and project population for the study area.

The U.S. Bureau of the Census is the primary source of enumerations, samples, estimates, and forecasts of population data. General sources of census data are cited in the following discussion. Planners can best learn about population data sources, however, by examining those and other publications and materials from the Census Bureau that apply directly to the study area being analyzed.

The decennial reports of the Census Bureau are based on enumerations and samples. Those containing data for small geographic areas—towns, counties, metropolitan areas, census tracts, enumeration districts, and blocks within those places—are of particular interest to planners. Since 1940, the census has issued bulletins on the number of inhabitants and the characteristics of populations for such small areas. Census of Population bulletins, along with a similar series for the Census of Housing, carry small-area data for counties and various minor civil divisions. Two other useful series of bulletins are the Census Tracts bulletins for metropolitan areas[2] and the Block Statistics bulletins for cities.[3] In addition to the Census Bureau, each state has one or more centers for the storage and dissemination of census data. Such centers serve as a source of both data and technical assistance in local demographic analysis and projection.[4]

The Bureau of the Census also publishes population estimates and projections in their Current Population Reports, series P-25. Estimates are made annually for states, metropolitan areas, and counties as well as the nation. Projections of population are made less often but still fairly regularly for the nation and for states. Although the census does not project for smaller areas such as metropolitan statistical areas (MSAs) or counties, many states make projections at the county level. At the very least, state projections offer control totals and the birth and survival rates needed for small-area projections. In addition, there is an office in each state government that participates in the Federal-State Cooperative Program for Population Projections and is a point of contact for local analysts (see note 4).

The Census Bureau presents not just a single forecast but a series of projections based on differing fertility, mortality, and migration rates. The user can pick the most plausible assumptions about those rates and then use the corresponding Census Bureau projection, which traces out their implications. In practice, many users simply take what the bureau calls the middle series on the assumption it is the most plausible. The planner is wiser, however, to pick the assumptions most appropriate for his or her study area, which may be subject to different death, birth, and migration rates than the parent region.

In addition to reports, census data are also available on magnetic tape and disks. These forms provide the capability to make detailed tabulations not included in published sources.[5] Many commercial software and data firms provide census data on disk. (See, for example, reviews of data and software by Klosterman 1985; Landis 1985; Levine 1985; Ottensman 1985; Brail 1987; and Langendorf 1987; although software changes so rapidly that the reader is advised to seek more recent assessments. The *Journal of the American Planning Association,* for example, regularly publishes such assessments.)

Some population projection techniques require data on vital statistics on births and deaths in order to calculate age, sex, and race-specific survival and fertility rates. These can be obtained in most states from the state's demographic data center or office for health statistics and from the National Center for Health Statistics. Those data are provided at the county level for three-year periods surrounding each decennial census and at the state level annually.[6]

In addition to the U.S. Census, virtually every state has an office of demographic and economic studies that performs analyses for the state legislative and executive branches. Those offices usually have highly qualified demographers and economists available for consultation, but they also publish estimates and projections for counties and other civil divisions. Other local agencies or divisions within the planning agency also often have relevant local data, particularly symptomatic data such as development permits, school registration, and utility hook-ups.

Methods and Techniques for Population Projection and Estimation

Planners use several approaches to estimating present population and forecasting future population.[7] Actual applications almost always use combinations of several approaches and techniques, but we have defined distinct categories for purposes of explanation.

1. *Trend extrapolation.* This approach examines trends and extends them into the future. It is applied to total population level, components of that total

(e.g., elderly), and sometimes to specific characteristics of the population (e.g., fertility). Extrapolation may be based on judgment, visually fitting lines to data on graph paper, or by mathematical formulas.

2. *Ratio-share techniques.* In this approach, the study area population is expressed as a ratio or share of the population of a larger geographic area, called a parent area. To estimate or project population for the study area, that ratio is multiplied by an independently derived population estimate or projection for the parent area.

3. *Symptomatic and statistical association techniques.* In this approach, a statistical equation or simple ratio is applied to indicators such as jobs, dwelling counts, housing starts, or school enrollment to obtain estimates or projections of population. Like the ratio technique, this approach requires a reliable enumeration, estimate, or forecast of indicators.

4. *Disaggregation of population change into component parts and simulation of the change in those components.* The population is divided into separate age groups, genders, and ethnic groups, called cohorts. Population change is divided into its components—births, deaths, and migration. Assumptions and change processes for each of these components are then addressed separately for each cohort. This approach is called the component, cohort-component, or cohort survival method.

5. *Joint economic-population techniques.* This approach projects population and employment in a coordinated, sometimes iterative, procedure. The population projection is based on employment and other economic analyses, and the economic projection is based on labor force–population indicators from demographic analyses.

6. *Holding capacity techniques.* Instead of economic and demographic processes, this technique focuses on the available space for employment or population. That is, it examines space and other resources available in a bounded geographic area such as a neighborhood, a city hemmed in by incorporated suburbs, or an island. Then it determines an upper limit, or holding capacity, based on multiplying a reasonable density of employment or population by the amount of space or other limiting resource such as sewer capacity. The population projection is some fraction of that ultimate "100 percent filled" holding capacity. Longer-range projections are larger fractions of holding capacity than near term projections.

Of these six approaches, all but the ratio-share technique assume that the study area is an independent economic, social, and demographic entity. That is, they are based primarily on what has happened in the study area itself in the past, what is happening, and what is projected to happen in the future, without respect to the parent area. That is not to say that the other techniques do not look to the parent area for clues about trends in causal factors and components of economic and population change.

The approaches for projecting future conditions are arranged in order of complexity except for the last approach, holding capacity, which is not necessarily more complex but rather a departure from the progression of population change simulation. Most are also applicable to estimating present conditions.

Trend Extrapolation

Trend extrapolation may be applied to both economic and population data. The implicit assumption in this approach is that time is a valid proxy for causal factors—births, deaths, migration, business starts and deaths, hiring and firing decisions, structural changes in the economy, and the like. In addition to projecting total population size, or amount of change, extrapolation can be applied to age groups, ethnic groups, and other subgroups and to variables incorporated into other methods (e.g., birth rates).

When applied to population size, extrapolation is best suited to shorter-range projections (ten years or less according to Shryock, Siegel, and Associates 1976, 443; Greenberg et al. 1978, 7); for slow-to-moderate growth areas; and for areas where historic census counts are the only reliable data available. It is also useful as a baseline projection against which to check the reasonableness of projections using other methods.

The quickest and simplest means of extrapolating past trends in population size and employment is by graph. Past population or employment data are plotted on the vertical scale, and time is plotted on the horizontal scale. The line fitted to the points on the graph by eye represents the analyst's best judgment about the past association between time and population or employment. The analyst then extends that line into the future to obtain a projection of population or employment.

It is a good idea to plot population or economic data on graph paper even when one does not intend to rely on the graph for making a projection. The graph produces a picture of what has happened over a historical period. It may suggest insights about the relationship between population size (or employment) and time. For example, the graph will show whether the relationship is linear or nonlinear (curved). It also is a way of answering other questions about the relationship, such as whether a nonlinear pattern becomes linear on semilogarithmic graph paper. Are the changes consistently in one direction, either up or down, even if unsteady in rate? If curved, is the line convex or concave? Do shifts in rate or direction occur at the same time as particular historical events that might have affected economic growth, migration, fertility, or mortality?

Of course, extrapolation lines may also be fit to the data mathematically, at least if the association of population or employment with time is fairly smooth. One of four common mathematical forms are generally used to describe historical population growth and extrapolate growth trends into the future:

1. the linear model,
2. the geometric or exponential model,

3. the modified exponential model, or
4. the polynomial model.

In addition, sometimes Gompertz or logistic models are considered (Keyfitz, 1972; Pittenger, 1976). These models translate into s-shaped curves. Because they require data covering an extended period, for which census data may not be available for small areas, the Gompertz and logistic models are seldom used for local planning.

The Linear Arithmetic Change Model   Mathematically, the linear model of population change uses the familiar general form:

$y = a + bx.$

The dependent variable, y, represents population level, birth rate, death rate, or other population characteristics that the analyst has shown to have a linear relationship with time. The constant a represents the value of that variable at the base year for the projection. The constant b represents the amount and direction of change in the population characteristic per unit change in time (usually either a year or a decade). Finally, x is the number of those units of time (years, decades) beyond the base year. When using the linear model to project population size, the form is:

(5.1) $P_{t+n} = P_t + bn$
where P_t = population in base year t;
P_{t+n} = projected population size at a future year, n units of time beyond base year t;
b = average increment of change in population size per unit of time; and
n = the number of time periods beyond base year t.

Simple linear regression may be used to calibrate the model.

The Geometric or Exponential Change Model   This model assumes that the amount of population growth over a unit of time is proportional to the size of the population at the beginning of the period. Population growth compounds like interest in a savings account. Although the rate of growth (like interest rate in the saving account) remains the same for each period, the absolute addition to population (dollars added to the savings account) gets bigger and bigger with each passing period because the rate is applied to a bigger and bigger population (saving account balance). The rate of growth is constant, whereas in the linear model it is the amount of growth that is constant for each period. That assumption is valid in the absence of shifts in the basic demographic components of births, deaths, and migration (Pittenger 1976, 47).

The form of the geometric model is:

$$(5.2) \quad P_{t+n} = P_t(1+r)^n$$

where P_{t+n}, P_t, and n are as in the linear model, and r is the rate of growth per unit of time.[8]

The geometric form in Equation 5.2 has an equivalent logarithmic form:

$$(5.3) \quad \log P_{t+n} = \log[P_t*(1+r)^n]$$
$$= \log P_t + [\log(1+r)]n$$

This form can be recognized as the linear model, and the ordinary least squares regression method of parameter estimation can be used to estimate $\log(1+r)$ (Pittenger 1976, 47–53; Keyfitz 1972). Equation 5.3 also represents a curve that plots as a straight line on semilogarithmic paper.

As one may see from examination of the graphic representation of the exponential growth curve in Figure 5-1, demographic conditions cannot sustain such a curve indefinitely. Eventually, the curve becomes incredibly steep, and the population exceeds any reasonable holding capacity of a finite geographic area, thus constituting an unrealistic projection. For this reason, where implications of the exponential model become unreasonable for the study area, other model forms, such as those following, become more appropriate.

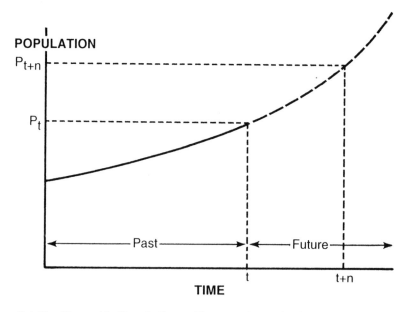

Figure 5-1. The Geometric Growth Curve. The rate of growth with respect to the base population at the beginning of each period is constant, but the absolute amount of growth becomes larger and larger through time as the population increases; similar to compounding interest in a savings account.

The Modified Exponential Curve If the analyst sees a pattern of smaller and smaller increments of absolute growth, as in Figure 5-2, the appropriate mathematical form may be the modified exponential model. This model assumes an upper limit on population size for the study area and is written as

$$(5.4) \quad P_{t+n} = K - [(K - P_t)b^n]$$

where P_{t+n}, P_t, and n are as before; k is the upper limit of population size for the study area, which the curve approaches but never quite attains; b equals the constant ratio (less than one) of change by which $(K - P_t)$ is reduced each successive time unit from its value in the immediately preceding time unit. Thus, P_{t+n} approaches K as n increases. That is, the equation projects P_{t+n} in terms of a constantly decreasing distance from the population ceiling, K.

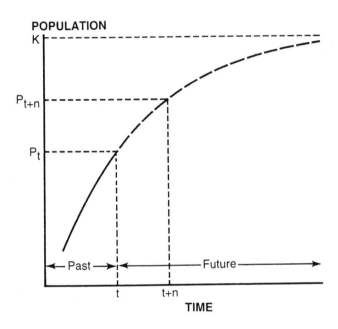

Figure 5-2. The Modified Exponential Curve. The increments of growth become smaller and smaller over time; the value K is an assumed upper limit that the population approaches but never quite attains.

The Polynomial Model of Population Change This model of population change permits more complicated curves than any of the models discussed above. At the same time, however, it has the least rationale behind it. For that reason it is more purely a mechanical fitting of a curve to data. The polynomial model is of the form:

$$(5.5) \quad P_{t+n} = P_t + b_1 n + b_2 n^2 + b_3 n^3 + \ldots + b_p n^p$$

The highest exponent indicates the degree of the polynomial. The linear model is a first-degree polynomial. A second-degree polynomial describes a curve with one bend, either convex (if b_2 is negative) or concave (if b_2 is positive). A second-degree polynomial could approximate the exponential or geometric curve, for example. A third-degree polynomial describes a curve that has two bends and could be used to approximate the Gompertz and logistic curves.

The polynomial curve is less rigid in its form than any of the previously described models. Therefore, it can better describe less regular growth patterns and patterns that include both decline and growth. On the other hand, the projections often produce unreasonable numbers if the analyst projects beyond a very short time frame.

Summary of Trend Extrapolation Trend models constitute a simple way to project population size and other population characteristics into the future using only data on past population. Population size is always a function of time, which serves as the proxy for the many factors that actually influence change in population size. Trend models are fitted to the historical association between time and population size; the models vary in shape to approximate the shape of the growth history.

For graphed models as well as the mathematical models, it is assumed that the better the fit of the curve to historical data (i.e., the better the fit to the empirical evidence), the better the model has captured the effects of the underlying forces. It is assumed further that the balance of basic demographic forces that held sway in the past will continue in the same balance into the future. The graphic version of a trend model may be modified by judgment, thereby reflecting departures from the past pattern of association between time and population size.

The basic problem with all trend extrapolation models is that they do not measure or identify underlying causal forces. The model only summarizes the net effect of many forces acting on population for the past period for which the model is calibrated.

The exclusive use of extrapolation models is justified when there is lack of data and time to formulate better population projection models and the analyst is interested primarily in the bottom line—total population. If the study area shows steady, slow-to-moderate rates of change in total population, and only total population projection figures are needed as inputs to projecting land and service needs for land use planning, extrapolation techniques may suffice. Another valid use of extrapolation is to provide a baseline projection, which is useful for comparison with the results of more complex techniques.

Ratio-Share

Ratio-share techniques also apply to both population and economic projection and estimation, although applications to population analysis tend to be less complex than those applied to employment analysis (chapter 6). Ratio-share techniques may either be applied in a single step from parent area to study area or in multiple steps through several layers of parent areas. In the single step-down, the ratio is established directly between the study area population and the parent area population, for example, the state or the metropolitan area. The forecast for the study area is then calculated by multiplying the parent area forecast by that ratio.

In the multiple step-down approach, a forecast for the largest parent area (e.g., the nation) is multiplied by ratios for one or more intermediate areas (e.g., census region or state). The study area forecast is then obtained by applying an appropriate ratio to the last of the intermediate areas, which itself was projected by the ratio technique. Pittenger (1976, 83), for example, suggests three possible chains to the county level (Figure 5-3). The first chain uses political jurisdictions entirely. The second and third chains introduce economic geographic areas.

In the simplest approach, the ratios are applied only to the areas in the chain leading directly to the study area without reference to the way other sub-areas of the system may be sharing in the parent area total. It is better practice, however, to apply ratios to all sub-areas of a parent area at each step. The results for the sub-areas are then adjusted to add up to the total for the parent area before proceeding to the next step down (or on the last step, before settling on the study area projection). Thus, if the planner were stepping down from the state to a particular metropolitan area, one calculates the projection for all metropolitan divisions and the nonmetropolitan portion of the state, then totals them and adjusts the figures proportionately to sum up to the state projection.

The ratio technique also may be applied to changes, as opposed to size, in population or employment. More specifically, the sub-area's share of the parent area change in population or employment is calculated and projected. The projection is based on a trend extrapolation of the study area's historical shares of the larger area's growth (Pittenger 1976, 98–101).

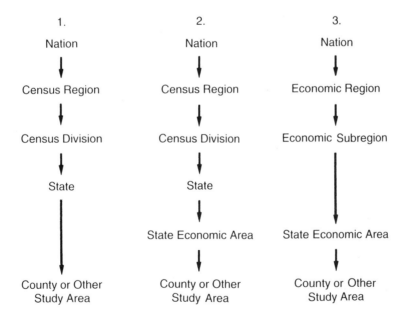

Figure 5-3. Three Possible Chains in the Multiple Step-Down Approach. The national projection is multiplied by its ratio to the next smaller region, which is multiplied by ratio to the next smaller region, and so on, until the analyst reaches a projection for the study area.

Ratio techniques are not limited to projecting total population or amount of change. They can be applied to population groups or to such components of population change as birth, death, and migration rates. For example, if parent area projections are available by age-sex-race cohorts, the ratio technique can be applied to obtain a similar breakdown for the study area.

Finally, the ratio technique may be applied to such attributes of a study area's population as auto ownership or average size of households. That is, a trend of ratios of average household size for the parent area to household size for a study area may be computed for a historical period, projected into the future, and then used to project present or future household size for the study area based on parent area projections (see the discussion on "Conversion of Population and Employment Projections" in chapter 6).

The ratio-share technique requires both a projection of the parent area(s) population and a projection of the parent-area-to-study-area ratios. The projection for the parent areas is obtained from a reliable source, for example, the Bureau of the Census or the state's office of demographic and economic analysis. Projection of the ratios is often by extrapolation (Pittenger 1976, 94–98). Care must be taken, however, to avoid projecting ratios that decline or increase to unreasonable values. The way to handle this problem is to assume that the ratios reach stability at a determined future date. Adjusting the complete set of sub-area ratios so that they are forced to total 1.0 also helps to avoid unreasonable future ratios. A second way is to project the ratios using a modified exponential curve, which limits the value the ratio may take.

When the ratio-share approach is applied to estimating population of the study area, it is referred to as *censal ratio method*. This method requires a previously prepared estimate of population for the state or other parent area. Analysts usually use the "provisional estimates" of population for states prepared periodically by the Bureau of the Census's Current Population Report, series P-25 publications, but states often prepare their own estimates as well.

Assessment of the Ratio-Share Method The ratio-share method requires three things: a reliable parent area projection or estimation, stability in historical trends of ratios, and confidence that the study area is and will continue to be an integral part of the parent area. This means that the method is inappropriate for study areas that differ economically or demographically from their states or other parent areas such that factors different from those determining the population of the parent area determine the study area's future. For example, ratio-share is inappropriate for a rural area of an urban state or an urban area of a rural state. Where the three requirements are met, however, the ratio-share approach has the advantage of simplicity and undemanding data requirements. Further, forecasts and estimates of parent areas, on which the method depends, generally are regarded as reliable because they are made by experts, who use the best methods and data for larger, and therefore more easily projected or estimated, populations.

Symptomatic and Statistical Association

This method is the most common approach that local planning agencies use for estimating current population (not for projection). It uses data that bear a close relationship to the population change, but which are more easily available. Such symptomatic data include recorded births and deaths for the study area, school enrollment, city directory listings, the number of electric meter, water meter, and telephone installations, dwelling counts, housing starts, voter registration, and other indicators. The suitability of indicator data is judged in terms of reliability, frequency, currency, and relationship to population. The symptomatic data must be available for at least the most recent census year (so that their relationship to population may be calibrated) as well as for the year for which the population is being estimated.

One symptomatic technique is called the *vital statistics rate technique*. Observing that the number of births and deaths occurring each year in a given area is roughly proportional to the size of the area's population, Bogue (1950, 149–63) developed this technique to use vital statistics data as a symptomatic measure of population change.

Bogue made rough tests, applying the technique to assorted geographical areas: states and census divisions, cities in three states where state censuses were available, and cities in California where special censuses were available at the time he was experimenting with the technique. Results indicated that the technique compared favorably with the migration and natural increase method. Generally, it showed greater accuracy in areas not subject to major population changes, in larger geographical areas, and in counties (rather than cities).

Composite methods comprise a second variation on the symptomatic technique. They use different symptomatic data for different age groups in the population. For example, Bogue and Duncan (1959; see also Morrison 1971) have used death statistics to estimate the "45 and over" population, birth statistics for the "18 to 44" and "under age 5" population, and migration and natural increase for the age "5 to 17" population. The results for the different age groups are then summed for an estimate of total population. Results of Bureau of the Census tests indicate that this method compares favorably with others (Zitter and Shryock 1964).

A third symptomatic technique is called *ratio-correlation*. This method employs the ratio principle but uses a multiple-regression equation in which the dependent variable is the study area share of the parent area population. The independent variables consist of the study area (county or metropolitan statistical area, for example) share of such parent area indicator attributes as births, deaths, school enrollment, labor force, housing starts, and other symptomatic data (Goldberg, Feldt, and Smit 1960; Pittenger 1976, 101–2).

The *dwelling unit technique* is a fourth variation on the use of symptomatic data. This approach is popular in planning agencies because they maintain statistics on building permits for new and converted dwellings in the normal course of their work. In this method, the ratio of the number of dwelling units to population at the time of the last census is applied to a current dwelling unit count to derive an estimate of the current population. Most applications assume the same average household size that prevailed at the time of the last census. For greater accuracy, trends of change in household size would be investigated and adjustments introduced if household size has changed significantly. This method has shortcomings where systematic reporting of building permits is not maintained throughout the study area. Differential reporting standards from one jurisdiction to another, and from one period to another, and the need to conduct field surveys in fringe areas where no building permit system exists undermine the accuracy of this method.[9]

Some analysts average results from several methods in weighted or unweighted combinations. The decision about what methods are averaged and what weights are used, if any, is based on tests of accuracy or on judgment (U.S. Department of Commerce, Bureau of the Census 1973, 757).

Techniques That Disaggregate Population into Component Parts: The Cohort-Component Approach

Disaggregation techniques in demographic analysis developed in two stages. First, Whelpton and Thompson (Whelpton 1928) separated population growth into its obvious components of births, deaths, and migration. They isolated trends separately in the three components and also by urban, rural, native white, foreign white, and nonwhite populations. This led to a much less deterministic conception of population change because one could tailor assumptions for each component and trace their implications and thereby explore assumptions behind growth.

As a second step to disaggregation, Whelpton divided the population into five-year age groups and introduced age-specific mortality rates adapted from insurance risk calculations. The method follows each age cohort through its life stages, applying the death and fertility rates appropriate for that age group at the time.

The contemporary synthesis of the cohort and the component innovations is called the *cohort-component method*. Conceptually, it is simply a logical simulation of aging, dying, birthing, and migration. Its advantages include the conceptual simplicity and directness with which assumptions may be changed and linked to demographic consequences. The projection can reflect the fact that each component of population change (births, deaths, migration) is determined by different factors, which may change in independent directions, and has different consequences for total population change. Furthermore, because of the cohort aspect, the effect of variation in birth, death, and migration rates by age (and even sex and race) also can be taken into account. Subtle but significant interactions between component change rates and the age structure of a population are captured. Finally, projection results are expressed for each age, sex, and possibly race cohort. Thus the projection includes specification of the structure of the population as well as population totals.

Methodologically, however, the cohort-component approach is considered the most complicated and sophisticated approach to projecting population because of the subtleties and complexities in estimating parameters and calculating their impacts. The cohort-component method is claimed to be the most widely used approach to regional population projections (Shryock, Siegel, and Associates 1976, 454). The availability of computer programs, moreover, is making its application even more feasible.[10]

The component concept is captured in the following equation:

(5.6) $P_{t+n} = P_t + B - D + IM - OM$

where P_t = population of the study area at the beginning of some time period t to n;

P_{t+n} = population at the end of the period;

B = number of births during the period;

D = number of deaths during the period;

IM = number of in-migrants to the study area during the period; and

OM = number of out-migrants to the study area during the period.

Until the 1990s, study-area out-migration and in-migration have not typically been treated separately. Rather, analysts have combined them as net migration, that is, the number of people who move into the study area minus the number who move out during the time period. More recent census data now allow the analyst to treat in-migrants and out-migrants as separate streams influenced by separate factors. Morrison (1975), Rogers (1990), and Isserman (1993) have pointed out that projections may differ on the average of 5 percent for a ten-year projection and 20 percent for a twenty-five-year projection. At this writing, practice still uses the concept of net migration, which is used in the approach explained below, but the reader should be aware that practice may be changing.

In even simpler versions of the model, a single component called *natural increase* may substitute for the separate components of births and deaths. Whether the method uses two components (natural increase and migration), three components (births, deaths, and net migration), or four components (in-migrants separated from out-migrants), assumptions must be specified for each component. Rates and other parameters reflecting those assumptions must also be projected for each component. Extrapolation and ratio techniques based on historical trends modified, perhaps, by judgment are often used to do that.

Cohort models start by dividing base year population into age groups, usually five-year age groups, into males and females and sometimes into two racial groups. Figure 5-4 illustrates a population pyramid for a hypothetical population. It is divided into ten-year age groups for simplicity of illustration; five-year age groups are usually used in practice. The horizontal bars to the left of the center vertical line indicate the population in each age cohort for males; the bars on the right for females. The length of the bar represents the number of people in that particular age-gender cohort.

The cohort-component method projects the population in each of these cohorts. To represent aging and mortality, the model survives and ages the population in

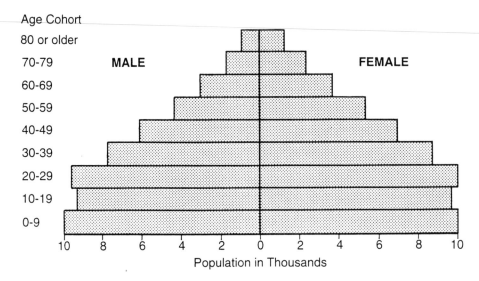

Figure 5-4. Population Pyramid. This graphic device shows the structure of a population and is used as a starting point for the cohort survival projection approach. This particular population pyramid divides the population into ten-year age cohorts for illustrative purposes and separates males from females. Adapted from Klosterman 1990, Figure 4.1, 55.

each cohort in increments of time equal to the age cohort interval, in this case ten years. Let $P_{f,c,t}$ indicate the population of females (f), in cohort c, at time t. The people in cohort $P_{f,c,t}$ in 1990 are in cohort $P_{f,c+1,t+1}$ in the year 2000. That is, ten years later they are ten years older. Thus, the cohort of females aged ten to nineteen, for example, in 1990, becomes the cohort of females aged twenty to twenty-nine in the year 2000. Because this model projects in ten-year intervals, a thirty-year projection takes three iterations. If the age cohorts were five-year age groups, a thirty-year projection would take six iterations.

The population, $P_{f,c+1,t+1}$, will be smaller than $P_{f,c,t}$ due to deaths that occur during the time, t to $t+1$, unless the number of in-migrants in the cohort exceeds the number who died. The model simulates this survival and aging process with the following equation:

$$(5.7) \quad P_{c+1,t+1} = P_{c,t} * s_{c-c+1}.$$

The survival rate, s_{c-c+1}, represents the probability of a person in cohort c surviving to be in the $c+1$ cohort ten years later. It is 1.0 minus the death rate. For example, if $P_{1,1980} = 1000$, and s_{1-2} is .9750, then $P_{2,1990} = 975$. Figure 5-5 depicts graphically what happens over one increment of time.

For the open-ended cohort at the end of the life-cycle (top of the pyramid), in this case the eighty-plus age cohort, the formula is slightly different.

$$(5.8) \quad P_{9,t+1} = (P_{8,t} * s_{8-9}) + (P_{9,t} * s_{9-9}).$$

The simulation of aging and surviving leaves the first cohort, the 0–9 age group,

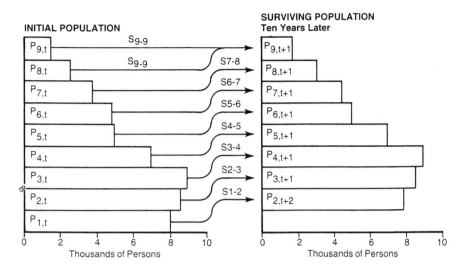

Figure 5-5. Surviving Population over One Period in the Cohort-Component Model. The diagram shows the combination of aging and survival that is simulated for a ten-year period, as people either die or age into the next-older ten-year cohort. Adapted from Klosterman 1990, Figure 4.4, 58.

empty at the end of the period because all the people in that cohort have either died or aged out of the cohort. That first cohort, $P_{1,t+1}$, is replaced by children born during the ten-year period and surviving to the end of the period. Births are simulated by the following equation:

(5.9) $B_c = \text{Pavg}_{f,c,t \to t+1} * f_{c,0}$

where B_c is the annual number of births to the population of women in age cohort c during the ten-year period t to $t + 1$. $\text{Pavg}_{f,c,t \to t+1}$ is the average number of women in cohort c during that period; the average is used because the number of women in the cohort changes from year to year during the time period. The parameter, $f_{c,0}$, is the fertility rate—the probability that a woman in cohort c will give birth in a given year. The total births for the ten-year period is

(5.10) $B_T = 10 * \text{Sum of } (B_c)$ over all child-bearing age cohorts.

Live births are then separated into males and females by multiplying by proportion who are male and proportion who are female. Finally, because some of the children die before the end of the period, the model uses the following equations to simulate that survival process:

(5.11) $P_{f,1,t+1} = B_{f,0} * s_{f,0-1}$
(5.12) $P_{m,1,t+1} = B_{m,0} * s_{m,0-1}$

Figure 5-6 diagrams the fertility component of the model.

Migration is the third component of population change represented in the

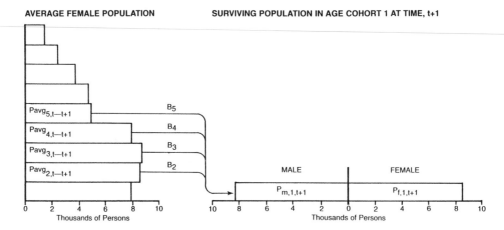

AVERAGE FEMALE POPULATION   **SURVIVING POPULATION IN AGE COHORT 1 AT TIME, t+1**

Figure 5-6. Projecting the Youngest Cohort in the Cohort-Component Model. Live births depend on the population of females in child-bearing ages and their fertility rates. Births are divided into males and females, who survive to become cohort 1, age 0–9, at the end of the ten-year period. Adapted from Klosterman 1990, Figure 4.5, 60.

model. Cohort component models usually use a net migration rate, which is calculated by dividing the net number of migrants by the "at risk" population. Population at risk is defined as the population of the study area at the beginning of the period, at the end of the period, or as an average of the two. Net migration may be positive for some cohorts and negative for others. For example, there might be a net out-migration of people between fifteen and thirty from a wealthy suburb and a net in-migration of people between thirty-five and sixty. Migration might be represented as follows:

$$(5.13) \quad Pmig_{for\,m,c,t-t+1} = Psurvived_{for\,m,c,t+1} * nm_{for\,m,c,t+1}$$

where $Pmig_{for\,m,c,t-t+1}$ is the projected number of net-migrants from time t to time $t+1$, female or male, in age cohort c at the end of the period; $Psurvived_{for\,m,c,t+1}$ is the population of males or females from the original population at time t calculated to have survived to cohort c at time $t+1$; $nm_{for\,m,\,c,\,t+1}$ is a net migration rate for males or females who are in age cohort c at the time $t+1$. Figure 5-7 depicts graphically how the model incorporates net migration. Instead of being incorporated as a rate, migration may be incorporated as a number that is calculated independently and added to or subtracted from survived population.

The critical task in cohort-component modeling is projecting the three component rates of change by age cohort and gender. Mortality is the most stable component and therefore the easiest to project (assuming no war, famine, or other local catastrophe). It also varies less from study area to study area as a ratio of the national or state mortality rate. For that reason, some cohort-survival projection computer programs build the mortality rates into the logical structure so that the analyst is not even expected to provide them (for detailed discussions of mor-

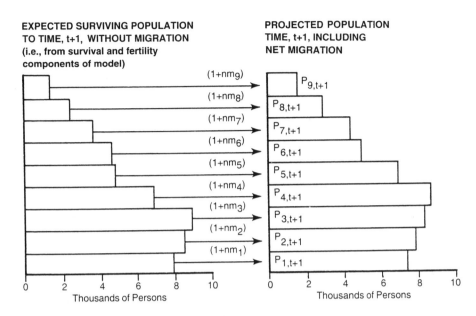

**EXPECTED SURVIVING POPULATION
TO TIME, t+1, WITHOUT MIGRATION
(i.e., from survival and fertility
components of model)**

**PROJECTED POPULATION
TIME, t+1, INCLUDING
NET MIGRATION**

Figure 5-7. Migration in the Cohort-Survival Model. Net migration, positive or negative, is added to the expected population resulting from aging, survival, and fertility simulations diagramed in Figures 5-5 and 5-6.

tality analysis, see Pittenger 1976, ch. 6; Shryock, Siegel, and Associates 1976, 444–45; Irwin 1977, 18–19; and Klosterman 1990, ch. 3).

Fertility fluctuates more widely over time and between geographic areas than does mortality. It is, therefore, less easy to project. Nevertheless, the Bureau of the Census makes projections of fertility at the national level—and usually at the state level—that can be used in making local projections. In projecting fertility for a study area, care must be taken to account for the changing nature of the population over the projection period. For example, a suburban or other fringe area may be changing from a generally rural population (usually with higher age-specific fertility rates) to a more urban-suburban population (usually with lower fertility rates). Of course, this same danger holds for projecting mortality rates, but to a lesser degree (discussions of the task of estimating fertility rates can be found in Pittenger 1976, ch. 7; Shryock, Siegel, and Associates 1976, 445–52; Irwin 1977, 16–17; and Klosterman 1990, ch. 4).

Migration poses the most difficulty in small-area population projection. The smaller the study area, the greater the problem. Nationally, more than 15 percent of the population will change their county of residence in a five-year period, the time period on which most cohort-component projection methods are based. In rapidly growing areas, migration rates are even higher. Not only is migration likely to involve a substantial proportion of the population, but it also fluctuates more widely over time than the other two components. Furthermore, it differs greatly among various age groups and frequently is negative for some age groups and positive for others. Finally, it can be calculated directly only at the decennial census, and then only as migration over the ten-year period. In spite of its critical role in projections for substate study areas, migration at that geographic scale receives little attention from demographers (methods for estimating migration can be found in Pittenger 1976, ch. 8; Shryock, Siegel, and Associates 1976, 452–53; Irwin 1977, 19–23 and Appendix H; and Klosterman 1990, ch. 5).

Making the task of projection even more challenging, the cohort-component method requires (almost always) that the fertility, mortality, and migration rates be age-specific, (usually) sex-specific, and sometimes race-specific. That is, each rate must be projected for each five-year age group of each sex. Usually there are seventeen such age cohorts, multiplied times two genders, and perhaps two races or ethnic groups.

There are variations on the general cohort-component model. Hamilton and Perry (1962) offer a simplified technique. The Bureau of the Census (1966) outlines a more complex method, using both in- and out-migration, that permits more detailed analysis of causation.

Using the Component Method in Estimation   When applied to estimation instead of projection, the component approach separates population change since the most recent census into its three components of births, deaths, and migration, but not into age cohorts; hence the title "component method" rather than cohort-component method. It is perhaps the most widely used approach for estimation at the regional, state, and local levels.

The component method derives a current estimate by starting with the enumeration of civilian population (not including military) at the time of the most recent census. It then computes natural increase since that time by adding births and subtracting deaths recorded in the study area since the census.[11]

Net civilian migration is computed next. It is based on comparing actual school enrollment in grades two through eight on the estimation date with what would be the expected enrollment in the absence of migration. Population age groups that would be in elementary grades two through eight on the estimation date are identified in the last census according to age at the time of the census. An expected (hypothetical, assuming no migration) school-age population is estimated by surviving and aging the children in the appropriate one-year age cohorts from the time of the most recent census to the date of the estimate. If the estimate is made in the last half of the decade, the children in the lower grades would not have been born at the time of the last census. Therefore, the children unborn at the time of the last census are estimated from recorded births. The resulting population, adjusted for a percentage of children not in school, is an estimate of the number of elementary school-age children based on natural increase alone. That enrollment based on natural increase alone is compared to actual enrollment figures, and the difference is presumed to be due to migration. Net migration of other, non-school-age groups, is estimated as a ratio to school-age migrants.

Next, the net shift between civilian and military, a special migration of sorts, is estimated and applied. Finally, the current military population stationed in the area is added to the civilian population to achieve an estimate of the total population for the study area.

This method of estimation requires more data than extrapolation methods, as well as careful logic to adjust figures to the exact dates of estimates and census and to adjust for military and for underregistration. It also relies on an accurate accounting for school-age children and on a stable relationship between school-age migration to total migration (perhaps not justified everywhere, for example Florida has elderly in-migration that is independent of the number of children in schools). Step-by-step illustrative examples of the method can be found in Morrison (1971, 100–116); Shryock, Siegel, and Associates (1976, 424–25); and U.S. Department of Commerce, Bureau of the Census (1973, 751).

Assessment of the Component Approach   The cohort-component approach has several strengths. It provides greater detail about population composition than other methods. That detail can be used in conjunction with age-specific participation rates to generate more sensitive projections of such things as labor force or school-age population. Even if the age-sex specific cohorts simply are added to obtain total population, the analyst knows that an accounting has been made for the subtle effects of the age-sex variation in rates of births, deaths, and migration through the projection period. The cohort-component method also allows more explicit assumptions about demographics and is therefore more open to examination, debate, and sensitivity testing. Finally, it allows the planner to focus on those components of change most relevant to the study area, for example, on migration and mortality in Florida.

On the other hand, the cohort-component method requires more extensive computations than other methods and also more data, some of which is difficult to obtain or project. It also becomes less valid as the study area becomes smaller because of decreased availability of vital statistics and migration data, decreased relevance of fertility, and the fact that migration begins to include short-distance moves.

It should be kept in mind that although the cohort-component method is conceptually superior to extrapolation and ratio-share methods, it remains essentially a computational procedure for determining the implications of assumptions about future birth, death, and migration rates. Those input rates are determined outside the model, usually by extrapolation and ratio projection techniques. Hence, the cohort-component projection is only as accurate as the inputs that the simpler extrapolation and ratio techniques project. Nevertheless, if the necessary data are available—and the analyst has confidence in them and enough time (and a computer program)—demographers prefer the component method.

Joint Economic-Population Techniques

The economy and demography of a study area are integrated, or at least linked, as we pointed out at the beginning of the chapter. The joint economic-population projection approach recognizes that linkage. Economic activity is presumed the fundamental engine driving growth, and these methods generally base population projection on the economic projection.

The extent of the linkage varies. At the very least, an analyst should compare the economic and demographic projections to assure compatibility. Two sets of ratios can be computed for past periods: one expresses employment as a percentage of total labor force, the other expresses labor force as a percentage of population. These ratios can be projected and applied to convert employment projections to population projections for comparison with results of other projection techniques. Beyond that, employment growth and wage rates can be used to establish migration coefficients in cohort-component population models, based on the theory that migration is mainly job-related in most places. Conversely, if employment and wages are projected to stagnate or decline, out-migration is assumed to increase and net migration may be negative.

Linkage between economy and population is more explicitly recognized in joint economic-population models. One commonly used version is the so-called OBERS model (chapter 6), which is important because state and federal agencies use it extensively and its results are widely available for substate areas and so become, at the very least, a good base projection for comparison with other projections.

Holding Capacity Approach

This approach goes by several names: *land use capacity, density, saturation,* or *carrying capacity approach,* as well as *holding capacity.* The projection is based on the physical space and institutional capacity of a bounded geographic area rather than on demographic processes. Holding capacity is a function of the available land, development regulations, infrastructure capacity, and housing density assumptions. Growth can be projected as a proportion of that holding capacity. Longer-range forecasts become higher and higher proportions of the holding capacity but never exceed it (for more complete discussions of the holding capacity approach, see Pittenger [1976] and Irwin [1977]).

This approach is applicable to neighborhood planning, central city planning, barrier island planning, and normative population projections. For normative projections, population level is regarded as a policy choice based on quality of life implications of high densities and population size in relation to services and environment.

Land use modeling is a related approach. That method assumes that a population projection for the study area has been made and focuses on the task of allocating the area-wide population totals to sub-areas, based partially on holding capacity of those sub-areas. In addition to holding capacity, however, this method bases allocation on such other sub-area characteristics as accessibility to jobs and shopping, availability of water and sewer, and other factors that attract or deter development.

Conclusion

The purpose of this chapter has been first to describe how economic and population information fits into the overall information system and land use planning and then to review the range of approaches for projecting future population and estimating present population. All the methods have limitations, and their results are uncertain. Fairly broad confidence intervals should be put around projections and estimates, regardless of the method used to obtain them.

In presenting population analyses, the planner should state assumptions, sometimes called *scenarios,* about demographic trends and specific parameters that determine the estimations, impacts, or projections. At one level, these should be easily interpreted by nonspecialists.[12] At a second, more technical level, the assumptions should be stated in sufficient detail (perhaps in an appendix) and in a form that enables an analyst to replicate the study.

Several scenarios should be developed. One might produce a "high plausible" projection, another a "low plausible" projection, the third a baseline (present rates or pure extrapolation of trends) projection, with a fourth being a "most likely" scenario. The most likely scenario may be regarded as a forecast, and the other three projections form a confidence interval or range of projections around the most likely forecast or perhaps a "preferred" projection.

Of the projection techniques, extrapolation is the most fundamental. Not only is it simple and quick, and therefore useful for a baseline projection, but it is also often used to estimate or project the parameters needed for the other methods, from the relatively simple ratio-share method to the cohort-component models. Next most fundamental is the ratio approach, which is useful as a primary technique when the study area is "like" its parent area. Like extrapolation, the ratio approach is also used to estimate or project parameters for more sophisticated methods. The cohort-survival method is the most valid approach conceptually. It allows sharper statements of assumptions about the future and produces more information on the structure of the projected population in addition to total population level.

NOTES

1. See Isserman (1984) for an insightful essay on the uses of population and economic forecasting in planning; the distinctions between projecting, forecasting, and planning; and the need to emphasize forecasting and planning rather than projection.

2. Census tracts are defined locally in consultation with the Bureau of the Census and consist of small divisions of counties or metropolitan statistical areas (MSAs) containing roughly 2,500 to 8,000 persons. Their spatial boundaries are drawn to encompass relatively homogeneous populations and held constant over time to permit comparisons from decennial census to decennial census. For more information, see U.S. Bureau of the Census, Census Tract Manual, latest edition, or the frontmatter of any MSA Census Tracts report of the most recent census.

3. Selected Census of Housing data have been published since 1940 for cities of fifty thousand or more on a block basis.

4. The Bureau of the Census can provide the addresses, telephone numbers, and contact people for the organizations that participate in the State Data Center Program.

5. Census of Population and Census of Housing data have been available in electronic format since 1970. Not only are the data more detailed than printed reports, but the tapes are also usually available ahead of printed reports. The data are for complete counts and for the 1 percent and 5 percent samples of population and housing units. They are available for large areas, such as states, but also for MSAs, urban places, counties, divisions of counties, census tracts, blocks, and groups of blocks. In addition, some data are available by the individual dwellings on which the data are collected. That allows the analyst to return to the original form of the data and summarize it in ways different from how the Census Bureau does it.

6. For example, see U.S. Department of Health and Human Services (1982) and Basic Automated Birth Yearbook (BABY).

7. For variations on this typology of approaches, see Pittenger (1976); Irwin (1977); and Hamburg et al. (1983).

8. There is a second form of this model, called the exponential form, where the rate is the instantaneous rate of change in population size with respect to time. The form of that model is $P_{t+n} = P_t e^{(r)n}$, where P_{t+n}, P_t, and n are as before; e is the irrational number and the base of natural logarithms, approximately 2.718; and r is the instantaneous rate of growth, a different value from the r calculated on a discrete time period for the geometric model. Generally, the geometric form is more convenient for population projection.

9. For other observations on the accuracy of the method, see Starsinic and Zitter (1968, 475).

10. For example, see Klosterman (1990) for a combined textbook and software program for cohort component analysis. Levine (1985) presents a microcomputer spreadsheet model.

11. For sources of annual vital statistics on births and deaths, see the latest publication of U.S. National Center for Health Statistics, *Vital Statistics of the United States*, latest annual report. Because there is a lag in publication for that report, local figures for the most recent two or three years must be obtained from the planner's own state health department or vital statistics office, or perhaps from local health agencies.

12. For example, the first-level scenario might be expressed in something like the following terms if one were using cohort-component methods: The <study area> will continue to experience mortality rates lower than those of the nation. Present differences will be maintained until the year 2000, when they will begin to converge on national rates, becoming equal to national rates by the year 2015. Fertility will rise from its present status of being lower than national levels to attain national average by 2010. Migration will continue to be positive in all age groups.

REFERENCES

Bogue, Donald J. 1950. A technique for making extensive population estimates. *Journal of the American Statistical Association* (45): 249–52.

Bogue, Donald J., and Beverly Duncan. 1959. A composite method for estimating postcensal population of small areas, by age, sex, and color. In *U.S. National Office of Vital Statistics, vital statistics—special reports*, 47: 6.

Brail, Richard K. 1987. *Microcomputers in urban planning and management.* New Brunswick: Center for Urban Policy Research, Rutgers University.

Goldberg, David, Allan Feldt, and J. William Smit. 1960. *Estimates of population change in Michigan: 1950–1960.* Michigan Population Studies no. 1. Ann Arbor: Department of Sociology, University of Michigan.

Greenberg, Michael R., Donald A. Krueckeberg, and R. Mautner. 1973. *Long range population projections for minor civil divisions: Computer programs and user's manual.* New Brunswick: Center for Urban Policy Research, Rutgers University.

Greenberg, Michael R., et al. 1978. *Local population and employment projection techniques.* New Brunswick: Center for Urban Policy Research, Rutgers University.

Hamburg, John, R., George T. Lathrop, and Edward J. Kaiser. 1983. *Forecasting inputs to transportation planning, National Cooperative Highway Research Program Report 266.* Washington, D.C.: Transportation Research Board, National Research Council.

Hamilton, C. H. and J. Perry. 1962. A short method for projecting population by age from one decennial census to another. *Social Forces* 41(2): 163–70.

Irwin, Richard. 1977. *Guide for local area population projections.* Technical Paper 39. Washington, D.C.: U.S. Department of Commerce, Bureau of the Census and U.S. Government Printing Office.

Isserman, Andrew J. 1984. Projection, forecasts, and plan: On the future of population forecasting. *Journal of the American Planning Association* 50(2): 208–21.

———. 1993. The right people, the right rates: Making population estimates and forecasts with an interregional cohort-component model. *Journal of the American Planning Association* 59(1): 45–64.

Keyfitz, Nathan. 1972. On future population. *Journal of the American Statistical Association* 67(3):347–63.

Klosterman, Richard E. 1985. An assessment of three microcomputer software packages for planning analysis. *Journal of the American Planning Association* 51(2): 199–206.

Klosterman, Richard. 1990. *Community analysis and planning.* Savage: Rowman and Littlefield.

Krueckeberg, Donald A., and Arthur L. Silvers. 1974. *Urban planning and analysis: Methods and models.* New York: John Wiley and Sons.

Landis, John D. 1985. Electronic spreadsheets in planning: The case of shift-share analysis. *Journal of the American Planning Association* 51(2): 216–24.

Langendorf, Richard. 1987. Statistical analysis on microcomputers. *Journal of the American Planning Association* 53(3): 368–82.

Levine, Ned. 1985. The construction of a population analysis program using microcomputer spreadsheets. *Journal of the American Planning Association* 51(4): 496–511.

Morrison, Peter A. 1971. *Demographic information for cities: A manual for estimating and projecting local population characteristics: A report prepared for U.S. Department of Housing and Urban Development.* Santa Monica: Rand Corporation.

———. 1975. Overview of population forecasting for small areas. RAND Paper Series no. P-5447. Santa Monica: Rand Corporation.

Ottensman, John R. 1985. *BASIC microcomputing programs for urban analysis and planning.* New York: Chapman and Hall.

Pittenger, Donald B. 1976. *Projecting state and local populations.* Cambridge: Ballinger Publishing Company.

Rogers, Andrei. 1990. Requiem for the net migrant. *Geographical Analysis* 22(4): 283–300.

Shryock, Henry S., Jacob S. Siegel, and Associates. 1976. *The methods and materials of demography (condensed editions).* Edited by Edward G. Stockwell. New York: Academic Press.

Starsinic, Donald E., and Meyer Zitter. 1968. Accuracy of the housing unit method in preparing population estimates for cities. *Demography* 5(1): 475–84.

U.S. Department of Commerce, Bureau of the Census. 1980. *Census of population.* Washington, D.C.: U.S. Government Printing Office.

————. 1966. *Current population reports, series P-25, no. 326.* Washington, D.C.: The Author.

————. 1973. *The methods and materials of demography,* by Henry S. Shryock, Jacob S. Siegel, and Associates. Washington, D.C.: U.S. Government Printing Office. (Condensed in Shryock, Siegel, and Associates 1976.)

U.S. Department of Health and Human Services, National Center for Health Statistics. Any Year. *Basic automated birth yearbook (BABY).* Washington, D.C.: U.S. Government Printing Office.

————. 1982. *U.S. decennial life tables for 1979–81.* Vol. 2, *State life tables, no. 34, North Carolina.* Washington D.C.: Public Health Service, National Center for Health Statistics.

————. 1987. *Vital statistics of the United States.* Washington, D.C.: U.S. Government Printing Office.

Whelpton, Pascal K. 1928. Population of the United States, 1925–1975. *American Journal of Sociology* 34(2): 253–70.

Zitter, Meyer, and Henry S. Shryock, Jr. 1964. Accuracy of methods of preparing postcensal population estimates for states and local areas. *Demography* 1(1): 227–41 .

6

The Economy

In the end, the best choice of a set of industry employment forecasts will depend upon a clear understanding of specific information needs and available resources, in addition to knowledge of the technical characteristics of the various alternatives.
—Goldstein 1990, 272

This chapter continues explanation of methods for analyzing and projecting growth and change in socioeconomic characteristics of the study area, shifting now to the economy of the community. Employment is an important determinant of population growth and change, as well as a direct source of demand for space, natural resources, and community infrastructure. The techniques for economic analysis and projection tend to be more complex versions of those used for population analysis. Thus we can build on explanations begun in the context of population projection. In practice, however, the planner would normally do an economic study before, or in conjunction with, the population study.

Economic Data

For land use planning, employment is the most useful measure of economic activity. Employment measures are obtained from four commonly used sources of national and subnational statistics: (1) Bureau of Labor Statistics (BLS) Employment and Earnings reports;[1] (2) the Bureau of the Census County Business Pattern reports prepared in cooperation with the Social Security Administration;[2] (3) the Bureau of the Census Economic Censuses;[3] and (4) the employment data in the Bureau of the Census decennial Census of Population reports (U.S. Department of Commerce, Bureau of the Census, 1992).

The first three of those sources report employment by location of the employer. The Census of Population, however, records employment by the employee's place of residence and is probably the source that local planning agencies use most often. All four series follow rigorous standards in collecting and maintaining the data, but the analyst must be sensitive to changes in definitions over time. All four sources use the industry breakdowns of the Office of Management and Budget's (1987) standard industrial classification (SIC) system, although not all have converted to the 1987 classification for the years before 1988. In addition to those federal agency sources, state employment security agencies publish so-called ES-202 quarterly reports of employment for all covered employment, available by individual counties and up to four-digit SIC detail. The *County and City Data Book* (Bureau of the Census 1988) is also a rich source of economic data for local study areas, but it is published irregularly.

For projections of employment, perhaps the single best source outside the local government is the OBERS regional projections produced by the Bureau of Economic Analysis (U.S. Department of Commerce, Bureau of Economic Analysis 1985, 1989). State employment security agencies also make projections, often by occupational categories as well as by industries for the state and for labor market areas (Goldstein 1988).

Methods of Analysis

Regardless of the particular methods used in economic analysis, Goldstein suggests principles to follow in economic studies. He first suggests that *the process should be analytical and systematic but not mechanical.* By analytical, he means analyzing the area's economy and key industries before engaging in the actual projections. Such a pre-projection analysis includes identifying special local factors or conditions that may require adjustments in rates or ratios derived from national data, adding special determinants of growth, and choosing projection techniques and parameters based upon the validity of their underlying economic assumptions as well as how well they fit the data. Post-projection analysis—reviews of results and corresponding adjustments to parameters of projection models—is also a part of being analytic.

Second, *the projection process should be cost-effective.* Cost-effectiveness includes devoting more attention to the more important and larger industries while deemphasizing other industries instead of spending equal time on each industry. It also requires evaluating differences in costs among techniques and input data, weighing expected gains in accuracy and validity against increased costs of better techniques and data.

Third, *the process should be pragmatic.* Projections should be designed to maximize usefulness to users and still be valid. Thus the analyst should know such needs of information-users as length of projection period (long-term for land use planners); geographical coverage (the study area); and industry detail (identifying industries by their land consumption, location, infrastructure, and environmental resource needs).

Typology of Approaches

The types of approaches for economic projection and impact assessment are similar to those for population analysis reviewed in chapter 5.

1. Judgmental approach
2. Extrapolation of trends
3. Ratio-share
4. Component techniques that disaggregate the economy into its component parts
   a. Economic base
   b. Input-output
   c. Single equation regression models
   d. Fully specified econometric models
5. Joint economic-population projection
6. Normative economic projection

Because economic extrapolation applies virtually the same methods as population analysis, with the same advantages and disadvantages, it is not discussed here (see chapter 5).

Judgmental Approach

This approach produces forecasts by polling a panel of experts. The methods for obtaining a group judgment about the future vary from single-round surveys, to multiround Delphi surveys, to group participation techniques. Experts typically include academics; research staff in state and local government; and research staff from banks, private consultants, and business and trade associations. They are chosen for their knowledge of a particular group of industries or the economy of the particular study area. The judgmental approach is usually used only in conjunction with one of the technical approaches discussed below, often in the review and adjustment of those approaches (Goldstein 1990).

Ratio-Share Techniques

The ratio, or step-down, approach for projecting employment for substate economic areas is increasingly appropriate for two reasons. First, the dependence of local economies on the national and international economy is increasing, even in the smallest economic regions and metropolitan areas. Second, carefully crafted projections for the nation and the larger regions that serve as parent regions in a step-down approach are increasingly available, for example, the OBERS model (U.S. Department of Commerce, Bureau of Economic Analysis 1985). National models also incorporate a larger number of variables than is possible at the state or substate level, and the data and projections are now more regularly updated. Thus, careful use of step-down ratios permits projection of local study area economic activity in considerable detail.

The usefulness of the ratio approach depends on the validity of the assumption that the ratio of parent area to local area employment remains constant or changes in a systematic manner that can be extrapolated. It also depends on historical data being available at the local level to establish the ratios at the "local end" of the step-down ladder. If those conditions are met, the approach is quite similar to the approach used in population projection (chapter 5), and the task is simple. (For example, see Krueckeberg and Silvers 1974, 416–18; or Greenberg 1972, 405–10 for application of ratio-share techniques to economic analysis.) To obtain the local area projection, the most recent ratio or extrapolated ratio—either for the total employment or for particular sectors of the economy—is multiplied by the projected parent area employment, usually a national projection for the reasons cited earlier.

Shift-share Analysis For economic analysis, the ratio approach is often refined to incorporate assessments of how particular industries in the study region might share differently in parent area growth (Perloff et al. 1960). Called "shift-share," this approach divides the study area's economy into its component industries and analyzes each separately. In that way, it might be considered as a component approach. It is used widely for urban economic development planning (Helly 1975), although not as widely as the basis for land use planning.

Shift-share projection begins with the simple statement that future employment equals present employment plus growth in employment. More specifically:

$$(6.1) \quad E_{i,r,t+1} = E_{i,r,t} + \Delta E_{i,r,t-t+1}.$$

$E_{i,r,t}$ is the employment level in industry i in study region r for time t; similarly for $E_{i,r,t+1}$, except that the time is $t + 1$. $\Delta E_{i,r,t-t+1}$ is the change in employment in industry i in region r from time t to time $t + 1$ (say from 1990 to the year 2000).

Shift-share analysis divides $\Delta E_{i,r}$, the change in employment in industry i for the study region r, into three components. The first component is the *national growth component:* the growth in industry i in region r attributable to overall change in national employment. This component of growth is the change industry i would experience if it equaled the rate of growth in total employment for the nation.

The second component is called the *national industry shift component,* or *industry mix component.* It adjusts the expected growth of industry i in the study region to reflect the shift in industrial mix for the nation, toward a larger share or smaller share for industry i relative to other industries. If industry i is growing faster than the economy as a whole, this factor is positive; if industry i is growing more slowly than the economy as a whole, it is negative. Thus, if the study region tends to concentrate its employment in industries that are growing faster than the national all-industry rate, it will grow faster than the national rate of growth.

The third component, the *competitive shift component,* represents the region's competitive advantage in industry i. It represents the study area's employment in industry i attributable to the region's competitive position in that particular industry compared to other regions of the nation.

The three components are expressed in the following form:

$$(6.2) \quad \Delta E_{i,r,t \to t+1} = E_{i,r,t}[(E_{n,t+1} / E_{n,t}) - 1]$$
Component 1 *nat. growth comp.*

$$+ E_{i,r,t}[(E_{i,n,t+1} / E_{i,n,t}) - (E_{n,t+1} / E_{n,t})]$$
Component 2 *ind. shift comp.*

$$+ aE_{i,r,t}[(E_{i,r,t} / E_{i,r,t-1}) - (E_{i,n,t} / E_{i,n,t-1})]$$
Component 3 *competitive comp.*

subscript
i = industry
r = geog. region
n = nation
t = time
e = employ.

The subscripts are as before, except that the subscript n is added to indicate that an employment figure is for the nation. The coefficient a in the third component is a correction factor to adjust for any differences in the length of the projection period, t to $t + 1$, compared to the length of the past period on which the competitive advantage is calculated, $t - (t - 1)$.[4]

For making projections, the national growth component and the national industry mix component are derived from a national projection. Usually the value for the competitive component is based on regional and national data for the most appropriate recent economic period for which reliable data are available and which reflects economic conditions and regional competitive advantages or disadvantages likely to occur over the projection period.

Assessment of the Shift-Share Approach   Sensitivity tests and comparisons against other projection approaches have been made for the shift-share model. Brown (1969–70) found shift-share projections actually less accurate than the simpler direct-share projections when applied to MSA study areas at the two-, three-, and four-digit SIC categories. The problem in shift-share was the instability of the competitive component; hence caution is required in selecting the historic time period for which local industry change is compared to the national change. In another test of a wide range of economic analysis methods applied to the New York metropolitan region, Greenberg (1972) also found instability in the competitive component, and several variants of the constant-share model yielded more accurate results.

Conceptually, shift-share is criticized on several grounds. First, local conditions are considered only in the competitive component (the constant-share approach lacks even that). Second, the two shift components are not independent of one another because some economic influences—for example, technological advances—affect both components. Third, changes in local industrial structure occurring within the calibration period affecting the competitive component may not be likely to occur in the future. Unless the analyst modifies the competitive component to reflect that fact, misleading results are possible.

In summary, shift-share analysis gets mixed reviews. Although instability in the regional competitive advantage component can be reduced by singling out the less stable industries for special analysis, shift-share requires backup investigations of the study area economy beyond mere examination of historical employment data. Planners continue to use the simpler constant-share model because it is simpler in concept, has less demanding data requirements, and yet yields favorable results in comparisons with the shift-share approach.

Component Methods

There are several types of component models—economic-base, input-output, single-equation regression, and multiple-equation, or econometric, models. These are discussed in turn, although econometric models receive less attention because local agencies rarely use them.

Economic-Base Analysis

Underlying economic-base analysis is the theory that the urban economy is made up of two components: basic economic activities, which produce and distribute goods and services for export outside the local region, and nonbasic activities, which produce goods and services for local consumption. Exported goods and services (e.g., autos or computers) are sent to purchasers out of the region, or they are sold within the study area to purchasers from outside the region (e.g., tourism or a university).

The economic-base concept holds that the basic sector is the key to an area's economic strength and its future. Exports bring money into the economy. Expansion in basic activity creates expansion in the nonbasic sector, especially in retail trade, construction, and local services for the local population and housing market. Decline in the basic sector has the opposite domino effect, leading to decline in the local economy.

Economic-base theory uses the multiplier implicit in the basic-nonbasic relationship. The ratio of basic employment (or income) to nonbasic employment (or income) is called the *economic-base ratio*. If, for the study area, for every one basic sector worker there are two nonbasic workers, the base ratio is 1:2. For every new job in the basic sector, two additional jobs are created in the nonbasic sector. The *economic-base multiplier,* however, is three. That is, when basic sector employment increases by one, a total of three new jobs are created—that basic job and the two nonbasic jobs.

Economic-base multipliers for urban regions typically range from two to nine, depending on the size of the region, the diversification of its economic base, and the level of detail to which industries are defined. Multipliers tend to be bigger for larger regions and more diversified economies and smaller for analyses based on more detailed breakdowns of industries. Some representative economic-base multipliers are given in Table 6-1.

By multiplying a projected or posited change in the basic sector by the base multiplier, an estimate of the total impact on the study area economy is computed. Arithmetically, the equivalent multiplier formula is

Table 6-1. Illustrative Base Multipliers for Some U.S. Areas

Place and Date	Mix of 1-/ 2-Digit	2-Digit	3-Digit	4-Digit	Comments
		SIC Code Level of Detail by Which Industries Are Defined			
Philadelphia (1977)	—	9.11	6.04	5.18	Large, diverse economy
Washington, D.C., MSA (1977)	—	2.97	2.81	2.80	Large but narrow economic base
Monmouth County, N.J. (1977)	—	5.16	3.88	3.50	Military area
Wilmington, N.C., SMA (1987)	6.85	—	—	—	Small metro, port and tourism economic base
Charlotte-Mecklenburg County, N.C. (1989)	5.76	—	—	—	Moderate size, diverse economy

$$(6.3) \quad \text{Base multiplier} = \frac{\text{Total employment}}{\text{Basic employment}}$$

from which we can derive

$$(6.4) \quad \text{Total employment} = \text{Base multiplier} * \text{Basic employment}.$$

The concept also can be applied to *change* in total employment caused by an increase (or loss) of jobs in the basic employment:

$$(6.5) \quad \begin{array}{c}\text{Change in}\\\text{total employment}\end{array} = \begin{array}{c}\text{Base}\\\text{multiplier}\end{array} * \begin{array}{c}\text{Change in}\\\text{basic employment}\end{array}$$

Performing an Economic-Base Study   Conceptually, the steps involved in an economic-base employment study are relatively straightforward. The first step is to identify which industries or proportions of industries are classified as basic, and which as nonbasic. Employment figures for past periods in each of the two sectors are then tabulated. The next step is to compute the base ratio and base multiplier using the preceding formulas. Finally, that base multiplier is applied in answering a planning question. That might involve assessing the impact of an expansion or contraction of a basic industry, making estimates of basic industry jobs required to reach the study area's target levels of total employment, or projecting future total employment based on projections of basic employment. Employment projections are then used to estimate demand for land; environmental resources (e.g., water supply or air quality); and public infrastructure (e.g., wastewater treatment or transportation).

Although the approach is conceptually simple, in practice there are difficulties in determining the appropriate study area (which in part determines what is an export and what is consumed within the study area) and measuring basic and nonbasic employment. Theoretically, there are the questions about the degree to which total employment and the growth of the economy really depend on so-called exports and on whether the ratios, which assume constant proportionality between basic and nonbasic employment, are valid into the future as the economy becomes larger and wages change and technology improves. There are ways to address issues of defining the study area and determining basic versus nonbasic employment.

Defining the Base Study Area   Ideally, the study area constitutes a commuter shed, that is, the area from which employees commute to jobs or a labor market area. A metropolitan statistical area (MSA), which the Bureau of the Census defines in part by economic interdependence and commuting patterns, meets that criterion. It would not be appropriate to use the economic-base concept for single counties or cities within an MSA. If the planning area is not metropolitan or is rural, the analyst can start with the labor market area. A trade area designation is another alternative, as defined in national studies, the Audit Bureau of Circulation (for newspapers), or by local credit or merchant groups.

Determining Basic versus Nonbasic Employment   Once the study area is decided, several techniques exist for dividing employment into basic and nonbasic sectors: the direct method, based on a survey of local firms; and several indirect methods, including the assumptions approach, the location quotient approach, the minimum requirements approach, and the Mather-Rosen approach (Isserman 1980, 32–53; Bendavid-Val 1983, 83–87).

The direct method is the most precise because it is based on a survey of local firms about the percentage of their sales during the preceding year that were local and nonlocal. The percentages are generalized to total employment figures for each industry to obtain totals for basic and nonbasic employment. The survey method is often impractical, however, because it requires considerable time, money, and survey expertise and may encounter response rate problems.

Indirect methods use secondary indicators of basic-nonbasic divisions. The first of the indirect methods, the assumptions approach, simply classifies certain entire industries as basic. A common assumption is that all manufacturing, agricultural, mining, and federal government are export industries, and all remaining economic activity is nonbasic. In small, isolated communities such assumptions are reasonable. In the majority of study areas, however, many industries have significant components in both the basic and nonbasic sectors. Depending on the peculiarities of the area, services normally thought to be basic may actually be export-oriented. For example, retail trade is often export-oriented in a tourist area. One variation on the assumption method uses judgment in assigning portions of industries to the two sectors. Additional variations exist. If time and data are short, the local economy simple, and the analyst is knowledgeable about it, the assumptions-by-judgment approach may be reasonable.

A second indirect approach uses the location quotient—a ratio of study area employment in a specific industry to study area total employment, divided by the same ratio for the nation—i.e., a ratio of ratios. It can be expressed as follows:

$$(6.6) \quad LQ_{i,r} = \frac{E_{i,r} / E_r}{E_{i,n} / E_n}$$

The subscript i indicates a specific industry, n indicates the nation, and r indicates the region under study. Assuming the ratio for the nation (in the denominator above) indicates self-sufficiency in industry i, a location quotient of 1 indicates the study area is just self-sufficient. If the quotient is greater than one, that is, if industry i's share of the study area's total employment is greater than industry i's share of national employment, the region is assumed to be exporting in that industry. An estimate of basic employment in the industry is calculated by first calculating the number of employees in industry i that would make the location quotient equal to 1.0 and then subtracting that number from the actual number of employees in the industry in the study area, $E_{i,r}$. Thus, unlike the preceding assumptions approach, no industry is presumed entirely basic. If the quotient is less than 1, the study area is assumed to be importing in that industry, and the number of basic employees is assumed to be zero.

This method has some implicit assumptions that are problematic. It assumes uniform demand in every study area across the nation and uniform productivity in industry i. It also ignores the proportion of national output that is for foreign consumption as well as national imports. Finally, it assumes that there is no cross-hauling, that is, no imports of the types of goods and services that are exported. Cross-hauling does exist, however, because of brand preferences and heterogeneous products and services grouped under each industry. Thus, the location quotient approach underestimates gross basic activity while also underestimating imports. Using two-digit- to four-digit-level SIC employment data achieves better accuracy under the location quotient approach than using single-digit SIC level data. In addition, federal government employment should be assigned entirely to the exogenous sector. Finally, the implicit assumptions can be relaxed by incorporating adjustments to estimate the variations in consumption and productivity among regions and to adjust for national net exports (Isserman 1977).

The minimum requirements approach is a variation on the location quotient technique. The main difference is that the study area's ratio of industry i employment to total employment in the region ($E_{i,r} / E_r$) is compared not to the nation but to study areas of similar size. Each industry's proportion (ratio) of the region's total employment is calculated for each region in the study area's class. The lowest ratio for each industry is selected to estimate the proportion of employment for an industry devoted to internal consumption for study areas in that class. Employment in excess of that proportion is presumed devoted to export.

This method relaxes the assumption, made in the location quotient approach, that consumption is identical across the nation for all types of study areas. Instead, local consumption is scaled to the study area's relative size. All other problems of the location quotient approach remain. In addition, this approach has the problem that the minimum case may not be "self-sufficient" at all, but a net importer, thus causing us to overestimate basic employment.

The fourth indirect approach is the regression, or the Mathur-Rosen, approach (Mathur and Rosen 1974, 1975). It uses a regression equation for each industry to estimate the fraction of the industry's employment devoted to export.[5] This approach also has weaknesses (Isserman 1980, 38–39). It overestimates basic employment and can generate negative fractions.

Empirical tests suggest no single best approach to assigning employment to basic and nonbasic fractions (Isserman 1980, 43–51). In fact, the best approach may be a combination of methods, depending on the industry and the particular study area. The employment of certain industries can be taken as entirely basic, for example, agriculture or federal government. For other industries, the location quotient, minimum requirements, and regression approaches are calculated and compared, discarding the results of regression and minimum requirements approaches that are lower than the location quotient result or using them to inform an assumptions approach. For a few key industries, it may be cost-effective to use the survey approach (Isserman 1980, 51–53; Bendavid-Val 1983, 85).

Application   In impact assessment, the base-service ratio is applied to the incremental employment represented by the opening or closing of a particular plant, for example. The multiplier is used to generate an estimate of the additional increase or decrease in nonbasic jobs.

For projection, we must have an acceptable independent forecast of national employment for the projection date, with breakdowns by the important local basic sectors. A constant-share or extrapolated-share multiplier is applied to corresponding national forecast levels to project basic employment in each local sector. The appropriate economic-base multiplier is applied to the projected local basic employment to estimate the nonbasic employment. In determining the base multiplier, the analyst may use a calculation based on a recent year or a projected multiplier based on extrapolation of trends. The allocation of nonbasic employment to particular industry categories is the final task. That allocation may assume the proportional breakdown among the industries that existed in a recent time period or be projected on the basis of special studies.

Assessment of the Economic-Base Approach   (Pleeter 1980, 17–18) The virtue of the economic-base model is its ease of implementation at reasonable cost. Although variation in complexity, validity, and cost exists within the approach, the equations and guidance for calculations are available in various textbooks. Data needs, which are modest, are available in published sources. The approach has limitations, however. Besides the practical classification problem, conceptual problems plague the economic-base method. One problem concerns the instability of the basic to nonbasic ratio for a study area. Over time, the multiplier changes. As a region develops a more diversified economy, more local products substitute for imports, and a higher multiplier will result. The multiplier may also have been calculated for a period when the nonbasic investment was lagging and not in equilibrium.

The economic-base approach also ignores the value of a region's service sector as an engine of regional growth; for example, education and cultural activities may lead to economic development. Pfouts (1960) points out that the region's propensity to import and its marginal propensity to consume are important regional income generators and "city builders." He also indicates that wages in the basic industry are important. Blumenfeld observes that the higher the degree of specialization and differentiation in the region, the higher the nonbasic share of employment. Thus, if the economy of an urban area is viewed as an integrated whole of mutually interdependent activities, "the distinction between basic and nonbasic seems to dissolve into thin air" (Blumenfeld 1955, 120–21).

Finally, the economic-base multiplier is an average for all basic versus all nonbasic sectors, but the multiplier actually varies by industry depending on wage levels and whether that industry tends to purchase inputs locally. Economic base does not allow those distinctions, hence the value of the next method, input-output.

Input-Output

The input-output technique is based on the theoretical work of Leontief (1936, 1951), for which he eventually received the Nobel Prize in 1973, and applications by others (e.g., Isard and Kuenne 1953; Miernyck 1964; Richardson 1972; Morrison and Smith 1974; Miller and Blair 1985; and Department of Commerce, Bureau of Economic Analysis 1986a,b). This approach represents the study area economy as a network of industries that purchase and sell goods and services among themselves and the outside world. Dollars flow among industries, representing the purchase of inputs and sale of outputs. The flows are expressed in tables and equations. Although the input-output method is more complex than shift-share and economic-base approaches, it is increasingly feasible for local agencies to use because of improved availability of data and microcomputer software.

Figure 6-1 illustrates a "transactions table," a format used to represent the structure of dollar flows in a study area economy. It lists purchasers across the top and suppliers along the side. Read horizontally, a row in the table shows output for a particular industry measured as dollars in sales to every industry in the study area; to consumers and other final purchasers in the region; and to exports. Read vertically, a column shows dollars spent by a particular industry for inputs from every industry in the local economy; for labor; and for imported supplies. The final demand columns on the right side of the table show purchases by households, governments, and investors within the region and purchases by all others outside the region. The charges against final demand in the bottom rows are payments for labor, taxes, and imports.

The input-output transactions table can vary in detail, depending on the needs of the study and the complexity of the study area economy. For example, the number of industries in the interindustry quadrant of the table may vary from

			Purchasing Sectors: Intermediate Industries						Purchasing Sectors: Final Purchase	
									Local	Export
			Industry 1	Industry 2	...	Industry j	...	Industry n	Households Gross Investment Government	Households Business Central Government
Supplying Industries and Sectors	Intermediate Suppliers: Processing Sector	Industry 1	x_{11}	x_{12}		x_{1j}		x_{1n}		
		Industry 2	x_{21}	x_{22}						
		⋮								
		Industry i	x_{i1}			x_{ij}				
		⋮								
		Industry n	x_{n1}					x_{nn}		
	Primary Suppliers: Final Payments	Local: Households, Gross Business Savings, Government								
		Imports: Labor, Transfer to Parent Companies, Central Government, Goods; Other								

Figure 6-1. Transactions Table Format. The dollar flows among sectors of the economy are represented in the body of the table, purchasing sectors are listed along the top of the table, and suppliers down the side of the table.

fewer than ten to more than five hundred. There may be only two sectors in the final payments and final sales quadrants—local and nonlocal—or there may be many sectors. The definition of industries and level of disaggregation are matters of judgment, reflecting characteristics of the local economy, the purpose of the economic study, data availability, time, and computing capability.

The primary advantage of input-output over the economic-base multiplier approach is that economic base calculates only one multiplier, whereas input-output calculates a multiplier for each industry. Input-output is able to trace how growth or decline in one industry differentially influences other industries. It takes into account that impacts are not limited to industries directly affected and recognizes that they are not felt evenly among all industries. For example, if the planner is considering the impacts of a proposed expansion of a particular industry, input-output indicates which other industries must expand, and by how much, to meet the needs of the proposed initial expansion of the one industry.

Employment Multipliers   Input-output tables represent the economy in the form of dollar flows, whereas for purposes of land use planning, we are usually interested in expressing projections and impacts in terms of employment. Thus, once an input-output table has been applied, it is necessary to convert the results to employment. The conversion is done using a ratio of employees to output, estimated from historical data on employment and dollar output. Let e_i be the employees per one dollar output of industry i. Then employment for industry i, E_i, is obtained by multiplying the estimated or projected output for industry i, X_i, by the multiplier, e_i. That is,

(6.7) $E_i = X_i * e_i$.

Employment can be summed over all industries to obtain total employment:

(6.8) $E_{total} = \Sigma_{all\ i} (X_i * e_i)$.

Using Input-Output for Projection   Forecasting with the input-output model includes three steps. The first step requires the proper definition of a study area, the appropriate level of industry breakdown, and the input-output coefficients for the study area to match that breakdown of industries. The second step is making or obtaining projections for each entry in the final purchasers (final demand) column of the input-output table. The third step is calculating a projected transactions table. All the coefficients in each column are multiplied by the given projections of final sales, or change in final sales, for the industry represented by the column. The resulting projection can be disaggregated by industry; further, total output by industry can be separated into output for final sales and output for interindustry processing.

Using Input-Output for Impact Assessment   Input-output is actually more suited to impact assessment than to forecasting. It can trace the ripple effect of a change in one industry through the other industries of the study area. Impact assessment can be either retrospective or prospective. In the former case, the analyst compares the effect of a past investment or other economic occurrence to what otherwise would have occurred. In the prospective situation, where the impact has not yet occurred, the analysis informs decision-makers about the effects of alternative futures. The economic events that can be assessed include changes in final demand for the products of any industry in the study area. In addition, competent analysts can also assess the effects of potential technological changes in an industry (e.g., substitution of inputs), changes in input sources (e.g., purchasing within the region compared to importing inputs), or the addition of a new industry (i.e., adding a new row and column into the table). Such uses involve creative changes in input-output tables.

In addition to impact assessment and forecasting, input-output analysis has value for its descriptive capabilities, which can be exploited in the pre-projection analysis for other forecasting methods. It presents information about the interindustry linkages in the study area's economy in a concise fashion and reveals the importance of particular industries and sectors.

Increasing Feasibility of Input-Output Analysis The use of input-output analysis in local-regional area economic analysis is increasing for two reasons. First, it is powerful, instructive, and flexible. The types and number of industries in the interindustry quadrant and the sectors in the final payments and final purchases quadrant can be adjusted to the analyst's purposes.

Second, use of input-output is becoming more feasible. Until the early 1980s, the high cost of surveys necessary to establish the transactions table, and the need for a high-powered mainframe computer to make the calculations precluded the use of input-output for small areas. Now, local study area input-output tables are available at reasonable cost, estimated from national input-output tables that are updated approximately every five years (the latest tables are for 1991 as of this writing).[6] Tests have shown that these regional multipliers obtained by adjusting the national input-output table according to the region's location quotients are similar to those based on expensive surveys of firms (Bureau of Economic Analysis 1986b). The analyses can also be run on a microcomputer.

Considerations and Problems in Applying Input-Output Analysis Like other methods, input-output has its drawbacks. First, the model assumes that present coefficients will remain constant under projected conditions. That may be reasonable for shorter-range impact assessment and projections, but it is problematic for longer-range forecasts required for land use plans. In the longer range, coefficients are affected by changes in relative prices, appearance of new industries, and technological change in production processes (Miernyck 1964, 37–40; Bendavid-Val 1983, 119). Prices change to reflect relative scarcity of inputs and cause industries to switch to alternative materials or change the balance between labor and capital inputs. New industries, especially where they substitute for existing industries (e.g., computers for office machines), make coefficients obsolete and misleading. New technology also changes the coefficients relating one industry to another. The greater the rate of economic change and innovation in the study area industries, the less reliable the technical coefficients for long-term forecasts.

The analyst does not necessarily have to assume that input-output coefficients remain constant, however. Observed trends can be used to make adjustments in the coefficients, although they remain a source of error. Price assumptions might be adjusted according to consumer price and other indices (Leontief 1951, 210–12).

Regional input-output analysis also requires separate and detailed projections or estimates of final demand sales data by industry, for consumption within the study area, and for export. Such data are commonly incomplete or unavailable and may have to be estimated in part. Finally, errors are compounded by all the cross-multiplying in the model.

Single-Equation Regression Model

The single-equation regression approach was developed by Harvey Goldstein and others at the University of North Carolina so state employment security agencies and occupational coordinating committees might improve industry and occupational employment projections using feasible techniques.[7] This approach is cost-efficient in comparison to other approaches and has good accuracy.

The single-equation regression model calibrates a separate regression equation for each industry in the study area. The dependent variable is the level of employment in the industry. The independent (predictor) variables are selected to be relevant for that industry. Thus, they vary from industry to industry. Each equation (industry) is solved independently, distinguishing this model from the more complex multiple-equation econometric model. Recursively related equations are allowed; employment in one industry can be projected in an equation for that industry and then used as a predictor variable in an equation for another industry.

The form of the equation is as follows:

(6.9) $E_{it} = a + b_{i1}X_{1t} + b_{i2}X_{2t} + \ldots + b_{in}X_{nt}$

where E_{it} is the estimated study area employment in industry i at time t;

$X_{1t} \ldots X_{nt}$ are values of predictor variables at time t;

$a, b_1, \ldots b_n$ are the regression model parameters that reflect the influence of the predictor variables on employment in industry i.

Ordinary least squares regression analysis is used to estimate the parameters of the equation, based on historical time series data on both the dependent variable, E_{it}, and the predictor variables, X_{1t} to X_{nt}. The calibrated equation is then used to project the level of study area employment in industry i at some future time based on projections of values for the predictor variables at that future time. Such variables may be known with certainty (e.g., elapsed time or year of projection); come from projections developed from other models; or may come from prior projections by other analysts (e.g., the state economist).

The choice of predictor variables is left to the analyst's judgment and usually varies among industries. Thus, the approach depends on whether the analyst has a good understanding of the study area and its industries. It also requires judgment in selecting predictor variables for the regression model for each industry and in applying regression model-building principles. A post-model projection adjustment step should be a part of the model-building process.

Data requirements limit application of the single-equation regression approach to labor market areas no smaller than county level; there are no suitable data for generating projections for portions of counties. A labor market area is where the large majority of labor demand and supply is located. Another way of character-

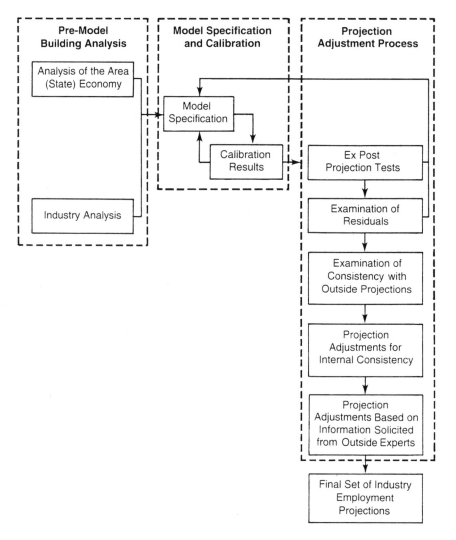

Figure 6-2. An Overview of the Single Equation Methodology. Adapted from Goldstein and Bergman 1983.

izing a labor market area is as an area in which change of residence would not, in principle, require a change in job location.

Figure 6-2 diagrams the steps in the single-equation regression model-building approach, which has three steps: premodel analysis of the study area economy, selection of predictor variables and calibration of the model, and post-projection adjustment of the model's projections. Those three steps are applied to each industrial sector.

Step 1: Pre-model Assessment of the Study Area Economy Step 1 involves analysis of the area's economy and its separate sectors. The principal objective is to classify each local industry by several criteria related to historical performance, relative importance in the local economy, and the market orientation of its products. That information is used to prioritize industry sectors, decide the appropriate level of detail at which to disaggregate the economy, and select appropriate predictor variables for each industry. Methods for generating information for the pre-projection analysis are not particularly sophisticated and include some approaches discussed earlier in this chapter: time-series trend analysis, economic-base analysis, location quotients, shift-share analyses, and telephone interviews with experts.[8]

Step 2: Specification and Calibration of the Model Step 2 involves choosing predictor variables and calibrating a regression model for each industry. Historical employment observations or estimates are required. They are obtained from the Current Employment Survey (CES 790) and Employment Survey (ES-202), which would cover most industries on an annual basis beginning with 1972. The CES 790 data are collected monthly by the Bureau of Labor Statistics from a sample of firms in each industry and are available at the state level and for selected metropolitan labor market areas.[9] ES 202 data are assembled quarterly by individual state employment security agencies from reports submitted by every firm covered by employment insurance and are available down to the county level. The CES and ES data do not cover agriculture, domestic workers, or self-employed workers. Decennial census and current population survey data are used for industries not covered by CES or ES.

Selection of predictor variables is based on principles of regional economics and labor economics. For export industries, predictor variables include:

1. outside (national or regional) demand for the industry's product (can be measured by projections of national industry employment);
2. regional share of overall national economic growth;
3. relative competitive advantages of the study area for the particular industry;
4. local area cyclical behavior, compared to national economic cycle; and
5. local interindustry product demand for the industry product.

The inclusion of a national industry employment predictor implies that the area industry employment growth rate *in part* reflects the national industry employment growth rate. It requires the availability of accurate and consistent national industry employment projections, generally available from the Bureau of Labor Statistics in their economic growth model package (U.S. Department of Labor 1980). The differences between area and national industry employment growth rates are explained by variables measuring predictors 2 through 5. Table 6-2 suggests empirical measures for each of several predictors of area employment for export-oriented industries.

Table 6-2. Classes of Predictor Variables for Models for Export-Oriented Industries

Determinant of Level of Industry Employment	Predictor Variables
Export product demand	U.S. industry employment
	Regional industry employment
Regional share of national economic activity	Regional/U.S. total employment
	Regional/U.S. manufacturing employment
	Regional/U.S. total personal income
Area competitive advantage	Area/U.S. average hourly wage
	Area/U.S. utility rates
	Area/U.S. value added per worker hour
	Area/U.S. median personal income
	Area/U.S. private capital spending for plant and equipment
Area cycle	U.S. unemployment rate
	Percent annual change in smoothed GNP
	U.S. business cycle employment fluctuation
Area interindustry demand	Area employment in related industries
Miscellaneous	U.S. defense spending
	Total state and local government spending
	State and local government spending for education

Source: Goldstein and Bergman 1983, Table 1.

For industries serving the study area, employment is determined by such factors as

1. area's demand for the products of the industry;
2. changes in industry productivity, technology, or consumer tastes (measured as a national average); and
3. area-specific business-cycle behavior.

For local serving industries, the model does not assume that area employment growth rate mirrors national growth rate. Local demand is assumed the primary predictor. Because historical data and projections are generally unavailable, that predictor is represented by such proxy variables as area population, personal income, total employment, or local export-oriented employment. Table 6-3 suggests empirical measures for each of several predictors for local serving industries.

Data sources for the measures suggested in Tables 6-2 and 6-3 are in the tech-

Table 6-3. Classes of Predictor Variables for Models for Local-Serving Industries

Determinant of Level of Industry Employment	Predictor Variables
Local product demand	Area population
	Area households
	Area personal income
	Area total employment
	Area employment in the industry
Industry productivity,	U.S. industry employment per capita
technology, or consumer	U.S. industry employment/U.S. total employment
preference change	U.S. industry employment per household
Area cycle effect	U.S. unemployment rate
	Percent annual change in smoothed GNP
	U.S. business cycle employment fluctuation

Source: Goldstein and Bergman 1983, Table 2.

nical appendices of Goldstein et al. (1982). The analyst selects predictors for each industry model based on the earlier, pre-model analysis of the area economy, subjective knowledge, and availability of data. The specified model is then subjected to calibration tests and to respecification based on the results of those tests. Goldstein and Bergman (1983, 61–83) provide guidance for interpreting regression model calibration results.

The simplest regression model specifications are those in which the predictor variables are either time, national employment, or state employment in the industry. If the only predictor is time, the model is reduced to a simple extrapolation model. If only state or national employment is used, the model is reduced to a constant-share model. If both time and national or state employment are used, the analyst assumes that some portion of the employment change is due to a change in state or national employment (and the study area's share of that national or state employment). The other portion is due to a linear function of time. The advantage of these simple model forms is that time is known with certainty, and national and state employment projections are usually readily available and based on sophisticated models applied by competent experts. The disadvantage of these forms is that they do not take other local factors into account. To overcome that disadvantage, the analyst can choose additional variables that are particularly relevant for each industry, thereby customizing each equation to the particularities of the industry being modeled.

At least five sources of information can help the analyst specify the appropriate equation for each industry: (1) results of the pre-model analyses of the area economy as a whole; (2) time plots of area industry employment, area share of national or state industry employment and industry share of total employment; (3) results of shift-and-share analyses of the components of study area employment change in the past; (4) informal knowledge of state and local experts; and (5) regression model calibration test results.

Step 3: Post-Projection Adjustment   After calibration, the models should be subjected to additional checks. Goldstein and Bergman do not recommend one best procedure. First, Goldstein and Bergman recommend ex-post projection tests of the model for a historical time outside the period for which the model is calibrated. Employment figures for a past period other than that used to calibrate the model are compared to predicted employment for that period.

Second, Goldstein and Bergman recommend examining the residuals (differences between actual industry employment and predicted values) for both the calibration results and the ex-post projections. If the pattern of residuals is nonrandom, models are respecified in an attempt to explain those residuals.

Third, the analyst evaluates the model projections for consistency with what the analyst subjectively knows about industry trends and with projections of other respected forecasters and other forecasting techniques. If results are not consistent, then the analyst considers respecifying the model once again or adopting an alternative projection technique for that industry.

Fourth, industry employment projections are adjusted to achieve consistency among industries and with state projections on an industry-by-industry basis. Goldstein and Bergman explain a preferred technique for that process (1983, 95–97).

Fifth, panels of users, industry experts, and experts on the overall economy evaluate the projections.

Econometric Models

Econometric models are sets of simultaneous equations that more fully reflect the complexity of relationships among economic variables and sectors in the economy than do the separate single-equation models. More sophisticated model-building and statistical techniques are required because of interdependence among the equations representing different aspects of the economy. The steps used in building the models are much the same as those for the single-equation models: data collection, model specification, calibrating and testing alternative specifications, development of forecasts, review and adjustment, and, finally, application.

Econometric models have excellent theoretical validity and ability to reflect assumptions about the future. They are expensive to build and maintain, however, and are low in comprehensibility. Evidence also suggests that employment forecasts from econometric models are not significantly more accurate than those developed from single-equation regression models, especially for projecting disaggregated industrial sectors as opposed to total employment (see, for example, Michigan Employment Security Commission 1984). Furthermore, most regional econometric models are generally designed to track movements within business cycles, and their theoretical strengths do not carry beyond the current business cycle to longer-range forecasting.

Although econometric models for substate areas are rare, except for the largest metropolitan regions, such a model should be considered if it exists for the planner's study area. It should have an appropriate disaggregation of industry sectors, be calibrated to longer projection periods, and meet acceptable validity standards as discussed under previous single-equation models. Even if the industry sector does not disaggregate the econometric model sufficiently, the forecasts could be used as control totals for another projection approach. If an appropriate econometric model is not already available for the study area, the development of such a model is probably not cost-effective.

Joint Economic-Population Approach

Planners should compare their economic and population projections for consistency. Beyond that, moreover, there is the joint economic-population projection approach. The best known of these is the OBERS approach, developed in the 1970s. OBERS is an acronym that stands for the Office of Business Economics and the Economic Research Service, which created the model. It is useful because it is applied widely to states, metropolitan statistical areas, and Bureau of Economic Analysis (BEA) economic areas across the nation; is prepared on a regular basis; and is readily available. Several federal agencies and some states use it for allocating funds.

OBERS is a chain of six models. The first three are economic and use the shift-share approach to project employment for agricultural, other basic industries, and nonbasic industries, respectively. The other three models project population. The labor force portion of the population—people from fifteen to sixty-four—is projected as a ratio of employment projections. The population age zero to fourteen is projected as a ratio of that labor force population under the assumption that those people are dependents of working households. The group aged sixty-five and over are projected by surviving the appropriate age groups from the most recent census enumeration.

Because it is both available and clear, OBERS is a good projection for local planners to use if there are no resources for local projections; it is also useful as a base line projection against which to compare the results of other approaches. However, it is purely mechanical (so that it can be applied consistently across the country) and lacks the benefit of local knowledge and judgment.

Normative Economic Projection

The normative approach bases the projection of future economic change on goals and objectives, rather than on trends and causal modeling. National economic projections or goals are allocated to regions using perhaps objective functions and linear programming. The objective, subject to internal consistency constraints, is to minimize the capital costs of achieving specified regional levels of income (Richardson 1973, 46).

Conversion of Population and Employment Projections into Socioeconomic Characteristics for Land Use Planning

Techniques for population and economic projection generally provide projections of numbers of people or numbers of employees, sometimes by age, sex, or race cohort, or by industry or occupation. The planner must eventually convert those projections into indicators more directly useful in land use planning; for example, number and size of households are used to estimate housing and land requirements.

Conversion techniques generally consist of rates, ratios, or proportions. A rate measures the incidence of events among a population, for example, labor participation rate is the fraction of population in the labor force. A ratio measures prevalence of something among the population, for example, the number of autos per household. A proportion measures composition of the population, for example, the proportion of the population that is school age. The population or employment level projected for a target year is multiplied by (or divided by) a rate, ratio, or proportion that represents a linear relationship between the population or employment size and the socioeconomic characteristics in which the land use planner is interested.

The methodology is simple, although the arithmetic computations may be complicated. Sometimes a socioeconomic characteristic or demand indicator is obtained in one step by multiplying the population or employment level by the appropriate rate, ratio, or proportion. The number of acres needed for a particular industry, for example, is estimated by dividing the projected employment in that industry by an average number of employees per acre. In other cases, it is more appropriate to make the conversion in several steps. For example, in the first step, a rate may convert a population level into a number of households, which may then be proportioned into households of several types (e.g., by income or size). This in turn is converted into required types of dwellings by multiplying the number of each type of household by specific dwelling type rates. Such conversion rates, ratios, and proportions may be applied either to the total population levels or to age-, sex-, or race-specific population groups as well as to such special populations as military personnel or college students.

The quality of the socioeconomic characteristics projections depends on *both* the accuracy of the population or economic projection and the accuracy of the projected rates, ratios, or proportions used to convert to socioeconomic characteristics. Inaccuracies are compounded if the ratios, rates, or proportions are used in series because one is multiplying error upon error (not merely adding them) (Alonso 1968). Given a population or employment projection of reasonable quality, the critical task becomes projecting the future values of the rate, ratio, or proportion multipliers. The techniques are the familiar ones: extrapolation of past trends, and study area, and study-area-to-parent-area ratios based on historical data and available projections of the multiplier for the parent area. Social scientists with expertise in the particular socioeconomic phenomenon should be consulted. See

Hamburg et al. (1983, 30–40) for detailed guidance in conversion of socioeconomic characteristics, particularly for transportation planning.

Conclusion

Economic and population estimates and projections help planners understand the present and future community for which they are planning, and the way it is changing over time. Thus, population and economic information components are fundamental elements of a planning information system. In the last two chapters, we have explained the types and sources of economic and population data and reviewed the range of approaches to estimating and projecting employment and population. We have also discussed rationales for choosing a projection approach suited to the situation and needs of a particular urban area. The choice depends upon the availability of a historical data series for the study area, the level of detail and accuracy required in the projection, the capability of the planning staff, and the time available to perform the analysis. Once an approach is chosen, the planner can turn to more detailed explanations of methodology in references cited in the text and listed at the end of the chapters.

Although population and the economy drive urbanization and development, information on the natural environment, land uses and the built-environment, infrastructure, and development policies are also important. Those components of the planning information system are covered in the next three chapters.

NOTES

1. The BLS Employment and Earnings series is based on a combination of sources: (1) labor force information obtained during one calendar week each month from a sample of nonfarm households made for the BLS by the Bureau of the Census; (2) payroll information obtained through monthly BLS mail questionnaires in cooperation with state agencies; and (3) unemployment insurance claim information collected weekly by the states for the approximately two-thirds of the nation's labor force covered by this system. Comparable data are available for labor market areas since 1939. The series is published by one-, two-, three-, or four-digit SIC categories for states and for 214 major labor areas. The level of detail depends on the numbers of various types of industries found in the area and what can be reported without disclosure of the operations of individual establishments. It is available on a year-by-year basis in the BLS's Employment and Earnings (U.S. Department of Labor, Bureau of Labor Statistics 1984 and annually).

2. This series is based primarily on FICA taxable payroll reports, but it makes use of supplemental information obtained in a special survey of multiple-location companies. The series was first published in 1946 and, beginning with the 1964 edition, has been published annually in volumes by state. It is also available on computer tapes. Mid-March employment data for the states, counties, and MSAs are shown in one-, two-, three-, and four-digit SIC categories, the level of detail depending on the number of firms in the area and what can be shown without disclosure of the operations of individual establishments. Data

for MSAs are shown at the two-digit level only. It provides an excellent basis for updating decennial data and for determining trends (U.S. Department of Commerce, Bureau of the Census 1987a).

3. The Bureau of the Census conducts these censuses of establishments every five years for years ending in the numerals two and seven (e.g., 1992). The data are available in report form, microfiche, and computer tapes. There are separate censuses for manufacturers, mineral industries, construction industries, retail trade, wholesale trade, and service industries. For a time, the various censuses were conducted in different years, but beginning in 1967 all have been conducted in the same year. These censuses do not include agriculture and forestry (covered in the Census of Agriculture), most transportation, most finance, insurance and real estate, certain service industries, and government (covered in Census of Governments). Among other information, the censuses include "value added," payroll, and the number of establishments, as well as employment. Data are available for cities and other places, counties, and MSAs, but the available statistics are fewer as the geographic level becomes smaller. More detail is available in microfiche and tape than in the published reports (U.S. Department of Commerce, Bureau of the Census 1987b).

4. The correction factor is calculated by the following formula:

a = the length of the future projection period, divided by the length of the past period on which the change is measured

$$= \frac{(t+1) - t}{t - (t-1)}.$$

The coefficient equals one if the two time periods are equal. For example, if the projection date, $t + 1$, is the year 2000, the base date, t, is 1990, and the past period for calibrating the region's competitive advantage, $t - (t - 1)$, is 1980 to 1990, the formula becomes:

$$a = \frac{2000 - 1990}{1990 - 1980} = 1.0.$$

If the calibration period was 1972 to 1980, $a = \frac{10}{8}$, or 1.25.

5. Using historical time series data, local employment in industry i is regressed on national total employment levels. The regression result is:

$$E_{i,r} = a_{i,r} + b_{i,r} E_n.$$

Then both sides of the equation are divided by $E_{i,r}$ yielding

$$1 = (a_{i,r} / E_{i,r}) + (b_{i,r} E_n / E_{i,r}).$$

The implicit assumption is that a proportion of the study area's industry i employment is sensitive to total employment in the nation and therefore basic (nonlocal), whereas the remaining, insensitive proportion is nonbasic (local). Thus the first term is the nonbasic fraction and the second term is the basic fraction.

6. One of the available models is the Regional Input-Output Modeling System (RIMS II) (Bureau of Economic Analysis 1986). It was developed in the 1970s at the Bureau of Economic Analysis in the Department of Commerce as RIMS, and enhanced later as RIMS II. The model is based on BEA's national input-output table, updated every five years, for 531 industries, and on their four-digit SIC county wage and salary data, which are used to adjust the national input-output table to reflect a particular study region's industrial structure and trading patterns. Tables of updated RIMS II multipliers may be

purchased from the Regional Economic Analysis Division of the Bureau of Economic Analysis.

Another input-output model, the Regional Science Research Institute (RSRI) model, can also be fitted to the particular study area and is also based on national input-output data (Regional Science Research Institute, n.d.). It calculates impacts on employment (including ninety-four occupational/skill categories), income, value added, and total output for 494 industries. The RSRI model allows for cross-hauling, which the RIMS II model does not, indicating that RIMS II may overestimate multiplier effects compared to the RSRI model.

7. Our discussion is based mainly on Goldstein 1990; Goldstein 1988; and Goldstein and Bergman 1983. Analysts who desire more thorough discussion of that research may also consult Goldstein, Bergman, and Paulson 1982, and Goldstein 1981.

8. One purpose of the pre-model analysis is to classify industries into those that are key (i.e., largest, fastest growing, undergoing the most technological change, or undergoing change different from the state); those that are least important (small, neither growing or declining nor departing from the state-share or stable trend in growth, not undergoing technological change); and an intermediate group. Goldstein provides a list of additional specific questions (1988, 17–18).

Another purpose is to classify each industry by its market orientation. Is it oriented to direct export, indirect export, or local final demand? If the industry is export-oriented, is the market regional, national, or international? If the industry sells its products to other local industries for further processing before export, that is, indirect export-oriented, what are those purchasing industries? If the industry primarily serves local final demand, does it sell to other firms or to consumers? What is the potential for import substitution to occur within the projection period? The market orientation helps the analyst identify the most relevant predictors for the regression equations, based on the incidence of final demand.

Location quotients and shift-share provide preliminary insight into determining the classification of each industry and the proportion of employment attributed to direct exports, indirect exports, and final local demand (Goldstein and Bergman 1983, 45–46). Less systematic procedures are used to determine the geographic scope of the market for export-oriented industries (Goldstein and Bergman 1983, 4–5).

9. The U.S. Department of Labor, Bureau of Labor Statistics publishes the monthly survey report for states and selected metropolitan labor market areas under the title "Employment and Earnings," <month>, and <year>. Each year's reports are identified as a separate volume that has twelve reports (e.g., January 1990 is Volume 37, number 1). Historical data are published periodically (e.g., see U.S. Department of Labor, Bureau of Labor Statistics 1984, *Employment, Hours, and Earnings, States and Areas, 1939–1982*, volumes 1 and 2, Bulletin 1370–17, U.S. Government Printing Office).

REFERENCES

Alonso, William. 1968. Predicting best with imperfect data. *Journal of the American Institute of Planners* 34(4): 248–55.

Bendavid-Val, Avrom. 1983. *Regional and local economic analysis for practitioners.* New York: Praeger Publishers.

Blumenfeld, Hans. 1955. The economic base of the metropolis. *Journal of the American Institute of Planners* 21(4): 114–32.

Brown, H. James. 1969–70. Shift and share projections of regional economic growth: An empirical test. *Journal of Regional Science* (9–10): 1, 1–18.

Goldstein, Harvey A. 1981. Occupational employment projections for labor market areas: An analysis of alternative approaches. Monograph 80. U.S. Department of Labor, Employment and Training Administration Research and Development. Washington, D.C.: U.S. Department of Labor.

———. 1990. A practitioner's guide to state and substate industry employment projections. *Economic Development Quarterly* 4(3): 260–75.

———. 1988. *Projecting industry and occupational employment for states and substate areas.* Chapel Hill: Institute for Economic Development, University of North Carolina at Chapel Hill.

Goldstein, Harvey, and Edward M. Bergman. 1983. *Methods and models for projecting state and area industry employment.* National Occupational Information Coordinating Committee. Chapel Hill: University of North Carolina at Chapel Hill.

Goldstein, Harvey A., Edward M. Bergman, and Nancy Paulson. 1982. *Methods and models for projecting state and area industry employment.* Final Report to the U.S. Department of Labor, Employment and Training Administration, Office of Research and Development. New York: Center for Social Sciences, Columbia University.

Greenberg, Michael R. 1972. A test of alternative models for projecting county industrial production at 2, 3, and 4-digit standard industrial code levels. *Regional and Urban Economics: Operational Methods* 1(4): 397–417.

Hamburg, John R., George T. Lathrop, and Edward J. Kaiser. 1983. *Forecasting inputs to transportation planning, national cooperative highway research program report 266.* Washington, D.C.: Transportation Research Board, National Research Council.

Helly, Walter. 1975. *Urban systems models.* New York: Academic Press.

Isard, Walter, and Robert E. Kuenne. 1953. The impact of steel upon the greater New York–Philadelphia region: A study in agglomeration projection. *Review of Economics and Statistics* 35(4): 186–97.

Isserman, Andrew M. 1980. Alternative economic base bifurcation techniques: Theory, implementation, and results. In *Economic impact analysis: Methodology and applications,* ed. Saul Pleeter. Boston: Martinus Nijhoff Publishing.

———. 1977. The location quotient approach to estimating regional economic impacts. *Journal of the American Institute of Planners* 43(1): 33–41.

Krueckeberg, Donald A., and Arthur L. Silvers. 1974. *Urban planning and analysis: Methods and models.* New York: John Wiley and Sons.

Leontief, Wassily W. 1936. Quantitative input and output relations in the economic system of the United States. *Review of Economics and Statistics* 18(3): 105–25.

———. 1951. *The structure of the American economy, 1919–1939.* New York: Oxford University Press.

Mathur, V., and H. Rosen. 1974. Regional employment multiplier: A new approach. *Land Economics* 50: 93–96.

———. 1975. Regional employment multiplier: A new approach. *Land Economics* 51: 294–95.

Michigan Employment Security Commission and the University of Michigan. 1984. *Alternative projections project for Michigan, final report.* Lansing: Michigan Employment Security Commission.

Miller, Ronald E., and Peter D. Blair. 1985. *Input-output analysis: Foundations and extensions.* Englewood Cliffs: Prentice-Hall.

Morrison, William I., and P. Smith. 1974. Non-survey input-output techniques of the small-area level: An evaluation. *Journal of Regional Science* 14(1): 1–14.

Miernyk, William H. 1964. *The elements of input-output analysis.* New York: Random House.

Office of Management and Budget, Executive Office of the President. 1987. *Standard industrial classification manual.* Washington, D.C.: U.S. Government Printing Office.

Perloff, Harvey S., Edgar S. Dunn, Jr., Eric E. Lampard, and Richard F. Muth. 1960. *Regions, resources, and economic growth.* Baltimore: Johns Hopkins University Press.

Pfouts, Ralph W., ed. 1960. *The techniques of urban economic analysis.* West Trenton: Chandler-Davis Publishing Company.

Pleeter, Saul, ed. 1980. *Economic impact analysis: Methodology and applications.* Boston: Martinus Nijhoff Publishing.

Regional Science Research Institute. N.d. *PC I-O: A regional impact model for the personal computer.* Peace Dale, R.I.: The author, P.O. Box 3725.

Richardson, Harry W. 1972. *Input-output and regional economics.* New York: John Wiley and Sons.

———. 1973. *Regional growth theory.* London: Macmillan Press.

U.S. Department of Commerce, Bureau of the Census. 1992. *Census of population.* Washington, D.C.: U.S. Government Printing Office.

———. 1987. *County business patterns.* CBP-87-01. Washington, D.C.: U.S. Government Printing Office.

———. 1988. *County and city data book.* Washington, D.C.: U.S. Government Printing Office.

———. 1987. *1987 economic censuses: Geographic reference manual.* Washington, D.C.: U.S. Government Printing Office.

U.S. Department of Commerce, Bureau of Economic Analysis. 1985. *1985 OBERS BEA regional projections: Economic activity in the United States.* Washington, D.C.: U.S. Government Printing Office.

———. 1986a. *Regional multipliers: A user handbook for the regional input-output modeling system (RIMS II).* Washington, D.C.: Superintendent of Documents, U.S. Government Printing Office.

———. 1986b. *RIMS II: Regional input-output modelling system.* Washington, D.C.: U.S. Government Printing Office.

———. 1989. Volume 1: *State projections to 2035.* Volume 2: *Metropolitan statistical areas to 2035.* Washington, D.C.: U.S. Government Printing Office.

U.S. Department of Labor, Bureau of Labor Statistics. Annual. *Employment and earnings.* Washington, D.C.: U.S. Government Printing Office.

———. 1984. *Employment, hours, and earnings, states and areas, 1939–1982.* Volumes 1, 2. Bulletin 1370-17. Washington, D.C.: U.S. Government Printing Office.

———. 1980. *Methodology for projections of industry employment to 1990.* BLS Bulletin 2036. Washington, D.C.: The author.

7

Environment

... the "environment" is where we all live; and "development" is
what we all do in attempting to improve our lot within that abode.
The two are inseparable.
—World Commission on Environment
and Development 1987, xi

For the land use planner, the natural environment is not only a source of land for future urbanization but also a set of resources to be conserved, natural functions to be maintained, and hazards to be avoided in order to achieve sustainable development. The complexities and contradictions inherent in the development–environment relationship challenge the planner to seek a working balance between productive uses of land and natural resources, maintenance of ecological functions, and protection of people and property from natural hazards. The goal is economic growth that is socially and environmentally sustainable, balancing economy and ecology.

Two major environmental concepts influence contemporary thinking about sustainable development (Ledec and Goodland 1988). The traditional concept is one of "environmental services," those beneficial functions (such as maintenance of water-flow patterns and recycling of wastes) that natural areas perform. The newer concept is one of "biological diversity," the full range of genetic diversity (plant and animal species and populations) and ecosystems (in which the plants and animals exist). Both are threatened by development because they are public goods that do not carry a market price tag. For example, the U.S. Fish and Wildlife Service has estimated that 30 to 40 percent of original wetlands in the United States has been lost and that destruction continues at three to four hundred thousand acres annually (Kusler and Kentula 1990, xiii). And several hundred species *a day* may become extinct over the next twenty to thirty years due to human activity (Ledec and Goodland 1988, 7). But these threats could be reduced by sensitive planning and determined implementation.

Environmental services are the economically valuable benefits to society that natural areas provide. These include creation and protection of soil, stabilization of water-flow patterns, amelioration of climate, breakdown of pollutants, recycling of wastes, provision of fish nurseries, and protection against weather damage (Ledec and Goodland 1988). For example, forests support agriculture by retaining water, preventing flooding, protecting watersheds, and reducing soil erosion and sedimentation. Wetlands regulate water flow by absorbing heavy rainfall and releasing it gradually, help maintain high-quality water supplies by naturally absorbing and breaking down pollutants, and support fisheries through provision of nurseries.

Biological diversity includes three elements: (1) the number and geographic distribution of ecosystems (communities of plants, animals, and their environments); (2) the number and geographic distribution of animal and plant species; and (3) the genetic variation within each species (Ledec and Goodland 1988). Because species extinctions are irreversible, preserving biological diversity keeps open important future options. Economically, biological diversity is valuable because many species of wild plants and animals are undeveloped resources with significant economic potential. Scientifically, biological diversity is valuable in studies of basic life processes. Esthetically, biological diversity is valuable as a source of beauty and wonder. Ethically, maintenance of biological diversity is important because nonhuman species have their own intrinsic value independent of any practical value for human beings.

Development–environment interactions may be positive or negative, but they are rarely neutral. Positive impacts of development are those that maintain biological diversity and environmental services. For example, an environmentally positive local land use plan would manage development so as to conserve:

1. areas of highly erodible soil through preservation of existing slopes and vegetation;
2. prime agricultural lands through encouragement of sound farming practices and location of future urban growth outside of farming areas;
3. watercourses, floodplains, and wetlands that make up natural drainage and aquifer recharge systems through conservation of such natural areas as forests and vegetated stream buffers that regulate water flow and adoption of impervious surface limits and other standards to regulate runoff from urban development;
4. airsheds with high air quality through location of such stationary sources as new power plants and transportation routes in downwind areas; and
5. habitats of rare or endangered species through maintaining a connected critical mass of natural areas adequate to support plant and animal populations.

Negative impacts of development are those that damage biological diversity and environmental services. The major sources of negative environmental impacts from urban land use are: (1) *displacement or damage of natural areas* by intruding development; and (2) *pollution of environmental media* (air, water, land) by such urban residuals as stormwater runoff or automobile and industrial emissions. In the case of displacement or damage, the primary remedy is to locate and manage future urban land uses so as to maintain the natural functions and biological diversity of the environment. In the case of pollution, the primary remedy is to reduce the generation of pollutants at the source as well as mitigate their environmental effects. To contain negative environmental impacts effectively, the planner must understand clearly the characteristics and functions of natural environmental systems. Environmental information is a critical component of the local planning information system.

Environmental systems are complex, however, and it would be a mistake to assume that the goal of land use planning should be simply to preserve all natural systems in their existing state. A noted ecologist points out that "ecological systems are dirty, changing, growing, and declining. That is the source of their resilience and diversity" (Holling 1978, 35). Holling suggests that the *variability* of ecological systems is valuable for self-monitoring and maintenance of resilience. He questions planning policies that attempt to reduce ecological variability in time and space in the name of environmental quality.

Environmental Information in the Planning Program

If one accepts the simple proposition that nature is the arena of life and that a modicum of knowledge of her processes is indispensable for survival and rather more for existence, health, and delight, it is amazing how many apparently difficult problems present ready resolution.

—McHarg 1969

To be useful for land use planning and change management, individual pieces of environmental information need to be coordinated to inform planning operations and decisions. Although not necessarily an environmental expert, the land use planner must make use of a wide variety of environmental data. This section proposes a framework for organizing the environmental information system so that it can be used for land use planning.

Environmental Inventory

An *environmental inventory* is a coordinated package of information on individual environmental features. The inventory is made up of maps, data series, regular (e.g., annual) reports, and special studies. It should contain sections for each element, including maps and attribute tables for land, water, air, habitats, and environmental policy. For each element, it should identify the natural environmental *analysis units,* for example, drainage basins for water-related features, airsheds for air quality, or patches and corridors for species habitats.

Certain features, such as soils, will be relatively stable over time. Others, such as land cover or water quality, may change extensively. For each section, the inventory should describe *baseline* conditions existing when the information was compiled as well as *changes* observed as the feature changes over time. One way of tracking change is to monitor development permits; others include periodic surveys and use of aerial photographs and remote-sensing data. If a GIS is available, then this will be the desired way of maintaining the environmental inventory. If no GIS is available, an atlas format should be used.

Assembling an environmental inventory requires gathering data on a number of environmental elements. Each individual environmental element may include valuable resources, important ecological functions, and dangerous hazards to human settlements. Before going into the technical aspects of environmental information, it is useful to review the positive and negative potential of the various elements.

Land   The inventory of land as an environmental element is concerned with soil and geology, topography and slope, and land cover and vegetation. Soil, the top layer of the earth's surface, is formed by the weathering of rocks (Marsh 1991). Soil contains air, water, and organic materials and is capable of supporting plant growth. This composition determines its resource value—its fertility for agriculture, forestry, and plant life, and its use as a construction material. Its important natural functions revolve around its drainage and filtering capacity and its bearing capacity, functions of its composition, slope, and underlying geology. Its hazards result from its susceptibility to erosion, slides, and collapse as well as its corrosivity and transportation and retention of chemical pollutants.

Water   The inventory of water features is concerned with surface streams and lakes, underground aquifers, floodplains and wetlands, and water quality. Water occupies that part of the earth's surface not covered by soil as well as many underground areas; it circulates between the earth and the atmosphere in the hydrologic cycle (Ortolano 1984). As a water supply resource, it provides life support for people, plants, and animals; it also serves as a transportation and recreation medium. The natural functions of streams and rivers are to concentrate and carry rainfall and form landscapes. Hazards include flooding and erosion of soil; water also absorbs, retains, and transports chemical pollutants.

Air   The inventory of air features is concerned primarily with air quality in terms of concentrations of pollutants harmful to human health. Air makes up the earth's atmosphere. As a resource, it provides oxygen for life support and serves as a transportation medium (Ortolano 1984). Its natural functions include the transmission of water through the evapotranspiration process and the ventilating movement of air currents through the atmosphere. The atmosphere contains gases that affect the transmission of radiant energy from the sun. Potential global warming from increases in atmospheric carbon dioxide is an important environmental problem. Hazards result from air-borne pollutants, as well as from high wind speeds generated from tornados and hurricanes.   *Sulfur fires*

Habitats   Habitat inventories deal with the distribution and character of plants and animals. *Vegetation* is the plant life that grows on the earth's surface (Marsh

1991), mapped through a land-cover inventory. As a resource, it provides food and timber for humans both through managed agriculture and through its natural processes, as well as food and habitat for animals. It is also important as an esthetic resource, a contributor to environmental processes, and a mitigator of damage from natural hazards. Its natural functions include absorbing air and water pollution, holding soil in place against erosion, and growing plant communities such as forests and meadows. Its hazards include certain poisonous species, toxic substances, and potential injury or damage from accidents, such as falling trees. *Wildlife* includes the animal populations of the earth (Spirn 1984), mapped through a wildlife inventory. As a resource, animals provide food for humans through animal husbandry and for other animals through the food web. The natural functions of wildlife include maintaining ecological communities and biodiversity. Their threats include potential for attacks on humans by some species, transmission of some diseases (e.g., rabies), and crop-damaging incursions into gardens and agricultural areas.

Environmental Policy In addition to environmental features, it is useful to assemble and maintain an inventory of current environmental policy. If this compilation of existing policy is keyed to environmental inventory and analysis, then it will be possible to assess the adequacy of existing policy to deal with environmental problems. Compiling the environmental policy inventory will require assembling information from existing regulations, procedures, programs, plans, and policies of a number of local, regional, state, and federal agencies responsible for environmental management. The inventory can be displayed in a matrix of environmental problems and related policies. Not only will such a matrix identify unmet problems and policy gaps, but it will also reveal conflicts among existing policies.

Environmental Analysis

Once environmental inventories have been prepared, then the data can be analyzed to generate planning and decision-support information. The environmental information module should be designed to facilitate environmental analyses done in the advance planning process in response to development proposals and in the normal course of monitoring environmental conditions. This chapter reviews environmental analysis approaches that are particularly useful for environmental planning and monitoring. Chapter 17 discusses applications of impact analysis in the overall context of evaluation and mitigation of development proposals. These approaches, which range from simple checklists to computer models, all seek to discover the critical interactions between development and the environment in order to devise more positive alternatives or recommended mitigation strategies. Before going into analyses, however, we turn to inventory and mapping approaches.

Inventorying and Mapping Environmental Information

The techniques of land use planning are primarily those of *spatial analysis*. . . . This places the concept of space in a relatively unique position in land use planning, for it must be viewed simultaneously as a primary property of all components in the landscape and as a principal resource in its own right.
—Marsh 1978, 7

Environmental inventories and maps are primary tools of the land use planner. They represent the characteristics and locations of—and connections among—environmental features in space. Data are collected in attribute files, which are keyed to map locations through identification codes. Basic environmental features to be included are topography and slope, soil, land cover, floodplains and wetlands, water quality, air quality, habitat, and composite landscapes.

Topography and Slope

Topographic maps represent the height of the ground surface above sea level, National Geodetic Vertical Datum, or some other baseline elevation. Each contour line on a topographic map represents a specified elevation. The difference in elevation between adjacent contours is the vertical "contour interval." The smaller the contour interval, the more detailed the information about the terrain on the map.

Topographic maps are necessary to calculate surface drainage patterns, slope, and solar aspect. The U.S. Geological Survey's 7.5 minute topographic quadrangle maps are very useful general maps for local planning, but their scale is too small to be used in connection with land ownership or parcel maps. Typically, they are published at a scale of 1:24,000 (1 inch = 2,000 feet), with a contour interval of 10 feet. For more detailed topographic information, local governments purchase topographic maps at larger scales with smaller contour intervals, for example, a scale of 1 inch = 200 feet, with a contour interval of 4 feet. These topographic maps are constructed by photogrammetric procedures from controlled aerial photography and may be overprinted on planimetric base maps or on orthophoto base maps that show groundcover and surface features.[1] Two types of planning maps can be generated from topographic information: the slope map will show ranges of steepness; the watershed map will show drainage basins (Figure 7-1).

Slope maps represent the inclination of the earth's surface. The closer the spacing of topographic contour lines (connecting points of equal elevation above sea level), the steeper the slope. Slope percentage can be computed by a simple formula:

$$\text{percent slope} = \frac{\text{change in elevation}}{\text{distance}} \times 100.$$

For land use planning purposes, slopes are often divided into ranges, such as gentle

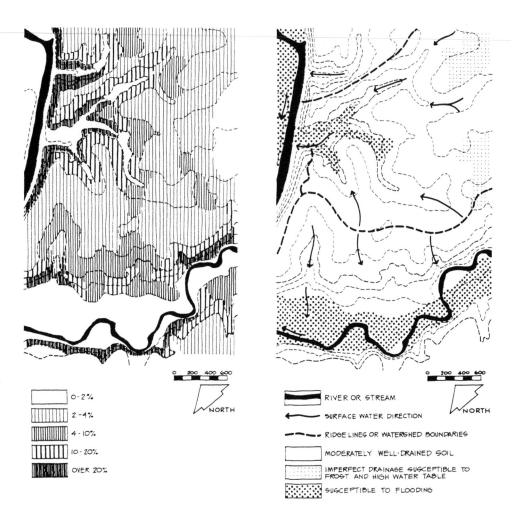

Figure 7-1. Slope and Watershed Maps. From De Chiara and Koppelman 1984, 196.

(under 5 percent), moderate (6 to 15 percent), steep (16 to 25 percent), and very steep (more than 25 percent). Land uses are limited by the steepness of slopes. For example, the maximum slope for roads is about 10 percent.

Watershed maps represent the locations of drainage basins. The top of a slope, or the drainage divide, forms the boundary of a drainage basin, one of the most important natural environmental planning units. Computer mapping systems that calculate slope can also generate maps of drainage basins to identify watersheds, steep slopes to show areas where development may be discouraged, solar aspect to show south-facing areas, and viewsheds to show potential areas where significant views should be preserved. The Geological Survey produces paper topographic maps and Computerized Digital Elevation Models (DEMs), which can show three-dimensional slope.

Soil

The most readily available source of soil information for the land use planner is the U.S. Department of Agriculture's Soil Conservation Service (SCS) county soil survey report. It includes general and detailed soils maps with information on bearing capacity, drainage capability, slope, and suitability for agriculture, forestry, wildlife, and urban uses. The soil survey classifies soils into series with similar profiles of topsoil, subsoil, and bedrock. Soil types are based on their relative content of sand, silt, and clay, which determines texture. Each soil series is named for the geographic location where it was first identified and its texture.

Soil maps in the county soil survey report are overprinted on aerial photographs. Land use planners use soil maps to identify areas of prime agricultural or forest land, good bearing and drainage capacity for development, septic tank suitability, depth to bedrock, and such potential hazards as flooding or slope failure. Digitized soil maps are available for some areas; other areas may have to digitize the soil maps for their jurisdictions for inclusion in computerized planning information databases. Figure 7-2 shows digitized versions of a general soils map and a hydric (water-bearing) soils map at the county level. The land use planner needs to compile soil features into a soil potentials map, which would show potential development areas where soils are suitable for building foundations, septic tanks, roads, and underground utilities, as well as nondevelopment areas with prime agricultural soils and wetland soils. A generalized soil potentials map can be constructed from the General Soils Map that the SCS publishes for each county.

Land Cover

Land cover is the vegetation or other material that occurs on the earth's surface (compared with land use, which describes human activity on the surface). General land cover mapping is done by analyzing aerial photographs and other remotely sensed data, such as satellite imagery, to classify land cover into various types. More detailed mapping of land cover, like land use, requires field inspection.

Land cover and land use are classified by hierarchical schemes going from the general to the specific. Of the various land cover classifications, one of the most well known is the Anderson et al. (1976) system, which combines classes of land use and land cover. It divides categories into "levels" that increase in specificity at each lower level. For example, Level I includes general categories such as urban, agricultural, forest, wetland, and the like. Level II is comprised of more specific categories, for example, it includes three types of forest land: deciduous, evergreen, and mixed. If more detail is needed, it is possible to break down these categories further into Level III types, which, for forest, might include such deciduous species as oak, maple, and hickory. A number of states have similar land use and land cover classification schemes, including Florida, Georgia, Maryland, Michigan, Minnesota, and Vermont.

Land cover maps have become familiar to land planners due both to advances

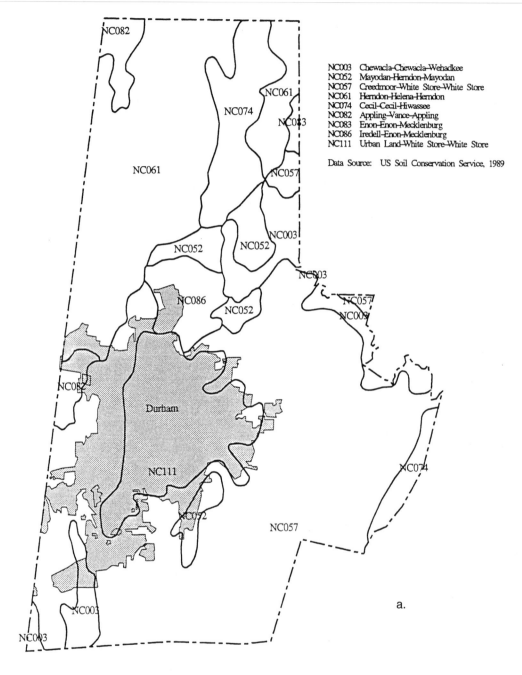

NC003 Chewacla-Chewacla-Wehadkee
NC052 Mayodan-Herndon-Mayodan
NC057 Creedmoor-White Store-White Store
NC061 Herndon-Helena-Herndon
NC074 Cecil-Cecil-Hiwassee
NC082 Appling-Vance-Appling
NC083 Enon-Enon-Mecklenburg
NC086 Iredell-Enon-Mecklenburg
NC111 Urban Land-White Store-White Store

Data Source: US Soil Conservation Service, 1989

a.

Figure 7-2. a. Digitized General Soils Map, Durham County, N.C. Identifies soil associations. b. Digitized Hydric Soils Map, Durham County, N.C. Identifies potential wetlands or flood-prone areas. Both maps provided by the North Carolina Center for Geographic Information and Analysis.

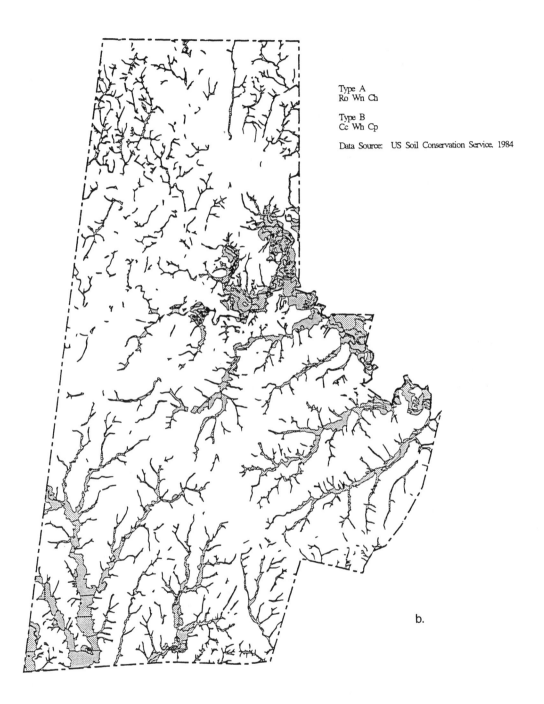

Type A
Ro Wn Ch

Type B
Cc Wh Cp

Data Source: US Soil Conservation Service, 1984

b.

in remote-sensing and increasing concern with ecology. Land cover maps generally must be prepared for the regional or local area because the only national inventories of land cover are those the Forest Service prepares of national forests. Land cover maps, however, are invaluable to the land use planner. They provide information about environmental resources such as agriculture and forestry, about different types of landscapes such as wetlands and grasslands, about animal habitats, and about the impacts of urban development upon the environment.

The typical land cover map is generated from inspection of aerial photographs to classify the local species; the map is then field-checked for the accuracy of its classes. Newer methods include computer generation from satellite data. The product will be a land cover map.

Floodplains and Wetlands

The Federal Emergency Management Agency (FEMA) publishes flood hazard boundary maps and flood insurance rate maps. The 1968 National Flood Insurance Act, administered by the Federal Insurance Administration within FEMA, provides a nationwide system of federal insurance for structures and property located in designated flood hazard areas. Under this flood insurance program, flood-prone lands—defined as those containing a hundred-year floodplain with a flooding probability of at least 1 percent a year—are mapped. Communities participating in the flood insurance program must regulate new floodplain development in order to reduce impacts of future floods, including requiring the first usable floor of a building to be elevated above the height of the hundred-year base flood elevation (Figure 7-3).

On flood hazard maps, the hundred-year flood zone is designated as the A zone. For coastal communities, a V zone also is designated to identify coastal high hazard areas where wave action raises the base flood elevation, requiring additional development safeguards. For land planning, this information should be compiled on a flood hazard map.

The loss of wetlands is recognized as a national problem. The presidential goal of no net loss of wetlands is supported by congressional adoption of the 1989 North American Wetlands Conservation Act, section 404 of the Clean Water Act, the 1985 Food Security Act, and other related acts. A number of states, such as Virginia, have enacted state wetlands protection laws. Although these various actions have created wetlands policies, however, local planners often must construct their own wetlands information base.

General wetlands maps are being compiled by the National Wetland Inventory of the U.S. Fish and Wildlife Service, according to a three-level classification scheme of systems, subsystems, and classes (Marsh 1991, 289). Under this scheme, Level 1 classes are marine, estuarine, riverine, lacustrine, and palustrine systems. Level 2 classes divide these further into subtidal, intertidal, and other subsystems. Level 3 classes include more specific characteristics such as rock bottom, unconsolidated bottom, and aquatic bed.

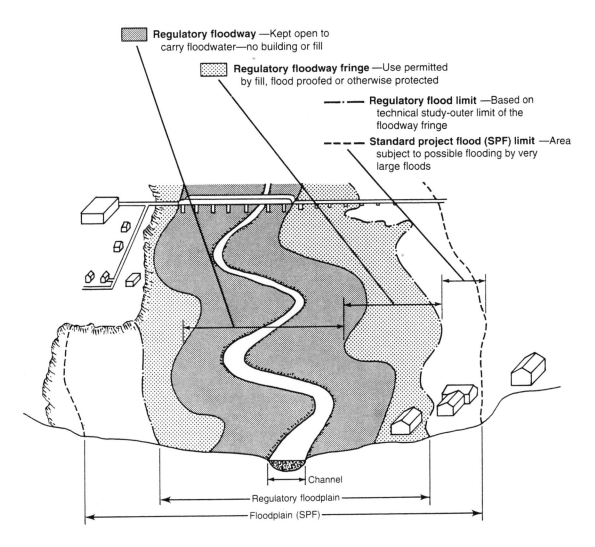

Regulatory floodway —Kept open to carry floodwater—no building or fill

Regulatory floodway fringe —Use permitted by fill, flood proofed or otherwise protected

Regulatory flood limit —Based on technical study-outer limit of the floodway fringe

Standard project flood (SPF) limit —Area subject to possible flooding by very large floods

Channel

Regulatory floodplain

Floodplain (SPF)

Figure 7-3. Flood Hazards Map. From Marsh 1991, 153.

Local wetlands can be mapped by use of aerial photography, hydrologic maps, and vegetation maps, supplemented with field verification. The result will be a wetlands map.

Water Quality

When residual substances that exceed the assimilative capacity of water are discharged into surface waters, problems of decreased fish propagation can occur, and humans can be threatened with disease. However, water quality problems also result from naturally occurring processes, such as eutrophication, which are accelerated by human activities. Major water quality problems include increased temperature, salinity, sedimentation, eutrophication, and toxic substances, as well as lowered amounts of dissolved oxygen (Basta and Bower 1982). A number of natural processes take place in water bodies, depending upon the hydraulic movement of water, and the chemical and ecological processes.

The Clean Water Act set a goal of making U.S. waters safe for swimming and aquatic life. The Environmental Protection Agency (EPA) was directed to develop national effluent standards. Point source dischargers are required to obtain permits and meet the standards. It has been harder to manage nonpoint pollution sources, such as runoff from farm fields and parking lots, however. Due to the complexity of the factors involved, it is usually not possible to provide single, comprehensive maps of water quality. Instead, the planner may find individual maps of water resource areas, such as fish nursery areas, and summary maps of state agency water quality designations based on an aggregation of indicators drawn from water sampling. An innovative analysis of North Carolina estuarine waters, for example, combines a number of factors to arrive at a proposed water use classification map (Clark 1990).

Air Quality

Air quality also results from a combination of natural and man-made factors. Natural factors include sunlight, wind, precipitation, vegetation, topography, water bodies, cloud cover, and temperature. Man-made factors include urban spatial patterns, human activities, raw materials for production, and time patterns of residuals discharge (Basta and Bower 1982). Resulting problems are acid rain, smog, and concentrations of particulates, sulfur oxides, carbon monoxide, nitrogen dioxide, ozone, hydrocarbons, lead, and other pollutants that affect human health, animal and plant life, corrode buildings, and destroy the ozone layer.

The Clean Air Act directs the Environmental Protection Agency to set air quality standards and provide emission control programs to monitor and mitigate air quality problems. A network of sampling stations has been established but due to the variability of air quality over time and space, and the difficulty of precisely identifying "airsheds," neither comprehensive nor summary maps of air quality are typically available to the local planner. Instead, data from sampling stations may be aggregated on a periodic basis to indicate the general level of air quality relative to human health risks.

Habitat

Locations of plant and wildlife habitats are important environmental information. Under the 1973 Endangered Species Act, federal agencies are required to protect all species of plants and animals facing possible extinction, and the U.S. Fish and Wildlife Service is charged with preparing a species recovery plan for any "endangered" or "threatened" species. As of 1989, there were 407 endangered species (249 animals and 158 plants in danger of extinction throughout all or a significant part of their ranges) and 128 threatened species (82 animals and 46 plants likely to become endangered within the foreseeable future) listed (Cairns and Crawford 1991, 122). The act makes it a crime to violate the endangered species regulations and supports the protection of critical habitats. The Fish and Wildlife Service analyzes the locations and habitats of listed species.

Researchers have studied the landscape as a mosaic of habitats ("patches" and "corridors") and flows of species, energy, and nutrients in order to determine the minimum habitat shapes and sizes to support particular species (Westman 1985, 469–70). Local planners may be able to obtain maps of the habitats of endangered species, although these are not routinely published and may be kept confidential in some cases to keep the species from being disturbed. However, habitats often coincide with streams and wetlands areas, and a generalized habitat map can be produced.

Composite Landscape Maps

Integrating the various environmental elements is important for the land use planner, who must produce a comprehensive change management strategy. Fragmentation of environmental management results from focus on one element, such as water, by a single-purpose bureaucracy. However, ecologists and environmental scientists emphasize the need for integrated environmental management that recognizes the connections between natural systems (Holling 1978; Westman 1985; Cairns and Crawford 1991). Landscapes are the composite features of the earth's surface, the sum of the parts that can be seen with the eye, including fields, hills, forests, lakes, and buildings (Steiner 1991, 4).

One way to integrate information about various environmental features is through composite landscape maps, which overlay layers of information on individual features. An example is the Metropolitan Landscape Planning Model (METLAND), which assesses "suitability" of each landscape planning attribute for (1) resource use (water, minerals, recreation); (2) hazard (air pollution, noise, or flooding); and (3) development suitability. The model judges "ecological compatibility" based on plant productivity classes, urban development extent, crop and forest potential indices, and soil erosion and runoff potential (Westman 1985). Because few local planners will have access to complex and expensive models of this type, simpler suitability analyses (such as those described in chapter 8) may serve most land use planning purposes.

Analyzing Environmental Information

Environmental analyses provide useful inputs to land use change management. Types of environmental analyses include environmental impact analysis, cumulative impact assessment, critical area analysis, and hazard analysis.

Environmental Impact Analysis

The National Environmental Policy Act of 1969 created the concept of environmental impact analysis, which has spread around the world. Originally aimed at requiring federal agencies to prepare environmental impact statements for actions that could significantly affect the environment, the concept also is in use by many states and local governments. Proposed public or private development projects trigger environmental impact analyses. Thus the focus is on potential negative impacts of the proposal or alternatives to the proposal and how they may be mitigated. When possible, we recommend that the land use planner look beyond the *individual* impact analysis (useful in reviewing a proposed project) to a *cumulative* impact assessment framework.

According to Burchell and Listokin (1975) the general structure of an environmental impact analysis is to describe

1. present conditions in the project area;
2. the proposed project;
3. probable short- and long-term negative and positive impacts of the proposed project;
4. alternatives to the proposal (engineering, design, location);
5. probable short- and long-term negative and positive impacts of alternatives; and
6. recommended action, including techniques to mitigate unavoidable negative impacts.

While environmental impact analyses may look at a variety of community impacts, our focus in this section is on natural environmental impacts. Four of the various environmental impact analysis techniques are especially useful: (1) the descriptive checklist; (2) the trade-off matrix; (3) the spreadsheet model; and (4) the overlay screening model.

Descriptive checklists provide systematic procedures for ensuring that all relevant impacts are examined for each proposed project that falls within the range for required environmental impact analysis (Burchell and Listokin 1975; Westman 1985). That range will vary with the size, type, and scope of the project; smaller projects are typically exempted. The checklist poses a series of questions about the impact of the project on the environment (e.g., will the project impede natural drainage patterns), as well as the impact of the environment on the project (e.g., will the project be subject to floods or mud slides). Checklist content should be determined by local environmental conditions. The general headings of an illustrative checklist might include:

1. Air quality impacts
   a. Public health
   b. Land use

2. Water quality impacts
   a. Groundwater
   b. Surface water
3. Soil erosion impacts
4. Ecological impacts
   a. Plant
   b. Animal
5. Noise impacts
6. Hazard impacts
   a. Natural
   b. Man-made

These would be amplified in terms of the particular local environment. For example, the air and water quality checklist could include the pollutants critical to the area; the plant and animal impacts could list the local threatened and endangered species; and the hazards could identify the types of natural (e.g., floods, slides, and earthquakes) and man-made (e.g., underground storage tanks and hazardous wastes) hazards.

Checklists have the advantages of promoting systematic thinking about impacts and summarizing effects in a concise format. However, checklist-based analyses may not be specific enough to capture all impacts, may not identify the interactions between effects, may overlook the distributional aspect of impacts, and may be so qualitative and subjective that their findings can not be replicated or tested.

Trade-off matrices link the substantive impacts of checklists to the affected groups. As proposed by Westman (1985, 159–62), a simple trade-off matrix would list the positive and negative impacts of each feature of a proposed project along the top (column) axis and the affected groups along the side (row) axis. It would express impacts in the cells in both verbal or qualitative terms and in monetary or physical units. Rather than assigning weights to impacts or to affected groups (as in the goals achievement matrix discussed in chapter 17), the weighting is left to decision-makers (see Table 7-1 for an illustrative trade-off matrix evaluating two airport plans).

Trade-off matrices have the advantages of clearly stating the effects of each impact on each affected group in whatever terms are appropriate, of permitting flexibility in using available information, and of avoiding the insertion of individual planner's judgments in determining the importance of groups or impacts. Disadvantages are the potential large size of the matrix and the difficulty of summarizing net benefits and costs because a grand total index is not calculated. However, the use of a grand total is not always a good idea because it obscures individual impact information and may distort the importance of various elements.

Spreadsheet models are a recent development in impact analysis techniques. They use the capabilities of spreadsheet programs, such as Lotus 1-2-3, rapidly to perform complex matrix relationships based on algebraic formulas that the user

Table 7-1. Illustrative Trade-off Matrix

Affected Groups	Impacts of Increased Air Travel				Noise			
	Benefits		Costs		Benefits		Costs	
	Plan 1	Plan 2	Plan 1	Plan 2	Plan 1	Plan 2	Plan 1	Plan 2
Air Travelers								
Monetary			$4.0M^a	$4.5M^a				
Physical	40,000 additional flights	50,000 additional flights						
Qualitative								
Nearby Residents								
Monetary							$1.2M^c	$1.3M^c
Physical								
Qualitative	Some added convenience of air travel by proximity to airport						Interruption to conversation; possible health effects; less adverse than Plan 2	Health and communication effects worse than Plan 1
Plants and Wildlife								
Monetary								
Physical								
Qualitative			Fewer birds killed by collision with planes	More birds killed by collision with planes			Noise effects on wildlife significant but less than Plan 2	Noise effects worse than Plan 1
Airplane Companies								
Monetary	$4.0M^a	$4.5M^a	$3.0M^b	$3.0M^b				
Physical	40,000 flights	50,000 flights						
Qualitative								

Source: Adapted from Westman 1985, 160.

a. Ticket sales; b. Operating costs; c. Potential property value loss puts in. They are particularly useful for calculating linked sequences of outcomes in large data sets, where the output from one formula is the input to a following formula. Their relative simplicity fits well with the types of database likely to be available in impact analyses.

An example of a spreadsheet model is the reservoir pollutant loading model created for computing the impacts of development management scenarios for the University Lake watershed in Orange County, North Carolina (Camp, Dresser and McKee 1989). Land use, soils, topography, and hydrology of the watershed were inventoried. Nonpoint pollutant loading coefficient estimates were prepared for different combinations of existing conditions. The spreadsheet was then used to compile total annual loads of phosphorus, nitrogen, lead, and zinc resulting from proposed development scenarios for the watershed, such as downzoning residential development from two-acre to five-acre minimum lots. It then was used to analyze various adjustments to the scenarios to mitigate the impacts of downzoning. The structure of the model includes different databases for existing conditions and each future scenario in terms of land use, soil types, and septic tank failure assumptions by sub-basin. The user selects the database to be used. Pollutant loading factors (pounds/acre/year) are used to compute pollutant loads for different land use categories based upon annual runoff volumes, mean pollutant concentrations, soil type, land use patterns, and base flow-water quality conditions.

Spreadsheet models have the advantages of user friendliness due to menu driven software; readily accessed data files; transparency of structure; rapid recalculation of the impacts of changes in the data, formulas, or parameters; and simplicity of construction and operation. Disadvantages are the necessity of considerable technical skill to set up the formulas and structure of the spreadsheet and the need to transform all data to similar units, such as dollars or amounts of a particular pollutant.

The *overlay screening model* is an offshoot of the overlay models developed by McHarg. It relies upon the cumulative impact analysis capabilities afforded by overlaying separate impact maps. Overlay screening models are useful in reviewing the aggregate impacts of pollution on such natural resources as groundwater.

An example of an overlay screening model is the EPA's DRASTIC model (Aller et al. 1987). This model assesses groundwater pollution potential in hydrogeologic settings of a hundred acres or larger using a numerical ranking system devised by an expert panel. It generates an index that shows the potential for contaminants released on the land surface infiltrating downward through the soil and vadose zone (the area above the water table that is not continuously saturated) and reaching the aquifer.

The acronym DRASTIC is derived from the first letters of the factors included. It is based on three elements: (1) weights, (2) ranges, and (3) ratings (Table 7-2). The model assigns weights to each of its factors and then rates the steps in the range for that factor on a scale from one to ten. For example, topography is given a weight of one (five is the highest), and each part of the topography range is given a rating, with the lower slope percentages rated the highest. The model simply adds the numerical values determined by multiplying each factor weight by the rating associated with a range value of that factor at the location being assessed.

Screening overlay models have the advantages of allowing an estimate of impacts in a complex system by combining separate estimates of impacts on individual factors, of being "transparent" in terms of the operations of the model, and

Table 7-2. Illustrative DRASTIC Model

Factor	Weight	Range	Rating
(D) Depth to water (feet)	5	0–5	10
		5–15	9
		15–30	7
		30–50	5
		50–100	3
		100+	1
(R) Net recharge (inches)	4	0–2	1
		2–4	3
		4–10	6
		10+	9
(A) Aquifer media (type)	3	Massive shale	1–3
		Metamorphic/igneous	2–5
		Glacial till	4–6
		Massive sandstone	4–9
		Massive limestone	4–9
		Sand and gravel	4–9
		Basalt	2–10
(S) Soil media (type)	2	Gravel	10
		Sand	9
		Peat	8
		Loam	5
		Clay loam	3
(T) Topography (% slope)	1	0–2	10
		2–6	9
		6–12	5
		12–18	3
		18+	1
(I) Impact of the Vadose Zone media (type)	5	Confining layer	1
		Silt/clay	2–6
		Shale	2–5
		Limestone	2–7
		Sandstone	4–8
		Basalt	2–10
(C) Hydraulic conductivity of the aquifer (GPD/FT^2)	3	1–100	1
		100–300	2
		300–700	4
		700–1,000	6
		1,000–2,000	8
		2,000+	10

Source: Adapted from Aller et al. 1987.

of being well suited to use in GIS operations, where the impacts can be rapidly calculated and recalculated. Disadvantages include the necessity to compile considerable data about the various factors, to use expert knowledge to estimate the weights, and to avoid the impression that the model outputs are absolute values rather than relative estimates.

Cumulative Impact Assessment

Cumulative impact assessment tracks the aggregate effects of individual impacts on the environment. Most environmental impact analysis techniques are geared to the effects of an individual project rather than to the effects of a comprehensive plan or a number of projects over time. A cumulative impact assessment uses an environmental inventory and regular environmental indicator monitoring, together with a running tabulation or modeling of the impacts of all existing and proposed projects, to look at the total effects.

Cumulative impact assessment is typically applied to multiple projects. For example, such an assessment could be done for a water supply watershed to report on the total deterioration in water quality due to development projects occurring over a multiyear period rather than simply the pollutants added by one proposed new project. This would give decision-makers a more complete perspective on the effectiveness of their water quality management policies.

Cumulative impact assessment can also be incorporated into the advance planning process. For example, a "prospective" cumulative impact assessment could be done during plan preparation to assess the probable impacts of implementing the plan's future land use proposals. Because of the uncertainty associated with plan implementation over a twenty-year period, the findings of such an assessment would necessarily be conditional and generalized. However, the process could be used to compare the likely impacts of different plan scenarios. It could also be made more specific by focussing it on intermediate geographic and time scales. For example, focussing on the territories of small area plans and/or the five-to-six-year period covered by capital improvement programs would allow greater analytical detail and make the assessments more feasible to conduct.

Cumulative impact assessment is not a simple technique due to complex natural system interactions. Contant and Wiggins (1990) point out that cumulative impacts result from both similar and dissimilar actions accumulating over space and time to produce natural systems changes that are both incremental and synergistic as well as immediate and delayed. They also note that some actions are *growth-inducing* and change potential future activity or natural system response. Ideally, planners would have complete cumulative impact monitoring and modeling systems (chapter 17). However, planning programs without sophisticated modeling capabilities can use basic environmental inventories, available data on environmental quality indicator changes, and running tabulations of individual project impacts to keep track of aggregate impacts.

Critical Area Analysis

The critical area concept appeared during the environmental quality movement of the 1970s as an outgrowth of our expanded understanding of the interaction between development and natural systems. The *Model Land Development Code* of the American Law Institute (1976) proposed state designation of "areas of environmental concern"; the Coastal Zone Management Act (CZMA) of 1972 required that states designate "areas of particular concern"; and the 1980 amendments to CZMA encouraged "special area management planning" (Godschalk 1987; Brower and Carol 1987). Critical areas are designated to conserve sensitive environments or natural areas such as wetlands, barrier islands, estuaries, endangered species habitats, or water supply reservoir buffers. Florida has used the critical area designation concept to initiate special resource management programs in a dozen areas. Maryland has designated as critical areas all land within a thousand feet of the Chesapeake Bay. The rationale is that such areas require special programs to manage conflicts between development and resource conservation.

Unlike impact analysis, which is a responsive technique, critical area analysis is a pro-active technique. The land use planner can use critical area analysis to identify in advance the areas that will need special management in order to protect their environmental services or biological diversity. For example, the areas within a mile of, or draining directly into, water supply reservoirs could be designated as critical areas and managed with special performance standards limiting impervious surface, stormwater runoff, vegetation clearing, and development density. In this way, the pollution filtering and runoff absorbing services of the natural environment could be maintained.

In order to ensure that critical areas are properly designated, inventories of the natural systems should be conducted. These inventories should cover the features described in this chapter and should be updated regularly. It may be necessary to defend the action in court, particularly if critical areas are downzoned, and a solid environmental database and process analysis will be required to demonstrate the reasonableness and public purpose of the action.

Hazard Analysis

Land use planners should anticipate the potential effects of hazards. Integrated hazard management is more efficient than single-purpose hazard management because some mitigation techniques can deal with more than one hazard.

Natural hazards directly related to land use planning include floods and hurricanes, earthquakes, landslides, and ground subsidence. The most regularly occurring natural hazards are floods, and, as previously discussed, a nationwide program provides maps of flood hazard areas for the local planner to incorporate readily into land use plans. Hurricane hazard areas also are mapped under the flood program; flood insurance rate maps show both A zones, where the hundred-year flood occurs, and V zones, where special hazards exist due to waves atop the base flood elevation. Additional hurricane hazard maps derived from the Sea Lake and Overland Surge from Hurricanes (SLOSH) program show the expected limits of flooding from each of the five categories of hurricane intensity.

Based on occurrence histories and seismic analysis, federal and state agencies have also mapped earthquake fault zones. Seismic risk mapping has been completed for Los Angeles, San Francisco, and the Wasatch Front (Provo, Salt Lake City, and Ogden) in Utah (Berke and Beatley 1992). However, there is no complete national earthquake hazard map series equivalent to the flood hazard maps. Earthquake hazard maps rely on information on seismicity (earthquake potential) and surface geology. They portray proximity to fault zones and identify earth areas subject to rupture, as well as ground-shaking, landslide, liquefaction, and flood. Preparation of earthquake hazard maps requires information concerning fault location and anticipated quake magnitude, fault displacement, earth deformation, and frequency of recurrence. When combined with land use maps, the degree of damage risk can be estimated (Blair and Spangle 1979).

Landslides and land subsidence hazard areas are not mapped at a scale useful for local land use planning under a national program, although federal and state agencies have mapped some individual high-risk areas. Landslide-prone areas result from combinations of slopes, soils, geology, and vegetation susceptible to movement resulting from impacts of heavy rains, ground tremors, forest fires, or other environmental shocks. For example, the San Gabriel Mountains of Los Angeles experience regular debris flows in which earth and stones stream down onto the urban plain. In Houston, the pumping of underground aquifers has resulted in major collapses of the earth over groundwater withdrawal areas. Land use planners in such areas need maps of these types of hazards in order to manage development safely.

Natural hazard maps can be compiled with the help of federal, state, and local emergency management agencies. They maintain records of past disasters as well as potential future disasters. By placing each type of natural hazard on a layer in a geographic information system, comprehensive hazard maps can be generated.

Man-made hazards often result from the leftovers or residuals from technological processes such as chemical production or inadequate waste disposal. Concentrations of hazardous wastes in soil or groundwater can pose public health threats as well as legal liability threats. The Resource Conservation and Recovery Act of 1976 sets forth requirements for hazardous waste generation, transportation, storage, and disposal. The "Superfund" Act, formally the Comprehensive Environmental Response, Compensation, and Liability Act of 1980 (CERCLA), sets forth requirements for cleanup of existing hazardous waste sites and liability provisions for potentially responsible parties. These include current and former property owners and lessors, hazardous waste generators, transporters, and disposers. The EPA maintains a list of hazardous waste sites, prioritized in terms of those most risky to human health and the environment, which included 1,143 sites as of 1988. Because the costs of cleanup and potential punitive damages often outweigh the value of the land, it is important to identify all existing and potential local hazardous waste sites in the planning information system.

A number of other pollution hazards exist. Underground storage tanks, especially those containing petroleum products, are potential hazards. Aging tanks develop leaks, and their contents can migrate into the groundwater, potentially polluting wells and drinking water supplies. Similarly, sanitary landfills containing solid wastes can discharge contaminated liquids, called "leachates," containing various pollutants. Agricultural fertilizers, pesticides, and livestock wastes, urban stormwater, septic tank drainfields, mineral extraction processes, and accidental spills can contribute pollutants.

Mapping local man-made hazards requires the planner to compile information from a number of sources. Environmental agencies can provide locations of known hazardous waste sites, as well as locations of aquifer recharge areas where pollutants can be introduced into the groundwater. Land use inventories can show locations of industrial and agricultural waste-generating operations. Public facilities maps can show locations of public water supply wells and reservoirs. Emergency management agencies can help document potential hazard areas due to transportation accidents.

NOTE

1. Chapter 4 discusses specifications for topographic, soil, and other types of computerized maps as recommended by the North Carolina Land Records Management Program (1987).

REFERENCES

Aller, Linda, et al. 1987. DRASTIC: A standardized system for evaluating ground water pollution potential using hydrogeologic settings. Ada, Okla.: Robert S. Kerr Environmental Research Laboratory, U.S. Environmental Protection Agency.

American Law Institute. 1976. *A model land development code.* Philadelphia: American Law Institute.

Anderson, James R., et al. 1976. *A land use and land cover classification system for use with remote sensor data.* Geological Survey Professional Paper 964. Washington, D.C.: U.S. Government Printing Office.

Basta, Daniel J., and Blair T. Bower. 1982. *Analyzing natural systems.* Washington, D.C.: Resources for the Future.

Berke, Philip R., and Timothy Beatley. 1992. *Planning for earthquakes: Risk, politics, and policy.* Baltimore: Johns Hopkins University Press.

Blair, M. L., and W. E. Spangle. 1979. *Seismic safety and land-use planning—selected examples from California.* Geological Survey Professional Paper 941-B. Washington, D.C.: U.S. Government Printing Office.

Brower, David J., and Daniel S. Carol. 1987. *Managing land-use conflicts: Case studies in special area management.* Durham: Duke University Press.

Burchell, Robert W., and David Listokin. 1975. *The environmental impact handbook.* New Brunswick: Center for Urban Policy Research, Rutgers University.

Cairns, John, Jr., and Todd V. Crawford, eds. 1991. *Integrated environmental management.* Chelsea, Mich.: Lewis Publishers.

Camp, Dresser & McKee. 1989. *Final report, University Lake watershed study.* Carrboro, N.C.: Orange Water and Sewer Authority.

Clark, Walter F. 1990. *North Carolina's estuaries: A pilot study for managing multiple use in the state's public trust waters.* Albemarle-Pamilico Study Report 90-10. Raleigh: UNC Sea Grant Program.

Contant, Cheryl K., and Lyna L. Wiggins. 1990. Toward defining and assessing cumulative impacts: Practical and theoretical considerations. In *The scientific challenges of NEPA: Future directions based on twenty years of experience.* Ann Arbor: Lewis Publishers.

De Chiara, Joseph, and Lee Koppelman. 1984. *Time saver standards for site planning.* New York: McGraw-Hill.

Godschalk, David R. 1987. Balancing growth with critical area programs. *Urban Land* 46(3): 16–19.

Holling, C. S., ed. 1978. *Adaptive environmental assessment and management.* New York: John Wiley.

Kusler, Jon A., and Mary E. Kentula. 1990. *Wetland creation and restoration.* Washington, D.C.: Island Press.

Ledec, George, and Robert Goodland. 1988. *Wildlands: Their protection and management in economic development.* Washington, D.C.: The World Bank.

Marsh, William M. 1978. *Environmental analysis for land use and site planning.* New York: McGraw-Hill.

———. 1991. *Landscape planning: Environmental applications.* 2d ed. New York: John Wiley.

McHarg, Ian L. 1969. *Design with nature.* Garden City: Doubleday.

North Carolina Land Records Management Program. 1987. *Technical specifications for base, cadastral and digital mapping.* Raleigh: North Carolina Department of Environment, Health, and Natural Resources.

Ortolano, Leonard. 1984. *Environmental planning and decision making.* New York: John Wiley.

Spirn, Ann Whiston. 1984. *The granite garden: Urban nature and human design.* New York: Basic Books.

Steiner, Frederick. 1991. *The living landscape: An ecological approach to landscape planning.* New York: McGraw-Hill.

Westman, Walter E. 1985. *Ecology, impact assessment, and environmental planning.* New York: John Wiley.

World Commission on Environment and Development. 1987. *Our common future.* Oxford: Oxford University Press.

8

Land Use

. . . the static concept of the city is no longer valid. It is constantly changing and growing, and, as it grows, it bursts its girdle and overflows into the countryside. The result is universally viewed with alarm as "urban sprawl," as being "neither city nor country."
—Blumenfeld 1967, 50

As a manager of urban change and growth, the land use planner looks at land through several perspectives. Land in its natural and urban states is both an input to, and a product of, the planning process. It is fought over by those who would change it through development and those who would stabilize it through maintaining existing and traditional uses. It represents potential opportunity for social and economic mobility or a potential disaster as an area for poverty and crime. In making plans to encourage the positive uses of land and to discourage its negative uses, the land use planner must build a knowledge base that encompasses the technical, social, economic, and institutional aspects of land use.

Four perspectives must be recognized in creating a land use information module: (1) land as functional space devoted to various uses; (2) land as a setting for activity systems; (3) land as a commodity to be developed; and (4) land as a perceptual image or esthetic resource. Taken together, these perspectives encompass many of the concerns (such as avoiding sprawl) and the values (such as preserving neighborhoods) that animate the land use game. Combined with information on population, economy, environment, and infrastructure, land use information provides intelligence on the dynamics of community change.

Functional space refers to the various uses, or functions, to which land is put. A number of dimensions of land use can be identified and recorded. We have previously reviewed the characteristics of land parcels, such as ownership and location (chapter 4) and environmental conditions, such as slope and soil type (chapter 7). Additional characteristics related to functional use are derived from structures placed on the land and from space use. Table 8-1 illustrates twenty-four functional space characteristics that could be associated with a single urban land parcel.

Viewed from a functional perspective, land use meets the demand for space fitted for urban settlement. It accommodates the needs for growth resulting from population and economic expansion. In that sense, the equation for determining

Table 8-1. Functional Space Characteristics

Parcel

Location	Area
Ownership	Assessed value of land
Zoning	

Environment

Slope	Soil type
Land cover	Wetlands
Floodplain	Hazards

Structure

Building type	Floor area
Ground coverage	Height
Number of stories	Condition
Assessed value of improvements	

Space Use

Existing use: primary and secondary	Intensity
Number of units	Number of residents
Number of employees	Planned future use

future land use is simple: *multiply the number of new households projected for the planning area by the number of acres needed per household.* Raw urban growth is not the only factor in the land use planning equation, however. As discussed in the previous chapter, land is also needed to meet the needs for environmental services and species diversity. Land is needed for agriculture to produce the food that feeds the cities. Extra land is needed to account for imperfections in the land market that keep it from satisfying demand on a one-to-one basis. The spatial equation gets more complex as more functions and conditions are added.

Land use is not a one-dimensional concept but rather a complex mix of various characteristics of ownership, physical environment, structures, and space uses (Table 8-1). In recording land use, the planner breaks it down into ownership units or parcels because these are the market units upon which development projects and land use changes are based. For each parcel, specific data are collected about its size, value, zoning, slope, soil, buildings, and existing and proposed uses. These data are primary inputs into the advance land use planning process.

Activity systems are the patterned ways in which households, firms, and institutions pursue their daily affairs within urban and regional areas. While land use data describe more stable characteristics, such as patterns of building and capital investment, activity data describe more dynamic aspects, such as patterns of commuting and visiting by land users. Activities include both the interactions that take place within particular urban spaces and those that take place between urban spaces. The most prominent urban activity systems are the regular journey-to-work movements of the area's work force. Knowledge of activity systems helps the planner understand household and business locational decisions and problems with existing land use arrangements.

Land use patterns are settings for activity. Social and life-sustaining activities pose demands on land use amounts, types, and locations. Land use arrangements determine social access, economic opportunity, travel patterns, and habitat survival. Proposals to change existing land use patterns should account for the potential disruption of current life settings as well as the creation of new settings. Viewed from this perspective, land use is a *dynamic set of stocks and flows* whose movements and frictions are in constant flux. Simplistic interventions into the arrangements of urban activity settings, such as occurred during the urban renewal program of the 1950s, may do more harm than good. As creators of new activity settings and conservers of existing settings, land use planners need accurate information on activity status and trends.

Developability of land is its capacity to be put to urban use. In its simplest meaning, developable land is vacant or underused land, without severe physical constraints, which is planned or zoned for more intense use and has access to the urban services necessary to support development. A more complete meaning of developability would include the land's market availability and the economic feasibility of developing it. Figure 8-1 illustrates the decreasing amount of land judged to be developable as more requirements are added to the definition. Public planning agency land information systems typically focus on the physical and regulatory characteristics of developability (numbers 1–4). Realtors and developers focus on these as well as the two market-oriented characteristics (numbers 5–6).

From the market perspective, land use is an exchange commodity whose value varies with its location, intensity, and relative scarcity. Home-buyers do not just think of their property as living areas, but also as investments on which they hope to turn a profit. Land use regulations typically require governing bodies to reject

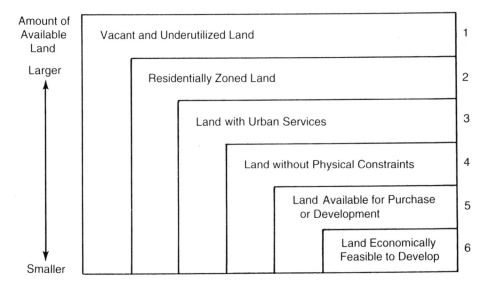

Figure 8-1. Levels of Developability. From Godschalk et al. 1986, 24.

proposed land use changes that will decrease existing property values on adjacent land. One of the paradoxes of land use is that the same homeowners' association that will fight fiercely for retaining existing residential land use patterns may turn around and offer to sell the neighborhood to the highest bidder for conversion to a commercial use. Another paradox is that government planners, because they do not include market considerations in their growth-management programs, do not provide strong grounds in their land use regulations for denying inappropriate large-scale speculative land development schemes. For example, many premature Florida subdivisions from the 1950s, still not built out forty years later, have complicated future planning and utility provision in their areas. Land use planners need to have a firm grasp on real estate implications.

Imageability of urban landscapes is their ability to provide a visible system for orientation, esthetic appeal, and social symbolism. As de Neufville points out, "The distinctive uses of land provide one of the lenses through which people interpret and evaluate the social milieu, and thus help to define and reinforce the social order" (1981, 35). Imageability can be used both to evaluate existing urban environments and to illustrate alternative future development scenarios. A related indicator of resident assessment of the community is *quality of life,* a synthetic rating that aggregates a broad spectrum of citizen concerns into an overall subjective image rating.

Positive outcomes from land use plans provide ample functional space for the community's needs throughout the planning period, maintain supportive settings for activities, enhance the commodity values of land over the planning area, and ensure that urban landscapes have high imageability. Negative outcomes reverse these benefits, incurring shortages of land that discourage or increase the cost of needed development, causing irreversible damage to neighborhoods or habitats, driving down the value of urban real estate so that owners and developers are unwilling to continue investing in the community, and resulting in unattractive, illegible community images.

Land Use Information in the Planning Program

Land use information, like environmental information, must be transformed from individual maps and studies into formats that can inform the planning process. A framework for organizing the land use database as a source of planning information includes inventories of land supply, land policy, and activities systems. Techniques for analyzing developability and imageability are also important.

Land Use and Activity System Inventories

A *land supply inventory* is a comprehensive database that relates the existing and projected supply of developed and developable land to infrastructure availability, environmental quality and constraints, and market trends. It should document the nature and condition of the present *built environment,* including the current stock of land uses and structures. It should consider the changes taking place in land use and built environment as new uses and activities supersede older ones. It should contain sections on land *available for development* for each urban land use type: residential, commercial, industrial, recreational, and public facilities. In areas where the jurisdiction also contains agricultural or forest lands, these types should be included. The inventory should be organized by the relevant planning scales (e.g., region, county, city, or neighborhood) and planning units (e.g., districts, watersheds, census tracts, traffic analysis zones, blocks, or parcels).

The land supply inventory must account for change over time. The initial inventory will portray *baseline* conditions, and annual updates will indicate observed *changes.* The minimum requirement is to maintain an accurate existing land supply database, which means that existing land use maps and tables must be regularly updated. This can be done through compiling building permits, certificates of occupancy, and subdivision approvals. It can also be done through field surveys although that method of inventory updating is expensive. Aerial photographs and remote-sensing images can also be used to update the inventory, especially for areas that include large amounts of agriculture or forest lands whose changes would not necessarily be visible from roads or urban permit records.

Other inputs to the land supply inventory are existing and projected infrastructure and market data. Engineering departments can supply infrastructure inventories, and capital improvement programs can indicate projected additions. Land value data can be obtained from the tax assessor, although market data must be obtained from the private sector. Multiple listing services can be scanned for current information, and market analyses performed for development projects can indicate anticipated future trends. If a GIS is available, it should be used to maintain the land supply inventory. Otherwise, an atlas and tabular database should be used.

A *land policy inventory* is a current compilation of the existing formal and informal regulations, procedures, programs, plans, and policies that affect land use in the local jurisdiction. Pulling this compilation together in an organized format will assist public and private decision-makers in understanding and complying with the intentions of the local land use management strategy. It will also serve as a comprehensive sourcebook of de jure (formally adopted) and de facto (used in practice) land use policy. As with the environmental policy inventory, it will be necessary to obtain the necessary information from a variety of government agencies at the local, regional, state, and federal levels. Because of the proliferation of regulatory programs, compiling this information will not be a simple task.

In addition to the primary source statements, the information should be summarized in a table or matrix. This summary should indicate the problem or need and the policy elements related to each. For example, the need might be to protect prime agricultural land. The policies might include the designation of, and limiting of urban development on, agricultural land by the comprehensive plan; the agricultural zoning category in the zoning ordinance; the subdivision regulation that requires a special use permit for new residential subdivisions at urban densities on prime agricultural soils; the county tax assessor's procedure for reduced tax valuation on property listed as active agriculture; and the state incentive program for soil conservation on prime agricultural land.

An *activity system inventory* is a database of urban land-using activity patterns, reflecting aggregate interactions between people and places over time. Activity system information, such as records of the pattern of journey-to-work commuting, describes the dynamics of urban movement by land-users. This information affects decisions about the more stable aspects of urban areas, such as locations of buildings and capital investments. Planners use activity system information to understand the macro implications of micro-level decisions by households and firms and to solve problems of inefficient existing land use arrangements.

Transportation studies provide the most common activity systems inventories, which illustrate the location, magnitude, and timing of the regular peak-hour morning and evening commuting patterns as well as other types of trips. Other types of activity system inventories can include recreational, social, and business activities.

Land Use Analysis

Developability analysis screens the land supply in order to locate areas suitable and desirable for future development or redevelopment. It can be used in plan-making and in development management. Developability analysis aims at maintaining a balance between the demand for developed urban land and the supply of available development sites during the planning period. It involves keeping a running tabulation of the impacts of all approved development proposals on the land supply inventory. For example, a developability analysis could show for a particular planning district how the projects approved during the current year have added to the available acreage of each type of land use, have decreased developable land, and have affected the capacity of the district infrastructure.

Three techniques, each using some of the same factors, can be used for developability analysis. Suitability analysis helps to find locations for various land uses. Carrying capacity analysis provides a comparison of demands posed by new land uses with the supply of available environmental and infrastructure resources in light of capacity restraints. Committed lands analysis allows a community to determine which of its public facilities have excess capacity, along with the value of the gains in efficiency that each additional customer would bring.

1. *Suitability analysis* identifies locations within the planning area that are best-suited to particular types of land use (Ortolano 1984). It involves overlaying maps of suitability measures, such as slope and highway access, to generate suitability scores for all sites within the planning jurisdiction for a particular use, such as shopping centers.
2. *Carrying capacity analysis* compares the demands of land uses with the ca-

pacity of natural or man-made systems to meet these demands (Godschalk and Parker 1975). It involves deriving critical thresholds of capacity, beyond which the system will suffer damage or breakdown, as the basis for recommendations on growth limits.

3. *Committed lands analysis* measures the change in production and delivery capacity of community facilities brought about by adding a new customer (Ford 1990). It analyzes location-related costs of public service delivery in order to delineate areas where the cost of adding a new customer is less than the value of gains in production efficiency from that customer.

Imageability analysis studies the perceptions of urban residents and visitors in order to determine how they visualize the cityscape (Lynch 1960; Nasar 1990). Planners use imageability studies to understand how their clients view their cities. Image information reveals a great deal about how people "read" urban form in terms of its legibility, attractiveness, and symbolism.

Image information is usually collected through personal interviews and surveys. Respondents are sometimes asked to draw maps of the major features of the cityscape as a way of collecting and comparing perceptual data.

Inventorying and Mapping Land Use Information

In setting up a land use information program, decisions must be made about the scales, planning units, and classification systems to be used and the types of maps to be produced. Ideally, these decisions will be coordinated with adjacent jurisdictions and with the regional planning agency so land use information will be compiled in similar formats suitable for sharing across jurisdictions. Because of the intergovernmental impacts of land use policies and decisions, regional compatibility of land use information is increasingly useful.

Information Units

The *scale* necessary to show the desired detail and specificity of land use information increases as the level of concern descends from the region to the county, city, neighborhood, and individual project. For example, a regional land use map might be presented at a scale of 1 inch = 2 miles; a county map at 1 inch = 1 mile; a city map at 1 inch = 1,000 feet; and a project map at 1 inch = 200 feet. With computer-assisted mapping programs, maps can be plotted at any desired scale. The more important issue is the scale of the source document from which the computer map was drawn, which will affect the accuracy of the map information. Transferring data from small-scale (regional) source maps to large-scale (project) finished maps can introduce serious inaccuracies.

Another important issue is the selection of *planning units*, or sub-areas, into which land use information is aggregated. Given the interdependence of planning databases, the definition of planning units should be done carefully. Planning units may be defined institutionally or ecologically (Table 8-2). Ideally, the planning units should "nest" into each other so that totals from smaller units can be added to obtain larger unit totals. Because traffic planners often collect useful small-area data, their traffic analysis zones should be nested into land use planning units. For example, a county's planning districts could be made up of groups of traffic analysis zones in order to use transportation data and modeling capabilities for land use planning. Nesting becomes difficult, however, when ecologically defined planning units, such as watersheds, are used in coordination with institutionally defined units. Ecological units typically do not match institutional boundaries.

Table 8-2. Planning Units

Institutionally Defined
Planning jurisdiction (county or city)
Planning districts (sub-areas of the jurisdiction)
Census tracts (defined by Census Bureau)
Neighborhoods or subdivisions (defined by development patterns)
Traffic analysis zones (defined by traffic engineers)
Blocks (defined by road rights-of-way)
Parcels (property ownership units)

Ecologically Defined[a]
Critical areas (defined by land cover, reservoir proximity, etc.)
Watersheds and drainage basins (defined by ridge lines)
Airsheds (defined by atmospheric conditions)
Habitats (defined by plant and animal species range)

a. Natural areas will often not fit into other planning units.

Land Use Data Acquisition

Systematically tracking land use change is the single most critical activity in maintaining a credible land use information system. In concept, this is simple; conduct a careful baseline survey of existing land use and then enter all changes as they occur. In practice, many planning agencies fail to enter changes and find it necessary to redo the baseline survey every time they need to update their land use inventory, an expensive and time-consuming process. We recommend a more systematic process of regular monitoring and updating.

Land use survey data can be collected through field inspections, cadastral file interpretations, or classifications of remote data from aerial photographs or satellite imagery. Change can be monitored through these methods and by collection of building permit and subdivision recording data. Often, several methods may be used together. For example, the initial data may be acquired through aerial photograph interpretation supplemented by field inspections for "ground truthing." The updating may be done by entering building permit and subdivision data on a monthly basis supplemented by annual comparisons with the tax assessor's files.

Field inspections are conducted either as "windshield surveys" from automobiles or by surveyors on foot in high-density areas such as central business districts. They involve physically sighting the use then recording it on a base map containing property lines and building footprints. Uses may be recorded either with notations signifying the actual use—such as "one family"—or with land use codes from the land classification system. The use of portable computer recording devices and global positioning systems (GPS) can increase the efficiency and accuracy of field work. During field surveys, it is also possible to record the condition of the buildings, perceptual data, and other information. These additional data usually are easier to gather in a separate survey, however. Complete community field surveys are expensive operations. Contemporary land use data collection frequently relies on cadastral files or remotely sensed data.

Cadastral file interpretations are conducted by extracting data about land use from the tax assessor's parcel ownership files. These files typically contain data for each tax parcel on the type of use or uses, parcel size, zoning, type and size of structure or structures, special conditions (such as agricultural status), and assessed valuation. Selected data can be classified and mapped to provide a graphic record of land use. Although this method is faster than complete field inspection, it may require spot field-checking to verify the data. Likely problems are out-of-date use listings, failure of the assessor's classification codes to match the planning classification codes, and missing data, such as square footage of use.

Classifications of remotely sensed data are conducted by inventorying aerial photographs or by analyzing the spectral "signature" of satellite imagery. Aerial photographs are most useful in classifying uses in built-up urban areas, where each building or structure may be identified. Satellite images are most useful in classifying areas that are nonurban or relatively homogeneous, where it is not difficult to assign a use category. They are not as effective in mapping densely developed, mixed-use areas where it has been difficult to assign a use due to the resolution limits of the images. The effectiveness of both photographs and images can be enhanced by combining them with field inspections or cadastral file interpretations. When obtained on a regular basis, aerial photographs and remote images are particularly effective in monitoring land use change because changes are relatively easy to spot from one set of photographs or images to the next.

Building permit and subdivision recording offer the opportunity to collect land use data from records that local governments maintain regularly. The legal requirements of obtaining a building permit before construction, an occupancy permit before moving into a new building, a site plan approval before developing a new area, and a subdivision approval before dividing land offer a built-in method of updating land use information. If the governmental departments responsible for each of these approvals share their information in an organized fashion, then it is not difficult to maintain an accurate running record of urban development use changes. Subdivision approvals signal the initiation of land conversion from rural to urban residential use. Building, site plan, and occupancy permit approvals indicate the construction or remodeling of structures. In addition to the standard development permits and approvals, land use change information can be obtained from engineering departments for public works projects, such as highways and dams, and from agricultural and natural resource agencies for changes in farm, forest, and resource uses. However, it is surprising how many governments do not systematically provide these data to their land information systems due to institutional inefficiency or narrow definitions of responsibility. One of the first steps in creating a planning intelligence system is to establish a working procedure for inputting approval and subdivision data.

Use Classification

For each existing and proposed land use, a complete information system would include data on its type, location, amount, condition, quality, timing, and cost. At the minimum, up-to-date type, location, and amount data are required for accurate land planning. While condition, timing, quality, and cost data also are useful, they have not been included in traditional land information systems. The form of this information depends upon the type of classification system used. Classification systems group similar categories of land use (activities, functions, and amounts) and land cover (vegetation and surface character) for purposes of planning, analysis, and record-keeping.

Type of land use is expressed through a hierarchical classification system in which more general classes are divided into levels of increasing detail. For example, in the Anderson et al. (1976) system, the most general level classifies land simply as urban; the second level breaks urban land into residential, commercial and services, and industrial; and the third and fourth levels allow for further subdividing each of these categories.

A major issue in specifying land use concerns how to describe the detailed subdivisions of the categories. For example, a residential structure for a single household could be classified as single family, townhouse or other attached single family, condominium townhouse, or rental townhouse. A residential structure for a number of households could be classified as multifamily, condominium garden apartment, rental garden apartment, condominium elevator apartment, or rental elevator apartment. These breakdowns are often related to the tenure of the use, whether it is an ownership, rental, or condominium unit.

To choose a particular classification system, the planner must first determine the purpose for compiling the land use information. If the information is only to be used for broad, large-scale planning, then a level one or two classification system may be adequate. For more detailed planning and land use regulation such as zoning, level three or four data will be needed.

The Anderson et al. land use and land cover classification system was designed for use with remote-sensor data.[1] This "resource oriented" system provides federal and state agencies with the basis for uniform categories at the generalized first and second levels as well as flexibility for regional and local agencies to adapt the third and fourth levels to meet their particular needs. Given the system's national orientation and its focus on remote-sensor data capture, many local planners will find that it contains a number of environmental categories—tundra, for example— not relevant to their areas; that it lumps some uses—such as industrial and commercial complexes—together into a single category that would more usefully be separated; and that it does not include density of residential uses. However, it can be adapted to fit local needs by leaving out unnecessary level one and two categories and adding detailed categories at level three. An adaptation of the Anderson system to meet the need for land classification in a typical county or small city is shown in Table 8-3.[2]

An earlier land use classification system was presented in the Standard Land Use Coding Manual developed by the U.S. Urban Renewal Administration and the Bureau of Public Roads in 1965. However, this manual was derived from the Standard Industrial Classification Code, which tends to overemphasize industrial uses, and it is not well suited to environmental data collection.

In practice, urban areas need classification systems that work for all public information users. In particular, the land planner, the transportation planner, and the tax assessor need a coordinated land use classification system because they should be able to share data. The system should be compatible with land use regulatory and computer record-keeping approaches and should be detailed enough to describe the use accurately, as well as its intensity and ownership in relation to spatial location. Urban-oriented land use classification systems will necessarily be more detailed than regional systems, but their primary classes should be similar enough so that urban data can be integrated into regional databases.

Location of land that has entered the development process may be expressed in terms of a street address, tax map and number, parcel identification number (PIN), or subdivision lot number. PIN numbers, based on a state plane coordinate system, incorporate the parcel centroid location as a locational device. Raw land or agricultural acreage location is often expressed by either a PIN number or a township/range/section number. Much of North America is divided into the township and range system, a rectangular grid based on parallels and meridians designated in degrees, minutes, and seconds. Each township is divided into thirty-six sections, one mile square, which can be further subdivided into quarter sections. Location at the aggregate level may also be expressed in terms of a planning unit such as a census tract or planning district. The Census Bureau's Topologically Integrated Geographic Encoding and Referencing (TIGER) system provides locational data in digital format for all 1990 census map features, 1980 and 1990 census geographic units (tracts and blocks), and political units (counties, cities, and minor civil divisions) (Klosterman and Lew 1992).

Amount of use is expressed as intensity of activity or density of development. For residential uses, amount can be measured in the number of units or people, but the usual measure is density (units per acre). Sometimes the density range is divided into low, medium, and high. Other places may divide the range into such numerical categories as one unit per acre or less, 1.1–5.0 units per acre, 5.1–10.0

Table 8-3. Land Use and Land Cover Classification System for County or Small City

Level 1	Level 2	Level 3
1. Urban	11. Residential	111. Residential one (<.5 du/acre) 112. Residential two (.5–2 du/acre) 113. Residential three (2.1–5 du/acre) 114. Residential four (5.1–10 du/acre) 115. Residential five (>10 du/acre)
	12. Commercial and services	121. General retail (CBD, shopping center, sales, and service) 122. Professional services and office 123. Mixed use (residential, commercial, and/or industrial)
	13. Industrial	131. Light industry/warehousing 132. Heavy industry 133. Industrial/research park
	14. Transportation, communications, and utilities	141. Transportation (road, rail, air) 142. Communications/utilities (water, sewer, and power plants, solid waste disposal, easements)
	15. Public or institutional	151. Parks, recreation, and public open space (ball fields, golf courses, etc.) 152. Institutional (schools, hospitals, churches, etc.)
2. Agriculture	21. Cropland and pasture 22. Orchards, groves, vineyards, and nurseries 23. Confined feeding operations (beef, hog, dairy, poultry) 24. Other agricultural land (barns, stables, research)	
3. Forest	31. Deciduous forest (70 percent lose leaves) 32. Evergreen forest (70 percent remain green) 33. Mixed forest (combination of deciduous and evergreen)	
4. Water	41. Streams, rivers, and canals 42. Lakes 43. Water supply reservoirs	
5. Wetland	51. Forested wetland 52. Nonforested wetland	
6. Barren land	61. Strip mines, quarries, and gravel pits 62. Transitional areas (e.g., cleared for agriculture or development)	

Source: Godschalk 1988.

units per acre, and more than 10.1 units per acre, depending upon local building practices. Another measure is floor area ratio (FAR), which describes the ratio of floor space in the building to the area of the lot. A third measure is lot coverage, which describes the percentage of the lot surface covered by a building or other impervious surface. For commercial shopping centers, the size may be described in terms of the market area of the center, for example, regional, community, or neighborhood.

Structural condition is a measure of the maintenance, repair, and safety of buildings on the site. For example, housing units may be classified as adequate, deteriorating, or dilapidated, depending upon the extent of serious defects they contain that make them safety hazards or unhealthy environments. They may be classified as in compliance or not in compliance with various structural regulations such as building codes, housing codes, zoning codes, and hazard ordinances. Structural condition is most often measured in older urban areas, where buildings may have deteriorated, or in hazard areas, where buildings may have to withstand extra structural stress.

Quality of use attempts to categorize the perceptual, architectural, or esthetic aspects of a site or area. It may include structural condition. Residential, commercial, and industrial areas could be distinguished in terms of their design quality as reflected in the condition or appearance of their buildings and grounds. In some cases, use conflicts could be identified as indicators of quality. For example, the conflicts brought on by surrounding heavy industrial uses could detract from the quality of a residential area. Because of the subjective nature of quality judgments, this measure is not often used in land use classification.

Timing applies to future use. At the most basic level, timing is simply a reflection of the uses anticipated to develop during the period that the future land use map covers. A finer classification of timing could be derived from the five-year capital improvement program for public facilities and from the growth-management program for private uses. For example, uses in a certain area may be programmed to coincide with the provision of infrastructure for that area. Timing also may be expressed in terms of land within an urban growth boundary, which is programmed for development during the planning period. Timing is not typically recorded in land use classification, but it is an important factor in plan implementation and development management and could be included in the land policy inventory.

Cost often is expressed in terms of assessed value for tax purposes because that information is available as a public record for both the land and structures. But other measures might also be used, such as replacement cost (for structures in a hazard area) or selling price (where real estate transaction data is available). Cost can be an indicator of the extent of private and public investment in a particular urban area. Cost information is not typically recorded in land use inventories, but it can be important in development management. For example, an analysis of assessed values in Lee County, Florida, found that 40 percent of the county's tax base was within the hundred-year floodplain, a fact that influenced hazard mitigation and land use policy recommendations in the comprehensive plan (Lee County 1989).

Land Use Mapping

Once land use inventories have been completed, the data are kept in both tabular and map form. The two basic types of land use maps show existing land use patterns and proposed future land use patterns.

The *existing land use map* records the arrangement of land uses, ownership units, and infrastructure in space. It organizes data from the various land inventories into a graphic display that shows urban patterns and relationships as well as urban problems and opportunities. As a map of existing conditions, it is important to keep current by recording land use changes and additions in a timely fashion and revising them at least annually, more often if significant or rapid change occurs. Many local planning departments fail to keep their land use maps up to date, largely because they have not built a system for incorporating building permit and tax assessor information into their mapping programs.

Existing land use maps should be produced at various scales, depending on the need for detailed information. More generalized maps, showing level one or two classifications, are useful for seeing overall urban patterns and relationships. For example, generalized maps would be helpful in developing a proposal for an urban limit line or a freeway corridor. More detailed maps, showing level three or four classifications, are useful in studying specific problem areas such as partially developed floodplains or changing neighborhoods.

Traditional maps of existing land use employ conventions developed for hand-drawn maps. Figure 8-2 shows a black and white version of a traditional, hand-drawn existing land use map that was originally reproduced in color in a comprehensive plan. The various shading patterns indicate different classes of land use, with darker tones for more intensive uses. Computer-drawn maps open new possibilities for both format and content. Computer-generated existing land use maps can integrate information from other sources, for example they can add data from traffic analysis zones or watersheds through an overlay technique to show not only land use but also infrastructure or environmental development capability. They also have the advantage of being more easily revised to show changes in future land use patterns or policies. And computer-generated existing land use maps can be produced from remotely sensed data, as in Figure 8-2a, which shows medium- and high-density urban or built-up land at the county scale. Such maps are especially useful for more general land classification planning.

A *land use report* accompanies the existing land use map to provide a quantitative breakdown of the map's graphic information. The land use report should be prepared in computer spreadsheet form to facilitate the recomputation of totals as changes are entered. It should break out uses (in acres and percents) by planning districts and jurisdictions.

Future land use maps are graphic records of the urban area's land use policy.

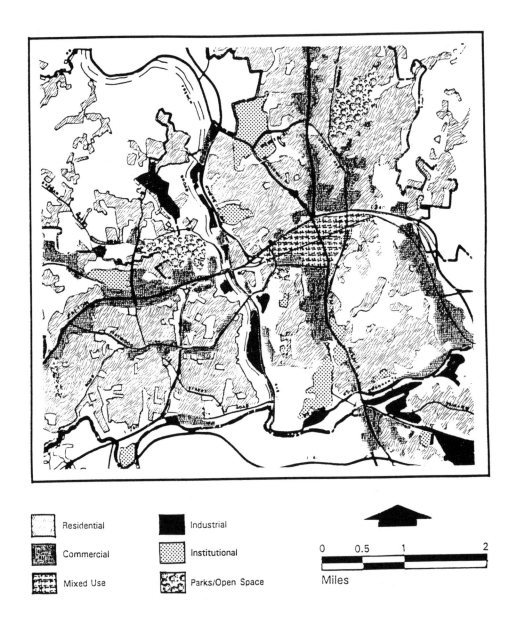

Residential Industrial
Commercial Institutional
Mixed Use Parks/Open Space

0 0.5 1 2
Miles

Figure 8-2. a. Traditional Existing Land Use Map, Central area of Asheville, N.C. Adapted from *Asheville City Plan 2010*, 93.

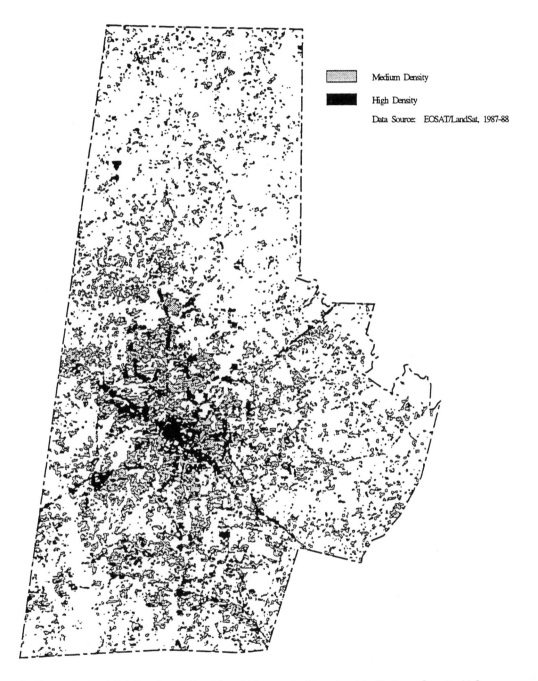

Medium Density

High Density

Data Source: EOSAT/LandSat, 1987-88

b. Computerized Existing Land Use Map. Urban or built-up land in Durham County, N.C. Generated from remotely sensed data. Provided by the North Carolina Center for Geographic Information and Analysis.

Although they are not likely to change as often as existing land use maps, they also should be updated regularly. Map revisions should be carried out after each revision of the future land use plan and after major land policy changes. The approved future land use map contains important planning intelligence for the planning information system. Later chapters discuss the preparation of a future land use map. Here we are concerned about it as an element of the planning information system.

As illustrations of adopted land use policy, future land use maps are important public information documents for developers, environmentalists, and urban households; they show the potential locations of urban change. In generalized form, they indicate where urban development is likely to occur during the planning period. In detailed form, they describe the types of land uses planned for each sub-area in the planning district. To guide the players in the land use game, future land use map graphics should communicate clearly the jurisdiction's policies and projections for the growth of an area.

Future land use maps use conventions similar to existing land use maps. Their patterns are more generalized and include such projected community facilities as planned arterial roads or parks. Traditionally, future land use maps have shown each projected future use in specific locations. This works well where development proceeds in a predictable fashion or where the future land use plan actually determines future growth patterns.

Management-oriented future land use maps can be less specific about exact locations of land use categories because in many cases it is difficult to anticipate how private development market will act some fifteen or twenty years in the future. Rather than pinpointing the precise locations of future commercial centers in the outlying areas of an urbanizing county, for example, the future land use map might show the extent of planned urbanization during the planning period within each planning sub-area or group of traffic analysis zones. The land use report accompanying the map would show overall commercial acreage totals allowed within the mix of urban land uses allocated to each sub-area for the planning period. These commercial acreage amounts would be controlled by estimates of need for commercial land derived from the overall county growth projections and allocated according to the goals of the plan. During plan implementation, approvals of commercial development within a sub-area that exceeded its planned total would be subtracted from commercial development allowed in other sub-areas to maintain the projected county total for the twenty-year future planning period.

Accompanying future land use maps are *land use policy reports* that document the quantities and locations of planned land uses by planning districts. These reports can include information about planned infrastructure in order to illustrate the jurisdictions' commitments to managed growth. They can be used to coordinate development regulations with future land use plans and to coordinate future development with management of critical environmental areas.

Activity Inventories

Activity inventories describe the way people use urban areas to conduct their daily affairs. Activity data are gathered through surveys, interviews, observations, and mechanical counts (Chapin and Kaiser 1979, ch. 7).

Household, firm, and organization activities can be analyzed through periodic activity surveys. Surveys of residential household activities ask respondents to record "time budgets," twenty-four-hour listings of all discretionary individual activities. Work is omitted, but all other activities are recorded, including shopping, recreation, socializing, and travel. Activity locations and frequencies also are noted. This information can be analyzed in connection with such household demographic characteristics as income, stage in the life-cycle, and ethnicity to generate archetypal activity patterns. Related information about the importance of dwelling unit and neighborhood factors and moving plans is helpful in analyzing quality of life and potential residential mobility.

Surveys of business and organizational activities ask respondents to describe their interactions with other establishments or clients. For example, a manufacturing plant would record the type, source, and means of transport of the raw materials it receives and the finished products it delivers during an average period. It would also provide data on employment, building and site characteristics, probabilities of expansion or relocation, and major factors affecting its location choices. This combination of activity data and location and space use criteria is helpful in dealing with development project requests and in preparing future land use plans for business firms and community institutions.

Transportation studies that document the time, location, origin/destination, and intensity of flows on urban road and transit systems are major sources of activity data. The tidelike flows of the morning and evening journey to work, which place the greatest demands on auto and transit capabilities, are relatively simple to record with mechanical counters. The less regular patterns of shopping and recreational trips require more labor-intensive origin/destination surveys and sampling procedures. Land use planners can learn about characteristics of urban travel important for land use planning from transportation studies, including time patterns, types of trips, modal distribution, environmental impact, and relationship between land use and transportation (ASCE 1986). This information is described more completely in later chapters. For now, we simply point out that transportation studies can offer a wealth of useful data to the land use information system, both on a small-area basis and on a systemwide basis. It is important to ensure that land use and transportation planning are carefully coordinated.

Social interaction studies show patterns of friendship and visiting in an area. Appleyard (1981) used social interaction studies in connection with perceptual studies to document the problems that automobile traffic causes in residential areas. He found that higher intensity traffic severely reduced neighboring and visiting within San Francisco city blocks (Figure 8-3). On a block with light traffic (two thousand vehicles a day, two hundred vehicles per peak hour), the inhab-

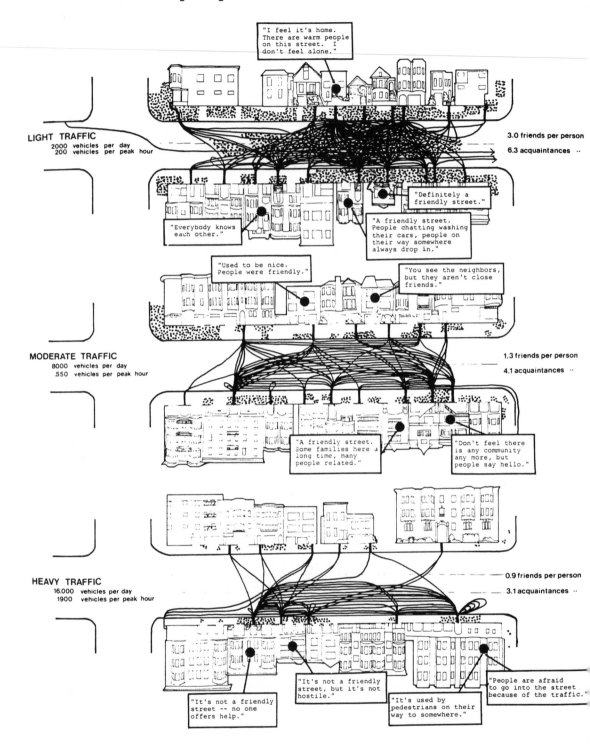

LIGHT TRAFFIC
2000 vehicles per day
200 vehicles per peak hour

3.0 friends per person
6.3 acquaintances

"I feel it's home. There are warm people on this street. I don't feel alone."

"Definitely a friendly street."

"Everybody knows each other."

"A friendly street. People chatting washing their cars, people on their way somewhere always drop in."

MODERATE TRAFFIC
8000 vehicles per day
550 vehicles per peak hour

1.3 friends per person
4.1 acquaintances

"Used to be nice. People were friendly."

"You see the neighbors, but they aren't close friends."

"A friendly street. Some families here a long time, many people related."

"Don't feel there is any community any more, but people say hello."

HEAVY TRAFFIC
16.000 vehicles per day
1900 vehicles per peak hour

0.9 friends per person
3.1 acquaintances

"It's not a friendly street, but it's not hostile."

"People are afraid to go into the street because of the traffic."

"It's not a friendly street -- no one offers help."

"It's used by pedestrians on their way to somewhere."

Figure 8-3. Impact of Traffic on Neighboring and Visiting. From Appleyard 1981, 21. Solid lines indicate household to household interaction; dots indicate sidewalk encounters.

itants had three times as many local friends and twice as many acquaintances as those on a block with heavy traffic (sixteen thousand vehicles a day, 1,900 vehicles per peak hour). Cross street patterns of neighboring and visiting were cut off by heavy traffic. On the street with light traffic, residents defined their home territory as including both sides of the street. On the street with heavy traffic, they perceived home territory in terms of their individual buildings or apartments. On the street with light traffic, the residents' maps showed much more detail of environmental features. On the street with heavy traffic, the maps showed traffic corridors packed with cars.

Analyzing Land Use Information

One of the functions of planning intelligence is to make sense of the information gathered in inventories. Developability analysis can guide decisions about where to direct future growth. Perceptual analysis can provide feedback on how citizens view the urban environment.

Developability Analysis

Studies of maintaining ample supplies of developable land typically are related to assessments of urban growth-management systems. For example, Dowall (1984) analyzed the tension between housing demand and land use control in the San Francisco Bay Area in terms of the effects of land use regulations on increasing new housing costs. Einsweiler (1979) argued that governments should analyze land supply needs in relation to demand, seeking to manage a market rather than implement a physical design. The assumed objective of such studies is to maintain supplies of developable land large enough to allow a competitive land market to operate. This requires that an "extra" amount of developable land, a "market" factor in addition to the projected demand, be included in future land use plans to account for market inefficiencies.[3]

Land use planners need accurate information about the supply of developable land within their jurisdictions in order to prepare land use plans and policies that effectively match land supply with future demand for developed urban space. Without this information they may overconstrict land supply, inflating land and housing prices and forcing desired development into other, less restrictive market areas. Or, at the other extreme, they may not constrain land supplies sufficiently to guide development into desirable growth patterns. The goal of a future land use plan is to determine not only what land should be available for urban development (usually a function of physical characteristics and infrastructure) during the planning period but also what land should *not* be available.

Four types of analyses can help in assessing land developability: land suitability models, carrying capacity analyses, committed lands analyses, and market forecasts.

Land suitability analysis is a procedure for mapping the variation in relative suitability for a particular land use across an entire jurisdiction or planning area (Ortolano 1984). This procedure is done for one land use at a time. It relies upon overlaying maps of physical, locational, or institutional attributes, such as soil type, distance from a highway, or zoning, to calculate suitability. The resulting suitability is expressed on a single scale that can be simply high, medium, or low, or it can be more elaborate, such as a numerical scale of one to ten.

For example, an industrial suitability analysis might be based upon slope, interstate highway access, and availability of water and sewer. Sites within the planning area that have moderate slope and are near the interstate and existing water and sewer lines would be rated as most suitable under this set of assumptions. It is important to understand that land suitability analysis is simply a systematic procedure for examining the combined effects of a related set of factors that the analyst assumes to be important determinants of locational suitability. Thus professional judgment in selecting and assigning importance to the factors in the model is of paramount importance.

The original procedure for land suitability analysis (McHarg 1969) relied upon overlaying hand-drawn, transparent maps on which the intensity or importance of a particular factor was shown in shades of gray, with the darkest gray representing the most intense or important degree of the factor. When the maps were overlaid, the darkest areas then showed the most suitable sites. Critics of this technique questioned its assumptions about the validity of adding quantities measured in different units, such as slope and erosion, and pointed out the difficulty of distinguishing among the various shades of gray when a large number of maps was overlaid (Ortolano 1984).

Contemporary land suitability analyses use computer-based mapping and combinatorial programs available in GIS software to handle the overlay and calculation procedure. In order to transform the scores associated with different factors, such as slope and sewer accessibility, into common units of measure, the factor scores are weighted before they are combined (Hopkins 1977). These weights should reflect the relative importance of each factor in determining suitability for the use under consideration.

The procedure for conducting a land suitability analysis, for example for light industrial sites, proceeds through a series of nine steps (Table 8-4).

1. Pick the land use to be analyzed (e.g., light industrial).
2. Determine the site attributes that determine suitability for that particular use (e.g., slope, interstate access, water and sewer availability).
3. Rank (rescale) the internal characteristics of each attribute, depending upon their contribution to suitability (e.g., slopes of 1 to 6 percent are given a higher rank, say 2, than steeper slopes of more than 6 percent, which are ranked lower, with a 1). Note that this rescaling involves aggregating the degrees of slope into classes. Choosing the number of classes and their included ranges is a matter of professional judgment, but in general it is preferable to keep the rankings simple both for procedural clarity and computational efficien-

Table 8-4. Suitability Analysis Procedure

Suitability Analysis for Industrial Development

Factors (Coverages)	Classes/Codes	Ranking Scores	Weights
Slope of the land (SLOPE)	< 5% / 1 5–15% / 2 > 15% / 3	5 3 1	1
Access to interstate highway (HYWBUF)	< 0.5 mile / 1 0.5–1 mile / 2 1–1.5 mile / 3 1.5–2 mile / 4 > 2.0 mile / 5	7 5 5 3 1	2
Access to water and sewer line (SEWERBUF)	< 500 feet / 1 500–2,640 feet / 2 2,640–5,280 feet / 3 > 5,280 feet / 4	5 5 3 1	3

Suitability Model
(Combination of attribute classes, ranking scores, and weights that identify degrees of suitability for locations for industrial development)

Degree of Suitability = (SLOPE x 1) + (HYWBUF x 2) + (SEWERBUF x 3)

Reclassification of Suitability Model Computation
(Assignment of ranges of values to degrees of suitabilty for the use, based on the outcomes of running the model for each location)

Scale Interval	Category	Suitability Degree (Description)	Map Pattern Number	Area (Acres)	Percent of Area
< 20	1	Least suitable	45	1,899	24.32
20–26	2	Less suitable	36	2,326	29.79
27–32	3	Suitable	47	3,046	39.01
> 32	4	Most suitable	14	536	6.87

cy. The rescaled site attributes should all have the same minimum and maximum values. Do not rescale one attribute on a scale of 1–3 and a second attribute on a scale of 1–9 because that weights the second attribute up to three times more when combined in the suitability analysis.

4. Weight each individual attribute in terms of its relative importance for suitability for the use under study (e.g., because interstate access is deemed twice as important for industrial location as slope, it is weighted 2, whereas slope is weighted 1. Similarly, availability of water and sewer is deemed three times as important as slope, so it is weighted 3).

5. Multiply each attribute rank by the attribute weight (e.g., the two classes of slope, 1 and 2, are multiplied by the weight of the slope attribute, 1).

6. Define the rules for the model to combine the weighted attributes into a sin-

gle suitability scale (e.g., addition, multiplication, or other algorithm). Following the advice of maintaining simplicity, we decide to add the weighted attributes to generate a single numerical score for each site in this case.

7. Reclassify the resulting range of numerical scores into a simplified composite suitability score (e.g., less than 20 is least suitable; 20–36 is less suitable; 27–32 is suitable; and more than 32 is most suitable). In reclassifying, try to ascertain what combinations of attribute values are represented by each suitability class. Remember that a class should not represent just a range of values on an abstract numerical scale and that thresholds between classes should not be arbitrary. The classes should represent selected combinations of conditions among the attributes, which are related to the suitability for the use under consideration. Thus, the prior rescaling, reweighting, and combinatorial rules are best kept simple to enable the planner to interpret the model's numerical results.

8. Transform the outcome into a suitability map by choosing a set of patterns to represent the different degrees of suitability (e.g., a darker pattern for the most suitable sites, grading to lighter patterns for less suitable sites).

9. Generate a statistical report showing for each suitability class, the site identification, number of acres, and other relevant data.

Most jurisdictions will use land suitability analyses for advising on site selection for projects, for considering alternative locations for impact studies, and for preparing future land classification and land use plans. Land suitability models also can be useful aids to negotiating settlements to land use conflicts, allowing the parties to test different settlement options (Godschalk et al. 1992). With a digitized parcel database and a GIS, the procedure is relatively straightforward. Even then, however, the planner will need to exercise judgment in devising analysis rules for dealing with parcels with wide ranges of attributes, for example, for averaging slope or other site conditions. Before a final model is selected, it will likely be run several times with different combinations of attributes, ranks, and weights in order to test its sensitivity and to evaluate the reasonableness of its outcomes.

Carrying capacity analysis is a method for studying the effects of population growth and urban development on ecological systems, public facility systems, and environmental perception. It seeks to demonstrate the impacts on public health, safety, and welfare of increases in the intensity of human use of natural resources and urban infrastructure. Originally, the carrying capacity concept was associated with managing ecosystems, such as rangelands where the number of cattle had to be limited to prevent overgrazing. From a planning viewpoint, carrying capacity can be defined as the ability of a natural or man-made system to absorb population growth, physical development, or intensity of use without significant degradation or breakdown (Schneider, Godschalk, and Axler 1978).[4]

For example, the comprehensive plan for Sanibel, Florida, a Gulf Coast barrier island, is based on population thresholds derived from the assimilative capacity of the wetlands to absorb additional pollutants and the evacuation capacity of the causeway in the event of a hurricane (Clark 1976). Sanibel's development regulations are specific to the island's different ecological zones, seeking to preserve their natural functions through limiting the location and intensity of development. Another example is the use of carrying capacity analysis for the Lake Tahoe region in California and Nevada, where the ultimate limit on population growth was derived from the water quality goals set for Lake Tahoe (Ortolano 1984). That study illustrated the limit on the expansion in capacity by means of public investment in facilities and services.

Early carrying capacity analyses relied on estimates and judgments of impacts on environmental systems. Current analyses use models that can be more precisely calibrated. For example, the impact of different land use density combinations was modeled for the University Lake watershed in Orange County, North Carolina (Camp, Dresser, and McKee 1989).[5] That model projected the amounts of four pollutants—total phosphorus and total nitrogen (affecting eutrophication), lead and zinc (toxic surrogates)—resulting from nonpoint source pollution that different watershed management strategies produced. Both structural and nonstructural best-management practices (BMPs) were analyzed. The two structural alternatives were onsite wet detention basins provided by developers of individual projects and a regional system of detention basins provided by the local government. The nonstructural practices were based on three future land use scenarios: two-acre single-family lots, five-acre lots, and variable-density clustered development equivalent to five-acre lot sizes. For each scenario, the impervious surface assumed for that density was used as the basis for determining the relationship between rainfall and runoff and the annual per-acre pollution discharges. The final plan adopted the five-acre lot BMP and the recommended water quality goal of preventing significant future deterioration.

The procedure for conducting a carrying capacity analysis varies according to the system whose capacity is at issue. For a natural system, such as a water supply watershed, an analytical approach similar to that used in the University Lake study is appropriate. First the *limiting factor, threshold,* or *environmental quality measure* and the *geographic unit of analysis* should be identified. This might be water or air quality of a certain level within a particular watershed or airshed. Then the *impact variable* should be defined. This could be increase in impervious surface leading to increased stormwater runoff or increase in carbon monoxide and particulates. Next, the *linkage* between the impact variable and the limiting factor should be quantified. This could be in the form of a spreadsheet model of pollutants generated by different land use configurations. Finally, alternative *scenarios* should be run to determine the changes in the limiting factor due to a range of impact-variable values.

For a man-made system such as a transportation, sewage treatment, or water treatment system, the analytical approach is more straightforward and in the nature of an engineering analysis. The limiting factor is usually a function of the system design. A road, for example, has a specified design capacity in terms of the number of vehicles per hour it can carry. The impact variable is based on the use of the system. For a roadway, this would be the number and speed of the automobiles. Linkage is spelled out in formulas that equate the number and speed of the cars with the characteristics of the roadway. Alternative scenarios could look at varying the modal split between automobiles and buses, at adding grade-separated interchanges, or at impacts of changing weather conditions.

When carrying capacity analyses are used to consider total populations supportable within a planning jurisdiction, then multiple limiting factors need to be considered. Nieswand and Pizor (1977) illustrate how water supply, water quality, and air quality constraints may support different population levels. In that illustrative case, water supply yield was the most limiting factor and determined the population capacity for the area.

For both natural and man-made systems, carrying capacity limits are not necessarily permanent. Increases in public investments can increase limits, as when septic tanks are replaced by a central sewage treatment system or additional lanes are added to a roadway. Limits may also be a matter of public discretion, as when governments set levels of service for public facilities and services. However, there also may be an inherent ecological or technological limit on how much capacity can be increased for each type of system.

The role of carrying capacity analysis in land use planning has changed since the introduction of the concept in the 1970s. Then, carrying capacity studies were rare and unique occurrences. Currently, capacity analysis is an accepted part of many planning studies, especially impact analysis studies and adequate public facility studies. Contemporary land use planning makes wide use of capacity studies to determine the type, location, amount, and timing of future development, as well as to calculate the type and nature of mitigation that should be conducted to offset the impacts of development projects on natural and man-made systems.

Committed lands analysis identifies locations where excess community service capacity exists and where the cost of additional distribution for each new customer is no greater than the value of the increased efficiency in producing the service. This marginal cost technique involves delineating the boundaries of these areas for each public service and then overlaying the maps to show aggregate committed lands areas. It highlights the benefits of clustering new development in areas that existing facilities already serve.

Ford (1990) gives an example of committed lands analysis. If each new user of a wastewater treatment plant would bring $1,500 in increased production efficiency (through making better use of plant capacity) and the cost of collecting sewage was $5 per lineal foot, then new users within three hundred feet of the existing sewerage network should be encouraged to connect to the system. The analyst would draw three-hundred-foot buffers around the existing sewerage mains to delineate the committed lands for sewage treatment. These, in turn, would be overlaid over water supply and fire protection committed lands to show where capital improvements should be provided next and where development should be encouraged. It is a technique to manage demand, based on making the most efficient use of public facilities.

Ford recommends using the "standard customer" as a basis for calculating production efficiency. For example, the standard wastewater treatment customer may be a single household that discharges two hundred gallons of wastewater a day. She arrives at the cost per customer by dividing the fixed annual operating costs of the treatment facility by the current number of customers. If there is sufficient excess plant capacity, then there is room for gains in efficiency and reductions in costs per customer by adding more customers. If the facility is within 10 percent of its engineering capacity, then committed lands analysis is no longer appropriate; a capital improvements expansion analysis is required.

Market forecasts attempt to project future land development. Simple forecasts rely on projections of past trends, population, and economic growth, along with information on development regulations, land use plans, and forthcoming development proposals, to estimate the location, type, amount, and cost of future development. More elaborate forecasts use models to simulate the growth of metropolitan areas. Older models relied on basic concepts of declining values of urban land as one moves outward from the central business district, based on concentric zones, on sectors oriented to radial transportation routes, or on multiple nucleuses (Chapin and Kaiser 1979, chs. 2, 14).

A prototype new generation model, the Bay Area Simulation System (BASS II), combines a detailed GIS land use database at the parcel level with a sophisticated spatial allocation model. This model seeks to emulate the behavior of private-sector developers as they screen potentially developable sites, called developable land units (DLUs), according to their likelihood of development and profit (Landis 1992). It assumes that the location and timing of land development decisions are almost entirely in the hands of private developers but that their decisions are constrained by government plans, policies, and regulations. Sites are developed or redeveloped in order of expected profitability. If there is insufficient developable land within a city or county to accommodate its forecast population growth, then the excess growth can spill over into a neighboring jurisdiction.

BASS II "grows" the ten-county San Francisco Bay Region by deciding how much new development to allocate to each DLU during a five-year period based on forecast population growth, DLU characteristics, and market clearing decision rules. The model structure includes four related models (Figure 8-4). The demand-side bottom-up population growth model generates five-year population forecasts for each city and county in the region. The supply-side spatial database generates the location and attributes of each developable land unit and displays the spatial growth pattern. The spatial allocation model scores undeveloped DLUs in order of profit potential and allocates forecast population. The annexation-incorporation model annexes newly developed DLUs to existing cities or incorporates them into new cities.

It will take time for advanced models such as BASS II to become widely avail-

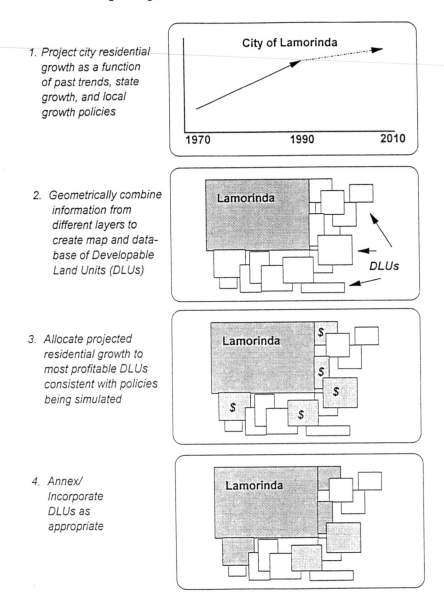

1. Project city residential growth as a function of past trends, state growth, and local growth policies

   City of Lamorinda

   1970   1990   2010

2. Geometrically combine information from different layers to create map and database of Developable Land Units (DLUs)

   Lamorinda   DLUs

3. Allocate projected residential growth to most profitable DLUs consistent with policies being simulated

   Lamorinda

4. Annex/ Incorporate DLUs as appropriate

   Lamorinda

Figure 8-4. Development Simulation Model Structure. From Landis 1992, 7.

able to land use planners. But the utility of such models is clear. Not only do they make use of precise GIS databases and private market logic, but they also allow planners to test the effects of alternative growth-management policies prior to adoption. Using a version of the model called the California Urban Futures Model, Landis (1993) tested the effects on regional development patterns of three types of scenarios: business as usual, environmental protection, and compact growth. For the fourteen-county Greater San Francisco Bay Region, he found that shifting to environmental protection policies would save some sixty thousand acres of agriculturally sensitive lands, whereas shifting to compact growth policies would save about 21,800 acres.

Perceptual Analysis

People's perceptions of urban areas are important determinants of travel behavior, locational choice, social relationships, and political action. Land use planners can maintain systematic perceptual information through the use of surveys and other procedures.

Planners need to understand the prevailing images of their cities in order to make plans that can fit the aspirations of residents, win political support, and be implemented. This entails studying residents' perceptions of neighborhood structure and social status. It means building perceptual maps of the area that translate standard land use symbols into social symbols. This type of information can be useful in formulating public policy to deal with land use problems. For example, Appleyard's *Livable Streets* study (1981) proposes a number of ways to reduce the negative impacts of traffic on residential neighborhoods based on his studies of household perceptions and activities. Without this type of information, the land use planner may misread the potential for future development and change within specific parts of the planning area. Four aspects of perception can be analyzed: legibility, attractiveness, symbolism, and quality of life.

Legibility of an urban area refers to the clarity of its spatial organization and the ease with which people can "read" its structure. A legible place is one that facilitates way-finding and identification of neighborhoods and other activity centers. Land use plans contribute to legibility by the way that land uses and transportation systems are integrated with each other and with the landscape to provide clear urban forms. Legibility can be analyzed through personal interviews and asking people to construct sketch maps of their communities.

Lynch (1960) developed the methodology for collecting peoples' mental maps of their urban environments. From these maps, he analyzed the legibility of the cityscape, the ease with which its parts can be recognized as belonging to a coherent pattern. He found that paths, edges, districts, nodes, and landmarks were consistent features of imageable cities. Alexander et al. (1977) have developed a "pattern language" based upon historic patterns of urban structure, use, and meaning. He and his colleagues (1987) have looked at processes to ensure that urban growth proceeds toward the creation of coherent wholes, with each increment of building guided by an overall vision of community form and space.

Attractiveness of an urban area describes the degree to which it is positively perceived. From a nonprofessional perspective, visual quality may be the most important influence on how people experience and respond to urban areas and planning initiatives.

Nasar (1990) analyzed the esthetic order of urban areas, based on resident and visitor opinions about attractiveness and ugliness. He used interviews of residents and visitors to determine composite maps of the most visually pleasant and unpleasant areas of Knoxville and Chattanooga. Respondents were not asked to draw maps, but simply to identify the five areas they considered most pleasant and unpleasant visually, to describe their boundaries, to name the physical features that accounted for their evaluation, and to tell what is most in need of visual improvement. Interviewers drew one map for each respondent and then overlaid maps to generate a composite (Figure 8-5).

Symbolism refers to the meanings that people attach to various parts of the urban area. Symbolism could be interpreted in terms of the environmental quality or cultural importance of certain places. Some observers have used the term *sacred places* to describe locations of high symbolic value in contemporary cities. An important aspect of urban symbolism is the implication of social status.

Perin (1977) identified the importance of social symbolism to city-dwellers, including their ascription of a symbolic "ladder of life" to the neighborhoods they pass through as their economic status increases. As Perrin notes, residential areas could be viewed as rungs on the ladder of life, ranging from "starter" rental houses or apartments in lower-status, less secure transitional neighborhoods to ownership of the "ultimate" residential addresses in stable, high-status neighborhoods. As a cultural anthropologist, she uses interviews with those engaged in urban development to analyze the social meanings of home ownership, sprawl, newcomers, mortgages, housing styles, forms of tenure, the life-cycle, status, and local control over zoning. Looking beneath the technical aspects, she sees the land

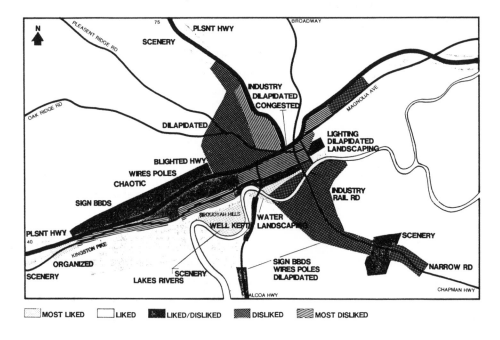

Figure 8-5. Evaluative Image Map. From Nasar 1990, 44.

use system as a translator of principles of social order into settlement patterns: "The cultural conceptions providing social meanings to newcomers and old-timers, renters and owners, those arriving and those arrived, high- and low-density settlements, stability and change, and suburbs and cities powerfully guide actual practice in land-use matters" (Perin 1977, 210).

Quality of life is a synthetic perceptual measure based on resident ratings of local trends of change over time in such factors as open space, urban design, crime, traffic, schools, and housing affordability. Ratings are compiled from regular citizen surveys so that changes in perceptions of quality of life can be monitored. By focussing on factors that government decisions can affect and asking whether these are expected to get better or worse, this approach reveals broad patterns of agreement in citizen perceptions of the community image.

Myers (1989) reports on a study in Austin, Texas, which found a consensus that seven factors were very important to quality of life. At least 85 percent of the respondents emphasized traffic, water quality, crime, jobs, schools, cost of living, and housing costs. The two highest priorities were the need to solve traffic congestion problems and the need to protect water quality in the natural environment. The study asked residents to rate the importance of different factors in forming a city's quality of life and to assess the rate of change in the factors. Myers suggests that growth management can affect quality of life by slowing the pace of change in a community.

NOTES

1. Planners who have attempted to classify land use and land cover from remotely sensed data have learned of the difficulties in identifying more detailed classes, such as level two and three, solely from the reflectance characteristics of the satellite data. The signatures of some uses are similar enough that they may be misclassified.

2. This system was developed to allow a regional agency to map both existing and future land use of its constituent governments on a GIS for analysis of land policy compatibility. It is an adaptation and renumbering of Anderson et al. (1976), leaving out rangeland, tundra, perennial snow or ice at level one, and some level-two classes such as dry salt flats and beaches. Level-three residential categories were developed to match local planning and zoning categories and were given numerical designations rather than names (such as "low" or "medium" density or "single" or "multiple" family) to fit as well as possible with the variety of density classes and labels in use locally.

3. The issue of how much extra land to add to projected future land use need has not been addressed thoroughly (Godschalk et al. 1986, 208–9). One rule of thumb is to allow an extra 25 percent of the projected need over a twenty-year planning period. San Diego (1985) adopted a policy of planning sufficient land for urbanization to accommodate the projected fifteen-year growth. The Metropolitan Council of the Twin Cities (1975) added a five-year surplus to projected demand in determining the amount of land planned for public services. Portland Metropolitan Service District (1979) allocated a land supply 15 percent over projected demand through the year 2000 in defining its urban growth boundary. However, Montgomery County, Maryland (1980) found no acceptable standard

for determining the correct ratio of land supply to market demand in order to provide sufficient market flexibility.

4. A more comprehensive approach to carrying capacity includes not only the common physical environmental definition familiar to planners but also a "perceptual" definition (the amount of activity or degree of change that can occur before we perceive the environment to be different) and an "institutional" definition (the ability of organizations to guide development toward public goals) (Godschalk and Parker 1975). Perceptual carrying capacity analyses have been conducted for degrees of crowding in recreation areas, stages of development intensity in urbanizing areas, and traffic intensities on urban streets (Appleyard 1981). Institutional capacity analyses are embodied in organizational audits.

5. The model was similar to the model used to analyze the Occoquan Basin in Fairfax County, Virginia, which supported the 1982 downzoning of that twenty-three-thousand-acre water supply watershed from one dwelling unit per acre to one dwelling per five acres (Fairfax County 1982).

REFERENCES

Alexander, Christopher, et al. 1987. *A new theory of urban design.* New York: Oxford University Press.

Alexander, Christopher, et al. 1977. *A pattern language: Towns, buildings, construction.* New York: Oxford University Press.

American Society of Civil Engineers. 1986. *Urban planning guide.* New York: ASCE.

Anderson, James R., et al. 1976. *A land use and land cover classification system for use with remote sensor data.* Geological Survey Professional Paper 964. Washington, D.C.: U.S. Government Printing Office.

Appleyard, Donald. 1981. *Livable streets.* Berkeley: University of California Press.

Blumenfeld, Hans. 1967. *The modern metropolis: Its origins, growth, characteristics, and planning.* Edited by Paul Spreiregen. Cambridge: MIT Press.

Camp, Dresser and McKee. 1989. *University Lake watershed study.* Raleigh: Camp, Dresser, & McKee.

Chapin, F. Stuart, Jr., and Edward J. Kaiser. 1979. *Urban land use planning.* 3d ed. Urbana: University of Illinois Press.

Clark, John. 1976. *The Sanibel report: Formulation of a comprehensive plan based on natural systems.* Washington, D.C.: The Conservation Foundation.

de Neufville, Judith Innes, ed. 1981. *The land use policy debate in the United States.* New York: Plenum Press.

Dowall, David E. 1984. *The suburban squeeze: Land conversion and regulation in the San Francisco Bay Area.* Berkeley: University of California Press.

Einsweiler, Robert. 1979. Increasing the supply of land in the fringe area. In *Reducing the development costs of housing actions for state and local governments.* Washington, D.C.: U.S. Department of Housing and Urban Development.

Fairfax County. 1982. *Occoquan Basin study.* Fairfax: Fairfax County Office of Comprehensive Planning.

Ford, Kristina. 1990. *Planning small town America: Observations, sketches and a reform proposal.* Chicago: American Planning Association.

Godschalk, David R. 1988. Region J land use and land cover classification system. Research Triangle Park: Region J Council of Governments.

Godschalk, David R., and Francis Parker. 1975. Carrying capacity: A key to environmental planning? *Journal of Soil and Water Conservation* 30(4): 160–65.

Godschalk, David R., et al. 1992. GIS as a tool for computer-assisted land use and environmental conflict resolution. *Photogrammetric Engineering & Remote Sensing* 58(8): 1209–12.

Godschalk, David R., et al. 1986. *Land supply monitoring: A guide for improving public and private urban development decisions.* Lincoln Institute of Land Policy. Boston: Oelgeschlager, Gunn and Hain.

Hopkins, Lewis. 1977. Methods for generating land suitability maps. *Journal of the American Institute of Planners* 43(4): 386–400.

Klosterman, Richard E., and Alan A. Lew. 1992. TIGER products for planning. *Journal of the American Institute of Planners* 58(3): 379–85.

Landis, John D. 1992. BASS II: A new generation of metropolitan simulation models. Working Paper 573. Berkeley: Institute of Urban and Regional Development, University of California.

———. 1993. *How shall we grow? Alternative futures for the Greater San Francisco Bay Region.* Berkeley: California Policy Seminar, University of California.

Lee County. 1989. *Lee plan.* Fort Myers: Lee County.

Lynch, Kevin. 1960. *The image of the city.* Cambridge: Harvard University Press.

McHarg, Ian. 1969. *Design with nature.* New York: Natural History Press.

Myers, Dowell. 1989. The ecology of "quality of life" and urban growth. In *Understanding growth management: Critical issues and a research agenda,* ed. David J. Brower, David R. Godschalk, and Douglas R. Porter. Washington, D.C.: Urban Land Institute.

Nasar, Jack L. 1990. The evaluative image of the city. *Journal of the American Planning Association* 56(1): 41–53.

Nieswand, G. H., and P. I. Pizor. 1977. How to apply carrying capacity analysis. *Environmental Comment.* December, 9–10.

Ortolano, Leonard. 1984. *Environmental planning and decision making.* New York: John Wiley.

Perin, Constance. 1977. *Everything in its place: Social order and land use in America.* Princeton: Princeton University Press.

Schneider, Devon M., David R. Godschalk, and Norman Axler. 1978. *The carrying capacity concept as a planning tool.* APA Planning Advisory Service Report no. 338. Chicago: American Planning Association.

9

Infrastructure and Community Facilities

Many of the design criteria for infrastructure investments in urban areas in the United States have been reduced to engineering rules of thumb and standard off-the-shelf designs. . . . While many of these rules have simplified design choices for engineering firms, they may also have removed planners and local government officials from an active part in the decision process. The initial design parameters for water, wastewater, and solid waste disposal systems (projections of future population and selection and planning of service areas) are more within the realm of the planner than that of the design engineer.
—Tabors 1979, 184

Urban land must have access to the network of public and quasi-public structures and services necessary for the operation, minimum health and safety, and desired quality of life in modern urban places. Although planners usually do not design the facilities, they must maintain accurate information about them in order to incorporate them into land use plans and coordinate development controls with a community's capability to provide urban services.

These public structures are called *infrastructure, community facilities,* or, sometimes, *commuity service facilities.* Generally, the term *infrastructure* is used to refer to public water and sewer facilities, highways, and public transportation, whereas the term *community facilities* refers to schools, parks, and other facilities that citizens actually visit. Sometimes "community facilities" is used interchangeably with "infrastructure" to designate the entire underlying public physical plant and system of services. We generally use the term *community facilities* to include both infrastructure and structures and places that serve people.

Community facilities are diverse. They include the streets, highways, expressways, subways and other public transit, rail line, passenger stations, freight yards, airports, parking lots and structures, and even bicycle and pedestrian paths of a city's circulation system. They include public utilities: water collection, treatment, and distribution; wastewater collection and treatment; and sometimes electrical distribution. They include schools, parks, fire and police stations, jails, libraries, convention centers, stadiums, and solid waste treatment and storage facilities. They may include hospitals, clinics, community centers, shelters, and other public and quasi-public facilities.[1]

Community facilities are important to planning in two ways. First, from the social use values perspective, they may both provide desirable services to, and impose undesirable impacts on, those who use the city. Thus, neighborhoods may lobby for a new park, but against a new arterial street. Second, from the market perspective, land, to be developable, must have access to a network of supporting infrastructure and community facilities. Property without infrastructure, such as road frontage, potable water, and waste disposal, has a low value in the land planning and development game. Areas remote from community services, such as schools and parks, also are less desirable for urban development. Thus, in terms of the land use game, infrastructure, from the perspective of both social use value and market value, is a higher-order chip that can literally change the game board on which the players move by adding or withholding new areas for urban development.

It is important to include service standards in the information system. They provide normative measures of desirable service levels that can be used to gauge the adequacy of existing facilities. For example, the fact that a highway is carrying two thousand vehicles per hour can be compared to its design capacity and a highway standard to arrive at the level of service that the road provides. The acres of land in community parks can be compared to the National Recreation and Parks Association standard of five to eight acres per thousand population to determine whether the level of recreation services is above or below that standard. Of course, standards should be a matter of conscious choice for the community; some localities may choose to provide higher levels of service than others, depending on their priorities and resources. In that sense, a service standard is both a technical and a political measure. The three most influential types of public facilities for urban development are transportation, water, and sewer facilities. In both a planning and a market sense, each must be brought to the site in an urban area in order for land to be suitable for development. Stormwater management, which must be provided within the planning area but not necessarily on each individual site, is also important to maintaining environmental quality and safety. Other facilities, including schools and park and recreation facilities, are less important in the market sense yet very important in creating social use value for community residents.

Infrastructure and Facilities Planning Information

Three types of information are proposed, similar to the inventory, cumulative impact assessment, and management strategy approaches recommended in chapters 7 and 8.

The *facilities inventory* collects and displays data on local public facilities that support land use planning. It should contain a section for each facility, including maps, and attribute tables organized by the relevant analysis unit, such as the transportation analysis zone (TAZ) for roads, the service area for water supply, waste disposal, and schools, and the drainage area for stormwater management. Both existing conditions and proposed changes should be covered.

The *cumulative impact assessment* for public facilities is an analytical procedure that monitors the aggregate effects of changes in supply and demand on the systems. It assesses such things as the impact of total increase in demand from approved development projects upon the service level of the facility, relative to critical capacity thresholds, for existing facilities, planned improvements, and expected deterioration in conditions. Basic assessments may simply tabulate projected demand increases and compare them to the design capacity of the facilities. Advanced assessments will model the impact of design changes to derive system adjustments as well as approaches to capacity limits.

Community facility management strategies may be part of the comprehensive plan, community facility plan, or capital improvement program, but they also should be a separate element of the information system. The purpose is to bring together in one place coordinated information on public facility growth plans, extension policies, and financing programs. Compiling this statement will require gathering data from the units responsible for the facilities, which could include authorities, service districts, and nongovernmental organizations as well as governmental public works and engineering departments.

Capacity and demand analyses are important to addressing so-called concurrency issues. Concurrency compares the availability and adequacy of service provision to the timing and amount of land use demand. A concurrency policy essentially requires that public facilities will be available concurrently with development, either through the government's capital improvements program or by the private sector, through development permit negotiation or exaction. Adequacy is defined in terms of the adopted level of service for each public facility. The objective of concurrency and adequate public facilities requirements is to ensure that localities do not incur large infrastructure debits as they grow. Rather, they must "pay as they grow" for necessary support facilities.

Transportation

Land use and circulation elements can be considered mismatched if the development permitted would overwhelm available and proposed transportation facilities, or if the size, configuration and location of transportation facilities do not correspond to what is needed for efficient circulation and access. This common problem may arise in a number of ways, including adoption of land use and transportation elements at separate times with little or no cross-checking; failure to estimate the trip generation implications of the land use element; overly optimistic forecasts of future transit use and ridesharing; and a tendency on the part of many lo-

cal governments to develop plans permitting levels of development far in excess of what realistically can be expected.
—Homburger et al. 1989, 33

Because of their interdependency, it is important to coordinate transportation and land use planning, beginning with inclusion of transportation information in the information system.

The purpose of transportation is to move people and goods safely and efficiently. For land use planning, the most influential transportation type is the automobile, which carries upward of 80 to 90 percent of urban trips (ASCE 1986, 118). City streets carry automobiles, trucks, emergency vehicles, and bicycles, providing access to all parts of the urban area. Rights-of-way carry public utility lines, including gas, sewage, stormwater, electric power, cable television, and telephone. In addition, as Voorhees et al. (1979) point out, streets also provide the space for public landscaping, the framework for urban design, and the context for urban history and symbolism.

Transportation Inventory

Streets are classified according to administrative authority and function. Administrative classes are related to the authority responsible for construction and maintenance: federal, state, county, or city. Functional classes are based on the use and design standards of each type of roadway.

There are four major functional types of roadways (Voorhees et al. 1979).

1. *Expressways or freeways* are controlled-access, multilane, divided highways devoted to high-speed, long-distance traffic movement with little or no access to adjacent land.
2. *Arterials* serve primarily to move traffic between principal traffic generators. Residential access is discouraged, but commercial access is allowed. Arterials should form an integrated system. They may be divided into major arterials and secondary arterials.
3. *Collectors* serve internal traffic movements within an urban area and connect it with the arterial system. They meet movement and access functions equally. They may be divided into major and minor collectors.
4. *Local streets* provide access to adjacent land as their primary function. They may be designed as grids, loops, or culs-de-sac.

Figure 9-1 diagrams this hierarchy of roadways. Table 9-1 specifies guidelines on function, speed limit, continuity characteristics, spacing, access to adjacent land, intersection spacing, right-of-way width, and maximum dwellings served for each level of roadway.

Roadway use is measured in terms of both the volume of vehicles per hour or day and the origins and destinations of the vehicles. Trip volume is counted by mechanical devices triggered by passage of vehicles. Counts are expressed in terms

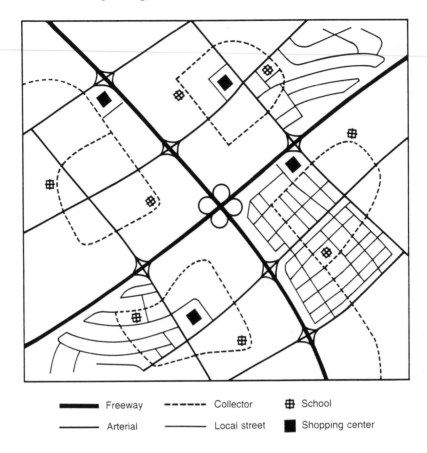

▬▬ Freeway	- - - - - Collector	⊞ School
▬▬ Arterial	▬▬ Local street	■ Shopping center

Figure 9-1. The Urban Hierarchical System of Roadways

of "peak hour volumes," determined during the time of day when most morning and evening journey to work and return trips occur, and of "average daily trips," defined as average twenty-four-hour volumes. Origin and destination counts are measured by surveys of drivers as they cross cordon lines within urban areas. Results are used to define trip generation factors for each type of land use. The Institute of Transportation Engineers publishes regular averages for trip generation by land use types. For example, the 1987 edition of *Trip Generation* lists the number of average weekday trip ends for a low-rise apartment as 6.6.

Roadway capacity is defined as the maximum number of vehicles that can be expected to travel over a given section of roadway or a specific lane during a given period under prevailing roadway and traffic conditions (Greenberg et al. 1984, 14). Prevailing roadway conditions include the road's characteristics, such as vertical and horizontal alignment, lane width, number of lanes, and types and numbers of intersections. Prevailing traffic conditions include usage factors at a particular time, such as traffic volume, turning movements, and conflicting pedestrian and bicycle movements.

The *level of service* of roadways is a measure of the effect on capacity of prevailing

Table 9-1. Functional Route Classification: Characteristics and Standards

Classification	Function	Speed Limit (mph)	Continuity	Spacing (miles)	Direct Land Access	Minimum Roadway Intersection Spacing	Right-of-way Recommended (feet)	Maximum Dwellings Served
Freeway and expressway	Traffic movement	45–55	Continuous	Variable	None	1 mile	150–300	NA
Primary arterial	Intercommunity and intrametro area Primary—traffic movement Secondary—land access	35–45 in fully developed areas	Continuous	1/8–1/4 (CBD) 1/4–1/2 (urban) 1/2–1 (suburban) 1–2 (rural)	Limited—major generators only	1/2 mile	110–140	NA
Secondary arterial	Primary—inter-community, intrametro area, traffic movement Secondary—land access	30–35	Continuous	1/8–1/4 (CBD) 1/4–1/2 (urban) 1/2–1 (suburban) 1–2 (rural)	Restricted—some movements may be prohibited; number and spacing of driveways controlled	1/4 mile	80–100	NA
Collector	Primary—collect/ distribute traffic between local streets and arterial system Secondary—land access Tertiary—inter-neighborhood traffic movement	25–30	Not necessarily continuous; should not extend across arterials	1/2 or less	Safety controls; limited regulation	300 feet	70–90	400–1,000 (for length of 1/2–1 mile)
Local	Land access	20–25	None, unless neotraditional grid pattern	As needed	Safety controls only	300 feet	30–60	50 (loop) 24 (cul-de-sac) N/A (grid)

Source: Adapted from Stover and Koepke 1988. Tables 4-1 and 4-3. See also Fernandez 1994 for local streets.

roadway and traffic conditions (Greenberg et al. 1984). Average operating speed is an indicator of level of service, with higher speeds indicating higher levels of service. Six roadway levels of service have been defined, ranging from A as the highest to F as the lowest (Table 9-2). Although service level C is the typical design goal, decision-makers may accept a lower level for peak hours in some situations. The major factor affecting level of service is traffic interruption from at-grade intersections.

A major source of transportation data is the transportation study. These are usually conducted by the Metropolitan Planning Organization, created under federal requirements for areawide transportation planning. The studies document

Table 9-2. Transportation Levels of Service

Level of Service	Expressways, Highways Streets[a]	Rail Transit[b]	
		Approx. sq. ft./ passenger	Approx. no. of passengers/seat
A	Free flow, limited only by alignment and speed limit; minimal delay	15.4+	≤ 0.65
B	Stable flow but presence of other vehicles noticeable; freedom to select speed relatively unaffected; slight decline in freedom to maneuver	15.2–10.0	0.66–1.00
C	Stable flow but freedom to select speed affected; maneuvering requires vigilance; comfort and convenience declines; vehicular conflict at many intersections	9.9–7.5	1.01–1.50
D	High density, still stable flow approaching unstable flow; speed and maneuvering restricted severely; poor comfort and convenience; small increases in flow cause operational problems; delays at intersections as long as two or more signal cycles	6.6–5.0	1.51–2.00
E	Operating level at or near capacity; speeds low but stable during off-peak hours; unstable flow with long queues at peak hours; maneuvering requires forcing others to give way; cross-street traffic has difficulty entering flow; comfort and convenience very low, frustration high	4.9–3.3	2.01–3.00
F	Forced flow or breakdown of operation; stop and go waves; back-ups through up-stream intersections; long delays through two or more cycles of traffic signals	3.2–2.6 (crush load)	2.01–3.80

a. Adapted from Transportation Research Board 1985.
b. Adapted from Rosenbloom, in So and Getzels 1988.

problems with existing roadways systems, such as poor levels of service on certain segments or at certain intersections. They also project future problems that may arise due to increased travel demand from changes in land use.

The planning unit for transportation studies is the transportation analysis zone (TAZ). These are defined as logical sub-areas of relatively homogeneous land uses for analysis of movement within, into, and out of the urban area. They vary greatly in size, normally including from 90,000 to 160,000 persons, but are getting smaller because computer-assisted database management and GIS are becoming more prevalent. They are often divided into smaller analysis areas and grouped into larger sectors or corridors of up to three layers of zone sizes so planners can focus on either a small area or the entire transportation system. The boundaries in at least one of the levels is increasingly based on census zones because it makes additional computer-based socioeconomic data available. In addition to automobile transportation information, the inventory should cover transit, bicycle, and pedestrian transportation. Published data for these systems typically will be less extensive and may require special surveys.

Transportation Impact Analysis

Automobile impact assessment includes both the impact of increasing travel demand upon the capacity of roadways to carry traffic and the impact of building new roadways upon adjacent land uses.

Assessment of roadway impacts is done both at the systemwide level and at the localized project level. Systemwide studies use network models to estimate the assignment of traffic increases to various roadway segments and compare the increased travel demand to the capacity of the segments. These models dynamically adjust demand as drivers respond to increased congestion by changing their paths through the system.

At the project level, traffic impact analysis is used to estimate whether the roadways in the area of a proposed major development will be able to handle the new traffic that the development generates, as well as existing traffic. This analysis can indicate if new roadway improvements or traffic controls are needed to accommodate the additional traffic. It can estimate the impact of through traffic upon local residential streets. It can assess fiscal and environmental impacts resulting from a proposed project's traffic and can be the basis for impact fee payments. The analysis is comprised of five steps (Greenberg et al. 1984, 3):

1. land use determination for the proposed project;
2. trip generation based on the character and intensity of proposed land uses;
3. percentage distribution of site-generated trips to major approach roads;
4. trip assignment of vehicle volumes to the roadway network and the development driveways; and
5. capacity analysis of the roadways to handle traffic from the proposed development.

Analysis of impacts of proposed new transportation facilities upon adjacent land uses is usually done with an environmental impact statement. Potential negative impacts on land use would be dividing or disrupting existing neighborhoods by major road corridors, increasing traffic volumes to unsafe levels on existing roadways, raising noise or air pollution to unhealthy levels, and cutting off important natural environmental corridors.

Transportation Management Strategy

Transportation plans delineate proposed improvements in the highway and public transportation systems and in total future transportation networks. They are normally regional in scale and include intergovernmental coordination between local governments and the state department of transportation. The plans indicate priorities and time schedules for improvements over a seven-year period or longer.

Transportation system management seeks to make existing highways and transit systems more efficient compared with building new facilities (Voorhees et al. 1979). It includes attempts to modify travel demand rather than accepting a fixed demand estimate. It provides for consideration of all travel modes and for implementation by both public and private sectors. Examples of strategies include encouragement of carpooling and use of transit to reduce traffic volumes, staggered work hours to spread peak hour demand, and adjustment of signals to make more effective use of existing roadway capacity.

Traffic control planning seeks to reduce impacts on residential streets and neighborhoods (Homburger et al. 1989). It may involve redesigning neighborhood streets and mitigating traffic impacts on collector or arterial streets in residential area to protect them from through and high-speed traffic. A variety of methods can be used, including changes in paving, landscaping, stop signs, speed limits, pedestrian priority, and street narrowing and closing.

Sewerage

The purpose of urban sewerage facilities is to collect wastewater from residential, commercial, and industrial establishments and transport it to a treatment plant, where the harmful constituents are removed before the effluent is discharged into a water course. The wastewater, or sewage, is carried through a branching network of sewer pipes that range in size from small house connections to large trunk and interceptor sewers. Interceptors connect directly to the treatment plant, whereas trunk mains connect to the interceptors (Figure 9-2). Sewer pipe systems are laid out to take advantage of gravity flow as much as possible. Where sewage must be moved against gravity, pumps are used to pressurize the collection systems.

The treatment plant removes solid and organic materials from the wastewater stream. Three levels of treatment can be employed: primary and secondary treat-

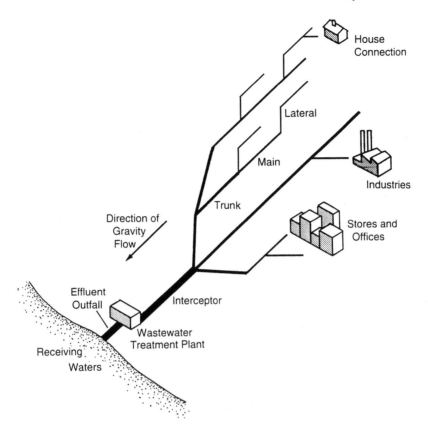

Figure 9-2. Schematic Diagram of Sewerage Systems. Adapted from Tabors, Shapiro, and Rogers 1976, Figure 2-2, 14.

ment remove solid and organic materials, and tertiary treatment removes such additional pollutants as compounds of phosphorus and nitrogen. The treatment process generates two waste products. Effluent is the treated wastewater that flows out of the treatment plant. It may be discharged to a water body, injected into deep aquifers, or reused for irrigation or other nondrinking purposes. Sludge is the solid residue of the treatment process. It may be buried in solid waste landfills or applied to the land as a soil conditioner for agricultural purposes.

Alternatives to central sewage treatment plants are small package treatment plants and individual septic systems. Often used to serve isolated or individual private developments, package plants have capacities of up to one million gallons per day and commonly provide secondary treatment. Package plants operate similarly to central treatment plants. Septic systems use a different type of treatment in which the wastewater is received in a septic tank, where the solids settle out and are decomposed by bacteria. The remaining liquids are discharged through underground drainage pipes, where they percolate into the soil and are purified further. Septic tanks typically serve single houses, although group systems are possible. They require cleaning every three to five years to remove accumulated solids. To operate effectively, septic systems must be placed in well-drained soils that support percolation. Both package plants and septic systems pose potential operations and maintenance problems and are not ideal long-range approaches where urban development is anticipated.

An important side effect of extending sewers to an area is to make possible its development at urban densities. Because individual septic systems can only be used in suitable soils and at low densities, they typically serve scattered rural or low-density suburban areas. Central sewerage facilities allow higher-density development, regardless of soil limitations. Thus, provision of sewerage can be a positive growth guidance tool. However, sewer extensions must be carefully integrated with the land use plan. As Tabors et al. note: "Sewerage facilities provide a *raison d'être* of their own; once in place, they set in motion a pathway of development difficult to divert and virtually impossible to guide" (1976, 8).

Sewerage Inventory

Inventory of the sewerage facilities of an area should include the location and capacity of central (sometimes called regional) wastewater treatment plants and the components of their collection systems. Components include pump stations and pressurized force mains, which move sewage against the force of gravity across ridgelines and over minimal slopes. The inventory should also record the current demand on the treatment plant as a measure of the percentage of plant capacity remaining. Data should be available from the treatment facility operators on flow (daily average, maximum, and minimum), biochemical oxygen demand (BOD), and other operational factors.

Because sewage treatment plants can not be expanded in small, inexpensive increments, it is important to anticipate expansion needs well in advance. When average daily flow approaches a specified threshold below the design capacity, then expansion plans should be carried out.

Levels of service standards for sewerage systems are usually expressed as the average sewage generation per person or establishment per day in gallons. They are derived from existing rates. For example, the sewerage level of service might be 115 gallons per capita per day.

An urban area might contain several sewerage service areas, depending upon the layout of the system. The inventory should include maps of these service areas. Maps should also be prepared showing the service areas of package treatment plants and areas served by septic tanks. This may require surveys of various sewerage service providers, governmental and nongovernmental, as well as local sanitarian and septic tank pumping firms.

Sewerage Impact Analysis

As with all infrastructure, sewerage systems both experience and cause impacts. The basic analysis of the impacts of growth upon sewerage systems is fairly straightforward. It takes into account both the amount and the location of projected demand. The cumulative amount of new demand is measured against the treatment plant capacity and collection system capacity and condition. The location of new demand influences additions to the service area through extensions of trunk lines. A more complex analysis might be required to assess the impacts of changing treatment needs, either due to new types of pollutants in the sewage stream or to new state or federal requirements for pollutant removal.

The analysis of the impacts of extensions of sewerage systems upon land use also is straightforward. The general assumption is that once an area is provided with trunk sewers, then all property within the area can be given sewer service. The impact then is the potential for development at urban densities. Coupled with this is the potential impact upon environmentally sensitive areas, such as water supply watersheds, which may have been protected from urban development in the past due to the lack of sewerage service.

Sewerage Management Strategies

Major management issues include whether mandatory hook-up to sewer lines as they are extended should be required, whether sewer extensions will be withheld to prevent premature urbanization or development of environmentally critical areas, and how the allocation of the costs of sewerage facilities will be divided among the public and private sectors. Other management issues include where sludge disposal will be permitted (land applications, landfills, or ocean disposal), whether advanced wastewater treatment will be required (e.g., to remove phosphorus or nitrogen), and whether multijurisdictional regional treatment facilities should be planned (rather than a proliferation of local individual facilities).

Water Supply

The purpose of a water supply system is to provide water for urban, agricultural, and industrial uses. This includes both potable water suitable for drinking and nonpotable water suitable for agricultural irrigation, industrial processes, golf course irrigation, and residential lawn watering. The majority of urban water systems provide only potable water, but dual systems are being developed in many water-short areas. These dual systems have two pipes, one for potable water and one for "gray" water that is not intended for drinking.

A potable water supply system consists of a supply source, a treatment plant, and a storage and distribution system. The supply source may be either surface water, such as a lake or river, or groundwater from an underground aquifer. The treatment plant removes impurities from the raw water and improves its quality. Users receive treated water through a network of storage facilities and pipes. Larger distribution mains carry water to demand areas and connect with smaller lines arranged in loops that allow circulation to areas that have the highest demand.

Water within the distribution system is under pressure to ensure adequate flow. Pressure is provided by storage tanks, located at elevations higher than the users, into which water is pumped. Demand varies during the day, with peaks in the morning and evening or when the system is used for firefighting.

Water Supply Inventory

[handwritten margin note: Safe yield - how much pressure can system take, & how much it can keep up with]

Inventory of water supply sources should record the storage volume of the supply reservoir and its safe yield (in million gallons per day), as well as the capacity of the storage facilities. Data should be collected on the location of water mains, and the system and its service area should be mapped. Where water is withdrawn through wells, the cones of influence of the wells should be mapped as an indicator of areas to be protected from harmful uses.

Level of service standards for water supply are based on historical average day demands, expressed in gallons per capita per day, such as 135 GPCD. Usually this average figure includes both residential and nonresidential consumption.

Water Supply Impact Assessment

Impacts on water supplies are caused by increases in consumptive demand for water, by pollution of water supply sources, and by droughts or other natural occurrences that reduce the availability of raw water. Demand increases are projected in the advance planning process, discussed in a later chapter. Pollution is assessed through water quality monitoring. Droughts and other natural occurrences are less subject to anticipation, so safety factors are included in system design to account for them.

Impacts caused by water supply development are similar to those caused by sewerage extensions in that they permit more concentrated urban development than do individual wells and septic tanks. Considerations in using groundwater supply sources also include drawing down the water table through withdrawals that exceed the capacity of the groundwater recharge. Lowered water tables can damage adjacent wetlands and cause land subsidence. *[handwritten: land sinks]*

Water Supply Management

One of the major management strategies is water conservation. This may be carried out through such demand limitations as restricted water use hours; through behavior changes, such as limiting water for bathing; and through system improvements, such as repairs to prevent leakage.

A second major management strategy focuses on water quality improvements. This includes preventing pollution from stormwater runoff, sanitary landfills, petroleum storage tanks, saltwater intrusion, and other sources.

Stormwater

The purpose of a stormwater system is to prevent environmental damage from flooding, stream erosion, and water pollution. It seeks to control storm runoff by means of land use controls, detention/retention of runoff, erosion control, and drainage (Whipple et al. 1983).[2]

Stormwater management is necessary in urban and urbanizing areas, where vegetation, porous soils, and other natural environmental features that reduce runoff are removed or covered over. Development can increase peak discharges two to five times, double runoff volumes, half runoff time to reach streams, increase frequency and severity of flooding, undercut banks, and widen stream channels. Stormwater management can be applied on a regional basis as well as individual sites. Its analytical methods rely upon the application of hydrological principles to calculate anticipated storm runoff. The frequency of rainfall is used with data on soil, land use, and ground cover to predict the movement of surface and underground water (Whipple et al. 1983).

Stormwater Inventory

The stormwater inventory compiles information about baseline conditions and problems. It is concerned with the pollution and flooding expected from runoff due to urbanization.

Pollution carried by stormwater runoff is called "nonpoint source pollution" to distinguish it from "point source" pollution from sewage treatment plants or factories. During the late 1970s, a series of best-management practices (BMPs) was developed for removing urban pollutants and protecting downstream aquatic life. These involved extra detention, retention, or infiltration of urban stormwater to enhance pollutant removal and provide additional stormwater management (Schuller 1987). They included extended detention ponds, wet ponds, infiltration trenches and basins, porous pavement, water quality inlets, and vegetative systems such as grassed swales, filter strips, marsh creation, urban forestry, and basin landscaping.

The many types of pollutants that stormwater carries include (Schuller 1987, 1.5–1.9):

—sediments, which cause increased turbidity;
—nutrients, for example, phosphorus and nitrogen, which cause eutrophication;
—bacteria, which cause public health hazards;
—dissolved oxygen depletion, which causes loss of aquatic life;
—oil and grease, which are toxic to aquatic life;
—trace metals, which are toxic to aquatic life and can contaminate drinking water;
—toxic chemicals, which present a public health hazard;

—chlorides or salts, which are toxic to many freshwater aquatic organisms at high levels; and

—thermal impacts, which can harm species adapted to cold waters.

The planning unit is the watershed, drainage basin, or catchment basin. The unit used depends upon the purpose of the analysis. Watersheds are used for analysis of larger systems, such as water supply reservoirs. Drainage and catchment basins are used for analysis of stormwater from development projects.

Level of service for stormwater management can be derived with respect to the discharge that a particular storm event generates. For example, the adopted level of service in Manatee County, Florida, is to require the rate of off-site stormwater discharge from new development to be equal to or less than the rate of discharge before development, based on a twenty-five-year-frequency, twenty-four-hour-duration storm event (Manatee County 1989, 11–19).

The stormwater management inventory collects data on the conditions that affect runoff, on the degree of flooding, on the types and levels of pollutants, and on the natural systems by planning units. Conditions that affect runoff include soils, slopes, ground cover, and rainfall records. Flood hazard data are derived from the flood history of the area, including the characteristics of the average floods and the most severe floods of record. Types and levels of pollutants are derived from water quality sampling and from the scientific literature.

Stormwater Analysis

Most methods of stormwater analysis are based on an equation called the "rational method" in which the calculation of peak runoff volume depends on the rainfall intensity, a runoff coefficient (porosity of the surface), and size of the watershed. Schuller (1987, 1.10) describes a simple method for estimating pollutant export from development sites smaller than one square mile in area. Whipple et al. (1983) describe a number of more complex models, including Storage, Treatment, Overflow, Runoff Model (STORM) sponsored by the Army Corps of Engineers and Storm Water Management Model (SWMM) sponsored by the EPA.

Stormwater Management Strategies

The basic regulatory standard for stormwater management is that the postdevelopment runoff rate from a site should not exceed the predevelopment runoff rate. Meeting this standard typically entails retaining runoff on site through BMPs, such as detention basins that limit outflow to a certain rate.

The three major alternative management strategies are: (1) systems of large-scale, regional detention basins; (2) small-scale, individual on-site detention basins; and (3) low-density land uses that limit runoff by holding down the amount of impervious surface on the land. Of the engineered strategies, the regional systems are the most efficient and reliable but the most expensive for the public to build and maintain. On-site systems pass construction and maintenance costs to the private sector but are not as efficient and reliable due to the decentralized design and upkeep responsibility. Once development has occurred under one of the engineered alternatives, it can not be reversed. The low-density land use alternative is the most conservative approach because it has low public costs, is reliable, and can be supplemented by or converted to engineered systems if necessary. The disadvantage of the low-density land use strategy is that it typically involves downzoning of land in the watershed, which can generate political conflict and legal challenges.[3]

Schools

Primary and secondary schools supply public education services to the community. Their construction is the responsibility of the local school system, which is usually separate from but related to the local government. Nevertheless, "the proper function and the best distribution of education services is possible only when planning for them is part of a larger process of community planning for growth and change" (Parsons and Davis 1979, 300).

The location of schools and the quality of their programs are major influences upon urban land use patterns, and accessibility to schools, adequacy of sites, and joint use as recreation sites or community meeting places are important considerations in land use planning. Since school integration has taken place, the traditional idea of a neighborhood school has been replaced by schools whose service areas or districts are more likely to be communitywide in scope. Still, schools are perceived as focal points for their neighborhoods and often serve dual functions as neighborhood playgrounds and meeting areas.

School Inventory

School sites are classified as elementary school, middle (or junior high) school, or high school. Community colleges are a possible fourth category. A school inventory should include a map of the school locations, a table of their capacities, and a tabulation of their attendance. It may also include the age and condition of the school facilities and the size and characteristics of their sites.

School Analysis

The basic analysis procedure is to compare school capacities with existing and projected attendance. Thus the impact of new development can be assessed against the ability of the school system to accommodate new pupils. Because schools also may be attractive to new development, a second type of impact analysis would look at the drawing power of schools for future residential areas. Location and site size standards for schools are discussed in chapter 15 (see also Engelhardt 1970, ch. 13).

School Management

Growing communities need locations for new schools. Declining communities may need to consolidate schools or reuse surplus school buildings. Existing schools may be expanded through additions or use of temporary classrooms. System demand and supply can be matched through shifting pupils from one school to another that has unused capacity. Demographic information and projections are critical to management decisions. Where school finance is an issue, developers may be required to provide school sites or funding as part of their development permit conditions.

Recreation

Planners have a primary role in the location, preservation, and design of open space and the development of recreational facilities, if not the delivery of social programs to serve the leisure needs of the public (Gold 1979, 273). The purpose of including consideration of recreation sites and facilities in land use planning is to provide for leisure activities through access to open space, natural areas, sports grounds, play areas, recreation centers, outdoor education, and the arts.

Recreation Inventory

The basic recreation inventory would include maps and tables describing the location, size, type, facilities, and characteristics of all recreation and open space sites and facilities. Facilities can be classified by function or dominant use, ownership, degree of intensity of use or development, or planning unit orientation. Gold (1979, 295) recommends using the planning unit orientation because it best relates to use patterns, public recreation systems, and private recreation activities. His categories include:

1. home-oriented spaces, associated with private living areas;
2. neighborhood spaces, associated with an elementary school, pedestrian-oriented, and serving a population of about five thousand;
3. community spaces, associated with a junior high or high school and a shopping or community center, serving three to six neighborhoods, pedestrian- or transit-oriented, and serving a population of about twenty thousand;
4. citywide spaces that serve the entire community, are auto- or transit-oriented and serve a population of a hundred thousand or more; and
5. regional spaces, resource-oriented areas that serve metropolitan needs with extensive activity settings and are accessible by private or public transportation.

(See chapter 15 for a discussion of standards for these categories of recreation facilities.)

Within this classification system, further breakdowns could be based on the type of recreation offered (active or passive) and the type of recreation site (natural resource-based or activity-based). It is also possible to distinguish between recreation sites and facilities and open space suitable for passive recreation and conservation uses. Open space can be classified as:

1. pastoral land preserved for management, protection, and prudent use of existing natural resources, such as public parks and forests;
2. utilitarian land reserved from intense development due to public safety constraints, such as flooding or airport flight paths;
3. corridor land preserved for maintenance of linear open space, such as stream valleys, ecological corridors, or scenic rights-of-way; and
4. multiuse open space land that serves more than one function, such as pedestrian greenways within utility easements or hunting areas within forests.

(See chapter 12 for another open space use classification system.)

Recreation Analysis

Analysis of recreation sites and facilities can be done in terms of the adequacy of the supply to meet existing and projected demand. It can also look at qualitative aspects of the recreation system, such as the nature of the experience of visiting a park and how the volume of other users affects that experience. This carrying capacity analysis will provide information on the satisfaction of recreation users with the degree of use or crowding, the feeling of security or threat, and the level of enjoyment or dissatisfaction. Surveys are useful to measure user preference and satisfaction for recreation activities and areas, participation, and demand. Information from surveys (such as attendance) can be combined with physical measures (such as the number of recreation sites per thousand population) to generate measures of effectiveness and levels of service. Gold (1979) recommends developing standards and levels of service based on the actual usage patterns of a community rather than on abstract national standards.

Recreation Management

Because leisure time and activities are not static, the management of recreation sites and facilities must respond to changing demands by adjusting programs or rules for using facilities rather than continually adding new recreation facilities and areas. Adjustments in hours of operation and staffing can compensate to some degree for demand increases. Seeking additional funding through impact fees or additional sites through development exactions can also expand the supply of facilities (Kaiser and Burby 1988).

NOTES

1. In some planning contexts, although not in this text, community facilities appropriately include private and quasi-private institutions, such as private recreation and social clubs, churches and synagogues, civic association facilities, and private schools.

2. A few older urban areas have segments of their sewerage system that combine stormwater with wastewater and treat it. In this text, however, we address sewerage and stormwater as separate systems, which is much more common.

3. An example of the application of the low-density land use strategy is the Occoquan Basin in Fairfax County, Virginia. This downzoning resulted in a number of lawsuits but was ultimately upheld by the Virginia supreme court (Tremaine 1987).

REFERENCES

American Society of Civil Engineers. 1986. *Urban planning guide.* New York: ASCE.

Engelhardt, Nickolaus L. 1970. *Complete guide for planning new schools.* West Nyack: Parker.

Fernandez, John M. 1994. Boulder brings back the neighborhood street. *Planning* 60 (6): 21–26.

Gold, Seymour M. 1979. Recreation space, services, and facilities. Ch. 10 in *The practice of local government planning,* ed. Frank So, Israel Stollman, Frank Beal, and David Arnold. Washington, D.C.: International City Management Association.

Greenberg, Froda, and Jim Hecimocvich. 1984. *Traffic impact analysis.* APA PAS Report 387. Chicago: American Planning Association.

Homburger, Wolfgang, Elizabeth Deakin, Peter Bosselmann, Daniel Smith, and Bert Beukers. 1989. *Residential street design and traffic control.* Englewood Cliffs: Prentice-Hall.

Institute of Transportation Engineers. 1987. *Trip generation.* 4th ed. Washington, D.C.: The author.

Kaiser, Edward J., and Raymond J. Burby. 1988. Exactions in managing growth: The land-use planning perspective. In *Private supply of public services: Evaluation of real estate exactions, linkage, and alternative land policies,* ed. R. Alterman. New York: New York University Press.

Manatee County. 1989. *The Manatee County comprehensive plan.* Bradenton, Fla.

Parsons, Kermit C., and Georgia K. Davis. 1979. Education services. Ch. 11 in *The practice of local government planning,* ed. Frank So, Israel Stollman, Frank Beal, and David Arnold. Washington, D.C.: International City Management Association.

Rosenbloom, Sandra. 1988. Transportation planning. Ch. 6 in *The practice of local government planning,* ed. Frank So and Judith Getzels. 2d ed. Washington, D.C.: International City Management Association.

Schuller, Thomas R. 1987. *Controlling urban runoff: A practical manual for planning and designing urban BMPs.* Washington, D.C.: Metropolitan Washington Council of Governments.

Stover, Vergil G., and Frank J. Koepke. 1988. *Transportation and land development.* Englewood Cliffs: Prentice-Hall.

Tabors, Richard D. 1979. Utility services. Ch. 7 in *The practice of local government planning,* ed. Frank So, Israel Stollman, Frank Beal, and David Arnold. Washington, D.C.: International City Management Association.

Tabors, Richard D., Michael H. Shapiro, and Peter P. Rogers. 1976. *Land use and the pipe: Planning for sewerage.* Lexington, Mass.: D. C. Heath.

Transportation Research Board. 1985. *Highway capacity manual.* Special Report 209. Washington, D.C.

Tremaine, J. Richard. 1987. Defending a major downzoning case: Aldre Properties, Inc. v. Board of Supervisors of Fairfax County, Virginia. *Proceedings* of Southwestern Legal Foundation. 17th Annual Institute on Planning, Zoning, and Eminent Domain. New York: Matthew Bender.

Voorhees, Alan M., Walter G. Hansen, and A. Keith Gilbert. 1979. Urban transportation. Ch. 8 in *The practice of local government planning,* ed. Frank So, Israel Stollman, Frank Beal, and David Arnold. Washington, D.C.: International City Management Association.

Whipple, William, Neil S. Grigg, Thomas Grizzard, Clifford W. Randall, Robert R. Shubinski, and L. Scott Tucker. 1983. *Stormwater management in urbanizing areas.* Englewood Cliffs: Prentice-Hall.

PART 3

Advance Planning

Determining land use can be considered the initial programmatic
decision in shaping the future of a human settlement.
—Lozano 1990, 131

This part of the book describes how to do advance planning, the second and perhaps the most basic of the four functions of land use planning enumerated in chapter 3: intelligence, advance planning, problem solving, and development management.

Purposes of Plans

Advance plans serve three purposes. One is to provide a process to make policy, that is, a process by which people of a community can take part, with elected officials and appointed boards, in generating and debating policy ideas. A second purpose is then to communicate that policy and intended program of action to property owners, developers, citizens, elected officials, appointed officials, and other affected parties. The plan should educate, inspire, and convince those parties. A third purpose is to help implement policy. Advance plans do that by becoming guides to elected and appointed public officials as they deliberate development decisions. Regulations may even incorporate plans as formal criteria for reaching decisions in issuance of permits. Plans also document the legal, political, and logical rationale behind the development management measures that implement policy.

Major Stages and Products in Advance Planning

The process of formulating and evaluating plans is organized into stages, each of which produces a particular type of plan or component of a plan. The sequence of stages and the plan products produced at each stage shows a progression from ends to means and from general policy to programs of specific measures. The stages, and chapters in which each stage is discussed are indicated below.

Stages in the Plan-making Process	Product Emerging from Each Stage

Stage 1: Direction-Setting (chapter 10)
Describing existing and emerging conditions, and
  causes
Setting goals

Formulating general policy: principles of land use
   design and action   Policy framework plan

(Chapter 11 provides overview of next two stages)

Stage 2: Land Classification Planning (chapter 12)
Above stage, plus:
Analyzing land demand and supply
Designating areas for natural processes
Designating areas for urban use
Designating areas for agricultural production   Land classification plan

Stage 3: Urban Land Use Design (chapters 13-15)
Above stages, plus:
Analyzing land demand and supply in more detail
Designating locations for employment and com-
   mercial centers
Arranging residential communities (housing and
   neighborhood facilities)
Designating locations for infrastructure and com-
   munity facilities   Urban land use design

Stage 4: Development Management Planning (chapter 16)
Above stages, plus:
Analyzing implementation factors
Setting procedural goals
Specifying components of management program
Specifying standards and procedures for those
   components   Development manage-
                                                        ment plan

---

All plans should have three components: facts, goals, and recommendations. Ideally, the evaluation of several alternative solution options should also be a part of the process, although it is often omitted from the final plan.

   Stage 1 includes three tasks: describing existing and emerging conditions and their implications; setting goals; and formulating land use design and development management principles, which we call land use policy. Direction-setting produces a policy framework that serves both as a community's interim plan and as a guide to further plan-making.

   Chapter 11 provides a preview of analysis and design steps common to both of the next two stages—land classification and urban land use design. We avoid repetition by describing these steps once instead of twice—once for land classification and again for land use design.

Stage 2 extends the policy framework to make the intended location and timing of urban development more explicit and to specify which land areas are so critical to protecting natural processes, agricultural production, and forestry that they need to be set aside and protected from development impacts. Compared to the policy framework stage, land classification planning adds a systematic analysis of demand for land by urbanization, conservation, and agricultural and forest uses and a spatial analysis of the supply of land, natural resources, and infrastructure to accommodate those uses. The plan includes a land classification map showing lands that should be converted to urban uses over the planning period (usually ten to twenty years), lands that should be conserved for natural processes, and lands that should be devoted to rural uses—primarily agriculture and forestry. Finally, the land classification plan states implementation policies for each land classification category, designed to bring about the spatial pattern of urbanization, rural production, and natural process conservation prescribed on the land classification map.

Stage 3 builds on the policy framework and land classification plan to specify the pattern of urban uses within the areas prescribed for urbanization in the land classification plan. The focus is on an optimal spatial organization of housing, retail shops, offices, industries, open space, parks, schools, transportation, and the like. The resulting plan is a map of the prescribed future land use pattern. Chapter 13 focuses on employment and commercial centers; chapter 14 on housing and neighborhood support facilities; and chapter 15 on community facilities and infrastructure. The land use design should be a holistic combination of all those land uses but dividing the whole into three separate major sectors of land use makes the book easier for practitioners to use as a reference and for students to follow as a textbook.

Stage 4 shifts emphasis to a shorter-range program of development regulations, capital improvements, and other means for local government to influence land use change to achieve the long-range land use design. Although the land classification plan and urban land use design plan include action-oriented policies, they are stated in general terms. The development management plan proposes more specific strategies and actions to be implemented over a shorter-range future. The development management plan often devotes closer attention to the timing of urbanization, particularly to balancing the public development of infrastructure with private development. There is also more attention to the quality and cost of development, at the project scale, and to desirable characteristics (such as procedural fairness) of government programs. The product of this stage is a package of capital improvements and development controls to be implemented over a period of five to ten years. The plan includes fairly specific standards and the procedures.

Land use plans are never permanent and are not the ultimate purpose of planning. They must be updated periodically to reflect changes in conditions and community values; they must continually be related to other community planning and action; and they must be creatively implemented. Updating should occur on a regular basis, at least every five years; some communities update annually in the form of a "plan report." Coordination with other plans and activities of local government continues during the updating and the implementation. The connections to transportation, water resource, and community facility planning and to economic and community development are especially important. Although these connections must be accounted for during the initial design of the plan, adjustments are necessary as these other plans, policies, and decisions become clearer.

Two components or orientations coexist in all four stages. The first is a vision of the future—what the community should become. The second is the specification of means to attain that vision. Both are important to good planning. Creating a vision of the future is stressed more in the initial steps, and creating a course of action to guide development and change is stressed more in later stages. In general, the stages and their product plans proceed from being ends-oriented to means-oriented, from longer-range to shorter-range planning and from the general to the specific.

Advance Planning as a Community Activity Involving Planners, Publics, and Elected Officials

The methods and techniques of advance planning are not limited to what planners do on note pads, drawing boards, and computers within agency offices. Instead, the planning process requires a wider participation on the part of other government employees, interested publics, elected officials, and appointees on advisory boards, all of whom contribute their own analyses, creativity, judgment, expertise, and communication skills. Participation is essential for achieving the community discourse discussed in chapter 2.

This text emphasizes the more technical aspects of methods and procedures that the professional planner would undertake as part of his or her role within the broader participatory planning process. Interest groups, individual citizens, and elected officials also participate in the technical procedures in many ways, and technical studies must fit into community discourse. Evaluation and choice, in particular, are part of that broader community planning discourse. The planner provides technical assessments of alternative statements of problems, alternative goals, alternative solutions, and alternative arguments. But in reaching decisions and actions, other participants in the discourse add assessments, argue them, and settle them.

Making a Work Plan

Each of the stages of advance planning should be preceded by a "plan for planning," something not discussed in these chapters. This work plan outlines how the planning team and the community will go about producing the policy framework, land classification, land use design, or development management plan. A work plan contains three elements.

1. A description of the scope, focus, and preliminary concept of the products envisioned as the major "deliverables" and the major tasks necessary to achieve them, including deadline dates.
2. A diagram or other device that presents the sequence of work elements to produce the products. It might consist of a flow diagram or bar chart on a time line representing the sequence of tasks, connections among them (which tasks are prerequisite to others, for example), and deadlines.
3. An element-by-element elaboration of the tasks, assignment of resources to them, and assignment of responsibility for them. These are not very detailed initially, but are expanded later to serve as a management tool as the time for each work element draws near.

Plan-Making as an Integrated Process of Analysis, Synthesis, and Implementation

By separating the plan-making process into chapters, it may appear that the stages and various tasks are separate and discrete. That is not the case. The tasks are interdependent, and the process employs considerable feedback. For example, the policy framework might well be modified and refined to reflect insights from the land use design stage and be more consistent with it.

Furthermore, we are describing a process that combines analysis with design. Although analysis is important to the process and actually absorbs the bulk of explanation in the following chapters, the planner cannot analyze his or her way to a solution. That takes design: the leap from analysis into the realm of invention and synthesis to produce solution ideas.

We take several approaches to communicating synthesis aspects of the land use planning process. First, chapter 3 on the land use planning program and this introduction to Part 3 establish an overall framework for the advance planning process (in fact, the reader may wish to review the "Advance Planning" section of chapter 3 before reading the following chapters and return to this introduction from time to time to help keep the larger framework in mind). Second, within the chapters, procedures are presented as parts of a larger process, and each chapter discusses how the parts must eventually be pulled together into a plan. In fact, specific synthesis methods are presented to help accomplish that.

By describing a four-stage approach to advance planning, we do not mean to imply that all four stages are absolutely necessary in every case. The policy framework is often integrated with the land classification plan or land use design. In other cases, a county planner may proceed directly from land classification to development management plan, skipping the land use design stage. A city planner may skip the land classification stage and focus on the land use design. Some communities skip both the land classification and land use design stages, although we do not recommend that approach because it lacks attention to spatial policy.

REFERENCE

Lozano, Eduardo E. 1990. *Community design and the culture of cities.* New York: Cambridge University Press.

10

Direction-Setting

More often than not a community relies on its planner to search for and articulate its aspirations. . . . Without clear goals, problem identification is no more than a statement of "existing conditions" without any sense of why these conditions constitute a problem.

—Leung 1989, 27

The purpose of direction-setting is to provide a clear, relevant basis for plan-making and later for evaluation and decision-making (Smith and Hester 1982; Vogel and Swanson 1988). It should enable the community to take control of its agenda and consciously orient it to long-range public interests rather than shorter-range issues and private ones. It should require officials, planners, and citizens to break out of their normal routine and away from incremental decision-making.

More specifically, we see direction-setting as helping planners, elected officials, appointed officials, and the community do three things: (1) understand current and emerging conditions; (2) determine goals to be pursued and issues to be addressed; and (3) formulate general principles to guide both further planning and day-to-day development management decisions. Three components of the policy framework plan emerge from direction-setting and parallel those three purposes.

1. A *fact component* describes existing and projected conditions indicating the relative seriousness of problems or degree of goal attainment and factors causing or otherwise contributing to problems, goal attainment, and land development.
2. A *values component* states goals, concerns, or issues, and priorities among them.
3. A *policies component* describes principles to guide planning, problem solving, and development management and setting priorities among issues and policies.

The three products of direction-setting may be assembled into a single policy framework and adopted formally. Alternatively, they may be separate reports, separately considered by elected officials and planning agencies. If there is a formal policy framework plan, later plans may simply summarize and refer to it. However, if the analysis of conditions, goals, and policies are produced and adopted in pieces, the planner should anticipate incorporating them into the land classification and/or land use design plan as described in following chapters. In either case they should be adopted in order to have legal and political standing as guides to development permit decisions, capital investments, and other local government decisions, as well as to problem solving and further plan-making.

Figure 10-1 diagrams the relationship among the three components of the policy framework plan and between that framework and later plans, problem solving, and land use management activities. Although we discuss fact-finding before goal-setting, the planner usually carries out these tasks somewhat concurrently. The investigation of conditions and causes reveals and elaborates on problems and otherwise feeds information to goal-setting, but at the same time the determination of community concerns, values, and priorities helps determine which facts and problems are relevant.

Initiating the advance planning process with direction-setting implies a ratio-

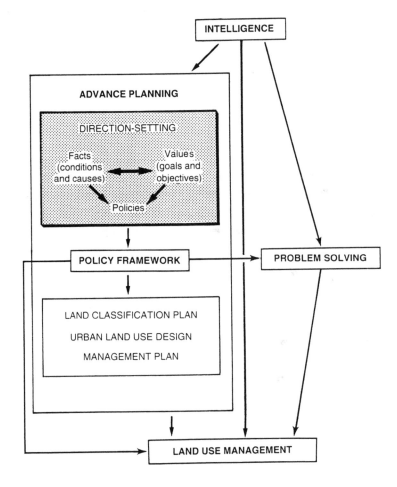

Figure 10-1. The Role of Direction-Setting in Advance Planning. The three components of direction-setting and its policy framework output are shown, along with their relationships to problem solving, land use management, and further stages of advance planning.

nal planning philosophy. That is, it assumes that ends should determine means and that planning is best initiated by defining the problem and setting a target. Feasibility is introduced later and is secondary to correctly specifying the problem and setting goals.

Participation is especially relevant to the direction-setting stage in advance planning. The validity, usefulness, and effectiveness of the output depends on the process being open to all individuals and groups that can affect or are affected by the land use management system and the future land use pattern. Thus, although the planner coordinates the process, it involves elected and appointed officials of the government as well neighborhood groups, civic groups, special interest groups, and general citizens. Those who have something at stake must be able to participate with a full awareness of their interests and have sufficient power to assure representativeness and equity in outcomes. For those reasons, we include techniques for facilitating participation in our approach.

In conjunction with participation, the process relies on several other resources: adequate and accessible information; a capability to query that database; and the "ordinary" knowledge brought to the process by elected officials, appointed officials, and other participants. Those elements are necessary for practical and effective discourse about problems, needs, aspirations, priorities, and alternative policies.

The Fact Component: Analysis of Relevant Conditions

The fact component of a plan can also be referred to as situational or environment assessment, fact-finding or findings of fact, problem analysis, scanning, analysis of relevant conditions, or information base. Whatever the terminology, facts have three ways to be relevant. First, some facts are relevant to goals. That is, they pertain to observations, assumptions, inferences, and deductions about problems, needs, and goal conditions. For example, facts may describe the number of dwellings in a floodplain. Second, other facts are relevant because they pertain to causal factors that bear on those problems, needs, and goal conditions. For example, the amount of land that has available public sewerage and is outside the floodplain bears upon how much development pressure exists in the floodplain. A third type of fact is relevant to the feasibility or effectiveness of potential solutions. Such facts may be about legal, political, and financial limits of the local government, or relations with neighboring governments, for example. All three types of facts should be in the analysis of existing and emerging conditions.

Facts differ along other dimensions, too. Some facts are observable and refer to past or present conditions. Other facts, however, are projected future conditions. Some are internal to the community, and some (such as the regional economy) are external but affect the community's present and future nevertheless. Some are directly controllable; they are sometimes referred to as policy facts or as de facto development policy. Others are not controllable but affect future conditions nevertheless and need to be considered in designing policy. Some facts derive from scientific knowledge, contributed mostly by planners and other professionals. Other equally relevant facts derive from ordinary knowledge, as opposed to scientific knowledge, and derive from personal experience, observation, and discussions with others.

In addition to information about conditions related to goals, causal factors, and feasibility, the fact component includes an explicit or implicit model of relationships between conditions and their causes or related conditions. The fact component should state whether and how conditions are related to other conditions, either as different facets of the same problem or as cause-effect. Planners' models of this structure of situations are based on scientific method to the extent possible. That is, they are based on formal processes of model specification, calibration, and testing by means of statistical analysis as discussed in chapter 4. But they are also based on theory and on ordinary knowledge.

The fact component of direction-setting contributes to planning in several ways. First, a clear picture of the situation helps determine issues and goals and priorities among them. Second, a sound analysis of conditions and causes contributes to finding good solutions. Third, a sound fact basis will help a plan stand up to legal and political challenges to implementation.

Determining the Scope and Focus of the Problem Analysis

There are two approaches to fact-finding and problem analysis. In the first, the planner explores and interprets conditions and relationships revealed in the information system. He or she is an independent analyst who identifies, clarifies, and quantifies existing and emerging problem conditions about which the community may be unaware or only faintly aware. The planner in this role is a scientific prophet who calls attention to facts about current conditions, trends, and likely future conditions. In strategic planning this track is referred to as scanning the external and internal environment to identify key factors and trends and determine how external forces will likely influence events for the community. The facts serve as inputs to goal-setting by apprising participants of present and emerging conditions and their implications.

In the second approach, the planner uses the participatory goal-setting results (discussed later in the chapter) to focus the analysis of facts. In this approach, the information system is used to clarify and quantify conditions related to those problems, needs, and aspirations identified by goal-setting participants. In other words, the relationship between facts and goals is reversed; goals define the scope and focus of the fact-finding task. The two approaches are not mutually exclusive and can be used in complementary fashion.

The analysis usually covers population and the economy and their implicit future demand for land and environmental resources, current uses of land and trends in land development, trends and conditions in the natural and built environment, capacity and condition of community facilities, regulations and incentives of the current land use management system, land supply for new development and re-development, federal and state policy directives and constraints, local governmental resources, and political factors.

Because advance planning is future-oriented, projected or possible future conditions are an important aspect of the fact component. Future conditions are represented through forecasting and scenario-building. Forecasting applies particularly to factors and conditions that are more or less foreseeable and can be estimated with projection techniques, such as ratios, extrapolation, and simulation (chapters 5 and 6). Scenario-building, on the other hand is a more exploratory representation of alternative futures that could, or in a normative sense perhaps even should, occur (Morrison, Renfro, and Boucher 1983). Scenario construction or writing sometimes uses participatory techniques. The participants might include professionals within the local government, experts in relevant fields from outside government, or elected and appointed officials—people who have special knowledge and perspective. Scenarios explore alternative futures, particularly in the external environment but also in the noncontrollable events within the community—for example, whether the economy will boom, grow slowly, or bust; whether tourism will continue to be the primary sector of the economy; or whether changing technology of on-site wastewater treatment will lessen dependence of development on the existence of public sewer services.

Scenarios can be used in conjunction with projection techniques to bracket the likely range of future conditions, using concepts of low end/high end projection, worst case/best case situations, or high impact/low impact possibilities.

Analyses of past, present, and emerging conditions can be published in separate reports, as separate volumes of a plan, or integrated with the goals and policies in a single report. The plan of Gresham, Oregon, is an example of both formats. First, Gresham published a separate volume called "Findings." It is a thick report, covering a comprehensive list of topics: community overview (history, regional context); the natural environment; physical environment (land supply characteristics, land use, transportation, and community infrastructure); social environment (population, labor, economic characteristics, housing, and social services); and the political environment (local government and intergovernmental organization). Appendixes contain much detail. In addition to that "Findings" report, however, Gresham includes summaries of the most salient "findings" with policies and implementation strategies in a separate summary volume, "Findings, Policies, and Implementation Strategies." For example, Table 10-2 later in this chapter illustrates such a linkage between findings, policies, and strategies.

The Values Component: Setting Goals and Priorities

Goal-setting involves identifying present and future problems, determining aspirations in the form of goals and objectives, and identifying strategic issues and priorities among them. A problem is an unsatisfactory condition, present or projected. A goal is an ideal future condition to which the community aspires. A goal is valued for itself, not as an instrument to achieve something else. It is usually expressed in general terms, using adjectives and nouns; it is usually not quantified. For example, a community might desire an esthetically pleasing downtown, high environmental quality, or equity. An objective is an intermediate step toward attaining a goal and is more tangible and specific. It is measurable and attainable. It is often time-specific, specifying attainment by the year 2000, for example. An objective may be one aspect of a larger goal. For example, water quality meeting EPA standards might be an objective under the goal of environmental quality. It may be one of several steps toward a goal; for example, reducing the number of dwellings in danger from the hundred-year flood to 450 dwellings by the year 2000, and 300 by the year 2005.

An issue is a concern about a condition or event likely to have an important impact on the ability of the community to meet its goals and where there is lack of consensus about what action to take. An issue agenda consists of higher-priority issues, calling for more or less immediate attention in the planning and governance process. For example, obsolete and undercapacity infrastructure, coupled with growth pressure, could be an issue. Thus, an issue has both problem and fact components as well as an implied aspiration component.

Five Types of Goals

Planners deal with five types of goals, which are classified by their source.

1. *Legacy goals* come from previously adopted and currently followed policy of the local government; they are a good starting point for the goal-setting process.
2. *Mandated goals,* "musts," come from state and federal policy and from the judicial system's interpretation of statutory authority and constitutional rights.
3. *Generic goals,* "oughts," come from political philosophy and the planning literature on good urban form, good land use management, and good governmental process.
4. *Needs are goals for accommodating change* and are derived from forecasts of population and economic change that must be accommodated.
5. *The community's concerns and aspirations,* "wants," are derived from a participatory goal-setting process.

The last of those five types is the most closely identified with any particular community. Those goals emerge from the participation of elected officials, appointed officials, interest groups, and citizens in the goal-setting process. They represent what the community uniquely values about itself, what should be conserved, what problems are of greatest concern, and what the ideal community of the future should represent. The other four types of goals should be considered during that participatory process, reviewed and modified, and then integrated with the community's unique goals in a coordinated statement. Figure 10-2 indicates the five sources of community goals and the idea that they must be merged through a participatory process into a coordinated goal statement.

Figure 10-2. Five Sources of Community Goals. The planner has a responsibility to introduce the first four types of goals (legacy goals, mandates, generic goals, and needs) and to organize a process to add a fifth type of goal (community aspirations and concerns) and synthesize goals from all five sources.

Legacy Goals   To derive legacy goals, the planner inventories goals that are explicit in current ordinances and plans and used by the local legislative body, appointed commissions, and operating departments. In addition, the planner may infer goals from patterns of past decisions by the local government. Legacy goals also come from previous stages in the current round of advance planning. For example, goals and action principles developed in the direction-setting process become goal inputs to the land use design, which in turn becomes an input to development management. Using legacy goals as a starting point simply acknowledges that every community has a history of deliberations that reflect its values and provides useful input to current goal-setting deliberations.

Mandated Goals   It is also the planner's responsibility to introduce federal- and state-mandated goals and policies into the community goal-setting process. These goals come from federal and state legislation, rules, and guidelines and from court rulings interpreting constitutional rights and statutory authority. The use of the adjective *mandate* does not mean that the community cannot interpret those goals, determine priorities, and otherwise modify mandates.

Mandated goals are particularly important in a growing number of "growth-directing" states that have state goals and policies to guide local planning and land use management (chapter 1). Examples at this writing include Oregon, Florida, Hawaii, New Jersey, Vermont, Colorado, Maine, Rhode Island, Georgia, and Washington. Additional states, such as North Carolina, California, and New York mandate goals and other requirements for particular substate areas that are of statewide concern, such as coasts, wetlands, or special areas (e.g., Adirondack Park in New York). In other localities, regional plans may be binding. For example, the Twin Cities Metropolitan Council Framework plan in Minnesota imposes a regional water and sewer extension policy on local jurisdictions.

Oregon provides a good illustration of mandated goals. That state establishes nineteen statewide policy areas. Each has a mandatory part, called "goals," which has the force of law, and another, nonmandatory part, called "guidelines." The state requires each city and county to have a comprehensive plan consistent with the statewide planning goals, and local plans are reviewed for such consistency and must be state-approved. Table 10-1 illustrates some of Oregon's goals, including several planning process goals.

New Jersey introduced a "cross acceptance process" through which governments at several different levels compare and coordinate planning policies to attain compatibility among local, county, and state plans. The process is intended to respect local planning prerogatives while simultaneously establishing the need for a regional and statewide approach to meet legislative mandates and state goals. Georgia requires coordination and approval at the regional planning agency level rather than by a state agency.

State-mandated goals often emphasize issues where the action of one jurisdiction affects neighboring jurisdictions, the interests of a larger region, or the state as a whole. For example, Florida imposes state policy on development affecting such "areas of critical state concern" as wetlands and water supply sources (in a state with scarce water) and on "development of regional interest" such as lower-income housing, airports, prisons, landfills, and other forms of development that meet a regional need but that local governments often try to exclude. Development of regional interest also includes large developments, such as large shopping centers, that may benefit local jurisdictions but have negative impacts beyond the jurisdiction.

Florida establishes both a state plan with goals and policies with which local governments must be consistent and a review process for approving local plans. The state goals and policies address a large number of topics, including land use, conservation, water resources, housing, and public improvements, as well as education, economy, health, and others. The state's land use goal, for example, specifies that "development shall be directed to those areas which have in place, or have agreements to provide, the land and water resources, fiscal abilities, and service capacity to accommodate growth in an environmentally acceptable manner." State policies under that goal include establishing a system of incentives and disincentives to encourage a separation of urban and rural land uses and devel-

Table 10-1. Selected Statewide Goals Mandated for Local Planning in Oregon

I. Planning Process Goals
1. A program that insures the opportunity for citizens to be involved in all phases of the planning process. Six components of such programs are specified: citizen involvement program, including an advisory committee, two-way communication, opportunities for citizens to influence particular steps in planning process, availability of technical information, mechanism for feedback by policymakers to citizen recommendations, and financial support.

II. Conservation Goals
1. Preserve and maintain agricultural lands. This goal defines agricultural lands, requires all jurisdictions to inventory them, and requires local policies and zoning to preserve and maintain them.
2. Conserve forest lands for forest uses.
3. Conserve open space and protect natural, scenic, and historic resources. This goal names twelve types of resources, establishes a process through which resources must be inventoried and evaluated, requires local government to choose one of three alternatives—preservation, allowing more important uses to destroy the resource, or establishing a balance between those two alternatives—and requires adoption of policies and ordinances to implement that choice.

III. Development Goals
1. Protect life and property from natural disasters and hazards.
2. Satisfy recreation needs and provide for siting of recreation facilities.
3. Diversify and improve the economy of the state.
4. Provide for housing needs of citizens of the state.
5. Develop a timely, orderly, and efficient arrangement of public facilities and services to serve as a framework for urban and rural development.
6. Provide and encourage a safe, convenient and economic transportation system.
7. Conserve energy.
8. Provide for an orderly efficient transition from rural to urban land use. This goal requires cities to estimate future growth and resulting need for land and then plan and zone accordingly. It specifies seven factors that must be considered in drawing up the urban growth boundary: accommodation of population growth; need for housing, employment, and livability; orderly and economic provision for public facilities and services; maximum efficiency of land uses; environmental, energy, economic, and social consequences; protection of the best agricultural lands; and compatibility of proposed urban uses with nearby agricultural activities.

oping a system of intergovernmental negotiation for siting locally unpopular public and private land uses. Local plans must be consistent with both state goals and state policies.

Perhaps more significantly, Florida establishes minimum criteria for determination of compliance. The criteria cover process, format, and content of local plans. Public participation criteria must be met for the planning process. With respect to format, the plan must contain certain elements, meet a particular time horizon, include implementation, and designate standards for public services. With respect to policy content, the future land use element must discourage proliferation of urban sprawl, for example. Florida is unique, thus far, in requiring that local plans include a capital improvements element and service standards for public services. Public facilities necessary to maintain adopted service level standards must be available when development impacts occur (something Florida calls a concurrency requirement). In fact, a community must adopt a land use management system that assures concurrency for roads, sanitary sewer, solid waste, drainage, potable water, parks and recreation, and mass transit (if applicable).

Judicial systems may also mandate goals defining the objectives local governments may pursue, the means they may employ, and allowable procedures for permits and other governmental decisions. Judicial mandates apply more to development control measures and practices than to land use design plans, however.

Generic Planning Goals Planning theory, political philosophy, the literature on good urban form (e.g., Lynch 1981; Jacobs and Appleyard 1987; Frank 1989; Mansfield 1990), and examples of good local plans that are recognized in the profession (e.g., award-winning plans in American Planning Association contests) all constitute a third source for community goals. Again, as is true for legacy goals and mandates from higher levels of government, it is the planner's professional responsibility to introduce and advocate generic goals, for often they reflect the interests (e.g., future generations) that the participatory process does not represent adequately.

Generic planning goals address matters of public interest and include economic efficiency, protection of constitutional rights, equity, choice, environmental quality, energy efficiency, quality of life, health and safety, effectiveness, and feasibility. They also include a valid participatory discourse for advance planning, implementation, and administration of the land use management system.

Economic efficiency means achieving maximum net economic benefit from a land use pattern, development processes, and development management measures. That is accomplished either by getting the most benefit for a given cost, finding the lowest-cost solution for a particular benefit, or getting the highest ratio of benefits to costs. With respect to the land use pattern, efficiency implies coordination of public and private development so that journeys of home-to-work, home-to-school, home-to-recreation, and home or work-to-shopping are short; industries have good access to the regional transportation network; land uses are located to be most easily served by water and sewer, transportation, and other services; and public and private operations are energy efficient. In other words, we seek a land use arrangement that is economical for the municipality to service and economically efficient for land users. It should be the case that no clearly better arrangements could provide more benefits without increasing costs, and no one could be made better off without making others worse off. With regard to land use control, efficiency implies use of measures that achieve the desired effect in the simplest manner with the least cost to government and the least interference with private choice. Efficiency in development practices means that they cause off-site nonmarket effects to be factored into development decisions. Ultimately, economic efficiency in land use means a development process, including regulations, that allocates resources to generate the highest utility.

Equity addresses the distribution of the costs and benefits of public policies. Equity is concerned with who gains and who loses. One interpretation of equity is captured in the benefit principle—those who benefit should pay the cost of government services and other actions. Another interpretation of equity is that benefits should be distributed according to need, but costs according to the ability to pay. A third is that benefits should go to those who contribute the most effort, talent, or other resources to a project; a matching grant program follows that principle. A fourth principle of equity is equal treatment, that is, benefits and costs should be distributed equally, regardless of ability to pay, need, or contribution. Such equality of treatment is also the concept behind "social equity," that is, equal access by all to judicial justice, education, safety, housing, and employment. These often conflicting equity concepts apply to land use management measures as well as land use designs.

Procedural fairness is a fifth principle of equity, and one particularly relevant to land use management and implementation strategies. That principle implies notification of all affected parties about impending plans and development decisions, ample and equal opportunity to argue one's case, and equal protection of the law in the sense of equal treatment of all persons equally situated.

The goal of *protecting constitutional rights* implies that the land use management measures pursue legitimate objectives, use means that have reasonable and efficient relation to those objectives and are not unduly repressive, refrain from taking property without due compensation, respect interests of other governments and residents in the region, apply equally and fairly to all people in similar circumstances, and do not discriminate unfairly against groups defined by race, color, creed, or gender. The protection of such rights is a fundamental public interest in American society and strongly felt by many residents. Yet, unless the planner raises it, this goal is not likely to come up in goal-setting but arise later, when specific measures are debated or later administered, or perhaps challenged in court. Rather than wait for them to arise later or to treat them as legal constraints, it is better to perceive constitutional rights as a goal up front during the direction-setting stage of the planning process.

The goal of *choice* implies providing a wide range of densities, locations, and development types so that residents and other land users can choose places to suit their tastes and pocketbooks. Choice, with respect to land use management, implies giving the regulated person, firm, or institution some flexibility in ways to meet requirements.

Environmental quality refers to the ambient quality of air, water, land and man-made environments (such as historic neighborhoods). It implies protection from harmful agricultural, industrial, and other urban societal processes. With respect to the design of future land use patterns, environmental quality implies protecting natural features, natural processes, and critical areas by allocating compatible uses to such areas. With respect to land use management, environmental quality refers also to performance standards that land users and land developers should meet.

Quality of life is a goal that reflects the noneconomic, less tangible, and less quantifiable well-being of a community—its general welfare. We are especially interested in *community* quality of life—those aspects of well-being, such as neighborhood quality or community character, that public policy affects directly—whereas many important quality of life aspects (e.g., marital harmony or friends) are not. Deteriorating quality of life is often cited as a primary reason for adoption of growth controls (Dowall 1984; Dubbink 1984). Popular books, such as *Places Rated Almanac* (Boyer and Savageau 1985) have also heightened public awareness of community quality of life issues. Quality of life can be measured by surveys asking people about their subjective well-being, particularly with neighborhood and community and public services. In contrast, the "places-rated" approach uses the weighted combination of objective indicators (e.g., Boyer and Savageau 1985; Park 1985) to indicate quality of life. Planners in Jacksonville, Florida, publish an annual "community report card" that lists seventy-four quantitative indicators of progress, a small number of which are chosen for special attention each year (Chambers 1992). Another approach uses the combination of subjective measures, along with a concept of community trends (Do you think that congestion is worse, compared to five years ago, or better?) and objective indicators (measuring congestion by actual observations of traffic and travel times) (Myers 1988).

Health and safety goals refer to health hazards and occasions for injury and to promotion of physical and emotional well-being. Regulations traditionally pursue this goal by setting minimum standards, but advance planning broadens the idea to include promoting what is desirable or even optimum, not just the minimum. Thus, planning involves not only "protection against" hazards to health and safety but also promotion of optimal living and working conditions.

Effectiveness and *feasibility* are goals that apply to development management measures. Effectiveness refers to the capability of a proposal to achieve its goal. The simple test is, Does the proposal do what it is designed to do? Does the land use design, for example, achieve the goals being pursued? Does the management system achieve the desired land use pattern? Does the implementation strategy achieve adoption and proper administration?

Feasibility, although a consideration in land use design, assumes greater salience in development management. Feasibility implies that the community is capable of carrying out a proposed plan, growth-management measure, or implementation action effectively. There are several aspects to feasibility: political feasibility (likely that officials will adopt and effectively enforce the proposal); legal feasibility (likely to withstand legal challenge in court); administrative feasibility (staff is capable of carrying out the proposed procedures); and financial feasibility (within ability of community to finance the proposal). Feasibility is not a rigid limit on what can be proposed, but a frontier to be pushed back to enlarge the realm of the possible.

Goals Representing Needs Implied by Community Change

The planner must forecast demographic and economic changes that determine "needs" for land, housing, water, transportation, schools, recreation facilities, wastewater treatment, solid waste disposal, and other community facilities and services. Translating growth and change into needs involves application of standards, which planners propose initially as options but which are then assessed and eventually chosen in a participatory goal-setting process. Standards are not simply accepted, except for those mandated by higher authority. While the methods of making population and employment projections are covered in chapters 5 and 6, and methods for converting such projections into space requirements and community facility requirements are covered in chapters 12 through 15, the initial estimates of needs and the choice of standards are direction-setting tasks. Those needs can then be balanced against other goals and costs, which may suggest a revision in projected population and employment or an adjustment in service levels and other standards.

Concerns and Aspirations Particular to the Community: A Participatory Goal-Setting Process

This fifth type of goal represents the community's particular aspirations, concerns, and priorities. Thus, this step in goal-setting should come after the other four types of goals have been introduced, and it includes integrating them in a coordinated statement.

The planner has several roles to play in this process. One is to introduce, advocate, and employ the generic planning goals discussed earlier and to advise on needs, mandated goals, and legacy goals. Another is to facilitate and coordinate the participatory process for assessing those goals and raising community-specific concerns and aspirations.

There are three angles from which to begin the participatory goal-setting process. One place to begin is with existing and anticipated problems, that is, undesirable conditions, such as deteriorating neighborhoods, sprawl, housing in floodplains, or poor water quality in a water supply reservoir. The goal is then to alleviate the problem. That approach is particularly suited to already built-up areas such as central cities but applies to some degree in any community. Another place to begin is with aspirations, that is, ideal future conditions. That approach applies to virtually any community—central city, growing suburb, or new community. It asks, essentially, What do we want to become? A third place to begin is with the array of legacy goals, mandates, generic planning goals, and projected needs. All three starting points are valid. And they are not mutually exclusive; all three are often used in conjunction.

The citizen participation movement that took hold in the 1960s often focused on participatory goal-setting. Participatory goal-setting faded in the 1970s with the decline of federal aid and its requirement for citizen participation. As critical planning theory caught hold in the 1980s, participatory goal-setting received renewed emphasis. Florida, for example, has enacted the Visions 2000 Act of 1986 (chapter 86-221), which provides funding to "encourage counties and municipalities to establish committees which will provide a forum to facilitate discussion of and community consensus about a direction for the future of the county or municipality. . . . such committees shall formulate goals and develop comprehensive short-term, intermediate-term, and long-term policies for achieving such goals. . . . it is intended to provide public statements of goals and policies reflecting the desires and will of the people" (cited in Vogel and Swanson 1988, 48–49).

The ideal participatory goal-setting process includes several steps—search, synthesis, and selection (Nutt and Backoff 1987). Search focuses on generating information and ideas. Synthesis focuses on finding patterns and themes and on improving understanding. Selection stresses the winnowing of ideas and the setting of priorities among goals, themes, and issues. It is the planner's task to help incorporate participatory techniques into a goal-setting process that covers all three steps: search, synthesis, and selection. Although some participatory techniques are particularly well suited to one of the steps, others can be used for several or all three steps. Techniques can also be combined to form a hybrid approach that covers all three steps.

Search Several techniques are especially suited to uncovering and elaborating ideas in the search step. They include interacting groups, silent reflective techniques, surveys, focus groups, and dialectic groups (Nutt and Backoff 1987, 52–53). The techniques of interacting groups emphasize face-to-face format and free-flowing, open-ended discussion. In brainstorming, one such technique, the planner keeps challenging the group to generate and modify ideas while postponing valuative judgments and criticisms (which tend to inhibit creative idea generation) (Osborn 1963).

Silent reflection techniques require each participant to identify goals, problems, and issues before group discussion begins. The intent is to avoid domination by more assertive people and to overcome barriers to candor and creativity by less assertive members. In the nominal group technique, for example, the participants first reflect silently; then they take turns revealing ideas (one idea per person per turn) until everybody's have been listed. Then participants discuss the ideas as a group to share judgments, improve understanding, make modifications, and consolidate the list. Finally, they rank the ideas individually and pool those rankings into a group ranking. (Delbacq and Van de Ven 1971) In brainwriting, sheets of paper with nominations for problems, goals, and issues are put in a central location in the room. A participant takes a sheet, adds his or her ideas, puts the sheet back, then takes another sheet returned by another member, and so on. Participants can add more ideas on fresh sheets, continuing until the ideas and comments (and participants) are exhausted (Gueschka, Shaude, and Schlicksupp 1975). As in the nominal group technique, participants take turns describing one idea at a time from lists, the group discusses and elaborates the ideas, and then assigns priorities by vote. In a variation called the nominal-interacting technique (Nutt and Backoff 1987), the nominal group or brainwriting approach is interrupted periodically to allow lobbying, perhaps during a thirty-minute break for refreshments, where participants can share opinions, exchange facts, challenge the views of others, and bargain.

Survey approaches, another search method, gather ideas and opinions by telephone, mail, or with representatives of reference groups without group interaction. They can be used alone to provide a barometer of opinion or as a reference point for an interactive group. In the Delphi technique (Dalkey 1972), the planner uses a series of questionnaires with a selective group of respondents. The first questionnaire solicits ideas and opinions and asks reasons behind them. Subsequent questionnaires collate the ideas and associated rationales, perhaps adding new information, and then feed them back to the group, without identifying authors of ideas and arguments, to set the stage for reconsidered responses. Each panel member reviews the logic behind the arguments of others and modifies his or her own arguments, opinions, and priorities in responding anew to the questionnaire. The process continues through several rounds until sufficient consensus is reached. Voting assigns priorities in the end.

In focus groups, outside experts describe opportunities and alternative aspirations and strategies to small groups of direction-setting participants selected to represent a cross-section of the population or particular sectors of the population. Ideas are presented to provoke discussion of values and choices and to assess the degree of support for the various positions and goals.

Synthesis For the synthesis step, there are yet other approaches, although the methods above do include a degree of synthesis. The planner might turn to the snowball technique, relevance trees, or policy capturing. These techniques are particularly useful for identifying patterns, themes, and generalizations from ideas produced by the search step. The snowball technique (Greenblat and Duke 1981) is a way to find labels that identify themes or generalizations to sum up ideas that come out of the search process in relatively unorganized form. Index cards are prepared, one idea to a card. Members attach the cards to a wall, group similar ideas, and then label the groups. Anyone can change any label or exchange cards among categories, merge categories, or create new groups and labels without discussion. Stable patterns often emerge that capture a synthesis or pattern. In the tree structure technique (Warfield 1976), participants use a paired comparison ranking technique to create a hierarchy of levels, and then subdivisions within the levels. Connections among levels show the relationships among goals, problems, and issues, perhaps identifying whether the relationship is causal or an order of priority/severity. In the paired comparison technique, each participant compares each idea with all other ideas on the list, inferring an overall order. The planner counts how many members judged an item to be more severe or of higher priority. By looking for patterns among the rankings, the planner and group might develop subdivisions within levels. After an initial ranking by participants and summary by the planner, the group can discuss the resulting structure and add more observations. The paired comparison procedure can then be repeated so that the ranking and subdivisions reflect more and more informed discussion.

Selection In the selection step, the planner may employ additional techniques, such as the estimate-discuss-estimate technique or Q-sort. In the estimate-discuss-estimate technique (Nutt and Backoff 1987, 55), participants make a preliminary estimate of priorities and nominate ideas to be dropped. Then reflection, discussion, and perhaps more searching for additional information focus on the tentative choices before a final determination is made. This can be considered a simplification of the Delphi technique.

Q-sort (Kerlinger 1973) is used when the list of items to be organized and selected is very long. Individuals first look for the most important, then the least important, item, switching back and forth until all the items have been categorized. The individual participants' orders of priority are then merged to form a group listing. Priorities can also be determined by rank weighting or other similar approaches.

There are several styles of participatory goal-setting: anticipatory democracy, the American assembly, and strategic planning. Anticipatory democracy emphasizes the value of the *process* over the content of the results. What counts most is not defining specific goals but the creation of a decision process in which all goals, no matter whose, are regularly reevaluated in the light of changing conditions. It is seen as a way to increase consciousness about the future of the community and increase popular participation and feedback.

The American assembly approach, on the other hand (Vogel and Swanson 1988) stresses attainment of consensus on the *content* of problems, goals, and policy as a common vision of the future. It focuses on a restricted agenda, a limited number of participants, and a limited time schedule. The participants isolate themselves for a brief period and produce a final report that represents the general group consensus.

Strategic planning, a third and more recent approach, (Sorkin et al. 1984; Bryson and Roering 1987; Bryson and Einsweiler 1988) limits participation to an even smaller group of citizens, focusing on reaching consensus by leaders in the private and public sectors. It emphasizes a concern for action and practical results. It begins with a scanning of the key factors and trends in external forces and an assessment of resources, strengths, and weaknesses of the community as bases for determining feasibility. It also emphasizes the selection of a few critical issues to focus upon, and in that sense is not comprehensive. Nevertheless, to the extent that we seek a planning process that extends to action, strategic planning can be an appropriate approach, particularly if the participants are fully representative of the community.

Participatory techniques must be applied through some group, and the selection of that group is significant. Some techniques are employed in interactive groups, which must be relatively small (e.g., committees, task forces, councils, and boards). Other techniques can apply to larger and less organized groups (e.g., public hearings and town hall forums). Other techniques might use the media (articles, notices, interviews and talk shows, presentations, newspaper supplements, and press releases) or surveys to reach the public at large.

Whatever the approach used, the validity and usefulness of goal-setting is threatened when it is not achieved through representative participation. One threat is that the results do not achieve commitment from important parts of the community. The other threat is that representation is flawed and an unrepresentative group engages in goal-setting in the name of the whole community. For the public interest to be served, the process must be under government or joint government-civic group ownership and broadly representative. Community goal-setting should be structured to assure that selected private groups do not control the public agenda for their own private interests. Leaders and citizens should be brought together in a way that gets them to put the interests of the larger community ahead of their own narrower interests. The mechanisms must focus attention on fundamental issues and critical choices about the community's direction.

The Goals Statement

The outcome of goal-setting is a goals statement. It can be long or short and can take several forms. For example, it can be organized by components of the land use design: work areas, living areas, open space areas, and so on. What follows are illustrative goal statements for living areas and commercial areas in a land use plan.

—*Goals for living areas:* A residential environment designed to fulfill human and social functions (shelter and related public services, child-rearing, social interaction, social participation, and leisure-time functions), with special attention given to (1) a range of housing choices for households of diverse economic, social, ethnic, and racial compositions; (2) safe neighborhoods with well-maintained housing, infrastructure, public amenities, and culturally significant landmarks and symbolic qualities; (3) accessibility to employment, shopping, education, recreation, and other activities; (4) attractiveness; (5) energy efficiency; and (6) cost-effectiveness for provision of infrastructure and public services.

—*Goals for commercial areas:* A system of shopping areas, coliseums, stadiums, and similar facilities accessible to public transportation as well as the regional highway system, located for convenient trips, located to serve all areas of the community, compatible with adjacent development, and attractive.

Some goals are more suited to a development management plan rather than the land use design. What follows are two examples of development management goals.

—Regulatory, taxation, fees, acquisition, and capital investment program should promote equity and constitutional rights of all segments of the community

with respect to the principles of equal protection, benefit, due process, reasonable means, and taking.
—Development control measures should be cost-efficient, simple in their procedures, reduce freedom and choice as little as possible, and allow flexibility in solutions to meet standards.

The Policy Component: Formulating Principles of Planning and Action

Policies constitute the third component of the policy framework, following the fact component and value component. Policies are principles of land use design or development management and are derived from goals but aimed more directly at what government can do to attain goals. Policies are expressed therefore in verbs rather than the nouns and adjectives used for stating goals and objectives. They also use such imperatives as *shall* and *should.* An example, related to the goal of an esthetically pleasing central business district, might be a policy to require new development on Main Street to provide pedestrian amenities and plant shade trees along the right of way. A policy does not normally specify the action to be taken. For example, it would not specify exactly how shade trees along Main Street would be required. It does not specify ordinance language or which particular parcels are affected. For example, a policy may be to extend water and sewer lines only to areas where revenues from user fees and taxes will exceed the costs of servicing the development. Policies can also be expressed as specific standards, however. A standard is a more specific version of a policy principle. For example, a standard may specify pin oak trees on Main Street to be consistent with existing trees on the street.

At the initial stages of advance planning, the policies will be very general and deal with fundamental questions. For example:

1. Growth: Will it be the community's policy to encourage growth, discourage growth, or encourage it under certain conditions? Should growth be low density or compact and high density?
2. Urbanization pattern: What pattern should be encouraged or discouraged in order to be consistent with policies above? These policies might address, for example, what minimum densities to encourage in transportation corridors if it is policy to encourage public transportation. Policy might address general shape (concentric, satellite, or linear) and grain (mixed land uses versus separated land uses, for example).
3. Environmental: What environmental qualities are most important to maintain?
4. Fiscal policy: How should the costs of development be distributed among various groups—existing residents, future residents, movers and new residents, development industry, landowners, others?

5. Transportation: Should public transportation be encouraged?
6. Infrastructure: How should private development be coordinated with the provision of public water, sewer, schools, and other community facilities?
7. Planning process: What is the schedule for completion of the plan, and what degree of participation is desired?
9. Land use and growth-management system: Will the emphasis be on regulation or some other approach, and on performance standards or design specification standards?

Sources for initial versions of policy parallel the sources for goals. Input policies include:

1. policy legacy—existing explicit and tacit policies of the community, derived from a search and inventory process;
2. state, federal, and regional policy mandates that are required to be followed by the local government; and
3. planning literature—examples from highly regarded policy plans of other communities and discussions in the literature.

Some of these "input policies" are only suggestive, and others, such as state policy in some "growth-directing" states, must be followed.

As in goal-setting, the planner needs to guide a community effort by planners, appointed officials, elected officials, and interest groups in reviewing the input policies, adding new policy based on goals, and synthesizing the results into a coordinated "output policy" statement.

The policy statement should make clear the linkage of policies to the goals they are meant to facilitate. To do that, policies should either be stated under each major goal, follow the same organizational scheme used for goals (e.g., physical, economic, or environmental), or in some other way clearly indicate which policies promote which goals. In that way, the decision-maker and policy users later can see the relevance of the policy. Table 10-2 illustrates one format to show linkages between goals and policies.

Table 10-2. A Policy Statement That Shows the Linkage among Findings, Policy, and Implementation Strategies

---

10.212 Soil Constraints
Findings
Above slopes of 15%, all soil types found in Gresham impose severe constraints for urban uses. Erosion and deposition caused by improper construction practices is a frequent problem on soils below 15%. Subsurface sewage disposal is not compatible with most soils in Gresham. (Section 2.220—Findings Document).

Policy
It is the City's policy to minimize development on soil conditions which may be hazardous.

Implementation Strategies
1. The Community Development Standards Document shall require that all development or alterations of hillsides with severe constraints upon urban uses (slopes between 15%-

Table 10-2, continued

35%) employ the most responsible construction, design, and management techniques possible to minimize hazardous conditions. This may include clustering of housing on gentler slopes, density reductions, etc.

2. The Community Development Standards Document shall establish erosion control landscaping requirements for parcels where the natural vegetative ground cover has been disturbed. The Community Development Code shall not permit land divisions in areas over 35% slope. Property which is entirely above 35% slope may be improved to the extent of one dwelling unit per existing lot of record. Subdivisions of land which are partially above 35% slope shall not develop the portions in excess of 35% slope.

3. The Community Development Standards Document shall discourage the use of subsurface sewage disposal systems and require connection to the City's sewerage system. Subsurface systems may be utilized as a temporary system if the City has committed service to the area within 5 years.

4. The City will coordinate its land development process with the U.S. Soil Conservation Service and seek that agency's assistance for proper soils management.

Source: Gresham, Oregon, *Gresham Community Development Plan,* vol. 1: *Policies and Summary* 1980, 11.

Summary and Conclusion

A policy framework plan, the product of direction-setting, has three components: goals, facts, and policies. Goals represent problems to be alleviated, aspirations to be achieved, or needs to be met. The fact component describes the conditions pertaining to problems, aspirations, and needs; causal factors relevant to those conditions; and factors that affect actions or their effectiveness. Facts and goals may be developed concurrently, each feeding information to the other. Policies are principles, based on both goals and conditions, that suggest likely directions for solutions but stop short of specifying actions. A policy framework creates the basis for further, more specific planning, but at the same time it is an interim guide to action.

The next few chapters will discuss two types of more specific land use policy plans: land classification plans and land use design plans. They will be based in part on the three components of the policy framework: goals, facts, and policies. In fact, planners often incorporate the goals, facts, and policies from direction-setting into those types of plans, thereby skipping formal adoption of a policy framework. What should not be skipped, however, is the conscious attention to setting goals and defining relevant conditions.

REFERENCES

Boyer, R., and D. Savageau. 1985. *Places rated almanac.* 2d ed. Chicago: Rand McNally.

Bryson, John, and Robert Einsweiler. 1988. *Strategic planning: Threats and opportunities for planners.* Chicago: Planners Press.

Bryson, John, and W. D. Roering. 1987. Applying private-sector strategic planning in the public sector. *Journal of the American Planning Association* 53(1): 9–22.

Chambers, Marian. 1992. Progress is Jacksonville's most important product. *Planning* 58(6): 20–21.

Dalkey, Norman. 1972. *Delphi.* Santa Monica: The Rand Company.

Delbecq, A., and A. H. Van de Ven. 1971. A group process model for problem identification and program planning. *Journal of Applied Behavioral Science* 7(4): 466–92.

Dowall, David. 1984. *The suburban squeeze.* Berkeley: University of California Press.

Dubbink, David. 1984. I'll have my town medium-rural, please. *Journal of the American Planning Association* 50(4): 406–18.

Frank, James. 1989. *The costs of alternatives development patterns: A review of the literature.* Washington, D.C.: The Urban Land Institute.

Gueschka, C., F. Shaude, and H. Schlicksupp. 1975. Modern techniques for solving problems. In *Portraits of complexity.* Columbus: Battelle Monograph Series.

Greenblat, C. S., and R. D. Duke. 1981. *Principles and practices of gaming simulation.* Beverly Hills: Sage.

Jacobs, Allan, and Donald Appleyard. 1987. Toward an urban design manifesto. *Journal of the American Planning Association* 53(1): 112–20.

Kerlinger, F. N. 1973. *Foundations of behavioral research.* 2d ed. New York: Holt, Rinehart, and Winston.

Leung, Hok Lin. 1989. *Land use planning made plain.* Kingston, Ontario: Ronald P. Frye.

Lynch, Kevin. 1981. *A theory of good city form.* Cambridge: MIT Press.

Mansfield, Howard. 1990. *Cosmopolis: Yesterday's cities of the future.* New Brunswick: Center for Urban Policy Research.

Morrison, J., W. Renfro, and W. I. Boucher. 1983. *Applying methods and techniques of futures research.* San Francisco: Jossey-Bass.

Myers, Dowell. 1988. Building knowledge about quality of life for urban planning. *Journal of the American Planning Association* 54(3): 347–58.

Nutt, Paul C., and Robert W. Backoff. 1987. A strategic management process for public and third-sector organizations. *Journal of the American Planning Association* 53(1): 44–57.

Osborn, A. F. 1963. *Applied imagination.* New York: Scribners.

Park, Siyoung. 1985. Quality of life in Illinois counties. *Growth and Change* 16(4): 56–69.

Smith, Frank J., and Randolph T. Hester, Jr. 1982. *Community goal setting.* Stroudsburg: Hutchinson Ross Publishing Company.

Sorkin, D. L., N. B. Ferris, and J. Hudak. 1984. *Strategies for cities and counties: A strategic planning guide.* Washington, D.C.: Public Technology Inc.

Vogel, Ronald K., and Bert E. Swanson. 1988. Setting agendas for community change: The community goal-setting strategy. *Journal of Urban Affairs* 10(1): 41–61.

Warfield, J. N. 1976. *Societal systems: Planning, policy and complexity.* New York: Wiley.

11

Overview of the Land Use Design Process

Essentially, land use planning is the art of matching different users of land to the supply of land, that is, the attainment of congruence between user needs and land supply by the proper siting and sizing of land uses.

—Leung 1989, 21

Of the two spatial policy plan formats, the land classification approach is less specific than the urban land use design about the particular land use at a location. That is, land classification differentiates where urban development should occur, and where land should be devoted to conservation or agricultural use, but it does not specify the spatial organization of living, working, shopping, and leisure activities within the urban sector. The urban land use design does that.

There is another distinction between land classification and urban land use design. Land classification planning emphasizes management of urban change and protection of environmental resources. That is, it specifies which presently rural land should become urban over the next ten to twenty years, and which land should not. Thus, it also seeks to protect important natural processes and productive agricultural and forest lands. With respect to our three-legged stool concept discussed in chapter 2, land classification is intended to manage the land market and land development process while protecting nature's values. It seeks to manage the growth machine.

The urban land use design, on the other hand, emphasizes "use values." It proposes a spatial arrangement that functions efficiently and promotes a high quality of life. It focuses on the day-to-day use of the city by people, firms, and organizations instead of the process of urban development by which the city changes over time. It emphasizes the values of the city's users (households, firms, and institutions) rather than its builders. It also reflects environmental values, however, by treating environmental processes as land users.

An agency may use both approaches or choose one. For example, an agency might employ a land classification plan without following up with a detailed land use design, proceeding instead directly to a development management program on the basis of the land classification plan. Regional agencies and counties often take that approach. In large, sparsely settled areas where open countryside is a goal, the urban land use design is less applicable than land classification. Alternatively, a community may choose to do urban land use design without a preceding land classification plan. Towns and cities are more likely than counties to take that approach. In the following chapters, we present an approach that incorporates both a land classification plan and an urban land use design in a two-stage sequence. A land classification plan is done first, then urban land use design builds upon it, designing a more specific arrangement of land uses, community facilities, and infrastructure.

The Land Use Plan-Making Process: A Sequence of Five Tasks

The process of designing either a land classification or urban land use plan can be pictured as a sequence of five tasks. The tasks apply to each land class or, in the case of land use design, each more specific land use type. Thus, the planner goes through the sequence several times, once for each land use category included in the plan. The sequence is not rigid; tasks may be undertaken in a different order and sometimes several tasks are engaged concurrently, and there is feedback between them. Nevertheless, each task plays a special role in the design process.

Task 1. Derive location requirements for the land use sector of concern. Develop principles and standards for locating the particular land use or facility and for the spatial relationships among uses. These principles and standards are based on goals and objectives and on locational preferences of households, firms, and other groups of land users.

Task 2. Map the suitability of lands for the particular use. Using the design principles and standards developed in task 1, make maps showing the variation in suitability for locating the particular land classification, land use, or community facility. The spatial pattern of suitability will depend on the spatial pattern of environmental factors (e.g., slope, soil qualities, and drainage characteristics), the pattern of existing and projected land uses, and transportation and other infrastructure systems mentioned in the principles and standards determined in task 1. Some locations will be suitable for more than one use.

Task 3. Estimate space requirements for the land user. Estimate the amount of land needed to accommodate the future level of activity expected for the particular land class, land use, or community facility.

Task 4. Analyze holding capacity of the suitable land supply. Determine the capacity of suitable areas to accommodate land use activities and facilities. Holding capacities may be expressed in such terms as dwelling units, households, number of employees, or simply as the number of acres suitable for the particular land use in different locations.

Task 5. Design alternative spatial arrangements of land classes or land uses. Develop alternative spatial arrangements for future development and redevelopment activity, specific sectors of land use, community facilities, and open space. This is the synthesis step, the most creative of the five tasks.

Figure 11-1 diagrams the sequences and relationships among the five tasks. In addition, the diagram highlights three important balances that are sought in land use planning. One such balance is between demand and supply. Dividing the diagram into a top half and a bottom half, the tasks in the top half emphasize analysis of *demand*—for space, location, and services generated by the land use system to be accommodated. The tasks in the bottom half analyze the *supply* of land, environmental resources, and infrastructure available to accommodate those demands. In the middle, between the top and bottom, is the design, or *synthesis,* by which demand and supply are brought into balance.

A second balance is struck between the left and right sides of the diagram. Tasks on the left constitute *locational* analysis (both demand and supply). Tasks on the right analyze *space* quantities (likewise, both demand and supply). Again, in the

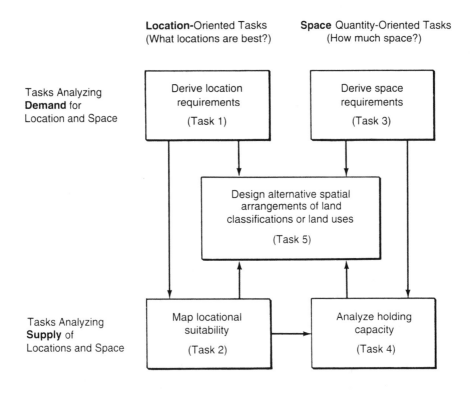

Figure 11-1. The Five Tasks for Land Classification and Urban Land Use Design. The diagram conceptualizes the sequence of tasks and the search for balance among demand and supply, location requirements and space requirements, and analysis and synthesis.

middle is the important task of *synthesizing*, or balancing, location with space quantity considerations.

The third balance, already implied by the first two, is between the *analytic* tasks at the four corners of the diagram and the *synthesis* task in the middle. Practical design is based on good analysis. Analysis can only go so far, however, and must be followed by creative design.

Task 1: Derive Location Requirements

Location requirements are principles for placing land uses in proper relation to each other and to physical characteristics of the land and for designing land use controls and development incentives to implement the land use plan. Principles are derived from the goals, objectives, and general policies in the policy framework plan. They may involve considerations of the danger to life and property from floods and other health and safety hazards; the vulnerability of important environmental processes to urban activities and construction practices; the need of people, firms, and institutions to interact and therefore to have accessibility to particular activities and facilities; the social, economic, and environmental compatibility of adjacent uses; and the economic feasibility of building in particular locations considering the soils and slopes on the site.

Design principles are often similar from place to place within the United States because the culture, technology, interpretations of the public interest, and even many specific goals and objectives, are shared. For that reason, we can discuss locational design principles and standards and expect the discussion to be relevant to the broad range of planning situations. Applications to other cultures, technologies, and governmental structures will require greater adjustments.

At the same time, variation exists even among communities in the United States, reflecting differences in relative importance among goals, fiscal capability, and cultural interpretations of such concepts as convenience. For example, one community may feel that taking more than twenty minutes to commute to work is unacceptable, whereas another accepts a forty-five-minute average work trip. The greater the community participation in formulating the goals and policies, the more unique those goals, objectives, and general policies, and, consequently, the resulting location principles. The planner should therefore not be too quick to impose the standards reviewed in this text without consideration of their relevance to the particular situation.

General Principles The idea of general principles for locational design apply to a land classification plan, an urban land use design, and a development management plan. For land classification planning, for example, the planner may derive locational principles for placing and delineating the urban transition area (where urban growth will be encouraged), the rural agricultural area, and the natural conservation areas. For the urban land use design, we may identify locational principles for work areas, living areas, shopping-entertainment-cultural areas, community facilities, agricultural and forestry areas, and natural ecological systems. Principles may also be developed for particular land uses, for example, multifamily housing or manufacturing. For growth-management systems, we might identify conditions that define where specific land use controls will be used.

Illustrative Locational Principles for the Land Classification Plan Natural conservation areas should be located where natural, recreational, productive, or scenic resources exist; where natural processes are vulnerable to urbanization and active agriculture and forestry; and where hazards pose danger to urban development. They may include water supply reservoirs and buffers adjacent to such bodies of water and the streams that feed them.

Built-up areas will be designated where development has already occurred at urban density and full urban services exist. Developed areas may be pierced by conservation areas such as open space systems along streams.

The urban transition areas should be located where urban services, including especially water and sewer, can be extended most easily and economically, where there are good existing or easily extended roads and other transportation, and where topography is not extreme. The urban transition area should not be located in hazardous areas, on land prime for agricultural or forest use, in highly vulnerable natural systems, or land needed as catchment area for a water supply reservoir.

Rural community areas should be located apart from the major urban concentrations and centered on already existing rural communities that may have low levels of urban services and no public water and sewer system but are suited for moderate levels of low-density residential growth and limited commercial development because of their market attractiveness, accessibility to employment, and soils suitable for on-site wastewater treatment.

The rural-agricultural-forestry areas should be located on lands with high productive potential for agriculture, timber production, or mining. Rural-nonagricultural areas might be lands where urban services would not be easily extended in the intermediate future but are not vital for agricultural production and do not contain environmental hazards or environmental features and processes vulnerable to urbanization.

Illustrative Location Principles for Urban Land Use Design The general principles for the land use design might be addressed to functional areas of an urban complex: work areas, living areas, shopping areas, community facility systems, and natural systems.

Work areas are those places devoted to employment in manufacturing, wholesale, trade, office, and service industries. They should be located in convenient proximity to living areas, where transit and thoroughfares can ensure easy access. They should also be convenient to other work areas as well as regional highway and public transport systems. They should be located away from vulnerable environmental systems and distributed to minimize concentrations of air pollution. Work areas should provide sites adequate in size, economical to develop for both the public and the private sector, and, except for heavy industry, attractively situated.

Living areas are the residential communities/neighborhoods and their accessory facilities such as neighborhood stores, local parks, and elementary schools. Living areas should be convenient to work, shopping, and leisure sites, as well as to public transport and thoroughfare routes, open spaces, and community facilities. They should be buffered from incompatible uses such as heavy industry and heavily traveled thoroughfares. They should contain small-scale recreation, shopping, office, and educational facilities. There should be a wide range of densities, housing types, and locations to offer wide choice. They should be in locations that are economic to develop and serve.

Areas for shopping, entertainment, and culture include major shopping and entertainment districts and such major educational, cultural, and recreational facilities as colleges, museums, concert halls, libraries, coliseums, and large, active recreation parks. These should be centrally located and convenient to living areas, served by public transit and the regional thoroughfare system. They should be of sufficient size and in locations to accommodate a wide range of goods and services activities and serve a variety of trade areas.

Community facilities include medical care facilities, police and fire stations, water and sewer plants, and airports and train stations. Such facilities should be located to be convenient to specific user groups and on sites economic for construction and of sufficient size to accommodate future expansion.

The transportation system should be safe, energy-efficient, comfortable, convenient, and multimodal if the urban complex is large enough. It should relate to the interregional highway, rail, air, and water transportation systems and located to serve but not disrupt work areas, living areas, and shopping-entertainment-cultural centers. Corridors for utilities and pipelines should be provided that are related to processing and storage requirements and to customer locations. Sites should be reserved for liquid and solid waste treatment and storage. Finally, sources for future water supplies should be delineated and controlled to protect watersheds and groundwater.

For agricultural areas, prime forest lands, and natural systems, see open space principles illustrated for the land classification plan in chapter 12. Major parks and large open spaces should be reserved in locations that take advantage of, as well as protect, natural processes, vulnerable environments, and unusual natural features, and to provide a variety of recreation opportunities. Wooded areas and other open space should also be located to provide definition to neighborhoods and districts as well as to moderate climate, noise, light, and air pollution; they should also provide access to open space. Most development should be kept away from environmentally hazardous areas such as floodplains, fault lines, steep slopes susceptible to sliding, and unstable soils. Lower-density development using on-site sewage treatment should be prohibited from areas of unsuitable soils. Present and future water supply drainage basins should be restricted to development compatible with protection of water quality.

Location Standards versus Principles Explicit "standards" can add meaning and usefulness to general principles. Thus "avoiding environmental hazards" might be stated more specifically as restricting development in the fifty-year floodplain. "Convenient proximity" or "easy access" is converted to a specific distance, measured in feet, miles, or travel time; for example, a half-mile service area for a neighborhood park. "Adequate size" might be converted to a specific number of acres; for example, a minimum of fifteen acres for a community park or 1.5 acres per one thousand population. "Economic to develop" might be stated as within the ridgelines defining a sewershed as drawn on a specific map. Standards can be mapped more precisely than the principles and therefore will provide a clearer basis for suitability analysis and design. They can also be assessed more easily to determine whether policy is being followed.

Some standards are established by law. They typically take the form of minimum standards necessary to protect the public health, safety, and general welfare. Minimum standards are particularly useful for land use regulations. For planmaking, however, we use a "desirability" standard not a "minimum" standard. A desirability standard establishes a quality somewhat above the minimum—something practicable to achieve but below an ideal.

Although most planning standards for land classification and land use design planning specify location directly, performance standards, which specify impacts, are also relevant, especially for the development management program. In performance standards, the emphasis shifts from direct specification of location characteristics to the specification of desired results while leaving open the means to achieving them. Thus, the location principles might delineate certain locations satisfactory for a land use, provided that development meet certain conditions through siting, engineering, or lowering density. For example, hillsides might be deemed appropriate for development, provided that land use controls restrict the amounts of impervious surface.

Task 2: Map Location Suitability

In this task, we map the implications of the location principles and standards developed in task 1, based on the spatial pattern of the factors cited in the principles. That is, based on soils, slope, floodplains, accessibility to current or projected employment, shopping, and leisure opportunities, accessibility to water and sewer lines, roads, and transit, and other data (and the way in which location principles refer to those data), we determine the relative suitability of locations for specific land use categories. The resulting maps show relative suitability of each unit of land in the planning jurisdiction for each type of land use, land classification, or community facility being specified in the land use plan.

A suitability map is not a design; it is only information for design. Suitability maps can only reflect existing facts and assumptions; they cannot reflect relationships among future land uses not yet allocated in the design. Also, the planner may only need to choose a small number of sites from a larger number of suitable sites, or he or she may need to determine which of several suitable uses for a given location will be encouraged there.

Task 3: Estimate Space Requirements

Having established in tasks 1 and 2 *where* land using activities and facilities should be located, we now shift to estimating *how much* land will be required. The bases for space requirements are projections of population and employment, studies of the densities of present and projected development, and policies about the future character of development (e.g., the mix of housing types and densities).

Space requirements are usually developed in several stages. In the first stage (the one accompanying the land classification plan and early stages of the urban land use design), we aim only for general approximations of the number of acres required for general land use categories (e.g., urban transition or residential development but not specifically multifamily versus single family residential needs). Later, in estimating space requirements for specific land use sector for the urban land use design, those initial estimates are reexamined, refined, and adjusted to reflect the specific character of desired development, consumer preferences, and suitability of the locations for various densities. For example, housing or industry located near the central business district might be allotted less space (higher density) than the same activity on the urban fringe.

In the first cut at space requirements, as applied to land classification for example, we might take the following approach. Existing gross densities of development are calculated. Population and employment projections are made. Those future levels of population and employment are multiplied by the existing density or an adjusted gross density to estimate the amount of land needed for the future urban transition area.

In the second cut, later in land use design for example, techniques for estimating space requirements share a common four-step pattern. The first step is a review of existing density characteristics for the particular land use and the variation in that density by age of development, development type, and central and peripheral locations. The second step is to decide upon the future level of population for residential areas and employment for employment centers. Projected trade area population, projected retail sales, and employment in particular sectors of the economy are the usual basis for the regional commercial activity centers. Those indicators of need are also used for community facilities (e.g., population for recreational facilities). In the third step, we derive space standards or proposed densities. We would consider existing densities and relative satisfaction with them, goals and higher-level policies, and trends in preferences and development. Space standards might be expressed in such terms as acres of industrial land per employee, acres of recreation or school site land per thousand population, square feet of retail space per dollar of sales volume or per consumer in the trade area, and so on. We would also specify minimum site size standards for such facilities as schools, shopping centers, industrial parks, and the like. In the fourth step, unit space requirement standards are multiplied by forecasted demand to obtain estimates of needed space. For example, if the space standard for an industrial sector is set at twenty-five employees per acre and the projected employment is ten thousand employees, then the implied space need is four hundred acres.

Task 4: Analyze Holding Capacity

The available land supply includes land in nonurban uses (e.g., agricultural uses), vacant land, and developed land slated for clearance or substantial rehabilitation. The planning jurisdiction is typically divided into planning districts, using neighborhoods, census tracts, or traffic analysis zones. The number of acres available is summarized for each planning district at each of several levels of suitability. Levels of suitability pertain to a particular land using activity that might locate in the planning district. If a GIS is used in the suitability analysis, holding capacity can be calculated for the suitability polygons determined by the suitability analysis, rather than by predetermined planning districts. Based on the standards for space consumption developed in task 3, the "suitable" acres can be converted to an equivalent number of dwellings, population, or number of employees. Alternatively, the conversion may wait until task 5, when holding capacity is balanced against demand for space. The outputs of task 4 are maps and tables indicating the holding capacities of each planning district or suitability polygon for different uses potentially located there. The information may be summarized for the planning area as a whole and for each of several subdivisions of that total area (e.g., built-up area and fringe area, or north, east, south, and west sectors). This task depends greatly on the vacant land analyses discussed in earlier chapters and on the suitability analyses.

Task 5: Design the Land Use Pattern

The previous four tasks are analytic. The fifth task requires inventing alternative land use patterns to accommodate the desired future population and employment while satisfying location principles, implications of suitability maps, space requirements, and holding capacities. Typically, the planner explores numerous schemes on tracing paper. There is no systematic way that we can suggest to do that.

Design ideas are tested by comparing the acres required for a use at a particular highly suitable location against the holding capacity of land at that location. As land is allocated to a use, it must be deducted from the holding capacity available for other uses. A sort of spatial accounting system is maintained on overlay maps and tables that do that. If deficiencies in land supply are encountered, some of the land allocated earlier in the design process, but suitable for a use being allocated later, might be reallocated to the new land use.

Shortages of suitable land might cause the planner to relax the standard of suitability, raise future densities, expand the planning area, or reduce the levels of population, employment, and other activity planned for the area. Generally, however, the limits of the planning study area are drawn sufficiently large initially so the balancing operation shows a surplus rather than a shortage of suitable land. Such a surplus is expected and is not a cause for reducing the planning area unless it taxes the data management capacities of the planning agency or exceeds the political reach of the government for whom the planning is being done.

An Appropriate Progression of Attention among the Various Land Uses

To avoid the complexity of dealing with all land classes or land uses at the same time, we suggest that the planner separate land uses into broad categories—first open space as separate from urban uses and then, within urban uses, regional activity centers for employment, commercial uses, and large-scale community facilities as separate from residential areas, including housing and local-scale community facilities (Table 11-1). The planner must pay attention to the overall design that combines all categories, but much consideration can be given first to each

Table 11-1. Recommended Order of Consideration for Categories of Land Uses for Land Classification and Urban Land Use Design

I. Open Space
Emphasis is on protecting critical environmental processes and also avoiding natural hazards, protecting economic natural resources such as agricultural and forestry land, providing regional outdoor recreation, and esthetic purposes.

II. Land for General Urban Transition
Emphasis is on delineating the area where policy should encourage new development over the next ten to twenty years.

III. Regional Activity Centers and Facilities
    A. Employment centers and districts
        1. Manufacturing and related activities
        2. Wholesaling and related uses
        3. Office employment centers
        4. Others particular to the area (e.g., research park or resort development)
    B. Regional commercial centers (mainly retail and services)
        1. Central business district(s)
        2. Satellite centers—older business centers, newer regional shopping centers, and multifunctional centers
        3. Highway-oriented centers
        4. Others, particular to the area (e.g., urban-oriented tourism)
    C. Regional recreational, educational, and cultural facilities

IV. Residential Communities
    A. Housing
    B. Local, population-serving activities and facilities
        1. Schools
        2. Local shopping
        3. Parks and neighborhood open space

category separately. The planner will further disaggregate the broad categories as plans and policies are refined. For example, open space for environmental protection might be distinguished from open space for recreational purposes.

Open space, which we recommend be addressed first, is a broad land use category that includes environmental processes (e.g., hydrology), hazards to urban development (e.g., floodplains), environmental resources (e.g., prime agricultural land and gravel deposits), cultural resources (e.g., a historic site), regional outdoor recreation sites, and areas where open space serves esthetic purposes (e.g., defining the edge of a neighborhood or providing foreground for a skyline view).

There are several reasons for beginning land use design with the allocation of open space rather than urban uses. For one thing, many of its location requirements can be expressed in terms of physical characteristics that already exist and are mapped in the land information system. By contrast, location requirements for human activities are highly interdependent and partially determined by where future employment and residential areas are located during the design process. Too, requirements for natural processes are less flexible than requirements for most urban uses; natural processes must occur where conditions permit and are not viable in different locations. In addition, technical, after-the-fact solutions to environmental problems are becoming increasingly costly and inefficient, and they are often ineffective. It is wiser to anticipate and avoid such problems through land use design. Yet another reason for designating open space first is that the market-oriented urban growth process does not provide sufficient open space in the right locations for environmental and recreational purposes. Thus, open space, particularly open space for natural processes, is vulnerable in the market-oriented urban development process and in a human values-oriented design process.

After open space uses, the planner should delineate those areas where new urban development should be encouraged. For the land classification plan, these are the urban areas and rural community areas. For the land use design, either after or instead of land classification the planner should designate locations for regionally oriented urban land uses and facilities. Those include several subcategories of uses: centers for employment in manufacturing, wholesaling, and regional and national office uses; regional commercial activity centers comprised primarily of retail and population-serving office uses; and regional facilities such as airports, waste-treatment plants, colleges, medical care centers, and the like.

After regional-scale activity centers and facilities, we recommend the planner designate the locations for residential communities. This includes not only housing but also local shopping and recreational facilities, elementary schools, other local facilities, and smaller-scale open space.

Summary and Conclusion

Both land classification and urban land use design require a similar pattern of tasks. It involves balancing location requirements against space requirements, demand against supply, and the needs of one land use against another. Four of the five tasks are analytic: formulating location requirements, mapping suitability of land, estimating space requirements, and calculating holding capacity of suitable lands. A fifth task is design, where the planner must synthesize the results of the four analytic tasks. The synthesis task is the kernal of land use design, but the preceding analyses provide information to assist design decisions and assure that they reflect goals and constraints.

In going about the land classification or urban land use design process, it is recommended that the classes or land use categories in the plan be divided into four categories: open space; urban transition; regional activity centers (including employment centers, regional commercial centers, and regional public facilities); and, finally, residential communities, including housing and local schools, shopping, and parks. It is also recommended that the designation of locations be done in that order: open space first, then urban transition land generally, then regional activity centers, and, finally, residential communities.

REFERENCE

Leung, Hok Lin. 1989. *Land use planning made plain.* Kingston, Ont.: Ronald P. Frye.

12

Land Classification Planning

. . . the Land Classification Plan identifies major directions of growth and indicates where future development should be limited because of the high cost of providing urban services, or for environmental reasons. In other words, the Plan indicates where urban growth would be compatible with the environment and with urban service capability, but it does not distinguish between residential, commercial or industrial development.
—Triangle J Council of Governments 1978, 3

A land classification plan is a spatially explicit statement of development policy. Like zoning, it divides a planning jurisdiction into districts. However, its classifications are not as specific as zoning categories, the districts are bigger, and the boundaries may not follow lot lines as they tend to do in zoning. Further, the classification plan states general policies for each type of district rather than specific restrictions on uses and structures. The land classification plan remains a statement of policy intent, not an ordinance.

Land classification concentrates future development into a few well-defined areas and delineates other areas where development should not occur. That strategy enables government to concentrate financial resources by providing services and utilities to limited, prespecified areas. It also relieves pressure on areas of environmental significance and areas particularly valuable for agriculture and forestry, where facilities will be withheld and development otherwise discouraged. Those districts where development is encouraged are appropriately sized to accommodate expected growth and expanded as necessary over time to respond to changes in growth rate.

Areas specified for urban growth are called by various names: urban areas, urban transition areas, development areas, or planned development areas, for example. Areas where development should not occur for environmental reasons are called conservation areas, open space, or areas of critical environmental concern, among other names. Still other areas, which are less environmentally critical but not suitable for immediate development, are often called rural areas. These areas are intended for agricultural or forestry activities. Some parts of the rural district may be intended as permanently hands-off for urban development. Other parts may be intended only as off limits for urban development for a time until more land for urbanization is required.

The concept of land classification is not new. One well-known early example, although not necessarily regarded as land classification, is Ian McHarg's approach to land planning (McHarg 1969 and earlier). He suggested dividing the planning region into three categories—natural use, production, and urban. Natural use areas have the highest priority and exclude even agriculture. Production areas, next in the hierarchy, include agricultural, forestry, and fishing uses. That is, production is used in the sense of producing food, fiber, and wood from the land, not industrial production. Urban areas are lands left over after allocating the two higher-priority uses. Urban areas are thus allocated to lands ill-suited for either natural processes or producing food and fiber.

In another example from the 1960s, Hawaii incorporated land classification into its state land use management program (Bosselman and Callies 1972; De Grove 1989). The state divides its land into one of four categories—conservation, agriculture, rural, and urban. In this case, policies for each class are backed with state regulations prohibiting certain uses and prescribing development practices for each class of land. Thus, land classification in Hawaii goes beyond the status of a policy plan and becomes the basis for land regulation.

A third early example of land classification is represented by the "development framework" policy plan of the Twin Cities Metropolitan Council in Minnesota. Developed in the 1970s, the development framework divides the seven-county metropolitan region into the metropolitan urban service area, free-standing growth centers, and the rural service area. The metropolitan urban service area is divided into the fully developed area (Minneapolis, St. Paul, and the inner ring of twenty suburbs) and the area of planned urbanization (other suburbs and land in the path of urban growth).

The districts in the land classification plan can be as few as the basic three or four, as in Hawaii or the Twin Cities, or as many as fifteen, as in the Orange County–Chapel Hill–Carrboro Joint Land Use Plan (1986). The classifications in that plan include urban, ten-year urban transition, twenty-year urban transition, rural buffer, rural residential, agricultural reserve, public interest, and water supply watershed areas. Those eight districts are supplemented by seven types of activity nodes centered on key highway intersections throughout the county—commercial transition, commercial/industrial transition, rural industrial, rural community, rural neighborhood, proposed urban commercial, and existing urban commercial nodes. Figure 3-3 in chapter 3 and Figure 12-3 in this chapter illustrate land classification plans.

The steps for designing a land classification plan follow the general approach described in chapter 11; specific techniques are suggested in this chapter for each step. The approach demonstrated for the open space and urban transition classifications can be adapted to narrower classifications.

The Overall Process for Land Classification Planning

The suggested land classification planning process is comprised of five steps: direction-setting (if not already done in a policy framework plan), formulating land classification categories to be used in the plan, mapping the land classifications, specifying implementation policies for each land class, and adopting and implementing the plan.

Direction-Setting

If direction-setting has preceded land classification, the starting points for land classification are the goals and objectives, analyses of relevant conditions, and general policies of the policy framework. If there has been no prior direction-setting, the land classification should begin with setting goals, analyzing relevant conditions, and developing general policies (chapter 11).

Formulate a Land Classification System

Next, the land classifications should be decided. They may be modified later in the process to reflect better understanding of problems and issues, but the planner must start with an idea of what land classifications he or she will be using. In some states, state government may specify the land classification system. For example, in counties covered by the Coastal Area Management Act in North Carolina, the state specifies a five-part classification system: urban, urban transition, rural, rural communities, and conservation (State of North Carolina 1985). Figure 12-1 diagrams a hierarchy of classification possibilities, based on a review of many plans. The terminology varies, and not all possibilities are represented.

Conservation areas are locations where development would jeopardize significant, scarce, or irreplaceable natural, recreational, scenic, and historic resources, prime agricultural and forest lands, or lands where natural hazards would jeopardize life and property and where long-term protection of the resource is deemed necessary. This is land, wetland, or water where development should either be prohibited or undertaken with considerable caution and under strict controls. Conservation areas are sometimes divided into three types. One type is "areas of critical environmental concern," such as floodplains, wetlands, stream networks, shorelines, water supply watersheds, and wildlife habitats where more rigorous regulation can be justified. A second type is prime resource lands, such as large-acreage tracts in commercial-scale productive agricultural or forest uses. The third type comprises less environmentally vulnerable areas, where development might be allowed under performance standards that protect natural processes.

The urban classification is the area where most urban growth is directed in the plan. It is often divided into already developed areas and (future) urban transition areas. The developed area is comprised of existing neighborhoods that the community wishes to protect, vacant lands suited for infill development, and neighborhoods and commercial areas where the community will encourage redevelopment. Urban transition areas are where rural-to-urban transition will be encouraged. These areas should either be relatively free of physical limitations and have urban services or be situated so that sewer, water, transportation, and other ur-

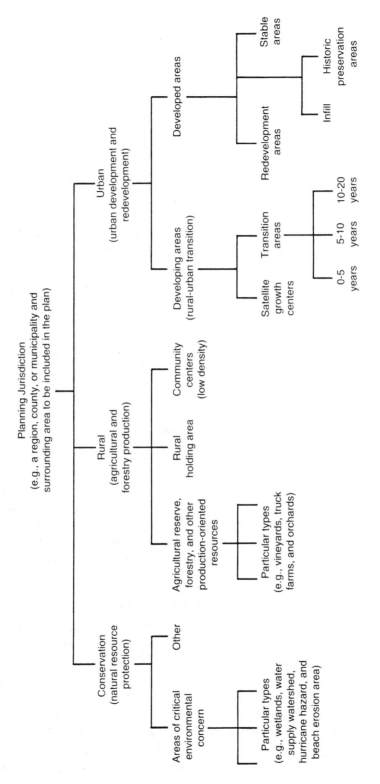

Figure 12-1. A Hierarchy of Land Classification Categories. Land classification schemes range from a simple division into three categories—conservation, rural, and urban—to more complex hierarchies, as shown by the options farther along the tree diagram.

ban services can be extended efficiently. Urban transition areas are sometimes divided into near-term development areas where utilities and services will be provided first and longer-term areas where they will be provided later. For example the transition area might be divided into five-year, five-to-ten-year, and ten-to-twenty-year service areas. Some plans provide for a third type of urban area, satellite growth centers, in specific locations within the rural area. A satellite growth center might represent a new town or other large planned unit development of mixed land uses, where urban level services are intended.

The rural classification comprises areas where development pressure is generally less intense, where urban services are not required nor easily extended and which may be in less productive agricultural, forestry, and mineral extraction uses and suitable for a modest amount of low-density employment and housing. Natural resources should not be so vulnerable as to be threatened by these rural and low-density urban activities, else an area is better defined as conservation. Rural areas may include important agricultural or forest areas but have been divided into small tracts not as suited to commercial-scale agricultural or forestry management. Some of these lands will eventually be reclassified into urban growth areas. For the time being, however, urban services are not provided, and urban density growth is discouraged. Within the rural area, land classification plans sometimes designate rural community nodes, or rural commercial or industrial nodes, where low-density residential, commercial, and industrial uses can be clustered that do not require urban infrastructure and services.

Formulate a Land Classification Plan Map

Once the classification system is decided, the planner must put it onto a map. This is essentially a design process that follows the five-task sequence outlined in the preceding chapter and summarized in Figure 11-1. It includes formulating location principles for each land classification, mapping suitability for each classification, projecting demand for development and converting it to space requirements, assessing holding capacity of suitable lands, and, finally, synthesizing those four considerations in the design task—drawing the classification map.

Formulate Implementation Policies for Each Land Classification

During and after mapping the land classifications, the planner formulates implementation policies to promote the desired uses in locations designated on the map. Those policies will commit public investments in roads, transit, sewers, water supply, schools, and other governmental services and facilities where urban development is desired. Policies will withhold public investment or increase its price substantially and add restrictions where development is not desired. The policies will also suggest regulations that prohibit development, reduce its density, or require site planning measures in conservation districts and other areas where development is not desired or where its side effects must be carefully controlled.

incentives to private developer to adopt this classification system

Finally, policies might suggest incentives for development, or nondevelopment, through preferential taxation, tax abatement, grants, preferential service provision, and other measures.

Combine the Results into a Plan for Publication, Adoption, and Implementation

The results of the preceding steps should be presented in a manner that facilitates public debate, evaluation, and choice of development policy. After adoption, the land classification plan should be published in a format that makes it clear and usable by elected and appointed officials, developers and others in the land development industry, and citizens.

Delineating Open Space

Let's say the planner and community have completed direction-setting tasks, adopted a policy framework, and decided to use the land classification approach as the next step in policy planning. In the remainder of the chapter, we will focus on designating two classifications—conservation areas and urban areas—in the land classification plan.

We use the more general term *open space* to refer to lands intended to conserve and protect valuable natural features and processes. Such processes perform useful functions for both nature and humanity and should therefore be allocated appropriate space in the plan and be protected through land use management measures. Examples of services performed by open space natural processes are water storage and purification, dispersal of atmospheric pollution, flood control, erosion control, topsoil accumulation, wildlife breeding and spawning, and wildlife and plant habitat.

Open space is sometimes also the location of natural hazards such as floods, earthquakes, hurricanes, mud slides or avalanches, tidal waves, and volcanic eruptions. Areas subject to such natural hazards might best be kept undeveloped in order to avoid loss of life, property damage, disruption to the economy and social structure of the community, and unnecessary development costs required to protect the development from the hazards. Open space might also include scenic, geological, ecological, or historic features that have cultural value. That is, open space contributes to social use values as well as environmental values.

Some agricultural and urban uses might have to be prohibited from some conservation areas or open space in order to protect natural processes from harmful effects of urbanization or to protect people and property from natural hazards. In other situations, however, development need not be totally prohibited from all conservation areas if site-development standards or best agricultural or forestry management practices will protect the environmental values.

Designating an area as a critical environmental area or conservation area in the land classification plan has five purposes.

1. It gives notice to landowners, developers, elected officials, and others about specific lands where natural processes and features are sensitive to certain human activities, and which therefore will be subject to regulation or acquisition.
2. It provides the legal and political basis for an open space protection program of regulations, acquisition, and other public actions, such as withholding sewer service.
3. It establishes priorities and focuses institutional attention and resources on locations where existing or potential problems are most significant.
4. It removes public subsidies to development in such areas (e.g., eliminating loans or grants for capital improvements on undeveloped barrier islands).
5. It provides a framework for dispute resolution.

The five-step land use design procedure outlined in Figure 11-1 in the preceding chapter must be modified in the case of open space allocation. Before undertaking that five-step process, the planner must first determine the purposes of open space, which are not as obvious as for other land uses. Second, space requirements and holding capacity analyses (tasks 3 and 4) do not apply to the same degree for open space as for urban growth. As a result, the sequence of tasks in delineating the conservation class in the land classification plan, or the open space uses in the more detailed urban land use design, is comprised of six steps.

Pre-design Task: Determine the purposes to be served by the conservation (open space) class.

Task 1: For each open space purpose, formulate locational principles and standards, including specification of human uses consistent with the open space purpose.

Task 2: Map suitable areas for accommodating each open space purpose by analyzing the land supply with respect to characteristics relevant to the principles and standards developed in task 1.

Task 3: Where a minimum size parcel is required for a particular open space use category, formulate minimum size standards (but not total amounts of space required because that concept does not apply for most open space purposes).

Task 4: Analyze the holding capacity of suitable lands by determining the size, shape, and other characteristics necessary to achieve the open space purpose.

Task 5: Make trial allocations of land to open space; that is, design an open space system. This is accomplished one open space purpose at a time but conscious of land that can serve multiple conservation purposes. This is regarded as "trial" allocation because we may modify it later to accommodate agricultural and urban uses.

Determine the Purposes to be Served by the Conservation Class

Open space is not a single homogeneous land use, but rather a broad sector of land uses. Thus, a first step is to decide the major categories of open space on the basis of the purpose to be served. The following open space purposes are derived from a survey of open space reports and plans. These categories are suggestive, not exhaustive, and may be modified for any particular community. Also, some lands may serve several purposes. Floodplains, for example, may also serve as wildlife habitats or as recreation sites.

1. *Protection of property and people from natural environmental hazards:* Areas that present danger from flooding, slides, quakes, shifting shorelines, and other natural hazards.
2. *Protection of natural resources and environmental processes:* Areas where natural processes are vulnerable to construction, urban land use activities, or agricultural, forestry, and mining activities. More specific purposes include preservation of estuaries, freshwater wetlands, unique forests, shorelines, special watersheds, and groundwater recharge areas. This purpose is the reverse of the first category of purposes, in this case protecting the natural environment from humanity rather than humanity from environment.
3. *Protection and management of natural resources for economic production:* Prime agricultural land, timber lands, mineral deposits (especially sand and gravel deposits near urban areas for the construction industry), fish and shellfish breeding grounds for the commercial and sport fishing industries, and water supply watersheds and groundwater recharge areas for aquifers used for public water supply. This category is distinguished from the second category by its concern for protection of economic rather than environmental values. Although in most plans, agricultural and forestry are accommodated in the rural classification, critical agricultural or forest land might be a special category of conservation. In urban land use design (see following chapters) agriculture may be a separate land use.
4. *Protection and enhancement of natural and cultural amenities:* Unique landscape features such as cliffs, bluffs, and other geologic formations; clear streams, rapids, and waterfalls; shoreland; pleasant scenes such as bridges, cemeteries, churches, and pastoral or sylvan landscapes; and foregrounds for vistas and panoramic views of such scenes. Such open space, unlike the first three categories, may require public access and infrastructure improvements.
5. *Protection or provision of outdoor recreation, education, or cultural facilities:* Places suitable for active outdoor recreation, trails, campsites, fairgrounds, zoos, golf courses, outdoor concert areas, and the like. These open spaces will require public access and, in many cases, public infrastructure.
6. *Shaping urban form:* Greenbelts, open space wedges and corridors, buffer areas, plazas and commons, construction setback lines, and other open space

to give imageability to the city. Together with the provision of natural amenities, this purpose is often associated with urban design. This purpose applies at many urban scales, from metropolitan form to green space within neighborhoods and commercial areas.

The first four purposes are most often associated with land classification planning; the fifth and sixth are more often introduced in follow-up land use design. The most critical conservation areas, for example, productive wetlands, endangered species habitats, or beach erosion zones, are sometimes designated "environmentally critical areas" or "areas of environmental concern" and receive special direct attention in follow-up development management programs. They may require special permitting procedures or be acquired outright.

Task 1: Formulate Locational Principles and Standards

While each community must decide its own principles based on its goals and objectives and its chosen open space purposes, the following list contains suggestive principles from which the planner can pick and adapt. Most are aimed at land classification and urban land use design, but some, particularly those at the end, apply to development management as well.

Illustrative General Principles (Regardless of Open Space Purpose)

1. Conservation lands should include major wetlands; undeveloped shorelands that are unique, fragile, or hazardous for development; critical wildlife habitats (i.e., habitats decisive to the survival of unique or endangered species or that contain an unusual diversity of native wildlife species); publicly owned water supply reservoirs and watersheds; state, federal, and other government controlled parks and forests; "areas of critical environmental concern" as defined by state or regional agency; floodplains; steep hillsides; mud slide areas; and lands containing significant natural, scenic, or recreational resources.
2. Compatibility principle: The proposed uses of an open space area must be (a) suited to the physical characteristics of the area; (b) compatible with adjacent land uses and features; and (c) compatible among themselves so that one particular use does not destroy the value of the site for other intended purposes.
3. Linkage or continuity principle: The value of an open space area may be significantly increased if it is connected to other open spaces in a multipurpose open space system.
4. Accessibility principle: Depending on the proposed function of an open space area, public access or the prevention of access can be quite important. For example, access is necessary for recreational sites, whereas denial of access may be necessary to preserve a natural process, for example, in wetlands.
5. Urban pressure principle: Open space priority is increased if urban development is imminent.

Illustrative Principle for Open Space Areas Intended to Protect Urban Investment and People from Natural Environmental Hazards Do not allocate urban development in floodways or floodway fringes in the land classification plan or land use design and prohibit encroachment in watercourses and floodways through regulations. Allowable uses might include those that do not reduce flood storage capacity; do not involve materials that are buoyant, flammable, explosive, or toxic; and have the lowest floor of any structure at least one foot above the level of the hundred-year flood.

Illustrative Principles for Open Space Areas Intended to Protect and Manage Valuable Natural Resources and Environmental Processes

1. Identify ecosystem units that can be used as basic planning units. One recommended approach is to base the ecosystem unit on the watershed concept, which represents the geographic delineation of particularly important natural processes such as stormwater run-off; is relatively easily identified and observed; is related to delineation of animal and plant communities and other natural resources and processes; and represents a basic physical system that must be considered in providing utilities to urban development (Wuenscher and Starrett 1973; Elfers and Hufschmidt 1975). As an alternative, the geographic units may be based on homogeneous environmental characteristics (e.g., soils and geology).

2. Preserve and manage vegetative cover, especially on steep slopes and along streams, to maintain natural infiltration and runoff processes; prevent undue erosion, sedimentation, and organic pollution of watercourses; stabilize stream banks; provide wildlife habitat; and control water temperature for fish. Standards for steep slopes vary from 10 to 25 percent grade and sometimes link percent of open space to steepness of slope, that is, the steeper the slope the greater the amount of open space required and the lower the overall density of development allocated in the land use design and allowed by the development management system. Standards for buffers along streams vary from fifty to three hundred feet.

3. Allocate wetlands and immediately adjacent areas to open space and apply special controls to those areas.

4. Preserve a few large areas rather than numerous small ones. Areas should be large enough to support wildlife that are of interest. This may vary from ten to fifteen acres for some wetland habitats (McCormick 1972) to several hundred acres for other forms of wildlife (Berry and Coughlin 1973, 3–14).

Illustrative Principles for Using Open Space to Protect and Manage Natural Resources for Economic Production

1. Allocate only lower-density development on major groundwater recharge areas and limit impervious surface through regulations.

2. Restrict development on sites having sand, gravel, rock, and limestone according to the following standards:
   a. X percentage (or absolute quantity) of these deposits should be preserved by withholding development;
   b. use such sites for various other open space purposes, both before and after mineral extraction, for example, parks, golf courses, lakes, or landfills (after extraction); and
   c. reclamation after mining should be required by regulation.
3. Future water supply watersheds should be preserved as open space in the land classification and protected through development management measures. For example, extra restrictions should be established on septic tank systems and landfills.

Illustrative Principles for Using Open Space to Protect, Provide, and Enhance Natural Amenities

1. Give highest priority to those areas having the rarest amenities, for example, very steep slopes; scarcer terrestrial habitats, lands, and streams (based on water quality, gradients, average floodplain width, average valley height and width, stream width, depth, and velocity, and stream-bed material); and esthetic properties such as visual pattern of streams and tributaries, serenity, naturalness, and geologic values (Dearinger et al. 1971, 49–52).
2. Provide ample physical and visual access to the amenity.

Illustrative Principle for Using Open Space to Provide and Enhance Sites for Outdoor Recreational, Educational, and Cultural Opportunities Distinguish user-oriented from resource-based urban recreation areas. User-oriented areas are located close to the users. Activities include tennis, golf, swimming, picnicking, and outdoor games, and the areas are used weekdays as well as weekends. Sizes of such sites range from one acre to one hundred acres. While resource-based areas should not be too far from the users, within one to two hours if possible, the higher priority is on locating where the best land/water resources exist. Activities include picnicking, hiking, swimming, hunting, fishing, camping, and canoeing. Such areas are generally used on weekends or one-day outings. The size of such areas ranges from one hundred to several thousand acres, for example, state parks and forest preserves. It is particularly the resource-based areas that can and should be allocated early in the land use design process because of its dependence on existing physical resources. Tentative locations for the user-oriented recreation areas might also be selected during land classification but not firmed up until the future population distribution is clearer. Allocation of space for community- and neighborhood-scale user-oriented recreation areas will be addressed in chapter 15; they are usually not part of the land classification plan.

Illustrative Principles for Using Open Space to Shape Urban Form

1. Use open space established for other purposes listed above whenever possible.
2. Establish clear edges to delineate communities, neighborhoods, districts, and other elements of urban form.
3. Use vantage points at high elevations, promontories, points, and other prominent locations to provide views.

In addition to locational principles, oriented to land use design and land classification, the planner will want to develop program design principles for the development management stage of advance planning. The seven principles that follow are adapted from Kusler (1980, 63–68).

1. Build on other local and state land use and resource management programs, such as zoning, subdivision regulations, floodplain and wetland legislation, and shoreland regulations. Combine and coordinate land acquisition, regulation, infrastructure, construction, and preferential taxation.
2. Balance public interests with private interests by allowing economic uses of the land and using performance standards rather than prohibiting marginal uses, and by complying with constitutional and statutory protection of citizens' rights, and generally ensuring fair treatment of affected parties, especially landowners.
3. Match the administration complexity of open space programs, standards, and procedures to staff resources while at the same time building staff expertise, using expert citizen groups, obtaining technical assistance, or requiring the developer to provide technical input. Build monitoring and enforcement into programs.
4. Seek cost-effectiveness by assuming reasonable data, analysis, administrative, and enforcement requirements; by sharing costs with other programs; and by shifting a portion of program costs to developers.
5. Involve and educate the public by using hearings, workshops, special committees, and other participatory mechanisms.
6. Set priorities; it will be impossible to address all open space issues or areas immediately.
7. Develop incremental approaches to achieving adequate control over open space lands by acquiring land by stages and designing a long-term capital improvement program.

Other principles for sensitive area program design and implementation can also be found in Kusler (1980, 1–6).

Task 2: Map the Suitability of Lands for Each Open Space Purpose

In this step, the planner uses the Geographic Information System to map the lands within the planning area that meet the location principles decided in task 1. Each open space classification has a separate suitability map. The mapping process involves weighing multiple variables pertaining to the suitability of a piece of land to the particular open space purpose and combines the results into one map for that purpose (chapter 8). For example, a map designed to help designate open space to avoid natural hazards might show the degree of risk of property damage based on a composite of floodways, floodway fringe areas, hurricane flood areas, earthquake subsidence and liquefaction zones, and other hazardous areas. There might also be composite maps that show areas that meet several open space purposes at the same time, making those areas even more important to designate for conservation.

Another type of suitability map, perhaps for a county or larger region, might identify ecosystems critical to multiple endangered or declining species. Such a map might use information from the Department of the Interior's proposed National Biological Survey to map species and ecosystems. Such environmental suitability maps could then be balanced against suitability maps for other open space purposes and for urbanization in devising a land classification plan.

Suitability analyses of land for open space purposes often consider other factors. For example, open space might be classified according to whether it is (1) already protected; (2) important but not yet protected and at the same time under urban development pressure and in danger of losing its capacity to serve open space purposes; or (3) unprotected but not under urbanization pressure so that it will probably continue to serve open space purposes without the need for governmental intervention in the short term.

An approach developed by Lane Kendig for Bucks County, Pennsylvania (Bucks County Planning Commission 1970) illustrates how a composite suitability mapping approach applies for county parks, but the idea can be adapted to other open space purposes. That approach, one of the earliest to incorporate a computerized GIS overlay technique, used seven criteria.

1. *Maximum utility:* A measure of the number of recreational activities for which the natural features of the site are suitable; the more open space uses of the site, the greater its suitability for park purposes.
2. *Esthetic quality:* A measure of amenity value due to the existence of cliffs, forest, water, historic association, and the like.
3. *Cost:* Appraised land value; the cheaper the land, the greater its suitability for acquisition.
4. *Supply and demand:* Measured as a ratio between the supply of available parks in the immediate vicinity and the demand for recreation based on a citizen survey and measured for sub-areas of the county; areas of high demand relative to supply are given higher suitability scores.
5. *Other facilities:* Measured as proximity to major existing recreation facilities; the higher the proximity, the lower the suitability for a new park at the location.
6. *Accessibility:* Measured as proximity to people and transportation facilities; the better the accessibility, the higher the suitability of the site for a park.
7. *Threat of loss:* Measured by potential for urban development; the greater

the threat of urban development, the higher the priority to acquire the site for park land.

The scores on each criterion at each location are multiplied by a weighting factor that reflects the planner's judgment about its relative importance to overall suitability. They are then summed to indicate overall suitability of the location.

Task 3: Formulate Space Requirements

Space standards are generally not relevant for open space intended to protect natural processes, avoid exposing development to natural hazards, or shape urban form. The amount of open space required for those conservation purposes is primarily the result of the pattern of physical determinants (e.g., how much land is in floodplains, or wetlands) coupled with the particular standards to be applied (e.g., more land would be in a hundred-year floodplain than in a fifty-year floodplain).

For recreational uses, however, space requirements are applicable. Three types of space requirements are used—number of recreation sites per thousand population, minimum site size for a type of recreation site, and aggregate recreation acreage per thousand population. Some of those standards are presented in chapter 15 on community facilities. Such standards, however, should be adapted to the community's leisure activity culture. Furthermore, factors such as the site's physical suitability for the recreational uses to be accommodated would be important in determining the amount of land needed.

Ecological principles may also suggest minimum acreage for certain wildlife and plant communities. In addition to space requirements, ecological principles may suggest patterns of open space, for example, arranging the space in corridors so that wildlife can move within and between territories.

Task 4: Analyze Holding Capacity

Like space requirements, this task is seldom relevant to open space allocation. With the exception of recreation lands, there is little need to compare the total amount of suitable land for open space with quantity of demand for such space; the suitability maps, in a sense, define both the demand and the supply side.

Task 5: Make a Trial Allocation of Land to Open Space Classifications

Based on the foregoing analyses, the planner now allocates land to open space purposes. Ideally, the planner explores several alternative designs. For each alternative, the planner draws the boundaries of the open spaces, calculates the land therein, and summarizes it in a table. Table 12-1 indicates one way to summarize open space allocations. Such a table should be accompanied by a map showing the locations and boundaries of open space classifications, perhaps with annotations about specific purposes served. The *xx*s used in Table 12-1 and in some other tables in following chapters merely indicate that figures on numbers of acres would be inserted in an actual case. The figures will vary from case to case, hence the use of xxs in the tables in this text.

Table 12-1. Open-Space Requirements by Type of Open Space, by Planning District

Geographic Area[a]	Primary Open-Space Purpose (acres)[b]			Total Open Space Allocated (acres)	(Optional) Net Remaining Vacant Land (by Category) Available to Other Land Use Sectors
	A	B	C . . .		
Central areas	XX	XX	XX	XXXX	XXXX
Fringe areas	XX	XX	XX	XXXX	XXXX
Outside of planning jurisdiction	XX	XX	XX	XXXX	XXXX

a. These geographic areas either may be large sections of the planning jurisdiction as shown (including a category "outside of planning jurisdiction" for such needs as water supply), or they may be smaller planning zones.
b. Open-space purpose categories will have been determined earlier. They will vary in number and content from place to place depending on local community values. Alternatively, the open space may be classified by relative priority (e.g., type A might be highest priority, not to be compromised by subsequent allocation of other uses, whereas type B might be second priority).

Until other land use categories are incorporated into the design, the allocation to open space remains tentative. Some of the land that seems best allocated to open space at this point may be found later in the design process to be even more appropriate as urban use. In other words, the benefit achieved by the open space use must eventually be balanced against the need of other land classifications for space.

The open space designations must also be tested for political acceptance in the context of the local government's regulatory authority and fiscal considerations. How far is the governmental jurisdiction prepared to go in regulating land areas for conservation purposes? If conservation areas are to be established through regulatory measures, do landowners have an economic use of their lands under the regulation? Or is a "taking" likely to follow a landowner challenge in the courts? Is local government prepared to purchase conservation easements or fee simple title to lands where regulations are not appropriate? Are there nonprofit conservancies or land trusts that could preserve such lands? Answers to such questions will assist the planner in determining which land and how much land is feasible to designate for open space conservation.

Allocating Urban Growth

The next stage in land classification planning, after open space allocation, is the designation of areas for urban growth: urban, urban transition, rural community, and satellite growth centers (if there are any), or some variation on those classes. In addition to delineating the districts, this stage involves determining the amount of urban growth as well as its distribution among the several land classifications. A sequence of five tasks delineates land classification areas to receive urban growth.

1. Formulate location principles for each classification to receive significant urban growth, for example, urban, rural, or rural community districts.
2. Develop a suitability map for each such classification.
3. Determine the amount of urban growth (population and employment) to be accommodated in the plan, distribute it among the land use classifications, and translate that growth into space requirements for each classification. If there are several districts within a class, for example, several satellite growth centers or several sectors of urban transition, determine the space requirements for each such district or sector.
4. Analyze the holding capacity of the suitable lands on the suitability map for each classification and district or sector within the classification.
5. Design the spatial pattern of classifications to receive urban growth, based on the suitability analyses and the area sufficient to absorb the determined amount of urban growth (i.e., meet space requirements).

Task 1: Formulate Location Principles

Location principles should be devised for each class whose purpose it is to accommodate urban growth. For purposes of explanation, we illustrate location principles for three such classifications—urban developed, urban transition, and rural community areas. The location principles that follow are illustrative only; they are neither comprehensive nor necessarily appropriate for every planning jurisdiction. Every community must derive location principles and standards from the goals, general policies, and the particular land classification system determined in preceding stages.

Illustrative Location Principles and Standards for Developed Areas The purpose of the urban developed area is to delineate areas and provide policy to guide continued development and redevelopment of existing built-up urban places and to protect neighborhoods from incompatible development. For example, developed areas may be more suitable for absorbing growth if they have:

1. infrastructure in good condition, with excess capacity; and
2. a supply of vacant buildable land.

Illustrative Location Principles and Standards for Urban Transition Areas The purpose of the urban transition class is to provide sufficient land for rural-to-urban transition beyond the already built-up areas.

1. Lands should not be subject to environmental hazards; thus flood hazard areas and extremely steep slopes are to be avoided.
2. Lands should avoid vulnerable environmental areas (wildlife habitats and wetlands, for example).
3. Lands should have public water and sewer systems already available or situated so that extension of infrastructure is economical.
4. Lands with better access to employment and shopping are more suitable.
5. Lands in the transition class should not be in strong contradiction to identified development trends.
6. Lands well suited to commercial agriculture or forestry should be avoided.

Illustrative Location Principles and Standards for Rural Community Centers
The purpose of the rural community class is to provide for clustering of lower-density land uses to help meet housing, shopping, employment, and public service needs within rural areas. They are not large enough, or dense enough, to justify public water and sewer service.

1. Locations on or near the regional highway network are more suitable than locations off the network.
2. Areas within prime agricultural or forest lands still viable for commercial-scale production should be avoided.
3. Areas with soils suitable for septic tank systems are more suitable.

Task 2: Develop a Suitability Map for Each Relevant Class

Using location principles such as those illustrated above and the spatial distribution of variables that measure such factors, the planner creates suitability maps for each class to which urban growth will be allocated, in this illustration, urban, rural, and rural community.

Task 3: Determine Space Requirements for Each Relevant Class

This task involves several subtasks: (a) determining the total population and employment growth to be accommodated; (b) distributing that growth to the several classifications; (c) determining number of acres necessary for each classification to accommodate the assigned growth; and (d) adding a safety margin to reflect uncertainty and avoid forcing up land prices by having a shortage of developable land (Figure 12-2). Space requirements will depend on the density assumed for development in each classification. The density of growth assigned to rural community and rural classes will be much lower than the densities of growth assigned to the developed or transition classes.

Subtask 3a: Determine the Amount of Population and Employment Growth to Be Accommodated in the Plan and Convert to Dwellings   The population and

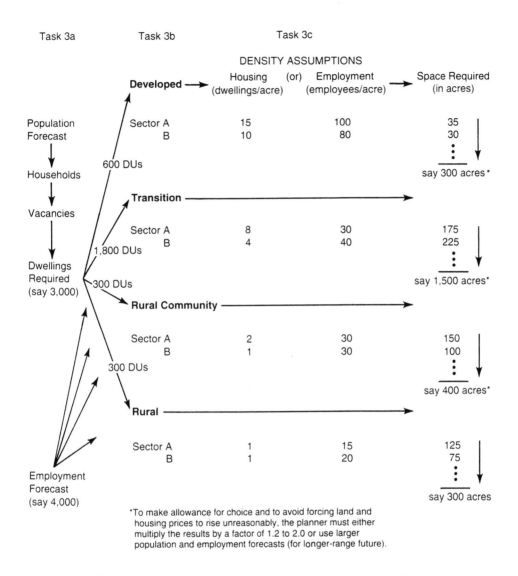

Figure 12-2. Diagram of the Steps in Estimating Space Requirements. The numbers are hypothetical and for illustration only.

employment projections developed as part of the analysis of relevant conditions in the policy framework are the basis for this determination. The population forecast is generally translated into households, which represent the demand for dwellings. That demand is multiplied by a factor that represents an allowance for vacancy. A 5 percent vacancy assumption, for example, would require the planner to divide the number of households by 0.95 to obtain an estimate of the number of dwellings required. For employment there is no need to convert to other measures.

Subtask 3b: Allocate the Growth to Different Land Classifications, and within Those Classifications, to Geographic Sectors (and Sometimes Concentric Rings)
The planner allocates the planned number of dwellings and the planned number of employees to the several land classifications that accommodate growth. For example, the distribution might be 20 percent to the developed urban area, 60 percent to the urban transition area, 10 percent to rural community centers, 10 percent to the rural area, and none at all to conservation areas. Then, for each of those classifications, except perhaps for the rural class, the planner might want to allocate a proportion of the growth for the class to the several geographic sectors within the class. For example, of the 60 percent allocated to the urban transition classification, 35 percent of it might be allocated to a northern sector, 25 percent to a western sector, and 20 percent each to eastern and southern sectors. These allocations to classes and sectors are based on examination of development trends, suitability maps for the classes, and land use design policy. The allocations may be adjusted later in the process in response to the results of the conversion to space requirements (task 3c) and the holding capacity analysis (task 4). The distribution of employment is made separately from population distribution.

Subtask 3c: Convert the Allocations of Population and Employment Growth to Space Requirements   To this point the planner has allocated dwellings and employment. Now those dwellings and employees must be converted to their implicit demand for acres of land. First, the planner must determine a gross density (i.e., including streets and some waste) for the dwellings in the particular classification and geographic sector and the employment type likely to be located there. The densities are based on existing densities in the vicinity, trends and projections, and desired densities in light of goals and policies. Densities will vary among communities and among land classification categories within communities. Next, the planner divides the number of dwellings and employment allocated to the area by the assumed gross residential and employment densities. The result is an estimate of the number of acres required in the particular classification, and perhaps by geographic sub-areas within the classification.

Subtask 3d: Adjust Estimate Upward to Provide a Safety Margin and Avoid Forcing Up Land Prices   The three previous subtasks render an estimate of minimum space requirements. However, those estimates must be adjusted upward for two reasons—to provide for choice of location and housing type among consumers and to avoid artificially increasing land and housing prices by severely limiting the supply of developable land. The allowance is generally made in one of two ways. One way is to add a percentage over the estimated minimum; that is, the minimum requirements are increased by anywhere from 20 percent to 100 percent, based on the planner's judgment about how much allowance is needed. The second approach is to use the growth levels expected five or ten years beyond the horizon period for the plan. Such an allowance to create an oversupply should be made in each of the land classifications and generally in each geographic sector of the total area covered by the plan.

A simpler, although cruder, approach would estimate total future urban space requirements by multiplying the current acres in urban land uses by a multiplier representing employment growth (for manufacturing, wholesale, and commercial land uses) and population growth (for all other land uses, including transportation). These acreage requirements would be adjusted upward to reflect uncertainty and avoid forcing up land prices, and then distributed between the developed area and urban transition classification.

Task 4: Analyze Holding Capacity

In this task, the planner estimates the amount of developable land in suitable areas for each class by small areas—planning districts or polygons formed through GIS overlays. It is summarized by annotations on suitability maps or in tables, or both. The actual amount of land available in each planning district, with characteristics that make it attractive and suitable for development, would be information similar to that which results from suitability studies discussed in chapter 8. This land supply analysis will be used to make each land classification district the appropriate size and to check against assigning more growth to a district than can be accommodated by the land supply there.

Task 5: Delineate Land Classes on a Map

The planner now takes the results of the four preparatory tasks and designs alternative land classification maps, specifying a pattern of areas best suited for accommodating urban growth. The alternative designs that come out of such a process should balance demand for space against the supply of suitable land; balance the need for good locations against the need for urban space; and balance the need for urban land against the need for conservation land.

One alternative should normally represent a more-or-less trend projection of urban development. That trend, or no-policy-change alternative, provides a baseline future against which to contrast other alternatives based more on goals and policies.

Formulating Implementation Policies

The land classification map should be supported by action policies to implement the plan. Generally, such policies are organized by land classification category. Thus, each classification is supported by its own set of mutually supportive policies. The following policy examples, applied to the urban transition district, illustrate the idea.

1. The community shall prohibit the use of septic tanks by new development (in order to discourage lower-density development in an area eventually intended for urban densities and to prevent having to replace on-site wastewater treatment with public sewerage later).
2. The community shall develop a capital improvements program for extending public infrastructure and community facilities in the urban transition area in a timely manner.
3. Land use controls shall require that adequate public facilities be available at the time of occupancy of new development, possibly through an adequate facilities ordinance or other forms of "concurrency requirements" (see Florida policies cited in chapter 10).
4. Zoning shall permit development at urban densities.

Bringing It Together

The land classification plan should consist of several parts:

1. an analysis of existing and emerging conditions;
2. goals and objectives;
3. general community policies;
4. a land classification map; and
5. implementation policies for each land classification.

The city-county plan for Lexington and Fayette County, Kentucky, provides an example of a land classification plan in the context of a traditional comprehensive planning approach (Figure 12-3). The planning jurisdiction, which covers all of the city of Lexington and Fayette County, is divided into three main classes: the urban service area, the rural use area, and special consideration areas (including environmentally sensitive areas and geologic hazard areas not shown in Figure 12-3). The special consideration areas penetrate the other two areas, and special overlay policies may apply there for development allowed in the underlying urban area or rural area. The urban service area is coordinated with the capital improvement program and defines the area where government is committed to providing sewer, water, police, fire, schools, street lighting, garbage collection, libraries, and transit. Other areas are defined where such facilities can be provided by the developer under an adequate facilities ordinance.

The urban service area is divided into six functional planning areas and further into sub-unit areas (in parentheses):

1. downtown core area (office and commercial core, mixed-use area);
2. employment centers;
3. urban activity centers, intended for high-intensity, nonresidential activities requiring high levels of accessibility;
4. existing neighborhoods (declining, stabilized, recently developed, transition);

5. urban growth area (partially developed, undeveloped); and
6. horse farms, to be protected from development where feasible, even though in the urban service area.

The functional planning areas each have implementation strategies for controlling change, based on physical characteristics, market conditions, and goals for the area. The Lexington-Fayette Urban County Planning Commission intends to review and adjust the shape and size of the urban service area boundary every five years. Their purpose is to expand the service area where and when necessary to assure a reasonable supply of land to accommodate anticipated growth and consumer choice and to allow for the efficient operation of a land and housing market.

The rural service area is further divided into rural activity centers, general rural use areas (including settlements, subdivisions, agricultural areas), and horse farms.

Because most of the growth is intended for the urban service area, a planning agency might supplement the land classification plan with a third-level refinement

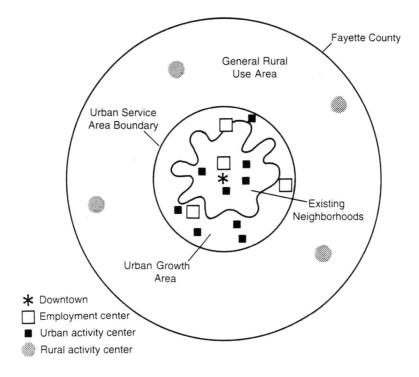

Figure 12-3. Functional Planning Areas Concept. There are three main classes for Lexington-Fayette County, Kentucky: urban service area, rural use area, and special consideration areas. The urban service area is divided into functional planning areas, such as employment centers, urban activity centers, existing neighborhoods, downtown area, and urban growth area. Special consideration areas (not shown) include environmentally sensitive areas, for example. From Lexington-Fayette Urban County Planning Commission 1980, 77.

of land use pattern and land use policy for the urban service area. The Lexington-Fayette County plan begins to do that, and the next several chapters in this text also discuss methods to do that through an urban land use design. Such a plan gives close attention to specific urban land use activities and their intensities. The land use design can then be followed up with a development management plan, outlining specific zoning or other development controls (chapter 16). The plan might also specify timing and geographic sequence to development within the urban transition district, implemented through a capital improvement program, timed development regulations, and refined service area policies.

Whatever the particular land classification system selected, it might be described in a table similar to Table 12-2 and might accompany the land classification map, summarizing the types of land classes, their purpose, locational principles, and implementation policy.

Summary and Conclusions

The land classification plan provides a balanced consideration of the needs of natural systems, human activity systems, and market systems. It seeks to preserve valuable, dangerous, or productive natural resources by prohibiting or restricting urban and agricultural development in those areas while promoting development on more suitable lands. It provides an opportunity for involving public interest groups and decision-makers in first-cut land use policy about the distribution of land resources before more detailed choices must be made in the land use design stage of the land planning process. It adds a definite spatial dimension to the policy framework.

Land classification provides a rationale for spatially differentiating development regulations and for locating public facilities and infrastructure. The land use design concept pursued in the following chapters builds on the land classification plan and emphasizes human systems and social values within the urban area. The planner might think of the land classification plan as a simple, loose-fitting dress for the future community, whereas the urban land use design addressed in the next several chapters is a more carefully tailored suit, and more attention has been paid to accessories.

Table 12-2. Summary of Land Classifications

Land Classes	Purpose	Characteristics	Services	Residential Population Density
Developed	To provide for continued intensive development and redevelopment of existing cities	Lands currently developed for urban purposes, with urban services available	Usual municipal or public services, including water, sewer, recreation facilities, police, and fire protection, etc.	Existing moderate to high density
Transition	To provide for future intensive urban development on lands that are most suitable and that are most likely to be scheduled for provision of necessary public utilities and services	Lands being developed for urban purposes but which do not yet have usual urban services, lands necessary to accommodate population growth for next ten-year period, lands which can be readily serviced with usual urban services, lands generally free from severe physical limitations for development	Usual municipal or public services to be made available at the time of development or soon thereafter	Moderate to high density land uses
Community	To provide for clustered mixed uses to help shopping, housing, employment, and public service needs within the surrounding region	Lands characterized by a cluster of residential and commercial land uses in rural areas	Limited municipal-type services such as fire protection, etc. may have public water but no public sewer systems. Public sewers possible only to correct an existing or projected public health hazard.	Clustered low density (suitable for private septic tanks)
Rural	To provide for agriculture, forest management, mineral extraction, and various other low-intensity uses on large sites, including residences	Lands identified as appropriate locations for natural resources management and allied uses; lands with high potential for commercial	Private septic tanks and wells. Other services such as rescue squad, police and fire protection, etc.	Low-density single-family residence on large sites to be determined by local conditions and planning standards

Table 12-2, continued

Land Classes	Purpose	Characteristics	Services	Residential Population Density
	where urban services are not required and natural resources will not be unduly impaired; to encourage preservation of scenic resources and guard against the premature or unreasonable alteration of irreplaceable, limited, or significant natural, scenic, historic, or other resources not otherwise classified	agriculture, forestry, or mineral extraction; lands with one or more limitation that would make development costly and hazardous; and lands containing irreplaceable, limited, or significant natural, recreational, or scenic resources not otherwise classified		
Conservation	To provide for effective long-term management of tracts of land consistent with their significant, limited, or irreplaceable natural, recreational, or scenic resources essentially undisturbed by human occupancy	Lands that contain major wetlands, undeveloped shorelands that are unique, fragile, or hazardous for development, necessary wildlife habitats, publicly owned water-supply watersheds and aquifers, large undeveloped tracts of forests with limited access, lands with one or more characteristics which would make development unwise, lands providing significant recharge to groundwater, and lands which contain significant natural scenic or recreational resources	No services and limited access only	Essentially no residential development

Source: State of North Carolina 1985.

REFERENCES

Berry, David, and Robert E. Coughlin. 1973. *Economic implications of preserving ecologically valuable land in Medford, New Jersey.* Philadelphia: Regional Science Research Institute.

Bosselman, Fred, and David Callies. 1972. *The quiet revolution in land use control.* Washington, D.C.: U.S. Government Printing Office.

Bucks County Planning Commission. 1970. *Computerized guidance system manual: Development of a computerized guidance system for planning in Bucks County.* Doylestown: The author.

Dearinger, John A., et al. 1971. *Measuring the intangible values of natural streams, part 1.* Lexington: Water Resources Institute, University of Kentucky.

De Grove, John M. 1989. Growth management and governance. In *Understanding growth management: Critical issues and a research agenda,* ed. David J. Brower, David R. Godschalk, and Douglas R. Porter. Washington, D.C.: The Urban Land Institute.

Elfers, Karl B., and Maynard M. Hufschmidt. 1975. *Open space and urban water management, phase 1: Goals and criteria.* Raleigh: Water Resources Research Institute of the University of North Carolina, The University of North Carolina.

Kusler, Jon A. 1980. *Regulating sensitive lands.* Cambridge: Ballinger Publishing Company.

Lexington-Fayette Urban County Planning Commission. 1980. *1980 comprehensive plan: Growth planning system.* Lexington: The author.

McCormick, Frank. 1972. *Ecological survey of the wetlands at Mystic Islands.* Highpoint: William F. Freeman Associates.

McHarg, Ian. 1969. *Design with nature.* Garden City: Natural History Press.

Orange County, Chapel Hill, and Carrboro, N.C. Planning Departments. 1986. *Orange County–Chapel Hill–Carrboro joint land use plan.* Chapel Hill: The authors.

Reichert, Peggy A. 1976. *Growth management in the Twin Cities Metropolitan Area: The development framework planning process.* St. Paul: Metropolitan Council of the Twin Cities Area.

State of North Carolina. 1985. *Administrative code, subchapter 7B—land use planning guidelines, coastal management.* The author.

Triangle J Council of Governments. 1978. *Land classification plan: Executive summary.* Research Triangle Park: The author.

Wuenscher, James E., and James M. Starrett. 1973. *Landscape compartmentalization: An ecological approach to land use planning.* Report No. 89. Raleigh: Water Resources Research Institute of the University of North Carolina, North Carolina State University.

13

Commercial and Employment Centers

Nature alone cannot create good industrial sites. . . . planning without an awareness of industry's needs, can destroy potentially excellent sites from what is almost always a limited supply.
—Muncy 1959, 5

Planning for commercial and employment centers is a challenge to find a fit between (1) land use type, (2) activity center type, and (3) location. That is, the planner must first estimate the locational needs and space needs of future employment and commercial land use activities (e.g., office uses); second, allocate them to appropriate activity center types (e.g., central business district and office parks); and, third, locate those land use/activity center combinations in a sensible spatial pattern, on suitable lands, and in proper relationship to the regional transportation, labor markets, and consumer markets. The triangle in Figure 13-1 suggests the simultaneous three-way fit that is the essential objective.

The planner needs to understand employment and commercial land uses and the hierarchical spatial structure of activity centers as a basis for designing a future land use pattern. Merely designating sites for commercial and employment activity in the plan will not meet the needs of these activities; what must be designed is a comprehensive network of locations and facilities.

The emphasis in designing the spatial structure of commercial and employment centers is on regional-scale activities and activity centers. Although community-scale and neighborhood retail and smaller private and public facilities are part of the employment and commercial land use picture, we postpone most of our attention of those more local-scale facilities until the next chapter on residential communities. Also, what we do here is suggest a generic approach; the planner will need to adapt the approach to the size of the urban area, its legacy of commercial centers and employment specialization, and the government's economic development emphases for the future.

The land use plan for employment and commercial centers, and for residential communities in chapter 14, seems to be pretty specific. The resulting plan should not be taken too literally, however, because it is not implemented directly by the local government that adopts the plan. Rather it is the development process in the land market game that will actually interpret the plan and the market forces to decide what gets built where. The plan essentially creates a framework for that market, together with the development management program, to implement, but it is just that—a framework.

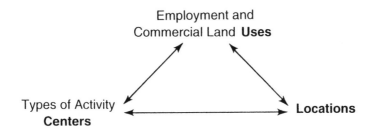

Figure 13-1. The Three-Part Challenge of Designing the Fit between Use, Activity Center Type, and Location. The planner simultaneously matches the different types of employment and commercial activities, or uses, with appropriate types of centers, at appropriate locations, to create an overall spatial structure.

Types of Land Use and Activity Centers

Types of Commercial and Employment Land Uses

In addition to transportation and parking, three types of uses occupy most of the land in employment and commercial areas: (1) *economic base employment* and related services; (2) regional-scale *retail and consumer services;* and (3) *community facilities.* Land uses associated with economic base employment include:

1. *Manufacturing:* The refining, fabrication, assembly, and storage of materials used in manufacture or produced on the site.
2. *Wholesaling and distribution:* Merchant wholesaling, manufacturer's sales branches, wholesale agents, brokers, and commission merchants, wholesale assemblers (most wholesaling involves warehousing and storage, some involves trucking terminals, and some involves only office and display space).
3. *Headquarters, developmental research, and back office activities* for manufacturing, wholesale, and other economic base industries.
4. *Nonlocal government activities* such as state government offices.
5. *Higher education.*

These economic base activities are not primarily oriented to local consumers and thus are less constrained in site selection by required access to local markets. However, they make very rigorous demands on access to utilities, the regional transportation network, and physical features of the land, such as level topography, large parcels, and visibility.

The nonbasic employment and population-serving activities include retail activities, personal services (e.g., cleaners, beauty salons, personal attorneys), and entertainment in the private sector. Public-sector consumer services, such as civic centers, sports arenas, museums, and community centers, also tend to locate in commercial centers with other population-serving activities. Transportation terminals are also likely to locate in such centers. In contrast to the more foot-loose economic-base activities, these consumer-oriented activities value access to local markets above all locational factors. Commercial services are automobile sales and repair establishments, building supply outlets, and other heavier commercial activity, which can be semi-industrial in character, that are also included under commercial activity.

Types of Activity Centers

The land use activities above locate in activity centers, which can be divided into two major categories: those that are primarily employment areas and those that are primarily commercial and civic activity areas. Economic-base employment tends to locate in employment areas, although finance and wholesaling may locate in what are primarily commercial centers (such as the central business district). Activities that serve populations tend to locate in commercial areas, although some retail and consumer and business services may locate in industrial parks. Both types of centers vary significantly, of course, in the size of the center and the size of its trade area, in density and mix of land uses, and in site design.

Employment Areas Areas devoted primarily to accommodating employment include industrial districts, industrial parks, office parks, planned employment centers, and a miscellaneous "other" category (Lochmoeller et al. 1975, 3–30; O'Mara 1982).

Industrial districts or areas—sometimes called manufacturing districts—typically consist of parcels that share an industrial zoning classification. Older industrial areas—established in the era before expressways—are usually located adjacent to ports and rail lines and have high site coverage and multilevel buildings. They often exhibit problems of structural obsolescence and incompatible mixtures of land uses (e.g., housing may be mixed in). Newer industrial districts typically consist of a mix of manufacturing plants, research and development laboratories, wholesaling office-warehouses, and some office buildings.

Industrial parks may also be called planned industrial districts, industrial estates, or, if they are oriented toward research laboratories and similar technological activities, research parks or R&D parks. More recently, business parks and office parks have been introduced, which deemphasize the industrial character of the land use activity and include a broader variety of industrial, wholesaling, and related business activities.

What distinguishes an industrial park from an industrial district is that the park is planned and developed as an optimal environment for industrial activities, or offices, and related service activities. The National Association of Industrial Parks specifies that the park also meet certain design standards for streets, utility systems, setbacks, percentage coverage limits, off-street parking, landscaping, building materials, signs, and appearance. The association also requires that the area be under one management, require design review, enforce restrictions on activities, and apply environmental standards (Lochmoeller et al. 1975).

The Industrial Research Council divides industrial parks into three categories—grouped by the standards they require of establishments (Conway et al. 1979, 37–39). The least restrictive category is an industrial district for heavy industry, which features large-scale development with access to rail, regional highway, and possibly a port. The second type of industrial park (with more restrictive standards) would likely be a distribution center or combined office-industrial center or office-distribution center. It has performance standards for noise, smoke, and other emissions, setbacks and buffer landscaping, off-street parking and truck loading, and controls over outdoor storage. The third type of park (with the highest site planning standards) would likely have offices, research and development laboratories, or light industry and would be lower density and place more emphasis on esthetic aspects of landscaping, building architecture, utilities, and loading and storage areas. It would constitute a more campuslike setting.

Planned employment centers are an extension of a mixed-use industrial park concept but are more carefully planned to facilitate interaction among activities within the center, including the sharing of facilities and materials-handling. Frequently, planned employment centers are larger, involve joint public-private investment, are located in prime locations close to markets and transportation, and are designed to minimize the need for vehicular movement within the center. Planned employment centers are also more likely than other types of centers to include consumer services for employees and even walk-to-work residences.

Planned employment centers include specialized industrial complexes of interrelated uses, such as research and technology parks, air cargo industrial complexes, and petrochemical complexes. The latter include chemical process plants that swap products by pipelines and the development-ecological complex, which combines industrial activity with waste processing, resource recovery, and energy utilization.

Industrial districts, industrial parks, and planned employment centers accommodate the entire range of manufacturing, warehousing, and distribution activities. Offices, either in office parks or as part of office-manufacturing or office-distribution combinations, are increasingly present in employment centers. Services for employees and visitors, including hotels and motels, restaurants, hair salons, drug stores, health centers, and recreation, are also emerging as important elements of employment centers.

The average-size industrial park is between 300 and 350 acres (Lochmoeller et al. 1975, 29–31). However, the range in size is great. About one-third are fewer than a hundred acres, and parks in excess of five hundred acres are relatively common. Large parks are warranted only at unique locations, such as in major metropolitan areas, near major transportation facilities such as large airports, and on large, level parcels in otherwise rugged landscapes. Usually, the public interest is better served by a wider distribution of sizes, locations, and types of employment areas in order to provide choices, reduce journeys to work, and avoid large concentrations of industrial and commuter traffic. The size at any particular location should be based on market demand for the particular type of park, allowance for expansion, and availability of land to be assembled. Table 13-1 provides some statistical information about sizes, densities, and parking requirements for industrial and office parks.

Table 13-1. Typical Characteristics of Industrial and Office Parks

Characteristics	Industrial Parks	Office Parks
Average size	300 acres	40 acres
Minimum recommended size	35 acres	none recommended
Typical floor-area ratios	0.1–0.3	avg. 5.7 for CBD; .27 otherwise
Typical employee densities	10–30/acre	none found
Typical parking spaces per employee	0.8–1.0	avg. 1.6 for CBD; 4.1 otherwise

Sources: For industrial parks, adapted from Lynch and Hack 1984, 306–11; for office parks, calculated from twelve case studies in O'Mara 1982.

Primarily Commercial Centers   Commercial centers are focal points for cultural, entertainment, and civic activities, as well as trade. They exhibit the highest concentrations of buildings and people, the highest land values, and the highest degree of interrelationship among land uses. In addition, commercial centers are very sensitive to access by consumers (i.e., residential areas), to locations of other centers, and to the transportation system. The appropriate number and types of commercial centers for a planning jurisdiction depends on the size of the population in the service area. For metropolitan areas, regions, and larger cities, commercial centers often include all of the following types:

A. Central business district(s)
B. Satellite business centers, including:
    1. Older business districts in the central city and older suburbs (often strip commercial developments)
    2. Shopping centers, usually planned projects under single ownership, divided into types by virtue of their size and the size of their trade areas:
        a. neighborhood shopping areas and centers, including convenience centers
        b. community-scale and discount shopping centers
        c. regional shopping centers
        d. super-regional, multifunctional shopping centers
        e. mixed-use development (MXD), often located within the central business district, incorporating office services, other employment, entertainment, lodging, and even residential and public/civic uses with shopping
C. Highway-oriented areas, generally at the edges of cities, including:
    1. Highway service areas (serving travelers)

2. Highway-oriented special purpose areas (e.g., clusters of auto sales and furniture establishments and off-price/outlet centers)

D. Other: convenience stores, strip commercial areas, fashion centers, industrial shopping centers (with a mix of retail, wholesale, and commercial services activities, perhaps dealing in lighting and plumbing supplies, building materials, millwork, catalog warehouse services, or auto specialty services), and isolated consumer goods and service businesses.

The central business district serves a large trade area, which usually exceeds the land use planning jurisdiction. In almost all cases it already exists, and the plan must deal with its future development and redevelopment, generally seeking to keep it compact, with small blocks and continuous retail frontage, integrating office employment, parking, and public transportation. Satellite centers accommodate businesses with smaller trade areas except for regional and super-regional shopping centers, which might actually exceed the trade area of smaller central business districts and host a range of activities beyond shopping—entertainment, cultural facilities, social and governmental services, office employment, and even civic events.

Satellite centers also serve establishments seeking lower-priced sites, escape from downtown congestion, and locations more convenient to suburban retail markets except for mixed-use developments. They are generally located in or near the central business district and developed more intensely (floor area ratio averaging 5.0), with taller structures, more vertical mixing, and more attention to pedestrian connections. Table 13-2 shows characteristics of the principal types of shopping centers, including the typical range of gross leasable area, size of site, population served, radius of market area, and leading tenant.

Highway-oriented business areas are less planned and less concentrated than satellite centers. One type provides goods and services to travelers and to others in automobiles. These land uses include fast food and other restaurants, service stations, and motels. Another type of highway-oriented business area consists of clusters of retailers that cater to comparison shopping by consumers and require large areas for display, for example, automobile sales and service areas, discount stores, furniture and appliance stores, and building supply centers. Because of their need for large sales areas, they cannot afford the rents per square foot in the central business districts and satellite centers that can be paid by stores (e.g., shoe stores) that use less space.

Matching Land Use Activities to Activity Center Type

The essential challenge is to allocate land use activities to different types of activity centers, at different locations, thereby forming a spatial structure of employment, retail activities, offices, and civic uses. The concept of combining land use type and activity center type is important to understand and can be illustrated for the case of office space. Unlike manufacturing and wholesale activities,

Table 13-2. Shopping Center Types and Characteristics

| Type of Center | Building or Sales Area (square feet) | | Site Area (acres) | Population Served | Radius of Market Area | | Leading Tenant | No. of Stores |
	Range	Typical			Minutes of Driving Time	Distance in Miles		
Neighborhood	30,000–100,000	50,000	2.5–10	2,500–40,000; 10,000 avg.	5–10	1.5	Supermarket	5–20
Community	100,000–300,000	150,000	10–30	40,000–150,000 50,000 avg.	10–20	3–5	Junior department store or variety store	15–40
Regional	300,000–1 million	400,000	10–60, usually 50+	150,000+	20–30	8+	One or more full-line department stores	40–80
Super-regional	500,000–1.5+ million	800,000	15–100+	300,000+	30+	12+	Three or more full-line department stores	100+
Mixed-use center (MXD)	500,000–2 million	1 million, 100,000–200,000 of which is retail	7–50, 15 avg.	—	mostly project based and nearby; some tourist and regional	—	Offices; one or more full-line department stores	—

Note: Parking spaces for shopping centers range from 3 to 5.5 spaces per 1,000 square feet of sales area, except for MXDs, which tend to be part of or adjacent to business centers with public transit service and contain 1.0 to 2.5 spaces per 1,000 square feet of floor space.

Source: Adapted from Casazza and Spink for Commercial and Retail Development Council, Urban Land Institute 1985, Tables 1.5, 2.2; Livingston 1979; Lynch and Hack 1984; Schwanke 1987, Appendix B; Witherspoon 1976.

which locate almost entirely in employment centers, and retail uses, which locate almost entirely in commercial centers, office space is spread across both types of development centers. Office space falls into five broad categories (O'Mara 1982, 39, 214).

1. *Professionals and major institutions,* which seek office space in centrally located prime sites, often in the central business district, for visibility, prestige, and convenience. This category includes many banking and other financial institutions, public relations and advertising firms, legal and accounting firms, and headquarters offices.
2. *General commercial office space,* for which prime location is less important but which still seeks good accessibility to transportation and markets. Suburban office parks and other sites near expressways are often suitable if adequate parking space is available.
3. *Medical office space* (including dental), which usually seeks locations near hospitals, either in medical office planned unit developments or on individual parcels.
4. *Quasi-industrial office space,* which often locates in industrial parks or planned employment centers, where performance standards exclude industrial uses incompatible with offices. Such office space may be used by industrial neighbors, which might include a mix of warehouses, distribution facilities, and light manufacturing concerns.
5. *Pure industrial office space,* which is built by large industrial corporations, often on their industrial property in industrial districts or in industrial parks.

These categories describe two types of office location requirements. One type requires little contact with the general public and is thus often better off in employment centers than commercial centers. The other type of office space is devoted to consumer services (some law and accounting firms are in this category) and would more likely locate in commercial centers in order to be accessible to clients. The land use plan should have activity centers that meet the needs of all types of office uses, as well as retail uses, industrial and wholesale employment, and community facilities.

The Plan-Making Process for Employment and Commercial Uses and Activity Centers

The main tasks are making preparatory analyses, formulating principles to govern land use and activity location, mapping suitability of the relevant land supply, designing a hierarchical spatial structure of employment and commercial centers, deriving space requirements for land uses and centers, assessing holding capacity of locations for proposed centers, and, finally, allocating space requirements to the centers, staying within their holding capacity constraints.

Conducting Preparatory Studies

The planner normally begins by reviewing studies of the urban economy and projections of employment and population. Studies of existing and projected land uses, transportation, and other infrastructure are also relevant.

Beyond those studies, the planner should analyze existing and emerging industrial, retail, and office land uses in existing and emerging employment and commercial centers. For the basic employment sector, such a study would analyze trends in production and organization as well as other factors that influence location and space requirements. For example, new industries may have different location and space requirements from existing industries. A separate but related study would analyze the physical characteristics of each existing employment center: delineating boundaries and potential adjacent areas for expansion, analyzing existing space use and trends, assessing the adequacy of space and services, estimating the linkages within and among employment areas, and assessing the center's accessibility to existing and proposed transportation, other utilities, and labor force. From these studies, the planner constructs a picture of the current structure of employment activity and current and emerging problems and opportunities.

A parallel series of studies is appropriate for commercial activities and centers. That is, the planner does studies of present and projected retail uses and consumer services as well as commercial centers. Greater attention would be paid to transportation (including traffic flow, parking, transit connections, and pedestrian flows) and consumer market (trade) areas than is the case for employment areas. Finally, a summary analysis is drafted on the combined structure of employment-oriented and commerce-oriented centers.

Formulating Location Requirements

In conjunction with the preparatory studies, the planning team should formulate location principles and standards for employment and commercial centers. Location requirements should reflect the community's goals and general policies as well as the findings of the preparatory studies. Location requirements reflect the particular community, but they also reflect considerations common to most U.S. communities. Thus, more explicit versions of the principles that follow are likely to be appropriate in most communities.

Employment Areas The following location principles illustrate the considerations that the planner should address, adapting them to the specific community's goals and concerns, the specific nature of the economy, and the physical geography.

1. *Appropriate terrain:* Reasonably level and well-drained land outside the floodplain is required. It should be not more than 5 percent slope. Occasionally, sites with steeper grades can be economically developed if the site is otherwise well located. For example, partly level and partly rolling terrain, with

trees, streams, and attractive landscape features, would be appropriate for headquarters office buildings or a low-density research development park.

2. *Range of locations:* A larger number of modest sized sites, distributed widely in space, is usually better than a few very large sites because they offer more choice to employers and better accessibility to employees.

3. *Different types of sites matched to types of employment centers:* Each of the various employment centers will have its own particular location requirements. For example, although heavy industry does not require attractive surroundings, offices, many light industries and wholesale-retail-distribution users want to locate in an area that will remain attractive. Thus, there should be sites to accommodate so-called nuisance industries, such as junkyards, construction equipment and materials businesses, fuel storage areas, decoplex complexes, and power plants, as well as sites that satisfy higher design standards.

4. *Sufficiently large vacant land areas:* Industrial parks and individual sites must be large enough to accommodate modern one-story buildings and accessory storage, loading, and parking areas. Areas should range in size from fifty to five hundred acres or more. Some may be formed through additions to existing employment districts.

5. *Access to transportation network:* The desired transportation system and the precise definition of access—distance to transit station, expressway interchange, railroad, port, or airport—may be different for each type of employment center and land use. For example, direct access to trucking routes and rail access is important for sites intended for warehousing and distribution uses. Highway sites should provide parcels ranging in depth from eight hundred feet up to two thousand or more feet from the road. Railroad sites should be at least a thousand feet in depth—and preferably two thousand feet or more—unless they are located in the central city.

6. *Visibility:* Some users and some types of employment centers desire prominent sites along freeways for public relations purposes.

7. *Access to labor force:* The planner may specify the characteristics of populations to which accessibility is desired.

8. *Availability of utilities:* In addition to water, sewer, electricity, and gas, the planner might specify special utility needs for particular industries or types of industrial areas. Some establishments drill their own wells for water supply and construct their own water and sewage treatment facilities. Some are such large consumers of power that utilities can be extended to even remote sites that are otherwise suitable.

9. *Compatibility with surrounding uses:* This criterion is especially applicable for heavy industrial areas and industrial processes with off-site noise, glare, odor, smoke, traffic, dangerous emissions, or waste storage areas. Compatibility is less critical for light industry, warehousing and distribution, office uses, or high-performance industrial parks. Truck and auto traffic generated by the employment center should not travel through residential areas.

10. *Compatibility with the natural environment:* Industries should avoid environmentally sensitive areas.

Commercial Centers Although particular standards are mentioned in the following list, the planner should derive standards for the specific circumstances in the community based on its goals and the scale and specific structure of the retail and services centers.

1. *Accessibility to the market area and direct access to traffic:* Accessibility is absolutely the top priority, although requirements vary from one type of center to another. For example:
   a. The *central business district* is located close to peak flow of auto, transit, and pedestrian traffic where retail, professional, financial, and related services can be conveniently accommodated and be accessible to public transportation, parking, and regional highways. Because the central business district already exists in most cases, these criteria apply to areas for expansion.
   b. *Satellite business centers* are located on major public transportation and auto routes, at intersections of major arterials serving the trade area population associated with the level of the center (from forty thousand to three hundred thousand people). The site should be large enough to accommodate not only the commercial activities but also parking, transit station, and other access to transportation network (from ten acres for a community shopping area, to fifty acres for a regional shopping center, to a hundred or more acres for a super-regional center).
   c. *Highway-oriented business centers* are located in outlying areas, adjacent to major highway, with adequate access to it and the regional highway network.
2. *Range of locations:* The range of sites should match the full range of types of business areas specified in the spatial structure hierarchy proposed for the land use design.
3. *Suitable terrain:* Sites should be reasonably level, well-drained land outside floodplains. (The central business district and other existing centers may not meet this criterion, but directions of expansion should consider terrain as well as such other amenities as visual and pedestrian access to water and other urban design features.)
4. *Availability of utilities:* Water and sewer are especially important. This criterion applies particularly to new sites in outlying areas not yet served by water and sewer.

Locational Suitability Analyses and Maps

This step involves an analysis of the land supply with respect to the location and site-size requirements derived above. Each type of center would have its own suitability map, plotting the implications of those location requirements for which data are available. Suitability maps might reflect, for example, the combined implications of relative proximity to expressways, interchanges, and railroads; proximity to existing or easily provided sewer and water services; suitability of the terrain; and proximity to traffic flow for commercial activity.

Schematic Design

At this point, after having studied location requirements and suitability maps but before deriving space requirements, the planner should develop a schematic design for the functional and spatial structure of employment and commercial areas. A schematic design focuses on finding a suitable location for each center and at the same time locating the centers in proper relationship to each other and to proposed future labor and consumer markets and transportation. The schematic design must, therefore, fit the residential and community facility designs addressed in the following two chapters.

The outcome of this step is a map with various centers shown as abstract symbols indicating locations only (not actual sizes and shapes), which will serve as the framework for the following steps. It is useful to specify this preliminary design before undertaking space requirements because the derivation of space requirements includes the allocation of floor space to various types of centers. That can be done more effectively if the planner has a sense of the number, location, and sizes of centers. Density standards may also partly depend on the proposed types, locations, and number of centers.

Space Requirements

Future space requirements are estimated somewhat differently for employment areas than for commercial centers.

Employment Areas Estimating the amount of land needed for employment areas in the land use design is generally done through four steps.

1. Determine the number of employees to be accommodated.
2. Develop future employment density standards, that is, employees per gross acre of employment center area.
3. Divide the future number of employees by density standards to estimate the number of acres that will be required.
4. Add a safety factor to accommodate the possibility that economic growth will be faster than expected or that densities will be lower than anticipated and to protect additional critical sites that will be required beyond the target year of the plan.

Employment Space Requirements Step 1: Determining the Future Number of Employees to Be Accommodated in the Land Use Plan The planned future number of employees is based on a combination of economic projections and economic development policy. Traditionally, land use planners have relied almost entirely on economic projection for estimating the employment-based demand for land. Over the past two decades, however, many planners have taken a less deterministic approach in which future employment is conceived as a combination of conscious policy choice, existing economic structure, and projection of trends. Thus, future employment levels, their distribution among economic sectors, their location requirements, and their requirements for space may reflect economic development policy for the community. This approach argues for inclusion of economic development planners on the land use planning team. For example, in Lee County, Florida, economic policy was to expand the manufacturing and related sectors of the economy to counteract a perceived overreliance on tourism, retirement, and related construction activities (Roberts 1983, 15–23).

Employment forecasts should be made for several sectors of the economy as well as for the economy as a whole. The most fundamental division is between basic- and nonbasic-sector employment. Beyond that, the breakdown of employment might separate out the largest sectors and particular target sectors of economic development policy. Finally, if the planning jurisdiction is large, perhaps a metropolitan region, an attempt should be made to allocate the employment to geographic sectors of the region. The geographic sectors can be defined in terms of radial sectors (e.g., north, east, south, west) and concentric rings (e.g., central city, suburban, and rural-urban fringe) or among service areas defined in the land classification plan. Table 13-3 illustrates a work table format for an allocation of future employment among a range of employment center types and general locations (built-up area versus outlying areas) in a hypothetical city. Note that the focus in this table is on economic base-oriented employment, not employment (such as retail and offices) that serves the population and will be discussed along with commercial centers.

Table 13-3. Allocation of Future Economic Base Employment by Type of Employment, Employment Center, and General Location

| | | Type of Employment Area | | | | | |
| | | Central Locations | | | Outer Locations | | |
Type of Employment	CBD	Industrial Districts	Industrial Parks	Other	Satellite Centers	Industrial Districts	Total
Intensive mfg.	0	800	200	0	0	0	1,000
Extensive mfg.	0	500	500	0	200	0	1,200
Warehouse/ distrib.	200	500	300	0	200	0	1,200
Office	500	100	500	0	200	0	1,300
Other	0	0	0	0	0	0	0
Total	700	1,900	1,500	0	600	0	4,700

Note: The figures in the table are illustrative only.

Employment Space Requirements Step 2: Develop Standards for Future Employment Densities The planner's estimate of future employment densities is based on existing densities in the study area, regional and national trends in various industries and for various types of employment centers, and community policy on economic development and land use.

For advance planning purposes, employment density is usually defined as gross density rather than net density. Net density is higher because it includes only the building site plus outdoor storage, parking, and loading areas but not undeveloped portions of the site, streets interior to the area and half the width of bounding streets, railroad spurs, and small, unusable parcels included in gross acreage. Net density also includes little space for expansion on site.

To determine and understand existing densities, a survey is desirable, but a short-cut method is more commonly used. For the more abbreviated approach, the planner uses existing land use data (acreage or floor area in various economic sectors) and data on the existing employment and then divides number of employees by number of acres. That information should be supplemented, where possible, with information on shortages and excesses in current space by industry and location; adequacy of the physical facilities for expected future economic activities (processing, assembly, storage); the likelihood of firms moving, expanding, or contracting; and the adequacy of parking, transportation, and other public and private services. The need to understand the area's existing industrial densities is another reason for including economic development planners on the land use planning team.

Density figures should be calculated, if possible, for each important sector of the economy—averaging the remainder for a residual "other" sector. Within these sectors, densities might also be categorized by type of employment center (e.g., industrial district, industrial park, multipurpose employment center, or central business district) and by general location in the urban region (e.g., inner city, suburban, or fringe). Variation in densities within an economic sector tends to be correlated with distance from the center of the urban area. For example, gross density in Charlotte, North Carolina, several years ago varied from 8.9 employees per acre in the outer, newer employment centers to 51 in the central business district (cited in Roberts 1983). Thus, the planner can estimate overall average density, densities of different types of employment center, density variation by location with respect to the city center, and perhaps separate industries into either low-density or high-density class.

Having examined the density characteristics of existing employment, the planner next develops density standards for the future. For existing industries, this generally consists of adjusting current densities based on trends and recent development examples. For example, a trend toward automated warehousing in the wholesale sector would increase the amount of land required per employee (decrease employee density) for the future. For new industries, density estimates are based on studies of cities where such activities already exist. In both approaches, economic development policy may suggest adjustments to promote economic goals. The appropriate number and types of density classes vary from one planning jurisdiction to another. Selection depends on the make-up of the economy (e.g., whether there is a large office sector or large manufacturing sector) and the variety of types of employment centers and locations. In areas under a hundred thousand population, a detailed breakdown by sector, type of employment center, and location is usually impractical and unnecessary. For larger places, the planner can begin with perhaps three to five density classes, increasing the number only if densities are found to vary widely. If two classes are used, they may simply be designated as either intensive (high-density) areas and extensive (low-density) areas or employment.

Lee County, Florida, for example, settled on a single density standard of seven employees per gross acre for the entire manufacturing sector, which was the focus of their economic development policy (Roberts 1983, 62–63). Other density standard examples are Charlotte, North Carolina (eight employees per gross acre) and Nashville-Davidson County (19.5 in 1970, decreasing to 13.4 in 1985) (Metropolitan Planning Commission of Nashville-Davidson County 1971; Roberts 1983, 58). Gross densities for industrial employment were found in a 1979 study of 18 cities to range from 3.3 in Phoenix to 24.4 in Seattle, with a median value of 8.4 (cited in Roberts 1983, 60). Standards projected for 1980 by the Urban Land Institute (Lochmoeller et al. 1975, 166–68), based on a survey of trends, are shown in Table 13-4.

Table 13-4. Employment Densities for Industrial Activities

Density Class	Employees per Acre		
	Net 1970	Gross 1970	Gross Projected for 1980
Intensive[a]	30	26	24
Intermediate[b]	14	12	10
Extensive[c]	8	6	8

a. Intensive industries include electrical equipment and supplies, instruments and related products, apparel and other textile products, and printing and publishing.
b. Intermediate industries include lumber and wood products, furniture and fixtures, primary metal industries, fabricated metal products, machinery (except electrical), miscellaneous manufacturing, food, textile mills, paper, chemicals, and rubber and plastic products.
c. Extensive industries include stone, clay and glass products, tobacco products, petroleum and coal products, leather and leather products, and wholesale trade.
Source: Lochmoeller et al. 1975, 166–68.

Again, it should be emphasized that densities will vary from place to place. Therefore, standards should be estimated locally and fitted to the breakdown of industries, centers, and general locations used in Table 13-3. It may not be that every cell in the table has a different density; the same density might be appropriate for several employment center types and locations. Table 13-5 illustrates density standards according to categories consistent with those in Table 13-3 for the same hypothetical city.

Table 13-5. Density Standards for Employment in the Land Use Plan by Type of Employment, Employment Center, and Location (employees per acre, gross densities)

| Type of Employment | Type of Employment Area | | | | | |
| | Central Locations | | | Outer Locations | |
	CBD	Industrial Districts	Industrial Parks	Other	Satellite Centers	Industrial Districts
Intensive mfg.	n/a	25	15	10	n/a	n/a
Extensive mfg.	n/a	12	10	10	8	n/a
Warehouse/ distrib.	10	10	8	10	8	n/a
Office	50	25	25	20	25	n/a
Other	30	10	10	10	10	n/a

Employment Space Requirements Step 3: Estimate Space Needs The next step is to divide the future expected employment in each density class by the density standard for that class: determining the gross acreage needed to accommodate employment in the class. The simplest approach is to do that for total future employment, including both jobs that survive from the present economy and new growth expected for the target year in each classification. The planner's estimate of additional acreage needed to accommodate employment is calculated by subtracting the present acreage in employment centers from the acreage projected to be needed for total future employment. Because not all existing plants and other facilities can be expected to rebuild to the normally lower-density standards during the planning period, that approach in effect introduces a built-in safety factor to allow for growth greater than forecasted. Another approach is to assume that existing employment will continue to occupy existing facilities at existing densities and to apply the future standards only to growth in employment. A third, more sophisticated, approach is to replace existing densities with two new ones: one to reflect the expansion, moving, and turnover that occurs within existing structures or expanded facilities on existing sites, and a second standard for employment in new structures. Table 13-6 illustrates the crude space requirements based on the employment allocation in Table 13-3 and the density standards in Table 13-5.

Space Requirements Step 4: Add a Safety Factor to Accommodate the Possibility That Employment Growth Is Greater Than Expected, or at a Lower Density Than Planned, and to Create an Industrial Reserve The addition of a safety factor is especially important in smaller urban areas where a single large new employer may by itself invalidate economic forecasts. It is also wise to protect prime industrial sites in anticipation of needs beyond the twenty-to-thirty-year target date

Table 13-6. Estimated Space Requirements (in Acres) for Employment Areas in the Land Use Plan

| Type of Employment | | Type of Employment Area | | | | | |
| | | Central Locations | | | Outer Locations | | |
	CBD	Industrial Districts	Industrial Parks	Other	Satellite Centers	Industrial Districts	Total
Intensive mfg.	0	32	13	0	0	0	45
Extensive mfg.	0	42	50	0	25	0	117
Warehouse/ distrib.	20	50	38	0	25	0	133
Office	10	4	20	0	8	0	42
Other	0	0	0	0	0	0	0
Total	30	128	121	0	58	0	337

of the land use, especially in regions where suitable land is scarce. In mountainous areas, for example, suitable land for economic development is scarce, and the protection of prime industrial land could be a matter of considerable long-run importance. There, the danger is that the scarce land for economic development will be taken by other uses in the short run, destroying the potentially better long-run utilization of the land for industrial uses. In level country, where a large supply of open land is adjacent to transportation and within reasonable range of existing utilities and labor market, the concept of an urban reserve beyond the target year of the plan is less appropriate. The amount of land required for the contingency of faulty forecasts and industrial reserve is largely a matter of local judgment; there is no standard practice.

The safety factor for space requirements may be added in one of several ways. It might be added to particular categories of employment centers, perhaps in a new row at the bottom of the equivalent of Table 13-6, or to specific centers and locations after the schematic design is fleshed out in Step 7. In the latter case, the safety-factor acres are added to the map first, then transferred to a summary table, and perhaps as a new row to the bottom of a revised version of Table 13-6.

The sample tables above are only suggestive; they have more columns and rows than is necessary for most planning jurisdictions. Fewer rows and columns, and different combinations of location and types of centers, may well be more appropriate in most places.

Space Requirements for Commercial Centers For purposes of the land use plan, a simple, broad-brush approach is generally used to estimate commercial space requirements. More detailed studies are useful in later refinements of the plan. On the demand side, they involve specialized investigations of retail, service, office, wholesaling, and other commercial functions, including market and purchasing power studies. On the supply side, they involve floor-area analyses, by ground area and above-ground floors, for individual centers as well as the study area as a whole, sometimes supplemented by studies of structures, parking, transportation, and urban design in particular commercial centers. For the long-range plan, however, the planner must distinguish four broad categories of commercial center occupants: retail, office, basic employment (wholesaling, and perhaps manufacturing), and public facilities (civic center or arena, open space, educational and cultural facilities, transportation terminals).

The derivation of future space needs for retail and office uses in commercial centers is different than the approach used for employment centers. Rather than being based on employment, it is based on projections for retail and office floor space, which in turn is based on population forecasts in the trade areas of the centers, and economic forecasts in the office sectors of the economy. Thus, if population growth of 35 percent is anticipated in the overall trade area, for example, retail and office space is expected to increase by 35 percent as well. If employment forecasts for medical professions, law, finance, insurance, real estate, and similar office-related categories of employment are dependable, they are preferable to population growth as the basis for office space needs. It is also preferable to base some of the highway-serving space requirements on estimates of transient population, especially in communities where tourism is an important sector of the economy. Other multipliers to consider are purchasing power (a combination of population, household income, and expenditure patterns), projected growth in the number of business establishments, and daytime population projections for the central business district and major centers.

Table 13-7 shows the steps in a procedure to calculate total future retail (step 1) and office (step 2) floor area requirements and allocate them to the various commercial and employment centers envisioned in the schematic land use design. Steps 1A and 2A estimate total retail and office floor area requirements respectively. Steps 1B and 2B then allocate those totals among the future centers proposed in the schematic land use design. The future distribution of space among centers is based on a number of factors, including the present proportionate distribution of space among centers (see proportions calculated in steps 1B-i and 2B-i); the schematic land use design; goals and general policies; judgments about local, regional, and national trends in shopping behavior and merchandising practices; the transportation plan; and standards about convenience in shopping and services. The figures in Table 13-7, like earlier tables in this chapter, are based on a hypothetical city.

The allocation of retail and office space to commercial centers implies such related space needs as parking, loading space, and landscaping. Some of the projected floor area can also be in floors above ground level, which would not take up ground space. Table 13-8 suggests a procedure to convert future retail and office-floor area (calculated in Table 13-7) into ground-area requirements that account for related space needs and the fact that some of the floor space is above ground level. Table 13-8 focuses on the central business district, but similar tables would be calculated for each center in the land use design scheme.

In steps 1 (retail) and 2 (office) of the table, total floor area is converted to required ground-floor area—the land needed for what is known as the building foot-

Table 13-7. Estimating Retail and Office-Floor Area Requirements for the Land Use Plan and Allocating Them among Commercial and Employment Centers (estimates are in square feet)

Step 1: Retail Floor Area
  1A. Estimating aggregate needs
   i. Total retail floor area in planning jurisdiction (base year)   910,000
   ii. Multiplier (1 plus population growth)   2
   iii. Total retail floor area, Year XXXX   1,820,000
  1B. Allocating total retail floor area among commercial centers and employment centers
   i. Present breakdown among existing centers (to use as one basis for allocation of future activity)

	Proportion	Square Ft.
CBD	0.7	640,000
Satellite Center A	0.3	270,000
Satellite Center B	0.0	0
Etc.	0.0	0
Highway clusters (as a class)	0.0	0
Employment Center X	0.0	0
Etc.	0.0	0
Neighborhood shopping (as a class)	0.0	0
Other	0.0	0
Total	1.0	910,000

   ii. Future breakdown among future centers in the land use design, by proportion, and implied future square footage

	Proportion	Square Ft.
CBD	0.6	1,092,000
Satellite Center A	0.2	364,000
Satellite Center B	0.0	0
Etc.	0.2	364,000
Highway Clusters (as a class)	0.0	0
Employment Center X	0.0	0
Etc.	0.0	0
Neighborhood shopping (as a class)	0.0	0
Other	0.0	0
Total	1.0	1,820,000

Step 2: Office-Floor Area
  2A. Estimating aggregate needs
   i. Total office-floor area in planning jurisdiction
       (base year)   300,000
   ii. Multiplier (population growth, or employment
        growth in financial, insurance, real estate, and
        related categories of employment forecast)   2
   iii. Total office-floor area, Year XXXX   600,000
  2B. Allocating total office-floor area among commercial centers and employment centers
   i. Present breakdown among existing centers (to calculate proportions as one basis for allocation of future activities)

	Proportion	Square Ft.
CBD	0.8	240,000
Satellite Center A	0.2	60,000
Satellite Center B	0.0	0
Etc.	0.0	0

Employment Center A	0.0	0
Employment Center B	0.0	0
Etc.	0.0	0
Other	0.0	0
Total	1.0	300,000

ii. Breakdown among future centers in the land use design: proportions determine future square footage

	Proportion	Square Ft.
CBD	0.70	420,000
Satellite Center A	0.15	90,000
Satellite Center B	0.00	0
Satellite Center C	0.05	30,000
Etc.	0.00	0
Employment Center A	0.00	0
Employment Center B	0.00	0
New Employment Center	0.10	60,000
Etc.	0.00	0
Other	0.00	0
Total	1.00	600,000

Note: Figures are illustrative only.

print. Steps 3 through 6 estimate additional ground area needed for parking, loading, waste, and landscape areas as well as a contingency factor. In step 3, the necessary ground area for parking to support retail and office-floor area is based on a desired or assumed ratio of floor space to parking space (adjusting for the fact that parking below ground and above ground does not require ground area). In step 4, ground area for loading and service areas is added as a percentage of retail-floor area. Ground area for landscaping and wasted land on retail and office parcels is added in step 5 as a percentage of ground-floor area. Step 6 adds a contingency factor, also on a percentage basis, to account for possible underprojections of retail and office use and possible erroneous assumptions about parking, loading, and landscaping. Finally, in step 7, the results of the preceding steps are summed and converted to the number of acres required in the target year in order to accommodate retail and office needs, including parking. The current number of acres in retail, office, and related parking in the central business district is subtracted from that estimated total future space requirement to estimate the required net increase in acres necessary to accommodate growth. Again, the figures in Table 13-8 are illustrative only, and are based on a hypothetical city.

Space requirements for other commercial centers envisioned in the future plan are estimated in similar fashion, but assumptions about total floor-space percentages, parking ratios, and perhaps loading, landscaping, and contingency space would vary from center to center and community to community. Regional shopping centers, for example, usually have a parking ratio of at least 1:1 and often close to 2:1, compared to a lower ratio generally provided in the central business district. Space for highway-oriented centers are more dependent on studies of inter- and intra-regional traffic as well as population in trade areas. Because highway uses tend to require greater space per customer, they may be forecasted separately.

Table 13-8. Calculating Ground-Area Requirements for Land Use Design, Central Business District (CBD) (for converting floor-area needs to total ground area in acres)

Step 1: Retail Ground-Floor Area Requirements	
Retail floor area in CBD (from Table 13-7)	1,092,000
Divide by assumed average number of floors in retail use	1.1
Ground-floor area requirement for retail use	992,727
Step 2: Office Ground-Floor Area Requirements	
Office-floor area in CBD (from Table 13-7)	420,000
Assume percent in office buildings (as opposed to floors in buildings above retail ground-floor space)	0.4
Total office use in office buildings	168,000
Divide by assumed average number of floors in office buildings	2.5
Ground-floor area requirement for office use	67,200
Step 3: Parking for Retail and Office	
Desired ratio for retail (multiply by total retail)	0.75
Parking space for retail use	819,000
Desired ratio for office (multiply by total office)	0.75
Parking space for office use	315,000
Total parking square footage for retail and office	1,134,000
Subtract underground and above-ground parking	100,000
Total ground area for retail and office parking	1,034,000
Step 4: Loading Area	
Assume certain percent of total retail area (adjust from current percent)	0.05
Loading area for retail uses	54,600
Step 5: Waste and Landscaping	
Assume certain percent of total retail and office ground-floor area (adjust from current percent)	0.2
Waste and landscaping area	211,985
Step 6: Contingency (Safety Factor)	
Assume certain percent of total steps 1-5	0.2
Contingency ground area	472,103
Step 7: Summarizing Total Ground Area Implied by Retail and Office Uses in CBD	
Retail use ground area (from step 1)	992,727
Office use ground area (from step 2)	67,200
Parking ground area (from step 3)	1,034,000
Loading ground area (from step 4)	54,600
Waste and landscaping (from step 5)	211,985
Contingency (from step 6)	472,103
Total square feet implied by CBD retail and office uses	2,832,615
Equivalent area in acres (divide by 43,560 sq. ft./acre)	65
Subtract current acres in retail, office, and related parking uses	25
Net increase to CBD in retail- and office-implied uses	40
Subtract available vacant acres in CBD (from land use survey)	10
Net surplus (deficit) acreage in CBD after allowing for retail and office growth to Year XXXX (negative number indicates implicit displacement in surrounding neighborhoods or industrial areas)	-30

Notes: 1. These calculations do not yet account for space required for new open space, civic functions and community facilities, transportation facilities, and residences.
2. Although this table is illustrated for the CBD, similar tables would be constructed for other centers proposed in the land use design.
3. Figures in the table are illustrative only.

The central business district, and some of the other commercial centers, will contain activities and facilities in addition to retail and office uses. Space for civic structures, arenas, residences, wholesale and industry, transportation, and open space will also have to be estimated and added to the overall space requirements. Some retail uses and population-serving offices will also locate in predominantly employment areas, such as mixed-use industrial parks, and space for such retail and office activities must be added to the basic employment space when calculating total space requirements for those employment areas. Techniques for other uses are addressed in other chapters, and Table 13-8 can be modified to add those space requirements as they are estimated. The sum of all these needs, for each center, constitutes the space requirement estimates for commercial centers and employment centers.

Holding Capacity Analysis

On the supply side, the planner measures the number of acres of suitable land available at each of the locations slated for an employment or commercial center in the schematic design. For existing centers, this analysis uses the preparatory studies discussed earlier. It focuses on vacant and underutilized space within the center, adjacent areas for possible transition to commercial or employment uses, and special situations that signal a potential future supply of space (e.g., underutilized warehouse space possibly suitable for office, retail, or residential space). Mitigation of crowded conditions may shrink the potential space available for new growth. When expansion of a commercial center involves encroachment into surrounding areas presently in noncommercial uses, adjustments must be made for losses in housing stock, other land uses, and vacant land. The final commercial center analysis is a summary of space deficits, surpluses, and opportunities for each existing center, constituting an assessment of capacity for holding additional office, retail, and other appropriate uses.

For sites of proposed new centers, the number of suitable acres is measured for each location. Sites can be shown on maps and annotated with notes about special conditions such as present and proposed availability of utilities and transportation. The amount of land available at each location, with the characteristics that make it attractive and suitable for a commercial or employment center, would be shown in a table.

Making the Trial Distribution of Space Requirements

In this near-final step, the planner matches the supply of suitable land in the proposed hierarchy of employment and commercial areas with the space needs of basic employment, retail, office, and other facilities to be located in such areas. Space needs are balanced against the holding capacity for each area proposed in the schematic design. The task combines assigning desired uses to suitable available space under the proposed schematic and holding capacity analysis; shifting some uses to centers with excess capacity (where it makes sense within the design concept); adjusting holding capacity and suitability by changing proposed boundaries or increasing density assumptions; increasing transportation and utilities services; and adjusting the design concept to add—or subtract—centers.

Where expansion of existing commercial and employment centers is proposed, care must be taken to assess impacts on adjacent neighborhoods. Expansion of the central business district and other centers in already built-up areas may conflict with neighborhood conservation objectives, and some resolution of the conflict must be achieved in the land use design. Possibly, the commercial or employment center can be developed more intensively to prevent it from spreading outward into residential areas or commercial uses, employment, and community facilities can be integrated with the neighborhood design.

The resulting distribution of space requirements can be summarized in an accounting table or checklist similar to Table 13-9. In addition to basic employment, retail, and office space, the table reflects the possible allocation of community facilities, civic uses, open space, and residential uses to the extent envisioned in the schematic design.

Sometimes in outer areas, general locations rather than specific sites might be designated for centers. A proposed center is indicated on the map merely as a symbol, such as a circle of appropriate size. Space requirements for such centers are deducted from the planning zones where the center is located. Specific siting, however, is either left to future planning at a more detailed level or to be decided during the urban development process as part of the review of specific development proposals by developers.

Summary

The design of employment and commercial areas for the land use plan is a complex task. It involves coordinating specific types of land use activities within a spatial system of multipurpose activity centers, each located in proper orientation to other centers, the transportation system, and to the residential communities of the area. The land uses include not only business activities but also civic uses, open space, community facilities, and even residences.

The tables suggested in this chapter help the planner account systematically for space needs and land supply. They are well suited to computerized spreadsheets, which can quickly trace the impacts of changes in density and spatial distribution assumptions on space requirements. The tables, of course, can be adapted to fit the planning situation. Similarly, the suitability analyses and the calculation of the holding capacity are compatible with computerized GIS. GIS overlay techniques can map the areas of suitable lands, in varying degrees of suitability, and also calculate the number of acres automatically. GIS also facilitates testing different weighting schemes for suitability factors to determine their implications on the spatial pattern and amounts of suitable lands.

Table 13-9. Work Table of Space Allocation for Employment and Commercial Centers

Type of Center and Use	Allocation		
	Acres[a]	Employment	Floor Area of Retail
Employment Centers			
Industrial District A			
Industrial uses	XX	XXX	
Other	XX	XXX	
Total	XX	XXX	
Industrial Park B			
Manufacturing	XX	XXX	
Wholesaling	XX	XXX	
Total	XX	XXX	
Industrial Park C			
Manufacturing	XX	XXX	
Wholesaling	XX	XXX	
Office	XX	XXX	
Total	XX	XXX	
Planned Employment Center			
Manufacturing	XX	XXX	
Wholesaling	XX	XXX	
Office	XX	XXX	
Retail	XX	XXX	XXX
Total	XX	XXX	
Commercial Centers			
CBD			
Retail	XX	XXX	XXX
Office	XX	XXX	
Wholesale	XX	XXX	
Civic	XX	XXX	
Transportation	XX		
Open Space	XX		
Other	XX	XXX	
Total	XX	XXX	
Satellite Center A			
Retail	XX	XXX	XXX
Office	XX	XXX	
Other	XX	XXX	
Total	XX	XXX	
Satellite Center B			
Retail, etc.	XX	XXX	XXX
Highway-Oriented Cluster A			
Retail, etc.	XX	XXX	XXX
Other (scattered, shown on an accompanying map)			
Manufacturing	XX	XXX	
Wholesale	XX	XXX	
Office	XX	XXX	
Retail	XX	XXX	XXX
Civic	XX	XXX	
Transportation terminals	XX	XXX	

a. Acreage figures are gross acres; they include land for streets and other rights-of-way and wasteland. Acreage for each use includes parking, loading, landscaping, and waste associated with these uses. Total acreages include contingency figures.

Following this design of the pattern of employment and commercial centers within the land use design, the remaining supply of vacant and renewal land is summarized as an available land supply for residential and community facilities, which have not yet been addressed. This land supply can be annotated on maps and in tables. In addition, the number of existing dwellings lost in conversion to employment and commercial space, and the land involved, should be summarized by planning district. These losses to existing housing supply must be replaced in planning for residential areas (chapter 14).

REFERENCES

Casazza, John A., and Frank H. Spink, Jr., for the Commercial and Retail Council of the Urban Land Institute. 1985. *Shopping center development handbook.* 2d ed. Community Builders Handbook Series. Washington, D.C.: The Urban Land Institute.

Conway, H. M., L. L. Liston, and R. J. Saul. 1979. *Industrial park growth: An environmental success story.* Atlanta: Conway Publications.

Livingston, Lawrence, Jr. 1979. Business and industrial development. In *The practice of local government planning,* ed. Frank So, Israel Stollman, Frank Beal, and David Arnold. Washington, D.C.: International City Management Association.

Lochmoeller, Donald C., Dorothy A. Muncy, Oakleigh J. Thorne, and Mark A. Viets, principal authors, with the Industrial Council of the Urban Land Institute. 1975. *Industrial development handbook.* Community Builders Handbook Series. Washington, D.C.: Urban Land Institute.

Lynch, Kevin and Gary Hack. 1984. *Site planning.* 2d ed. Cambridge: MIT Press.

Metropolitan Planning Commission of Nashville-Davidson County. 1971. *Analysis of employment and land use relationships* Nashville: The author.

Muncy, Dorothy A. 1959. *Industrial land development.* Technical Report No. 2. Baltimore: Baltimore Regional Planning Council, Maryland State Planning Commission.

O'Mara, W. Paul, for the Industrial and Office Park Development Council and Commercial and Retail Development Council of the Urban Land Institute. 1982. *Office development handbook.* Community Builders Handbook Series. Washington, D.C.: The Urban Land Institute.

Roberts, Thomas H. and Associates. 1983. *Industrial land use needs in the Lee County comprehensive development plan.* Decatur, Ga.: The author.

Schwanke, Dean, principal author, for the Urban Development/Mixed-Use Council of the Urban Land Institute. 1987. *Mixed-use development handbook.* Community Builders Handbook Series. Washington, D.C.: The Urban Land Institute.

Witherspoon, Robert E., Jon P. Abbett, and Robert M. Gladstone. 1976. *Mixed-use developments: New ways of land use.* Washington, D.C.: The Urban Land Institute.

14

Residential Areas

[This concept of land use organization is] named the urban village. "Urban" implies density, efficiency, diversity, balance. "Village" implies cohesiveness, compactness, a manageable scale.
—Council on Development Choices for the '80s 1981, 59

Of all the land use sectors, the residential sector is the largest user of urban space; it constitutes from 30 to 50 percent of developed land in an urban area. Moreover, in addition to dwellings, residential areas contain other uses that support the day-to-day life of households—schools and day-care centers, local [+ police, fire, hospital] shopping, playgrounds and open space, churches, clubs, and community centers, and a circulation network for pedestrians and bicycles as well as automobiles and perhaps public transportation. In other words, residential areas are minicommunities within the larger urban community, so the planner must think not just of allocating housing, but of designing a variety of living environments to provide choices for households with varied values, needs, and abilities to pay. Yet these communities are not self-sufficient, either; they must be spatially related to each other, to the regional network of employment and commercial centers, and to the open space system.

The function of a residential area is to support the needs of residents in a way that also furthers such community goals as environmental quality and efficiency in governmental services. Neighborhoods serve the following functions (Richman and Chapin 1977; Richman 1979, 450–52):

1. *Shelter*, which encompasses the traditional concern of housing, and basic services, such as water, sewer, and electricity.
2. *Security*, providing a safe, stable, and ordered setting free of danger from traffic, violence, criminal actions, and other physical and psychological hazards.
3. *Child-rearing*, facilitating transmission of values through family, neighbors, peer groups, churches, community organizations, schools, and play space.
4. *Symbolic identification*, providing a sense of place, belonging, pride, and satisfaction to the resident.
5. *Social interaction*, providing personal associations through social networks, organizations, and physical facilities.

6. *Leisure*, providing recreation, entertainment, cultural, and educational facilities, and programs and open space.
7. *Accessibility*, providing access to employment, shopping, and personal services required to maintain a household, as well as to regional-scale entertainment and leisure opportunities.
8. *Financial investment*, protecting the large financial stake in the residence, which often serves as an investment for future financial security for the homeowner.
9. *Public efficiency*, minimizing public or societal costs associated with meeting the needs of households, including the costs of water and sewer, garbage and trash collection, fire and police services, education, recreation, transportation, and the costs of maintaining public capital improvements such as streets and sidewalks.

The land use design should organize residential areas to serve these functions.

Residential Design Concepts

A number of physical design concepts have been proposed to promote the social and other functions of residential areas. They are useful for analyzing demand for community facilities and as models for organizing the residential sector of a land use plan.

One such design concept is the neighborhood unit principle, which has been widely used for a long time. First conceived by Clarence Perry (1929) the neighborhood unit consists of one thousand to five thousand people, has clear boundaries, contains pedestrian paths connecting a public elementary school and recreation facilities, and incorporates a connected open space system. In one example, Clarence Stein and Henry Wright applied Perry's concept to the design of Radburn, New Jersey. Radburn opens the front doors of houses to an open space/pedestrian path network and the back doors to parking and the street. Thus, there was a separated, dual system of circulation. Figure 14-1 diagrams several versions of this more traditional neighborhood planning concept, including both Perry's and Stein and Wright's schemes.

Certain aspects of the traditional neighborhood concept have been criticized for stifling the kind of interactive social community life available in traditional city neighborhoods by removing pedestrian activity from the street, and for limiting the neighborhood to a single—residential—use with a limited range of housing types. The notion of a homogeneous neighborhood population to foster face-to-face contact, socialization, and social participation has also been criticized on several counts. First, such a neighborhood encourages income and class exclusivity as well as racial, ethnic, and economic segregation (Isaacs 1948). In addition, by being incorporated into Federal Housing Administration guidelines, the concept encouraged the production of vast areas of look-alike subdivisions. More fundamentally, social science analysis since Perry first outlined the neighborhood con-

Figure 14-1. Versions of the Neighborhood Unit Concept.

a. (right) Clarence A. Perry's Plan. Perry was one of the first to give some consideration to the physical form of the neighborhood unit. It is substantially the same as in Stein's diagram but suggests that the maximum radius for walking be only one-quarter mile. Accepting the practice that was and still is prevalent, shopping areas are situated at intersecting traffic streets on the outside corners rather than at the center of the unit. From Gallion and Eisner 1986, 300.

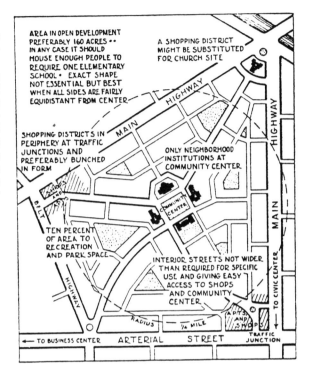

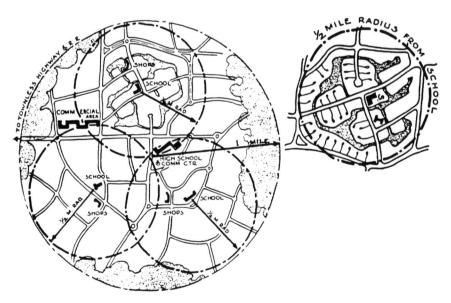

b. (above) The Neighborhood Unit—Clarence Stein's Conception. These sketches are Clarence Stein's determinations of the proper design of the neighborhood unit. In the diagram on the right, the elementary school is at the center of the unit and within a half-mile radius of all residents in the neighborhood. A small shopping center for daily needs is located near the school. Most residential streets are suggested as culs-de-sac or dead-end roads to eliminate through traffic, and park space flows through the neighborhood in a manner reminiscent of the Radburn plan. The diagram on the left shows the grouping of three neighborhood units served by a high school and one or two major commercial centers, the radius for walking distance to these facilities being one mile. From Gallion and Eisner 1986, 299.

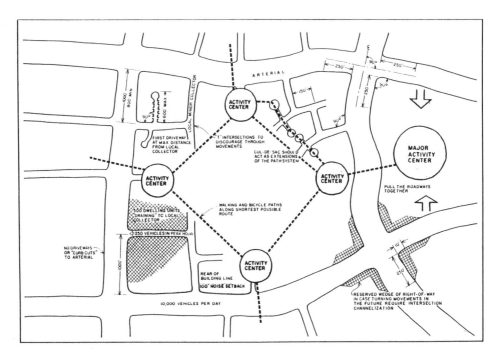

c. (above) A concept for the plan of Flower Mound New Town by R. H. Pratt Associates and Alan M. Voorhees and Associates from the basic theories of Richard Llewelyn-Davies. From Barnett 1982, 145.

cept has shown social interaction to encompass an activity space larger than the neighborhood and to be quite variable in size—depending on socioeconomic class, stage in the life cycle, and ethnic background of residents (Richman and Chapin 1977).

A more recent, and significantly different, neighborhood design concept is the neotraditional neighborhood (Krieger 1992). Like Perry's neighborhood concept, this design proposes a walkable community in conjunction with public spaces and institutions to encourage social interaction and a sense of community. In addition, the neotraditional neighborhood concept encourages a gridlike street and lot pattern found in traditional city and town neighborhoods and includes stores and jobs within the neighborhood. Also, its streets are designed for pedestrian movement and play as well as access to residences, thereby reducing the primacy of the automobile. The concept incorporates a regulatory code with highly specific standards to control the implementation of the plan, featuring minimum densities (not maximum as is usual for zoning regulations) and required minimum amounts of land in commercial, civic, and employment activities. For example, in Duany and Plater-Zyberk's proposal for a 350-acre new community in Gaithersburg, Maryland, there are 1.2 million square feet of shopping and 900,000 square feet of commercial office space, along with 1,600 dwellings of various sizes and types and a school, parks, and cultural center.

A related, more urban, concept is the "pedestrian pocket," sometimes called a transit-oriented development (TOD) (Kelbaugh, ed. 1989; Calthorpe 1990). A TOD is a cluster of housing, retail space, and offices within a quarter-mile of a transit station. It contains a mix of two- to three-story walk-ups, a mixed-use "main street," day-care facilities, open space, regional shopping mall or "back office" employment center, and a transit station. The idea is to weave together the currently isolated land use components of a suburban environment. A TOD ranges from fifty to a hundred acres in size, smaller than a new town but more heterogeneous and larger than many planned unit developments (PUDs). It contains about two thousand dwellings and about a million square feet of commercial and employment activities. It is meant to be home to a mix of income groups and household types—young singles, married couples, families with children, empty nesters, and the elderly. A typical design program for a sixty-to-ninety-acre pedestrian pocket might include a light rail station; 750,000 square feet of office space; sixty thousand square feet of neighborhood shopping; a thousand parking places; four hundred units of townhouses/duplexes; fifty single-family detached dwellings; 150 units of elderly congregate living facilities; two day-care centers; and community facilities such as a police station, fire house, town hall-type meeting space, post office, library, and churches; and twelve acres of parks and recreation facilities. Figure 14-2 illustrates the pedestrian pocket concept. The upper part of the figure diagrams the TOD concept, and the lower part suggests how a hierarchy of TODs might be organized around a public transportation system. Sacramento, California, is promoting the TOD concept in its land use plan and proposed development management program (Sacramento County 1990).

The planner must also recognize the continuing attraction of the suburban neighborhood model, which consists of low-density homogeneous neighborhoods comprised of single-family dwellings, lawns, garages and carports, curving streets, and culs-de-sac. Schools, office parks, shopping centers, and recreation areas are located within convenient distance for commuting by automobile. This model promotes mobility through the use of automobiles; thus it incorporates garages and driveways into residential layouts and generous off-street parking at shopping, employment, and other destinations. The suburban model more or less assumes the traditional middle-class household with two parents, children, and several cars. It has been criticized for creating auto-dependency, and isolating children, the elderly, and others who cannot drive or cannot afford a car.

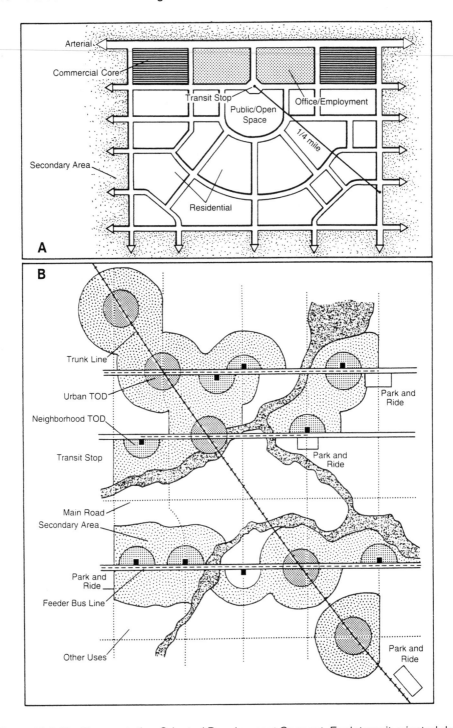

Figure 14-2. The Transportation-Oriented Development Concept. Each transit-oriented development (TOD) of 50–100 acres is a cluster of housing, retail space, offices, and civic uses centered on a transit station. TODs would be strung like beads along transit lines. From Sacramento County 1990, 4–5.

The planner uses design concepts such as the neighborhood concept, neotraditional neighborhood, pedestrian pocket, suburban subdivision, planned unit development, apartment project, or others as modules for planning residential areas. (See De Chiara and Koppelman 1982, 551–72 and De Chiara 1984, ch. 1 for additional concepts and discussion of residential planning units.)

Beyond those design modules, however, the planner needs concepts that weave those neighborhood-size residential units into the larger-scale residential community. The arrangement of TODs illustrated in the bottom half of Figure 14-2 illustrates such a connective, community-building concept. Another model is the hierarchical concept of neighborhood-village-town used in the design of the new town of Columbia, Maryland (Figure 14-3a-f). The concepts of, from smaller to larger, housing cluster (diagram a), neighborhood (diagram b), village (diagram c), and town (diagram d) form a nested system of spatial communities. The sizes of neighborhoods

Figure 14-3. (below and following page) A Hierarchical Nested Pattern of Residential Community Units. Housing clusters are grouped into neighborhoods, which are grouped into villages, which are grouped into a town. Neighborhoods, villages, and the town all have centers of commercial and civic activities. From Hoppenfeld 1967, 389–409.

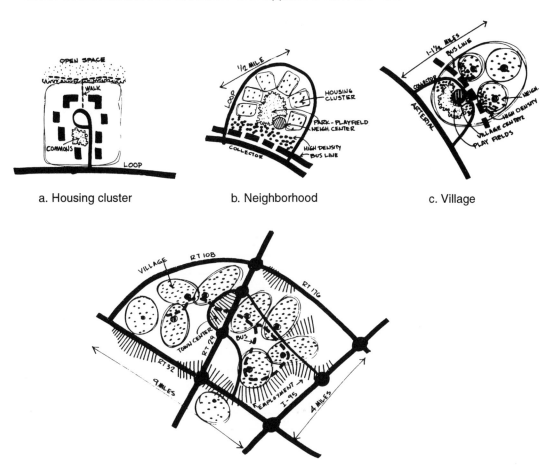

a. Housing cluster   b. Neighborhood   c. Village

d. Town

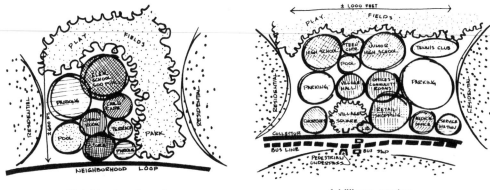

e. Neighborhood center   f. Village center

and villages are determined by the nature and size of commercial areas and community facilities to be located there—particularly schools in the case of Columbia (Hoppenfeld 1967, 406). A neighborhood center (diagram e) consists of a kindergarten through fifth grade elementary school supplemented by a day-care center, a small store, a multipurpose meeting room, park and playgrounds, and serves particularly the most place-bound residents—mothers and young children. A village center (diagram f) contains a junior or senior high school, a cluster of local shopping establishments, community service facilities and institutions, and recreation facilities to provide the basic goods and services to support households in a trade area population of ten to fifteen thousand. Pedestrian and bicycle, automobile, and bus circulation networks link the parts of the community.

The Planning Process

The tasks for designing residential areas are like those already applied to open space and commercial and employment centers in the preceding chapters. They include formulating location requirements, mapping the suitability of vacant and renewal land, deriving space requirements, analyzing holding capacity of suitable lands, adding local shopping and other population-supporting uses and facilities, and, finally, synthesizing all those considerations into a land use design.

Task 1: Formulating Location Requirements

Location principles apply to in-fill development in built-up areas, to the reuse of land in renewal areas, to partially developed areas, and to entirely new development on the rural-urban fringe. Location principles derive from local goals and higher-level policy and consumer preferences. Because each community should develop its own location principles, the following examples should be considered only as illustrative.

For Developed Areas

1. Residential communities will be protected from incompatible uses and intrusion of unnecessary traffic.
2. Community facilities will be located to create reasonable service areas—some metropolitan in size, some community scale, and some neighborhood-serving; and provide reasonable accessibility for existing neighborhoods.
3. Proposed changes to neighborhoods and communities must reflect community needs concerning housing types, commercial uses, and public facilities. They must also be sensitive to residents' values, life-styles, and activity patterns, and to the symbolic values of existing physical features and locations.

For Newly Developing Areas

1. Residential areas will be located to be accessible to activity centers.
2. Residential areas will be located in areas with excess capacity in community facilities and in areas that can be served most efficiently by extending existing facilities or constructing new facilities.
3. Residential areas will be built at densities and in spatial patterns that encourage energy-saving and congestion-reducing travel behavior, for example, using public transportation, carpooling, taking shorter trips, and walking and biking.
4. Housing will be located in hospitable micro-climates to save energy in heating and cooling.
5. Residential areas will be located out of floodplains and away from fragile ecosystems.
6. There will be a reasonable range of choice, among housing and neighborhood types, for all income groups.

For Community Service Facilities   (See also chapter 15):

1. Transportation, water and sewer, and other community service facilities such as parks and schools, will be accessible at a level of service established by community goals.
2. Local (neighborhood and community-scale centers) shopping facilities will be available at convenient locations, with adequate access and parking, and will be visually attractive. Neighborhood centers will be within walking distance or within convenient driving distance in low-density areas. Community-serving centers will be on public transportation routes and located on a major thoroughfare, preferably near major intersections and interchanges, with due consideration for buffering from adjacent residential areas.
3. Churches, community centers, clubs, and other local community-serving institutions will have land reserved in convenient locations, on circulation networks.

Task 2: Plotting Suitability for Residential Area Development

In a manner similar to what was done for commercial and employment centers, the planner maps the relative suitability of vacant and renewal land in built-up areas, developing areas, and new areas scheduled for future development in the land classification plan and preliminary land use design scheme. Suitability patterns are based on the geographic pattern of the factors cited in the location principles derived in step 1. Maps may differentiate between types of housing; for example, the map of relative suitability for high-density housing will differ from the map describing suitability for large-lot, single-family dwellings on septic tanks because these two types of residential development seek different features. Separate maps may also be prepared for local support facilities—local shopping centers, schools, playgrounds, and the like.

Task 3: Deriving Space Requirements for Residential Areas

The analysis of space requirements generally includes the following steps (subtasks 3a-d).

Inventory – Smart Growth requirement

a. Analyze quantity, types, density, cost, condition, and location of existing housing, and trends with respect to new housing.
b. Estimate the total number of new dwellings required to house the future population of households.
c. Estimate the proportions of the total that will be required for each of several future dwelling types, densities, and perhaps neighborhood types (e.g., suburban versus neotraditional neighborhoods); convert the proportions to quantities of dwellings.
d. Convert the quantity of dwellings, by housing type, to acres of land required, by housing type.

The analyses for these tasks use data previously collected and stored in the information system.

Subtask 3a: Analyze the Number of Dwellings, Types, Densities, Prices, Conditions, and Locations of Existing Housing and Trends in the Housing Market

This first task is an analysis of the current situation, including both the present status of the housing supply and trends of new development, conservation, and redevelopment. The analysis of current status focuses on the existing number of dwellings, existing acreage in residential use, and prevailing densities—by dwelling type and location (usually by planning districts or neighborhoods). Planning districts or neighborhoods are often grouped into city sectors, usually central and outer districts, and sometimes by direction from the center (e.g., north, east, south, and west). Dwelling counts come from the information system, special housing or land use surveys, or perhaps an estimate updated from the most recent decennial census. Acreages come from a land use survey or parcel-based information system. Densities (net) are calculated by dividing the number of dwellings by corresponding acreages for relevant sub-areas of the planning jurisdiction. Table 14-1 illustrates one way to summarize the present housing stock using four typical classes of housing; the types may vary from community to community. The housing types should correspond to designations used in the land use or housing survey for the information system. Additional types may be added later in the analysis as it shifts toward estimation of the future. Note that the figures in Table 14-1 should be regarded as illustrative only.

A second part of the current situation analysis examines trends in the housing market, represented by recent construction of new dwellings and conversions in the existing stock. Table 14-2 illustrates one format for representing the results of such an analysis. The table is compiled from development permits or from a land use survey and usually covers a five- or ten-year period. When read horizontally, the table shows the relative proportion in each housing type, as well as the total number of dwellings, in any particular sub-area (e.g., neighborhood or planning district). The types of housing could include planned unit developments, pedestrian pockets or neotraditional neighborhoods, typical suburban subdivisions, and mixed-use commercial developments instead of or in addition to the types shown in the table. When read vertically, and used in conjunction with a map of the neighborhoods or planning districts, the table indicates locational trends for each type of housing or neighborhood. Such information indicates the direction of growth and change.

Other analyses are often added, including studies of structural conditions, neighborhood conditions, and socioeconomic changes in resident populations of neighborhoods. Studies are sometimes made to estimate losses from the present housing inventory due to conversion to other uses, clearance for new public facilities, or likely condemnation. Those losses will have to be made up in the plan (subtask 3b). That information also estimates the amount of land thereby made available for other uses or new residential development. Thus, there are deductions of housing stock, but additions to available land supply for new uses, for which the planner must account in the plan-making process.

Subtask 3b: Estimating the Total Number of New Dwellings Required to House the Future Population of Households   The first step in this subtask is to project the future population of households—the basis for housing demand. A household is simply a group of persons who occupy a housing unit. It is often, but not always, a family (two or more persons related by blood, marriage, or adoption and residing together). It may include unrelated persons who share the dwelling with a family (e.g., lodgers, employees, foster children), or it may be a single person living alone or a group of unrelated persons sharing a dwelling. Thus, population must be converted to households. The key factor in making that conversion is estimating future average household size, which is based on local trends and regional, state, and national studies. The average household size implicitly reflects assumptions about future life-styles (marrying behavior, group living, or doubling up) as

Table 14-1. Current Stock of Dwellings, Acreage in Residential Use, and Net Densities by Housing Type

Planning District, neighborhood, etc.	Single-Family Detached[a]			Row/Townhouses[b]			Garden Apartments[c]			Multistory Apartments			Total		
	DUs	Acres	Density	DUs	Acres	Density	DUs	Acres	Density	DUs	Acres	Density	DUs	Acres	Density
Central City															
1	120	13	9.2	0	0		10	2	5.0	40	2	20.0	170	17	10.0
2	105	20	5.3	25	3	8.3	25	2	12.5	100	5	20.0	255	30	8.5
3	135	41	3.3	200	16	12.5	250	15	16.7	75	4	18.8	660	76	8.7
4	420	97	4.3	300	22	13.6	225	13	17.3	0	0		945	132	7.2
5	675	169	4.0	0	0		0	0		0	0		675	169	4.0
6	345	92	3.8	0	0		0	0		0	0		345	92	3.8
7	215	66	3.3	100	7	14.3	50	3	16.7	0	0		365	76	4.8
Subtotal	2,015	498	4.0	625	48	13.0	560	35	16.0	215	11	19.5	3,415	592	5.8
Fringe Area															
8	60	25	2.4	0	0		0	0		0	0		60	25	2.4
9	55	44	1.3	0	0		0	0		0	0		55	44	1.3
10	30	28	1.1	0	0		0	0		0	0		30	28	1.1
11	0	0		0	0		0	0		0	0		0	0	0.0
12	25	16	1.6	0	0		0	0		0	0		25	16	1.6
13	15	16	0.9	0	0		0	0		0	0		15	16	0.9
14	10	10	1.0	0	0		0	0		0	0		10	10	1.0
15	5	6	0.8	0	0		0	0		0	0		5	6	0.8
16	45	35	1.3	0	0		0	0		0	0		45	35	1.3
17	0	0		0	0		0	0		0	0		0	0	0.0
18	0	0		0	0		0	0		0	0		0	0	0.0
19	10	9	1.1	0	0		0	0		0	0		10	9	1.1
20	20	19	1.1	0	0		0	0		0	0		20	19	1.1
21	10	9	1.1	0	0		0	0		0	0		10	9	1.1
22	0	0		0	0		0	0		0	0		0	0	0.0
23	0	0		0	0		0	0		0	0		0	0	0.0
Subtotal	285	217	1.3	0	0	0	0	0	0	0	0	0	285	217	1.3
Total	2,300	715	3.2	625	48	13.0	560	35	16.0	215	11	19.5	3,700	809	4.6

Note: Figures in this and other tables are illustrative only.

a. Single-family detached housing could be split into several density classes.
b. Attached housing includes duplexes, townhouses, and row houses.
c. Ground-floor and walk-up apartments.

Table 14-2. Recent Trends in New Additions to Housing Stock, 19XX–19XX

Planning District	Total Number DUs Added in Zone	Percentage of Planning Area Total	Conversions	Single Family Detached Low Density (1 DU/acre)	Med. Density (1-3 DU/acre)	High Density (3-6 DU/acre)	Attached Dwellings Duplexes, Townhouses	Multifamily Garden Apartments	Multistory Apartments
Central City									
1	20	2	10	0	0	10	0	0	0
2	42	4	0	0	0	12	15	15	0
3	150	15	10	0	0	15	0	50	75
4	320	31	0	35	50	65	70	100	0
5	250	25	0	70	130	50	0	0	0
6	75	7	0	10	45	20	0	0	0
7	100	10	10	0	0	30	10	50	0
Subtotal	957	94	30	115	225	202	95	215	75
Fringe Area									
8	30	3	0	10	10	10	0	0	0
9	5	0	0	0	5	0	0	0	0
10	2	0	0	0	2	0	0	0	0
11	3	0	0	0	0	3	0	0	0
12	0	0	0	0	0	0	0	0	0
13	3	0	0	0	3	0	0	0	0
14	5	0	0	0	5	0	0	0	0
15	5	0	0	3	2	0	0	0	0
16	10	1	0	5	5	0	0	0	0
17	0	0	0	0	0	0	0	0	0
18	0	0	0	0	0	0	0	0	0
19	0	0	0	0	0	0	0	0	0
20	0	0	0	0	0	0	0	0	0
21	0	0	0	0	0	0	0	0	0
22	0	0	0	0	0	0	0	0	0
23	0	0	0	0	0	0	0	0	0
Subtotal	63	6	0	18	32	13	0	0	0
Total	1,020	100	30	133	257	215	95	215	75
Percentage by housing type			3	13	25	21	9	21	7

well as family size. Dividing the population forecast by average household size yields a forecast of the future number of households needing housing. That number constitutes an "unadjusted" housing need for the target year (Table 14-3, lines 1–3).

Table 14-3. Derivation of Total New Dwelling Units Required, 20XX

Sequence of Steps	Illustrative Results
1. Population forecast for Year 20XX	20,000 people
2. Divide by future average household size	2.7 people/household
3. Equals: rough estimate of housing needs at end of planning period	7,407 households
4. Divide by (1 – vacancy rate) (e.g., 1 – .04 = .96)	0.96 vacancy rate adjustment
5. Yields an adjusted estimate of housing stock required at end of period to meet needs	7,716 future dwellings
6. Minus existing housing stock	3,700 existing stock
7. Yields an estimate of new additions required beyond the existing housing stock	4,016 additional dwellings required

8. Plus losses to existing stock that must be replaced
  Fire, etc. 100
  Urban renewal, etc. 50
  Conversion to non-residential use 125
  Abandoned 50
  Other 25
	350 dwellings to be replaced

9. Result: An adjusted estimate of required additions to housing stock.	4,366 new dwellings to be added by Year 20XX

The planner next adjusts that projection upward to reflect vacant housing stock; that is, vacant housing is necessary for a housing market to operate and must be added to the number of households to estimate number of dwellings needed. The vacancy adjustment is made by dividing the number of households by a factor obtained by subtracting an assumed future vacancy rate from 1.0. For example if the vacancy rate is 4 percent, the factor would be 1.0 minus 0.04, or .96. If the projected number of households is 7,407 (as in line 3 of Table 14-3, for example), then the adjusted estimate of housing need is 7,407/0.96, or approximately 7,716 dwellings required for the target population. About 309 of those dwellings would be assumed to be vacant.

Next, the planner deducts the present stock from projected aggregate need, which results in an estimate of required additions to the housing stock. If the present stock is 3,700 dwellings, then the required additions would be 4,016, that is, 7,716 minus 3,700 (lines 5 through 7 of Table 14-3).

That figure must be adjusted further to reflect losses of dwellings over the planning period. For example, dwellings may be abandoned, destroyed by fire or other catastrophes, eliminated through urban renewal, highway construction, or other public improvement programs, converted to such nonresidential uses as offices or day-care centers, or combined into larger units. The planner estimates the number of losses, using trends, governmental plans, and judgment. The total of those losses must then be added to the estimated number of additional housing required during the planning period. Thus if the planner judges that 350 dwellings will be lost through various causes, the estimate of need for additional housing is expanded from 4,016 above to 4,366 dwellings (lines 8 and 9 of Table 14-3).

Subtask 3c: Distribute Additions to Housing Stock among Various Housing Types   In this step, the planner divides the total housing construction needs into housing types and calculates, roughly, how much total land will be required. For the general land use plan, this is usually based on an analysis of trends, informed by the land use policy established earlier in the process and influenced by a specific vision for the future (e.g., compact city or spread-out city). In more detailed studies, an analysis of consumer preferences might be included. Trends in housing types can be obtained from a study of housing construction over the past five to ten years (Table 14-2). Trends may be adjusted to reflect community policy, which may, for example, encourage higher proportions of lower-cost housing, mid-density housing, in-fill housing, or neotraditional neighborhoods. The first column in Table 14-4 shows the number of dwellings in each principal type of new housing to be accommodated in the future land use plan. The categories are combinations of housing types and density; thus there might be both a low-density, single-family category and a high-density, single-family category. (Note that the numbers of dwellings in column 2 sum to the estimate of required additions to the housing stock calculated in Table 14-3.)

Table 14-4. Allocation of New Dwelling Units by Housing and Density Types

Housing Types	Assumed Density (DUs/acre)				Acreage Requirements		
	DUs	Net	Gross	Neighbor-hood	Net	Gross	Neighbor-hood
A. Conversion from other uses	128	20	16	13	6	8	10
B. High-rise apartments	319	35	28	24	9	11	13
C. Walk-ups	921	25	20	17	37	46	54
D. Townhouses/rowhouses (lower density)	203	15	12	10	14	17	20
E. Townhouses/rowhouses (high density)	204	9	7	6	23	29	34
F. Single family detached (higher density)	2,022	4	3	2.3	506	674	879
G. Single family detached (lower density)	569	2	1.5	1	285	379	569
Total	4,366				879	1,165	1,580

The third, fourth, and fifth columns in Table 14-4 record the planner's estimate of average density in dwellings per acre for each category of new housing. The assumed densities are expressed as both net density (column 3), gross density (column 4), and neighborhood density (column 5). Net residential density refers to the number of dwellings per acre actually in residential use, and gross residential density includes that land area plus associated streets, alleys, and other rights of way, as well as any residual undevelopable land parcels. Thus, gross density is generally 17 to 20 percent lower than net density for the same group of dwellings because it includes more land in the denominator of the ratio of dwellings to land. (And net density is 20 to 25 percent higher than gross density.) Neighborhood density, in column 5, includes not only the streets and other land included in calculating gross residential density, but also space for local shopping, schools, neighborhood park, streets and pedestrian ways, parking, and more or less permanently vacant land. The net density concept is most useful in estimating space needs and holding capacity in developed or partially developed areas, where streets and other infrastructure are already available and development will be primarily on single parcels. Gross density and neighborhood density are more useful for matching space needs to holding capacity in areas that are largely vacant and require extension of streets and other infrastructure and community facilities.

In a sense, the figures in Table 14-4 represent standards for the future land use plan. In making judgments about densities in that table, the planner might consult Table 14-5, which indicates some typical urban residential densities (see also DeChiara 1984, 21–23; DeChiara 1990, 186–89). The densities will also vary from planning jurisdiction to planning jurisdiction. For example, those in Table 14-5 represent study areas that are more urban in character; densities would usually be lower in smaller cities and in fringe areas. Studies of existing densities, recent trends in density, and the sizes of subdivided but undeveloped lots give clues to probable densities for future development, at least for the next decade or so. In the longer run, for special sites and for special housing policies (e.g., encourag-

Table 14-5. Typical Residential Densities for Common Housing Types

Households per Acre Housing Type	FAR[a]	Net	Gross	Neighborhood
Single family	≤ 0.2	≤ 8	≤ 6	≤ 5
Zero lot-line, detached	0.3	8–10	6–8	6
Two-family detached	0.3	10–12	8–10	7
Rowhouses	0.5	15–24	12–20	12
Stacked townhouses	0.8	25–40	20–30	18
3-story walkup apartments	1	40–45	30–40	20
6-story walkup apartments	1.4	65–75	50–60	30
13-story walkup apartments	1.8	85–95	70–80	40

a. FAR = floor-area ratio.

Source: Adapted from Lynch and Hack 1984, Table 5, 253.

ing transit-oriented pedestrian pocket development), the planner may propose significantly different density standards and development forms.

Subtask 3d: Convert the Dwelling Unit Allocations among Housing Types to Space Needs In the final step for calculating space requirements, the planner divides the number of dwellings required in each housing-type category by the average net density, average gross density, and neighborhood density to estimate the land requirements for each category of residential development. (See the last three columns in Table 14-4.) Later in the design process, the planner can choose the most relevant density concept—net, gross, or neighborhood density—for the situation being considered. For example, if filling out a relatively built-up neighborhood, the planner might apply net density. Gross density or neighborhood density would be more appropriate for newly developing areas on the urban fringe.

Task 4: Analyze the Holding Capacity of the Suitable Land Supply

The fourth major step in designing the residential sector of the land use design is to establish the holding capacity of suitable vacant or renewable land. Holding capacity, usually expressed as the number of dwellings that vacant and renewal land will accommodate in the proposed residential densities, is usually calculated by planning district or neighborhood.

In largely undeveloped areas, gross density or neighborhood density should be used to account for land to be used for streets and supporting facilities. The holding capacity analysis should also discount lands unavailable for development as defined in chapter 8 (e.g., lands being withheld from the market).

To calculate the dwelling unit holding capacity of an area, the number of suitable acres in an area is multiplied by the density standard appropriate for that location according to the design scheme being explored. For example, if there are two hundred acres of suitable land in a neighborhood/district, and the residential density desired for that area is eight dwellings per acre, the holding capacity is 1,600 dwellings. The number of suitable acres is measured from the suitability map or taken from a summary table of that map, and the density standards are taken from Table 14-4; the results can be organized in a table similar to Table 14-6. The holding capacity is not calculated for all possible residential types in each planning district, but just for housing types consistent with the preliminary schematic design. Thus, not every cell in the table need be filled out. A supplementary working map is also helpful, which identifies the neighborhoods or planning districts for which holding capacities are being calculated.

Task 5: Allocating Housing to Residential Areas

The fifth task of the residential planning procedure is to flesh out the schematic land use design by distributing new dwelling requirements to various suitable ar-

Table 14-6. Approximate Holding Capacity of Vacant-Renewable Land Suited for Residential Development by Several Types of Dwellings, by Planning District, 20XX

Planning District, Neighborhood, and Other Useful Sub-area Designation	No. of Suitable Acres	Number of Dwelling Units by Density Type[a]						
		A	B	C	D	E	F	G
Central City								
1	10	200	350	250	150	90	40	20
2	25	500	875	625	375	225	100	50
3	65	1,300	2,275	1,625	975	585	260	130
4	175	3,500	6,125	4,375	2,625	1,575	700	350
5	40	800	1,400	1,000	600	360	160	80
6	20	400	700	500	300	180	80	40
7	40	800	1,400	1,000	600	360	160	80
Subtotal	375							
Fringe Area								
8	200	3,200	5,600	4,000	2,400	1,400	600	300
9	250	4,000	7,000	5,000	3,000	1,750	750	375
10	250	4,000	7,000	5,000	3,000	1,750	750	375
11	60	960	1,680	1,200	720	420	180	90
12	65	1,040	1,820	1,300	780	455	195	100
13	300	4,800	8,400	6,000	3,600	2,100	900	450
14	350	5,600	9,800	7,000	4,200	2,450	1,050	525
15	180	2,880	5,040	3,600	2,160	1,260	540	270
16	400	6,400	11,200	8,000	4,800	2,800	1,200	600
17	450	7,200	12,600	9,000	5,400	3,150	1,350	675
18	25	400	700	500	300	175	75	35
19	250	4,000	7,000	5,000	3,000	1,750	750	375
20	300	4,800	8,400	6,000	3,600	2,100	900	450
21	600	9,600	16,800	12,000	7,200	4,200	1,800	900
22	250	4,000	7,000	5,000	3,000	1,750	750	375
23	200	3,200	5,600	4,000	2,400	1,400	600	300
Subtotal	413							
Planning Area Total	8,635							

a. Convert number of acres to number of DUs by dividing acres by density; net density for central city and gross density for fringe area.

eas. The allocations should follow the goals, policies, location requirements, and design concepts of the schematic plan, meet the quantitative dwelling and space requirements, and stay within holding capacity constraints. Existing neighborhoods are filled out or redeveloped. New neighborhoods are created. In both existing and new areas, the planner needs to consider the rate at which the areas ought to develop and the amount of land that should remain undeveloped at the end of the planning period, available for development beyond that time. Depending on the design concept, some of the housing may be allocated to mixed-use centers, and, conversely, some employment and commercial activities may be allocated to residential communities, especially if the design features transit-oriented development or neotraditional neighborhoods. Residential land is allocated at two conceptual levels.

1. Neighborhood-sized modules or other community concept units (e.g., pedestrian pockets) include not only a sizable number of dwellings but also an assumed mix of dwelling types and community-serving public and private facilities such as parks, schools, and local shopping. Gross neighborhood densities are used for space requirement purposes. Locations of facilities within the neighborhood might be indicated as abstract symbols (e.g., squares or circles) or not indicated at all. This approach might be used in those parts of the planning jurisdiction that are still vacant or sparsely developed.
2. Individual dwellings are more appropriate for filling out existing communities and areas already under active development. Facilities also would be located on an individual basis in such areas. For example, single parks or schools would be assigned fairly specific locations. Gross residential densities are generally used unless almost all or most local streets necessary to serve building sites already exist.

The results of this spatial allocation/design process are checked against the requirements in Table 14-4; the holding capacities in Table 14-6; and the location requirements, goals, and policies formulated earlier. The allocations are then summarized in working tables like Tables 14-7 and 14-8. Table 14-7 summarizes the spatial allocation of new dwellings and residential acreage within holding capacity constraints of suitable land in each planning district. Table 14-8 summarizes the planned distribution of dwellings and population for the target year, compared to the current number of dwellings and population.

The present distribution of population could be based, at least in part, on U.S. Census and local population estimates rather than relying on dwelling counts multiplied by an average household size for the district. Future and current average household size could vary from district to district within the planning jurisdiction. The future distribution includes existing dwellings expected to remain in residential use at the end of the planning period, as well as the dwellings added during the planning period. The table also converts the dwelling distribution to an estimate of population distribution. Population also reflects an adjustment for vacant dwellings; that is, a portion of the housing stock is presumed not to have occupants. The spatial distribution of population and households is useful for designing and evaluating plans for community facilities, retail activities, and commercial centers, both regional and local.

A reminder: These results are still considered tentative, pending review and revision after further design decisions are made about local shopping and community service facilities, and refinements are made to the plans for open space, employment, and commercial areas.

Table 14-7. Spatial Allocation of New Dwelling Unit Requirements, by Density Type, 20XX

Planning District	No. of New DUs from Conversion and New Construction by Density Type							No. of New DUs Total	Acreage for Additions to Housing Stock							Total
	A	B	C	D	E	F	G		A	B	C	D	E	F	G	
Central City																
1	X	X	X	X	X	X	X	X	X	X	X	X	X	X	X	X
2	X	X	X	X	X	X	X	X	X	X	X	X	X	X	X	X
3	X	X	X	X	X	X	X	X	X	X	X	X	X	X	X	X
4	X	X	X	X	X	X	X	X	X	X	X	X	X	X	X	X
5	X	X	X	X	X	X	X	X	X	X	X	X	X	X	X	X
6	X	X	X	X	X	X	X	X	X	X	X	X	X	X	X	X
7	X	X	X	X	X	X	X	X	X	X	X	X	X	X	X	X
Subtotal	X	X	X	X	X	X	X	X	X	X	X	X	X	X	X	X
Fringe Area																
8	X	X	X	X	X	X	X	X	X	X	X	X	X	X	X	X
9	X	X	X	X	X	X	X	X	X	X	X	X	X	X	X	X
10	X	X	X	X	X	X	X	X	X	X	X	X	X	X	X	X
11	X	X	X	X	X	X	X	X	X	X	X	X	X	X	X	X
12	X	X	X	X	X	X	X	X	X	X	X	X	X	X	X	X
13	X	X	X	X	X	X	X	X	X	X	X	X	X	X	X	X
14	X	X	X	X	X	X	X	X	X	X	X	X	X	X	X	X
15	X	X	X	X	X	X	X	X	X	X	X	X	X	X	X	X
16	X	X	X	X	X	X	X	X	X	X	X	X	X	X	X	X
17	X	X	X	X	X	X	X	X	X	X	X	X	X	X	X	X
18	X	X	X	X	X	X	X	X	X	X	X	X	X	X	X	X
19	X	X	X	X	X	X	X	X	X	X	X	X	X	X	X	X
20	X	X	X	X	X	X	X	X	X	X	X	X	X	X	X	X
21	X	X	X	X	X	X	X	X	X	X	X	X	X	X	X	X
22	X	X	X	X	X	X	X	X	X	X	X	X	X	X	X	X
23	X	X	X	X	X	X	X	X	X	X	X	X	X	X	X	X
Subtotal	X	X	X	X	X	X	X	X	X	X	X	X	X	X	X	X
Planning Area Total	128	319	921	203	204	2,022	569	4,366	X	X	X	X	X	X	X	X

Note: Totals match those at the foot of Tables 14-3, "Derivation of Total New Dwelling Units Required," and those in Table 14-4, "Allocation of New Dwelling Units by Housing and Density Types." Planning district totals should be less than or equal to the holding capacities shown in Table 14-6.

Table 14-8. Future Distribution of Population by Planning Sub-area, 20XX

| Planning District | Current | | | By End of Planning Period | | | | |
	DUs	Average Household Size	Population	Existing DUs Remaining by 19XX	DUs Added	Total DUs	House-hold Size	Population
Central City								
1	170	2.7	459				2.7	
2	255	2.7	689				2.7	
3	660	2.7	1,782				2.7	
4	945	2.7	2,552				2.7	
5	675	2.7	1,823				2.7	
6	345	2.7	932				2.7	
7	365	2.7	986				2.7	
Subtotal	3,415		9,221					
Fringe Area								
8	60	2.7	162				2.7	
9	55	2.7	149				2.7	
10	30	2.7	81				2.7	
11	0	2.7	0				2.7	
12	25	2.7	68				2.7	
13	15	2.7	41				2.7	
14	10	2.7	27				2.7	
15	5	2.7	14				2.7	
16	45	2.7	122				2.7	
17	0	2.7	0				2.7	
18	0	2.7	0				2.7	
19	10	2.7	27				2.7	
20	20	2.7	54				2.7	
21	10	2.7	27				2.7	
22	0	2.7	0				2.7	
23	0	2.7	0				2.7	
Subtotal	285		770					
Total	3,700		9,990	3,350	4,366	7,716	2.7	20,000

Notes: Although this process is crude, it is considered sufficiently accurate for the generalized character of the land use plan.
1. Columns 1 through 3 show the existing situation.
   a. Column 1 is a summary of the dwelling unit count appearing in Table 14-1.
   b. Column 2 figures are estimated by methods described in chapter 5.
   c. Column 3 is derived from the population data or calculated from columns 1 and 2, after adjusting column 1 for vacancies.
2. Columns 4 through 8 approximate dwelling counts and population by the end of the planning period.
   a. Column 4 total comes from Table 14-3.
   b. Column 5 numbers come from Table 14-7.
   c. Column 6 represents the sum of entries in columns 4 and 5.
   d. Column 7 shows estimated future average household size based on housing types and expectations about how the the planning sub-areas are more likely to attract families with children compared to households without children.
   e. Column 8 computes an estimate of the population by planning district, multiplying entries from columns 6 (adjusted for vacancies) and column 7.

Task 6: Adding Local Support Facilities to Create Residential Communities

Residential communities should consist of more than housing. They need local shopping and banking, personal care, and entertainment facilities; community service facilities such as schools and playgrounds, community centers, and police and fire stations; institutions such as churches, synagogues, and clubs; and open space for recreation and environmental protection. Although residential unit concepts are not rigidly defined by distances to these facilities, the hierarchy of shops, schools, recreation areas, and other service facilities should be compatible with the spatial distribution of housing, and they become a part of the design of residential areas. Although public facilities require more detailed consideration during capital improvement programming, and are also addressed in chapter 15, they are introduced here in the context of residential area design.

Local Business Location requirements for local business areas are suggested earlier in this chapter under general location requirements for residential areas and in chapter 13 in terms of space requirements. Standards, such as those suggested in Table 14-9, and Table 13-2, also serve as guides to location and space requirements (De Chiara 1984, 234–38). Those principles and standards should be assessed in the light of the existing pattern of neighborhood and community-scale business centers and residents' satisfaction with shopping opportunities they provide, and against the preliminary design for the commercial spatial structure.

Table 14-9. General Space Requirement Standards for Neighborhood and Community Shopping Centers

Selected Neighborhood Population Sizes in Residential Communities of 30,000–50,000	Acres of Combined Community-Neighborhood Shopping Area per 1,000 Population for Given Parking Ratios[a]		
	1:1	2:1	3:1
5,000	0.5	0.7	0.9
2,500	0.6	0.8	1.0
1,000	0.9	1.1	1.5

a. Parking ratio is here defined as the square feet of parking space for every square foot of floor area.

For each residential community module (neighborhood, village, or other residential design unit) the planner must estimate total space requirements and find locations for local business. The population figures in Table 14-8 are useful for calculating trade-area population as a basis for calculating space requirements for local shopping. For completely new residential areas, the specific locations of local shopping areas are sometimes deferred for subsequent, detailed planning at the time the area begins to develop. Meanwhile, in the land use plan, the local shopping area is designated as a circle or other symbol indicating a general but not specific location. In those cases as well, neighborhood densities can be used to allow for the space required for local shopping.

Schools While schools are taken up in more detail under community facility design in chapter 15, that design process should be integrated with residential area design. The locations of schools are determined by a mix of education policy and land use principles, with education policy being the dominating factor. For example, educational policy determines the span of grades served by schools (kindergarten through sixth, seventh through ninth, and tenth through twelfth grades or kindergarten through eighth and ninth through twelfth grades, for example) and optimum enrollments per facility. Policy also determines the types of activities to be accommodated on school sites, including whether the sites are available for recreational activities, community meetings, and adult education. The amount of land required by each school site is determined by the size of enrollment, facilities desired, and school system standards. However, such things as the catchment area of each school are also at least partly determined by land use factors—including the density of school age population, housing densities, and traditional distance standards of land use planning.

Although schools are not necessarily as central to residential planning concepts as they once were (e.g., in Perry's neighborhood concept), they are still vital elements in residential area planning. This is especially true for residential areas intended primarily for households with children.

Recreation and Open Space Recreation, the third type of local support facility, is also taken up in Chapter 15. The related topic of neighborhood open space design (chapter 12) is also relevant. Since neighborhood playgrounds are sometimes integrated with elementary school grounds and community recreation facilities sometimes integrated with junior and senior high school facilities, recreation and open space planning are sometimes coordinated with school planning.

Other Local-Serving Facilities Private institutions such as churches and clubs, public community facilities such as libraries and community centers, and public safety facilities like police and fire stations are also important in making residential areas more livable. Space in appropriate locations for such facilities should be built into the residential area design, and requirements and incentives for such local support facilities should be built into the development management measures later.

Task 7: Synthesizing and Summarizing the Residential Area Design

The integration of housing, infrastructure, local retail and consumer services, and local community facilities takes several rounds of mutual adjustments in the pattern of housing and community facilities. Land for community facilities, for example, reduces holding capacity for housing (Table 14-6), which can change the designed distribution of dwellings. That, in turn, changes population catchment areas for community facilities and local businesses. A work table like Table 14-10 can be used to keep track of adjustments during the design process and to summarize the results. As usual, there should be an accompanying annotated working map showing the same sites to indicate spatial relationships and approximate catchment areas of individual facilities.

When the residential sector design is fairly settled for a particular land use design alternative, the results are summarized in a work table something like Table 14-11. Land for local supporting community facilities is aggregated into a single community facilities category (column) in the table. Land for streets and highways, incorporated into gross residential density for much of the residential design process, is separated out into a transportation column.

Table 14-10. Allocation of Land to Local Community Facility Uses, by Planning Sub-areas, 20XX

| Planning District | Total Land Suitable for Residential Communities | Space Requirements of Community Facilities | | | | | Vacant and Renewal Land Remaining for Residential Use |
		Local Business	Schools	Recreation	Other	Total	
Central City							
1	X	X	X	X	X	X	X
2	X	X	X	X	X	X	X
3	X	X	X	X	X	X	X
4	X	X	X	X	X	X	X
5	X	X	X	X	X	X	X
6	X	X	X	X	X	X	X
7	X	X	X	X	X	X	X
Subtotal	X	X	X	X	X	X	X
Fringe Area							
8	X	X	X	X	X	X	X
9	X	X	X	X	X	X	X
10	X	X	X	X	X	X	X
11	X	X	X	X	X	X	X
12	X	X	X	X	X	X	X
13	X	X	X	X	X	X	X
14	X	X	X	X	X	X	X
15	X	X	X	X	X	X	X
16	X	X	X	X	X	X	X
17	X	X	X	X	X	X	X
18	X	X	X	X	X	X	X
19	X	X	X	X	X	X	X
20	X	X	X	X	X	X	X
21	X	X	X	X	X	X	X
22	X	X	X	X	X	X	X
23	X	X	X	X	X	X	X
Subtotal	X	X	X	X	X	X	X
Total	X	X	X	X	X	X	X

Table 14-11. Derivation of Gross Space Requirements for Entirely New Residential Communities in Selected Planning Districts

| Planning Sub-area | Net Acreage Allocations | | | | | | | | Community Facilities | Allowance for Streets | Gross Acreage Requirements |
| | Residential Use by Density Type | | | | | | | | | | |
	A	B	C	D	E	F	G	H			
Central City											
1	X	X	X	X	X	X	X	X	X	X	X
2	X	X	X	X	X	X	X	X	X	X	X
3	X	X	X	X	X	X	X	X	X	X	X
4	X	X	X	X	X	X	X	X	X	X	X
5	X	X	X	X	X	X	X	X	X	X	X
6	X	X	X	X	X	X	X	X	X	X	X
7	X	X	X	X	X	X	X	X	X	X	X
Subtotal	X	X	X	X	X	X	X	X	X	X	X
Fringe Area											
8	X	X	X	X	X	X	X	X	X	X	X
9	X	X	X	X	X	X	X	X	X	X	X
10	X	X	X	X	X	X	X	X	X	X	X
11	X	X	X	X	X	X	X	X	X	X	X
12	X	X	X	X	X	X	X	X	X	X	X
13	X	X	X	X	X	X	X	X	X	X	X
14	X	X	X	X	X	X	X	X	X	X	X
15	X	X	X	X	X	X	X	X	X	X	X
16	X	X	X	X	X	X	X	X	X	X	X
17	X	X	X	X	X	X	X	X	X	X	X
18	X	X	X	X	X	X	X	X	X	X	X
19	X	X	X	X	X	X	X	X	X	X	X
20	X	X	X	X	X	X	X	X	X	X	X
21	X	X	X	X	X	X	X	X	X	X	X
22	X	X	X	X	X	X	X	X	X	X	X
23	X	X	X	X	X	X	X	X	X	X	X
Subtotal	X	X	X	X	X	X	X	X	X	X	X
Total	X	X	X	X	X	X	X	X	X	X	X

Beyond the Preliminary Plan

The levels of analysis described in the foregoing studies and in chapter 15 are suitable for preliminary land use plan-making. Although the basic rationale is the same in more advanced studies, more precise estimating techniques are used, which generally require the skills of people trained and experienced in housing analysis and community facility planning. For example, a more thorough housing market analysis would be made, the condition of the housing stock and public improvements would be assessed, and deficiencies identified in neighborhood facilities—especially in older areas—and it would define residential areas where rehabilitation or selected clearance is indicated to retain a viable living environment. These investigations would provide a more exacting assessment of the number of existing housing units surviving through the planning period and the amount of freed-up land available for renewal. A study of recreational needs would incorporate user surveys and a participatory approach. For schools, the planner would employ more detailed forecasts of school-age population and would analyze the existing school plant more carefully. For local shopping, a detailed survey of existing floor space used by local businesses and a study of purchasing power would be made. We provide discussion of more detailed analyses for shopping and community facilities in other chapters, but we can indicate the nature of more refined housing analyses here.

A housing market analysis is essentially a more thorough analysis and projection of supply and demand conditions than has been outlined for general purpose land use planning. The most important elements added to the housing analysis are (1) an analysis of the housing inventory by rent and price categories compared with rent-paying and purchasing ability of subgroups of the populations; (2) a study of housing features, consumer preferences that affect demand for those features, their prices, and consumer financial ability and willingness-to-pay; (3) a study of the special needs of low- and moderate-income households, the elderly, minorities, growing families, and other special groups; and (4) a study of low-cost and subsidized housing stock and production, compared to need, including possibly an assessment of "fair-share" allocation of low- and moderate-income housing to submarkets of the region. The studies define deficits in housing supply, identify causes of inadequate supply, and suggest mitigation strategies. They cover qualitative as well as quantitative aspects of supply and neighborhoodwide aspects as well as dwelling unit aspects.

For the land use planner, the studies should include attention to the intermediate-range and long-range future and to spatial submarket areas (geographic sectors, communities, and neighborhoods). Although they emphasize a market orientation rather than longer-range land use planning objectives, housing studies can help the planner frame the assumptions about future housing and neighborhood types as well as density standards for residential area designs. The planner should also explore housing and neighborhood design possibilities beyond the realm of existing options and trends.

Summary

By this point in the land use design process, trial residential area designs have been added to the earlier designs for the open space system and the commercial and employment structure. Alternative residential sector designs address both the arrangement of dwellings and supporting uses *within* residential communities as well as spatial relationships of those communities to the regional structure of commercial and employment areas, transportation networks, and open space. Residential designs incorporate not only housing but also the private and public infrastructure of local community facilities and services such as local shopping, recreation and leisure, transportation, schools, and employment. The entire arrangement is designed to support public interest objectives of security, financial investment, social interaction, socialization, symbolic identification, and public efficiency.

REFERENCES

Barnett, Jonathan. 1982. *An introduction to urban design.* New York: Harper and Row.

Calthorpe, Peter and Associates. 1990. *Transit-oriented design guidelines.* Final public review draft, September 1990. Sacramento: Sacramento County Planning and Community Development Department.

Council on Development Choices for the '80s. 1981. *The affordable community: Growth, change, and choice in the '80s.* Washington, D.C.: U.S. Government Printing Office.

De Chiara, Joseph. 1984. *Time-saver standards for residential development.* New York: McGraw-Hill Book Company.

De Chiara, Joseph, and John H. Callender. 1990. *Time-saver standards for building types.* 3d ed. New York: McGraw Hill.

De Chiara, Joseph, and Lee Koppelman. 1982. *Urban planning and design criteria.* New York: Van Nostrand Reinhold Co.

Gallion, Arthur B., and Simon Eisner. 1986. *The urban pattern: City planning and design.* 5th ed. New York: Van Nostrand Reinhold Company.

Hoppenfeld, Morton. 1967. A sketch of the planning-building process for Columbia, Maryland. *Journal of the American Institute of Planners* 33(6): 398–409.

Isaacs, Reginald. 1948. The neighborhood theory: An analysis of its adequacy. *Journal of the American Institute of Planners* 14(2): 15–23.

Kelbaugh, Doug, ed. 1989. *The pedestrian pocket book: A new suburban design strategy.* Princeton: Princeton Architectural Press.

Krieger, Alex, ed., with William Lennertz. 1992. *Andres Duany and Elizabeth Plater-Zyberk: Towns and town-making principles.* Cambridge: Harvard University Graduate School of Design.

Lynch, Kevin, and Gary Hack. 1984. *Site planning.* 3d ed. Cambridge: MIT Press.

Perry, Clarence. 1929. *Neighborhood and community planning: The neighborhood unit.* New York: Regional Plan of New York and Its Environs.

Richman, Alan. 1979. Planning residential environments: The social performance standard. *Journal of the American Planning Association* 45(4): 448–57.

Richman, Alan, and F. Stuart Chapin, Jr. 1977. A review of the social and physical concepts of the neighborhood as a basis for planning residential environments. Mimeographed manuscript. Chapel Hill: Department of City and Regional Planning, University of North Carolina.

Sacramento County. 1990. *Land use element of the County of Sacramento general plan.* Final public review draft, September 1990. Sacramento: Sacramento Planning and Community Development Department.

15

Integrating Community Facilities with Land Use

The planning process, operating through a professional planning staff and/or a citizen-based planning and zoning board, should direct the laying of the pipe; if it does not, the laying of the pipe is likely to direct the planning of the community.
—Tabors, Shapiro, and Rogers 1976, 2

Community facilities are increasingly being recognized as a vital element of a land use or comprehensive plan. Florida, for example, requires that every locality's comprehensive plan contain a capital improvements element designed to consider the need for, and the location of, public facilities (De Grove and Stroud 1988).

Although considered as a separate land use sector in this chapter, community facilities are also integral parts of commercial centers, industrial and office parks, and residential communities, and they must be planned as such. For example, a civic center, transit stations, and governmental offices may be part of the central business district. Freight terminals, railroad marshaling yards and service facilities, port installations, power plants, and gas works might be studied and located in conjunction with industrial centers. Other facilities, such as cemeteries, waterworks, sewage treatment plants, power substations, landfills, and airports, have special location considerations, however, and are better handled somewhat separately.

The purpose of this chapter is threefold. First we describe traits that distinguish community facilities from the commercial, employment, and residential land use sectors that we have discussed in the previous two chapters. Second, we explain how to adapt the general land use design process to community facilities. Third, we discuss several specific facilities: transportation, sewerage, water supply, schools, and recreation. There is insufficient space to consider the complete range of urban public investments, but these are the ones most often included in land use and growth-management plans.

Important Traits of Community Facilities

Community facilities have traits that significantly affect how local governments plan for them. These traits include (1) their dual purpose of providing services and guiding development; (2) their mutually dependent relationship with private land uses; (3) wide variation in the number of people served and size of service area for a facility; (4) divergent user groups; (5) facilities' uneven impacts on non-users; and (6) public responsibility that extends beyond planning and into management. Each characteristic has implications for land use planning.

1. *The dual purpose of community facilities in land use planning: providing services and guiding development.* The more fundamental purpose of community facilities is to service properties, firms, and people. At the same time, however, some facilities (e.g., public sewerage) influence the location and density of private-sector development. From the service perspective, the planner designs the types, locations, and sizes of facilities to best meet present and future need for services. From the development guidance perspective, the planner considers how location, size, timing, service area, and price of facilities determine whether it attracts or repels development or redevelopment. For example, the availability of public sewer services will increase the market attractiveness of undeveloped land. A solid waste facility, nuclear power plant, or other facility that creates off-site nuisances or hazards, on the other hand, often makes nearby lands less attractive to development or redevelopment. Facilities with the greatest potential development impact include water and sewer systems, highways and interchanges (compared to local streets), transit stations, airports (for employment, not housing), and convention centers or stadiums (for commercial development).

2. *The mutual dependency between land uses and community facilities.* The community facility-private land use relationship is a two-way street. On the one hand, projected population and employment levels and the distribution of land uses determine the number, sizes, and general locations of community facilities. On the other hand, efficiency in operation of facilities requires particular densities and spatial patterns of land use and coordination among different community facilities. For example, transit lines and stations imply a minimum density housing and employment within a quarter mile of stations and in the transportation corridor being served, as well as the need to concentrate employment at a few centers that can be served by transit. Public sewerage requires a minimum density of housing to justify the public's capital investment in lines and treatment plant. Facilities serving crowds require top-level transportation service; in fact, most community facilities, right down to neighborhood parks and schools, should be related to streets and pedestrian-bicycle routes.

3. *Variation in size of user community and area served.* Some facilities, such as airports and wastewater treatment plants, serve large areas and populations, whereas other facilities, such as elementary schools and neighborhood parks, serve small populations and areas. Some types of facilities are organized into a hierarchy of sites to serve progressively larger service areas. For

example, regional parks, forest preserves, and zoos serve entire regions; community parks serve a city or sector of a city; and neighborhood parks and tot lots serve small populations within walking and biking distance.

4. *Selectivity of user populations*. Many community service facilities are not used by everyone in their geographic service area. Schools, parks, mental health clinics, and community centers, for example, all have special clienteles within their service area. In locating and sizing such facilities, planners need to be sensitive to the spatial distribution and relative density of user groups, not just population generally.

5. *Uneven distribution of external effects of facilities*. Community facilities often have negative impacts on nearby properties, people, firms, and institutions, which may not use the facility. A wastewater treatment plant or a solid waste facility has odors, a nuclear power plant poses potential danger to people in the vicinity, and a prison or public housing project may be perceived to depress property values nearby. These adverse side effects generally decline with distance from the facility, thus greatly harming some members of the community while benefiting others.

6. *Potential for conflict*. The combination of selectivity of user populations (where some people use the facility and appreciate its benefits while others do not) and the uneven distribution of negative external effects (nearby land and users bear the nuisance or danger or depression on land value) combine to create the potential for community conflict over facility location and design. The potential for conflict increases because community facilities result directly from public officials' decisions.

7. *Public decision responsibility, and therefore planning, extends beyond the land use plan and land use management considerations*. It extends to capital programming, revenue planning, budgeting, engineering design, maintenance and repair, and management of services.

The Community Facilities Planning Process

The five-step planning process introduced in chapter 11 requires modification for community facilities in ways different from the modifications incorporated for land classification, commercial and employment centers, and residential areas. First, the planner requires the support of a special planning team for community facilities. Second, the scope of goals and policies are extended to include maintenance, financing, rehabilitation, and management, as well as size and location. Third, space and location requirements take on a different nature. Fourth, the exploration of alternatives is modified to consider optimization modeling and the addition of financing, repair and maintenance, and management aspects. Fifth, evaluation and impact assessment, connected with conflict resolution, is an added step.

Organizing the Planning Team and Process

Community facilities planning requires a team approach, preferably including participation by both providers and users of community services. Providers include engineers responsible for designing the facilities, service provider-managers, such as the recreation director and school system superintendent, a finance official, and representatives of general management, as well as the planning director or his or her representative. Users may be represented by representatives from town advisory boards, neighborhoods, and special interest user groups such as the elderly or active recreationists.

In Dayton, Ohio, a "capital allocation committee" constitutes the planning team and is charged with achieving balance among the different service systems and between service levels and financial resources (Riordan et al. 1989, 23). In Hillsborough County, Florida, an "infrastructure and growth management team" represents providers and development management officials more than users. It is led by an assistant county administrator and, in addition to facility operators, has representatives from departments of growth management, planning and zoning, and development review, all of which are involved with development exactions by which facilities are provided as part of private development process (Bourey 1989, 39–40).

Direction-Setting

General goals and land use policies discussed in earlier chapters are now supplemented by policies relevant to repair, maintenance, expansion and rehabilitation, financing, interfacility capital improvement priorities, and management of service delivery. In particular, for land use planning purposes, the planning team should recommend levels of service, as expressed in standards about quantity of facilities, capacity, accessibility, site characteristics (e.g., level land versus steep land), minimum site size, and coordination among types of facilities and between facilities and other land uses.

Table 15-1 illustrates the types of community development policies that are particularly relevant for land use planning. Additional principles and standards for

Table 15-1. Illustrative General Policies for Community Facility Planning

1. The city will ensure that prime commercial/industrial acreage is served with necessary infrastructure. (This is an example of a development management policy, in contrast to a service-oriented policy. It has implications for both location of commercial/industrial acreage and service area delineation.)
2. The transportation system should be multimodal, including transit, automobile, bicycle, and walking. It should provide safe, energy-efficient, convenient movement of people and goods. It should relate to the interregional transportation system: air, highway, rail. It should be located and designed to serve but not disrupt existing and future neighborhoods and employment/commercial centers. (An example of general-level policy addressed to the specific facility, transportion.)

Table 15-1, continued

3. Community facilities involving structures, parking, or active recreation should be located on land of no more than 5 percent slope, capable of being graded without undue expense. Direct access should be provided to major road and transit routes, with direct connections to residential communities.

    Cultural facilities, large churches, and spectator sports facilities: level sites in central locations but out of highest value areas, adequate to accommodate buildings, parking, and landscaping and with due consideration to approaches and general amenity of surroundings.

    Similar sorts of principles would apply for other community facilities.
4. The city will require development-impacted roads to meet minimum level of service of D (somewhat congested but still functioning) in approving new developments.
5. For road improvement allocations, priority will be given to projects designed to raise levels of service on roads currently below D in level of service.
6. The capital investment committee will use three criteria to evaluate the relative merit of each capital project (for indicating priorities among projects).
    a. Capital investments will foster the goal of economic vitality.
    b. Capital projects that implement an approved plan will receive priority.
    c. Priority will be given to projects that directly support development efforts in areas with a majority of low- and moderate-income households.

Note: Additional principles and standards for specific facilities are introduced in later sections of the chapter.

specific facilities are introduced in later sections of the chapter. The location and space requirements that will also be discussed constitute a form of policy because they imply the choice of a service level.

Direction-setting should also include an infrastructure inventory (chapter 9) and assessment. The inventory should include the number, capacity, location, and condition of facilities. When compared to standards of service, the inventory helps pinpoint specific facilities and service areas with shortages or excess capacities, potential for expansion, potential for improvement and modification, priorities for replacement, as well as service life expectancies.

Location and Space Requirements

One of the most important tasks in community facility planning is to decide on location and sizing principles, based on standards and priorities for levels of service decided in the direction-setting stage. There are two general approaches to deriving such requirements or needs: the per capita requirement approach and the demand assessment approach.

The per capita requirement (or standards) approach is the simplest of the two approaches and is appropriate in long-range land use planning for all but the most sophisticated planning programs. This approach simply multiplies a future population level by a predetermined standard expressed as the desired quantity of community facilities per capita. It involves a projection of future population for a target year, selection of a per capita standard, and calculation of overall quantity or size of facilities (by multiplying target population by the per capita standard).

The choice of standards, or level of service, is obviously critical to this approach (see De Chiara 1984, and De Chiara and Koppelman 1982, for a collection of standards for many public facilities). That choice should be a conscious one for the community. It should not simply accept, uncritically, the standards recommended by such professional and trade organizations as the National Recreation and Park Association. Such standards inevitably incorporate the judgment, and sometimes the bias, of the organization. Instead, the local planning team generally consults the recommendations of the relevant organizations, reflects on present levels of satisfaction relative to present facility capacities and locations, and considers the community's financial capability and competing needs in establishing standards.

For example, Houston, Texas, decided on a standard of 2.5 acres of community park per one thousand population. A projection of a population of two million for a target year yields a "need" of five thousand acres for community parks. Their minimum size standard for a community park is ten to forty acres, with an ideal size of one hundred acres. The Houston accessibility policy is a community park within three miles of almost every residence (i.e., a three-mile service radius) (City of Houston, Department of Planning and Development 1987).

The demand approach is more involved but more realistic. It is based on investigation of current use of facilities and consumer preferences and determines how much of a community service people desire, given relative costs. Although this approach is not cost-effective for initial long-range land use planning, it is well suited for highly skilled planning agencies in later rounds of comprehensive planning, capital improvement planning, and specific community facility plans that incorporate financial, expansion, repair, maintenance, and management aspects.

In the demand approach, such factors as income and other characteristics of user groups, prices of services, and other variables are used to determine how demand for services varies with price and characteristics of users. At its most sophisticated, the approach involves regression analysis of current and preferred use of services by different user groups at different prices and service levels. In the absence of actually doing such a study locally, a planner might adapt the findings of existing studies made in other communities to assess the reasonability of the results of the simpler standards approach. The demand approach could incorporate accessibility considerations, although it usually does not.

· for more stagnant, land locked communities (built-out)
· system is defined - reorient existing facilities

Designing Alternatives

Designing the spatial pattern of community facilities generally follows the five-step approach introduced in chapter 11 and followed in the previous chapters on land classification, commercial, industrial, and residential land uses. In other words, the planner derives locational and space requirements for each type of facility from goals and policies and does a locational suitability analysis. Holding capacity is not generally a salient consideration. In most cases, it is not a single facility that must be located, but a coordinated system of facilities. For example, it is not a single park location that must be specified, but a hierarchical pattern of parks of neighborhood, community, and regional scale. Thus, based on goals and objectives, locational and space requirements, and locational suitability analyses, the planner actually designs alternative spatial patterns of "point facilities" (e.g., parks or schools) and networks of "linear facilities" (e.g., sewers or roads).

The design process generally follows what is sometimes called a heuristic process. That is, higher-level and higher-priority facilities are assigned locations first. Then surrounding areas are assigned to each facility's service area until the minimum or maximum user population is reached or a maximum service radius is reached for that facility. If the maximum service radius is not exceeded by the distance at which minimum user population is reached, unserviced areas are added until either maximum user population or maximum radius is reached. When a reasonable pattern of facilities is created in that fashion, the remaining unserviced areas are added to the nearest facility with excess capacity or with the potential to be expanded. The process is guided by the goals and objectives, the number of facilities to be located, minimum capacity and site size standards, minimum site sizes, and a maximum service radius for each type of facility.

Computerized mathematical models for locating community facilities have been developed since the seventies that allow a more systematic approach to design for agencies capable of using the models. They include optimization models, dynamic programming models, and welfare maximization models. Optimization models minimize the cost of a community facility system, subject to satisfying demand for services. Dynamic programming models introduce a time schedule for completing the system facilities. Welfare maximization models seek to optimize community welfare goals beyond accessibility and costs (Lim 1986). We anticipate continued development of such models and increasing feasibility for application by planning agencies with high levels of technical capability. In that respect, modeling for community facilities is ahead of modeling for industrial, office, retail, and residential land uses.

Although other community facilities and infrastructure are also considered in land use planning, the most relevant for long-range planning are transportation, sewerage, water supply, schools and recreation.

Transportation Facilities

The need to coordinate land use and infrastructure is nowhere stronger than it is for transportation facilities. From one perspective, existing and future land use is an input to transportation planning because the transportation system should be designed to serve people, firms, and other organizations; land use creates the demand for travel. From the opposite perspective, however, locations and densities of residential areas and activity centers should be designated to facilitate efficient transportation. Transportation improvements also alter accessibility of land parcels, and thereby their potential for development and redevelopment; transportation, in other words, virtually creates (with the water and sewer system) the supply of land for urban development. This perspective suggests designing the transportation system to promote a desirable land development pattern, for example away from environmentally vulnerable areas and toward locations where other community services can be provided more economically.

Land use and transportation planning have tended to be separate operations in practice, however. Transportation planning has tended to assume the future land use pattern as a given, usually based on market projections of land use rather than a land use plan. The transportation system thereby reinforces past development trends, not the land use plan. Land use planning, for its part, often merely accepts much of the proposed transportation system as an input determined by others rather than a plan element to be coordinated jointly with land use.

Ideally, one can conceive of a "spatial structure planning" approach, which would merge land use with multimodal transportation planning. Less ideally, but more realistically, we suggest a collaborative land use and transportation planning approach. It seeks to balance the use of land use policy as an input to transportation planning with a realization that transportation is a determinant in land use projection and the land use plan. Communities such as Portland, Oregon, Atlanta, Georgia, Sacramento, California, Montgomery County, Maryland, the research triangle region of North Carolina, and Florida communities (by virtue of state requirements for infrastructure concurrency) are exploring coordinated land use-transportation planning. See, for example, the land use element and the circulation element of the Sacramento comprehensive plan (County of Sacramento 1992a).

The Intermodal Surface Transportation Efficiency Act (ISTEA) and the Clean Air Act Amendments of 1990, working in combination, have the potential of further reshaping the collaboration of transportation planning and land use planning (see "Future Trends" in chapter 1). The ISTEA first and foremost requires a more comprehensive, multimodal, system management approach to transportation planning. Moreover, metropolitan planning organizations, which are responsible for long-range transportation planning and for shorter-range (three-year) transportation improvement programs, must now consider land use and development, energy conservation, and environmental protection, especially air quality, in their planning. In doing so they must determine the size and shape of the future urbanized area, that area forecasted to become urbanized within the next twenty years (a twenty-year growth area, similar in concept to the transition area in the land classification plan described in chapter 12) (Transportation Research Board 1993).

Planning Methodology

During policy framework planning and early rounds of land use design, transportation "sketch planning" and "land use strategy planning" can take place concurrently (Hutchinson 1974). The planning team of course will need to include transportation planners because of the technical nature of that planning process. Alternative land use/transportation concepts are specified in sketch form to explore interactions between, and implications for, transportation, activity systems, land development, and other infrastructure and community facility plans. Transportation implications are explored using simplified trip generation, trip distribution, and modal split analysis for each alternative. In the opposite direction, the costs, accessibility, and land development impacts of the transportation alternatives are analyzed using simplified land development modeling.

Figure 15-1 diagrams the flow of planning activities in a collaborative long-range transportation/land use planning approach. The approach has three major components: specification of the future urban spatial structure of land use and transportation, forecasting travel demand, and testing the plan.

The *specification of the future urban spatial structure* integrates several orientations to the future. One orientation is to project the future distribution and intensities of population, employment, and economic and social activity centers, perhaps using land use modeling to extrapolate land market trends, assuming a particular future transportation system. That approach, minus the feedback of transportation system impacts on land use, dominates conventional transportation planning. In the approach recommended here, however, it is balanced against two other approaches. The second orientation is to specify a future land use design, reflecting a conscious policy choice about a desirable future urban form instead of an extrapolation of market trends as input to transportation planning. A third orientation is to incorporate the design of a future transportation system in the design of the future urban form. This approach constitutes what might be called a "future urban spatial structure design approach," which incorporates both land use design and transportation system design and both the impacts of land use on transportation and transportation on land use.

The transportation system component in the design should be multimodal, that is, it should include public transportation, where relevant, and eventually incorporate consideration of taxicabs, bicycles, pedestrians, car pools and van pools, transportation management strategies, and parking.

The roads component of the urban spatial structure is a network of arterials, collectors, and local streets, as well as on-site circulation (chapter 9). At the level of long-range and intermediate-range land use and transportation planning, the emphasis is on the arterial and collector systems. Local streets, which provide access to properties, would not be shown on the land use plan. Arterials would be designed to connect proposed commercial centers, employment centers, major regional facilities, and residential communities, and to serve most of the trips entering and leaving the urban area and those passing through it. Collectors provide for movement within residential, industrial, and commercial areas. They penetrate but should not continue through residential areas, serving to collect traffic from local streets and pass it through to the arterial system as well as serve local shopping and similar trips. They usually are not shown in the land use plan

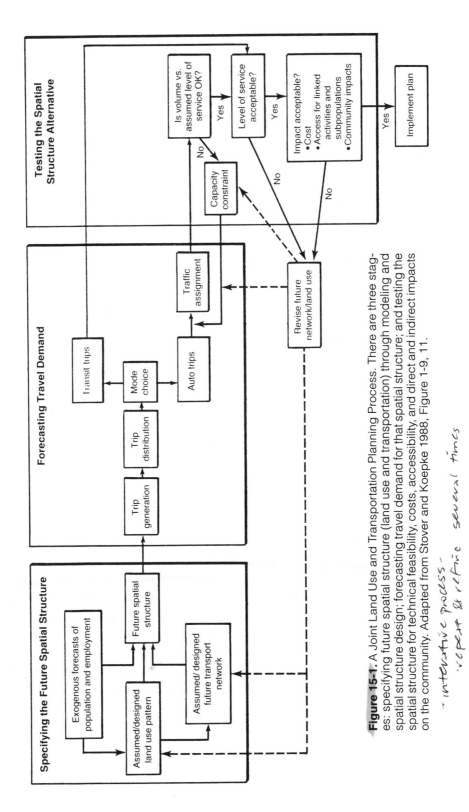

Figure 15-1. A Joint Land Use and Transportation Planning Process. There are three stages: specifying future spatial structure (land use and transportation) through modeling and spatial structure design; forecasting travel demand for that spatial structure; and testing the spatial structure for technical feasibility, costs, accessibility, and direct and indirect impacts on the community. Adapted from Stover and Koepke 1988, Figure 1-9, 11.

"interactive process:
  repeat & refine several times

or comprehensive plan, but should be, at least in schematic format, so that they guide development permit review (Figure 9-1).

The public transportation component of the urban spatial structure design can be divided into distribution systems, feeder systems, and line-haul systems based on their function. The spatial relationships of the three systems to the overall transit system are illustrated diagrammatically in Figure 15-2, along with the general characteristics of each part. The distribution system distributes people from where they get off the line-haul system to their destination and takes people around (circulates them) within major activity centers. The feeder system is a combination of a residential collection system and short lines connecting to the longer line-haul system. The line-haul system connects feeder systems to distribution systems and is the most likely to require a high-speed, exclusive right-of-way.

Policy about availability of alternative transport modes and levels of service for each is a necessary input to combined transportation-land use planning. For example, the Transportation Research Board's *Highway Capacity Manual* (1985) defines six levels of service that describe congestion and speeds for highways. A similar six-level scale of passenger loading standards exists for public transport. Figure 9-1 provides both the highway and public transport standards corresponding to levels of service.

In relating long-range land use design to long-range transportation planning, the planner could well begin with the major activity centers. These include the central business district and satellite commercial centers, major office centers, industrial parks and districts, and other employment centers, airports, and other concentrations of activities that are the major destinations of trips. The proposed locations and sizes of these major centers should reflect transportation policy as well as land use policy. In a transit-oriented scheme, for example, fewer and more densely developed centers would be appropriate, with less space for parking and streets. The hierarchy of commercial and employment centers should be coordinated with the hierarchical network of highway and public transportation. More detailed planning, beyond the long-range land use plan, would address major points of ingress and egress to the centers, transportation terminals, parking, and the channelization of traffic flows. With respect to residential land use, major highways and transit lines should bound rather than penetrate neighborhoods, with the exception of transit stations.

Forecasting travel demand involves four steps, all based ultimately on the land use pattern and travel behavior. First, the analyst generates trips, based on the activities represented in the future land use pattern. Second, the trips are distributed among destinations, also represented in the land use pattern. Third, trips are split among several travel modes, primarily auto and public transportation. Finally, trips are assigned to specific routes through the highway and public transit networks.

In the first step, the number of trips generated or attracted is a function of the population and land use characteristics of traffic zones. For more detailed planning, beyond the long-range land use or transportation plan, trip generation models may reflect individual household behavior rather than aggregate or average

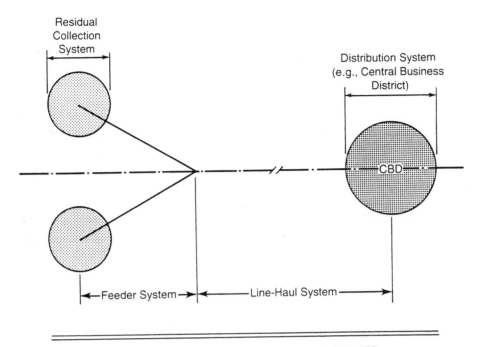

SYSTEM COMPONENTS

TYPE OF CHARACTERISTIC	DISTRIBUTION SYSTEMS	FEEDER SYSTEM	LINE-HAUL SYSTEMS
Network	Loops, shuttles, or very small networks	Limited network up to few miles	Linear or radial routes up to several miles
Typical station spacing	1/4-1/2 miles	1/4-1/2 miles	1/2-3 miles
Service	Scheduled or demand-responsive	Scheduled	Scheduled
Area of service	High-density areas of small activity centers	High-density urban areas, large activity centers, or low-density suburban areas	Areas with population density above 5,000 per square mile

Figure 15-2. Diagrammatic Layout and Characteristics of a Transit System's Components. The transit system consists of a combination of residential collection and feeder systems, linked to longer line-haul systems, which connect to systems that circulate people within major commercial and employment centers. Adapted from Yu 1982, Figure 13-2 and Table 13.1, 207.

household characteristics of a traffic zone. The Institute of Transportation Engineers (ITE) publishes and updates a manual that gives the number of trips generated by, and attracted to, ten major types of land uses and numerous subcategories of those ten categories. The ten major categories are residential, industrial, agricultural, office, retail, services, institutional, medical, recreational, lodging, and port and terminal, which are compatible with most land use classification schemes.

In the second step, trip distribution reflects the spatial distribution of employment, shopping, and population represented by the future land use design. That is, trips will tend to be attracted to nearer rather than farther places, where the trip purpose (say, employment or shopping) can be satisfied and be attracted to places with greater employment or shopping opportunity rather than places with fewer jobs or shops.

The third and fourth steps, modal split and traffic assignment to links in the transportation networks, are more purely transportation-oriented methodology. Those two steps, along with the earlier trip distribution step, require at least a preliminary transportation system design.

Some places, such as Portland and Sacramento, are incorporating characteristics of neighborhood-scale urban design into simulations of transportation behavior. Pedestrian orientation (presence of sidewalks, short blocks, and ease of street crossing, for example), presence of public transportation, housing densities, and the mix of retail and employment and other destination opportunities are presumed to affect trip generation and distribution as well as modal split. Public transportation oriented developments (TODs) are integrated into the land use element and circulation element of the Sacramento County General Plan, and their influence on transportation behavior is accounted for (Sacramento County 1992b). In Portland, transportation models are adjusted to reflect "pedestrian environment" near transit lines.

Plan testing involves recalculating trip generation, distribution, and modal split after adjustments in land use and transportation designs (and, in later stages of planning, system operating and congestion management policies). Adjustments in the land use projection and design should reflect assessment of transport system performance in terms of congestion and travel times, as well as assessment of accessibility for neighborhoods and activity centers in the land use design. Relative development and operation costs should also be assessed. Finally, the impacts on neighborhoods, environment, and development potential of land should be assessed. These assessments are used to suggest modifications in both land use and transportation elements of the spatial structure plan.

A coordinated land use-transportation planning approach suggests the need for land use and transportation models that are able to receive inputs and outputs from one another. Such combined land use and transportation models have been under development since the early 1970s (Putman 1983; Webster et al. 1988; de la Barra 1989; Batty 1994; Wegener 1994). Klosterman (1994a, 5) and Batty (1994) find that integrated urban models that examine the interaction between land use and transportation are in actual use in seven of the ten largest metropolitan areas of the United States. Outside of those large metropolitan cases, however, U.S. planners have seldom used fully integrated models in practice over the past twenty years. While substantial progress has been made in theory and model specification, large-scale urban models are still difficult to adapt to new settings because of data quality, inadequate model calibration, and insufficient documentation (Klosterman 1994b, 42–43) and because of their complexity, costs, and computer requirements—and perhaps also for lack of faith (Webster et al. 1988, 4). Klosterman notes that land use outputs have been more plausible than travel predictions (1994b, 42), and that performance declines at higher levels of disaggregation. Nevertheless, modelers predict that large-scale urban models are likely to be much more important for future land use-transportation planning practice than they have been in the past twenty years because they help the planner achieve consistency between land use activity, physical development, transportation networks, travel, population, and employment components of urban change (Putnam 1983, 43; Klosterman 1994a, 5; Wegener 1994).[1]

Although the emphasis here has been on the long-range, macro-system, capital investment approach to transportation/land use planning, a comprehensive planning process also includes attention to the short-range, micro, and operational management approaches (Transportation Research Board 1993; Meyer 1986, 124–25). On the land use planning side, those extensions of the planning process shift attention to the type, intensity, and location of activities in the immediate vicinity of transportation facilities and to site design requirements for parking and transit facilities. On the transportation planning side, the process includes short-term programming of incremental improvements to transportation systems (TIPs) and transportation systems management (TSM) to get the most out of the current system. TSM identifies traffic engineering, public transportation, regulatory, pricing, management, and operational improvements to the transportation system. Emphasis may also be applied to parts of the transportation system, for example to specific transportation corridors; to specific individual traffic generators such as spectator sports facilities, industrial parks, and shopping centers; to major land development projects, urban revitalization projects, and joint transportation-real estate developments; or to congestion management strategies to reduce pollution emissions.

More recently, there has emerged a more sophisticated model for comprehensive, short-and-long range, transportation-land use planning, called a congestion management program (CMP), which is now required of California cities and counties (Congestion Management Agency, Santa Clara County, California, N.d.). The California 1991 legislation requires a congestion management program (under penalty of loss of the locality's share of state gas tax revenues) that specifies both level-of-service standards and programs of action. Certain elements are required in a CMP: roadway system definition and traffic level of service standards, transit service (if relevant) and standards, transportation demand management and trip reduction plan to improve levels of service, land use impact analysis to analyze transportation impacts of land use decisions, a prioritized capital improvements element, a monitoring and conformance element, and a deficiency plan for addressing facilities that do not operate within the adopted level-of-service standards.

Water and Sewer

Water supply and wastewater treatment are both linked strongly to land use planning. The capacities and spatial configurations of water and sewer systems are based on the amount, type, and location of urban development to be served; and at the same time, the amount and location of urban development depends on the availability of water and sewer. There can be no significant development at urban densities without both water and sewer.

Water Systems

Water supply planning begins with the intermediate- and long-range (up to fifty years) projection of future demand based on projected population and employment, and in some cases specific industrial uses (see Dzurik 1986, 286–89, and Boland et al. 1981 for reviews of forecasting techniques). Studies have shown population to be a reliable overall water use indicator. Thus, the most commonly used technique is to multiply projected population by a per capita water use coefficient that incorporates water use by nonresidential uses. Sometimes this method is refined by using separate per capita coefficients for residential population, commercial, industrial, and public employment and adding in specific uses such as thermal power stations or heavy water using industries, such as textiles or food processing.

Typical water demand in the United States is 150 gallons per capita per day (GPCD): fifty-five in domestic (residential) use, twenty in commercial uses, fifty in industrial uses, and twenty-five in public and unaccounted uses. Total use varies from place to place, however, from fifty to 250 GPCD. Differences are attributable to climate, per capita income, annual rainfall, and types of industry. If a community has little or no industrial uses, for example, the total water demand might be considerably less than 150 GPCD. Therefore, an analysis of local usage and the projected industrial employment mix is useful (Goodman 1984, 88–90).

A public water system is normally economical at densities greater than a thousand persons per square mile; that is, average lot size of 1.5 acres or smaller or minimum gross densities of 0.6 dwellings per acre. At densities of less than five hundred persons per square mile, public water supply is rarely justified.

Water supply planning involves the assessment of ground water and/or surface water supplies and the design of means to capture, treat, and distribute the water to users. In many situations, reservoirs are needed to regulate and store surface water flows. Reservoir capacity usually provides not only for active water storage, but also for sediment collection and possibly for hydropower production, recreation, and flood control (see Dzurik 1986, for techniques for calculating storage requirements).

Land use planning can play a role in water supply protection strategies. Land use regulations can help protect the water quality of aquifer recharge areas and water supply reservoir watersheds by prohibiting industrial and other uses that threaten water quality and requiring site design practices to reduce erosion, sediment, and pollutants in stormwater runoff. Land use planning can also prevent premature abandonment of a water source. Land use planning for watersheds of future water impoundments can assure their future viability (Burby et al. 1983; Kaiser 1986).

Sewerage

As noted in chapter 9, *sewerage* refers to the system of pipes and facilities required to transport, treat, and discharge wastewater from residential, commercial, and industrial establishments. The size and shape of a sewer service area is governed by the need to design the collection system to service existing development, reach land that is presently being developed, and yet also reach out to areas designated for future development in the land use plan. Unlike the lattice pattern of a water distribution system, sewer lines follow a hierarchical, or treelike, pattern laid out to allow wastewater to flow from the house, store, office or industry by force of gravity to the treatment plant, which is suitably located to discharge effluent at acceptable levels into receiving waters. Force mains and pumping stations can be used to move wastewater under pressure against the force of gravity over a ridge line, allowing for transfer of sewage between natural drainage basins.

Planning for wastewater collection, treatment, and disposal requires assessing existing facilities and water quality conditions in potential receiving waters; estimating future need (wastewater volumes based on population and economic projection); designing the collection system (in conjunction with land use design); and locating and designing a treatment facility (Carver and Fitzgerald 1986, 378–406).

An assessment of the operation, excess capacity, and condition of present facilities and environmental conditions establishes one baseline for planning. It should cover private, on-site systems and small community package plant systems, as well as public systems, and include a study of receiving waters and lands for wastewater effluent discharges and solid waste disposal, including waste loading conditions, resulting water quality conditions, and implied assimilation capacities of existing and potential receiving waters.

Forecasting future needs for wastewater collection and treatment involves projecting population and employment in general, as well as employment in industries with heavy wastewater treatment requirements. The geographic distribution of that demand, as represented by land use models and tentative land use design alternatives, is an important aspect of the study. Population, employment, and land use are then converted to wastewater loads. The simplest approach, suitable for general land use planning, is to base wastewater generation on water use. Generally, planners multiply water demand by a coefficient of .60 to .80 to obtain wastewater demand, based preferably on a study of local data (Tabors et al. 1976, 28).

If water demand is broken down by land uses, which is recommended, then the ratio can vary across those uses. Houston, for example, multiplied residential water demand by .80 to obtain wastewater collection and treatment needs; office demand by 1.0; and retail demand by .5 (City of Houston 1987). Another approach is to use figures from comparable communities. The U.S. Environmental Protection Agency has recommended designing interceptor sewers on the assumption of 100–125 GPCD for residential areas (Tabors et al. 1976, 29). As in water systems, the design horizon is long range, commonly fifty years for major sewer lines and twenty years for treatment facilities, with allowance for treatment plant expansion being factored into the calculation of plant site size.

Location of wastewater treatment facilities is critical to both wastewater planning and land use planning. Desired gravity flow of sewerage systems restricts the number of appropriate wastewater treatment plant locations. Because of odors and a generally negative image, sewage treatment plants are ill-suited near existing or planned residential and commercial areas. Thus, coordinating land use and wastewater facility planning is vital. In fact, preliminary wastewater planning should precede the land use planning for residential, office, commercial, and industrial sectors to the extent that geographic areas most easily sewered by gravity flow from existing and potential new treatment plant sites are delineated in suitability maps.

Minimum densities to make public sewerage feasible are normally higher than what is needed to justify a public water system. Densities of 2,500 to 5,000 persons per square mile are normally required; that is, average lot size of no more than one-half acre, and gross densities of at least two dwellings per acre. At densities of fewer than a thousand persons per square mile, public sewerage is rarely justified (Carver and Fitzgerald 1986). Of course, public sewerage may be justified at lower densities to prevent a health hazard.

· Sewer system higher density requirement to make things efficient. Thus,

Joint Water and Sewer Considerations

A small number of water and sewer utilities is preferable to a multiplicity of uncoordinated systems. Independent companies or municipal departments may result in insufficient capacity in some areas. Where practical, interconnection between water distribution lines and between wastewater treatment systems is recommended (De Chiara and Koppelman 1982, ch. 16).

A master plan for utilities may be coordinated with the land use plan. It shows future needs and facilities in relation to urban growth and water resources. The water master plan should be developed in connection with a sewerage master plan and should encompass long-range watershed needs, storage facilities, and flood control. Pipe networks, pumping facilities, treated water storage needs, and fire protection demands should also be considered. The master plan should include a long-range capital improvement and financial plan.

The community should have a definite policy for extending water and sewer systems. Although economy in capital investment and system operation is important, growth-management considerations should also count. The policy should include regulations calling for mandatory, not voluntary, connection of new development to public water and sewer within service areas to facilitate system planning and financing and to control growth. The policy should incorporate financial arrangements where new lines cross vacant areas and where oversized pipes are installed in anticipation of future urban growth.

For further guidance on planning water and sewer facilities, see the American Society of Civil Engineers' *Urban Planning Guide* (1986, chs. 12, 14), and Tabors, Shapiro, and Rogers (1976).

Schools

Schools should be considered in land use planning even though the local school system is governed by a separate elected board in most cases and several school systems may exist within the planning jurisdiction. The school board or boards, administrative officials, and representatives of parent-teacher groups should be part of the design team.

Location and Space Requirements

Almost all school site selection standards in the literature originate from the baby boom of the late 1940s and the 1950s and school boom that followed in the 1950s and 1960s (Seelig 1972). Thus they assume more children in a household than tends to be the case now. They are also influenced by the neighborhood concept, based on an assumption that most students will walk to school and that schools are neighborhood-oriented. Although pedestrian-oriented schools are still desirable, especially for the lower grades, school plant technology and educational policy now imply larger schools with more special facilities and higher enrollments at each site. That, together with smaller average household sizes and low-density housing in many areas, creates a larger geographic service area for each type of school than traditional standards represent. As a result of these changing conditions, the development of location and space standards for particular jurisdictions depends heavily on the participation of the school planning team. General standards, such as those in Table 15-2, should be used only as starting points for local standard-setting. The land use planning team is ultimately interested in establishing local standards for the number of school sites, service radiuses, and minimum desirable site size, which depend on local development densities and average number of school-aged children per household. Standards might well vary within the planning jurisdiction. Table 15-2 includes some of the assumptions behind the suggested location and space requirement standards, which should help the school facility design team adjust the standards to conditions and educational policy in their community. The planner might also consider school site criteria suggested by Engelhardt (1970, illus. 13-1) and in Council of Educational Facilities Planners, International (1991).

Table 15-2. Suggested Standards for Siting Schools

	Nursery School	Elementary School	Junior High School	High School
Assumed Population Characteristics	60 children of nursery school age per 1,000 persons or 275–300 families	175 children of elementary school age per 1,000 persons or 275–300 families	75 children of junior high school age per 1,000 persons or 275–300 families	75 children of high school age per 1,000 persons or 275–300 families
Size of School				
Minimum	4 classes (60 children)	250 pupils	800 pupils	1,000 pupils
Average	6 classes (90 children)	800 pupils	1,200 pupils	1,800 pupils
Maximum	8 classes (120 children)	1,200 pupils	1,600 pupils	2,600 pupils
Population Served				
Minimum	4 classes: 1,000 persons (275–300 families)	1,500 persons	10,000 persons (2,750–3,000 families)	14,000 persons (3,800–4,000 families)
Average	6 classes: 1,500 persons (425–450 families)	5,000 persons	16,000 persons (4,500–5,000 families)	24,000 persons (6,800–7,000 families)
Maximum	8 classes: 2,000 persons (550–600 families)	7,000 persons	20,000 persons (5,800–6,000 families)	34,000 persons (9,800–10,000 families)
Area Required				
Minimum	4 classes: 4,000 ft.^{2}	7–8 acres	18-20 acres	32–34 acres
Average	6 classes: 6,000 ft.^{2}	12–14 acres	24–26 acres	40–42 acres
Maximum	8 classes: 8,000 ft.^{2}	16–18 acres	30–32 acres	48–50 acres
Radius of Area Served				
Desirable	1–2 blocks	1/4 mile	1/2 mile	3/4 mile
Maximum	1/3 mile	1/2 mile	3/4 mile	1 mile
General Location	Near an elementary school or community center	Near center of residential area; near or adjacent to other community facilities	Near concentration of dwelling units or near center of residential area; away from major arterial streets	Centrally located for easy access; proximity to other community facilities advantageous; adjacent to park area

Note: Such standards are good starting points for local standard-setting but should be adjusted to reflect local education policy, proposed residential densities in the land use plan, and the average number of school-age children per household locally.

Source: De Chiara and Koppelman 1982, 374–75.

Methodology

The planning process involves a study of the existing school plant, a projection of enrollments, development of location and space requirement standards, and the design of a spatial pattern of school sites.

The first step, a study of existing schools, involves plotting trends of past enrollments for each school, for each neighborhood or other residential community unit, and for each administrative jurisdiction (public, private, and parochial), an inventory of school capacities measured in numbers of classrooms, existing and projected physical plant conditions, and sizes of school sites and their potential for expansion and remodeling. A review is also made of existing and proposed policies with respect to the progression of grade levels included in elementary, middle or junior high, and high school levels (6-3-3, 8-4, or 5-3-4, for example) and the community's policy about joint use of schools for recreation, community meetings, and other functions.

The second major step is to project future enrollments according to the anticipated future grade level organization (e.g., 6-3-3), by neighborhood, planning district, or other suitable geographical unit. Methods for projecting population by school-age composition are discussed in chapter 5. The projections may have to be adjusted to reflect the proportion of children expected to attend private and parochial schools at each level if those enrollments are significant. The resulting projections of future total enrollment are broken down by elementary, junior high or middle school, and senior high school levels, and by public and private systems (assuming both systems are substantial). Total enrollment, by school levels, is then distributed to geographic areas, based on the population distribution implied in the land use design for residential areas (chapter 14). Adjustments in school-age population may be made to reflect variation in household size by housing types; adjusting upward for predominantly single-family detached housing and downward for predominantly multifamily housing (chapter 14). This approach is satisfactory for designing the pattern of school sites in the general land use plan but should be adjusted later in more detailed studies for more detailed school planning and capital improvement programming. The result of this step is a spatial distribution of demand for school space by grade level.

In the next step, existing school locations are examined with respect to their capacity, condition, and accessibility for the distribution of projected future school enrollment. The planner must assess the potential for expanding and otherwise adapting existing school buildings and sites and also assess the availability and suitability of vacant or renewable land for new sites. Location and space requirements are applied, including acceptable walking and bussing radiuses, minimum site size standards, and number of sites required. On the basis of those considerations and basic goals, the planner designs a pattern of school sites, including specification of existing sites to be retained, enlarged, otherwise modified or abandoned, as well as new sites. School sites to be abandoned become potential sites for other uses.

The product of the school system design stage is a map of sites. The map would indicate location, type, and name of sites and be cross-referenced with a table listing the sites and indicating for each site, its size, site procurement status, and the number of classrooms and other facilities existing and proposed, and a time period for proposed development.

Further References

For further information about school plant planning principles, and locational and space standards, see De Chiara and Koppelman (1982), especially the summary table of site standards; Seelig (1972), especially the discussion of standard-setting and a table of eight different sources for standards on site size; and Engelhardt (1970, ch. 13) for a "scorecard" for rating specific school site alternatives.

Recreation Facilities

Recreation land use actually encompasses a wide range of facilities, each having its own location and space requirements. There are, for example, recreation facilities with small service areas—tot lots, playing fields, local parks, and recreation centers—that need to be coordinated with residential and school plant planning. Downtown parks, while serving open space needs, also call for sites that are highly accessible to pedestrians. At the regional scale, there are spectator sports facilities: ball parks, stadiums, arenas, and other facilities for sports events and exhibitions, most of which require locations directly accessible to transit and major highways. Regional recreation facilities that require suitable physical environment, as well as good access to the regional transportation system, include golf courses, race tracks, fairgrounds, botanical gardens, and zoos. Forest preserves and country parks require large sites and specific environmental features, with capital improvements for picnicking, hiking, nature walks, boating, informal games, and other forms of outdoor active and passive leisure activities for individuals, families, and larger groups.

Principles and Standards for Recreation Facilities

The standards most widely accepted by local governments are from the National Recreation and Park Association (NRPA) (Lancaster 1983). The NRPA suggests standards for a hierarchical classification system (Table 15-3): minipark, neighborhood park, community park, regional park, regional park preserve, linear park, special use, and conservancy. For each component in the recreation facility system, the table suggests maximum desirable service area, minimum desirable site size, minimum desirable total acres per one thousand population, and other desirable features. More than one component of a recreation system may occur within the same site. As a general minimum, the NRPA recommends a core system of parkland, with a minimum of 6.25 to 10.5 acres of developed open space per thousand population. In addition, regional recreation and open space of fifteen to twenty acres per thousand population is recommended. The NRPA supplements the guidelines shown in Table 15-3 with suggested standards for nineteen specific recreation activities such as tennis and baseball (Lancaster 1983, Appendix A).

The NRPA stresses that although their recommendations are called standards, they should be viewed as "guides" for a community to use in developing its own standards. Those standards should reflect the needs of the people in the specific service area, be realistic and attainable, and be acceptable to elected and appointed officials and the public. The NRPA even suggests procedures for assessing recreation demand, reviewing local responsibilities, and assessing attraction potential of specific facilities at particular sites. It also emphasizes the importance of integrating such procedures into a planning process (Lancaster 1983). Table 15-4 provides an example of standards adapted by the District of Columbia from the NRPA national guidelines.

Recreation facility plans generally reflect the hierarchical nature of the recreation and open space system. Miniparks, for example, are small parks or open spaces and may be called "tot lots" or "block and street space" (the term used by District of Columbia in Table 15-4). They serve very small user groups, and not every community sees a need for this niche in the system.

Neighborhood parks serve a walking population (up to one-half mile) of all age groups, but primarily the elderly and children, and provide for both active and passive recreation. Facilities may include playgrounds, playing fields and courts, benches and tables, and natural open space. Indoor facilities are sometimes included.

Community parks provide facilities that are too expensive or require too much space to be provided in every neighborhood, although there may be overlap in the functions served. They are generally at least ten acres in size and may be as large as seventy-five acres, with a service radius of two miles or more. They are more likely to include picnicking areas, a swimming pool, lighted ball fields and courts, a community center, recreational and educational programs, and parking. They should be located near major streets but still allow pedestrian access.

Regional and metropolitan parks are large (a minimum of a hundred acres) and serve populations that would spend up to an hour's driving time to reach them. The size and facilities vary more widely than for smaller parks. In addition to facilities found in community parks, regional parks may include nature centers, trails, boating, a golf course, small zoos, and sports centers, for example. Responsibility for them may be shared among several jurisdictions or be held by a regional authority or a county government.

Additional special facilities may be appropriate to the jurisdiction but are not usually geared to population ratio standards or maximum service radiuses. Such facilities might include linear open space, parkways, and greenbelts, which might contain only hiking, riding, and biking trails, boat ramps, and scenic overlooks.

Table 15-3. Recreation and Open Space Standards Suggested by the National Recreation and Park Association

Component	Use	Service Area	Desirable Size	Acres per 1000 population	Desirable Site Characteristics
Local or close-to-home space					
Minipark	Specialized facilities that serve a concentrated or limited population or specific group such as tots or senior citizens	Less than 1/4 mile radius	1 acre or less	0.25 to 0.5	Within neighborhoods and close to apartment complexes, townhouse development, or housing for the elderly
Neighborhood park/playground	Area for intense recreational activities such as field games, court games, crafts, skating, and picnicking; also for wading pool and playground apparatus areas	1/4 to 1/2 mile radius to serve a population up to 5000 (a neighborhood)	15+ acres	1.0 to 2.0	Suited for intense development; easily accessible to neighborhood population; geographically centered with safe walking and bike access; may be developed as a school-park facility
Community park	Area of diverse environmental quality; may include areas suited for intense recreational facilities, such as athletic complexes, large swimming pools; may be an area of natural quality for outdoor recreation, such as walking, viewing, sitting, picnicking; may be any combination of the above, depending upon site suitability and community need	Several neighborhoods, 1 to 2 mile radius	25+ acres	5.0 to 8.0	May include natural features, such as water bodies, and areas suited for intense development; easily accessible to neighborhood served

Total close-to-home space = 6.25 to 10.5 acres per 1000 population

Regional space					
Regional/metropolitan park	Area of natural or ornamental quality for outdoor recreation, such as picnicking, boating, fishing, swimming, camping, and trail uses; may include play areas	Several communities, 1 hour driving time	200+ acres	5.0 to 10.0	Contiguous to or encompassing natural resources
Regional park reserve	Areas of natural quality for nature-oriented outdoor recreation, such as viewing and studying nature, wildlife habitats, conservation, swimming, picnicking, hiking, fishing, boating, camping, and trail uses; may include	Several communities, 1 hour driving time	1,000+ acres, sufficient area to encompass the resource to be preserved and managed	Variable	Diverse or unique natural resources, such as lakes, streams, marshes, flora, fauna, and topography

active play areas; generally 80% of the land is reserved for conservation and natural resource management, with less than 20% used for recreation

Total regional space = 15.20 acres per 1000 population

Space that may be local or regional and is unique to each community

Linear park	Area developed for one or more varying modes of recreational travel, such as hiking, biking, snowmobiling, horseback riding, cross-country skiing, canoeing, and pleasure driving; may include active play areas. (Note: Any activities included for the preceding components may occur in the linear park.)	No applicable standard	Sufficient width to protect the resources and provide maximum use	Built on natural corridors, such as utility rights-of-way, bluff lines, vegetation patterns, and roads, that link other components of the recreation system or community facilities, such as schools, libraries, commercial areas, and other park areas
			Variable	
Special use	Areas for specialized or single-purpose recreational activities, such as golf courses, nature centers, marinas, zoos, conservatories, aboreta, display gardens, arenas, outdoor theaters, gun ranges, or downhill ski areas, or areas that preserve, maintain, and interpret buildings, sites, and objects of archaeological significance; also plazas or squares in or near commercial centers, boulevards, and parkways	No applicable standard	Variable depending on desired size	Within communities
			Variable	
Conservancy	Protection and management of the natural or cultural environment with recreational use as a secondary objective	No applicable standard	Sufficient to protect the resource	Variable, depending on the resource being protected
			Variable	

Note: Although called "standards," the NRPA stresses that they should be viewed as "guides" for a community to use in developing its own standards.

Source: NRPA-suggested classification system (Lancaster 1983, 56–57).

Table 15-4. Summary of Recreation Standards for the District of Columbia[a]

Area Category	Size of Area (acres)	Capacity[b] (in persons)	Maximum Service Radius
1. Block and street space			
a. Play and decorative areas	≤ 0.60	60	2 blocks
b. Miniparks	0.60	110	3/8 mile
2. Neighborhood playgrounds	3–5	264	3/8 mile
3. Community recreation centers	10–15	420–820	A number of neighborhoods
4. District recreation centers	≥ 25	867	All or parts of a service area
5. Large urban parks	≥ 400	8/acre[c]	All or major sections of the city

a. These standards illustrate the modification of NRPA national guidelines to meet the specific local conditions and values.
b. Total capacities are based on the capacity of the modules used in each recreation area.
c. The typical capacity for large urban parks is based on the standard for picnicking, which is eight persons per acre.
Source: Lancaster 1983, 70.

Special recreation facilities may also include zoos, ice skating rinks, stadiums, beaches, amphitheaters, botanical gardens, arboretums, historic sites, and cultural centers.

Some of the space requirements for neighborhood parks could be satisfied by playgrounds on elementary school sites, and some requirements for community center and playing field needs could be satisfied at junior, middle, and high school sites. Such coordination assumes cooperation among school boards, municipalities, and recreation agencies.

Designing the Recreation Facility System for the Land Use Plan

Referring to the open space pattern, the system of existing and proposed school sites, and existing recreation facilities, the planner and community facility planning team develop a schematic plan of recreation sites. Attention in the suitability analysis should be given to surplus public lands, abandoned school sites, and tax-title lands as potential sites. The result is a scheme of sites dimensioned according to the locally adopted standards for minimum desirable site sizes. The total acreage is a balance between the total population ratio standard and land supply constraints.

Miniparks and some neighborhood parks, especially those in areas to be developed in the future, and drainage and other small-scale elements of the open space network may be designated by a symbol indicating the type of facility and general location in the land use plan. Typically, development regulations specify standards for providing such facilities in subdivisions, planned unit developments, and other projects, with exact locations and site planning being determined during the permit review and approval process.

Further References

The National Recreation and Park Association (Lancaster 1983) provides an excellent review of procedures for adapting recreation standards to local situations and suggests ways to integrate those procedures into a three-level planning process: policy plan, site plan, and operation and maintenance plan. Gold (1980) describes a more refined recreation planning and design process, including supply and demand analysis and the formulation of action alternatives.

For a guide on assessing whether a specific recreation project is appropriate and feasible for a community, see Kelsey and Gray (1986). For example, should a community of thirty thousand build an eighteen-hole golf course? Where are appropriate sites, will there be sufficient use, how financially feasible is it, and what will be the impact on the community?

For guidance on a more detailed demand analysis and economic evaluation, see Hendon (1981), who covers leisure behavior by different user groups, consumer demand, public investment, and public efficiency evaluation. Richman (1979) proposes a social performance standard approach to recreation planning.

Summary and Conclusions

Community facilities and infrastructure are vital aspects of the land use plan and development management. However, they need the attention of a special facilities team during the planning process, and the planning process extends to maintenance, financing, rehabilitation, and management of facilities, not just their initial size and location. Although a per capita standards approach is appropriate for general land use planning purposes, a more refined assessment of demand is needed in later rounds of comprehensive planning.

One set of issues in coordinating land use and public facility planning revolves around priorities for the types, timing, and location of facilities, and who shall pay for them. Because these public facilities are expensive and should be provided concurrently with private development or in advance, local governments may have trouble paying for them. One public planning and management tool to be used to address this situation is the capital improvements program (CIP), a five-year schedule of governmental capital improvements. By requiring elected officials to back up public facility plans with realistic financial plans, the CIP creates the discipline necessary for deciding priorities. The development management plan (chapter 16) incorporates a CIP; in Florida, local governments are required by the Growth Management Act to include a CIP in their adopted comprehensive plans (De Grove 1993).

Another example of incorporation of community facility planning into a future land use plan is the future land use element of the Reedy Creek Improvement District Comprehensive Plan (Sedway Cooke Associates 1991). This plan for the Disney World area near Orlando, Florida, estimates the "development maximum" increments for each type of land use for future five-year periods. For example, one million square feet of office use is the maximum projected between 1991 and 1996. This is the demand side of the analysis, which is then balanced against supply-side analysis of urban services. In analyzing the infrastructure supply, the Reedy Creek plan establishes "development thresholds" based on plans for service availability of roads and public transportation, water, wastewater treatment, solid waste, drainage, and parks over the same five-year periods. The service availability is established in a capital improvements program for the first five years and in the traffic and infrastructure elements of the general plan beyond the first five years. These plans are based on the land use design as well as financial and other factors. Service availability is converted to development thresholds by using service generation factors for each land use type. For example, a square foot of office space generates daily some 0.0146 trips, 0.18 gallons of water use, 0.15 gallons of wastewater, and 0.01 pounds of solid waste. In this way, concurrency between private-sector growth and public infrastructure is achieved. This planned concurrency is also addressed in development permitting procedures, where proposed projects are checked against service availability. If service consumption exceeds the threshold capacity, either the project is scaled down or a public-private plan is devised to increase service availability beyond the planned thresholds.

Local government is also increasingly turning to private funding sources to assist in public facility finance. Traditionally, developers have paid for the facilities within their projects. More recently, local governments have turned to impact fees which require private developers to pay some portion of the impact of their projects on off-site public facilities, for example on the need for a wastewater treatment plant, schools, or larger-scale recreation facilities. While the main reason for these approaches has been to help pay for public infrastructure by shifting costs to the private sector, they should be governed by the land use plan. Otherwise, as Kaiser and Burby (1988, 117) point out "developers' willingness to pay the costs of new infrastructure and impact mitigation gives them virtual carte blanche over the character, location, and density of development." This issue concerns not only who pays for facilities, but also whether the public sector or the private sector determines when and where growth is to occur.

The question of whether land use should precede or follow provision of public facilities is moot for the planner. Infrastructure can induce urban development (Tabors, Shapiro, and Rogers 1976) and should be planned with that in mind. On the other hand, land use generates demand for new roads and public transportation. In practice, land use and public facilities should be planned together.

NOTE

1. Readers interested in exploring the topic of land use-transportation modeling should consult a symposium on large-scale urban models in the *Journal of the American Planning Association* 60(1). For example, see Klosterman 1994a, 1994b; Wegener 1994; Batty 1994.

REFERENCES

American Society of Civil Engineers, Urban Planning and Development Division. 1986. *Urban planning guide.* Rev. ed. ASCE Manuals and Reports on Engineering Practice, no. 49. New York: The American Society of Civil Engineers.

Batty, Michael. 1994. A chronicle of scientific planning: The Anglo-American modeling experience. *Journal of the American Planning Association* 60(1): 7–16.

Boland, J. D., D. D. Baumann, and B. Dziegielewski. 1981. *An assessment of municipal and industrial water use forecasting approaches.* Fort Belvoir: U.S. Army Corps of Engineers, Institute for Water Resources.

Bourey, James M. 1989. Managing growth and infrastructure development. In *Capital projects: New strategies for planning, management, and finance,* ed. John Matzer, Jr. Washington, D.C.: International City Managers Association.

Box, Paul C., and Joseph C. Oppenlander. 1976. *Manual of traffic engineering studies.* Washington, D.C.: Institute of Transportation Engineers.

Burby, Raymond J., Edward J. Kaiser, Todd L. Miller, and David H. Moreau. 1983. *Protecting drinking water supplies through watershed management: A guidebook for devising local programs.* Ann Arbor: Ann Arbor Science. Reprint. 1986. Raleigh: Water Resources Research Institute.

Carver, Paul T., and A. Ruth Fitzgerald. 1986. Planning for wastewater collection and treatment. In American Society of Civil Engineers, *Urban planning guide.* Rev. ed. ASCE Manuals and Reports on Engineering Practice, no. 49. New York: The American Society of Civil Engineers.

City of Houston, Department of Planning and Development. 1987. *Planning policy manual.* Houston: The author.

Congestion Management Agency, Santa Clara County, California. N.d. Congestion management program of Santa Clara County: Executive summary. San Jose: Congestion Management Agency.

Council of Educational Facility Planners, International. 1991. *Guide for planning educational facilities.* Columbus: The author.

De Chiara, Joseph. 1984. *Time-saver standards for residential development.* New York: McGraw Hill.

De Chiara, Joseph, and Lee Koppelman. 1982. *Urban planning and design criteria.* New York: Van Nostrand Reinhold Co.

De Grove, John M., and Nancy E. Stroud. 1988. New developments and future trends in local government comprehensive planning. *Stetson Law Review* 17(3): 573–605.

de la Barra, Tomas. 1989. *Integrated land use and transport modelling: Decision chains and hierarchies.* Cambridge: Cambridge University Press.

Dzurik, Andrew A. 1986. Water resources planning. In American Society of Civil Engineers, *Urban planning guide.* Rev. ed. ASCE Manuals and Reports on Engineering Practice, no. 49. New York: The American Society of Civil Engineers.

Engelhardt, Nickolaus L. 1970. *Complete guide for planning new schools.* West Nyack: Parker.

Gold, Seymour M. 1980. *Recreation planning and design.* New York: McGraw Hill.

Goodman, Alvin S. 1984. *Principles of water resources planning.* Englewood Cliffs: Prentice-Hall.

Hendon, William S. 1981. *Evaluating urban parks and recreation.* New York: Praeger.

Hutchinson, B. G. 1974. *Principles of urban transport systems planning.* Washington, D.C.: Scripta.

Institute of Transportation Engineers. 1987. *Trip generation.* 4th ed. Washington, D.C.: The author.

Kaiser, Edward J. 1986. Is your water supply protected? *Carolina Planning* 12(2): 50–52.

Kaiser, Edward J., and Raymond J. Burby. 1988. Exactions in managing growth: The land-use planning perspective. In *Private supply of public services: Evaluation of real estate exactions, linkage, and alternative land policies,* ed. Rachelle Alterman. New York: New York University Press.

Kelsey, Craig, and Howard Gray. 1986. *The feasibility study process for parks and recreation.* Reston: The American Alliance for Health, Physical Education, Recreation, and Dance.

Klosterman, Richard E. 1994a. Large-scale urban models: Retrospect and prospect. *Journal of the American Planning Association* 60(1): 3–6.

———. 1994b. An introduction to the literature on large-scale urban models. *Journal of the American Planning Association* 60(1): 41–44.

Lancaster, Roger A., ed. 1983. *Recreation, park and open space standards and guidelines.* Washington, D.C.: National Recreation and Park Association.

Lim, Gill C. 1986. Community service facilities planning. In American Society of Civil Engineers, *Urban planning guide.* Rev. ed. ASCE Manuals and Reports on Engineering Practice, no. 49. New York: The American Society of Civil Engineers.

Meyer, Michael D. 1986. Urban transportation planning. In American Society of Civil Engineers, *Urban planning guide.* Rev. ed. ASCE Manuals and Reports on Engineering Practice, no. 49. New York: The American Society of Civil Engineers.

Putman, Steven H. 1983. *Integrated urban models: Policy analysis of transportation and land use.* London: Pion Limited.

Richman, Alan. 1979. Planning residential environments: The social performance standard. *Journal of the American Planning Association* 45(4): 448–57.

Riordan, Timothy, Maria E. Oria, and Joseph P. Tuss. 1989. Dayton's capital allocation process. In *Capital projects: New strategies for planning, management, and finance,* ed. John Matzer, Jr. Washington, D.C.: International City Managers Association.

Rosenbloom, Sandra. 1988. Transportation planning. In *The practice of local government planning,* ed. Frank S. So and Judith Getzels. Washington, D.C.: International City Managers Association.

Sacramento, County of. 1992a. *Land use element of the County of Sacramento general plan.* Revised final public review draft (Aug. 4). Sacramento: The author.

———. 1992b. *Circulation element of the County of Sacramento general plan.* Revised final public review draft (July 15). Sacramento: The author.

Sedway Cooke Associates. 1991. *Reedy Creek Improvement District comprehensive plan.* San Francisco: Sedway Cooke Associates.

Seelig, Michael Y. 1972. School site selection in the inner city: An evaluation of planning standards. *Journal of the American Institute of Planners* 38(5): 308–17.

Stover, Vergil G., and Frank J. Koepke. 1988. *Transportation and land development.* Englewood Cliffs: Prentice-Hall.

Tabors, Richard D., Michael H. Shapiro and Peter P. Rogers. 1976. *Land use and the pipe.* Lexington, Mass.: D. C. Heath.

Transportation Research Board, National Research Council. 1993. *Transportation plan-*

ning, programming, and finance. Conference Proceedings, Circular no. 406. Washington, D.C.: The author.

———. 1985. *Highway capacity manual.* Special Report no. 209. Washington, D.C.: The author.

Webster, F. V., P. H. Bly, and N. J. Paulley, eds. 1988. *Urban land use and transport interaction: Policies and models.* Report of the International Study Group on Land Use/ Transport Interaction (ISBLUTI). Aldershot, England: Avebury.

Wegener, Michael. 1994. Operational urban models: State of the art. *Journal of the American Planning Association* 60(1): 17–29.

Yu, Jason C. 1982. *Transportation engineering: Introduction to planning, design, and operations.* New York: Elsevier North Holland.

16

Development Management Planning

Every government that zones land, or makes public capital investments, or acquires land for public purposes, or taxes land for service, or in any other way attempts to influence private development is operating a development management system. . . . The concept of management must come at such time as the public truly attempts to take charge.
—Einsweiler et al. 1978, I-15–I-16

This chapter extends the advance planning process to include designing the combination of regulations, public investments, and other measures to influence the rate, amount, type, location, cost, quality, and impact of development. Such a development management plan logically follows the land use design, and is intended to implement it.

Some planners suggest that land use design is not a necessary precursor for formulating the development management program (e.g., The American Law Institute 1976; Brower et al. 1984). They suggest that it is reasonable to skip land use design and proceed directly from the analysis of conditions and the setting of goals to the design of a program of regulations, public investments, and other actions. That may be appropriate where no particular future pattern of development need be envisioned. For example, a regional policy plan or a state plan might leave the specification of spatial patterns of development to local governments. For a local government, however, the specification of a future spatial pattern is strategically important, and the land use design records and communicates that spatial policy. Thus, in the planning process recommended here, the land use design is a vital precedent to the development management plan.

At the same time, the land use design and the development management plan should be mutually supportive. Development management is intended to implement the land use design, the land use design can help implement development management. It does that by providing rational, legal, and political bases for regulations and public investments proposed in the management program. In fact, the land use design policies and standards are sometimes incorporated directly into development management as explicit criteria for development permits and public investment decisions. The land use plan itself can also be adopted as a component of the development management program.

Description of a Development Management Plan

As suggested in chapter 3, the development management plan is primarily a sequence of actions, supported by appropriate analyses and goals, to be taken by specific agencies of local government over a three- to ten-year period. Ideally, a development management plan might include most or all of five components (adapted from a review of such plans, see especially American Law Institute 1976; Breckenridge, Colorado 1978; Gresham, Oregon 1980; Wickersham 1981; Hardin County, Kentucky Development and Planning Commission 1985; Sanibel Planning Commission 1987).

1. *A section on existing and emerging development conditions.* (This is an extension of similar sections in the land use design or land classification plan, but with a focus on development processes, the political-institutional context for development management, and a critical review of the existing development management system).

2. *A section on goals and/or statement of legislative intent,* including the land use design as a goal form, but also including management-oriented goals and policies.

3. *A program of actions*—the heart of the plan—including the following:

   a. *A development code,* probably in outline form. Such a code might integrate improved versions of existing subdivision, zoning, and other development regulations, or propose a fresh unified code. The outline should include (1) procedures for permit review and decision-making (perhaps at several levels of complexity to match scale and type of development being proposed and the sensitivity of the proposed location); (2) standards for type of development, density, allowable impacts, and/or performance standards (varying perhaps by sensitivity of proposed locations); (3) site plan, site engineering, and construction practice requirements; (4) exactions and impact fee provisions; (5) incentives to encourage particular development types, site designs, and construction practices; and (6) delineation of districts where various development standards, procedures, exactions, fees, and incentives would apply.

   b. *A program for the expansion of urban infrastructure and community facilities and their service areas.* Such a program should include (1) the sequence, timing, and geographic boundaries of each stage in the expansion; (2) standards and procedures for deciding modifications in sequence and areas served; and (3) distribution of the responsibility and costs of infrastructure and services between public and private sectors over time (i.e., the program should specify which facilities will be built by the private sector as exactions to development permits and which will be built by the public sector through its capital improvement program; see element 3); and (4) incentives and regulations (coordinated with the development code above) to assure adequate facilities are provided by the combined public- and private-sector efforts. This element could include annexation policies and plans.

    c. *A capital improvement program.* This program grows out of the urban infrastructure and community facility expansion program and acquisition program and focuses on the public-sector investment strategy. It includes a financial plan for arranging debt financing and raising revenues. It might be a two-stage plan: a short-term program covering about five years that specifies locations, development, and financing in more detail (showing who will be responsible for which improvements) and a longer-term program in less detail.

    d. *An acquisiton program.* This is a program to obtain property rights (in fee simple and by easements) by purchase, gift, or exaction, to provide open space, protect the environment, and obtain lands for future public improvements.

    e. *Other components,* depending on the community situation. For example, there might be an affordable housing program, an urban revitalization program for specific neighborhoods and commercial centers, a historic preservation program, or an environmental conservation program.

4. *Official maps.* Such maps are intended to be given official status as indicators of legislative intent and as parts of ordinances, with force of law. These might include goal-form maps (e.g., land classification plan or land use design); maps of zoning districts, overlay districts, and other special areas for which development types, densities, and other requirements vary; maps of urban services areas; maps showing scheduled capital improvements; and other maps related to development management standards and procedures.

5. *An outline of relevant federal, state, regional, and neighboring local government measures* and the way they coordinate with the remainder of the local development management plan.

The Five Dimensions of a Development Management Plan

The program of actions, the heart of the development management plan, should specify five dimensions: content, geographic coverage, timing, assignment of responsibility, and coordination among the parts.

Content is the most basic dimension. It refers to the specification of program components and for each component the standards and procedures that govern action. Standards are concrete interpretations of goals and policies, whereas procedures are vehicles to apply them. Content specifies what will be done by government and what is allowed to be done by private property owners, developers, and land users—and under what conditions. Components of the development management program generally include measures in the categories suggested previously for the program of action, or perhaps organized under other categories, for example:

1. *Regulations* are expressions of government's police power. They apply restrictions on development and land use and may exact public capital improvements or impact fees as a part of development approval. Among these measures are zoning and subdivision regulations, unified development ordinances, development timing ordinances, interim development regulations, building codes, housing codes, public health regulations, hazard area ordinances (e.g., flood hazard ordinance), critical environmental areas regulations, or environmental impact ordinances. They also include incentive regulations, linkage ordinances, and adequate facilities or concurrency requirements, which incorporate features of capital improvements, acquisition, and taxes listed below.

2. *Capital improvements* contribute directly to urban development in the form of infrastructure and community facilities to service properties, neighborhoods, and land use activities. They may be provided by the private sector through exactions or incentives incorporated in regulations, or they may be provided through the public sector under its power to spend. Capital improvements include the complete range of infrastructure and community facilities discussed in chapter 15.

3. *Acquisition* measures acquire property rights to provide sites for future community facilities, public access to open space, or to prevent certain types of private development or uses on the property. The acquisition may be by expenditure of public funds (the power to spend), acceptance of gifts of property rights, acceptance transfers from other public and quasi-public agencies, or acceptance of dedications of property through exactions or incentives. Acquisition may include all the property rights incorporated in a piece of real estate (acquisition by fee simple) or include only some of the property rights (easements), leaving the remaining rights with the property owner. Acquisition measures include advance purchase of sites for community facilities and purchase of development rights (PDR) to protect critical areas from development. Acquisition can be linked to regulations in such measures as transfer of development rights and exaction requirements in regulations.

4. *Taxes and fees* must primarily be used to raise revenues based on property value, development impact, or use of services, but they also can incorporate development incentives or disincentives. Examples of measures with such a development management purpose are: preferential assessment for property taxes, tax abatement, tax increment districts, service district fees, impact fees, and land transfer taxes.

Several governmental powers are often incorporated within the same measure, or in complementary measures. For example, a development code that requires dedication of open space actually combines regulation with the acquisition of property; a development code that requires the building of a collector road, transit stop, or major extension of a sewer line would combine regulation with the provision of public capital improvements; and a development control that offered a tax rebate for rehabilitation of deteriorating structures in certain neighborhoods would combine regulation with taxation.

Table 16-1 lists measures often found in local governmental development man-

Table 16-1. Development Management Measures

Category and Measure	Development Dimension Influenced					
	Type	Location	Density	Timing	Cost	Design
Regulations						
Zoning	1	1	1		2	1
Subdivision regulations					1	1
Planned unit development (PUD) regulation	1	2	2			1
Unified development ordinance	1	1	1		1	1
Building code					2	1
Public health regulation			2	2	2	1
Adequate public facilities		2	2	1	1	1
Rate of growth ordinance				1		
Hazard area ordinance	2	1	2			1
Critical areas standards	1	1	1		2	2
Linkage ordinance	2	2	1		1	
Environmental impact assessment requirement	2	2	2			1
Incentive regulations			1			1
Urban growth boundary		1	2	2		
Best management practices						1
Transfer of development rights	1	1	1		2	
Public Spending						
Capital Improvements:						
Infrastructure	2	2	2	2	2	1
Community facilities				2		1
Service area	2	1	2	2	2	
Acquisition:						
Advance land acquisition		1		2	1	
Purchase of development rights	1	1	1			
Taxation/Fees						
Preferential assessment	2	2		1		
Service district	2	2	2		1	
Impact fees	2	2	2	2	1	
Land transfer tax			2		1	
Tax increment financing	1	1	2	2	1	1

Note: Individual measures are grouped by their primary category, although many measures have elements of more than one category. Measures usually adress more than one, but not all, dimensions of development. Cost refers to either private-sector or public-sector cost, and design refers to site design and neighborhood amenity features. A "1" indicates that the development dimension specified is a primary target of, and is significantly influenced by, the measure listed to the left. A "2" means that the dimension is not a primary purpose of the measure and that influence of the measure on that aspect is secondary.

agement programs. Measures are listed under their primary heading although many incorporate features of several governmental powers. The table also suggests the dimensions of development most appropriately targeted by each measure—type of development, location, density, timing, cost, and quality.

There are other ways of categorizing development control measures. For example, Deakin (1989, 5–6) groups them by purpose:

1. limitations on the level of intensity of development permitted (e.g., zoning);
2. stringent design and performance standards (e.g., planned unit development regulations, performance zoning);
3. shifting costs from the public sector to the project (e.g., impact fees and exactions);
4. reductions in the supply of developable land and/or restrictions on the locations where development is permitted (e.g., zoning, urban growth boundaries); and
5. reductions in the amount of growth permitted, overall or per unit time (e.g., annual permit caps, concurrency requirements).

Beatley and Brower (1987) group development-management measures into strategies: controlling the rate of growth, delineating urban growth boundaries and preferred growth areas, controlling impacts through performance requirements and point systems, small area planning (e.g., neighborhoods, special environmental areas), and regional approaches (e.g., regulations for developments of regional impact). Comprehensive coverage of development management measures can be found in Mandelker and Cunningham (1990), Rathkopf and Rathkopf (1986), Rohan (1978), or Schiffman (1983).

Geographic coverage is a second major dimension of the development management program that should be specified in the plan. This is the mapping aspect, and its inclusion is recognition that, until the program is defined on maps as well as in text, the design of the development management program is incomplete. Maps should show locations of proposed infrastructure; boundaries of urban service areas and areas where different infrastructure extension payment provisions apply; areas where different impact fees or service fees apply; zoning districts and other areas where restrictions apply (e.g., floodplain regulations or conservation zones in transfer of development right schemes); and areas where incentives apply (e.g., enterprise zones or receiving zones in transfer of development rights schemes). Different measures may be applied in different parts of the community, or there may be geographic variation in the standards a measure imposes.

Timing, the third dimension that should be specified in a development management plan, refers to the scheduling of implementation for the various components. Timing is determined by the desired effect on pace of development, governmental priorities, resource limitations, and requirements for mutual implementation of measures (e.g., a downzoning of a commercial area concurrent with an incentive zoning scheme that allows higher density as a bonus in exchange for private provision of public amenities).

Assignment of responsibility for designing more specific standards and procedures, shepherding their adoption, and implementing development management components is the fourth dimension of the program design. It is likely that responsibility for development management is shared among several agencies of a county or municipality and also among several special-purpose local governments with overlapping geographic jurisdictions. Increasingly, development management involves even neighboring governments in an intergovernmental or regional approach. The plan should specify which agency has lead responsibility, or (in some cases) which agencies share responsibility, with respect to design, adoption, and operation of components.

Coordination of the various parts of the program is the fifth important dimension of design. The parts must work well together. Excessive time delays, added development costs, unnecessary governmental costs, duplication of permit procedures and requirements, and inconsistent requirements can disrupt a management strategy, diminish results, harm community commitment, and bring on lawsuits and unnecessary adversary relationships between various stakeholders. Coordination should incorporate relationships with programs of federal, state, regional, and neighboring local governments.

Table 16-2 summarizes the five dimensions that should be specified in a development management plan: content (components of the plan), geographic coverage, timing of implementation, distribution of responsibility for implementation, and coordination among the parts.

The ideal development management plan as described is only suggestive. Its precise nature and components should be adapted to the particular planning situation. The plan for Gresham, Oregon (Table 3-2) illustrates one community's version of the development management plan. The Sanibel, Florida, plan is another example. It includes (1) goals and objectives and statement of legislative intent in a preamble; (2) findings from studies of growth, land use, environment, and public facilities; (3) comprehensive land use design and elements of the cap-

Table 16-2. The Five Dimensions of a Development Management Plan

Dimension	Meaning
Content	The components of the development management program and the procedures and standards of each component
Geographic coverage	A mapping of the area to which each component, requirement, or procedure applies
Timing	Schedule and sequencing of implementation of the various components in the program
Distribution of responsibility	Assignment of responsibility for designing, adopting, and implementing each component
Coordination	Making components compatible and mutually supporting

Note: The dimensions define the important aspects of a program or an individual component that should be specified in the design process.

ital improvements program; (4) a development code (including both procedures and development standards, which vary by districts and are shown in official maps); and (5) official maps. The official maps include a permitted uses map, an allowed development intensity map, and a map of ecological zones; these three maps are the primary spatial bases for development regulations (Sanibel 1987).

Overview of a Planning Methodology

Designing a development management plan requires the planner to broaden goals beyond those generated in the land use design process and work more closely with new stakeholders in the land use game. Goals and policies must now address political and legal issues, such as the concept of constitutional rights. The planner must also deepen his or her understanding of the urban development process that the development management program will influence the political-institutional context within which implementation takes place. Finally, the development management plan requires more conscious balancing among the various stakeholders in the land use game: developers and property owners, environmentalists, neighborhood residents, employers and businesses, governmental officials, and future residents. All are affected more directly by the development management program than by a land use design. Putting a development management program into place entails a three-stage process.

1. *Initial steps* involve assembling a core planning team, formulating a working statement of the planning situation, and designing a work plan. Initial steps may also involve official approval of the outcomes of those steps by the chief executive or legislative body.
2. *Direction-setting* is an extension of the framework of goals, facts, and policies discussed in chapter 10. The goals component addresses specific management issues and reinterprets some goals originally conceived in the narrower context of land use design. For example, efficiency and equity are now extended to land use control procedures and standards. The fact component is now focused on factors in the land development process to be influenced by the management program, and the political-institutional system, which must adopt and implement the program. Attention is also given to an analysis of the community's existing development management program, which is both a starting point for the design of a new program and, at the same time, a source of development management problems. The policies component now adds principles to guide the design and implementation of a development management system.
3. *Design, assessment, and adoption* include formulating development management program alternatives; assessment, refinement, and synthesis of those alternatives; making choices among them; and adopting ordinances, administrative procedures, resolutions, and other official legislative acts that will

constitute the future development management program. Thus, the planning process, including the planner's participation, extends beyond the design of the management program and into the debate and adoption process, where elected officials and their constituents further refine and select alternatives.

Following adoption, implementation involves putting adopted legislation into practical operation—administering and coordinating the various measures, monitoring compliance by private- and public-sector development, assessing development projects and impacts, negotiating development permits, building capital improvements, facing legal challenges, monitoring and assessing development consequences, and postimplementation adjustments in land use controls. To some degree, implementation contributes to the design or redesign of the development management program. Although implementation is a part of development management planning, this chapter covers only the first three stages. Implementation is treated in following chapters.

Participation

The ideal development management planning process involves many people in addition to the core planning team. The technical contributions of the planner are embedded in a broader community process involving participation by various agencies, officials, interest groups, and general citizens. The work plan, developed as one of the initial steps, should specify participants, modes of participation, and points in the process where participation should occur. For example, affected parties can help point out the weaknesses and strengths of the existing development management system during the direction-setting stage. They can assess program proposals and voice preferences in the adoption process.

Figure 16-1 diagrams the three stages, as well as implementation, their components, and the relationships among them. The reader should not infer a perfect linear progression, where one stage is completed before the next one starts. The stages and studies described here are all necessary but may occur in a different sequence, at different levels of rigor, and be revisited in order to update, refine, or refocus earlier studies.

Stage 1: Initial Steps

The initial three steps are designed to get the development management planning process off to a quick start. Results are not intended to be definitive, and these steps should not take long. The tasks are:

1. assembling a core planning team and supplementary groups;
2. formulating a working description of the planning situation (the planner may start this step while assembling the planning team, but it should be completed by that team, not the planner); and

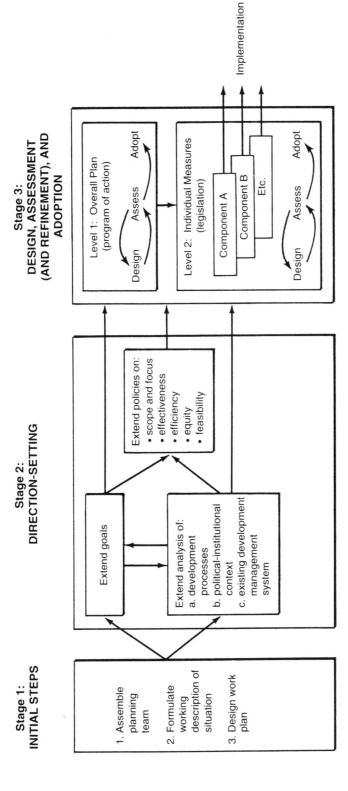

Figure 16-1. The Three Stages of Development Management Planning. Initials steps are followed by direction-setting, followed by the design-assess-adopt stage, at two levels.

3. formulating a work plan to create and adopt a development management program.

Assembling a Core Planning Team

The core planning team should be led by the planner, city or county manager, his or her designate, or another professional in development management. The team might include a city or county attorney (because ordinances, procedures, and standards must be legally defensible) and one or more representatives of prospective implementing bodies, for example, the inspection department (because those who must implement the program should be involved in its design). There may also be a planning consultant who is expert on development management. The core team members are largely professionals and experts; they will be responsible for professional leadership, technical expertise, and most day-to-day planning.

The core team might be supplemented by an advisory or steering group appointed by the local legislature to provide policy oversight, approvals of key products, and advocacy during the adoption and implementation stages. This group might consist of representatives from interest groups affected directly by land use management (e.g., development industry and environmental interests), representatives from the planning board and other formal advisory boards, and possibly a representative from the local legislative body itself. Although mechanisms and procedures for participation, and the stages in the process where it should take place, are specified in the work program, possible players might be identified during the initial task of formulating the planning team.

The composition of the core team and steering group may change slightly as the scope and focus of the land use management program is defined in the initial working statement and work plan, or even later. It might be appropriate, for example, to add a representative of the water and sewer authority to the core team if water and sewer extension policy becomes key to the development management strategy. Or, the community might seek a representative from an adjacent local government for the steering group if an intergovernmental strategy is important. In the plan-making steps taken up in the rest of the chapter, the steering group is consulted each step of the way.

Formulating a Working Description of the Planning Situation

This step might also be called a "development threats and opportunities analysis." Using available data, studies, and plans, the planner and core team describe the conditions, trends, problems, policies, and other factors relevant to planning a development management program. This might be done in a two- or three-day charrette by the core team after one or two planners do the preparatory work of pulling together relevant information. The steering group might then review the output, which might be revised by the core planning team. The purpose is to quickly form a preliminary understanding of the planning situation, and an information base for the work plan and initial stages of direction-setting. For the most part, data should be extracted from available plans, reports, and databases.

The description of the existing situation should include both facts and values. The fact component emphasizes three urban systems: the urbanization process, the political-institutional system, and the present land use management program. The analysis of the urbanization factors would describe development trends and problems, make projections, assess the strength or weakness of particular development markets, and anticipate issues. The analysis of the political system would summarize factors affecting the feasibility of particular land use management measures; for example, geographic extent of territorial jurisdiction and legal authority and the capability of local agencies to administer certain types of land use controls. Finally, the analysis of the existing land use management program would summarize the procedures, standards, spatial extent of application, and responsible governmental agency for each element in the program and the perceived problems with any parts of the program.

The values component of the problem statement would summarize goals to be achieved, issues to be addressed, problems to be solved, and policies to be followed, much of it extracted from existing plans and from the core team or steering group.

Formulating a Work Plan

Based on the preliminary working statement, the planner and the core team can develop a work plan containing three elements.

1. A statement describing the scope, focus, and preliminary concept of the land use management program. This statement should incorporate the major goals, issues, and problems to be addressed; aspects of urbanization to be influenced; areal extent of coverage; organizations to be involved in implementation; and also perhaps suggest the types of measures contemplated and how they would be organized into a land use guidance strategy. The statement should also specify the nature of participation in the process and designate who will be involved. The entire core planning team should be involved in determining this statement, and the steering group should review it. The proposal might need to be approved by the planning board or legislative group.
2. A general diagram of mile-posts, or other device, that presents the sequence of work elements necessary to produce and adopt the plan.
3. An element-by-element elaboration of the work program, describing the tasks involved and assigning resources and responsibility.

These three tasks—forming a planning team, formulating an initial working statement of the planning situation, and creating a work plan—constitute the first stage in formulating and implementing the development management plan. Together with the information system and the land use design plan, it becomes the basis for the remaining stages.

Stage 2: Direction-Setting

This stage involves three tasks: extending goals, analyzing relevant community systems in more depth, and formulating general policies to guide development management. This stage may also include creating an inventory of potentially applicable ideas for measures and strategies.

Extending Goals

Setting goals for development management requires that the planner extend concepts of public interest established during the land use design. The goals of efficiency, economy, and equity, for example, take on added dimensions. Until now, they have referred to the land use pattern; we must now consider the efficiency, economy, and equity of regulations and other means to accomplish land use goals, policies, and the desired land use pattern. For example, development controls impose administrative costs on government. They also create windfalls (undeserved benefits) to some property owners adjacent to new sewer lines and roads, but subject others to wipeouts (undeserved costs) from new regulations.

A new public interest, the protection of people's constitutional rights, must be added. Constitutional rights are not ordinarily affected directly by the land use design, and therefore did not come into play during that stage of advance planning. Yet, constitutional rights represent fundamental goals of American society, strongly held by citizens and judicial systems and directly affected by governmental regulations, infrastructure investments, property acquisitions, and taxes and fees.

The goal of protecting constitutional rights goes beyond legal defensibility (Godschalk et al. 1979). That is, such rights should be an explicit aspiration of the development management system, not just a legal constraint. To promote this goal, land use management tools must pursue the legal goals of due process, equal protection, just compensation, and regional general welfare. That is, government's development management actions should have legitimate objectives, have a reasonable and efficient relation to those objectives, be nonrepressive, take no property without due compensation, respect interests of other governments and residents in the region, apply equally and fairly to parties in similar circumstances, and avoid discriminating unfairly. These become policy guidelines for the design of a development management system.

Two other goals—effectiveness and feasibility—are also particularly applicable to development management. Effectiveness speaks to the capability of the proposed management program to actually influence development and achieve the land use design and policies; that is, to have the desired effect. Feasibility is the likelihood of the community actually adopting and effectively administering the overall strategy and individual measures.

These new goals for development management focus on generic concepts such as efficiency, equity, effectiveness, and constitutional rights, not so much on unique community aspirations. Thus, the planner can take the lead in drafting such goals and deriving policies from them; then the core planning team can discuss, revise, and approve them as guiding principles.

Situation Analysis

The situation analysis extends the "initial steps" analyses of the urban development market, the political-institutional context, and the existing or de facto development management system.

Development Market Study   It is absolutely necessary to understand the public/private urban development process, because the effectiveness of regulations and other development management measures will be determined by their interaction with that process, especially with the private development market. The planner, therefore, studies growth trends and potential, differentiated by geographic areas within the planning jurisdiction and by development type. She or he also seeks to understand development decision-making and the way in which they react to governmental interventions. The analysis will be important to the design of standards and procedures that are effective, efficient, and equitable. If the development market is relatively weak, for example, regulations may be ineffective. If the market is strong, however, more restrictive regulations and greater exactions are feasible and effective. For example, in a strong market, the community can require open space dedication or open space impact fees without dissuading new housing.

Political-Institutional Study   Second, the planner must understand the political-institutional context within which a community adopts and operates a development management program. Studies should examine legal, financial, administrative, and political resources and constraints that largely determine what is adoptable and capable of being administered effectively and efficiently. They should examine the existing and potential boundaries of jurisdictions, the responsibilities and powers of various agencies, and intergovernmental relations among adjacent and overlapping governments. These studies are not intended to define inflexible constraints or to prejudge what is feasible and what is not. A solution estimated to be less feasible initially is not necessarily abandoned if it has high marks on effectiveness, efficiency, and equity. Instead, the planner can use knowledge about the political-institutional context to develop a better implementation strategy.

The legal component of these feasibility studies examines the constitutional, statutory, and judicial factors that shape a local government's authority to the use of private property, build infrastructure and acquire property rights, generate revenues through taxes and fees, and, in the case of state and regional agencies, influence the actions of local governments. A report for Fairfax County, Virginia (Freilich 1973) is an example of such a study. It advises planning and legal staff of the county on procedures and standards to make a growth timing program legally defensible, based on an analysis of statutory authority and case law in Virginia and ordinances from other localities. It also provides drafts of elements of an interim development ordinance, adequate facilities ordinance, low- and moderate-income housing requirements, and an open space ordinance. Such studies help the planner devise a legally defensible development management system that promotes constitutional rights. See also Blaesser and Weinstein (1989), who offer "constitutional decision tree" tables that can be consulted in designing land use controls.

Assessment of the Existing Development Management System   This study examines how local government influences development: regulations, incentives, capital improvements, taxation, and pricing policies. They include not only what is on paper, but also the way in which ordinances and policies are administered in the field. They should include any important federal and state programs and laws (e.g., environmental laws or state planning mandates) that affect local development or local development management. In addition, the studies should include a review of regulations and policies of neighboring jurisdictions and of intergovernmental programs in which the local government participates. Viewed as a whole, all those components, whether consciously designed or not, constitute the de facto development management system to be assessed.

The purpose of this analysis is to determine how well the various components of the de facto development management program are working and how feasible it is to change them. For example, federal, state, or regional policies may be relatively "unchangeable," but the study should include an assessment of the feasibility of changing them. Existing development management measures consistent with goals and policy, and which either work well or have the potential to do so with adjustments, form a basis for new, improved alternatives. Thus, most development management program designs incorporate appropriate parts of the existing system.

Formulating General Development Management Policies

The third part of direction-setting is formulating general policies to guide the design and implementation of a development management system. Development management policies might cover scope and focus, effectiveness, efficiency, equity, and feasibility, paralleling topics covered under goals.

Considerations and Policies about the Scope and Focus of the Land Use Management Program   These policies define the targets of the program, for example, location, density, timing, amount, or quality of development. Although the first attempt at scope and focus was one of the initial steps, this follow-up takes advantage of the improved understanding gained by the situational analysis that has taken place since that initial working statement. For example, the planning team might determine to what extent the development management program will address the following dimensions of development: amount of urbanization to be allowed; its spatial pattern; density of development and intensity of activity; timing of development; balance between private development and supporting public development of infrastructure (concurrency) and among various sectors of land use (e.g., employment and residential); site design and development practices; distribution of costs of infrastructure and services; types of public facilities and services to be included in the development management program, their locations, and levels of service; the geographic area covered by the development management measures; impacts on environment, infrastructure, quality of life, and local government's fiscal health; and specific additional land use issues, for example, historic preservation, economic development, revitalization of the central business district, watershed protection, or group homes.

The scope and focus principles might also suggest strategic orientations (e.g., an emphasis on requirements versus incentives, regulations versus infrastructure extension and service policy, performance approach versus design specification, and minimal intervention versus aggressive intervention in the private- and public-sector development process). Finally, they might suggest which governments and agencies will participate in administering the program.

Effectiveness policies suggest design principles that will increase the probability of having the desired effect on the amount, type, location, density, timing, cost, and quality of development and redevelopment; the location and amount of urban services; protection of the environment; and other dimensions of urban change.

Location principles suggest the spatial configuration of controls, incentives, and service districts included in the development management system. They would parallel and support the land use design. A development management principle might be to discourage development on septic tanks in areas scheduled to be serviced with water and sewer within a given number of years.

Space and service requirement principles are of three types. One type prescribes the demand for services to be met through the capital improvement program and exactions provisions in development regulations. They might apply to water supply, wastewater collection and treatment, parks, schools, solid waste disposal, and transportation, for example. These are expressed in such capacity measures as millions of gallons per day.

A second type of space requirement principle is aimed at assuring adequate quantities of land for private development, located appropriately with respect to necessary services and the land use design scheme and subject to appropriate controls. Table 16-3 suggests one way to specify such space requirements (in that case, by sewershed service areas). Urban service districts and land use control districts would be defined to delineate areas where full-service urban development would be encouraged.

A third type of space requirement principle would specify upper and lower

Table 16-3. Illustrative Land Requirements, in Acres, for Full-Service Urban Development

Sector of Planning Jurisdiction	Land Required (with full service and land use controls)		Land Supply with Current Urban Services	Future Service/Control Area	
				Additional Acres Needed	Additional Acres Needed
	by 2005	by 2015		by 2005[a]	by 2015
Sewershed/ Service Area A	4,600	5,800	3,000	2,200	3,400
Sewershed/ Service Area B	3,200	4,200	3,300	400	1,400
Sewershed/ Service Area C (Future)	0	800	0	400	1,200
Total	7,800	10,800	6,300	3,000	6,000

a. Includes a five-year contingency quantity to maintain sufficient land supply to avoid pressuring land prices upward. Before the year 2005, developers would still be allowed to develop outside the Year 2005 Service/Control Area but within the Year 2015 Service/Control Area, provided they build the infrastructure to service such development adequately.

threshold sizes for areas scheduled to receive particular treatments, for example, urban renewal areas and planned unit developments. Such principles would assure that the area in question is small enough so that resources are sufficient to complete programs in a timely manner, but also large enough to obtain economies of scale and overcome negative influences.

Timing principles apply to the sequence and pace of adoption and implementation. For example, a policy might prescribe the pace of expansion of wastewater treatment capacity and sewer service area. See Table 16-3 for a way to present the staged increase in land demand for a service district. Timing principles may also suggest the chronological coordination of actions with respect to each other or with respect to a triggering event, for example, to install preferential assessment of land in conjunction with a development timing ordinance.

Site design and development practice principles address issues not generally reflected in a land use design. They would suggest facility standards, performance standards, and required construction practices. For example, they might encourage multiple use of parking lots, prohibit direct access of commercial establishments to major thoroughfares, require erosion and sedimentation controls on construction sites, require dedication of open space in residential subdivisions, or require retail, office, and multifamily developments to provide transit stops.

Focus areas call for special measures in specific geographic areas. The basis for such areas and corresponding principles might be critical area designations in the land classification plan or renewal-rehabilitation-conservation areas in the land use design. Beyond those areas, which are designated in the plan, other focus areas might be determined by comparing the plan with maps of projected development. In areas where projected development conflicts with the land use design, special development management attention is called for. Some of these areas will require stimulation of new development where it is not otherwise likely to occur; other areas will require actions that discourage development. Principles for revitalization of Neighborhood A, where houses are still in early stages of deterioration, might differ from principles for Neighborhood B, where more serious deterioration has occurred and there is little market demand.

Efficiency. Ends do not necessarily justify any and all means. A desired land use pattern must be judged against the costs of achieving it and the distribution of those costs. One principle might be that the development management program should employ the least costly measures and interject the least interference with the land market, consistent with achieving the control necessary to serve the intended purpose. For example, where the objective is safety alone, regulation of site design and construction and practices in the floodplain is more appropriate while achieving the purpose than public acquisition of floodplain land, because regulations are far cheaper. Also, where building elevation requirements will achieve the public safety purpose in the floodplain, there is no need to prohibit development altogether. Facilities and requirements serving several purposes are preferable to single-purpose measures. For example, an open space exaction requirement for new development might be designed and administered to meet both recreation, ecology, and flood protection purposes.

Equity. Effectiveness, economy, and efficiency must be balanced against equity. The following principles illustrate policies that promote equity.

1. Measures should cause as few windfalls and wipeouts as possible, regardless of legality.
2. Costs should be distributed to those receiving the benefits (the benefit principle), or costs should be shared equally (equality principle), or costs should be born by those most able to afford them (ability-to-pay principle); communities must choose among these differing concepts of equity.
3. Benefits should be distributed equally (the equality principle), or should be in proportion to effort, contribution, potential, or other measure of merit (the "just deserts" principle); again communities must choose.

Feasibility principles suggest ways to help achieve legal, fiscal, administrative, and political feasibility. For example, methods and studies employed in land use design and development management program design should be systematic, rigorous, and replicable, especially if aggressive development management is contemplated, in order to establish a sound basis for governmental action. There should be a logical consistency among findings of studies, the public purposes being sought, and proposed measures in order to avoid challenges of arbitrariness or unreasonable means. Development management measures should be explicit about intent, geographic coverage, who is to be affected, standards that must be met, what can and cannot be done, procedural requirements, and time schedules for implementation to address challenges of arbitrariness. The cost of proposed capital improvements and of administering regulations, incentives, and other measures must be within the fiscal capability of the government. The complexity of measures and the skills called for in their administration should be within the capabilities of the staff and other officials who must operate them. The development management program must be able to muster the support of elected officials, a coalition of stakeholders, and the public.

Stage 3: Design, Assessment, and Adoption

This stage begins with the design of alternative development management programs for review and assessment by the core planning group and advisory group of stakeholders and community officials, followed by refinement of leading alternatives, followed by adoption. It includes the design and adoption of specific ordinances, administrative procedures, resolutions, and other official legislative acts, as well as an overall development management strategy. Thus, the advance planning process, and the planner's participation in it, extends from the general level of a development management program through the crafting of specific measures, and from the design of alternatives through the adoption process. Actually, the planner's role should continue into implementation as well (Figure 16-1), but that is addressed in the next chapter.

Design

Design occurs on two levels (see the "Design, Assessment, and Adoption" box in Figure 16-1). The first is at the level of overall program design. At this level, the planner formulates a coordinated package of regulations, incentives, capital improvements, and revenue components, including suggested linkages among components and perhaps even intergovernmental coordination. Variation in application among geographic areas within the planning jurisdiction would be indicated, along with a timetable for implementation of the various components. The plan should also assign responsibility for detailed design and operation of the program's components to the appropriate agencies and should estimate personnel and other resources necessary for implementation. Procedures and standards might be suggested in general terms.

On a second, more detailed level, development management design involves writing legislation that defines procedures, standards, and administrative rules to be followed in implementing the legislation, and establishing sanctions with a specificity sufficient for administration as well as legal defensibility. We emphasize level-one design in this text, but the second, more specific, level is just as important.

Level-one development management planning is still very much in the advance planning mode; it takes a comprehensive perspective and is still a statement of intent. Level-two activities extend almost into the realm of implementation. The outputs go beyond statements of intent and specify actual procedures and standards that mandate governmental action to facilitate or restrict private- and public-sector development and use of land. Yet level-two activity is also advance planning, to the degree that it is a conscious, systematic implementation of level-one plan-making, rather than a response to immediate problems and political opportunities.

Design, both level one and level two, should specify content, geographic coverage, timing, responsibility, and coordination among the parts of the development management program, as discussed earlier in the chapter.

Assessment

Assessment, as part of design, entails projecting and then evaluating consequences for a design alternative. That dual analysis—projection and evaluation—applies to the overall program (level-one design) and to individual components (level-two design). Assessment is made with respect to the stated goals; efficiency, equity, and feasibility of the program; and complementarity (or lack of it) between tools. It applies to side-effects as well as main effects and to qualitatively measured as well as quantitatively measured impacts. Assessment involves not only the planner and core planning team but also other participants, particularly as the adoption stage approaches at either level one or level two.

There is a dual purpose to assessment. The first purpose, most closely related to design, is to provide information for refining alternatives. Thus, in Figure 16-1 an arrow leads from assessment back to design, both at level one and at level two. We incorporate assessment with the design step because a feedback-redesign-reassessment cycle should be regarded as part of the process of formulating good alternatives.

A second purpose of assessment is to help make choices among alternatives. Choices are made first to select better alternatives during the design refinement process and, later, to choose an alternative for adoption. Assessment in this sense is preparatory to, or perhaps even integrated with, the adoption process. Suggestions about methods to use in assessment are in chapter 17.

Adoption

The general level (level-one) design may be adopted by resolution as community policy, similar to the land classification plan or land use design. Many individual components, however, are adopted as official legislation, attaining the force of law.

Although the assessment and adoption process involves additional important participants, including legislative officials, citizens, and interest groups, the planner and core planning team should continue to participate. Design continues in the form of modifications to development management measures during—and as a result of—debate toward adoption.

Summary

The purpose of this chapter has been to extend the advance planning function to the design and adoption of a development management program. The management program is a combination of measures designed to achieve the goals, policies, and land use pattern decided in the land use design. We have proposed a three-stage process: (1) initial steps; (2) direction-setting; and (3) design, assessment, and adoption.

Initial steps, the first stage, includes assembling a core planning team, formulating an initial working description of the planning situation, and designing a work plan. The initial steps may also involve official approval of those three outputs by the community executive or legislative body.

Direction-setting, the second stage, includes formulating goals and guiding principles especially relevant to development management—goals of effectiveness, efficiency, equity, feasibility, and the protection of constitutional rights, for example. This stage also includes an analysis of the urban development process through which any management program must work, the political-institutional system through which it must be adopted and implemented, and the existing development management program, which may provide the framework for a new program.

Stage three, the design, assessment, and adoption of a development management program, includes the design of a program (level one) and specific components of that program (level two). This stage includes the assessment and subsequent refinement of those alternatives; making choices among them; and, ultimately, adopting ordinances, administrative procedures, resolutions, and other official legislative acts that will constitute the future development management program. Thus, the planning process, including the planner's participation, extends through community debate and adoption of development management measures.

Development management planning does not stop at adoption. Implementation—putting adopted legislation into practical operation—is a vital follow-up stage. It includes administering and coordinating the various measures, monitoring and assessing their operation, implementing the capital improvement program, monitoring and assessing actual development results, negotiating development proposals, and facing legal challenges. Implementation also includes ongoing adjustments in operation of the program; to that degree, implementation is part of design and redesign.

REFERENCES

The American Law Institute. 1976. *A model land development code.* Philadelphia: The author.

Beatley, Timothy, and David J. Brower. 1987. *Managing urban growth.* Chapel Hill: The Center for Urban and Regional Studies, the University of North Carolina.

Blaesser, Brian W., and Alan C. Weinstein, eds. 1989. *Land use and the Constitution: Principles for planning practice.* Chicago: Planners Press.

Breckenridge, Colorado. 1978. *Breckenridge development code.* Breckenridge: The author.

Brower, David J., Candice Carraway, Thomas Pollard, and C. Luther Propst. 1984. *Managing development in small towns.* Chicago: Planners Press.

Brower, David J., David R. Godschalk, and Douglas R. Porter. 1989. *Understanding growth management: Critical issues and a research agenda.* Washington, D.C.: The Urban Land Institute.

City of Sanibel, Florida. 1987. *Comprehensive land use plan.* Tallahassee: Municipal Code Corporation.

Deakin, Elizabeth. 1989. Growth controls and growth management: A summary and review of empirical research. In *Understanding growth management: Critical issues and a research agenda,* ed. David J. Brower, David R. Godschalk, and Douglas R. Porter. Washington, D.C.: The Urban Land Institute.

Einsweiler, Robert C., Robert H. Freilich, Michael E. Gleeson, and Martin Leitner. 1978. *The design of state, regional, and local development management systems.* Minneapolis: Hubert H. Humphrey Institute of Public Affairs, University of Minnesota.

Freilich, Robert H. 1973. *The legal basis for a growth control system in Fairfax County, Virginia.* Fairfax County: Board of Supervisors.

Godschalk, David R., David J. Brower, Larry D. McBennett, Barbara A. Vestal, and David C. Herr. 1979. *Constitutional issues of growth management.* Washington, D.C.: Planners Press.

Gresham, Oregon, Planning Division. 1980. *Gresham community development plan.* Gresham: The author.

Hardin County, Kentucky, Development and Planning Commission. 1985. *Development guidance system.* Hardin County: The author.

Mandelker, Daniel R., and Roger A. Cunningham. 1990. *Planning and control of land development.* 3d ed. Charlottesville: The Michie Company, Law Publishers.

Rathkopf, Arden H., and Daren A. Rathkopf. 1975. *The law of zoning and planning.* 4th ed. Vols. 1–5. New York: Clark Boardman Company.

Reichert, Peggy A. 1976. *Growth management in the Twin Cities metropolitan area: The development framework planning process.* St. Paul: Metropolitan Council of the Twin Cities Area.

Rohan, Patrick J. 1978. *Zoning and land use controls.* Vols. 1–6. New York: Matthew Bender and Company.

Sanibel Planning Commission. 1981. *Comprehensive land use plan.* Sanibel, Fla.: The author.

Schiffman, Irving. 1983. *Alternative techniques for controlling land use: A guide for small cities and rural areas of California.* Davis: Institute of Governmental Affairs, University of California at Davis.

Wickersham, Kirk, Jr. 1981. *The permit system.* Boulder: Indian Peaks Publishing Co.

PART 4

Development Management and Problem Solving

This section covers a potpourri of techniques used in implementing the plan, operating the development management program, and solving problems unforeseen during advance planning. Although many of these techniques involve more art than science, together they offer the planner the possibility of a more objective and systematic basis for managing land use change. The unifying thread in this section is the notion of implementation as a process of ongoing evaluation and mitigation, budgeting and planning, conflict resolution, and problem solving. Although our treatment of these techniques is necessarily less detailed than those of advance planning, we felt it important to include them to illustrate the ongoing nature of the land use game. The techniques are presented in two chapters.

In chapter 17, "Evaluation and Impact Mitigation," we discuss the family of techniques that can be used to assess plans and development proposals, along with approaches to impact mitigation. Evaluation and mitigation are grouped into one chapter on the presumption that most evaluation results in recommendations for mitigation. This mitigation may be in the form of changes to a land use plan or conditions on a development proposal. The combination of evaluation and mitigation enables a balancing of stakeholder interests and public interests during the planning and development processes.

In chapter 18, "Implementation," we explain a number of individual techniques used to carry out plans and development management objectives on a day-to-day basis. These include capital budgeting, small-area or district planning, conflict resolution, quick problem solving, and preparation for legal challenges. The assumption is that these ongoing activities can help the planner adapt to the inevitable changes that occur once the advance plan and development management program are adopted, maintaining the intent of the goals and objectives in the face of new conditions and demands.

17

Evaluation and Impact Mitigation

Evaluation is an elastic word that stretches to cover judgments of many kinds. . . . What all the uses of the word have in common is the notion of judging merit. Someone is examining and weighing a phenomenon . . . against some explicit or implicit yardstick.
—Weiss 1972, 1

Two key land use planning game activities are judging the impacts of plans and development proposals on various stakeholders and then mitigating the negative impacts to an acceptable level. Land use changes inevitably involve impacts. Systematic and objective assessment of these impacts not only gives decision-makers important information for their deliberations, but also points out options for impact mitigation. The land use planner constructs and applies evaluation procedures and identifies and proposes mitigation alternatives.

Plan evaluation methods assess the impacts of proposed and adopted plans. They estimate the degree of achievement of goals and objectives, the distribution of benefits and costs, and the feasibility of implementation. They range from informal and subjective assessments to rigorous, analytical models that attempt to quantify plan results. Two types of plan evaluation are discussed in this chapter. Preadoption evaluation methods are used during plan preparation to provide information about plan design and alternative selection. Postadoption evaluation methods are used following plan adoption to assess the implementation effectiveness of the plan in achieving its goals and objectives as a guide to further plan amendment.

Development proposal evaluation methods assess the impacts of proposed public and private land use changes in light of plan objectives. They consider both local and communitywide impacts. Two types of development proposal evaluation methods are discussed in this chapter. Individual proposal impact assessments are used to review single land use change proposals. Cumulative impact assessments are used to consider the aggregate impacts of a series of land use changes.

Mitigation methods seek to reduce negative impacts from future development or from hazard threats. They may be used to mitigate impacts on the environment, community facilities, social factors, or hazard conditions. Often, an outcome of the evaluation process is a recommendation for changes or conditions of approval that mitigate the negative impacts of a plan or development proposal.

Plan Evaluation

Plan evaluation is the systematic assessment of environmental, social, economic, fiscal, and infrastructure implications of land use and development management plans. In theory, evaluation is the rigorous, quantitative comparison of alternative plans in light of their potential or actual achievement of preferred goals and objectives. In practice, however, evaluation takes many forms. It may be used to assess outcomes resulting from both alternative and single plans. It may be informal as well as formal and qualitative as well as quantitative.

Evaluation Methods

All evaluations seek to learn what difference plans make, although the methods used vary from simple visual comparisons to elaborate modeling analyses. In choosing an effective evaluation method, the planner considers appropriateness for purpose, credibility of outcomes, feasibility of application, and acceptability to the community. An appropriate method is suitable for its evaluation purpose, producing information that will facilitate informed public decisions about adopting or amending the plan. A credible method produces consistent results with reasonable levels of confidence in its accuracy. A feasible method is one that is practical to carry out, given the resources at hand. And an acceptable method is understandable and plausible to decision-makers and the public. To illustrate the application of these choice criteria to the range of evaluation methods available, Table 17-1 lists factors to be considered in selecting an evaluation method.

Simple *visual comparisons*, where two alternative plans are laid side by side and assessed relative to each other, are appropriate in the concept design stage of land use planning. If alternative plan schemes are prepared at the same scale, then

Table 17-1. Evaluation Methods Selection Factors

Method	Appropriate for Assessing	Credible When	Feasible for Use with	Acceptable When
Visual comparison	Concept design stage	Alternative schemes available	Basic design skills	Images comparable
Numerical indicators	Goals and objectives setting	Measures available	General planning skills	Numbers comparable
Goals-achievement	Distribution cost/benefit	Weights consistent	Special analysis skills	Weights plausible
Single-function model	Functional analysis	Model well specified	Basic modeling skills	Output applicable
Linked models	Comprehensive systems	System linkages known	Advanced modeling skills	Confidence in links

visual comparisons should be effective in conveying the major differences that result from applying a particular design principle, such as prohibiting development on prime agricultural lands or minimizing extension of trunk sewers. The easiest-to use for comparing two-dimensional plans, visual comparisons are feasible for a planner who has basic land use design skills. If well prepared, visual comparisons are acceptable to nonprofessional audiences, who can readily grasp the differences in visual images. An example of a visual comparison, showing a site after conventional development (Figure 17-1) and after creative development using residential and commercial cluster plans to achieve the same level of development (Figure 17-2), is used effectively by Yaro et al. (1989) to make the case for changes in development regulations in order to preserve rural character.

Tables of *numerical indicators* present tabulations of plan outcomes or impacts according to goals and objectives. They are appropriate for comparing plan and development management alternatives. If the numerical measures are available or can be derived, then these indicators are effective comparison tools. They are feasible to apply by the general planning professional and often are compiled into convenient checklists (Schaenman 1976, 27–34). If their output numbers are comparable, they should be acceptable to decision-makers as guides to choice among alternatives. Table 17-2 illustrates some of the environmental, esthetic, and cultural indicators that might be included in an impact checklist for evaluating land development (Schaenman 1976, 27–28). Schaenman's complete list also includes public and private services, local economy, and other social impacts.

In order to sharpen the focus of numerical indicators, the planner can propose standards or "targets" for acceptable impacts. Schaenman (1976, 7) suggests that these targets be included in comprehensive plans to indicate tipping points or thresholds to allow cumulative effects to be monitored and assessed. For example, once a certain level of agricultural land loss was reached, new subdivision policies would go into effect. An illustrative indicators table comparing two plans with respect to loss of agricultural land and need to extend trunk sewers is shown in Table 17-3. It shows that neither Plan A nor Plan B meet the target for agricultural land preservation, while only Plan A is within the target for length and cost of trunk sewer extensions.

Goals-achievement matrices (Hill 1968) extend the numerical indicators approach to include both the costs and the benefits of achieving particular goals and the distribution of these costs and benefits to different population groups. They are appropriate where it is important to analyze who benefits and who pays for achieving selected goals under alternative plans. Because they involve the use of weights for both the individual goals and the importance of each goal to each interest group, their effectiveness depends upon the accuracy of weight assignment, a task Hill gives to the decision-makers. Although goals-achievement matrices are appealing in the abstract because they show the incidence of plan impacts, their feasibility is limited by the degree of specialized cost/benefit analysis required, as well as by the potential difficulty of assigning consensus weights and the poten-

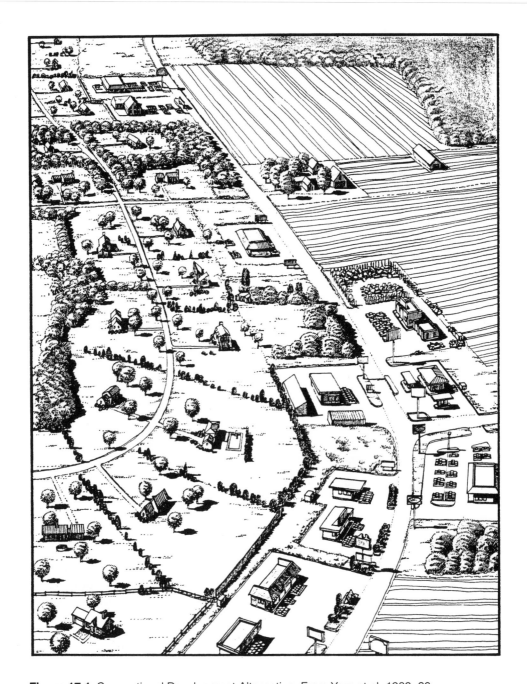

Figure 17-1. Conventional Development Alternative. From Yaro et al. 1989, 30.

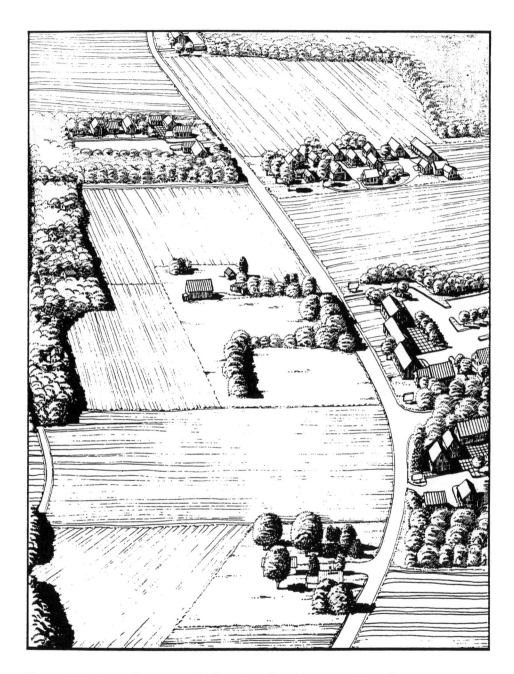

Figure 17-2. Cluster Development Alternative. From Yaro et al. 1989, 31.

Table 17-2. Illustrative Land Development Impact Measures

Impact Area and Sub-areas		Usually Applicable to Evaluating				Bases for Estimates
				Small to Medium		
		Comprehensive Plans, Cumulative Effects, Large Rezonings	Residential Rezoning	Commercial-Industrial Rezoning		
Preferred Measures	Fallback Measures					
Natural Environment **Air Quality** **Health** Change in air pollution concentrations by frequency of occurrence and number of people at risk	Change in air pollutant concentrations relative to standards Change in pollutant emissions relative to emission "budgets" or targets	X		X		Current ambient concentrations; current and expected emissions; dispersion models; population maps
Nuisance Change in occurrence of visual (smoke, haze) or olfactory (odor) air quality nuisances and number of people affected	Change in likelihood that air quality nuisances (qualitative judgment) will occur or vary in severity	X		X		Baseline citizen survey; expected industrial processes; traffic volumes
Water Quality Changes in permissible or tolerable water uses and number of people affected for each relevant water body	Change in water pollutant concentrations (relative to standards) for each water pollutant Change in amount discharged into body of water relative to effluent "budgets" for each pollutant	X		X		Current and expected effluents; current ambient concentrations; water quality model
Noise Change in noise levels and frequency of occurrence and number of people bothered	Changes in traffic levels, sound barriers, and other factors likely to affect noise levels and perceived satisfaction	X	X	X		Changes in nearby traffic or other noise sources and in noise barriers; noise propagation model or nomographs relating noise levels to traffic, barriers, etc.; baseline citizen survey of current satisfaction with noise levels

Wildlife and Vegetation			
Change in diversity and population size (abundance) of wildlife and vegetation (including trees) of common species	Changes in amount and quality of (a) habitat by animal type; (b) green space; or (c) number of mature trees	X	X	Wildlife and vegetation inventory; expected removal of cover or changes to habitats
Change in numbers of rare or endangered species	Same as above	X	X	Same as above
Natural Disasters			
Change in number of people and value of property endangered by flooding, earthquakes, landslides, mudslides, and other natural disasters, by frequency of occurrence	Change in flooding frequency	X	X	Floodplain and other hazard maps; changes in local topography and sewering; change in percent permeable cover; stream flow and hydraulic models
	Change in percent of land with impermeable cover relative to "budgeted" levels	X		
Esthetics and Cultural Values			
Attractiveness			
Change in number and percent of citizens satisfied with neighborhood appearance	Disturbance of physical conditions considered attractive; removal/improvement of conditions rated unattractive	X	X	Baseline citizen survey of ratings of current attractiveness and identification of problems and assets; visual simulation of proposed development using retouched photos, drawings, or 3-D models for assessing future preferences by a sample of citizens
View Opportunities			
Change in number or percent of citizens satisfied with views from their homes (or businesses)	Number of households (or businesses) whose views are blocked, degraded, or improved	X	X	Baseline citizen survey; geometric analysis of structures to identify view opportunities before and after development
Landmarks			
Number and perceived importance of cultural, historic, or scientific landmarks to be lost, made less accessible, or made more accessible	Rarity of landmark and distance to nearest similar examples of landmarks to be lost (or made more accessible)	X	X	Inventory and importance ranking of landmarks; survey of citizens and scholars regarding importance

Note: For other impact measures, see Schaenman 1976.   *Source:* Adapted from Schaenman 1976, 27–28.

Table 17-3. Illustrative Numerical Indicator Targets

Indicator	Plan A Impact	Plan B Impact	Target
Remaining agri- cultural land	250,000 acres; 60% of present	125,000 acres; 30% of present	Preserve 312,500 acres agricultural land: 75% of present supply
Trunk sewer extensions; amount and cost	4 miles; $1.2 million	8 miles; $2.4 million	Maximum of 5 miles length: $1.5 million total cost

tial distortion of final scores resulting from the weighting process. Whether their outputs would be acceptable depends upon the willingness of decision-makers and interest groups to accept a weighted index of goals achievement.

An illustrative goals-achievement matrix, in which raw and weighted costs and benefits have been aggregated into comparative scores for two goals and three groups for Plans I and II, is shown in Table 17-4. In this illustration, under Plan I the raw total benefits of Goal A (40) outweigh the raw costs (20) by two to one. Under Plan I, the raw benefits of the more important Goal B (40), however, are only half its raw costs (80). Based on raw scores, in terms of incidence under Plan I, Group X is the most disadvantaged, scoring 50 on raw costs and only 10 on raw benefits. Group Y is the advantaged, with raw scores of 50 on costs and 60 on benefits, and Group Z is equally advantaged, with no raw costs and a raw benefit score of 10. When the weights of Goal A (2) and B (4) of Plan I are multiplied times the raw scores, however, then Group X's benefits are 40 versus costs of 180; and Group Z's benefits are 20 versus costs of 0. Finally, when the relative weights of the groups are included, then the relative ranking based on benefits minus costs shows Groups Y and Z each with scores of +40 and Group X with a score of −140. Because overall weighted costs outweigh overall weighted benefits by 360 to 240 for the two goals evaluated, Plan I would not be acceptable. Under Plan II, by

Table 17-4. Illustrative Goals-Achievement Matrix

Incidence	Goal A (rel. wt. = 2)			Goal B (rel. wt. = 4)		
		Costs/Benefits			Costs/Benefits	
	Rel. Wt.	Plan I	Plan II	Rel. Wt.	Plan I	Plan II
Group X	1	10/0	5/10	1	40/10	10/10
Group Y	3	10/30	10/25	2	40/30	20/10
Group Z	2	0/10	5/10	3	0/0	10/10
Raw totals		20/40	20/45		80/40	40/30
Weighted totals		40/80	40/90		320/160	160/120

Summary Index (including Goals A and B)
Costs   Plan I = 360   Plan II = 200
Benefits   Plan I = 240   Plan II = 210

comparison, overall weighted benefits outweigh costs by 210 to 200 for the two goals evaluated. Plan II would be acceptable.

Single function models display the interactions among factors related to a particular activity or function. Thus, a transportation model includes all the inputs and outputs of a transportation system. Similarly, a land suitability model includes the factors that define suitability for a particular land use. These models can be used for both design and evaluation.

A single model is appropriate for analysis of a particular function, such as transportation, land use, stormwater runoff, or air pollution. It will be an effective evaluation tool if the model is well specified and includes all the relevant factors, relationships, and weights so that it accurately portrays the workings of the functional system under various conditions. Single models are feasible for use by planners who have basic modeling skills, especially where the model is available in a standard commercial software package, such as the TransCAD transportation model. Single models are acceptable to decision-makers and citizens when outputs are produced in forms applicable to the issues at hand. For example, a stormwater runoff model that allowed comparison of peak runoff under different density conditions would be useful in comparing the effects of alternative land use density policies.

Linked models bring together several individual models within a coordinated system, where the outputs of one model may become the inputs of another. For example, a linked model system might include models of transportation, land use, and air quality. Outputs of the transportation and land use models would become inputs to the air quality model. Its outputs, in turn, could feed back into the land use model. However, when computer models feed from one to another, the linked model set must reflect an internally consistent weighting system so that the output of each model remains in the "evaluation space" as it becomes input into the next model.

Linked models are appropriate for use in evaluating comprehensive systems. They are effective if the factors and relationships are correctly specified, a more difficult task for linked than single models. Their feasibility depends upon the availability of advanced modelers, along with the resources to carry out extensive data gathering and analysis. They will be acceptable to the degree that there is confidence in the validity of the links among the submodels.

Plan Evaluation Issues

Because land use plans are comprehensive and have wide-ranging effects, plan evaluation can be a very complex process. Among the issues confronting the evaluator are what types of measures to use (e.g., absolute numbers, dollars, or percentage of change); whether to weight certain elements (e.g., to give a higher value to selected objectives, indicators, or impacts); and whether or not to aggregate results into summary measures or to leave them as individual indicators.

The complexity of the cause and effect relationships may lead the evaluator to believe that the only appropriate and effective methods require complicated analytical methods. However, because plan evaluation is still a young field and its products are relatively unproven, it would be wise to err on the side of simplicity and reliability. Thus, we suggest that it is not necessary to convert all measures to a single metric, that weights be used sparingly if at all, and that results be shown as individual indicators rather than aggregated into possibly misleading single supermeasures.

Types of Plan Evaluations

The two major types of plan evaluations are preadoption evaluations used to aid in deciding between proposed alternatives or in comparing the effects of a proposed land use design with a continuation of present development trends, and postadoption evaluations used to assess the effectiveness of an adopted plan in achieving its goals and objectives in order to aid in fashioning plan amendments.

Preadoption Evaluation Before adoption, plan evaluation is both a design and a decision-making tool. The planner can use evaluation to compare design alternatives and suggest design improvements. The decision-maker can use evaluation to test policy alternatives in order to choose among them.

Simple visual and numerical comparisons can illustrate the strengths and weaknesses of proposed concept or sketch plans. A typical approach is to project historic development patterns through the planning period to show the "trend" outcome (a straw man with obvious defects) and to compare this with the more desirable development patterns expected to result from the "plan" outcome. A rarer approach compares a series of plan proposals that embody different, but desirable, combinations of priorities, layouts, or development management schemes. Although this multiple-plan comparison offers more choice, it requires more planning and evaluation effort and may be more confusing to decision-makers. However, computerized design techniques should reduce the effort required to prepare alternative plans, and more experience in assessing alternatives may educate decision-makers to cope with genuine differences.

An example of a county-level land use plan evaluation that relied on simple visual and numerical comparison of alternatives is the Volusia County [Florida] Coastal Management Element (Sedway Cooke Associates 1989). Three alternative plans were drawn:

1. continuation of past development practices;
2. prohibition of future development outside existing urban areas; and
3. limiting expansion of urban areas to adjacent areas where natural resource losses could be mitigated.

Sketch plans showed decision-makers the obvious defects of the first two alternatives. Continuing past practices would encourage sprawl and destroy valuable wetlands and environmental resources. Prohibiting any growth outside current urban areas would make it impossible to accommodate projected growth. This led to a focus on the third alternative, which directed growth to less environmentally sensitive locations adjacent to existing urbanized areas (Figure 17-3, Godschalk 1992).

It is also possible to use models to evaluate plans before adoption. *Communities*

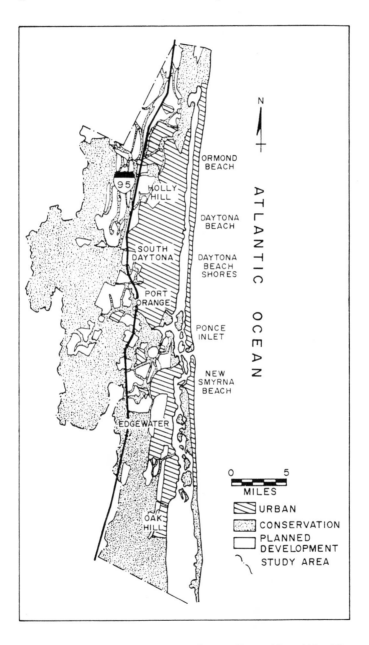

Figure 17-3. Generalized Volusia County Coastal Land Use Plan. From Godschalk 1992, 371.

of Place, the 1991 Interim Development and Redevelopment Plan for the State of New Jersey, was evaluated with a number of independent simulation models (Rutgers University 1992). The 1989 New Jersey State Planning Act required an impact assessment before the final vote on the state plan by the State Planning Commission. The assessment compared outcomes under the plan with trend projections based on continuation of historic development patterns. It allocated the expected twenty-year growth in population, households, and jobs under the different locational criteria of the plan and the trend scenario. Although the plan did not contain a land use map or proposed densities, it did contain performance standards oriented toward more clustering, multifamily, and mixed-use development at higher densities. The evaluators used these criteria to infer future land use patterns.

The impact assessment concluded that the plan will bring substantial benefits that traditional development will not. For example, the plan will result in more jobs being located in cities and suburban and rural centers, rather than scattered in suburban and rural areas generally. It will consume 127,000 acres less in land to accommodate the same number of households and jobs. It will save $740 million in road costs and $440 million in water supply and sewer infrastructure costs. Due to increased densities in centers, housing affordability will increase under the plan, contrary to the typical assumption that growth controls raise housing costs (Rutgers University 1992).

It is instructive to review the New Jersey State Plan assessment approach as a potential catalog of assessment criteria and evaluation models. The models used in New Jersey included:

1. Population projection/land capacity
2. Fiscal impact
3. School capital facilities
4. Agricultural lands
5. Transportation infrastructure (road and transit)
6. Water and sewer demand
7. Water cost
8. Wastewater cost
9. Econometric
10. Housing demand/supply
11. Housing and property development cost
12. Economic impact
13. Water pollution
14. Air pollution
15. Frail environmental lands
16. Quality of life
17. Intergovernmental coordination
18. Linkage/feedback/evaluation

Postadoption Monitoring and Evaluation After a land use plan has been adopted, it is important to track its implementation to see how its proposals work in practice. Schaenman (1976, 4) criticizes the lack of postadoption evaluation by practitioners: "Most communities rarely if ever undertake retrospective evaluations. This eliminates a crucial type of feedback needed for decision-making; most communities are continually making predictions about development impacts, but not testing their accuracy." Unlike an architectural plan for a building, a land use plan is expected to change over time and never to be completed fully. Thus, the land use planner must monitor the plan's implementation and evaluate its effectiveness in order to recommend additional implementation actions and periodic plan revisions. Ragatz (1983, 1) notes, "Failure to monitor plan implementation leads to plan obsolescence and to abandonment of the plan as a policy document for local decision-making."[1]

Monitoring and evaluation is the process of compiling information on the outcomes resulting from implementation of a land use plan and development management program. It is used to measure progress in achieving goals, objectives, and policies; to identify revisions needed to respond to changes in local and regional conditions; and to provide information on trends and conditions. Where the plan is done under state planning guidelines, monitoring and evaluation can help assess compliance with state objectives.

Monitoring and evaluation are closely connected to planning information systems activities. Data collection and analysis are at the heart of the process, supporting plan preparation, implementation, and updating. Referring back to the planning information system concepts of chapter 4, the first need is to collect appropriate "data," which are then processed into relevant "information," which becomes the basis for "intelligence" that can guide decisions. Figure 17-4, adapted from Ragatz (1983), illustrates this sequence. Data are collected on both "conditions," such as housing and land use inventories, and "decisions," such as approvals of zoning changes or development projects. These data are processed into information about "trends" over time and compared with plan objectives and targets. Such trends can be the basis for intelligence analyses about the need to adapt plan policies to achieve objectives more effectively. For example, if the land inventory and decision-monitoring showed that demand for developable land was exceeding projections, leading to a potential shortfall in supply, then the growth boundary and infrastructure provision policies could be adapted to meet the new projected needs.

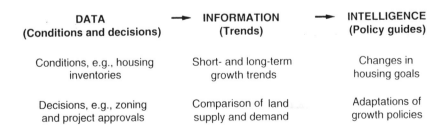

Figure 17-4. Monitoring and Evaluation Activities. Adapted from Ragatz 1983, Figure II-2.

The first step in designing a monitoring and evaluation system is to select the plan objectives to be tracked. Ragatz (1983, 130–31) suggests that factors to be considered in this selection include:

1. local importance of the objective, such as forest protection;
2. frequency of the issue, such as requests for conditional uses on forest lands;
3. level of confidence in the implementing measures, such as policies to maintain forestry production;
4. dollar savings from maintaining current data inventories (rather than collecting data from scratch for each new study), such as the number of forest acres lost annually to urban development; and
5. value of using data from the monitoring program for nonplan uses, such as tax assessment or economic development.

Because most jurisdictions will not be able to monitor all objectives, the selection process should identify priority objectives. They should stress the more important objectives, more frequent issues, lower confidence implementation measures (where lower certainty of outcomes may require more frequent evaluation of development management measures), higher cost inventories, and higher other use values. As described in Part 2, we recommend that data be maintained on land use, development approvals, community facilities, housing, employment, and sensitive environmental areas as a minimum monitoring and evaluation database. This will allow ongoing comparison of supply and demand and assessment of goals achievement.

The second step is to identify data sources, select data items to be collected, and establish a collection and recording procedure. Sources will consist of both locally collected and state and federal published data. A checklist will help to organize data sources.[2] Data items chosen will depend upon the detail of measurement to be undertaken. For example, if building permits are to be monitored, then a simple approach would tally the number of permits issued by type (residential, commercial, office, industrial) per year. A more detailed system would break down the types into more detail (e.g., single family, multifamily, and mobile home residential and square footage of commercial); specify location by planning district or traffic analysis zone; and record the data on a more frequent basis (e.g., monthly). Collection and recording procedures will depend upon the type of planning information system in use. Local governments with computer networks can set up automatic transfers of relevant data, for example, from tax assessment and building permit records. For those with manual information systems, periodic data collection procedures should be established.

Development Proposal Evaluation

Development proposal evaluation is a procedure for assessing the impacts of proposed public and private land use changes in order to provide information to decision-makers charged with reviewing and approving the changes. Such land use changes include requests for rezonings, variances, subdivision plats, special exceptions, special uses, planned unit developments, cluster developments and similar private-sector applications. They also include public-sector proposals for infrastructure and public facilities projects.

In chapter 7, we discussed techniques for environmental impact analysis and, in the previous section of this chapter, the techniques for plan evaluation. Many of those techniques are also applicable to development proposal evaluation. However, development proposal evaluations look at more than environmental impacts and are more geographically focused than plan evaluations. Because of their broad scope and site-specific impacts, as well as their more immediate action implications, development proposal evaluations can be very controversial.

Rather than responding in an ad hoc fashion to each land use change proposal, impact analysis offers a fair and consistent way to provide decision-makers with measures of likely impacts from carrying out the proposals. The assumption is that better decisions can be made if the parties involved understand the likely impacts. Schaenman (1976, 16) notes that "informed impact evaluations may shoot down bogeymen, get discussions focused on the relevant issues, and encourage an openness in decision making." However, it should also be recognized that publication of impact analysis findings can lead to increased opposition to development proposals on the part of those interests most affected.

Impact analysis techniques can be divided into two types. Individual proposal analyses, the most common, look at the effects of single projects as part of the development review process. Cumulative impact analyses are not found often in practice, even though they are provided for in the National Environmental Policy Act regulations. They look at the consequences of a series of development proposals or plan alternatives.

Individual Proposal Impact Assessment

According to Schaenman (1976, 53), "The bread and butter use of a measurement system . . . is the review of individual development proposals." Typically, such proposals occur in the form of project approval applications during the implementation stage of a land use plan. However, they may also occur during the consideration of plan alternatives, particularly for small-area plans.

The general steps in carrying out an individual development proposal impact analysis include seven procedures.[3]

1. *Describe the proposal,* including its objectives, site location, design, construction, land uses, features, history, and other relevant characteristics.
2. *Identify alternatives,* including reducing negative impacts through other means of obtaining the objectives, such as different technology, location, and design, as well as the postponement and no-action alternatives.
3. *Select impacts to be evaluated,* using a checklist to identify potential signifi-

cant impacts, based on the type of proposal, as well as to identify available and missing data needs.

4. *Scope out potential impact characteristics*, including both individual and cumulative impacts, in terms of their causal mechanisms, geographic extent, duration, amount, permanency, growth-inducing effects, links to other impacts, and potential mitigation actions.

5. *Gather data*, including meetings with proposer and interested parties, impact map preparation, site visits, and data collection from agencies and published sources.

6. *Analyze the proposal and alternatives*, including impact measurement, review of fit with comprehensive plan, and mitigation formulation.

7. *Present the analysis,* including the reviewer's recommendations, using terms that decision-makers and interested parties can understand, showing how the proposal relates to the long-range land use plan, and acknowledging areas of uncertainty and scientific disagreement.

For example, in assessing a proposal to rezone an area from agricultural to residential and to subdivide it for a traditional, single-family development project, the planner would first prepare a complete description of the proposal. This could include:

1. the present land use of the parcel and adjacent areas;
2. existing and proposed infrastructure and public facilities;
3. history and characteristics of the site;
4. environmental features;
5. proposed nearby projects;
6. relationship to the comprehensive plan and future land use plan;
7. relationship to the capital improvements budget and program; and
8. specific features of the proposed development.

Next, the planner would identify alternatives to the proposal. These might include retaining the area in agricultural use (the no change alternative), delaying the rezoning until sewer mains are extended to the area (the postponement alternative), or substituting cluster development for the traditional, large-lot subdivision proposed.

Then, the planner would select impacts to be evaluated. In this case, negative impacts might affect water quality from stormwater runoff, air quality from increased traffic, agricultural production from removal of prime agricultural land, fiscal resources from demand for additions to infrastructure and public services, biodiversity from developing within a stream valley wildlife corridor, and historic resources from demolishing a pioneer farmstead and part of a Civil War fortification. Positive impacts might include additions to the housing supply, increases to the tax base, and improvements to infrastructure and public services by the developer's construction of an arterial road to serve the project and a golf course open to the public. Adequate data typically are available from the developer's traffic im-

Is it relevant to the comprehensive plan?

pact study, site analysis, and engineering studies on expected traffic, slopes and drainage, land cover and specimen trees, water supply, and waste disposal. Additional data might need to be collected on air and water quality impacts, endangered plant and animal species, and agricultural production.

To scope out potential impacts, the planner would consider the fit between the proposal and the comprehensive plan. If the area proposed for rezoning was designated as a future residential area, then the type, density, and timing of the development would be checked against the plan recommendations. The addition of new housing units would be reviewed in terms of potential for increasing demand for new commercial development in the area. The extension of an arterial road and trunk sewer line would be assessed in terms of inducing additional residential and commercial development on adjacent lands.

To gather data, the planner would meet with the developer to collect additional information on the timing of the project, proposed environmental protection measures, and buffering or other impact mitigation possibilities. Meetings might also be held with project neighbors to learn of their concerns and perceptions of potential impacts. A base map of existing land use in the area would be consulted to assess the project's potential impacts on, and compatibility with, surrounding property and public facilities. A site visit would be conducted to the project area and its surrounding environment to view existing uses, environmental conditions, and potential development problems and opportunities, such as protection of significant historical structures or Native American cultural sites. Data on air and water quality, and endangered species would be collected from state environmental and natural heritage agencies. Agricultural data would be collected from the county extension agent.

To analyze impacts of the proposal, the planner might compile numerical indicators in the form of a tradeoff matrix (chapter 7). This could show the benefits and costs of the traditional subdivision plan as proposed versus a cluster plan that contained the same number of units and a delayed development plan that did not proceed until the area was scheduled for development under the growth-management program. All three plans could be compared with the goals, objectives, and policies of the land use plan. Mitigation measures could be described in order to maintain the on-site stream valley wildlife corridor and historic areas through clustering, to reduce traffic and air quality impacts by extension of ride-sharing and high-occupancy vehicle lanes to the area, to use impact fees to pay for off-site infrastructure costs, and to encourage replacement of the lost agricultural production areas on outlying fallow lands.

To present the analysis, the planner could prepare a written report and a handout containing the trade-off matrix. This could be supplemented with overhead transparencies showing the major impacts on an area impact map and with slides of the existing uses on and adjacent to the site. It could conclude with a recommendation on the request, including whether to approve it as submitted, to approve with specified mitigation conditions, or to deny.

Cumulative Impact Assessment

Cumulative impact assessment compares the aggregate demand from proposed plans or projects with the aggregate supply of facilities and resources after existing urban area demands have been subtracted.[4] Rather than considering individual proposal impacts in isolation, cumulative impact assessment looks at each new proposal in light of information from continuous monitoring and comparison of demand and supply. Cumulative impacts can affect natural resources, infrastructure capacity, natural hazard vulnerability, visual quality, and other community facilities and resources. For illustrative purposes, we focus here on environmental impacts, but the technique applies to many other types of impacts.

Procedures for cumulative environmental impact assessment are not as well developed as those for individual proposal assessment. Among the difficulties are lack of information on previous development projects and environmental parameters, lack of identifiable natural system thresholds and operational ecosystem impact models, and lack of management techniques for controlling cumulative impacts.

As Contant and Wiggins (1991, 303) state, "To be comprehensive, . . . an approach for considering cumulative environmental impacts of individual project proposals must include mechanisms that capture the interrelationships of development activities and the complexities of natural systems' responses to perturbations." Their approach to analyzing cumulative impacts involves tracking development and natural systems in parallel (Figure 17-5).

Development activities are monitored both in terms of past and current proposals and in terms of socioeconomic factors affecting the type and nature of future development actions. Data from the monitoring are used in regional land use development models to forecast future development actions and regional structural changes and to identify the incremental and growth-inducing effects of particular projects.

Natural systems are monitored to establish baseline conditions so that time-series data could be used to identify the type and magnitude of changes. These data are used in models of individual natural systems (e.g., wetlands, airsheds) or in ecosystem models that include more than one natural system (e.g., linked air and water quality models to forecast acid rain impacts). These models look at the natural systems' response to impact "crowding," in which the system is unable to recover from a series of "nibbling" impacts close together in time or space before new impacts occur. They identify unanticipated responses in which an incremental impact produces a larger effect than earlier impacts or exceeds a system threshold or stability boundary. They forecast systemic changes from "time-delayed" impacts where the initial effect appears benign but later becomes serious (as in cancer), from the accumulation of effects due to "cycling" where the natural balance is changed over time due to repeated impacts (as in forest clear-cutting where new species are introduced), and from structural alterations (as in damming a waterway).

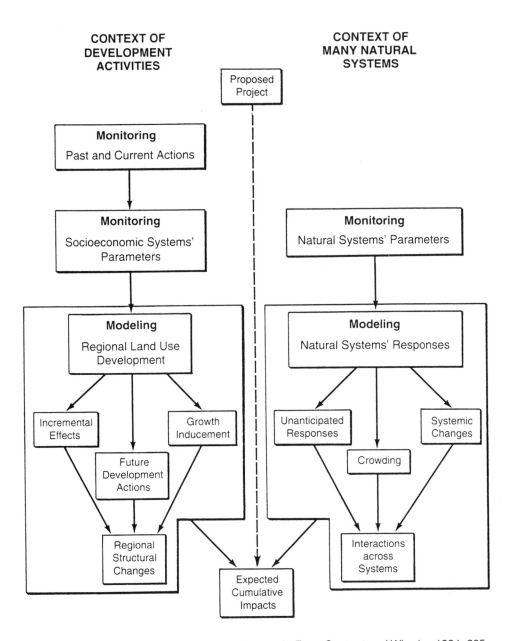

Figure 17-5. Cumulative Impact Analysis Approach. From Contant and Wiggins 1991, 305.

Dickert and Tuttle (1985) applied a cumulative impact assessment approach to a coastal wetland in California. Their analysis of the Elkhorn Slough attempted to avoid the problem of modeling a system threshold beyond which irreversible damage would occur by assuming "historic land disturbance targets" based on the maximum amount of bare ground present in the subwatersheds at any point within the preceding fifty years. They assumed that if other conditions remain the same, then similar rates of watershed change will result in acceptable wetland impacts similar to those of the past. They used aerial photographs to identify the amounts of bare ground within each subwatershed. As adopted in the Monterey County coastal plan, their system allows additional development to be permitted where existing use falls below target levels. Where existing use exceeds target levels, no new development is permitted until the amount of bare ground in the subwatershed is reduced through revegetation or mitigation measures such as erosion controls.

A start toward establishing a cumulative assessment process is to set up a land supply monitoring system (chapter 4). The illustrative system maintains data at both the parcel and the project level in order to monitor existing and proposed land use. It compares development "demand" from residential and employment uses with infrastructure "supply," in terms of the capacity of transportation routes, water supply, waste disposal, and schools within planning sub-areas.

To build a comprehensive impact assessment database, the planner needs to add data on other features. Besides transportation, the database should include the other major infrastructure types (chapter 9), land supply (chapter 8), environment (chapter 7), the economy (chapter 6), and population (chapter 5). It should also include any measurement thresholds established by design, law, or policy. For example, such thresholds could include the capacities of utility systems (design threshold), the allowable carbon monoxide standard for air quality (legal threshold), or the level of service standard adopted for arterial roads (policy threshold).

Microcomputer spreadsheet models are useful techniques for organizing cumulative impact data. Using one of the commercial spreadsheet packages, these models can contain baseline data on all impacts of interest, along with thresholds and policy targets. Data gathered in development and environmental modeling can be entered into the spreadsheets, which would be programmed to calculate the remaining capacity for the systems being analyzed. The spreadsheets can be used to answer "what if" questions, such as what if new sewer mains were extended into a certain fringe area. For more complex interactions, other types of models would be needed. Econometric, land use, transportation, air quality, and water quality models can all provide inputs to the spreadsheet for calculating cumulative impacts. In many local jurisdictions, such advanced models will not be available. However, they could be operated by regional agencies, whose territory might correspond more closely to natural systems boundaries.

The Coastal Population/Development Information System of the North Carolina Division of Coastal Management provides an example of a regional agency's approach to cumulative impact assessment. Population and development information in the twenty coastal counties is collected and analyzed on a small watershed basis. The watersheds used as the units of analysis are five thousand- to fifty thousand-acre hydrologic units as mapped by the U.S. Soil Conservation Service and provided in digital form. The objective is to develop methods to analyze and predict the impacts of population growth and development on coastal water resources to identify areas experiencing significant adverse cumulative impacts. Data are maintained in a GIS and related database management system. Two types of "growth impact coefficients" will be created. Primary impact coefficients will describe the effects of population growth on such parameters as number of acres of agricultural land converted to residential uses; secondary coefficients will attempt to relate growth changes to impacts on water quality, such as the change in loading rate of phosphorus to coastal estuaries as a result of land converted to residential uses.

Impact Mitigation

Mitigation is advance action taken during plan preparation and implementation or project review to reduce the impacts of future development or threat from natural hazards. In the context of environmental impacts, mitigation may imply land use changes to buffer natural areas from impacts, or it may imply the restoration or replacement of affected areas, such as wetlands. In the context of impacts on community facilities, mitigation may imply the provision of new infrastructure or the payment of an impact fee toward increases in facility capacity. In the context of social impacts, mitigation may imply changes in the project density, layout, or location. In the context of natural hazards, such as floods, mitigation includes actions taken before the disaster strikes to prevent or reduce the effects of the disaster. Mitigation recommendations are derived from the findings of development proposal evaluations and advance plans. Land use changes create many types of impacts. We review here only a selection of potential impacts to illustrate mitigation possibilities.

Environmental Impact Mitigation

Development proposals involve a variety of environmental impacts, ranging from on-site damage to ecological systems to areawide effects on air and water quality. We focus on the on-site impacts as those most likely to be mitigated during the project review process. Although erosion and wetland damage are not the only on-site environmental impacts, they are two of the more prevalent.

Erosion due to grading, removal of vegetation, new construction, and added impervious surface results in the loss of on-site soil, the flow of sediments into streams, and the increase of sheet-flow water volumes leaving the site. Mitigation measures include slope stabilization, sediment retention, and slowing of surface runoff. Their effectiveness depends upon effective enforcement of permit conditions and monitoring of performance (Burby et al. 1990).

New construction activities in or near wetlands can also result in loss of wetlands. In this case, mitigation can take the form of moving urban uses away from wetlands or buffering wetlands from development. It can also take the form of wetland restoration and creation, whose purposes are to:

1. reduce the impacts of activities in or near wetlands;
2. compensate for additional losses;
3. restore or replace wetlands already degraded or destroyed; and
4. serve new functions, such as wastewater treatment, aquaculture, and waterfowl habitat (Kusler and Kentula 1990).

The record of success in wetlands restoration and creation is mixed. The probability of success has been highest in coastal, estuarine, and freshwater marshes. Less success has been achieved with sea grasses and forested wetlands. Success often depends on the long-term ability to manage, protect, and manipulate wetlands and adjacent buffer areas; thus, ongoing monitoring is a critical need. This means that a detailed plan, with clear, site-specific goals and attention to wetland hydrology, is necessary. Table 17-5 lists existing conditions that should be included in evaluation of proposed mitigation sites where wetlands are to be created (Josselyn, Zedler, and Griswold 1990, 15).

Community Facility Impact Mitigation

Development proposals place new demands on transportation, sewerage, and water supply systems, as well as on such public services as fire and police protection, libraries, recreation, and education. The impacts may result in reduction of the available capacity of these infrastructure and facility systems to handle the demand from users. Mitigation often takes the form of directly providing additional system capacity or paying a fee or tax to the local government so they can add to system capacity.

Impact fees are charges imposed on development to help pay the public costs of off-site service provision beyond typical on-site subdivision exactions for roads and utilities. They are assessed according to the dollar value of the burden that a development proposal places on community facilities. They formalize the negotiation process that often occurs between a developer and a local government over what contributions the project should make toward mitigating its impacts.

The courts have set guidelines for the use of impact fees (Metropolitan Area Planning Council 1989, 15):

1. New development must require that the present system of public facilities be expanded.
2. The fees imposed must not exceed a proportional fair share of the costs incurred in accommodating the new users of the system.
3. The fees must be earmarked and spent for the purposes for which they were charged.

The details of design and administration of impact fees are complex, combining legal and fiscal analyses. We do not go into these matters; a number of sourc-

Table 17-5. Illustrative Wetland Mitigation Checklist

Feature	Description	Product
Site history	Past uses of site, including past functioning as wetland	Description, map, or photographs illustrating historic uses
Topography	Surface topography, including elevations of levees, drainage channels, ponds, islands	Topographic map with 1-foot contour intervals, 1 inch to 100 or 200 scale
Water contour structures	Location of culverts, tide gates, pumps, and outlets	Elevations for all structures, size and type of structure, current operational status
Hydrology	Description of hydrologic conditions affecting the site	Water budget for site, including inflow, precipitation, evaporation, and outflow; tidal range; history of sandbar closure
Flood events	Current potential for flooding by high flows, extreme tides, and storms; adequacy of any external or internal levees	Evaluation of current flood control protection using appropriate runoff models
Sediment budget	Analysis of sediment inflow, outflow, and retention	Evaluation of historic sedimentation rates and those projected due to watershed development
Edaphic characteristics	Description of existing soils with analysis of suitability for supporting wetland plants	Presence of hydric and non-hydric soils, salinity, and toxic compounds in filled areas
Existing wetland characteristics	Determination of Corps of Engineers jurisdictional wetlands, if any	Boundary map illustrating wetland extent on mitigation site
Existing vegetation	Description of existing habitat with analysis of degraded areas and any habitat with current high value to wildlife	Vegetation map with list of dominant species and location of non-native nuisance species and species of regional concern
Existing wildlife	Description of wildlife using the site, indicating species that may be displaced by mitigation activity	Listing of wildlife known to use site, especially species of special concern (including rare and endangered)
Adjacent site conditions	Analysis of wildlife habitat adjacent to site, indicating those species likely to benefit or be impacted by the mitigation	Map showing site in reference to surrounding habitats, preferable National Wetlands Inventory maps; list of species benefited or impacted

es in the literature provide comprehensive treatments.[5] However, we note that applications of exactions, such as impact fees, serve land use and development mitigation purposes beyond meeting fiscal needs. As shown in Figure 17-6, these include ensuring adequate quality of infrastructure/built environment, accommodating growth, achieving efficiency of the public-private development process, and furthering equity in urban development (Kaiser and Burby 1988, 115).

Relationships between Goals and Functions of Exactions

Goals

Ways in Which Exactions
Can Affect the Goals

Adequate quality of
infrastructure/built environment

Accommodation of growth

Efficiency of "public-private"
development process

Equity in urban development

Requiring features of development
(beyond what market requires)

Allocating costs of required features

Providing flexibility

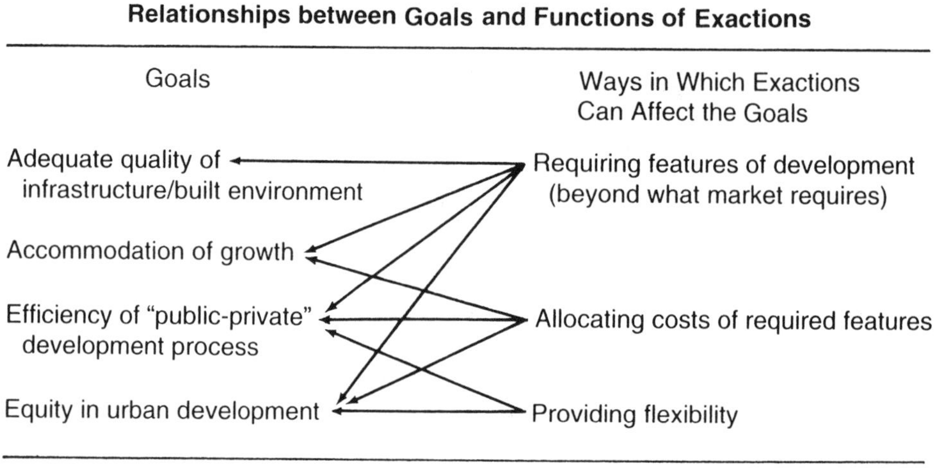

Figure 17-6. Exactions and Land Use Objectives. From Kaiser and Burby 1988, 115.

Social Impact Mitigation

New development proposals almost invariably result in protests from adjacent residents about the impacts of additional activity, traffic, and noise. In addition, large-scale projects may result in displacement of existing uses, changes in air quality, demographic shifts, and new patterns of access. Mitigation focuses on changes in the proposed development, such as building location, activity buffering, and street layout, which will alleviate impacts.

Figure 17-7 shows the relationship between physical aspects of a proposed development project and social factors (Christensen 1976, 3). Impacts occur at both the neighborhood and community scales. They include both perceived, subjective impacts, and measurable, objective impacts. Perceived negative impacts include beliefs that development brings decreases in environmental quality, quality of life, and public safety. The planner can create objective measures of these factors and others to add objectivity to the public debate and illustrate opportunities for mitigation. As Christensen (1976) notes, data sources include census block data, surveys, and direct observation. Mitigation recommendations can stem from review of project redesign possibilities, based on early feedback from neighborhood residents and project critics.

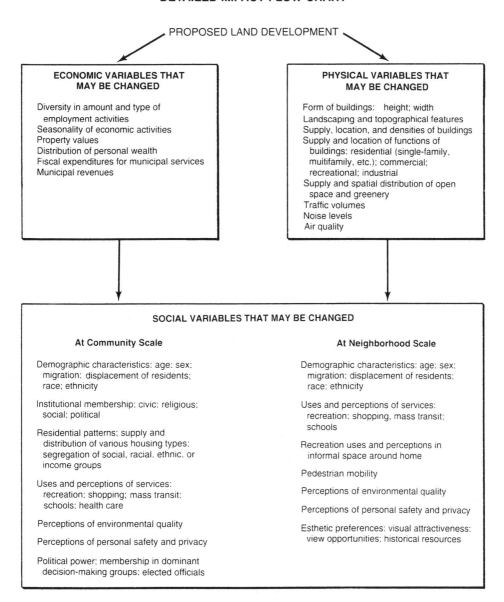

Figure 17-7. Social Impact Relationships. From Christensen 1976, 3.

Hazard Impact Mitigation

Development in or near floodplains can result in loss of life, property damage, and increased downstream flooding. Mitigation has been used to contain flood hazards through structures such as dikes; to protect people and property in flood-prone areas through flood insurance, building elevation, and floodproofing; and to limit the development of flood hazard areas through zoning and subdivision regulations. These actions change the nature of the flood threat, decrease vulnerability to flood damage, and reduce exposure to the flood hazard. In 1990, the Federal Emergency Management Agency (FEMA) initiated the Community Rating System, which rewards local hazard mitigation efforts by reducing federal flood insurance premiums in communities that adopt mitigation policies. The following list illustrates local hazard mitigation measures that can be taken under a development management program, along with potential mitigation objectives for each measure (Godschalk 1991, 136).

Measure	Mitigation Objective
Land use management	Direct development to safe areas
Building codes	Resist hazard stresses
Zoning ordinances	Restrict hazard area density
Subdivision regulations	Hazard-resistant infrastructure
Hazard analysis/risk mapping	Identify hazard areas
Hazard information systems	Increase buyers' risk awareness
Public education	Improve disaster understanding
Monitoring/inspection	Track regulatory compliance
Hazard land acquisition	Convert to open space/recreation
Relocation	Move vulnerable uses to safety
Tax incentives/disincentives	Encourage use of safer locations
Disaster insurance	Compensate economic losses

A local government may face multiple hazards. The development management program should consider all potential hazards and develop a comprehensive approach to mitigation as part of an integrated emergency management system. It is likely that some of the same measures will mitigate more than one hazard. For example, identifying flood, landslide, and earthquake hazard zones and separating them from urban service areas can reduce exposure to multiple risks.

Like all development management actions, recommendations for hazard mitigation measures must consider both the technical and the political feasibility of adoption. For example, it might be less difficult to persuade local officials to adopt hazard overlay districts with density bonuses for mitigation than to adopt a more complicated and uncertain program of development rights transfer. Constructing a matrix of hazards faced and potential mitigation tools is a useful technique for looking comprehensively at elements of a mitigation program. As shown in Table 17-6, the tools and hazards matrix can identify opportunities to create multipurpose mitigation tools (Godschalk 1991, 154). It can be used to display both estimates of the effectiveness of individual measures and the feasibility of their adoption.

Table 17-6. Tools and Hazards Matrix

Tools	Flood	Earthquake	Landslide	Hurricane	Nuclear Accident	Toxic Spill
Land Use Plan						
Urban services areas	+	+	+	+	+	0
Hazard zone identification	+	+	+	+	+	+
Evacuation plan	+	+	+	+	+	+
Reconstruction plan	+	+	+	+	+	0
Hazardous materials transportation	0	0	0	0	0	+
Zoning						
Hazard overlay districts	+	+	+	+	+	0
Mitigation performance standards	+	+	+	+	0	0
Hazard mitigation bonus	+	+	+	+	0	0
Nonconforming requirements	+	+	+	+	0	0
Subdivision Regulations						
Hazard disclosure	+	+	+	+	+	0
Hazard area dedication	+	+	+	+	0	0
Soil reports	0	+	+	0	0	0
Building Code						
Elevation requirements	+	–	–	+	0	0
Wind resistance requirements	+	+	+	+	0	0
Public Health Regulations						
Hazard overlay districts	+	+	+	+	+	0
Construction standards	+	+	+	+	+	+
Public Facility Programs						
Siting requirements	+	+	+	+	+	0
Capital improvement programs	+	+	+	+	+	0
Land Acquisition						
Hazard/open space	+	+	+	+	+	+
TDR (transfer of development rights)	+	+	+	+	+	0
Taxation						
Preferential hazard assessment	+	+	+	+	+	0

Note: + = complementary; 0 = neutral; – = conflicting.

NOTES

1. Much of this section on monitoring is adapted from the comprehensive plan monitoring guide compiled by Ragatz (1983) for use by Oregon communities in complying with state-mandated goals.

2. The Urban Institute has published a series of practice-oriented impact measure-

ment publications. They contain various checklists of impacts and bases for estimates (sources of data). See Christensen (1976) for social impacts, Keyes (1976) for environmental impacts, Muller (1976) for economic impacts, and Schaenman (1976) for land development impacts. The emphasis is on evaluating individual development proposals, but the methods also apply to evaluation of land use plans.

3. These steps are similar to those of the environmental impact analysis presented in chapter 7.

4. This definition is adapted to the local planning context from the definition of cumulative impacts in the National Environmental Policy Act (CEQ 1978, 56004): "the impact on the environment which results from the incremental impact of an action when added to other past, present, and reasonably foreseeable future actions."

5. See, for example, Nelson (1988), Frank and Rhodes (1987), Alterman (1988), and Snyder and Stegman (1986). The chapters on these topics in Nelson (1988) are particularly useful for the practical aspects of design of an impact fee ordinance, calculation of fees, and administering fee programs. For a land use planning perspective, see the chapter by Kaiser and Burby in Alterman (1988).

REFERENCES

Alterman, Rachelle, ed. 1988. *Private supply of public services: Evaluation of real estate exactions, linkage, and alternative land policies.* New York: New York University Press.

Burby, Raymond, et al. 1990. A report card on urban erosion and sedimentation control in North Carolina. *Carolina Planning* 16(2): 28–36.

CEQ [Council on Environmental Quality]. 1978. National Environmental Policy Act—final regulations. *Federal Register* 43(230): 55978–56007.

Christensen, Kathleen. 1976. *Social impacts of land development: An initial approach for estimating impacts on neighborhood usages and perceptions.* Washington, D.C.: The Urban Institute.

Contant, Cheryl K., and Lyna L. Wiggins. 1991. Defining and analyzing cumulative environmental impacts. *Environmental Impact Assessment Review* 11(4): 297–309.

Dickert, Thomas G., and Andrea E. Tuttle. 1985. Cumulative impact assessment in environmental planning: A coastal wetland watershed example. *Environmental Impact Assessment Review* 5(1): 37–64.

Frank, James E., and Robert M. Rhodes. 1987. *Development exactions.* Chicago: Planners Press.

Godschalk, David R. 1991. Disaster mitigation and hazard management. In *Emergency Management: Principles and Practice for Local Government,* ed. Thomas Drabek and Gerard Hoetmer. Washington, D.C.: International City Management Association.

Hill, Morris. 1968. A goals-achievement matrix for evaluating alternative plans. *Journal of the American Institute of Planners* 34(1): 19–29.

Josselyn, Michael, Joy Zedler, and Theodore Griswold. 1990. Wetland mitigation along the Pacific Coast of the United States. In *Wetland creation and restoration: The status of the science,* ed. Jon A. Kusler and Mary E. Kentula. Washington, D.C.: Island Press.

Kaiser, Edward J., and Raymond J. Burby. Exactions in managing growth: The land-use planning perspective. In *Private supply of public services: Evaluation of real estate exactions, linkage, and alternative land policies,* ed. Rachelle Alterman. New York: New York University Press.

Keyes, Dale L. 1976. *Land development and the natural environment: Estimating impacts.* Washington, D.C.: The Urban Institute.

Kusler, Jon A., and Mary E. Kentula, eds. 1990. *Wetland creation and restoration: The status of the science.* Washington, D.C.: Island Press.

Metropolitan Area Planning Council. 1989. *Impact fee primer: A manual for local officials.* Vol. 1. Boston: The author.

Muller, Thomas. 1976. *Economic impacts of land development: Employment, housing, and property values.* Washington, D.C.: The Urban Institute.

Nelson, Arthur C., ed. 1988. *Development impact fees: Policy rationale, practice, theory, and issues.* Chicago: Planners Press.

New Jersey State Planning Commission. 1991. *Communities of place: The interim state development and redevelopment plan for the State of New Jersey.* Trenton: The author.

Nicholas, James C., ed. 1985. *The changing structure of infrastructure finance.* Cambridge, Mass.: Lincoln Institute of Land Policy.

Ragatz, Richard L., Associates. 1983. *Comprehensive plan monitoring: Guidelines and resources for Oregon communities.* Portland: Oregon Department of Land Conservation and Development.

Rutgers University. 1992. *Impact assessment of the New Jersey interim state development and redevelopment plan.* Prepared for the New Jersey Office of State Planning. Rutgers: Center for Urban Policy Research.

Schaenman, Philip S. 1976. *Using an impact measurement system to evaluate land development.* Washington, D.C.: The Urban Institute.

Sedway Cooke Associates. 1989. *Volusia County coastal management element.* San Francisco: The author.

Snyder, Thomas P., and Michael A. Stegman. 1986. *Paying for growth: Using development fees to finance infrastructure.* Washington, D.C.: Urban Land Institute.

Weiss, Carol H. 1972. *Evaluation research: Methods of assessing program effectiveness.* Englewood Cliffs: Prentice-Hall.

Yaro, Robert D., et al. 1989. *Dealing with change in the Connecticut River Valley: A design manual for conservation and development.* Cambridge, Mass.: Lincoln Institute of Land Policy.

18

Implementation

Planning is the premediation of action;
management is the direct control of action.
—Harris and Batty 1991

Attempting to control the action of the land use game during implementation poses many opportunities for conflict. Because each player tries to win as much as possible for his or her interests, the planner as game manager must spend a lot of time mending fences and keeping the peace. Although there are always some conflicts over the design and content of the advance plan, there are usually many more conflicts during plan implementation as players learn more about the plan's specific effects on their individual properties, projects, and proposals for stability or change.

One of the major plan implementation approaches is development management. In practice, development management is carried out with a selection of implementation tools (for example, regulations and incentives) within a program tailored to the context of a particular jurisdiction. A basic premise of development management is that government must be a major player in the land use game in order to balance public and private gains and maintain a fair development process. These objectives will not necessarily be achieved by market forces alone, but will require the use of government authority to plan, regulate, tax, purchase land, and build facilities.

As distinct from periodic plan and development management program preparation efforts, the implementation of the development management program involves a number of ongoing, day-to-day activities. These activities combine planning and administration. They fall more into the adaptive management side than the rational design side of planning. They are shaped by procedures and standards but call upon the planner to be flexible and creative as well as fair and objective. They are process-oriented in that their outcomes are intended to guide immediate actions or decisions. They not only require the planner to follow rules and policies, but also to reinterpret and rewrite these rules and policies from time to time.

In chapter 16, we discussed the design of a development management strategy or plan as part of the advance planning process. In this chapter, we will review some implementation techniques for putting a development management program into operation and adjusting it to particular situations. These include capital budgeting, small-area planning, conflict resolution, problem solving, and coping with legal challenges.

Capital Budgeting

Capital budgeting is the selection of public physical improvements, based on available fiscal resources and the five-year capital improvements program, to be included in the jurisdiction's annual budget (So 1979). The capital budget contains those facilities programmed for the coming fiscal year. Traditionally, the purpose of the capital budget was financial control, but contemporary budgeting may also be a planning and communication tool. Preparation of the capital budget is an opportunity to educate the community and its decision-makers about implementing the priorities of the advance plan and capital improvements program and to demonstrate the usefulness of the planning information system, particularly on capacity thresholds of community facilities.

The annual capital budget adds flexibility to the five-year capital improvements program included in the comprehensive plan. As Brevard notes:

> Conventional plans often include an implementation element that is intended to bridge the gap between the strategic foundation of the plan and current (that is, budgeting) needs. However, these are usually little more than static expressions of the long-term strategy; that is, they prescribe actions which are sensible only so long as the originally conceived strategy remains sensible. . . . When these conditions change (as they inevitably must), a program of specific near-term facility investments that is derived from the plan is likely to become obsolete. Consequently, conventional approaches to planning are normally not resilient enough to retain their usefulness as a source of capital budgeting. (1985, 370–71)

Capital budgeting has a number of benefits relative to development management implementation. It gives both public and private decision-makers a basis for making related land use and project design decisions. It implements the more general long-range proposals of the advance plan, translating them into short-range, growth-management actions. It offers an opportunity for government officials, market representatives, and special interest groups to debate near-term fiscal policy, as well as a programmatic framework to record and organize their decisions. It contributes to sound financial management, comparing expected expenditure needs with returns from property taxes, general obligation and revenue bonds, fees and charges, assessments, and other revenue sources.[1] Finally, it enables localities to coordinate capital investment decisions with such community development policies as neighborhood revitalization or acquisition of open space.

The capital budgeting process is a combination of technical planning and politics. As So (1979) points out, operating bureaucracies within local government have their own capital project priorities, which may not be the same as those in the land use plan. They play the budget game with their requests, asking for more than they expect to get, lobbying for current rather than long-range needs, and establishing relationships with elected officials to get votes for their priority items. Also, the timing of investment decisions is not always neat and rational. Campaign promises, emergencies, new state or federal mandates, and neighborhood priorities can skew the timing for capital facilities. Finally, the bargaining between elected officials and interest groups that promote or oppose certain improvements must be taken into account. Elected officials value flexibility. Often they are reluctant to commit themselves to a five-year capital improvement program and may seek to bump projects up or back as pressures and opportunities change. They seek to keep tax rates down and spread capital improvements throughout the jurisdiction, whether or not these aims fit well with rational budgeting decisions.

A number of factors shape the decision environment for facility planning. In addition to political factors, rational investment analysis must compete with organizational values and reward systems, pet projects, perceptions of financial and image factors, and the tax and regulatory environment (Figure 18-1). As Brevard (1985, 45) observes, "The decision environment more or less automatically crys-

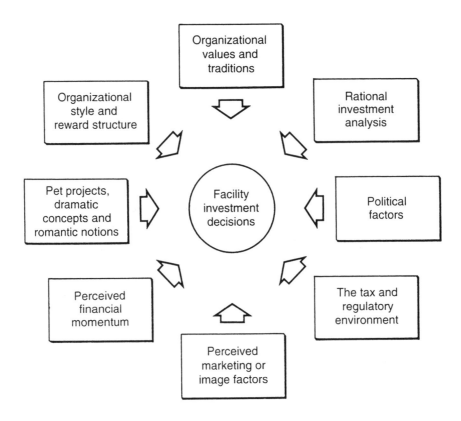

Figure 18-1. Facility Investment Decision Environment. From Brevard 1985, 44.

tallizes in a way that tends to promote certain short-run objectives as determined by the organization's culture."

To counteract dominance of short-run views and organizational competition, Brevard recommends a facility planning strategy that restructures the organizational context to support planning. He suggests creating a "matrix organization" for facility planning. This draws staff members from various departments into a facility budget planning group, where their primary loyalty is to the group's proposal rather than to their home department. Along with the planner, the group could include staff from the engineering, finance, legal, and management departments. The planner would ensure that the short-range goals of the budgeting process are connected with the long-range goals of the advance plan and capital program.

Brevard also recommends reorienting planning methods to create information categories that correspond to decision issues. Information is formatted so as to provide "action-advice" for decision-makers. For example, in the case of a decision about expanding an existing public facility, decision-makers would be provided with thorough evaluations of comparable alternatives so that they can decide on the basis of clear cost and benefit tradeoffs. This information is generated through an approach called "tactical planning," which analyzes the details and linkages of facility programming decisions (Brevard 1985). The elements of tactical planning include six steps.

1. *Strategic target.* Facility improvements needed to respond to long-range objectives, such as meeting demand for solid waste disposal during the twenty-year planning period.
2. *Facility option catalog.* Alternatives to improve elements of the facility system, evaluated in terms of effectiveness (capital and operating costs, performance level, coordination with other elements, external impacts on environment or safety, and ease of construction staging to meet demand changes).
3. *System development packages.* Desirable combinations of facility options assembled into comprehensive, coherent, and internally consistent facility configurations to meet long-range capacity objectives.
4. *Staging paths.* Alternative financing schedules for each system package, including different patterns or programmed sequences of resource expenditures necessary to reach the total capital outlay needed, which might vary significantly when the discounted, or time-value, of capital expenditures is taken into account.
5. *Monitoring program.* A system for collecting data on the performance of key facilities in order to evaluate the relationship of demand to capacity thresholds and the lead time necessary to bring needed capacity increases on line, so as to assess time pressures on facility improvement decisions.
6. *Capital plan and budget.* Specific, well-documented facility project proposals, which can result in an adopted statement of managerial intentions car-

rying the full weight of the organization's decision-making authority, a "legitimized plan" that includes goals, priorities, and implementation means.

By tailoring the capital budgeting process to respect long-run planning goals and objectives, it becomes a critical means of preventing obsolescence of the plan and development management program. By giving decision-makers tightly structured system development packages with clear financial schedules, the capital budgeting process counterbalances some of the political bias affecting budget decisions. Another approach for relating long-term planning goals to more immediate public concerns is the small-area planning process.

Small-Area Planning

Small-area planning is the process of developing detailed plans for sub-areas of the jurisdiction, based on the overall land use plan as well as on discourse with local interests to set specific community development priorities. Small-area planning can be seen as "stepping down" from the more general areawide plan to deal with the nitty gritty details of neighborhoods and specific parts of the urban area. Because these plans are closer to home for citizens, they typically inspire more focused debate than plans at the scale of the city or county. They are an important way of implementing areawide plans, translating more general policies into action recommendations, and building consensus among land use game players for these actions. As Sedway observes:

> Planning for a district—that is, a *portion* of a municipality—cannot be perceived simply as comprehensive community planning at a lesser scale. . . . Three unique requirements characterize planning for a district or a part of a community: the need to relate closely to the residents or users, of the district; the need to define carefully the boundaries of the district; and the need to relate the district to its larger setting in terms of circulation, open space, natural resources, visual form, land uses, and public services and facilities. (1988, 95)

The scale of small-area plans is midway between the scale of community plans and the scale of project plans. Where a community plan policy might tend to gloss over differences among sub-areas in order to achieve a general goal, small-area plans highlight the unique characteristics of each sub-area. By working at a larger scale than the community plan, the small-area plan can use analytical techniques from site plans, such as studies of land cover and land use, slope, drainage, and development suitability. The small-area plan can go into the detailed problems of existing use and activity patterns, community services and facilities, and changing trends and conditions. It can explore the impact on the sub-area of implementing such general plan recommendations as road construction or open space preservation.

The planner can use small-area plans for a variety of purposes. They may be used to tackle particular problem areas, such as declining inner-city neighborhoods or obsolete commercial strips. They may be used to scope out future development possibilities in growing fringe areas, including transportation corridors, where future development would benefit from a planned pattern of infrastructure. They may be used for environmentally critical areas, such as water supply watersheds or wetlands, which need special management. They may be applied on a jurisdictionwide basis as a neighborhood planning tool to work out plans for all the subareas over time.

Certain prerequisites are needed for small-area planning (Sedway 1988). First, the comprehensive community plan should be adopted as a guide for sub-area planning. Community support is essential to ensure that property owners and tenants support the planning process. A small-area advisory committee can provide advice and serve as a sounding board. A technical advisory committee can bring together the various government departments and agencies whose cooperation is needed.

The process of small-area planning is similar to that of community planning, although the focus is much more detailed. Figure 18-2 is an overview of the small-

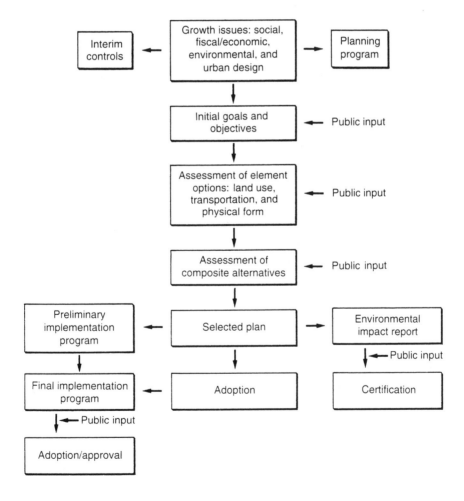

Figure 18-2. Small-Area Planning Process. From Sedway 1988, 96.

area planning process. It begins with design of a planning/study program with a work and staffing schedule, district boundaries, and identification of major development management issues. Initial goals and policies are defined with public participation. A data inventory and analysis is undertaken to describe existing conditions in terms of land use, circulation, visual form, economic conditions, housing, community facilities, regulatory adequacy, and available financial resources. The scope and format of the plan are defined on the basis of the inventory and analysis, and the work program is refined to focus on the identified problems and opportunities.

Small-area alternatives are developed for community review. Sketch plans address varying land use mixes and densities, alternative circulation and parking patterns, urban design choices, and implementation feasibility. Sketch plans can be done in stages. The first stage might be to explore particular sites or projects of significance, such as a transit-oriented commercial area or a potential new park and recreation facility. The second stage could then explore land use, transportation, and urban design options for the entire small area.

Based on response to the alternatives, a draft plan is prepared and evaluated. It should include an implementation program and an analysis of environmental impacts. Following public review, this draft is converted into the final plan for adoption by the governing body. Once adopted, the small-area plan becomes the basis for capital budgeting, review of rezoning and site plan requests, and for public and private project development.

An example of a small-area plan for a fringe area of a small city is shown in Figure 18-3 (Chapel Hill 1992, 18). This area contains some residential subdivisions, a school, farmland, and a quarry. It is located at the entrance to the city. The plan proposes a mixed-use village, including higher-density residential uses, a school, and a small office and commercial center. Outside the village, uses include low-density residential, preservation areas along the streams, preserved viewsheds along the major roads, and maintenance of some farming areas. The small-area planning process that generated this plan also was a useful vehicle for addressing a number of conflicts about future land use in this location.

Conflict Resolution

The land use game is rife with opportunities for conflict. As Godschalk et al. (1979, 21) observe, "In devising a growth-management program, one of the crucial concerns is whether the program reaches a fair compromise among the conflicting needs and demands of developers, current residents, potential residents, people of lower-income or minority groups, local business people, surrounding communities, and the local government."

Sometimes conflict can be useful in making decision-makers aware of unrecognized impacts on community groups and in leading to more balanced develop-

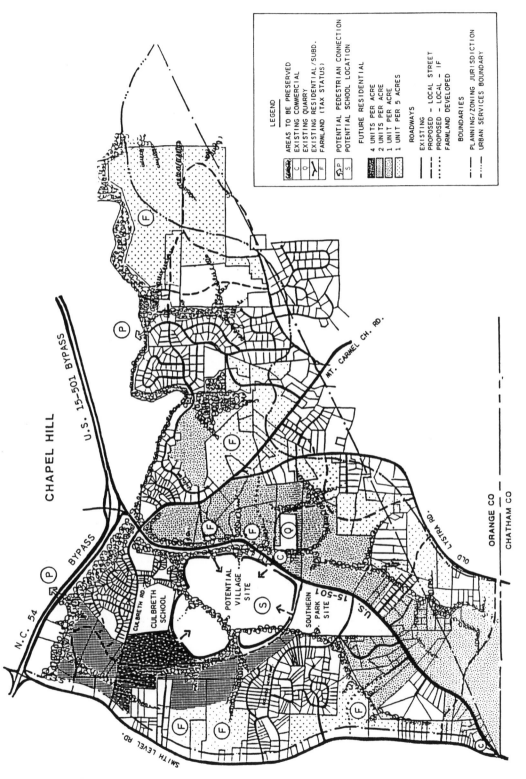

Figure 18-3. Illustrative Small-Area Plan. From Chapel Hill 1992, 18.

ment proposals. More often, conflict is destructive, leading to a spiral of increasing hostility, polarization, and adversarial proceedings (Figure 18-4). The wise planner is aware of impending conflict and uses proactive dispute resolution techniques to avoid the spiral of unmanaged conflict by building consensus whenever possible. As Carpenter and Kennedy (1988, 17) note, "The lesson of the conflict spiral is not that its progress is inevitable but that it is predictable when nothing is done to manage the conflict."

Designing a Conflict Management System

Given the frequency of conflict over land use decisions, planners should design conflict management approaches to deal consistently with disagreements. Three linked factors are important in the design of such approaches: the negotiation technique, the negotiation forum, and the intensity of conflict. Figure 18-5 illustrates a conflict management approach that ties techniques and forums to conflict intensities. As conflicts escalate, more formal resolution measures and settings are required for resolution.

Dispute resolution techniques range in formality from simple, face-to-face negotiation among affected parties to contracting with a professional outside mediator or arbitrator. Susskind and Cruikshank (1987) identify the range of techniques as:

1. *Direct, or unassisted, negotiation,* in which the parties get together on their own to work things out.
2. *Facilitation,* in which a third party assists in making the negotiation process work, through helping with procedures, communications, and logistics.
3. *Mediation,* in which the third party helps with both the process and the substance of the proposed agreements, meeting privately with each side as well as in joint sessions and seeking to craft win-win agreements that meet their joint interests.
4. *Arbitration* may be nonbinding, in which case a private judge or panel listens to both sides and suggests a solution that the parties can accept or reject. If the arbitration is binding, the arbitrator's decision is final.[2]

Dispute resolution forums, the types of settings in which conflicts are addressed, range from informal meetings among planners, developers, and citizens to hearings that judges and attorneys conduct according to strict legal procedures. Many disagreements can be headed off at their early stages through preliminary proposal reviews in the planner's office or at planning board work sessions. More difficult conflicts can be tackled in special work groups or task forces. Intergovernmental organizations, such as councils of government, can be neutral settings for negotiation or mediation involving elected officials. More formal administrative hearings before a hearing officer or lawsuits before a judge tend to encourage adversarial rather than negotiation behavior.[3]

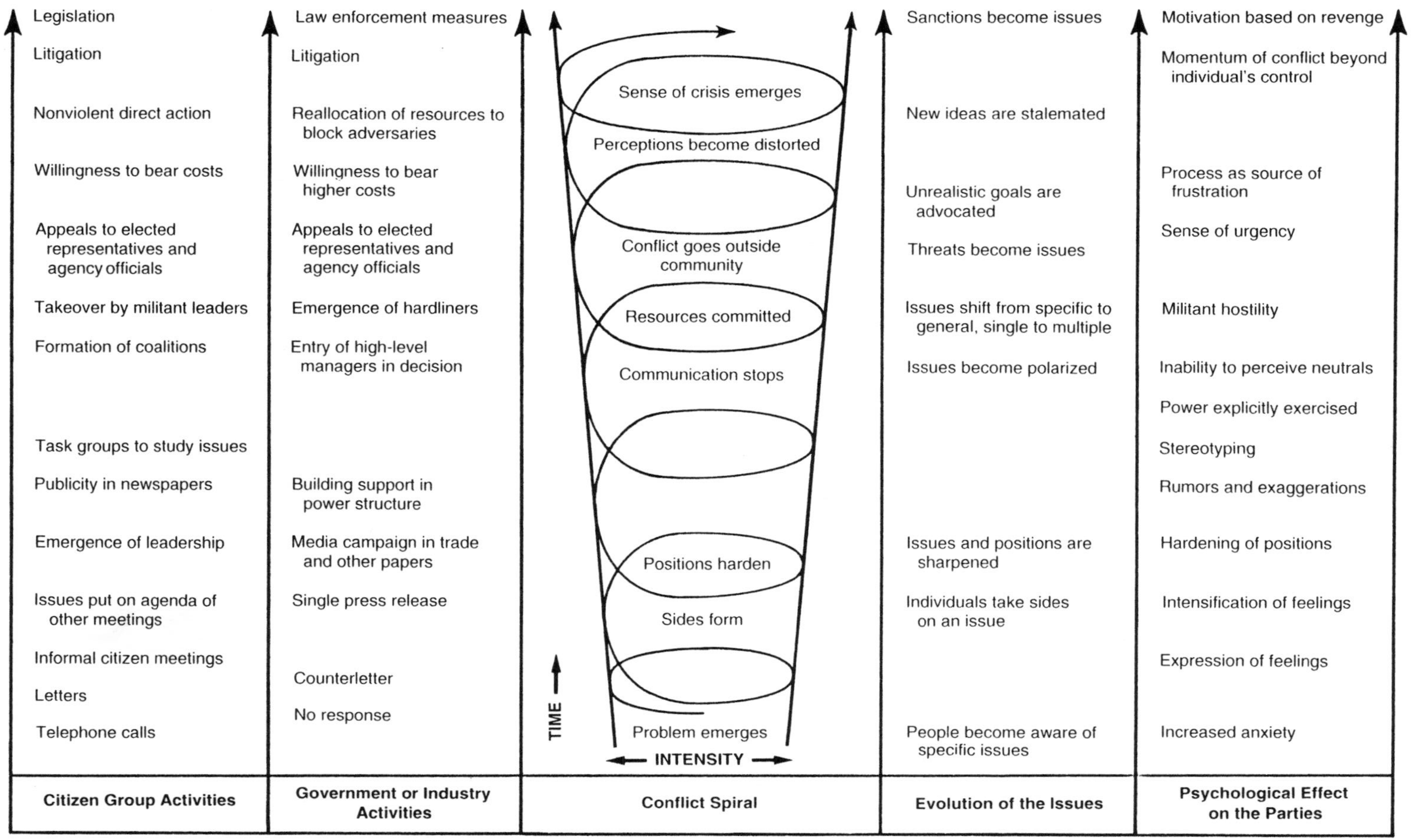

Figure 18-4. Spiral of Unmanaged Conflict. From Carpenter and Kennedy 1988, 12.

Citizen Group Activities	Government or Industry Activities	Conflict Spiral	Evolution of the Issues	Psychological Effect on the Parties
Legislation	Law enforcement measures		Sanctions become issues	Motivation based on revenge
Litigation	Litigation			Momentum of conflict beyond individual's control
Nonviolent direct action	Reallocation of resources to block adversaries	Sense of crisis emerges	New ideas are stalemated	Process as source of frustration
Willingness to bear costs	Willingness to bear higher costs	Perceptions become distorted	Unrealistic goals are advocated	Sense of urgency
Appeals to elected representatives and agency officials	Appeals to elected representatives and agency officials	Conflict goes outside community	Threats become issues	Militant hostility
Takeover by militant leaders	Emergence of hardliners	Resources committed	Issues shift from specific to general, single to multiple	Inability to perceive neutrals
Formation of coalitions	Entry of high-level managers in decision	Communication stops	Issues become polarized	Power explicitly exercised
Task groups to study issues				Stereotyping
Publicity in newspapers	Building support in power structure			Rumors and exaggerations
Emergence of leadership	Media campaign in trade and other papers	Positions harden	Issues and positions are sharpened	Hardening of positions
Issues put on agenda of other meetings	Single press release	Sides form	Individuals take sides on an issue	Intensification of feelings
Informal citizen meetings				Expression of feelings
Letters	Counterletter	Problem emerges	People become aware of specific issues	Increased anxiety
Telephone calls	No response			

INTENSITY →

TIME

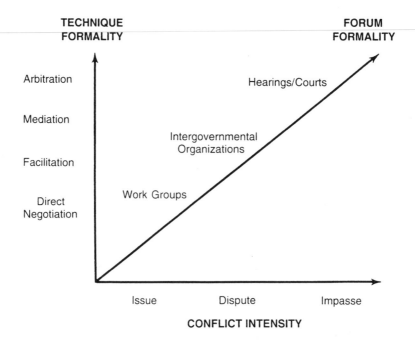

Figure 18-5. Linked Conflict Management Approach. From Godschalk 1992, 369.

Conflicts differ not only in terms of substance but also in the intensity of the disagreements. Assuming "conflict" as the generic term for disagreement, three different intensity levels can be defined (Godschalk 1992, 369).

1. *Issues* are technical problems involving moderate levels of disagreement, susceptible to solution through informal negotiation or facilitation among planners and affected interests within a semiformal process or organization, such as a work group.
2. *Disputes* are unresolved issues that have become politicized and escalated to substantial intensities of disagreement. They require formal negotiation or mediation involving planners, elected officials, and affected interests within existing governmental organizations or conflict management groups.
3. *Impasses* are stalemated disputes involving overwhelmingly intense disagreement, in which good faith efforts have broken down and formal arbitration in a hearing or courtroom setting is required for resolution.

Conflict Resolution Principles and Analysis

Underlying most successful conflict resolution is a change of mindset toward building consensus and seeking joint gains rather than beating the other side. The most cogent expression of this mindset is principled negotiation, a technique based on meeting the affected parties' real interests rather than their blustering positions. The technique consists of four principles (Fisher, Ury, and Patton 1991).

1. *Separate the people from the problem.* Be tough on the substantive elements of the problem. Be sensitive to the feelings and perceptions of the people in order to create a positive, problem solving relationship in which you work side-by-side to resolve the conflict.
2. *Focus on interests, not positions.* Ask why. Probe beneath positional statements to identify the underlying interests of each party. State the problem in terms of common and conflicting interests rather than artificial bargaining positions.
3. *Invent options for mutual gain.* Avoid premature judgment, searching for a single answer, assuming a fixed set of benefits, and letting the other side look out for itself. Invent new options through brainstorming, create a variety of possibilities, broaden the benefits by dovetailing shared and differing interests, and make it easy for the other side to agree by building good options for them.
4. *Insist on using objective criteria.* Do not accept arbitrary demands based on the wills of the parties. Search for verifiable objective criteria that apply equally to all sides in order to measure the fairness and effectiveness of agreements.

Translating principled negotiation into development management implementation involves applying the framework from Figure 18-5 to your governmental setting. To build an effective conflict management capability, four guidelines should be helpful (Godschalk 1992).

1. *Build negotiation-friendly climates and procedures.* Develop a constructive problem solving climate by educating public officials and interest groups on the values of principled negotiation. Design procedures to deal with various conflict levels, building on existing organizations and resources. Lay out ways for notifying stakeholders of perceived conflicts, convening meetings to explore issues, and using alternative conflict management forums and techniques.
2. *Identify issues early and deal with them forthrightly.* Screen the local situation regularly to uncover differences of opinion about planning and development management implementation. Identify technical problems that are amenable to settlement at an early stage through informal negotiation. Create an early warning system for potential conflicts.
3. *Recognize disputes and provide settings for resolution.* Once an issue has blown up into a dispute, through going public in the press, provide a neutral forum where it can be tackled. If necessary, involve the affected decision-makers in direct negotiation. Arrange for facilitation or mediation support when direct negotiation is unable to resolve the dispute. Provide politicians with incentives and level playing fields where principled negotiation can work.

4. *Invest in good tools to find solutions and joint gains.* The information systems and analytical techniques described in this book can be instrumental in breaking deadlocks over planning and growth-management conflicts. Problem definitions, simple tradeoff matrices, and spreadsheet models are all means to highlight positive joint gains. Planners who understand both the process of dispute resolution and the substantive issues of land use planning can create ongoing conflict management systems to cope with persistent development conflicts.

The stakeholder analysis is a technique that can be used to prepare for negotiation. This is an advance scoping of the interests of those affected by a plan or proposal and how they are likely to respond to it.[4] A "stakeholder" is any affected person, group, or organization. A stakeholder analysis looks at who the key players are, what they need, what they can contribute, what power they have, and what their influence pattern is.

Table 18-1 (Buckley 1985, 56–57) illustrates a framework for recording the findings of a stakeholder analysis. This analysis looked at stakeholders concerned with a public/private development project in the Republic Square District of Austin, Texas. Data for a stakeholder analysis can be acquired through personal interviews, surveys, or group discussions with representative stakeholders. It can be checked against the analyst's own estimates. A benefit of stakeholder analysis is that it puts the planner into the shoes of other players and provides insights into their likely interests and behavior. Thus equipped, the planner is able to be more effective in managing conflicts and creating joint gains.

Problem Solving

In the course of managing land use change, the planner will confront many difficult problems not necessarily anticipated by the advance plan. In analyzing these problems, Patton and Sawicki (1986, 4) state, "Success is measured by the quality of public debate and the efficacy of the policy adopted. Therefore, basic analysis must be responsive to the policy problem. Methods must be selected for their ability to attack the client's problem in the time available without obfuscation."

Solution of unanticipated problems calls for skills in "quick and dirty" analysis and recommendation formulation. We define this activity as problem solving—the systematic analysis of day-to-day problems in light of feasible alternative solutions. Although effective problem solving is both a political and a technical skill that transcends simple analysis, systematic analytic techniques can improve the process.[5] We focus on defining the problem, assuming that a problem well specified becomes more amenable to solution.

A penetrating problem definition can highlight the critical variables that can be affected by government action. Patton and Sawicki (1986, 107) observe that

Table 18-1. Illustrative Stakeholder Analysis Framework

Stakeholder	Interests/Expectations Needs	Resources to Contribute	Power		Who Influences the Stakeholder	Whom the Stakeholder Influences
			Adoption	Implementation		
State government University of Texas Austin Community College	Attractive environment Security/safety Institutional needs met Housing A 24-hour environment	Influence Joint ventures, possibly in teleconferencing facilities Office of video production space Housing mortgage finance programs	+	+	Strong community groups Private interest groups City	Member institutions Strong community groups Private interest groups
City of Austin	Diversified housing Public improvements Retail amenities Designation as a special district Cultural uses Height, view corridors Scale and density	Urban Development Action Grants Influence and support Condemnation/eminent domain Land writedowns Bonds Community Development Block Grants Land Tax abatement Zoning Capital and operating budget Designation as a special district Special assessment anticipation notes Tax increment financing Marketing/promotion Signage Public transit	N	N	Institutions Community groups Private interest groups Voters	Institutions Community groups Private interest groups Voters

Table 18-1, continued

Stakeholder	Interests/Expectations Needs	Resources to Contribute	Power		Who Influences the Stakeholder	Whom the Stakeholder Influences
			Adoption	Implementation		
Private Developers	Diversified housing Demolition and site control Retail/commerical center Recreational facilities Public improvements	Equity/syndication Track record/expertise Links with financial community "Vision"	0	+	Uncertain	Uncertain
Minority Groups	Housing development Commercial development Public improvements Recreational space and community facilities Involvement and direct participation in development initiatives Employment training and job placement	Strong links with the political community In-kind services Publicity/marketing Small business	+	+	Minority development and financial community	Minority development and financial community City council and politicians
Special Interest Groups	"Appropriate" scale and density Transformation/traffic Effect on neighborhoods View corridors Open space	No fiscal support	+	++	Uncertain	City departments City council Mayor

Note: ++ = very powerful; + = powerful; 0 = not powerful; N = key actor with ability to veto.

"a convincing problem statement can focus resources of many groups on an important problem." They suggest that the problem definition process follow seven steps.

1. Think about the problem, including making the values explicit.
2. Delineate the boundaries of the problem, in time, history, and location.
3. Develop a fact base, focused on the key variables or criteria (the central "nuggets").
4. List goals and objectives in measurable form.
5. Identify the "policy envelope," the range of factors to be studied.
6. Display potential costs and benefits to those affected.
7. Review the problem statement to ensure it allows for action and potential solutions.

Among the basic techniques for land use and environmental problem definition are back-of-the-envelope calculations to estimate the size of the problem, decision tree analysis to identify the key attributes of alternatives, and operational definition to create workable measures. One other task of problem definition, the analysis of relevant political factors, has previously been discussed in this chapter under the heading of stakeholder analysis.

Back-of-the-Envelope Calculations

Back-of-the-envelope calculations are aimed at establishing key dimensions of the problem and checking numerical estimates against known reference points. They attempt to answer questions about the size of the problem or proposal, how many people are affected, how much it will cost the community, and what its spillover effects will be.

For example, if a downtown office project's backers ask to have the city's parking requirements waived, the planner might do the following quick calculations. The proposed office building will include 30,000 square feet. This translates into space for about 250 employees at an average office size of 100 square feet plus circulation, storage, and common areas. Assuming that 75 percent of the employees commute to work by private cars, then up to 188 parking spaces could be demanded. An adjacent, underused public parking lot has about 70 spaces available. Thus, a reasonable first-cut alternative to eliminating all parking might be to ask the developer to provide a minimum of 120 spaces on-site and to lease an additional 70 spaces from the public parking lot.

Decision Tree Analysis

Decision tree analysis is a technique that is useful where the choice of alternatives is uncertain, showing decision-makers the potential consequences of safe and risky decisions. Its value is to structure the problem so that critical components can be identified and analyzed. It graphs the alternatives, including the estimated probabilities of each, and their outcomes (Patton and Sawicki 1986).

The elements of the graph include decision nodes, uncertainty or probability nodes, outcome branches, terminal nodes, and consequence branches (Figure 18-6). In the example shown, the question is whether to abate taxes to encourage downtown development. If the decision is to do nothing (the safe decision), then development may occur anyway. This is the best consequence because it costs the city nothing to achieve the goal. However, if development does not occur, then this is the third-best consequence because the goal of development is not achieved. If the decision is to abate taxes (the risky decision), then development may occur. This is the second-best consequence, achieving development but at the cost of lost taxes. Finally, if taxes are abated and no development occurs, then this is the worst consequence because revenues are lost and the goal is not achieved.

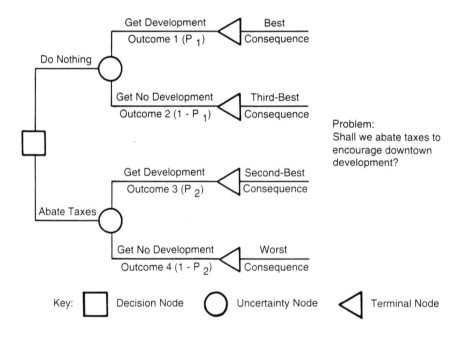

Figure 18-6. Decision Tree Graph. From Patton and Sawicki 1986, 115.

Estimated probabilities can aid in deciding which alternative to choose. Note that the probabilities for each pair of outcome branches should add up to 1.0 (certainty). In practice, it will be difficult to estimate probabilities of future actions with precision. The planner can either choose to omit probabilities and simply use the decision tree graph to highlight the structure of the problem and alternative outcomes or estimate probabilities in more general terms (such as alternative A is twice as likely as alternative B).

Operational Definition

Operational definition means translating a problem statement or objective into measurable terms. This is similar to expressing a plan objective in measurable terms so that its achievement can be monitored. A good operational definition is clear, derived from available or collectible data, and focused on the central nugget or criterion of the problem.

For example, if the problem is to enact a land use policy that will support a light rail transit system, then one issue is what residential and employment density will be needed at which locations relative to the system to provide an adequate ridership base. In this case, the planner might discover from the literature that the critical locations are those within one-quarter mile of the transit stops (walking distance) and that the minimum residential density needed in this area is twelve units per acre. The operational definition of a feasible transit stop land use policy would then be: an area of one-quarter-mile radius within the transit corridor whose average residential density is or can be regulated so as to be at least twelve units per acre.

Legal Challenges

Development management programs are often challenged in the courts. No matter how effective the conflict resolution effort, not all parties will always be willing to agree to negotiated settlements. To be on the safe side, the planner should be prepared to defend development management plans and decisions before a judge in court. Lawsuits are not necessarily catastrophes; they may turn into opportunities to educate the community about the value of the plan and its underlying principles.

Planners are not expected to be legal experts. If you are involved in a law suit, your attorney will deal with the legal arguments. However, you should be aware of the types of legal challenges that your plan and development management program may face.[6] You should be able to provide your attorney with the planning rationale to show a judge that your actions were reasonable and supported by facts. You should be prepared to testify on behalf of your plan and program. To ensure that your development management actions are defensible and that your testimony is effective, you should:

1. *Document all plans and decisions thoroughly.* Nothing beats a written record for demonstrating that there was a reasonable process based on valid data and analysis behind the government's action. Keep a clear paper trail of relevant memos, studies, and meeting minutes. Remember that your files may be subpoenaed and combed through by opposing lawyers, so do not include extraneous materials that may muddy the water but do not omit any information on which you relied for your conclusions or recommendations.

2. *Be prepared to explain your logic.* It is not easy to educate a judge or jury on planning methods and techniques. You should couch your explanations in clear and simple language, omitting planning jargon. The best approach is to start with a very basic description of what you did and then add the necessary qualifications and special circumstances. An apt metaphor may help to convey your point. Think of your audience as beginning students of the topic and offer them a patient, straightforward first course.

3. *Use graphics to support testimony whenever possible.* The abstract concepts of planning come alive much better when they are shown in diagrammatic or pictorial form. Sketch plans, process diagrams, and simple charts can communicate a lot of information in an understandable fashion. Often you can use existing graphics to make your point, sometimes adding annotations to point out key factors. If possible, use color in your graphics. This not only helps to make the point, but it also engages the esthetic sense of your audience more completely.

4. *Summarize your data in table format.* Long pages of numbers are not appropriate to communicate numerical findings. Pick out the key criteria and develop summary tables that illustrate the important relationships. Simple tables can be blown up into exhibits large enough to be read by the courtroom participants. Use large, bold face type. Always indicate your sources.

5. *Be honest.* It is tempting to try to cover up your mistakes. But, if asked, you should own up to your failures as well as your successes. Because of sunshine laws and public information laws, planners work in fishbowls. A good attorney can usually dig up enough information to discredit you as a witness unless you are scrupulously honest in your testimony. This does not mean that you cannot make a strong claim for the correctness of your analysis or conclusion. It does mean that you should admit to the gray areas in your findings or to the projections that were off the mark.

NOTES

1. For a review of some contemporary alternatives for infrastructure finance, see the chapters in Nicholas (1985). Although the major focus is on impact fees, the authors also review the relationship of community planning to infrastructure funding and the use of special districts.

2. Binding arbitration is rarely used in public disputes because most public officials cannot legally delegate their authority to an arbitrator. Nonbinding arbitration has taken the form of "mini-trials" in some cases, in which the expectations of the parties are examined in light of what would likely happen in court if they went to trial. The outcomes of mini-trials can provide parties with more realistic grounds for seeking negotiated solutions.

3. Not all conflicts can be resolved through bargaining and mediation. Some may have to be adjudicated. Dispute resolution works best when conflicts do not involve all or nothing philosophical or ideological value differences.

4. Stakeholder analysis is also used in strategic planning to identify the criteria that

stakeholders use to assess the performance of the planning unit and estimate how well the unit is performing according to these criteria (Bryson 1988).

5. Much of this section on problem solving draws upon Patton and Sawicki (1986). Their focus is on simple methods of policy analysis, which are limited in scope and time, directed at a particular problem and client, and assume a political approach to implementation. They contrast these methods with comprehensive planning, which they see as broad in scope and time, directed at overall functions and a community client, and assuming apolitical implementation. What they term as *policy analysis,* we call *problem solving.* And we do not assume apolitical implementation. The land use game would not exist without politics.

6. For reviews of the basic types of legal challenges and their planning contexts, see Godschalk et al. (1979) and Blaesser and Weinstein (1989).

REFERENCES

Blaesser, Brian, and Alan Weinstein, eds. 1989. *Land use and the Constitution: Principles for planning practice.* Chicago: Planners Press.

Brevard, Joseph H. 1985. *Capital facilities planning: A tactical approach.* Chicago: Planners Press.

Brower, David J., David R. Godschalk, and Douglas R. Porter. 1989. *Understanding growth management: Critical issues and a research agenda.* Washington, D.C.: Urban Land Institute.

Bryson, John M. 1988. *Strategic planning for public and nonprofit organizations.* San Francisco: Jossey-Bass.

Buckley, Michael P. 1985. Stakeholders analysis applied to the Republic Square District, Austin, Texas. In *Managing development through public/private negotiations,* ed. Rachelle Levitt and John Kirlin. Washington, D.C.: Urban Land Institute.

Carpenter, Susan L., and W. J. D. Kennedy. 1988. *Managing public disputes: A practical guide to handling conflict and reaching agreements.* San Francisco: Jossey-Bass.

Chapel Hill. 1992. *Small area: Plan southern area.* Chapel Hill: The town.

Fisher, Roger, William Ury, and Bruce Patton. 1991. *Getting to yes: Negotiating agreement without giving in.* 2d ed. New York: Penguin Books.

Godschalk, David R. 1992. Negotiating intergovernmental development policy conflicts: Practice-based guidelines. *Journal of the American Planning Association* 58(3): 368–78.

Godschalk, David R., David J. Brower, Larry D. McBennett, Barbara A. Vestal, and Daniel C. Herr. 1979. *Constitutional issues of growth management.* Rev. ed. Chicago: Planners Press.

Harris, Britton, and Michael Batty. 1991. Locational models, geographic information and planning support systems. Paper presented at Regional Science Meeting, New Orleans, Nov. 7–10.

Nicholas, James, ed. 1985. *The changing structure of infrastructure finance.* Cambridge, Mass.: Lincoln Institute of Land Policy.

Patton, Carl V., and David S. Sawicki. 1986. *Basic methods of policy analysis and planning.* Englewood Cliffs: Prentice-Hall.

Sedway, Paul H. 1988. District planning. In *The practice of local government planning,* ed. Frank So and Judith Getzels. 2d ed. Washington, D.C.: International City Management Association.

So, Frank S. 1979. Finance and budgeting. In *The practice of local government planning,* ed. Frank So, Israel Stollman, Frank Beal, and David Arnold. Washington, D.C.: International City Management Association.

Susskind, Lawrence, and Jeffrey Cruikshank. 1987. *Breaking the impasse: Consensual approaches to resolving public disputes.* New York: Basic Books.

Index

Access: to commercial areas, 326; to employment centers, 325; as "good" city form, 43; to open space, 298, 302

Activity centers: access to residential areas, 349; economic base, 317; employment projections for, 324; holding capacity of, 323, 337; location requirements for, 324–26; matching land use to, 321–23; multipurpose, 338; planning process for, 323–28; preparatory studies for, 323; schematic design of, 327; spatial structure of, 316; suitability analyses of, 326–27; transportation planning for, 379; trial distribution of space requirements for, 337–38; types of, 316–23; urban, 310

Activity systems: inventories in, 199–201, 213–15; land as setting for, 197–98; theories of, 43, 44–45

Advance planning: capital improvement programs for, 253; as community activity, 254–55; development management in, 74, 253, 398, 417, 454; direction-setting in, 258–59; fiscal policy in, 274; four-stage approach to, 255; future conditions in, 261; goal-setting in, 252, 261–74, 457, 458; in land use planning programs, 62–63, 79; policy legacy in, 275; policy-setting in, 274; products of, 251–54; purpose of, 251; role of capital budgeting in, 455; role of planners in, 416; stages of, 251–54

Aerial photography, 109; of environmental conditions, 175; inventories of, 204; of land cover, 179; in land use information systems, 200, 203; of wetlands, 183

Agenda for the 21st Century (Agenda 21), 21

Aging, as component of population measurement, 133–35

Agriculture, Census of, 168n3

Agriculture: functional space for, 197; and growth allocation, 306; in land use planning, 290; locational design of, 283; and open space planning, 297

Air quality, 21, 25, 174, 184; impact analysis of, 186; inventory of, 175

Airsheds, 174, 184

American assembly (goal-setting technique), 272

American Institute of Certified Planners, 32n10

American Law Institute, 73, 192

American Planning Association: awards by, 66, 70; journal of, 122

Anderson (et al.) system of land cover classification, 179, 205–6, 225n2

Anticipatory democracy (goal-setting), 272

Aquifers, 175

Arbitration, of conflict resolution, 462, 472n2

ARC/INFO (geographic information system), 95, 99

Army Corps of Engineers, 12, 242

Asheville, N.C.: land use map of, 210

Assumptions approach, to employment analysis, 152

ATLAS thematic mapping program, 94, 113n3

AUTOCAD (computer assisted design), 94, 113n3

Back-of-the-envelope calculations (problem-solving), 469

Base maps, 98, 441; cartographic, 109, 110; orthophoto, 109, 110, 177; planimetric, 177. See also Maps

Bay Area Simulation system (BASS II), 221

Beatley, Timothy, 403

Bergman, Edward M., 163, 164

Best-management practices (BMPs), 219

Biochemical oxygen demand (BOD), 238

Biological diversity, 172, 173

Block Statistics bulletins, 121

Blumenfeld, Hans, 155

Bogue, Donald J., 131

Brainwriting (goal-setting), 270

Brevard, Joseph H., 455, 456–57

Brower, David J., 403

Building permits, as source of land use data, 204

Bureau of the Census: censuses of establishments, 168n3; data provided by, 120–22, 130, 142n4, 145, 167n1; fertility projections of, 137

Bureau of Economic Analysis, 165, 168n6

Bureau of Labor Statistics, 145; data provided by, 161, 167n1, 169n9

Business districts, central: accessibility to, 326; land use planning for, 320, 321, 368; space requirements for, 335, 336; transportation planning for, 379

Business districts, local: location requirements for, 362–63; in residential area design, 364

Business Economics, Office of, 165

Bus service, community, 111

Cadastral files, interpretation of, 203, 204

Cadastral maps, 110

Calibration, of models, 161, 163

California Urban Futures Model, 222

Calvert County (Maryland) Comprehensive Plan, 66, 67

Capital budgeting, 423, 455–58; definition of, 455; political process of, 455–56; in rational planning, 39; small-area planning and, 460; tactical planning for, 457–58

Capital improvement programs, 3, 29, 111; in advance planning, 253; budgeting for, 455–56; in development management plans, 75, 78, 399, 400, 401, 415–16, 418; governmental, 393; and land supply inventories, 200; and land use change management, 36; for public facilities, 230, 393; role of cumulative impact assessment in, 191; and urban growth, 310, 312

Capital investment, 197; and infrastructure programs, 22, 25

Carpooling, 236

Carrying capacity analysis: institutional, 226n4; of land use, 50, 56n11, 201–2, 218–20

Carrying capacity: concurrency policies for, 219–20; factors limiting, 219–20; of recreation sites, 244. *See also* Holding capacity

Causal factors (fact-finding), 259, 260, 276

Census of Agriculture, 168n3

Census of Housing bulletins, 121, 142n3–5

Census of Population bulletins, 121, 142n5

Census of Population reports, decennial, 145, 161, 168n3

Census Tract bulletins, 121

Census tracts, 141n2

Census, U.S., 90; of 1980, 104, 206; of 1990, 103, 206; digital format of, 24, 122, 206; use in land allocation, 359

Census zones, use in transportation planning, 235

Change: institutional, 97; as unit of analysis, 41. *See also* Land use change

Chapel Hill, North Carolina: small-area plan for, 461

Chapin, F. Stuart, Jr., 44

Charlotte, North Carolina: employment density of, 329, 330

Checklists: for environmental analysis, 186–87; for impact analysis, 439–40, 451n2; for impact mitigation, 427, 429–31

Cities. *See* Urban areas

Citizens: role in advance planning, 254; role in development management, 417; role in direction-setting, 257, 259; role in goal-setting, 269; role in land use planning, 4, 81

Citizens' groups. *See* Interest groups

Clark, John, 56n11

Clean Air Act, 21; 1990 amendments to, 27, 375

Clean Water Act, 21, 184; wetlands in, 182

Coastal Barrier Resources Act (1982), 12

Coastal management programs: evaluation of, 434, 435; federal funding for, 15, 16; state-run, 13, 30n5

Coastal Population/Development Information System (North Carolina), 444

Coastal Zone Management Act (1972), 11, 13, 30n5, 31n8, 192

Cohort-component method (of population projection), 132–38, 139, 141; software for, 142n10

Cohorts (population groups), 123; in population-economic projection, 166; in population measurement, 132–38; in ratio-share techniques, 130; survival projections for, 136, 141. *See also* Population

Columbia, Maryland: neighborhood design in, 347

Commercial centers, 20; advance planning for, 253; community facilities in, 368; density of, 338; floor-area analysis of, 332, 333–35; future land use maps of, 212; goals for, 273; ground-area requirements for, 335, 336; highway-oriented, 320–21, 326, 335; holding capacity analysis of, 337; impact on residential areas, 338, 348, 359, 366; land use planning for, 316, 317, 320–21, 324, 326, 332–37; location requirements for, 326; office space in, 323; overbuilding of, 20; satellite, 378; in small-area plans, 460; space requirements for, 285, 338, 339; spatial structure of, 323; suitability analysis for, 326–27, 338; water supply for, 382. *See also* Employment centers

Committed lands analysis, 201, 202, 220

Communities: acceptance of change, 38; builders of, 30n4; control of agenda by, 257; future vision for, 254; goals of, 262, 268–69, 281, 341, 349; impact mitigation for, 448; input policies of, 82; local support facilities for, 362–63; measures of change in, 116; plan evaluation by, 437; quality of life in, 267–68; recreational facilities for, 244, 300, 389; service facilities for, 349, 362–63; social use values of, 16–17, 40,

115, 229; standards of, 269; use of open space, 298, 303; use of planning intelligence, 112. *See also* Neighborhoods
Communities of Place (New Jersey), 435–36
Community facilities, 228–30, 245*n1;* advanced planning for, 366; analysis units of, 229–30; capital improvement programs for, 393, 394; cumulative impact assessment for, 442; demand approach to planning, 373; design process of, 373–74; in development management plans, 399; dual purpose of, 368, 369; efficiency of, 369; as element of intelligence, 87; goals of, 374; impact mitigation for, 446–48; impact on nonusers, 369; infrastructure of, 366; inventory of, 229–30; land supply for, 340, 363, 364; land use planning for, 229, 317, 368, 369, 393; levels of service for, 373; locational design of, 283; locational requirements for, 252, 349, 372–74; for neighborhoods, 359; as part of commercial areas, 368; per capita approach to planning, 372–73, 393; plan evaluation for, 438; planning information for, 229–35; planning process for, 370–74; planning team for, 371, 393; potential for conflict over, 370; and private land use, 369; providers of service to, 371; role in residential area development, 363, 364; schools as, 243; service areas for, 369, 374; space requirements for, 285, 372–74; traits of, 368–70; transportation services for, 374–82; uneven effects of, 368, 370; users of, 369–70, 371; variation in areas served, 369–70. *See also* Infrastructure; Public facilities
Community Rating System (FEMA), 450
Commuter rail access, 111
Commuting, patterns of, 197
Competitive shift component, of economic analysis, 148
Composite landscape maps, 185
Composite methods (symptomatic measuring technique), 131
Computer assisted design (CAD), 94, 95, 113*n3;* in mapping, 99; for plan evaluation, 433, 434; for TIGER files, 104; of transportation systems, 433
Computer programs. *See* Software
Computers: mainframe, 95; use in planning information systems, 93–94. *See also* Databases; Microcomputer technology; Technology
Concurrency policies, 219–20, 230, 265–66, 394; in development management plans, 403; and land use management programs, 413; and urban growth, 310
Conflict: disputes in, 464, 465; issues in, 464, 465; spiral of, 462, 463
Conflict resolution, 3, 22–23, 432, 460, 462–

66; impasses in, 464; information systems in, 466; in land classification, 296; in land use planning, 6; legal procedures for, 462, 473*n6;* mediation of, 462; principles of, 464–66; in rational planning, 39; stakeholder analysis in, 466, 467–68, 469, 472*n4;* techniques for, 455, 462, 464. *See also* Problem–solving
Congestion management programs (CMP), 381; funds for, 27
Congress, U.S.: involvement in land use planning, 25–26
Consensus-building, 3, 23; in land use change management, 35, 36, 53–54; in land use game, 458; planners' role in, 29, 30, 53–54, 79–80; principles of, 464; in rational planning, 39, 40
Conservation, environmental, 25, 173; state-mandated, 13; of water, 240
Conservation areas: classification of, 292, 295, 296, 298, 309; economic use of, 304; in land use planning, 290; purpose of, 297–98. *See also* Critical areas, environmental; Environment
Constant-share model, of economic analysis, 149–50, 154
Constitutional decision trees, 412
Constitutional rights, protection of, 267, 405, 410
Consumer services, types of land use for, 317, 323
Content theories, of urban change, 40–42, 56*n6*
Control theories, of land use, 56*n7*
Control, as characteristic of "good" city form, 43
Conversion techniques, definition of, 166
Corporatism, 23
Cost-effectiveness, in economic analysis, 146
County Business Pattern reports (U.S. Bureau of the Census), 145
Critical areas, environmental, 290; analysis of, 185, 192; classification of, 292, 296, 298; in development management plans, 401; and growth allocation, 185, 192; plan evaluation for, 438; small-area plans for, 459. *See also* Conservation areas; Environment
Cross-hauling (of industrial exports), 153, 169*n6*
Cumulative impact analysis. *See* Impact analysis, cumulative
Current Employment Survey (Bureau of Labor Statistics), 161, 169*n9*
Current Population Reports (Bureau of the Census), 121, 130

Data: acquisition of, 99, 103–4, 203; attribute, 99, 105; classification of, 103; for development management planning, 408–9; employment, 145–46; environmental, 174–76; graphic, 99; for impact assessment, 440–41, 442, 444, 448; for legal challenges, 472; organization of, 105–6; primary, 120; in projections, 120; quality of, 105; retrieval and analysis of, 64, 120–21; secondary, 120; for single-equation regression analysis, 161–63; for small-area plans, 460; soft, 47; symptomatic, 131. *See also* Information systems; Intelligence collection

Data analysis: models for, 64; for plan evaluation, 437–38; as rational planning process, 39

Database management programs: in land use planning, 24, 94, 98; software for, 94, 113*n2*

Databases, control of, 90; decentralized, 96–97; for development management planning, 409; housing, 26; for impact assessment, 187, 189, 444; interdependence of, 202–3; of land parcel records, 98, 99, 101, 106, 107, 111; object-oriented, 95; of land supply, 199–200; relational, 106; role in intelligence gathering, 63–64; as source of planning information, 199; spatial, 63, 221. *See also* Computers; Information systems; Microcomputer technology; Records

Dayton, Ohio: planning team of, 371

Deaths. *See* Mortality

Decision-making: in development management plans, 411; homogeneity of groups in, 16; in land use change management, 56*n4*; politicization of, 6

Decision tree analysis, 412, 469–70

De facto development policies, 259

De Grove, John, 13

Delphi surveys (economic analysis), 147, 271

Demand and supply: of land, 252, 280, 289, 302; for public facilities, 442

Demographic forecasting. *See* Forecasting, population

Density: gross and net, 355, 356, 357, 359, 364. *See also* Holding capacity

Design format (policy planning), 70–73

Design, land use. *See* Land use design

Detention basins, 219, 242

Developability analysis (land use), 201–2, 215–23, 225*n3*; carrying capacity in, 218–20; perceptual, 223–24; steps in, 216–18

Developable land units (DLUs), 221

Developers, 115; of community facilities, 394; consensus-building with, 53; expectations of, 28; role in land use planning, 8–9, 80, 405; use of future land use maps, 212

Development: codes for, 75, 399, 401–2, 405; conditions for, 399; control measures for, 403, 412; cost of, 253, 403; fees for, 73; im-

pact mitigation for, 425, 446–51; impacts of, 173–74; infrastructure as prerequisite to, 30*n3*; and land use change management, 52; mixed-use (MXD), 46, 48, 320, 351, 358, 436; monitoring of, 442, 451*n1*; of open spaces, 295, 299; opposition to, 22–23, 26; public subsidies for, 296; purchase of rights to (PDR), 401; regulations for, 253; residential, 111, 118; role in land use planning, 198; rural-to-urban, 42; simulation models of, 221–23; socioeconomic factors in, 442; spatial patterns of, 398; standards for, 399, 400, 415; sustainable, 50–51, 52, 172; as threat to environment, 172, 173–74, 408; timing of, 403, 413; transit-oriented (TOD), 345, 346, 347, 380

Development management plans, 73–75, 79; acquisition programs in, 400, 401; adoption of, 405–6, 416–17, 418; advance planning in, 454; assessment of, 405–6, 417, 418, 423; capital improvement in, 75, 415–16; components of, 399–400, 418; constitutional rights in, 410; content of, 400–401; coordination of components, 401, 404; core planning teams for, 405, 406, 408, 409, 416; description of, 399–405; design of, 412–17, 418; direction-setting in, 253, 405, 410–16, 418; economic efficiency in, 266; effectiveness of, 410, 411, 417, 418; equity in, 417, 418; evaluation of, 425, 438–51; as extension of planning, 78; fact component of, 409; feasibility of, 268, 410, 411–12, 415–16; five dimensions of, 400–405; formulation of work plan in, 408, 409; geographic coverage in, 403, 415, 416, 417; goal-setting in, 273–74, 399, 410–11, 417; governmental regulations in, 401, 402; implementation of, 415, 418, 423, 454; initial steps in, 405, 406–9, 418; intelligence gathering in, 40; and land use design, 398; in land use planning programs, 63, 64, 78–79; legislative intent of, 399, 416, 417, 418; location standards in, 284, 298; maps for, 400; methodology of, 405–17; modification to, 75–76; for open space, 301; origins of, 64–65; participation in, 406; policy component of, 274; political-institutional context of, 409, 411; problem solving in, 76; program of actions in, 399; selection of alternatives in, 405–6; situation analysis in, 411–12; special consideration areas in, 75, 81; standards in, 400, 401, 404, 415; values component of, 409; working descriptions for, 406, 408–9. *See also* Land use management programs

Development management programs: assessment of, 412; feasibility of, 417, 418; formulation of, 412–16; hazard mitigation in,

450; legal challenges to, 455, 471–2; monitoring of, 437–38, 451n1; role of capital budgeting in, 455

Development markets, 8; in development management plans, 409, 411; and land use planning, 8–10, 28, 47; regulation of, 20

Dickert, Thomas G., 443

Digital elevation models (DEMs), 108, 178

Digital line graphs (DLGs), 104, 108, 113n5

Direction-setting (advance planning), 83, 251–52, 258–59; for community facilities, 371–72; in development management plans, 405, 410–16, 418; and land classification, 292; purpose of, 257

Disaggregation: of industry, 157; in urban areas, 381

Disaggregation techniques, of population analysis, 123, 132–38

Discourse: in land use game, 53; in land use planning, 39, 82; model, 53–55; in rational planning, 54

Disney World (Orlando, Florida), 393–94

Dispute resolution. *See* Conflict resolution

District of Columbia, recreational facilities of, 389, 392

Districts, in land classification formats, 66, 68, 74

Dowall, David, 47–48, 215

Downzoning, 48, 189, 192; in development management plans, 403; to low-density use, 245n3; of watershed areas, 226n4

Drainage basins, 174, 242; locational design for, 283; maps of, 178

DRASTIC (overlay screening model), 189–91

Dwellings. *See* Housing

Dwelling unit method, of symptomatic measuring, 131

Earthquakes, 193, 295

Earthquake zones, maps of, 302

Ecological systems. *See* Conservation areas; Critical areas, environmental; Environment

Economic analysis, 145–46; competitive shift component of, 148; component methods of, 150–65; constant-share model of, 149–50; cost-effectiveness in, 146; econometric models of, 164–65; estimates in, 120; for impact assessment, 157–58, 452n2; input-output technique of, 155–59; judgmental approach to, 147; and land use studies, 119–20; methods of, 146–50; national industry shift component of, 148–49; normative approach to, 119; and population studies, 115–16, 139–40; pragmatism in, 146; ratio-share techniques for, 147–48; shift-share approach to, 148–50, 169n8; single-equation regression model approach to,

159–64; state, 122; typology of approaches in, 146–47. *See also* Forecasting, economic; Employment analysis

Economic-base analysis, 150–55, 161; assessment of, 154–55; defining study area of, 152; steps in performing, 151–52

Economic-base multipliers, of employment, 150, 154, 155, 157

Economic Censuses (U.S. Bureau of the Census), 145

Economic projection: conversion into socioeconomic characteristics, 166–67; for employment centers, 328; normative, 165; ratio-share techniques of, 128. *See also* Forecasting, economic; Population projection

Economic Research Service, 165

Economy: balance with ecology, 172; as element of intelligence, 87; problem analysis of, 260; role of open space in, 297, 299–300; service sector of, 155

Ecosystems. *See* Conservation areas; Critical areas, environmental; Environment

Educational facilities. *See* Schools

Efficiency: in development management plans, 410, 411, 418; economic, 266; as "good" city form, 43; in land use management programs, 415

Effluent, discharge of, 237. *See also* Wastewater

Einsweiler, Robert, 215

Elkhorn Slough, California: wetland analysis of, 443

Emergency management systems, 450; computer files of, 104

Emission control programs, 184

Employment: in advance planning, 253; basic and nonbasic, 149, 151–54, 168n5, 317, 328; decentralization of, 55n3; and demand for land, 328; economic-base, 317, 318, 328; economic-base ratio of, 150; locational needs of, 252, 316; national growth component of, 148–49; plan evaluation for, 438; role in population growth, 145; sources of data for, 145–46; space requirements for, 285, 308, 309, 316, 328; spin-off, 118; and urban growth, 305, 306–7

Employment analysis: assumptions approach to, 152; location quotient approach to, 152–53, 169n8; Mather-Rosen approach to, 152, 154; minimum requirements approach to, 152, 153–54; multipliers in, 157; ratio-share techniques for, 147–48; single-equation regression model of, 159–64

Employment and Earnings Reports (Bureau of Labor Statistics), 145, 167n1

Employment centers: access to, 325; compatibility with residential areas, 366; density standards for, 327, 329–31, 338; economic projection for, 328; holding capacity analysis of, 337; impact on residential areas, 338, 359; in land classification plans, 310; land use planning for, 316, 317, 318–20, 338; locational design for, 282–83; location requirements for, 324–25; space requirements for, 327–32, 339; spatial structure of, 323, 380; suitability analysis for, 326–27, 338; transportation planning for, 378. *See also* Commercial centers

Employment projection: for activity centers, 324; for commercial areas, 333; economic-base multipliers in, 150, 154; in land use studies, 119; uses for, 151

Employment Survey (ES-202), 161

Empowerment Zones, 26

Endangered species, 51, 184–85

Enterprise Communities Program, 26

Entrepreneurs, role in land use planning, 8, 9

Enumeration (data measurement), 120

Environment, 173; analysis of, 174, 176, 185–94; baseline conditions in, 174; carrying capacity analysis of, 219; compatibility with employment centers, 326; cumulative impact assessment of, 185, 191; effect of population on, 218; as element of intelligence, 87; hazard analysis of, 185; integrity of, 49–51; in land use change management, 49, 185; in land use design process, 278, 288; mapping of, 99, 101, 177–85; open space as protection for, 295, 299; planning units of, 299; pollution of, 173–74, 184, 189, 240–42; simulation models of, 64; state management of, 13; threats to, 21, 172; variability of, 174. *See also* Conservation areas; Critical areas, environmental; Natural resources

Environmental groups. *See* Interest groups, environmental

Environmental impact, 452n2; statements of, 49; of transportation systems, 236, 380; variables effecting, 219

Environmental impact analysis, 186–91, 444, 452n3; cumulative, 185, 186, 191; descriptive checklists of, 186–87; overlay screening models of, 186, 189–91; spreadsheet models of, 186, 187, 189; and transportation impact analysis, 236. *See also* Impact analysis

Environmental inventory, 174–76, 177, 191

Environmental management, policy frameworks for, 274

Environmental planning, in development management plans, 74, 172, 400; goal-setting in, 267; inventory of policy in, 176; by local government, 18; use of computer mapping in, 99, 101, 177–85

Environmental Protection Agency (EPA): effluent standards of, 184; hazard records of, 193–94; national standards set by, 11; and policy change, 16; sewerage recommendations of, 384; stormwater management of, 242

Environmental services, 172–73

Environmental values: and land use, 4, 24, 91; in land use change management, 42–43, 49–51; role of open space in, 295, 299

Equity: in goal-setting, 266–67, 410; of impact fees, 448; in land use management programs, 415, 417, 418

ERDAS (GIS programs), 99

Estimate-discuss-estimate technique (goal-setting), 272

Estimation (data measurement), 120

Eutrophication, 183

Exactions. *See* Impact fees

Expert systems, 102, 113n4

Expressways, 231

Extrapolation. *See* Trend extrapolation

Fact-finding, 257, 259–61

Fairfax County, Virginia: feasibility studies in, 411–12

Feasibility: in development management, 268, 410, 411–12, 417, 418; in fact-finding, 259, 260; of hazard mitigation, 450; of land use management programs, 415–16, 417

Federal Emergency Management Agency (FEMA), 182, 450

Federal government. *See* Government, federal

Federal Housing Administration, guidelines for neighborhoods, 342

Federal-State Cooperative Program for Population Projections, 122

Feminists, as urban theorists, 46

Fertility: projections of, 137; scenarios of, 142n12

FICA taxable payroll reports, 167n2

Field inspections, for land use data, 204

Fish and Wildlife Service, U.S., 172, 182; protection of endangered species, 184–85

Floodplains: classification of, 182, 192–93, 242, 292; computerized mapping of, 101; and cost of land, 208–9; effect of development on, 173; federal regulations concerning, 11; hazard mitigation in, 449–50; inventory of, 175; in land use management programs, 415; maps of, 182–83, 192; stormwater management in, 242; as wildlife habitats, 297

Floor-area analysis, 208; for commercial areas, 332, 333–35

Florida: Coastal Management Plan, 55; concurrency system of, 22, 375, 394; goal-setting of, 269–70; growth management policies of, 13–14, 393; land use plans of, 368; mandated goals of, 264–65; use of critical area analysis, 192

Focus groups (goal-setting), 271

Ford, Kristina, 220–21

Forecasting: economic-population approach to, 165; of employment, 328; long-range, 117, 158; margin of error in, 118; of market, 221; and projection, 117; and scenario-building, 261; of travel demand, 378, 380–81

Forecasting, economic, 87, 116–17; OBERS approach to, 165; purpose of, 116; role in land use planning, 141n1. *See also* Economic projection

Forecasting, population, 115–17; for commercial areas, 333; housing requirements for, 351–57; OBERS approach to, 165; purpose of, 116; role in land use planning, 141n1. *See also* Population projection

Forest areas, 172; and growth allocation, 306; in land use planning, 290; locational design for, 283; monitoring of plans for, 438; as recreation sites, 300

Forest Service, U.S., 49; inventories by, 182

Frieden, Bernard, 48

Friedman, John, 77

Functional space, 196, 310–11; characteristics of, 197

Functional theories, of land use change management, 56n4

Future goal forms, 66; in development management plans, 73; in land use design, 70; origin of, 64; use in problem solving, 76

"Fuzzy gambling," as planning theory, 30n6

Gaithersburg, Maryland: community planning in, 345

Games, ecology of, 30n2

GBF/DIME (Geographic Base File/Dual Independent Map Encoding) files, 104

Gender, role in urban land use, 46

Gentrification, and neighborhood theory of land use, 46

Geographic identifiers (computer mapping), 99

Geographic information systems (GIS), 3, 24, 56n3, 89; for activity center planning, 338; and Anderson system, 225n2; definition of, 95; for development simulation, 221, 222; in environmental planning, 175; file format of, 106; and holding capacity analysis, 309; integration of, 101; in land suitability analysis, 216, 218, 286; in land supply inventories, 200; for open space planning, 301–3; planners' knowledge of, 29; in transportation planning, 235; triangulated irregular net-

work (TIN) technique of, 108; use of vector systems, 99. *See also* TIGER GIS system

Geological Survey, U.S.: mapping programs of, 108, 113n5, 177, 178; TIGER files of, 104

GIS. *See* Geographic information systems

Giuliano, Genevieve, 55n3

Global positioning systems (GPSs), 204

Global warming, 175; effect on wetlands, 21

Goal forms. *See* Future goal forms

Goals, 276; in advance planning, 252, 261–74; community concerns as, 262; definition of, 262; in development management plans, 399, 410–11; in fact-finding, 259, 260; forecasting for, 116; generic, 262, 266–68; for land use, 82, 281; legacy, 262, 263, 266; linkage of policies to, 275–76; for living areas, 273; long-range, 457, 458; mandated, 262, 263–66; needs as, 262; for small-area plans, 460; statements of, 273–74; types of, 262–70

Goals-achievement matrices (plan evaluation), 427, 432–33

Goal-setting: choice in, 267; in development management plans, 273–74, 428; economic efficiency in, 266; equity in, 266–67; feasibility in, 272; health and safety in, 268; incentives for, 264; participatory, 269–70, 272–73; in policy planning formats, 66; and problem analysis, 260, 261; protection of constitutional rights in, 267; quality of life in, 267–68; in rational planning model, 38; search in, 270–71; selection in, 270, 272–73; surveys in, 271; synthesis in, 270, 271–72

Goldstein, Harvey A., 146, 159, 163, 164

Good city form, 43–44, 266

Government, federal: deregulation by, 19, 25; devolution of responsibility, 19, 20, 25; response to social trends, 18; role in land use planning, 10–12

Government, local, autonomy over land use, 10; computer files of, 104; conflicts among, 15; development codes of, 75; development of community facilities, 394; effect of federal policy on, 11; growth-managing, 14–15; hazard mitigation by, 450; in land use game, 112; monitoring of plans by, 438; need for planning standards, 20; role in development management, 398, 400, 401, 402–3, 411, 412; role of planning department in, 81–82; use of information systems, 92, 93

Government: mandated goals of, 263–65; role in development management, 410, 454; role in land use planning, 8, 9, 10–16

Government, state: effect of federal policy on, 11; land classification systems of, 292; role in land use planning, 9, 12–14

Grants, federal, 11; economic basis for, 116, 120

Green party (Europe), 26

Gresham, Oregon: advance planning by, 261; development management plan of, 74–75, 404

Grid outputs (computer mapping), 95, 99

Groundwater, hazards to, 194. *See also* Water

Growth-accommodating localities, 15

Growth-accommodating states, 14

Growth management: conflict resolution in, 460, 462; impact assessment of, 441; and land use planning, 368; legal issues concerning, 29; by local government, 14–15, 18, 19–21, 200; policy frameworks for, 274, 275; role of capital budgeting in, 455; by state government, 19–21; and water supply, 385

Growth-managing states, 12–14

Habitats: classification of, 292; inventory of, 175–76; maps of, 184–85. *See also* Environment

Hall, Peter, 56n3

Hawaii, use of land classification, 291

Hazards: analysis of, 185, 192–94; cumulative impact assessment for, 442; in development management plans, 401; and goal-setting, 268; to habitats, 176; impact mitigation for, 449–51; impacts of, 187; in land use design, 281; maps of, 185; overlay districts for, 450

Hazards, man-made, 25, 193–94; mapping of, 194; to soil, 175

Hazards, natural, 172, 192–93; and growth allocation, 306; in land classification plans, 295; maps of, 302; protection from, 297, 299

Highway Capacity Manual (Transportation Research Board), 378

Hillsborough County, Florida: planning team of, 371

Historic preservation: in development management plans, 73, 81, 400; by local government, 18

Holding capacity, 126; of activity centers, 323, 337; analysis of, 279, 286, 289; for community facilities, 373; for housing, 357, 363; of open space, 296, 303; and population projection, 123, 124, 140; of residential areas, 348, 357, 358; and urban growth, 305, 309. *See also* Carrying capacity; Density

Households: activity surveys of, 213; definition of, 351; density of, 308; as measure of functional space, 197; new dwelling requirements for, 351–54, 355, 360

Household size: and allocation of land, 359; as population measurement device, 132; and school planning, 385

Housing, affordable, 17, 56n3; in development management plans, 73, 400; and the market, 48; state-mandated, 13

Housing: databases of, 26; density of, 140, 355–57, 360, 369; in development management plans, 401; holding capacity for, 363; plan evaluation for, 438; and population studies, 119; role in residential area development, 363; spatial allocation for, 253, 260, 359, 366; subsidized, 18, 23, 366

Housing market, 48; analysis of, 365, 366; role in residential area development, 350–51

Housing supply: additions to, 355–57; advanced planning for, 365; loss of, 340, 354–55; for residential areas, 351–61; vacant, 354, 359

Housing types, 351–52; in residential areas, 251, 342, 349, 353, 355–58; space requirements for, 357

Housing and Urban Development, Department of (HUD), 19

Houston, Texas: community facilities planning in, 373; sewerage system of, 384

Howard County (Maryland) General Plan, 70, 71–72

Human activity systems, 43, 44–45. *See also* Activity systems

Human ecology theories, 41

Hurricanes, 192–93, 295

Hurricane zones, maps of, 302

Imageability analysis (land use), 202

Impact analysis, cumulative: in advance planning, 191; definition of, 442, 452n4; of environment, 185, 186, 191; models of, 444; of public facilities, 230

Impact analysis: of the environment, 176; input-output technique in, 157–58; of noise, 187; plan evaluation for, 436; in rational planning, 39; techniques of, 439; time-delay in, 442; variables in, 219. *See also* Environmental impact analysis; Economic analysis

Impact analysis, of individual projects, 186, 439–41, 452n3; characteristics of, 440; checklists for, 439–40, 451n2; and comprehensive plans, 441; data gathering for, 440–41; proposals for, 439, 440

Impact fees: for community facilities, 394; in development management plans, 401, 403; equity of, 448; guidelines for, 446, 448; for infrastructure, 441, 472n1; ordinances for, 452n5; for recreation, 244; use by local government, 15

Impact mitigation, 425; checklists for, 427, 429–31; for community facilities, 446–48; data sources for, 448; of hazards, 449–51; social, 448–49, 452n2; targets for, 427, 432

Implementation: conflict during, 454; of development management plans, 415, 418, 423, 454; of land use planning programs, 439; as process of evaluation, 423; techniques for, 454

Incentives, 11; in development management plans, 399; for goal-setting, 264

Industrial districts: density standards for, 329, 330; land use planning for, 318, 319

Industrial parks: community facilities in, 368; density standards for, 329; land use planning for, 73, 318–20; location requirements for, 325; mixed-use, 337; office space in, 323; transportation planning for, 378

Industrial Research Council, 319

Industrial reserves, 331–32

Industry: disaggregation of, 157, 165; econometric models of, 164; in economic-base studies, 151, 153–54; export-oriented, 161, 162, 169$n8$; input-output analysis of, 155–57; local-serving, 162–63, 168$n5$; location requirements for, 325; market orientation of, 169$n8$; predictor variables for, 161–63; premodel analysis of, 161, 169$n8$; role of open space in, 297; single-equation regression model studies of, 159–64, 169$n7$; space requirements for, 285, 286; suitability analysis for, 216

Information base (fact-finding), 259

Information systems: accessibility of, 98; capture of data in, 103–4; centralized, 95; computerized, 89–90; in conflict resolution, 466; data quality of, 105; decentralized, 96–97; design of, 98–102; distributed, 95–96; expert, 102, 113$n4$; governmental, 90; hardware/software selection of, 93–94; implementation of, 97–98, 112; interests served by, 92–93; interpretation of data in, 106–7; in land use game, 111–12; of local governments, 87; management issues of, 91–98, 113$n1$; manual, 89; maps in, 107–8; mixed control of, 93; module design of, 102–8; organization of, 95–97, 105–6; political support for, 97; population-economic information in, 167; public, 91; purpose of, 90; querying of, 101; scope of, 99; service standards for, 229; as sources of planning intelligence, 111–12; staffing of, 98; transportation information in, 231; use in development management planning, 409; use in plan evaluation, 437–38. *See also* Data; Intelligence; Land use information; Records

Infrastructure, advance planning for, 253; for commercial areas, 326; coordination with land use, 374; cumulative impact assessment for, 442; deficits in, 22, 25; effect of federal devolution on, 19; as element of intelligence, 87; for employment centers, 325; financing of, 48, 441, 472$n1$; impact assessment of, 444; impact fees for, 441; in land supply inventories, 200, 372; land use planning for, 9, 393; locations for, 252; management of, 88; mapping of, 88; planning information for, 229–35; policy framework for, 275; and population studies, 119; as prerequisite to development, 30$n3$; and private development, 56$n10$, 219–20, 230, 265–66, 394, 403, 413; role in residential area development, 363, 366; simulation models of, 64; small-area plans for, 459; standards for, 229; state-mandated, 13; and survival of neighborhoods, 46; and urban growth, 110–11, 208, 305, 306, 399. *See also* Community facilities; Public facilities

Input-output technique, of economic analysis, 155–59; adjustments to coefficients in, 159; defining study area of, 158; for impact assessment, 157–58; problems in application of, 158–59; for projection, 157; technological change in, 158–59; transactions in, 155–57

Input policies, 65; in advance planning, 275; of communities, 82

Institute of Transportation Engineers (ITE), 232, 380

Institutions: control of planning information systems, 92; interdependence with government, 24–25

Institutions, financial: role in land use planning, 9, 19

Intelligence: artificial, 102; definition of, 61, 89; socioeconomic impact assessment in, 118–19; strategic, 111–12; users of, 93

Intelligence collection, 40, 79, 83, 87; for plan evaluation, 437–38; by planning departments, 81–82. *See also* Data; Information systems; Land use information; Records

Interest groups: advocacy of individual values, 52; mobilization of, 25; opposition to development, 22–23, 26; role in advance planning, 254; role in capital budgeting, 455; role in development management, 417; role in direction-setting, 259; role in land use planning, 7, 80

Interest groups, environmental: role in land use policy, 17, 28, 405; use of future land use maps, 212

Intergovernmental organizations: planners' understanding of, 411; role in conflict resolution, 462; role in planning, 3

Intermodal Surface Transportation Efficiency Act (ISTEA), 26–27, 32$n9$, 375

Interstate highway system, 12

Judicial systems, mandated goals of, 266
Justice, as characteristic of "good" city form, 43

Laissez-faire, in land use planning, 14
Lake Tahoe region, carrying capacity analysis of, 219
Land: amount of use, 206–8; as commodity, 112, 196, 198–99; cost of, 208–9; demand and supply of, 252, 280, 289, 302; developability of, 215–23; employment-based demand for, 328; as esthetic resource, 196, 208, 223, 302; as functional space, 196–97; hierarchical classification of, 205–6; inventory of, 175, 437; location records of, 206
Land classification, 205–9, 225$n1$, 287–88; accommodation of growth in, 305, 306, 308–9; districts in, 74; formats of, 66, 68–70; formulation of system in, 292–94; geographic sectors of, 308; hierarchies of, 292, 293; origin of concept, 290–91; standards for, 284, 296; types of, 304–5, 313–14
Land classification plans, advance planning for, 252, 253, 255; categories in, 292; components of, 310; definition of, 290; formulation of, 291–95; future development in, 290; goals of, 310; implementation policies for, 292, 294–95, 309–10, 310; locational principles for, 282, 296, 298; mapping in, 292, 294, 309, 310; open space in, 295–304, policy framework plans in, 257–58, 276, 312; publication of, 295; purpose of, 312; for residential areas, 350; space requirements in, 285; tasks in, 288–89; and urban development, 278, 279; use of development management plans, 278
Land cover: classification of, 179, 205, 207; inventories of, 176, 182; maps of, 179–82; role in space management, 299
Landis, John D., 222
Land market, 198–99; in land use management programs, 415; modeling of, 118; regulation of, 40; social values associated with, 91; theories of, 40; and urban growth, 306, 308, 316; value of, 16, 28, 53. See also Market
Land owners, role in land use planning, 8–9
Land parcels: characteristics of, 196; computerized mapping of, 98, 99, 101, 106; identification number (PIN) for, 106, 107, 109, 110, 206; in open space, 296; transportation facilities to, 374
Land records management programs, 87, 98; in North Carolina, 108–9, 211; specification–based, 108–9; use of aerial photography, 109
Land records offices, computer files of, 104
Landscapes: maps of, 185; urban, 199

Landslides, 193
Land supply: changes in, 200; for commercial centers, 338; and demand, 252, 280, 289, 302; in development management plans, 403; effect of transportation services on, 374; effect on design, 286–87; holding capacity of, 357, 358; inventories of, 199–200; monitoring of, 87, 110–11, 199, 444; for residential areas, 340; spatial analysis of, 253, 305; suitability maps for, 323; and urban growth, 308–9
Land use: acquisition of data for, 203–5; and activity centers, 197–98, 321–23; activity patterns of, 197, 201, 213–15; baseline surveys of, 203, 350, 441; carrying capacity analysis of, 50; classification of, 205–9, 225$n1$, 287–88; control measures over, 47–48; control theories of, 56$n7$; density of, 103, 111, 117, 140, 285, 413; developability analysis of, 215–23; and environmental values, 4, 24, 91; goals for, 410; growth projections for, 87; impact of sewerage on, 238–39; impact of transportation systems on, 374, 376, 377, 381, 394; integration of values in, 51; intelligence systems for, 87; inventory of, 199–215; legislation concerning, 20–21; location requirements for, 279, 288, 289; low-density strategy for, 243, 245$n3$, 282; mapping of, 64, 87, 209–12; measurement of, 206–8; misallocation of, 70; modeling of, 64, 376, 383, 394$n1$, 442; national strategy for, 32$n8$; ownership records of, 106; patterns of, 286–87; perceptual analysis of, 223–24; premature, 73, 199; quality of, 208; role of community facilities in, 369; social use of, 42, 91, 112, 213–15; space requirements for, 279, 280, 288, 289; spreadsheets of, 209; suitability analysis of, 50, 80, 201, 215–18, 302, 373–74; timing of, 208, 413, 414; types of, 205–6, 317–23, 380; values of, 42–51
Land use change: aerial photography of, 204; evaluation of, 438–51; impacts of, 425; modeling of, 101, 118; monitoring of, 88; planning information on, 90; role of information systems in, 89, 91; Rudel's theories of, 41–42; variables in, 101. See also Change
Land use change management: adaptive technique of, 37; effect of technology on, 36; and market failure, 47–48; methods of, 36; models of, 52–53; political interests in, 41, 42; as practice rationale, 35–42; redistribution of power in, 48; sequential interactions in, 42; theories of, 56$n4$; use of maps in, 185
Land use design, advance planning for, 254,

255; for commercial areas, 333, 340; and development management plans, 398, 404–5, 409; feasibility in, 268, 281; format for, 66, 70–73; formulation by planners, 286–87, 289; future goal forms in, 70; holding capacity in, 286, 289, 357; location requirements for, 281–84; location suitability of, 284–85; neighborhoods in, 358; open space in, 303–4; policy component of, 274; policy framework plans in, 258, 276; and population measurement, 140; principles of, 252, 281; for residential areas, 342–48, 350, 357–58, 363–65; sequence of tasks in, 279–89, 294, 296; space requirements for, 285–86; synthesis in, 281; transportation planning in, 375–78, 380. *See also* Development management plans; Land use planning

Land use design, urban, 252; accommodation of growth in, 312; categories of, 287; locational design in, 281–82; locational standards for, 282–83, 298; role of agriculture in, 297; role of land classification plan in, 312; space requirements in, 285; use values in, 278, 279

Land use game, 5–8, 30*n1–2*; conflict in, 460; consensus-building in, 458; control of, 454; dissemination of information in, 64; evaluation of impacts in, 425; infrastructure in, 229; integration of values in, 51; and land use change, 37; market in, 112; planning discourse in, 53; players in, 6–9, 111–12, 405, 454; political dimensions of, 455–56, 473*n5*; problem solving in, 75; role of information systems in, 111–12; role of planners in, 6–8, 54–55, 79–80, 81, 454; social use in, 18, 112; use of information modules in, 196

Land use information, 104; analysis of, 215–25; classification of, 205–9; data acquisition in, 203–5; mapping of, 202–15; modules of, 196; in planning programs, 199–202; regional compatibility in, 202; units of, 202–3. *See also* Data; Information systems; Intelligence; Records

Land use management programs: core planning team for, 408, 413; development principles in, 414; effectiveness of, 413; efficiency of, 415; equity in, 415; feasibility of, 415–16; focus areas in, 414–15; location principles in, 413; scope of, 412–16; service requirements in, 413–14; site design in, 414; space requirements in, 413–14; timing principles in, 414; working description of, 409. *See also* Development management plans

Land use planning, activity centers in, 318, 323; capital budgeting in, 455; carrying capacity analysis in, 220; choice in, 267; for commercial centers, 332–37; for community facilities, 6, 229–35, 368, 369; competition in, 6; context for, 5; coordination with infrastructure planning, 374; core planning team in, 405, 406, 408, 409; critical theory of, 39; current trends in, 18–19; density standards for, 329–31, 356; and development markets, 8–10; economic planners in, 328; economic projections in, 166–67; for employment centers, 316, 327–32; employment data in, 145–46; environmental data in, 174–76; environmentally positive, 173–74; evaluation of, 425, 433–34; evaluation of methods, xiv, 425; "fiscalization" of, 19, 22; for future, 25–27, 209, 212, 265; governmental trends in, 10–16; incremental theory of, 39, 82; normative theories of, 37, 39, 56*n4*; past trends in, 17–18; policy frameworks for, 275; political process of, 6, 10, 30*n1*, 409; population information in, 116–20; projections for, 117–18; rational model of, 37–40; for recreational facilities, 388–93; for residential areas, 348–65; schools in, 243–44, 385–88; sewerage in, 236–40, 383–85; societal trends in, 17–18; space requirements in, 327–37; and special interests, 16–17; steps in, 279–87; stormwater management in, 241; strategic model of, 39–40; suitability mapping in, 323; synthetic aspects of, 255; technological trends in, 36; theory base for, 3; transportation systems in, 230–36, 374, 380; units of, 202–3; updating of, 253–54; use of database management programs, 24–25; use of information systems, 199–202; use of maps, 279; use of population projections, 166–67; use of visual comparison, 426–27, 428; water supply in, 239–40, 382–83. *See also* Land use design; Plan design; Plan evaluation; Planning

Land use planning programs: advance plan-making in, 62–65; development management in, 63, 78–79; evaluation of, 436; four functions of, 61–79, 81; impact assessment of, 441; implementation of, 439; intelligence function of, 61–64; for local governments, 4; methodology of, 82; monitoring of, 437–38; postadoption evaluation of, 436–38; problem-solving in, 63, 75–78. *See also* Planning programs

Land use policy, 199; for community facilities, 371–72; dynamics of, 15–16; formats of, 66–73; housing supply in, 355; intergovernmental, 15; land classification in, 66, 68–70, 312; problem solving in, 471; regional, 398;

reports on, 212; role of inventories in, 200–201; shopping areas in, 362–63; wastewater in, 383

Lane Kendig (Bucks County, Pennsylvania), 302

Lee County, Florida: economic policy of, 328; employment density of, 330

Lee, Douglas B., Jr., 47–48

Legal challenges: preparation for, 423; types of, 473n6

Leisure. *See* Recreational facilities

Lexington and Fayette County, Kentucky: land classification plan of, 310–12

Livable Streets (Appleyard), 223

Local government. *See* Government, local

Locational analysis (land use), 279, 280

Locational design (land use): general principles of, 281–82; for work areas, 282–83. *See also* Land use design

Location quotient approach, to employment analysis, 152–53, 161, 163, 169n8

Logan, John, 41, 45, 46, 48

Long, Norton, 30n2

Los Angeles metropolitan area, air quality of, 11

LULUs (locally unwanted land uses), 26

Lynch, Kevin, 36, 37; "good" city form theory of, 43–44; on planners' values, 56n12; theories of land use change management, 56n4; on urban environment, 223

Management and Budget, U.S. Office of: Standard Industrial Classification system of, 145–46, 149, 153, 167n1–2, 168n6, 206

Mandates, government, 13, 264–66, 275

Maps: accuracy of, 101, 105, 202; for activity centers, 326–27; cadastral, 110; composite, 101; coordinate systems of, 108, 178; of development management plans, 400; digital elevation models (DEMs), 178; environmental, 177–85; features of, 107–8; of future land use, 209, 212; of hazards, 182–83, 192–93; of holding capacity, 286; hydrologic, 183–84; of land cover, 179–82; of landscapes, 185; of land use information, 202–15, 441; of location suitability, 284–85; of open space, 296; overlay, 101, 216, 302, 309, 338; perceptual, 223; registration systems for, 100–101, 106; scale of, 107–8, 202; of sewerage, 238; of soil, 110, 179, 180; topographic, 110, 177; use in intelligence, 89; use of remote sensing, 182; use with geographic referencing systems, 108; of wetlands, 182–83. *See also* Base maps; Suitability maps

Maps, computerized, 94, 99–101; accuracy of, 108; file format of, 106; geographic identifi-ers in, 99; land use data in, 209, 211; outputs of, 95; raster programs, 95; use in land suitability analysis, 216

Market: and community facilities, 229; effect on land use, 3–4, 42, 47–48; failure of, 47–48; forecasts of, 221; management of, 9; role in development management, 454; role in land use planning, 8–10, 16, 41, 42. *See also* Land market

Marxian theories, of urban development, 41, 56n3

Mass transit, 17; computer models for, 106; federal initiatives for, 26; local planning for, 18. *See also* Transportation systems

Mathematical models: for population change, 124–28

Mather-Rosen approach, to employment analysis, 152, 154

Matrices: goals-achievement, 427, 432–33; organizational, 457; tools and hazards, 450–51; tradeoff, 187, 188, 441, 466

McHarg, Ian, 291

Mediation, of conflict resolution, 462, 472n3

Metropolitan areas: employment centers in, 328; state-mandated planning for, 13; transportation surveys of, 44. *See also* Urban areas

Metropolitan Council of the Twin Cities, 225n3

Metropolitan Landscape Planning Model (METLAND), 185

Metropolitan planning organizations (MPOs), 27; as source of transportation data, 234–35

Metropolitan statistical areas (MSAs), 121, 142n5; Census Tract reports of, 141n2; employment data for, 167n2, 168n3

Microcomputer technology: effect on land use planning, 25, 40; for impact assessment, 444; use in planning information systems, 94. *See also* Computers; Databases; Technology

Migration, 131; civilian to military, 138–39; as component of population change, 135–36, 137–38; of elderly, 139; job–related, 140; measurements of, 133, 138; scenarios of, 142n12

Mitigation. *See* Impact mitigation

Model Land Development Code (American Law Institute), 192

Models: calibration of, 161, 163; for community facilities, 374; computerized, 101–2, 118; for cumulative impact assessment, 444; for data analysis, 64; econometric, 164–65; for economic analysis, 147; of environmental impact, 187, 189–91; of land suitability, 215–18; of land use, 383, 442; of mortality rates, 133–35; of natural systems, 442–44; of neighborhoods, 345; for plan evaluation, 425, 433, 435–36; of pollution, 189; for simulation of development, 221–23; of spatial allocation, 118, 221; of stormwater management, 106, 242; urban, 221–23; of water quality, 106

Models, of population change, 221; exponential, 125–27, 142n8; geometric, 124, 125–26, 142n8; linear arithmetic, 124, 125, 127; polynomial, 125, 127–28. *See also* Population

Molotch, Harvey, 41, 45, 46, 48

Montgomery County (Maryland): land supply monitoring system of, 110–11, 225n3; transportation planning in, 375

Mortality rates: age-specific, 132; models for, 133–35; scenarios of, 142n12

Multiple Listing Service (real estate), 26

Myers, Dowell, 225

Nasar, Jack L., 223–24

National Association of Industrial Parks, 318–19

National Environmental Policy Act (1969), 21, 452n4

National Flood Insurance Act (1968), 182

National Geodetic Survey, 109

National Geodetic Vertical Datum, 110, 177

National industry shift component, of economic analysis, 148–49

National Recreation and Park Association (NRPA), 373, 388–91, 393

Natural increase method, of population measurement, 133

Natural processes: advance planning for, 252, 253; in land classification plans, 295, 296; monitoring of, 442–44

Natural resources: cumulative impact assessment for, 442; economic use of, 299–300; effect of development on, 173; efficient use of, 49; in land use design, 283, 288; in land use planning, 291; open space for, 299; organization of files on, 106; preservation of, 51, 297; and sustainable development, 50–51. *See also* Environment

Neighborhoods, 18, 56n9; activity surveys of, 213; community facilities for, 229, 253, 359; density of, 345, 356, 357, 359; functions of, 341–42; goals for, 273; housing for, 358, 359; impact mitigation for, 448; impact of commercial centers on, 338; impact of transportation systems on, 214, 223, 380; in land classification plans, 310; in land use design, 358; location requirements for, 349; neotraditional, 344–45, 350; "pedestrian pocket," 345, 346, 347, 351, 357, 359; and population studies, 120; public efficiency of, 342, 367; recreational facilities for, 244, 300, 389; revitalization of, 415, 455; role in direction-setting, 259; role in land use plan-

ning, 80; scale of, 56n8; schools in, 385; small areas planning for, 458; social, 43, 45–47, 341, 344; socioeconomic change in, 351; spatial requirements for, 362, 363; suburban model of, 345; threats to, 46; transportation systems for, 345, 347; unit principle of, 342–44. *See also* Communities; Residential areas

New Jersey: mandated goals of, 264; state land use plan, 40, 436

New Zealand Resource Management Act (1992), 51

NIMBY (not in my backyard) campaigns, 26

Nominal group technique (goal-setting), 270

North American Wetlands Conservation Act, 182

North Carolina Coastal Area Management Act, 292

North Carolina Division of Coastal Management, 444

North Carolina Geographic and Information Analysis Office, 109, 180, 211

North Carolina Land Records Management Program, 108–9, 194n1

Numerical indicators (plan evaluation), 427, 432–33, 441

OBERS model of economic-population forecasting, 140, 147, 165. *See also* Forecasting

"Object-oriented" software, 95

Objectives, definition of, 262

Occoquan Basin (Fairfax County, Virginia), 226n4

Office parks: land use planning for, 319; transportation planning for, 378

Office space, 321; floor area of, 333; types of, 323

Officials, government: adoption of policy plans, 65; direction-setting role of, 257; expectations of planners, 28–29; in land use game, 112; role in capital budgeting, 455, 456; role in development management, 417; role in land use planning, 4, 7, 8, 80, 254, 405; use of information systems, 92–93

Open space: accessibility of, 298, 302; capital budgeting for, 455; compatibility principle of, 298; continuity principle of, 298; definition of, 295; delineation of, 295–304; development management of, 301; holding capacity analysis of, 296; in land use design process, 283, 287, 288, 289; in land use management programs, 415; in land use planning, 290; locational standards for, 298; maps of, 296; National Recreation and Park Association standards for, 390–91; for natural amenities, 300; as protection from hazards, 299, 303; for recreational activities,

300, 363, 388, 389; for residential areas, 359, 362, 366; role in urban form, 301; social use values of, 295; space requirements for, 296, 303; suitability of use, 301–3; trial allocations of, 296, 303–4
Orange County–Chapel Hill–Carrboro (North Carolina) Joint Land Use Plan, 291
Oregon, mandated goals of, 264, 265
Output policies, 66; definition of, 65

Paired comparison technique (goal-setting), 271–72
Parks: land allocation for, 359; land use planning for, 389; locational design for, 283; standards for, 229
Patton, Carl, 77, 466, 469, 473n5
Perceptual analysis (land use), 223–24
Perin, Constance, 224–25
Perry, Clarence, 45, 342, 343–44, 363
Pfouts, Ralph W., 155
Pinchot, Gifford, 49
PIN. *See* Land parcels
Places Rated Almanac, 268
Plan design: as integrated process, 255; as rational planning process, 39. *See also* Land use planning
Plan evaluation, 426–38; data analysis for, 437–38; goals-achievement matrices for, 427, 432–33; issues in, 433–34; linked models of, 433; methodology of, 426–33; models for, 425, 433, 435–36; numerical indicators of, 441; postadoption, 436–38; preadoption, 425, 434–36; priorities in, 438; single function model of, 433; types of, 433–38; use of numerical indicators, 427, 432–33; visual comparison method of, 426–27. *See also* Land use planning
Planned unit developments (PUDs), 345, 351, 357, 359; evaluation of, 439
Planners: advocacy of goals, 266, 410–11; analysis of political conditions, 411; as communicators, 80; and community aspirations, 269; consensus-building skills of, 29, 30; in core planning team, 408; direction-setting role of, 257; economic skills of, 116; ethical codes for, 32n10, 55; expectations of government officials for, 28–29; and federal social programs, 18; government, 199; and impact mitigation, 425; intelligence gathering function of, 63–64; knowledge of real estate market, 199; market-oriented, 7, 10, 112; need for vision, 29; physical, 45; pressures on, 27–31; role in advance planning, 254, 416; role in conflict management, 462; role in consensus-building, 29, 30, 53–54, 79–80; role in development management, 78, 405, 406; role in impact assessment,

441; role in implementation, 454; role in land use game, 6–8, 54–55, 79–80, 81, 112, 454; role in legal challenges, 471–72; role in problem solving, 76–77, 260; and social use values, 47, 112; technical competence of, 30; values of, 54–55, 56n12
Planning: for activity centers, 323–28; change management in, 55n2; evaluation of, 425; formulation of principles for land use in, 323; intergovernmental, 416; long-range, 6; plans for, 254; policy framework for, 275; preparatory analyses for, 323, 324; rational/adaptive model of, 38–39; tactical, 457–58; theories of, 37–40. *See also* Land use planning; Rational planning; Strategic planning
Planning boards (local government), 81
Planning departments (local government), 81–82; control of planning information systems, 92
Planning discourse, model of, 53–55
Planning programs: environmental information in, 174–76; land use information in, 199–202; organization of, 81–82; purpose of, 251. *See also* Land use planning programs
Planning team, core, 405, 406, 408, 409; assessment of development management plan, 417; goal-setting by, 411
Point systems, 403
Policies, as component of policy framework, 274–76
Policy analysis: influence on development management, 65; "quick," 77–78
Policy envelope, 469
Policy facts, 259
Policy formats, 65; verbal, 66, 67
Policy framework plans, 252, 253, 254; fact component in, 257, 259–61; modification of, 255; policy component of, 257, 274–76; role of land classification in, 312; use in deriving location requirements, 281; values component in, 257, 261–74
Pollution: inventory of, 175; loading models of, 189; monitoring of, 240; point/nonpoint source, 184, 241; of stormwater, 241–42
Polygon outputs (computer mapping), 95, 99, 286, 305, 309
Polynomial model, of population change, 125, 127–28
Population: as basis for spatial allocation, 359, 361, 362; cohorts within, 123, 130; data collection on, 102; disaggregation of, 123, 132–38; effect on ecosystems, 218; as element of intelligence, 87; as a function of time, 128; growth models of, 221; impact analysis of, 444; as labor market, 115; migration of, 131; military, 139; natural in-

crease of, 131, 132; as predictor of water use, 382; problem analysis of, 260; pyramid model of, 134; and recreational site planning, 389; and school planning, 385, 388; and sewerage planning, 384; space requirements of, 285, 308, 309; spatial distribution of, 119–20, 121; and urban growth, 305, 306–7. *See also* Forecasting, population

Population projection: for community facilities, 372–73; component method of, 138–39; conversion into socioeconomic characteristics, 166–67; data for, 131; economic analysis for, 123; economic-population technique for, 139–40; graphs for, 124; holding capacity techniques for, 123, 124; models of, 124–25, 127–28; ratio-share techniques of, 128–30; role in land use planning, 141$n1$; statistical association techniques for, 131–32; symptomatic techniques for, 123, 131–32; trend extrapolation for, 122–23, 124–28. *See also* Forecasting, population

Population studies: and economic studies, 115–16, 139–40; estimates in, 120; and land use studies, 119–20; normative approach to, 119; sources of data for, 121–22; state, 122

Portland Metropolitan Service District, 225$n3$

Portland, Oregon: transportation planning in, 380

Postprojection analysis, economic, 146

Poverty reduction programs, 18

Poverty, urban, 23–24

Predictor variables: for industry, 161–63; in single-equation regression analysis, 159, 160

Private sector: role in land use planning, 56$n10$; use of information systems, 93. *See also* Public/private partnerships

Problems: analysis of, 259, 260–61; definition of, 466; goals in, 469; operational definition of, 471

Problem solving, 40, 466, 469–71, 473$n5$; back-of-the-envelope calculations in, 469; in development management plans, 423; by expert systems, 102; feedback from, 79; in land use planning programs, 63, 75–78, 79; quick, 423, 466; steps in, 76, 77–78; techniques for, 455. *See also* Conflict resolution

Projection. *See* Economic projection; Employment projection; Forecasting; Population projection

Property rights, acquisition of, 400, 401

Public discourse, in land use planning, 39, 82

Public domain, turbulent nature of, 36

Public facilities: adequacy of, 230; construction of, 12; cumulative impact assessment for, 230; definition of, 228; development packages for, 457; effect of population growth on, 218, 369; impact mitigation for, 446; inventories of, 229–30; local, 362–63; management of demand on, 221; planning strategy for, 456–58; as source of land use data, 205; and urban growth, 310. *See also* Community facilities; Infrastructure

Public investment policies, 63

Public/private partnerships, 24–25; and community facilities, 369; conflict resolution in, 466; for development, 20, 26, 56$n10$, 78, 400, 406, 411, 417; efficiency in, 266; impact fees for, 448; in land use change management, 48

Publics: expectations in land use planning, 28; role in advance planning, 254; use of information systems, 91

Q-sort technique (goal-setting), 272

Quadtree programs (computer mapping), 95

Quality circles, 82

Quality of life, 47; goal-setting for, 267–68; and imageability of landscape, 199; studies of, 104, 268; urban, 225, 228

Questionnaires: of Bureau of Labor Statistics, 167$n1$; in goal-setting, 271

Radburn, New Jersey: residential design of, 342

Ragatz, Richard L., 437, 438, 451$n1$

Raster mapping programs (computer mapping), 95

Rate, definition of, 166

Ratio-correlation (symptomatic measuring technique), 131

Ratio, definition of, 166

Rational/adaptive model (of planning), 38–39

Rational investment analysis, 456

Rational planning, 37–40, 56$n5$; goals in, 82; and planning discourse, 54. *See also* Planning; Strategic planning

Ratio-share techniques: for employment projection, 147–48; for population projection, 123, 128–30, 130, 141

Records, organization of, 105–6. *See also* Databases; Information systems

Recreational facilities: activity-based, 244; analysis of, 244; classification of, 388, 389; design of, 392; impact mitigation for, 446; in land use design process, 288; land use planning for, 244–45, 368, 388–93; locational design of, 283; management of, 244; needs surveys of, 366; for neighborhoods, 342; open space for, 363; protection of, 297; regional, 388; in residential areas, 362, 366; schools in, 243; service standards for,

229; space requirements for, 303; special, 389, 392; standards for, 388–92; user-oriented, 300

Reedy Creek Improvement District Comprehensive Plan (Orlando, Florida), 393–94

Regional activities, design for, 287, 288, 289

Regional Input-Output Modeling System (RIMS II), 168n6

Regional planning agencies, computer files of, 104, 109

Registration systems, 100–101, 106

Relevance trees (goal-setting), 271

Remote sensing: classification of data from, 204, 205; use in maps, 182

Republic Square District (Austin, Texas): public/private development of, 466

Research parks, land use planning for, 318

Research Triangle Park, North Carolina: transportation planning in, 375

Reservoirs, 382

Residential areas: access to activity centers, 349; advanced planning for, 365–66; compatibility with employment centers, 325, 359, 366; density of, 349, 350–51, 352, 355–57; development of, 111, 118; and employment centers, 338; environmental considerations for, 349, 362; functions of, 341–42; goals for, 273; gross density of, 359, 364; holding capacity of, 348, 357, 358, 359; housing supply for, 351–61; in land classification plans, 282; land supply for, 340; land use design for, 287, 288, 289, 342–48, 366; land use plans for, 316; local support facilities for, 362–63; locational design of, 283; location requirements for, 348–49; older, 365–66; open space in, 359; planning process for, 348–65; recreation sites in, 362, 366; schools in, 363; shopping centers for, 362–63; social function of, 341, 342; space requirements for, 348, 349, 350, 362; submarket areas of, 366; suitability analysis for, 348, 350; synthesis of design for, 363–65; trial designs for, 366. See also Neighborhoods

Resource Conservation and Recovery Act (1976), 193

Revenue-sharing, 116

Right-of-way, 231

Roadways: arterial, 231; capacity of, 232, 235; classification of, 231, 232, 233, 378; collector, 231; in community facilities planning, 376–78; impact analysis of, 235–36; level of service of, 232, 234–35. See also Transportation systems

Rouse, James, 30n4

Rudel, Thomas K., 30n1, 41–42, 56n7

Runoff. See Stormwater

Rural areas: allocation of land for, 304–5; classification of, 68, 70, 282, 294, 310, 311

Sacramento, California: transportation planning in, 380

Sagalyn, Lynne, 48

Sampling (data measurement), 120

San Francisco Bay Area, 215, 221

Sanibel, Florida: comprehensive plan for, 218–20; development management plan of, 404–5

Satellite business centers, 326; transportation planning for, 378

Satellite growth centers, 305, 320, 321

Satellite imagery, 179, 203, 204, 225n1

Sawicki, David, 77, 466, 469, 473n5

Scale, of maps, 107–8, 202

Scanning (fact-finding), 259, 260

Scenario-building, participants in, 261

Scenarios, of population trends, 141, 142n12

Schaenman, Philip S., 427, 437

Schools: advanced planning for, 366; analysis of, 243; enrollment figures of, 138–39; inventory of, 243; land use plans for, 243–44, 359, 368, 385–88; location requirements for, 385–86, 387; management of, 244; mapping of sites for, 388; planning methodology for, 387–88; and population density, 385; in residential areas, 363, 366; role in neighborhood planning, 45; in small-area plans, 460; space requirements for, 285, 385–86, 387

Sea Lake and Overland Surge from Hurricanes (SLOSH) program, 193

Sensitivity tests, for shift-share analysis, 149

Septic systems, 237–38; prohibition of, 310

Service areas: for community facilities, 369, 374

Service areas, urban, 310, 312, 399, 403; in development management plans, 399; growth of, 311; land use policies for, 312

Settlement policies, 25, 56n12

Sewerage, 111; alternative treatment methods, 237–38; carrying capacity analysis of, 219; federal initiatives for, 26; federal regulations concerning, 11; impact analysis of, 238–39; impact mitigation for, 446; inventories of, 238; management strategies for, 239; planning for, 236–40, 368, 383–85; standards for, 229, 238; stormwater in, 245n2; and water supply, 384–85

Shift-share analysis, 148–50, 161, 169n8; correction factor in, 149, 168n4

Shopping centers: advanced planning for, 366; characteristics of, 322; land use planning for, 320, 321; and residential areas, 349, 362–63, 366; space requirements for, 335, 380

Sierra Club, 26
Silent reflection (goal-setting), 270
Simulation. *See* Models
Single-equation regression model, of employment analysis, 159–64; data requirements of, 160–61; postprojection adjustments to, 164; predictor variables in, 159, 160; premodel assessment of study area in, 161, 163, 169n8; specification of model in, 161–62
Slope. *See* Topography
Sludge, disposal of, 239
Small-area plans, 118, 191, 403, 439, 458–60; in capital budgeting, 460; goals for, 460; implementation of, 423, 455, 460; prerequisites for, 459; scale of, 458
Snowball technique (goal-setting), 271
Social neighborhoods, land use theory of, 43, 44–45
Social networks, urban, 56n9
Social use values: of communities, 16–17, 40, 115, 229; and land use, 3, 42, 43–47; and land use change management, 36, 37, 56n3; of open space, 295; and quality of life, 47
Socioeconomic analysis, 87, 118–19; population-economic projections in, 166–67
Software: for cohort-component method of measurement, 133; for planning information systems, 94–95, 113n2. *See also* Computers; Databases; Microcomputer technology; Technology
Soil: inventory of, 175; maps of, 110, 179, 180
Soil Conservation Service, U.S., 110, 444
Soil erosion, 173; impact analysis of, 187
Spatial analysis: computerized, 94, 99–101, 163, 221; of land supply, 221, 253, 305; models of, 221; of population, 119–20
Spatial structure: of activity centers, 316; of commercial centers, 323; for development, 398; for employment centers, 323, 380
Special consideration areas (land classification), 68, 70, 75, 81, 310
Spreadsheets. *See* Databases
Stakeholder analysis (conflict resolution), 466, 467–68, 469, 472n4
Stakeholders, definition of, 466
"Standard customer," 221
Standard Industrial Classification system (SIC), 145–46, 153, 167n1–2, 206; in shift-share analysis, 149; use in economic-base analysis, 153; wage and salary data in, 168n6
Standard Land Use Coding Manual, 206
State Consolidated Transportation Program, 111
State Data Center Program, 142n4
State employment security agencies, data provided by, 161

States: census data of, 121, 122; growth-accommodating, 14; growth-managing, 12–14, 264–65, 275. *See also* Government, state
Statistical association technique (population projection), 131–32
Stein, Clarence, 342
Storage, Treatment, Overflow, Runoff Model (STORM), 242
Stormwater: combination with wastewater, 245n2; inventory of, 241–42; pollutants of, 241–42; rational method of analysis, 242; runoff of, 242–43
Stormwater management: computer models for, 106; in land use planning, 241–43; standards for, 229; strategies for, 242–43
Storm Water Management Model (SWMM) of EPA, 242
Strategic planning, 39–40, 56n5; in goal-setting, 272; problem analysis in, 260. *See also* Planning; Rational planning
Stream buffers, 173, 299
Streets. *See* Roadways; Transportation systems
Subdivisions records, as source of land use data, 204–5
Subsidies, federal, 11–12
Suitability analysis (land use), 50, 201, 215–18; for community facilities, 373–74; of open space, 302; for urban growth, 305, 309
Suitability maps, 284–85; for activity centers, 326–27; for land supply, 323; for open space, 301–3; for residential areas, 357; for urban growth, 305, 306. *See also* Maps
Superfund (Comprehensive Environmental Response, Compensation and Liability Act), 21, 193
Symbolism, of urban areas, 224–25
Symptomatic techniques, for population estimation, 123, 131–32

Tactical planning, monitoring programs of, 457–58
Tax assessor files, as source of land use data, 203–4, 208
Tax ordinances, in development management plans, 73, 401
Technological change, 3; and input-output analysis, 158–59; and land use change management, 36
Technology: communications, 24, 25; effect on land use planning, 17, 18; interdependence in, 24, 26. *See also* Computers; Microcomputer technology
Thematic mapping programs, 94, 95, 99, 113n3. *See also* Maps, computerized
TIGER GIS system, 24, 103–4; land location records in, 206; use for parcel data, 107;

use of Census data, 103. *See also* Geographic information systems (GIS)

Time-series trend analysis, 149, 161, 168*n5*

Tools and hazards matrix, 450–51

Topography: in land classification plans, 282; maps of, 110, 177–78; overlay screening models of, 189–90

Tourism, 333

Trade-off matrices, 441; in conflict resolution, 466; for environmental impact analysis, 187, 188

Traffic: analysis of, 438; automobile, 231; impact mitigation of, 448; level-of-service standards for, 380, 381; zones, 378, 380. *See also* Roadways; Transportation systems

Transactions tables, in input-output analysis, 155, 156, 157

TransCAD transportation model, 433

Transportation analysis zones (TAZs), 44–45, 47, 230, 235

Transportation improvement programs (TIPs), 27, 381

Transportation Management Areas (TMAs), 27

Transportation Research Board, 378

Transportation systems: activity surveys of, 213, 214; alternative, 378; carrying capacity analysis of, 219; for commercial centers, 317, 332–33, 338; for community facilities, 349, 374–82; components of, 376, 378, 379; for employment centers, 325; federal initiatives for, 26–27; impact analysis of, 235–36; impact mitigation for, 446; impact on land use, 376, 381, 394; impact on neighborhoods, 380; inventory of, 231–35; in land use change management, 56*n3;* in land use planning, 230–36, 377, 368, 380; locational design of, 283; management of (TSM), 381; management strategy for, 236; models of, 433; multimodal, 374, 376; planning for, 44–45, 167, 375–76, 380–82; policy framework for, 275; for recreational facilities, 388; for residential areas, 111, 366; sources of data on, 234–35; standards for, 229. *See also* Mass transit; Roadways; Traffic

Travel demand, forecasting of, 378, 380–81

Tree structure technique (goal-setting), 271

Trend extrapolation, for population projection, 122–28, 129, 130, 141

Trend projection, for plan evaluation, 434, 436

Trip generation (transportation planning), 232, 235, 376, 378, 380

Tuttle, Andrea E., 443

Twin Cities Metropolitan Council Framework plan, 264, 291

Universal Transverse Mercator systems, 99, 108

University Lake watershed (Orange County, North Carolina), 189, 219, 226*n5*

Urban areas: attractiveness of, 223; classification of, 206, 292, 294, 295; components of economy in, 150; econometric models of, 164–65; economic growth of, 23–24; effect of communications technology on, 24; efficiency of, 43; as "growth machines," 41; growth models for, 221–23; imageability of, 199, 202; land use activity patterns in, 201; land use classification of, 68, 290; land use design for, 252; legibility of, 223; organic models of, 45; political-institutional system of, 409, 411; quality of life in, 228; service districts for, 48; spatial form of, 40, 376; stormwater management of, 241; symbolism of, 224–25; travel characteristics of, 213; vitality of, 43; water supply for, 239–40. *See also* Metropolitan areas; Urban development

Urban areas, transitional: classification of, 292, 294, 312; design for, 282, 285, 287, 288, 289; in land use planning, 290, 291, 304, 305–6

Urban change, 3; management of, 278; theories of, 40–42, 55*n3*

Urban development: deal-making in, 48; ecological theories of, 41; full-service, 414; location of, 48; policy frameworks for, 274; space requirements for, 413–14; theories of, 41. *See also* Urban areas

Urban form: role of open space in, 297–98, 301, 303; spatial structure of, 376; theories of, 43–44

Urban growth: allocation of land for, 304–9; boundaries of, 32*n9,* 403; in development management plans, 409; in land classification plans, 311; in land use management programs, 413; location principles for, 305–6; margins of safety for, 306, 308–9, 327, 331–32; space requirements for, 306–9; standards for, 305; suitability analysis for, 305; suitability maps for, 306; theories of, 3; zoning for, 310

Urban Institute, 451*n2*

Urban Land Institute, 30*n4*

Urban land use design. *See* Land use design, urban

Urban limit lines, use by local government, 15

Urban renewal: in development management plans, 400; federal subsidies for, 18; and neighborhood theory of land use, 46

Urban Renewal Administration, U.S., 206

Urban service areas. *See* Service areas, urban

Urban social disintegration, and land use planning, 26

Urban sprawl, containment of, 13, 44, 196

Urban stress, 115

Variances: evaluation of, 438–51; requests for, 81
Vector mapping programs, 95, 99
Vegetation, inventory of, 175
Verbal policy formats (policy planning), 66, 67
Village centers, 347, 348; spatial requirements for, 362
Visions 2000 Act (Florida), 269–70
Visual comparison (plan evaluation), 426–27, 428
Vitality, as characteristic of "good" city form, 43
Vital statistics, 142*n11;* rate technique of, 131
Volusia County, Florida: coastal management plan of, 434, 435

Waste management: engineering solutions to, 21; federal initiatives for, 26; by local government, 18
Wastewater: combination with stormwater, 245*n2;* land use management programs for, 414; in land use planning, 382, 383–84; treatment of, 236–37, 239, 310
Water: assimilative capacity of, 183; classification of use, 184; inventory of, 175; measurement of demand for, 382, 384; standards for, 229
Water quality, 25, 183–84; changes in, 174; computer models for, 106; impact analysis of, 187; jurisdictional disputes over, 15; in land use planning, 75

Watersheds: carrying capacity analysis of, 219; classification of, 292; cumulative impact assessments of, 191, 444; in land classification formats, 70; land use planning for, 73, 383; maps of, 177, 178; in open space management, 300; small-area plans for, 459; in stormwater inventories, 242
Water supply: impact assessment of, 240; impact mitigation for, 446; inventory of, 240; in land use planning, 239–40, 368, 382–83; management of, 240; and population density, 382; and sewerage, 384–85; small-area plans for, 459
Wetlands: benefits of, 173; carrying capacity for, 219; classification of, 292; destruction of, 172, 182; effect of development on, 173; effect of global warming on, 21; federal regulations concerning, 12; impact analysis of, 240, 443–44, 446, 447; inventory of, 175; in land classification formats, 70; maps of, 101, 182–83; small-area plans for, 459
Whelpton, Pascal K., 132
Winston-Salem–Forsyth County (North Carolina), land classification program of, 70
Work areas. *See* Employment centers
Work plans (advance planning), 254–55
Wright, Henry, 342

Zoning: in development management plans, 399, 401; industrial, 318; for urban growth, 310

EDWARD J. KAISER, AICP, is professor and chair of the Department of City and Regional Planning at the University of North Carolina at Chapel Hill, where he teaches land use planning and quantitative methods. He has served as coeditor of the *Journal of the American Planning Association* and been vice president of the Association of Collegiate Schools of Planning and of the North Carolina chapter of the American Planning Association and vice chair of the Chapel Hill planning commission. He received a planning Ph.D. in 1966 from the University of North Carolina and a bachelor of architecture in 1958 from the Illinois Institute of Technology.

DAVID R. GODSCHALK, AICP, is Stephen Baxter professor of planning in the Department of City and Regional Planning at the University of North Carolina at Chapel Hill. He has served as chair of the department, editor of the *Journal of the American Institute of Planners,* planning director of Gainesville, Florida, and vice president of a Tampa planning consulting firm. Holder of the Service Medal of the American Institute of Planners and the Distinguished Professional Achievement Medal and the Elected Official Award of the North Carolina Chapter of APA, he has been a member of the national governing boards of the American Planning Association, the American Society of Planning Officials, and the Association of Collegiate Schools of Planning. He received a Ph.D. in planning in 1971 and a master's degree in 1964 from the University of North Carolina, a bachelor of architecture in 1959 from the University of Florida, and a bachelor's degree from Dartmouth College in 1953.

F. STUART CHAPIN, JR., AICP, is Alumni Distinguished Professor Emeritus of the University of North Carolina at Chapel Hill. He has served as director of the Center for Urban and Regional Studies at UNC, regional planner for the Tennessee Valley Authority, director of planning for Greensboro, N.C., and on several national committees, including Lyndon Johnson's Task Force on Cities. He is a past president of the Association of Collegiate Schools of Planning and has received its Distinguished Educator Award among other national honors, including the American Planning Association's Distinguished Service to Education in Planning Award and the American Institute of Certified Planners' Planning Pioneer Award. He wrote the original edition of this text in 1957, its second edition in 1965, and its third, with Kaiser, in 1979. He received a bachelor's degree from the University of Minnesota in 1937, and, from MIT, a bachelor of architecture in planning in 1939 and a master's degree in planning in 1940.

University of Illinois Press
1325 South Oak Street
Champaign, Illinois 61820-6903
www.press.uillinois.edu